CW00765605

MIMESIS
INTERNATIONAL

LITERATURE
n. 9

José Paulo Cavalcanti Filho

FERNANDO PESSOA
A QUASI MEMOIR

MIMESIS
INTERNATIONAL

Original title: José Paulo Cavalcanti, *Fernando Pessoa – uma quase autobiografia*, originally published in Portuguese by Porto Editora © José Paulo Cavalcanti Filho 2019. 7th edition revised by the author.

Translated by Filipe Faria.

www.mimesisinternational.com
e-mail: info@mimesisinternational.com

Isbn: 9788869771811
Book series: *Literature* n. 9

P.I. C.F. 02419370305

TABLE OF CONTENTS

ACT III
IN WHICH HIS MANY TASTES
AND TRADES ARE DESCRIBED

ACT IV
IN WHICH HIS DISQUIET
AND FATE ARE RETOLD

To Maria Lectícia

I offer you this book because I know it is beautiful and useless.
May it be yours like your very Hour.

The Book of Disquiet ("Peristyle"), Bernardo Soares

With special thanks to Teresa Bonafede

Your ships, Lord, didn't make a greater voyage
than the one made by my thought,
in the disaster of this book.

The Book of Disquiet, Bernardo Soares

A REVISED EDITION

The first commitment of every memoir lies with the truth. Even when one is fully aware that, in spite of all one's best efforts, it is not always possible to attain. Or, perhaps, there is no one truth, may the good Lord have mercy on our souls. Thus, I could but humbly strive for the most humanly possible accuracy. Even after this book's first edition, in May 2011. In that endeavour, I counted upon the contributions of both good and will. Many friends, who took this task upon them as if it were their own. And critics (not many, fortunately), invariably of the kind that thinks of themselves as *specialists* – perhaps on account of my not belonging to their inner circles. As if these humble authors were encroaching upon their self-appointed demesne. And with language more appropriate to college students, who could well do with a couple of grey hairs. Be that as it may, my thanks to all of them. For helping this book be accurate. On such critics, Pessoa had the following to say in an (undated) letter to an English editor: "I am not so prideful as to fully disregard an opinion contrary to my own, nor as humble as to fully accept it". Thus, I made corrections when it felt appropriate. And didn't, when it wasn't the case.

An example of the former came from an observation by the esteemed Ana Rita Palmeirim, granddaughter of José Coelho de Jesus Pacheco. There were ever doubts concerning C. Pacheco – who signs the poem "Para além d'outro oceano" – being a heteronym of Fernando Pessoa (which, at first, seemed a most reasonable assumption to me). However, after the book's first edition, Ana Rita found in her grandfather's estate a draft of that very poem – scrawled all over, with verses added and removed. And brought that information to my knowledge. Without a doubt, it had been the poem's author.

An example of a refused observation was a rather rude post calved at a blog in Lisbon. Blogs, as we know, tend to make heroes of the War of Troy out of the puniest of men. Veritable colossi, fearless and brave. That particular diatribe's author claimed that Father Mattos, whom I had labelled as a heteronym, had been a real person. According to the sage, he had gone by the name of Father José Lourenço Matos (only one "t") – born on the 7th of December 1893, in the village of Folques (Arganil, Portugal), where he died on the 11th of December

1916. The same man who, according to the blog, had written for the newspaper *A Palavra.* The blogger, however, seemed unaware that that particular newspaper had been made of foolscap folio, like the one children write in. Written with a pencil. By Pessoa himself. Crossing the father's date of birth with those of Pessoa's writings attributed to that particular heteronym (1902), one quickly concluded that, in order for the good blogger to be correct, that meant a 9 year-old priest had somehow managed to have been ordained, written seven books, fought the monarchy, been arrested and sent into exile. Laughable.

The reader will, in this new edition, be privy to a number of addenda of the Portuguese version of this book (which was rather well received on the other side of the ocean), and many others which followed. And more will surely follow, provided there is need and time for them in this vast and senseless life of ours. That being said, it is with satisfaction that I say that, essentially, nothing has really changed. One last thing that needs to be said is that this book should be taken as what it is – another proof of devotion and veneration of the absolute genius that Fernando Pessoa was and will ever be.

JPCF, 13th of June, 2013

PRESENTATION OF THE BRAZILIAN EDITION

José Paulo Cavalcanti Filho says that, in a letter to João Gaspar Simões, dated 17/10/1929, in which he ponders the matter of prefaces, Pessoa writes: "I think it is preferable not to have a preface at all". Even so, here it is, fully aware as I am that this task is "most onerous indeed for the freely acknowledged limitations of my competence". But let it be written that, in this journey that now has begun, I "have strenuously sought the truth".

I fully concur with these words written by Pessoa, agreeing with them in gender, number, degree and case. In this rather brief journey I now begin, I shall endeavour to express my sincere appreciation, and how pleasant it has been to consort with the immense Portuguese Poet. How satisfying it was to be led by the experienced hand and inquisitive mind of a 'pessoan' whose peerless curiosity brought me to paths I thought I'd never tread. Despite my long convivial relationship with at least four of those multiple creators of poetry, along with an expert crafter of prose – he too, a poet – called Bernardo Soares, who, although but a "semi-heteronym", was the one who tried to make "a memoir bereft of facts, my lifeless story". And managed to write one of the most intriguing work in all of literature in Portuguese: *The Book of Disquiet.*

This book that José Paulo Cavalcanti Filho puts in our hands is not, according to him, "what Pessoa said, when he said it; it is what I wish to say, in his words. If it's in quotes, it was him, without them, it was me".

These quotes work just like a new mask of sorts, only this time applied to the face of the author of this new book; a mask of which, when removed, he might say, as Álvaro Campos did: "Thus, I am the mask", indissociable as it has become to his true self.

By narrating the final days of Pessoa, Cavalcanti gets ever closer to him, suffering physical pain with him, the moral pain of solitude. Before that, he'll have visited the houses the poet lived in, seeking, in his own words, "to experience the limits of his fate", and feeling that "his figure was slowly taking shape". The brief paragraph is concluded with these exquisite words: "As if, in every corner, he were escaping from the shadows, unnoticed".

Also, this punchline that reads both serious and jocular: “So much so, that I saw him at Chiado, close to the corner of the Bertrand bookshop. My friends swore it wasn’t him, but what do they, poor souls, know of ghosts”.

Cleonice Berardinelli
February 2011

PRESENTATION
OF THE PORTUGUESE EDITION

A monumental 'quasi-memoir'

The first and most fundamental biography of Fernando Pessoa was penned by João Gaspar Simões, in 1950. Robert Bréchon's *Estranho Estrangeiro* followed in 1996. The first photobiography, by Maria José Lencastre, came out in 1984, and the last one was published by the hand of Richard Zenith and Joaquim Vieira in 2008. This book by José Paulo Cavalcanti Filho (JPCF) is a wholly different beast – both in intent and depth of investigation and creativity. The author essentially provides us with undistilled Pessoa, bringing down whatever might separate the poet's life (and his characters') from his work. The work is the man, and the man is the work – from the very personal perspective of this "quasi-memoir's" author.

At length, JPCF writes: "It isn't what Pessoa said, when he said it; it is what I wish to say, in his words. If it's in quotes, it was him, without them, it was me". And so, "these quotes work just like a new mask of sorts, only this time applied to the face of the author of this new book", in the words of the great lusitanist and "pessoan" Cleonice Berardinelli in the presentation of the Brazilian edition – which, not even a year after its release, has already gone back to print for the sixth time, selling over 30 thousand copies.

These hundreds of pages, which, at times, can be read as a romance, add much to what we know of Pessoa's existential path and that of those closest to him, as well as – paradoxical as it might sound – to what we know of the characters he created and/or the figures, facts and real events that were the foundation or 'inspiration' for what he created.

Besides the rigour and "orthodoxy" of certain classifications and opinions, Cavalcanti presents a number of revelations, whether it's the "biography" of heteronyms, sub-heteronyms, "or characters, or masks, and the like", or pointing out where we might find the "tobacco shop", who its owner was (Alves), and who Esteves was. He regales us with characters and situations of Pessoa's body of work, and assures us that "Porto-style tripe" was the writer's favourite dish, who he ate it with, and goes into the details of the very recipe.

Always writing with intelligence, as befits the outcome of a serious investigation, the author is nevertheless still able to draw controversial conclusions while unveiling the details of Pessoa and his life: Family, hangouts, friends, girlfriends (both real and imagined), houses, jobs, crafts, temperament, habits, demeanour, esoteric world, books, magazines, etc. And his thesis, which could be nothing other than controversial, is that the brilliant poet actually had little imagination, as the situations and characters he created derive largely from his own life – "family, friends, writers he admired, initiation rites".

To wit, an absolutely unusual book, extraordinary and "passionate", for only a passion bordering on obsession for Fernando Pessoa could have led an eminent Brazilian – not a literature specialist by any means, but a lawyer and specialist of other *arts* – to dedicate four hours a day for eight years to write it, to say nothing of his numerous travels, mainly to Lisbon. But was it ever worth it!

José Carlos de Vasconcelos

PRÆLUDIUM
(PREFACE)

A preface is never a good thing...
But, sometimes, much like immorality,
a preface is a necessary thing.
Annotation by Ricardo Reis,
for a presentation by Alberto Caeiro

This book is "the biography of one who never had a life". A mere "presentation of sorts" of the man and his work. Of the work that is the man. An attempt at understanding the mysteries behind that "character of an unwritten romance", who "could be the night just as well as the dawn". In the words of the heteronym Vicente Guedes: "This book isn't his: It is him". In a letter João Gaspar Simões, who was to be his first biographer (17/10/1929), "reflecting upon the matter of prefaces", Fernando Pessoa suggests: "I find it preferable not to have a preface at all". Even so, here it is. Even knowing this task is "most onerous indeed for the freely acknowledged limitations of my competence". But let it be known that, in this journey we now begin, I have "ardently sought the truth".

In another letter, this one to the Azorean poet Armando César Côrtes-Rodrigues (19/01/1915), Pessoa admits he envies "those whom one can write a biography about, or who can write their own". After all, *poets have no biography of their own. Their work is their biography* – says Octavio Paz in a book about himself. *Nothing in their lives is surprising, nothing at all, other than their poems.* "I have become a life one reads about". And *I find it hard to believe that anyone could ever better speak of Fernando Pessoa than himself,* according to Eduardo Lourenço. *For the simple reason that it was Pessoa who came up with the method of speaking about himself by the way of those others he became.* And so it will be in this book, in which the object of the biography will become a "future historian of his own sensations". Pessoa himself bequeathed us a "memoir bereft of facts, my lifeless story"[1]. "Fragments of a memoir", as it stands in the *Book of Disquiet.*

1 As per Bernardo Soares, elaborating upon this point: "These are my confessions, and, if I say nothing in them, it is because I have nothing to say". Which brings us to an episode which took place in 1878, when Porto's Ernesto Chardron Bookstore and Publishing House (now Lello

"A memoir of one who never existed", as per Vicente Guedes' presentation. A memoir penned by two, perhaps. Or, even better, a quasi-memoir.

After all, Pessoa wrote in life close to 30 thousand papers, with the topic invariably being himself or those close to him – family, friends, writers he admired, initiation rites. The rough equivalent to 60 books, all 500 pages long. So many, that, in a magical moment, I realized I could tell his life with those words. Using not only those he wrote in chronological order, much like a diary, much like in conventional memoirs, but saying what I wanted to say, as if he were writing it – since I'd be using the words he did write. Let us take, for example, his last months. He knew the end was nigh and began to organize his papers and writing in a frenzy. With not a single line of dismay – that ever present companion of announced death – to speak of. And so, to address that particular period of time, I mainly used texts dating from 1916-1917, when he experienced a series of so-called "psychological crises", and used a similar approach for all highlights of Pessoa's trajectory. Thus, this book isn't what Pessoa said, when he said it; it is what I wish to say, in his words. If it's in quotes, it was him, without them, it was me. Not all quotes are sourced, as there are far too many of them – except for poems, titles (or dates) and the heteronyms that signed them. As Pessoa himself imagines in "Steps of the Cross" (XI), "I'm not the one writing. I am the canvas / And an unseen hand colours someone in me". Here, mine is that hand.

This isn't a book meant for specialists, as they already have far too many pages to fall back on. Those who count the octosyllabic poems, year by year – three in 1919, six in 1920, and so on – or the modal adverbs used, equivalent to 2,94% of the sentences in Pessoa's body of work; or those who study the use of the vocative in his verses, or examine each and every word in *The Message,* to conclude that the book contains ten with 13 syllables; or those who argue that castles, swords, gladii and assorted patterns expressed therein are *phallic symbols;* or those who equate Bernardo Soares' *paradigmatic horizon that modifies the black hole of melancholy's blinding light* with the theories of a German philosopher of the Frankfurt School, or with the *lituraterra* of psychoanalysis; or those who discuss the number of times (125) the word "heart" is used. For the record, much more frequent is the word "sea" – it is used 35 times in *Message,* 46 in "Maritime Ode", his longest poem, and 13 others in a fragment of "Ode to the sea", penned by the semi-heteronym Alexander Search, and many others. I stopped counting when the number approached two hundred. Nor do I propose a new interpretation of Pessoa, of which there are many, for all tastes. To wit, the goal of these good pages is to be a mere guide for those who have yet to be initiated in Pessoa.

Bookstore) asked Eça de Queiroz for a small biographical text to be included in his books. In November of that very year, Eça told Ramalho Ortigão the words which Pessoa would eventually also utter: *I have no story, I am like the Republic of Andorra.*

It wasn't always easy to recreate the environments in which he lived. Such was the case, for example, when I tried to find the A. Caeiro pharmacy – "the letterhead of which", Pessoa wrote in a letter to Côrtes-Rodrigues (04/10/1914) "I happened to spot" as he drove down Avenida Almirante Reis. He thought it funny, as the "A" might have stood for "Alberto", the first name of his Caeiro heteronym. But he never bothered to verify that. And there are hundreds of pharmacies in the several kilometres that avenue runs through. I spoke to the owners, none of which could recall any by that name. There are no records in the neighbourhood's archive of finances. Nor at the national Pharmacy association. Lisbon's historical archive has two photos of old pharmacies in its files, the ones numbered 46 and 78, with no record of names. 46 was a modern pharmacy last time I checked, one "Confiança"; 78 no longer even exists. The Pharmacy Museum mentions another one, numbered 22, with an exterior décor in the shape of a cut stone palm tree. I went to its location, where one can now find Café Palmeira dos Anjos, between a photo shop and Pastelaria Liz; there, at the old corner wall, one may still find the relief of a snake coiled around a palm tree – as opposed to the chalice that is the symbol of pharmacies. I was ready to give up on the notion of it having ever existed – something that often happens when dealing with Pessoa – until, upon perusing Portugal's yearbook of commerce of 1922, I chanced upon *António Joaquim Caeiro, pharmaceutico, Avenida Almirante Reis 108-D.* António, and not Alberto. End of chase.

In other occasions, I was able to skirt around hurdles. Such was the case when I went for the first time to Pessoa's place of birth. Having been informed that the chime of the Basilica of Our Lady of the Martyrs rang at midday, I arrived ten minutes earlier, as I wanted to be where his room was at the time, to make sure that it was actually possible to hear the chimes and see the Tagus from there. At the ground floor of the building in question, at the time a subsidiary of Fidelidade Mutual Seguros, there was only a security guard, one Fernando José da Costa Araújo. I explained why I was there, showed him a sample of the book and asked permission to go up. With me were Maria Lectícia, my wife, and Duda Guennes, Brazilian journalist and a dear friend who had been living in Lisbon for over 30 years. But Mr. Araújo, looking rather unfriendly, simply said:

> "I'm not allowed to let you up, sir."
> "Then could I please speak to the head of the company?"
> "I'm not allowed to do that for you."
> "Then could you please call your secretary, or some other employee who can?"
> "You should call home office, sir."
> "Could you please give me the number?"
> "I'm not allowed to do that."
> "Then could I please borrow your phone book?", I asked, pointing at it.
> "I'm not allowed to do that."

Then, as fate would have it, right after the utterance of this last sentence, we heard the bells chime – the first "of your clangs, resounding across the sky". I needed to be there, so I told the gentleman: *"Please call police to arrest me, because I'm going to the fourth floor without your permission"*. And so I did. To see the shining Tagus from that floor and the unceasing sound of ringing bells. When I went back, the security guard stood at the elevator, looking rather aggravated.

"Did you just go up without my permission?"
"I did."
"What should I do now, then?"
"You can call the police, I'll wait for them, we'll explain what happened and they will decide if I should be arrested or not. Or you can just let me go."
"I don't know, sir."
"Well, I do."

With this, I bid him a good afternoon and went away. In the crisp air of than wintry midday, the bells of Pessoa's *village* sounded again. I thanked them with overwrought reverence, as if they were doing so for my sake. People in the street thought it funny.

I sought his trails for many, many years; and once, in Paris, I was convinced I'd found at the time still an unknown piece of his past. His best friend, Mário de Sá-Carneiro, with whom he had exchanged many letters, had lived there. 216 of those remained, all saved by Pessoa. The fate of those he wrote himself is unknown. He wrote to *monsieur le Gérant* of the Hotel de Nice, where Sá-Carneiro had been lodging when he committed suicide, asking him for their return (16/09/1918). With no reply forthcoming, Carlos Alberto Ferreira (Sá-Carneiro's friend and later Portugal's consul at Nice) claimed to have stored in a briefcase the contents of the room's drawers the day after the funeral, including a great number of letters. Later, upon returning to the hotel, he could no longer gain access to them. Perhaps they had stayed with businessman José de Araújo, who had provided for the burial, he thought. But, if that had been the case, one would have heard of said letters by now. According to Manuel Jorge Marmelo, some went to the hands of English astrologer Aleister Crowley – who had confessed so and *whose lips had widened, in what could have been a smile of satisfaction, triumph, mockery, or something else.* All in jest, of course. The most likely event is that the letters remained in the briefcase in which Sá-Carneiro stored his belongings, and which the hotel kept as lien for the unpaid debt. And, when it was returned to Sá-Carneiro's father, years later, nothing remained in it other than tatters of clothes and scraps of moth-gnawed paper, the sad remains of his lost son. I tried to retrace Sá-Carneiro's steps; and, asking my way around, I got to the nice Moroccan lady, Mme. Fatima

Hannouf, the current proprietor of the hotel – now named *des Artistes.* She confessed to having stored several letters she found, written in other languages and unclaimed in all the years she had been there. I thought I might actually find Pessoa's correspondence (or part of it), and so I nervously perused the papers with trembling hands, comparing the handwriting with other letters he had written in that period. They weren't his. But it had been worth a try. "Everything is worthwhile".

This edition has been conceived mainly for a Brazilian audience. Thus the detailed character pointers and the bits of Portuguese history contained herein. To ensure an easy reading, I have updated the spelling and explained in parenthesis () or brackets [] the translations and the meaning of words and idioms in his sentences whenever they deviate from the norm. The poems (and prose texts) in English and French have been translated as literally as possible, without any concern whatsoever for the rhyming and aiming only to be faithful to them; and are only partially transcribed – with indications that allow readers to consult the sources. For the sake of some unity of effect in this book, I endeavoured to emulate his writing style whenever possible, avoiding adjectives and following the rhythm of his prose. Saramago, in the beginning of his *The Gospel According to Jesus Christ,* uses 21 commas before a period (17, in *Cain*). I mostly do without them. In the case of Pessoa, on average, there are two per sentence. Ideas that slide in three waves. Thus this peculiar style, when I write in between his quotes, so as not to break the rhythm of reading. Also, the use of quotes in Latin, which he was rather fond of – inspired by an old professor at Durban High School, headmaster Willfrid Nicholas. Observations concerning the wording of other verses come in the form of footnotes, as proof that, beyond his inspiration, Pessoa was a stickler for perfect form. And his texts were chosen by me according to purely *personal* preferences, as Millôr Fernandes suggested I put it.

This book began when I set out to discover how many of his heteronyms there had been. For that reason, the *biographies* of all are featured. For Pessoa, they were his masks. "I took off the mask and put it on again. That's better. Thus, I *am*[2] the mask". This is a recurring theme in his writings: "How many masks wear we, and undermasks?", as he says in the eighth of his 35 sonnets. In the death masks of Ancient Egypt, the eyes of pharaohs were pierced in preparation for the future of shadows that had been promised to them. The same dead man in "a world that were anything other than a world". In Greek theatre, on the other hand, actors (all of them men) were converted into characters represented

2 According to Cleonice Berardinelli, this verse of 1934 is usually found in books as "Assim *sem* a máscara" ("Thus, *without* the mask") instead of "*sou* a máscara" ("I *am* the mask") due to an erroneous transcription of a manuscript attributed to Álvaro de Campos. My attempts to verify the original at Lisbon's National Library were unsuccessful.

by masks – in Greece, *prosopon;* in Rome, *persona,* person, Pessoa. It wasn't by random choice that Brazilian poet Ronald de Carvalho dedicated his book to *Fernando Pessoa, esquisito escultor de máscaras* (odd sculptor of masks), his heteronyms. Little by little, the creator and his creations become hard to tell apart. "When I wanted to take off the mask, it was stuck to my face". Robert Bréchon, one of his biographers, claims that *one can't very well take off any of his masks without ripping off his own flesh.* There were at least 127 of them, giving shape to the painful mosaic of his true face – if he even had one.

I wish to thank those friends who accompanied me in this journey. In Portugal, president Mário Soares, Ana Rita Palmeirim, António de Abreu Freire, Augusto Duarte Rozeira de Mariz, Fernando Ronto, Maria Manuela Nogueira, Rosa Dias Murteira (Pessoa's niece) and her husband (Bento José Ferreira Murteira), Luís Miguel Nogueira Rosa Dias (Pessoa's nephew), Miguel Luso Soares, Maria da Graça Borges Queiroz Ribeiro (Ophelia Queiroz's great-niece), professor Henrique Veiga de Macedo, Manuel Monteiro Grilo, Pedro de Azevedo, Barão Abel (and Zira) de Santiago; the astrologer Paulo Cardoso; journalists Duda Guennes, João Paulo Sacadura, Joaquim Vieira, José Carlos Vasconcelos, Ronald de Carvalho and Victor Moura Pinto; writers Jerónimo Pizarro, José Blanco; professor Luís Felipe Teixeira, D. Marcus Noronha da Costa, Richard Zenith, Teresa Rita Lopes, Teresa Sobral Cunha and Yvette Centeno. Also Victor Luís Eleutério, for the corrections pertaining to historical data and Lisbon's geography. To my friends at the Torre do Tombo, at Lisbon's National Library, the Casa Fernando Pessoa (especially Teresa Diniz d'Almeida), Lisbon and Porto's registry offices. In France, while tracing the steps of Sá-Carneiro, Maria Lia and Jean-Paul le Flaguais. In Brazil, due acknowledgment to professors Carlos Roberto Moraes, Francisco Trindade (Chicão), José Maria Pereira Gomes, Lúcia Figueiroa, Othon Bastos, Paulo Meireles, Pedro Arruda, Samuel Hulak, Saulo Gorenstein and Vital Lira, who helped me better understand who he was and why his end came about. For mythology, Lawrence Flores Pereira. For Latin, Francis Boyes and father Theodoro Peters. To Cleonice Berardinelli, Edson Nery da Fonseca, Eduardo Lourenço, Mário Hélio and father Daniel Lima, Pessoa experts, for the conversations. To Alberto Dines, Antônio Portela, Fábio Konder Comparato, Janio de Freitas, Joaquim Falcão, Juca Kfouri, Marcelo Tas and Marcos Vilaça, for their observations. And many, many more.

I first met Fernando Pessoa in 1966, through the voice of João Villaret. It was the beginning of a passion that, to this day, bewitches and oppresses me. I do have the feeling that I liked him even more at the time. Maybe because such is the way of passion, before it inevitably cools off; either that or, much like the river in his village, he simply belonged to very few people. Little by little, we became closer. Today, I read sentences of his as if I had been there when he penned them, and I actually feel what his reaction might have been to any given everyday fact. And I was far from the only one to whom it happened. Jorge Luis Borges, 50 years after Pessoa's death, asked: *Let me be your friend;* and Luis Ruffato recalls how it was *autumn and blue when I first introduced myself to Fernando Pessoa.* Deep down, it's as if he still were alive. I think that will always be the case in books such as this, which set out to tell the story of a life. As years went by, I came to better understand this restless man, his fragile body, the anguish of his soul, the grandiose scope of his oeuvre. In Lisbon, I got to speak to people who had met him. To touch papers written by him with my own fingers. To visit the houses he lived in. To imagine that I was seeing him write *The Keeper of Sheep* in front of the writing desk in his room. Deep down, I now realize, I wanted to feel the boundaries of his fate; and, at every step of that journey into the past, it was as if his figure were taking shape. As if, in every corner, he were escaping from the shadows, unnoticed. So much so, that I saw him at Chiado, close to the corner of the Bertrand bookshop. My friends swore it wasn't him, but what do they, poor souls, know of ghosts.

"Each of us is a speck of dust that the wind of life lifts and then lets fall". Aren't we? "Gods are friends of the hero, and take pity on the saint; but the only one they truly love is the genius"; and few indeed are those who, chosen by the gods, attain "the other thing that shines at the bottom of all longing like a *possible diamond* in a cave one cannot reach". Touched by eternity. "More alive after death than while they lived". We see them from afar, reverential, "in a vast silence like a god asleep". And, among them, undoubtedly the body, the mind, the kindling and the fire that is Fernando Pessoa.

> Lord, my step is at the Threshold
>   Of Your Door.
> Make me humble for that which I am about to bequeath…
>   Let it remain, here
> This work, which is yours and begins from me
>   And ends in You.
> The rest is just me and the worldly wilderness…
>   And that which I am to reveal.
>
> *Preface – Prayer*, Fernando Pessoa

JPCF, 13th of June, 2011

ACT I

IN WHICH HIS FIRST STEPS AND PATHS ARE RETOLD

Quomodo fabula, sic vita; non quam diu, sed quam bene acta sit, refert
(Life is like a fable; it matters not how long it is, but that it be well narrated) Seneca

PARADISE LOST

If, after I die, they should want to write my biography,
There's nothing simpler.
I've just two dates – of my birth, and of my death.
In between the one thing and the other, all the days are mine.
Detached Poems, Alberto Caeiro

Birth

"Today, a ray of light dazzled itself with clarity. I was born". Then, "as if a window had been opened, daybreak broke in". It is Wednesday, the 13th of June 1888. The ample apartment, fourth floor left[1], exhibits bourgeois luxury – incompatible with the scarce means of the family inhabiting it. Instead of windows like those of the floors below, this one has doors shielded by small iron counters. The Tagus can be seen from two of them "over a couple of low-set houses". The entrance in the form of a varnished porch and the large stairway with iron handrail give the building an aristocratic look – built in a style that to this day is called *número 4 de polícia.* Situated at the Largo de São Carlos, in front of the São Carlos National Theatre, the most opulent and elegant of its kind in Lisbon. Guests celebrate in the "shadowed dining room" between dark furniture, dressers, settees, "armchairs, drapes, carpets", china cabinets and a "sleepy clock" that decorates "the old wallpaper".

It's *three twenty in the afternoon,* according to his birth certificate[2]. But the actual time might have been another. In a letter penned in English to the editor of *British Journal of Astrology* (08/02/1918), he says: "The date of birth is close enough, and the time was hedgingly indicated as *around* 15h20. That said, a

1 In Portugal, apartments are always characterized – left, front or right – according to the stair or elevator's exit on the floor. In this case, to the left of one who is looking outside from inside the building.

2 On the 21st of June 1888, number 20, in the Basilica of Our Lady of the Martyrs. This because, ever since the Council of Trent, these records were kept at parishes, and only after the Republic (1910) did they become the purview of registry offices.

The building where Pessoa was born

couple of months ago, while reading Sepharial's *New Manual of Astrology,* I tried to apply the principles explained therein in order to obtain a more accurate indication. The number that came up pointed, rightly or wrongly, to 15h12[3] as the time of my birth. I questioned my family on the matter – exacting as the matter of minutes was for them to pinpoint – and the consensus was that I had been born a little before 15h15, which brings this exercise of estimation to a likely probability. I am rather behind on the recent developments concerning timekeeping and its recording, and so entrust you with the task of a final rectification". Portuguese astrologer Paulo Cardoso, when comparing the calculations of the Sun's transit (and its arrival at the horoscope's Mid-Heaven) with Pessoa's life, told me in rather assured terms that he had been born at 15h22. Two minutes after the official time.

3 Shortly before this (1916), after a séance, the heteronym Henry More had already pinpointed the time to "3h12 pm".

I know how to have the initial awe[4]
Which a child would have if, being born,[5]
Would notice truly it was born…
I feel born at every moment
To the eternal novelty of the world…[6]

The Keeper of Sheep, Alberto Caeiro

From the building, one has a nice overview of the entire city. "Lisbon's houses descend in steps, stopping at the edge of my emotion, and my emotion is called the Tagus". The Largo de São Carlos is all theatre, on one side; and a building, on the other. These days, the ground floor of that building hosts the Marc Jacobs store, with a panel about Pessoa (by Alexandre Paulo), and, on the remaining floors, we have a law firm. At the front, a bronze statue of Pessoa (by Belgian sculptor Jean-Michel Folon) and four trees that had been previously uprooted and replanted. Below the theatre, the square itself, sloping, with a fountain in the middle, in which I counted 35 steps from each opposite end to the other. To the right, when coming out of the building, one sees the elevated Paiva de Andrada street, accessed by a small stairway; to the left, on the side overlooking the river, is Serpa Pinto street. A number of small houses dot the space between that street and the Basilica of Our Lady of the Martyrs, so close to his room, that young little Fernando could hear the Christmas carols that churchgoers sing to this day:

Little shepherds of the desert
O baby Jesus
From the rod the staff was born
High goes the Moon

On Christmas night
Ho, festive lads
May God bid you a good evening
To those living in this house

These houses are tall, indeed
O noble house
Departed are they from the East
Alas, thus end the Holidays.[7]

4 In a first version, "I know how to *hold myself in awe*"

5 After perusing the originals, Teresa Rita Lopes holds this to be the correct wording – *would have* instead of *has,* as we see in all publications of the poem since Ática's 1946 edition.

6 In a first draft, Pessoa writes and strikes through in succession: "To the *serene, future, sudden, great, complete"* until arriving at *"eternal* novelty of the world".

7 According to a leaflet handed out during mass, "Primeira Cantata de Natal", composed by Fernando Lopes-Graça (1906-1994). The same who, coincidentally, published in *Presença* #48 (June 1936) *Uma canção de Fernando Pessoa musicada por Fernando Lopes-Graça* (*A Song*

Sitting on chairs in front of their front doors, as if there were nothing more important, neighbours chat in lively fashion. In the world of the arts, conversation topics are no longer about opera, seeing as the lyrical season of São Carlos had just ended in April. No, what is all the rage is the suicide of the lyrical singer Bastia, renowned prima donna who had great success at the local stage, and who couldn't get over having gained weight and no longer being able to play the roles meant for slimmer women; that, and the release of the newest book penned by he who is "the most striking example of Portuguese provincialism", (José Maria d') Eça de Queiroz (1845-1900). The book at the issue was *The Maias,* a *romance on the uselessness of life,* according to Casais Monteiro, and a story in which the young and wealthy Carlos Eduardo da Maia seduces Maria Eduarda, unaware that she is his sister. But, on that afternoon, the one topic that mattered was the feast of Saint Anthony all over Chiado – a neighbourhood which Eça defines (in *Prosas bárbaras)* as *the cream of the crop of dissipated grace* – but especially there, close to Largo de Camões, among those inhabitants known as hailing from the Two Churches – Loreto (*the Italians',* as it's called) and Encarnação.

Along the windows, a veritable festival of quilts and colourful towels. The streets are festooned with *vistões* (strings of small flags), bouquets of lemon balm are sold in stalls, along with little jars of basil for good luck or to give to one's sweetheart (Saint Anthony *is* the patron saint of marriage, after all), bunches of flowers *(festões)* and laurels (with box tree, lavender and bay leaves). Rosemary and myrtle burn in fires, there is dancing in the streets, balloons, and half a dozen fireworks in accordance with the revelries of the time. Children ask for *a coin for Saint Anthony*[8], and girls sing a number of songs with a refrain in common: *Saint Anthony, Saint Anthony, dear, please find me a husband of good cheer.* The following day, Lisbon's *Correio da Noite* gives note of his birth in its first page, in the section *Crónica elegante* (Elegant Chronicle).

---

by Fernando Pessoa Composed by Fernando Lopes-Graça), which was actually a poem (untitled, 15th of January 1912) and begins with the verses *Place your hands on my shoulders.../ Kiss my forehead.../ My life is rubble.*

8 This tradition dates back to 1755, the year in which Lisbon was destroyed by an earthquake, after which small altars were erected by children to ask passers-by for contributions. In time, those coins, which were initially meant to help rebuild the churches, began to remain in the children's pockets. Despite being Portugal's most popular saint, and having been born in Lisbon, Saint Anthony isn't the city's patron saint, an honour which was bestowed upon Saint Vincent, whose feast takes place on the 22nd of January. Born in Huesca, in the Pyrenees (Spain), Saint Vincent was declared the patron saint of Lisbon in the first Portuguese dynasty. Tortured by the Roman emperor Dioclecian, he nevertheless managed to keep a strange smile on his face and died smiling. His cult spread out during Muslim rule in the Iberian Peninsula. His body, found on a rudderless barge, was being guarded by two crows, which are now part of Lisbon's crest. He is also the patron saint of Bern, Charlone, Faro, Magdeburg, Milan, Saone, Zaragoza and Valencia. The kingdom of Portugal had two saints: Mary Immaculate, thus proclaimed in 1646 by John IV (The Restorer); and Saint Anthony, for whom children still ask for coins, proclaimed *Portugal's secondary patron* by Pope Pious XI, in 1934.

CORREIO DA NOITE

N.º 2:522 | **Assignatura—Paga adiantada**—Lisboa: anno, 3$600 réis: semestre, 1$800; trimestre, 900—Provincias: anno, 4$300; semestre, 2$000; trimestre, 1$000—**A correspondencia** dirigida (franca de porte) á P. de Luiz de Camões, 6, 2.º | LISBOA — Quinta-feira, 14 de junho de 1888 | **Publicações**—No corpo do jornal pagarão: na 1.ª pagina, 100 réis a linha; na 2.ª e 3.ª, 60 réis—**Annuncios**—20 réis a linha—**Numero avulso**—No dia da publicação, 10 réis; nos outros, 20 réis—**Numero telephonico, 83.** | ANNO VIII

Explicações

Não ha rasão de reparo em se haver chegado a ponto de harmonia na questão parlamentar. Podia continuar essa situação anomala e quasi indecorosa de se perderem sessões e sessões da camara electiva, sem nada se resolver, sem nada se votar, palavreando-se muito, fazendo-se discursos largos e aperfeiçoando-se o systema de obstruccionismo politico que estava sendo uma *feelle* muito usada na nossa vida parlamentar? Evidentemente não podia.

O governo tinha á sua disposição fartos recursos para resolver de maneira favoravel e airosa a pendencia que se debatia entre os mais directos representantes da soberania nacional.

Mas o presidente do conselho quiz fazer a derradeira tentativa de paz e conciliação e appellou para o patriotismo dos partidos. Não se fez um perfeito accordo politico, na significação que estas palavras recebem da historia dos partidos nos ultimos annos. Abriu-se uma tregua, breve e rapida, mas proveitosa para todos e para todos digna e honrada, tregua sem outro alcance que não seja o encerramento proximo do parlamento. Os partidos ficam no seu logar de combate. Não se tomou nenhum [...]tuguez e com o respeito que a todos devem merecer os altos serviços feitos ao paiz pela poderosa e energica intelligencia do grande luctador.

Crise ministerial em Hespanha

As ultimas noticias que nos chegam do paiz visinho declaram acceite a demissão de Martinez Campos, visto que não foi possivel resolver o general a desistir do seu proposito. A affeição pessoal de alguns dos membros do gabinete pelo iniciador da restauração dynastica e o manifesto desequilibrio de elementos politicos pela attitude do general, levaram o governo a pedir a demissão collectiva.

A regente acceitou a demissão, mas encarregou logo o sr. Sagasta da organisação do novo gabinete que certamente será constituido por elementos de conciliação liberal.

Os telegrammas que se referem a este assumpto, são os seguintes:

Madrid, 12.
O gabinete reunido em conselho acaba de acceitar a demissão do general Martinez Campos. Está pois, ao que parece, aberta a crise ministerial. Corre que ámanhã serão suspensas as sessões das côrtes, até á resolução da crise. *(Havas).*

Madrid, 13.

[...]tam communicações que lhe permittam explorar o interior e transportar para a costa os abundantes productos da sua industria agricola e do seu commercio com o gentio.

Agora que o districto de Lourenço Marques se vae transformando e accordando para a vida commercial, graças ao caminho de ferro, que lhe permitte derivar para o seu porto as correntes de riqueza que a inveja e a cubiça sangravam no interior, agora que já se reconhece a necessidade de atravessar o valle do Zambeze com uma linha ferrea, que não só attesta a nossa posse, mas affirma os propositos do governo em valorisar aquellas vastissimas regiões da Africa oriental, é justo que o governo attenda tambem na provincia de Angola ás condições em que se encontra Mossamedes, com o seu extenso e formoso planalto, onde se criam todos os fructos europeus, e onde o clima permitte todos os commodos e vantagens dos povos do meio dia da Europa.

O que falta a Mossamedes é unicamente o transporte facil para o littoral e o meio economico de estender as relações commerciaes com o interior. E' esse o grande beneficio que a linha agora proposta para estudos, poderá realisar.

[...]sequencia das doenças da sua gente e da escassez de viveres; o major Barteloit enviou um mensageiro á costa para pedir novas instrucções a Londres. *(Havas).*

"ESTIMAREI"
Sociedade secreta no Porto

A policia d'aquella cidade principiou a levantar um auto de investigação ácerca d'uma sociedade secreta que tinha suas parecenças com a quadrilha dos Terriveis, do celebre Sonriano.

Já foram interrogados alguns dos socios, e outras pessoas.

A sociedade tinha adoptado a divisa *Estimarei*, que ultimamente começou a apparecer pelas paredes das casas e pelos muros do Porto, escripta a giz ou a carvão.

Os dizeres do diploma eram os seguintes:

«O ex.mo sr. . . . é approvado e nomeado socio activo e gosará de todas as garantias estipuladas nos estatutos, ficando sujeito igualmente aos deveres que são inherentes a esta nomeação. (a) Presidente. (a) Vice-presidente. (a) Secretario».

Estes diplomas eram encimados por um balão, em cujo bojo se lia a palavra *Estimarei*.

Eis algumas informações que colhemos nos jornaes do Porto:

A Sociedade do *Estimarei* tem cerca de quatro annos de existencia, e é composta de mais de cincoenta membros, alguns bastantes conhecidos.

Os estatutos marcavam, como fins d'esta associação secreta: as patus[...]

CHRONICA ELEGANTE

Fazem annos ámanhã:

As ex.mas sr.as:

D. Aurora C. dos Santos.
D. Anna Margarida de Espregueira.
D. Maria Rosa de Jesus Vaz de Carvalho (Monção).

E os srs.:

Anselmo Sousa Mattos (Almeirim).
Antonio Affonso Velloso (Freixo).
Conde da Azenha.
Caetano Beirão.
Ignacio Augusto de Vadre e Mello (Andaluz).
João Lobo da Silveira Guedes Pacheco (Alvito).
João Gomes da Silva.
Sebastião Perestrello de Vasconcellos.
Vicente Affonso.
Visconde do Desterro.

Faz hoje annos o nosso amigo sr. João Nunes Ribeiro Montanha.

Regressaram de Madrid os srs. Miguel Queriol, dr. Nuno Porto e sua ex.ma esposa.

A ex.ma esposa do nosso amigo e collega do *Diario de Noticias*, Joaquim Pessoa, deu hontem á luz um menino.

Os nossos parabens.

O sr. visconde de Nazareth parte brevemente com sua familia para as Caldas da Rainha.

[...]defeza de Moraes e da de Vaquairo, o sr. Vicente Gonçalves.

Tanto a defeza como a accusação prescindiram das que faltaram.

Finda a chamada, o sr. dr. Carvalho Teixeira apresentou em juizo uns documentos de defeza dos reus; em seguida passou-se á lista do jury que ficou constituido da seguinte fórma:

Jurados

Augusto Joviano Candido da Piedade, amanuense do tribunal de contas.
—Arthur da Fonseca, commerciante e proprietario.
—Antonio Costa Aureu, proprietario.
—Antonio Henrique Galhardo Quadros, empregado no banco hypothecario.
—André Meyrelles de Tavora Canto e Castro, proprietario.
—Gaspar Candido da Graça Correia Fino, empregado no ministerio das obras publicas.
—João Pereira Rangel, empregado publico.
—Manuel Thiago Henriques Delgado, professor de latim.
—José Dias Silva, padeiro.
—José Clemente Faria, empregado no Asylo de mendicidade.

Pela accusação foram recusados os srs. José Joaquim de Freitas, José das Neves e Antonio Vicente da Costa.

Pessoa's birth in the news

Pessoa's village

"From my village I see as much of the universe as can be seen from the Earth". The "village" being Lisbon, of course. But not quite Lisbon, as, at the age of 7, Pessoa moves to Africa and will only return when he is 17, all but a grown man for the standards at the time, "as much a stranger here as everywhere else". He studies with his mother, because, at the time, children didn't go to school before the age of 7 or 8. And he plays around the building. His horizons are narrow and close in scope. The world he knows is that little space he has at hand. "The village I was born in was the Largo de São Carlos" – he confesses in a letter to João Gaspar Simões (11/12/1931). *Ah, yes! He would say that all the time, and also that the Largo de São Carlos was the village he had been born in* – according to Teca, his sister Henriqueta Madalena. Journalist and writer Luís de Oliveira Guimarães (1900-1980) confirms: *When I first met him, I asked "Where were you born?". To which he replied: "I was born in a village with an opera house. A village called São Carlos".* It was to be his first homeland, painfully abandoned. "I love those solitary squares that intersperse streets with little traffic". From there, "one may ponder infinity. An infinity with warehouses below, granted, but with stars at the end". The image of one such square, as if it were "a clearing at a village", will forever be treasured by the child.

O church bell of my village,
Each of your plaintive tolls
Filling the calm evening[9]
Rings inside my soul.

And your ringing is so slow,
So as if life made you sad,[10]
That already your first clang
Seems like a repeated sound.

However closely you touch me
When I pass by, always drifting,[11]
You are to me like a dream –
In my soul your ringing is distant.[12]

With every one of your clangs
Resounding across the sky,
I feel the past farther away,
I feel nostalgia close by.

Untitled (1911),[13] Fernando Pessoa

That bell lay far away from the hinterland town he dreamed of ending his days in. "The bell of my village, Gaspar Simões, is that of the Basilica of Our Lady of the Martyrs, in Chiado" (letter from 11/12/1931). From the side windows of his apartment, one could see its belfry — two bells on one side, one larger than the other; above them, a small globe, a palm tree and a black iron cross; plus a smaller bell to the side, set apart from the others. The narrow Serpa Pinto street is the only thing separating him from "the old alcove of my lost childhood". In those days, while in his room, he could almost feel the bells physically as they toll, even if only memories remain.

Ring, bells, ring - ring out clear!
Perhaps by the vague sentiment that you raise -
I know not why - you remind me of my infancy.
Ring, bells, ring! Your soul is a tear.
What does it matter? My childhood's glee -
You cannot call it back to me.

The Bells, Alexander Search

9 In a first version, "*slowly ringing* in the calm evening"

10 According to experts on Pessoa, in this verse, there would be an ellipse of the word "slow" of the previous verse; the intended meaning would thus be *slow and sad with life.*

11 In a first version, "You do not sound to me like a monk", and then "When I pass by, *sad and* drifting".

12 In a first version, "your ringing is *ever* distant".

13 The poem Pessoa sometimes refers to as "The Villager" had a first draft dated 8th of April 1911. The definitive version was published in 1914, in the *Renascença* magazine.

Although his mother wasn't religious, he was baptised in that church (21/07/1888) by monsignor António Ribeiro dos Santos Veiga. His godparents were his aunt Anica, Ana Luísa Xavier Pinheiro Nogueira (married to agronomist João Nogueira de Freitas), his mother's only remaining sibling – her brother, António Xavier Pinheiro Nogueira, died single (in 1883) at the age of 19; and a relative, army general Cláudio Bernardo Pereira de Chaby – who fought at the Little Civil War, was a member of the Lisbon Academy of Science and was the uncle of the great actor Chaby Pinheiro, the fattest in Portugal's history. Pessoa would later write to the church's prior, complaining that baptism was carried out at such an early age and claiming that "baptism implies the victim's integration in the Catholic Church". Probably because he felt he had been unduly compelled, as his paternal ancestors were Jewish. In his diary, in an entry dated the 26th of May 1906, he says "I have started writing the letter". A draft of 1907, with the prior as recipient, is classified as *letters sent or to be sent* with the stamp of the heteronym C.R. Anon. Later, he would confess to having been born at a time "in which most of our youth had lost the faith in God, for the same reason that their elders had had it without quite knowing why". He would keep his distance from Catholicism, although he felt Christ's presence as his last hour drew near, as one can see in this poem honouring the Lamb of God:

> The King speaks, and a gesture of his fills all,
> The sound of his voice transmutes all.
> My dead King is more than just majestic:
> He speaks the Truth with his mum mouth;
> His tied hands are Freedom.
>
> *Untitled* (1935), Fernando Pessoa

Portugal

The country, with its 5 million inhabitants, had a foreign debt to the tune of 20 thousand contos de réis. The economy lies in shambles. Despite the paucity of the public coffers, the government acquires the manuscripts of the House of Pombal – despite them having no mention of the war waged against the Jesuits, who had been banned from the country since the 3rd of September 1759. Minister Joaquim Augusto de Aguiar had issued a decree on the 19th of December 1834, that all religious orders were to be extinguished, an act which earned him the cognomen of *friar-killer.* Now, with the country plunged in a deep moral crisis, the Society of Jesus makes another foray into Portugal. But the hate directed at Jesuits and nuns still burns strong, and a national campaign aims to prevent the sisters hospitallers from returning to the country. In 1888, kings seem to be an endangered species all over Europe. Germany has just lost two of its emperors. Brazil's has taken ill. Umberto II of Italy seriously so.

Leo XIII would soon meet the God he had always dreamed of. Few are those still unaware that the Republic's red is now staining the white and blue of the flag of the dying monarchy in Portugal. That year, the royal family travels to Marseille, fleeing the searing heat of Summer. The queen heads to Paris to make the dress in which she is to witness the wedding of her brother, Amadeu, duke of Aosta, with princess Laetitia. Prince Pedro Augusto decides to marry princess Joséphine, niece of the king of Belgium. Among the many reasons for his choice was the fact that his Belgian cousin was willing to take on the wedding expenses. Newspapers speak of the treasury's depleted coffers, of a ruinous comedy of grandeur and the old king's flatulence.

The long and paternal reign of Luís I (The Popular), who had been sitting on the throne since 1861, is on its death rattle. In the streets, the people sing *La Marseillaise.* In another year, in 1889, so would the Brazilians, in the first month of the Republic. In Europe, following a unique logic of power, the decision is made to split the African continent with no regard to the territories Portugal still held there. In London, *The Times* announces that Morocco will be handed over to Spain, Tripoli to Italy, the oasis of Figuig and an area above Niger to France. Great Britain would get Egypt and the bay of Lourenço Marques, with no compensation to be paid, plus the consolidation of British territories in the gulf of Guinea. In exchange, it would cede the Wahlfish Bay to Germany, which would also retain the area of Lagos. The British ultimatum still held further humiliation for Portugal, which later on (11/01/1890) would lose some more of its African possessions. Corruption festers in every layer of society. The sudden and mysterious enrichment of minister Emígdio Navarro in less than two years is rather puzzling. His expensive chalet at Luso could be evidence of commissions handed to him due to the work done at Lisbon's harbour. Manuel Pinheiro Chagas, writer and member of the Regenerator Party, is assaulted with an iron cane by an anarchist, right at the entrance to the Parliament. The country undergoes a series of popular uprisings. The monarchy is in its death throes.

Lisbon

For many, the Romans' *Felicitas Julia* is still Lisbon, *queen of cities*, as Camões had dreamed in *The Lusiads* (Canto III); whereas, for Pessoa, it was "the one Portuguese city one can consider *grand* without eliciting laughter with such an adjective", an "eternal truth, empty and perfect"[14]. Unlike the rest of the country,

14 Not all heaped such praise on it. In *A formosa lusitânia,* Catharina Carlota Lady Jackson has the following to say about the city: *One can compare the Tagus to a pretty tulle veil covering the face of an ugly woman. Lisbon is a disappointment. There are no monuments here, no grandeur, no civilization, no society. Words of popular novelist Camilo Castelo Branco, in a recent novel of his.* As it so happened, Castelo Branco had been hired to make the Portuguese version of that book, and remarked in a footnote that: *With all due respect for the illustrious foreign lady's*

it is experiencing undeniable progress. Rossio was finished in 1870, with the old D. Pedro IV[15] square as foundation. The city, which, in 1864, had 200 thousand inhabitants, now boasts an extra 100 thousand – 330.964, according to the official census of 1890. In 1865, regular shipping lanes to Porto are inaugurated. It is now also possible to travel in animal-drawn public transportation between nearby Sintra and Colares. In 1888, carts with barrels of water are no longer sufficient to wash the rubble of so many public works. The Portuguese Company of Public Lifts draws up a project for a lift that goes up from the Mouraria to the Costa do Castelo. The Palace of Calhariz burns down, and the government gives up the notion of installing the Justice Department there. In the name of progress, a transportation monopoly is consolidated, at the expense of smaller transportation companies. The construction of the Campo Pequeno plaza begins, a space meant for bullfighting (inaugurated in 18/08/1892). Construction engineer Henrique de Lima e Cunha proposes the construction of an underground railway system which would eventually become Lisbon's subway (and which only became a reality in 29/12/1959). The Lisbon Shopkeepers' Commercial Association wants shops closed on Sundays.

Habits change. Now, carnival is celebrated with battles of flowers and squirt guns – much like at the Bois de Boulogne or the Jardin des Tuleries. Women's hats imitate those worn in Paris. Life is a calm affair, consisting of waking up late, taking a nap, badmouthing others and going to bed early. Men wear gaiters and take their hats off whenever they come across wives and mothers, who get the honorific of *dona;* or women of easy virtue, affectionately referred to as *perdidas* (lost). In the streets, misery and luxury mingle. To the poet's eyes, Lisbon would ever be two cities: One real on the outside, where it survives laboriously; the other delirious on the inside, in which its tormented soul is consumed.

> Lisbon and its houses,
> Multicoloured
> (…)
> I wish to broaden my sight with that what I imagine
> Across fantastical palm forests,
> But there is no more to be seen.
> (…)
> Without me, it is lonely, as I forget when I sleep
> Lisbon and its houses,
> Multicoloured.
>
> *Untitled* (11/05/1934), Álvaro de Campos

---

words, the translator declares he has no recollection of having written the sentences to him attributed by her, and perfectly recalls not having written them. Castelo Branco died, blind, in São Miguel de Seide, with actress Ana Plácido by his side.

15 Emperor Pedro I, in Brazil.

São Carlos Theatre

São Carlos Theatre

The São Carlos "is at my feet". This theatre was opened on the 30th of June, 1793, with Cimarosa's *La ballerina amante,* at a time in which women weren't allowed on Portuguese stages, and their roles were played by men with high-pitched voices. Thus it was until 1800, when the prohibition was revoked by Maria I (The Mad Queen) – described by historian Rocha Martins as *dishevelled, pale, cognizant of the sin she lived in, and seeing but figures out of hell all around her.* In that theatre, Pessoa would later on watch shows on his feet, as was the wont of those who paid cheaper tickets. Three arches guard the entrance, with two other side doors (which had originally been meant as windows) and a gaslit façade – the city would only have public illumination in 1902, by the hand of the United Gas and Electricity Companies (which would take another two years to timidly reach the houses). On the first floor, in perfect symmetry with the ground floor, three doors lead to a small terrace with two windows on each side. On the second, two other windows and a clock – "the clock strikes, today is gone"[16]. Up above, the royal crest and an inscription in Latin, which pays homage to the one who gave the theatre its name (abridged):

16 A bit of wordplay with the homonym "strike" by heteronym Alexander Search, ambiguously conveying the notion that the clock struck today and forced it to leave.

To Carlota, princess of Brazil by virtue of her royal progeny, dedicated by Lisbon's citizens in their solicitous love and lasting loyalty to the august house. Year of 1793.

"Carlota" is, naturally, Carlota Joaquina Teresa Cayetana de Borbon y Borbon[17], promised at the age of ten to João VI (The Merciful), third son of Maria I. What none could have foreseen was that, later on, that Spanish nymphomaniac from Aranjuez would cheat on her husband with pretty much every mulatto in Rio de Janeiro when, in 1808, the royal family came to visit this land she so hated. *How awful; I'd rather Luanda, Mozambique or Timor,* were her words upon arrival. As punishment, Brazil's tropical heat left her rough face pockmarked and, according to some versions, facial hair. *When searching for lovers, she would pay their appearance no real heed. Anyone would do, provided their shape was reasonably similar to that of a man* – as per the words of her contemporary, historian Luiz Edmundo. *She was almost horrific, dwarfish, bony and miserable,* according to Octávio Tarquínio de Souza. On the 25th of April 1821, she would return to Lisbon with her husband and nine children (only five of which legitimate), she hit one shoe against the other and said: *I'll bring none of Brazil's memories with me, not even in my shoes.* She left and took with her a good part of the royal treasure, more than 50 million cruzados withdrawn from the Bank of Brazil – which she all but bankrupted. To compound her misery – perhaps as punishment – she did not have a happy ending, for, having dreamed of being queen of Spain, regent of River Plate or empress of Spanish America, she would live out the rest of her days as an exile at the Palace of Queluz. *The Shrew of Queluz,* as she was known. And ended up committing suicide. To the chagrin of her unfortunate husband, who had passed away four years earlier (fat, suffering from varicose veins, haemorrhoids and unceasing headaches), she was buried next to him at the monastery of São Vicente de Fora. But that particular story was never of any interest to young Pessoa, who saw the theatre as merely his "backyard". Which is why he treasures "the childhood memory of a theatre in which the blue lunar scenery represented the terrace of an impossible palace". Much farther away, there was the dream and "the old quiet house, close to the river". Time passes by, and the scenery doesn't change. The theatre carries out its role as such. The Tagus remains the same. Only the man will be different.

17 The homage is justified, even if it hadn't been inaugurated on her birthday, since, according to Iberian tradition, everyone celebrates two dates: The anniversary *(cumpleaños)* and the saint's day *(el día del santo).* Even when there's no exact correspondence – such as, in the absence of a female saint with the honouree's name, a male one will do just as well. And one of Carlota's dates happened to coincide with the day which pays homage to Saint Charles Borromeo – who, unlike that tawdry lady, had *humilitas* (humility) as his motto.

Origins of the name

The firstborn's birth always holds special meaning for a religious family. Especially when it takes place during the feast day of the place of birth's saint. This one would be no different. The mother decides to pay homage to a distant relative, one Teresa Taveira Martins de Bulhões. But Fernando – the name of the lady's son – according to old Iberian superstition, was a designation for an acolyte of the Devil; which was why, upon being ordained Franciscan in Coimbra (1220), the son of *dona* Teresa renounced such primitive name and adopts the name of António, from the Latin *Antius* (he who is at the forefront). Born on the 15th of August 1195 (or perhaps even earlier), he lived a pure life and died in his sleep. Naked, as was his wont, in spite of the cold. On the 13th of June (1231), much like the day Pessoa would be brought to the world, he utters his final words: *I can see my Lord;* and children scream in the streets: *The saint is dead, the saint is dead*[18]. The deceased was Saint Anthony, who would become Lisbon's (where he had been born) and also Padua's (where he died, in the hermitage of the commune of Camposampiero). Canonized by pope Gregory IX, on the 30th of March, 1232, he ended up quartered in the interests of the faith: His left forearm and jaw were sent to a village near Marseille, while his body remained in the crypt of a reliquary close to Padua, keeping tongue and teeth (none of which had cavities).

Anthony is also known as the *Fighting Saint,* due to the episode in which he faced demons who were biting, goring and clawing at his body, until a flash of light sent them scurrying away. Recognizing Christ, he said: *Why weren't you here to avail me when this began?* And the Lord spake: *I was here, watching you fight. As you availed yourself well, I shall make your name famous.* For being a *fighter,* his miraculous flag is said to have rallied Portuguese troops to victory in the Restoration war against the Spaniards of the marquis of Caracena. Later, *for such patriotic service,* he was anointed brigade captain by Pedro II (The Peaceful)[19] – 437 years after his death. And entitled to a salary, which was religiously paid to the Franciscan order[20]. Pessoa reveres him, and always carries an engraving of the saint in his pocket – radiating silver from the head,

18 His feast takes place on this day because Catholic tradition celebrates mainly the days their saints and martyrs die in, with the sole exception of John the Baptist.

19 The Portuguese Pedro II, obviously, seeing as the Brazilian Pedro II, son of the Brazilian Pedro I and the archduchess Maria Leopoldina, was never king of Portugal.

20 With no separation between church and state in Portugal, it was commonplace for the court to name a military saint for religious orders. In Brazil, Saint Anthony is the perpetual councilman of Igarassu (Pernambuco), thus named by José I on the 23rd of November, 1754, and his salary is paid to this day by the Chamber of Councilmen (who currently seek to do away with the obligation), and attained the rank of soldier at Paraíba and Espírito Santo, of captain at Bahia, Goiás, Minas and Rio, colonel at São Paulo, and general of the Brazilian army, in 1890, by the direct order of marshal Deodoro da Fonseca, first president of the republic, and was then assigned to paid reserve. There are 71 cities in Brazil with Saint Anthony's name.

and with Baby Jesus with a sceptre and a royal crown in his left arm. "A Saint Anthony irrevocably conceived as an infantile teenager".

In his last days, Pessoa sought for similarities with the saint, such as the fact that the number 7, sacred in its own right, is the result of casting out nines from their respective births – the saint's 1195 (as was then thought) and Pessoa's 1888. 7 was also the sum of the year of the saint's death, 1231 (no argument here), but not the poet's, 1935 – but, at the time, that could not be known. Both also shared the importance of tropical storms in their lives. Horror and suffering for Pessoa, a design from heaven for the saint. The latter travelled to Moorish Africa in 1220, aiming to be martyred – anticipating the saga Sebastião I would carry out three centuries later. In Morocco, he preaches to the Saracens and falls seriously ill. Returning to Coimbra, he is nursed back to health, and, on account of said storms, he would end up in Sicily, which he takes as a sign and then decides to dedicate the rest of his life to that new land God had taken him to. Despite all these similarities, deep inside, Pessoa feels different that the other Anthony blessed by God. "Amongst the *saints*, who are the truly great *men of action*, for they act with all their emotions, not just some of them, this sense of the nothingness of life leads to the infinite. They garland themselves in night and stars, anoint themselves with silence and solitude". Whereas "amongst the great men of inaction, to whose ranks I humbly belong, the same feeling leads to the infinitesimal; feelings are pulled taut, like elastic bands, the better to observe the pores of their false, flabby continuity. At such moments, both types of men long for sleep". Except the saint's pure dreams are quite different from the dark nightmares that assail the poet's sleepless nights.

On his mother's passport (dated 07/01/1986), which was issued for her trip to Durban, we can find the note *accompanied by her 7 year-old son, Fernando;* his birth certificate also simply says Fernando. Fernando Nogueira Pessoa can only be read on his identity card (number 289.594, issued on the 28th of August 1928, at the age of 40); on a letter to the minister of Trade and Communication, in which he required the patent of a different kind of yearbook (16/10/1925); and in an application with which he applied for the job of curator for the Museum of Cascais (15/09/1932). Fernando, in honour of the saint's certificate of baptism; Nogueira, from his mother's side; and Pessoa, from his father's, "a noble surname which came from Germany to Portugal, but it is not known by whom".

Two surnames pointing to Sephardic[21] descent. But, for his family, he would always be both Fernando and António. Much like many other Antónios who were also born on that day. António, the name the other Fernando (de Bulhões)

21 Sephardic Jews hail from Portugal and Spain (known in the Iberian Peninsula as *"Sefaradim"*, from the Hebrew *Sefarad),* and then spread throughout the Mediterranean, Northern Africa, the Middle East, Brazil and Mexico. They had their own Hispanic language, *ladino.* Different from the Ashkenazim, which hailed from Germany and Central Europe, who speak the medieval dialect Yiddish, that to this day is spoken by over a million people.

– the one whose name had been paid homage to – had also taken. Thus, we have Fernando António Nogueira Pessôa on the Queen Victoria Memorial Prize, on his diploma of the University of the Cape of Good Hope, on a "biographical note" written by him, on the funeral notice provided by the funeral home Funerária Barata, on the death certificate of the 7th registry office of the parish of Mártires, and in each and every publication in which his full name is credited. Pessoa himself says so quite clearly: "I am my friend Fernando António Nogueira Pessoa". But, in the realm of literature, he'd end up being just Fernando Pessoa. His middle names were dropped, as was his "surname's caret", so he'd "disadapt from that which is useless, which adversely affects my name on a cosmopolitan level" – for him, a decision which would entail "a great change in my life". The last letter he signs with a caret on "Pessôa" was penned on the 4th of May 1916, and the first he does so without it dates from the 4th of September 1916, in which he claims to be "rebuilding" himself – both written to Côrtes-Rodrigues. Perhaps to be recognized as an English writer, as English names tend not to have accents. Thus, Fernando Pessoa.

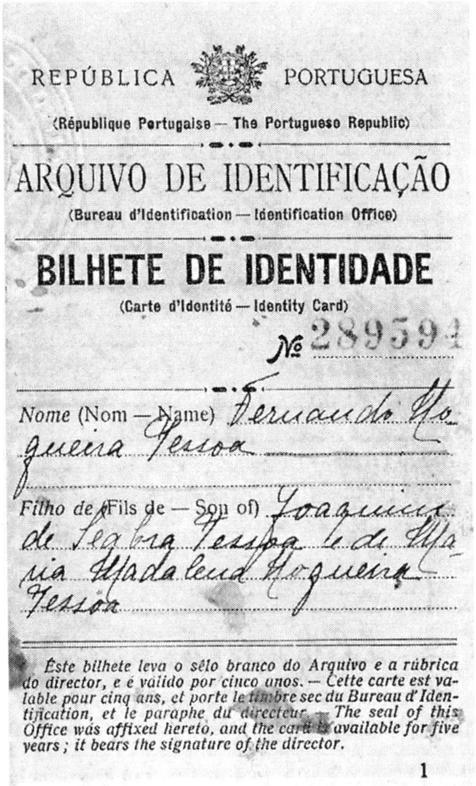
REPÚBLICA PORTUGUESA
(République Portugaise — The Portuguese Republic)

ARQUIVO DE IDENTIFICAÇÃO
(Bureau d'Identification — Identification Office)

BILHETE DE IDENTIDADE
(Carte d'Identité — Identity Card)

№ 289594

Nome (Nom — Name) Fernando Nogueira Pessoa

Filho de (Fils de — Son of) Joaquim de Seabra Pessôa e de Maria Madalena Nogueira Pessôa

Êste bilhete leva o sêlo branco do Arquivo e a rúbrica do director, e é válido por cinco anos. — Cette carte est valable pour cinq ans, et porte le timbre sec du Bureau d'Identification, et le paraphe du directeur. — The seal of this Office was affixed hereto, and the card is available for five years; it bears the signature of the director.

1

Identification

His father

Joaquim de Seabra Pessôa was born on the 28th of May 1850, in the parish of Santa Maria Maior de Lisboa. Son of Dionísia Rosa Estrela de Seabra Pessôa (1823-1907), from Santa Engrácia, Lisbon; and general Joaquim António de Araújo Pessôa (1813-1885), from Santa Maria, Tavira (Algarve) – a liberal opponent of the supporters of Miguel I (the Absolutist) in the 19th century's civil war, decorated for bravery with honours such as the badge of the Tower and the Sword[22]. Both shared Galician descent. The father spoke and wrote fluent French and Italian, but had no degree to speak of. Upon baptising his son as Fernando, he defined himself as a *civil servant.* A modest servant, he was deputy head of the Accounting Department (having attained the role of first officer upon his death) of the Secretariat of Ecclesiastical Affairs and Justice, today the Department of Justice. He works nights since the age of 18 at the board of *Diário de Notícias,* at the time, the most widely read in Lisbon[23]. He even wrote small and unpretentious music reviews, all of them unsigned, and almost all of them based on whatever was playing at the nearby theatre. He left behind 16 books with clippings of those reviews – from 1875 to 1892, when he could no longer write – and actually published a pamphlet on Wagner's *The Flying Dutchman.* He left Pessoa early, but would be a constant presence in his heart. "Of my father, I know but his name, they told me he was called God".

His mother

Maria Magdalena Pinheiro Nogueira was born on the 30th of December 1861, at the feet of Monte Brasil, in the parish of Sé, at Angra do Heroísmo, Azores[24]; and would take the surname Pessôa upon marrying her husband at the Basilica of Our Lady of the Martyrs, on the 5th of September 1887. Her family claimed noble descent of the Azorean isles of Terceira and São Miguel, and had influential friends, such as the poet Tomás (António) Ribeiro (Ferreira), who would become Porto's councilman; or he who would become the first president

22 His family took great pride in his feats, such as having taken part in the pursuit of "Remexido", the nom de guerre of José Joaquim de Souza Reis, a famed guerilla fighter and supporter of Miguel I in the Algarve, who was killed on the 2nd of August 1839.

23 Almost none of the newspapers, magazines, schools, coffee shops and libraries of Pessoa's time still exist today. Those cases will be duly pointed out in this book, such as *Diário de Notícias,* which still operates at Avenida da Liberdade, 266, in Lisbon.

24 From the Portuguese *açor* (goshawk), a hawklike bird of prey. But the origin of the name of the nine isles (which form the archipelago) lies not in the bird, as explained by António Cordeiro in 1789, but rather in the name given them by Mediterranean peoples, who knew the isles as *Azzurri* (blue), due to the waters' colour. Thus, *Azor, Açores,* the Blue Isles. The name "Terceira" is owed to the fact that the isle in question was the third to be settled (after Santa Maria and São Miguel) by the Fleming Jacob van Brugge.

Pessoa's mother and father

of the Portuguese Republic, Manuel de Arriaga. Her father, Luís António Nogueira (1832-1884), born in Angra do Heroísmo and with a Law degree from Coimbra, came to the continent upon being named secretary-general of Porto's Treasury Department (in 1864), and came to Lisbon right after to occupy the role of director-general of the Civil and Political Administration of the Kingdom's Ministry. At home, Dr. Luís would often play the roles of several characters and their mannerisms, a theatrical proclivity he would bequeath the grandson he never got to know. Maria's Mother, Magdalena Amália Xavier Pinheiro (1836-1898), from Matriz, Velas, provided her daughter with a dapper British education at Miss Calf's British college, at the Rua do Alecrim. The epitome of a cultured woman of the *belle époque,* her daughter reads, writes verses, plays the piano, knows Latin and speaks fluent French, as well as English, which is taught to her by master Júlio Joubert Chaves, preceptor of princes Afonso and Carlos – the latter would become king, on the 28th of December, 1889. She is *of the home,* as expected of wives hailing from good families. But so gifted and educated, that her family sometimes laments the fact she wasn't born a boy. "The mother is stronger in us than the father".

His grandmother Dionísia

The mad grandmother, in the middle, and Pessoa's aunts

With the parents, of whom he always claims to be the "legitimate son", lives his paternal grandmother – in the eyes of Joaquim Pessoa, a *silly and demented* lady. It is the dear, mad and toothless grandmother Dionísia[25], 64 years old at the time of Pessoa's birth.

In pictures when she was young, what we see is a lady with a placid, sad look on her face; in the later ones, an old lady with undeniable signs of dementia. On the 3rd of May 1895, she would be admitted for the first time at the Rilhafoles[26] mental hospital. She would return to the family home on 14 June, but, at the request of her daughter, she went back to medical care on September 3, and would thenceforth alternate between the hospital and home – at first with

25 The name came from another grandmother, Dionísia Maria Rita Oliveira de Seabra, daughter of nobleman João de Oliveira Delgado.

26 The origins of the name lie in the 17th century, at a time in which a legion of tinkers plied their trade there in tinplate. The bellows used to keep the furnace's embers aglow produced a grinding (*rilhado,* in Portuguese) sound which was as characteristic as it was unpleasant, and the constant grinding of bellows *(rilhar de foles)* ended up giving the place its name of *Rilhafoles.*

Pessoa's mother, then with her aunts. Dionísia suffered from *alternating madness,* talking to herself while sitting in corners and indulging in obscene speeches – so often, that she sometimes has to be locked in her room. To say nothing of her seething, indiscriminating hatred for all children. All, except for little Fernando, for reasons that have yet to be disclosed. Two maids, Joana and Emília, live in the house and care for the child, which they get attached to. "It reminds me of my old maid telling me fairy tales", "tell me tales, maid…"

> So much I've loved…
> Today, nothing remains.
> Sing to me, my maid,
> Here next to my bed
> A sad song.
> (…)
> Sing it in my ear
> And I shall fall asleep…
>
> *Untitled* (04/11/1914), Fernando Pessoa

His father's death

Pessoa's father had tuberculosis from an early age – the same illness that had already fatally befallen José, his only brother. Afraid to infect his family, and in search of nature and fresh air[27], on the 19th of May 1893, he goes to the hot springs at Caneças, in the outskirts of Lisbon. But, for all the good weather and the massive dosages of quinine and arsenic, everyone can see he's a corpse in the making. *He was coughing his lungs right out of his mouth,* in the words of Gaspar Simões. Dr. João Gregório Korth, a friend of *dona* Maria's family in the Azores, wants to ensure he lives out his final days in comfort and offers him a stay in his farm at Telheiras – at the time, a small rural village between Campo Grande and Lumiar. Joaquim Pessoa heads there with a handmaid and Madalena, his mother-in-law. His wife remains in Lisbon with his son, *Fernandinho* (as she likes to call him), as the family wants to prevent him from coming into contact with the illness. Thus, the child is surrounded by women – mother, grandmother, maids and the sisters of Pessoa's maternal grandmother (Rita, Maria, Adelaide and Carolina). There is also his father's second cousin, Lisbela da Cruz Pessoa, childless, who inherited the surname Tavares Machado from her husband – the dear and caring aunt Lisbela, who

27 At the time, it was standard practice. Pernambucan poet Manuel (Carneiro de Sousa Bandeira (Filho, 1886-1968), for example, tried a cure at Clavadel, Switzerland (1913), returning the next year to flee the war and because he was disabused of the notion. He ended up cured after his stays at Quixeramobim (Ceará), Pouso Alto (Minas) and Teresópolis (Rio).

came from her village near Tavira to help the household. Wife and son will only visit the ailing father a few times. He writes her simple letters which always begin with *my dear Maria* and end with *so long.* Maria keeps them rolled up with a blue ribbon over a note – *letters to give to Fernando when the time comes to entrust them to him.*

Letters from Pessoa's father

The poet will keep those letters all his life, as if they were relics. But neither his father nor his absence would last much longer, as, despite all the care he was subjected to, the disease progresses. Such is his weakened state, that he can't even attend his son's 5th birthday.

> In the days when they used to celebrate my birthday,
> I was happy and no one was dead[28].
> (…)
> When I came to have hopes, I no longer knew how to have hopes.
> When I came to look at life, I'd lost the sense of life.
> (…)
> What I am today is they've sold the house[29],

---

28 *No one,* because, at the time of that particular birthday (13/06/1893), his parents, three brothers, two grandmothers, his uncle, the two great-aunts who were closest to him and a good number of friends were all still alive.

29 Here but a metaphor, as none of the houses Pessoa lived in were ever sold, by him or his family, since they were all rented.

And all of them are dead.
What I am today is outliving myself like a cold match…
(…)
Stop, my heart!
Don't think! Leave thinking to the brain!
O my God, my God, my God!
Today I don't have birthdays.
I last.
The days add themselves to me.
I'll be old when I get there.
Nothing else.
(…)

Birthday[30], Álvaro de Campos

His father would return to Lisbon on the 12th of June 1893, having already abandoned all hope, and would die the next day, at 5am, at "the dawn of that sad hope". *Without sacraments,* according to the death certificate. He was only 43. Just like the magical numbers of Saint Anthony, 4 plus 3 equals 7. "Today, morning came, and I am sad. The child went silent". For Eduardo Lourenço, *Fernando Pessoa's spiritual and carnal adventure boils down to the endless search for his father,* this despite him being a figure *that doesn't even appear in his oeuvre.* Thus, like a dark cloud that comes when least expected, "suddenly, I am alone in the world". Him and his mother. *Dona* Maria, following the rules of proper mourning, does without her lace chokers, grosgrain silk dresses and fashionable bonnets, and wears only crepes and black. The following month, she pays tribute to her husband in verse:

Sad and alone! Two words
That contain such bitterness
To be alone and feel in one's soul
The cold of the grave.
(…)
Sad and alone! Two words
That summarize but one – longing!
To know how big the world is,
Is to not see its vastness.

30 The poem's originals contain a false date – the 15th of October 1929. Pessoa himself explains, in a letter to Gaspar Simões (04/07/1930): "I wrote those verses on my birthday (my own), which is to say on June 13; but Álvaro [de Campos] was born on October 15, and so I erred on the side of accuracy". It was published in *Presença* #27, dated June/July 1930.

His childhood

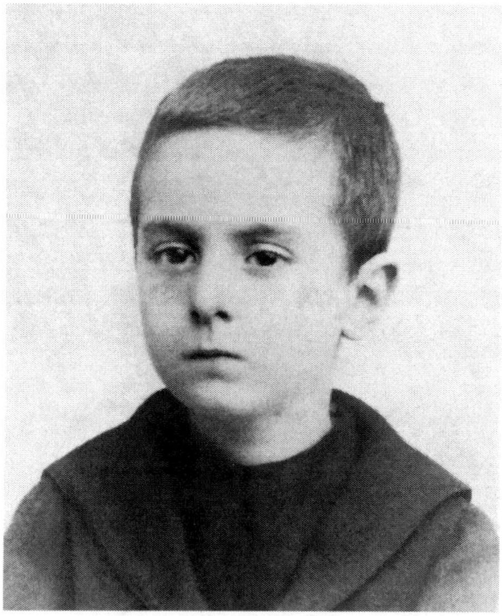

Pessoa at the age of 7

Despite that tragedy, he has "a serene childhood". And a lonely one, too. "It is not – no – the longing for my childhood that which I don't miss: It's the longing for the emotion of that particular moment". *Horret animus meminisse* (the soul trembles to recount), quoth Virgil. During those times, he played with a rubber ball which "rolls through the precipice of my interrupted dreams", a yellow jockey, a blue horse "that appears over the wall", tin soldiers, brass and paper ships. He "would love to see once again only wooden ships and sailing vessels"; even knowing that "we will never again have those hours, or that garden, or our soldiers and our ships". There is no record of him having had any friends during that time. Someone his age he could talk to or play with. To face loneliness, "my biggest dream was to have a dog". All he gets is a wooden one. Green. For other children, that might have been scant reward, but, for him, "all toys become living things and form a parade: Horses and soldiers and dolls". Just as if he had written it. "God created me to be a child, and a child I remained forevermore. But why did he let Life beat me and take my toys away, and leave me all alone?"

In a later annotation in French, he had the following to say of himself, as if speaking of someone else: "At the age of 7, he evidences a rather reserved demeanour, not at all childlike. He likes to play on his own. To those traits must be added plenty of angry urges, bordering on hate, and much fear". Thus, "tears well up in my eyes, and, together with the taste of chocolate, the flavour of my past happiness is mixed". This is the past he would constantly hark back to in his imagination. "Yes, once I belonged here; today, however new a landscape might be to me, I return from my first sight of it a foreigner, a guest and a wanderer, a stranger to all I see and hear, old man that I am". In "The hour of the devil", his description is precise: "I never had a childhood, nor adolescence, and consequently a virile age I could attain. I am the absolute negative, the incarnation of nothing. That which one wants and can never get, that which one dreams of but can never exist – therein lies my null kingdom and sits the throne I wasn't given". In a letter dated 14/03/1916, he asks Sá-Carneiro: "The child I was, does she yet live or has she died?" And carries on living his life, until, little by little, "the corpse of my bygone childhood" starts lagging behind. "Tomorrow, so too will I be what no longer walks these streets, and which others faintly recall with *I wonder what happened to him?"*

How many years have I
frittered away, dreaming!
How much of my life was
But the living lie of
Some imagined future!
(...)
I spent all that I never had.
I am older than my years.
The fantasy that sustained me -
The queen upon my stage;
Standing naked, her reign is over.
(...)
I am the future dead,
Only a dream connects me to myself -
A dark and dragging dream
Of what I might have been -
A wall in my deserted garden.

The Scaffold, Fernando Pessoa

Dona Maria and her loneliness

His mother had led a *sad and lonely* life for a long time, much like in the verses she composed in honour of her dead husband; but, still a young woman, she ardently yearns to begin anew her interrupted life. After a distant courtship, as was customary at the time, she knew little of what it felt like to be next to a man, and was resolutely determined not to live out the rest of her days as a widow. And so, after a year of mourning, she takes her colourful dresses out of the wardrobe. She wouldn't have to search long for a man, as one would soon enter her life, one João Miguel dos Santos Rosa – born on the 1st of December 1850, a navy commander and harbourmaster of Lourenço Marques (today's Maputo, capital of Mozambique). Their first date takes place in October 1894, *in a famous elevator ride* – according to Teca, her daughter. They would soon speak again, as she recalls, during a ride on an *americano*[31]. The commander right then allegedly told a friend of his: *See that blonde? The only way I won't marry her is if she doesn't want to. Dona* Maria did want to, and so their relationship began. Such is the effect of the military man on her, she regains her inspiration to write poems – now sighing for the man who was to be the father of her future children:

> On that very day we met
> When I looked at you askance, afraid to betray my heart
> I felt my soul had been bound to yours
> I wanted you! And you? You did not even try to run!

However, she would live as a single woman until the end of 1895, as it just wasn't proper then to remarry so soon. The commander would be good for her heart and her purse, as the family's routines had changed. The humble sum she received from the local mount of piety after her father's death in 1884 was no longer enough to afford the house, as prices had gone up – especially after having lost her first husband and his double salary as a public servant and music critic; and only after remarrying would she inherit a couple of additional rents from her mother. Five months after becoming a widow, just so she could have a bare minimum of financial resources, she auctions off part of her most valuable belongings. Pessoa kept the list of those goods, which was signed by an appraiser named António Maria Silvano – a general and distant cousin of hers, and eventual tutor of grandmother Dionísia's inventory; after which *dona* Maria, her two sons and her insane mother-in-law moved on the 15th of November 1893 to a modest place that was more compatible with her means. At the time (21/01/1893), Pessoa's brother Jorge Nogueira Pessoa had already been born, still at the Largo de São Carlos. Baptised on the 13th of May 1893 at the Basilica of Our Lady of the Martyrs (registered on sheet 7 of Book X), his godparents were aunt Lisbela and João Nogueira de Freitas, married to aunt Anica.

The new address is Rua de São Marçal, 104, 3rd floor – a bare building, with a wooden staircase and windows bereft of the aristocratic balconies of the Largo de São Carlos. Today, nothing as much as alludes to Pessoa having lived there. A couple of steps away from that building, there is the Praça das Flores, triangle-shaped and with a fountain in the middle, one of Lisbon's most romantic nooks. The Tagus follows him, "ancestral and silent", as it could be

31 Name given to a rail-borne horse-drawn vehicle.

sighted from his room, over the roofs and far away. Much like before, there was also a bell (although farther away than the previous one) at the Estrela Basilica. The following year (1894), on the 2nd of January, his brother Jorge dies in that address. Having been conceived during an advanced stage of his father's illness, and being of fragile constitution, he doesn't survive the many vaccines he's forced to take. According to Teca, *Jorge, who also suffered from tuberculosis, had been vaccinated against smallpox, which caused a shock in his system.* The world Pessoa lives in now consists of himself and *dona* Maria. "When a mother cradles a dead son, so do we all cradle a dead person". With his brother in his thoughts, he would then write poems such as "Inscriptions" (VIII)[32], as well as this one:

Mother, give me once more
My dream.
It was so beautiful, mother,
That I cry for having had it...
I want to go back, mother,
And pick it back off my path.
I know not where it lies
But it is there.

And shines where I cannot see it...
My dream, mother,
Is my younger brother.

Untitled (1916), Fernando Pessoa

The first verse

In the beginning of 1895, *dona* Maria already knows she is going to remarry. And live abroad. The family must decide who will keep little Fernando. The first candidate is great-aunt Maria Xavier Pinheiro, known for writing pitiful romantic poems and for singing love songs all the time, married to Manuel Gualdino de Cunha – *Taco,* as Pessoa called him – a navy officer who supported the October Revolution of 1846. Childless and already disabused of the notion of having any, the couple quickly take to the child. Gualdino was so fond of little Fernandinho, he indulges his every whim, even going to the circus. "I never feel so close to the truth [...] as on the rare occasions when I go to the theatre or the circus". So much so, he fondly recalls Little Walter, famous Spanish clown, which he once saw live at the

32 *Scarce five years passed ere I passed too./ Death came and took the child he found./ No god spared, or fate smiled at, so/ Small hands, clutching so little round.*

Coliseu: "Quite splendid". He would later confess: "When I was a child I was amused by the Sunday circus every week. Today I'm only amused by the Sunday circus of every week of my childhood". The second candidate is aunt Anica – who conveyed such wish in order to allow her sister to begin a new life, in a new land, with a new husband. And also for the child's sake, as the future stepfather, despite presenting himself as a *friend of the family* for all social purposes, had been straightforward in how he felt, as was the wont of a military man: He wanted Fernando far away. Preferably in the Azores. Pessoa's mother asks him how he feels, and, at the age of 7 (26/07/1895), he conveys his choice in a quatrain dedicated "to my dear mummy": "Here I am in Portugal/ Land where I was born/ Although I really like it/ I love you much more".

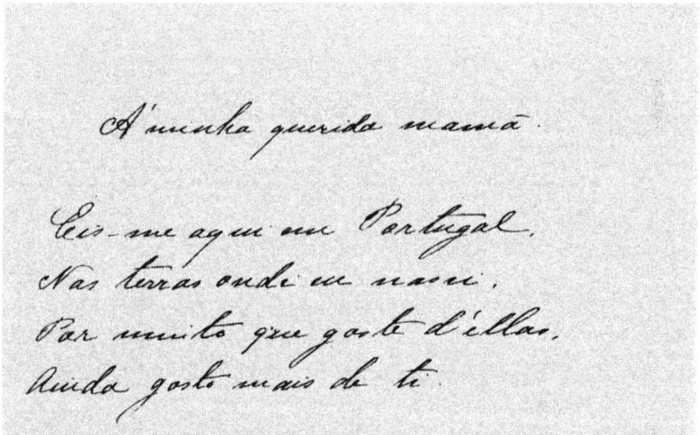
A minha querida mamã.

Eis-me aqui em Portugal,
Nas terras onde eu nasci.
Por muito que goste d'ellas,
Ainda gosto mais de ti.

Fernando Pessôa.
26-7-95.

Pessoa's first verses

Pessoa would afterwards apologize for having addressed his mother in such familiar fashion. When hearing such words, *dona* Maria is moved and plants a kiss on his forehead. And realizes she has no choice but bring him with her. She writes the verses in a notebook and signs them as *Fernando Pessôa* in almost premonitory fashion, still with the caret, but without the rest of the name. She will keep it for the rest of her life, along with what little jewellery remained her – and it only came to light when the family was rummaging through her belongings in search of documents that might help complete the inventory's formalities. The day of departure draws near. "My belief and my garden were taken from me. My childhood, my day and night, all seized. They took away the forest of my childhood".

> The room is closed for ever now.
> My heart is now buried alive.
> My heart is closed for ever now.
> The whole room is buried alive.
>
> *The broken window*, Fernando Pessoa

His mother's second marriage

Pessoa's mother and her second husband

The second wedding takes place on the 30th of December 1895, a discreet and bare affair that also marks her 34th birthday, at the church of São Mamede (and not in the one where she first married), before a marble Holy Mary sculpted by Bernini. The groom is represented by his brother, general Henrique Rosa – with whom Pessoa would later have lively literary discussions, get to know Lisbon's poets, and take up the art of drinking. The commander had become Portugal's interim consul at Durban, South Africa, on the 5th of October 1895. Portly, square-faced and heavily moustachioed, he little resembled Pessoa's fine-featured father. Pessoa calls him "daddy" or simply "father"; and, especially during the first years, appears to even like him:

My stepfather
(What a man! such spirit! such heart!)
Reclined his ample body
Built like that of a calm, hale athlete

On the biggest armchair
And listened, smoking and brooding
And his blue gaze was colourless.

Untitled (undated), Fernando Pessoa

On the 20th of January 1896, they depart from Lisbon; the now married mother, her son, and uncle Manuel Gualdino – as it just wasn't proper for a respectable lady to travel on her own. They first travel to Funchal, Madeira, and, on the 31st of January, they depart towards Durban. "My childhood passed like the smoke of a steamship at high sea". The child trembles just thinking of the journey. "My heart is like a mad admiral who abandoned the sea". At the age of 14, and in a still rather juvenile style, he recalls those days:

The ship departs, I choke back tears
Which give birth to cruel longing in my heart;
I am solely afflicted by the memory that, soon,
Your charms will no longer be seen by me.
(…)
The ship sails away on its lengthy journey:
By way of goodbye, I send her a sigh,
As she sobs her goodbye to me.

Untitled (undated), Fernando Pessoa

Uncle Taco would soon go back to Portugal and sends his nephew newspapers from Lisbon. From that moment on, in a strange land, it will be just the three of them, mother, stepfather and "the child that died to life and wonderment". "That which I was and will never be again". That first childhood of Pessoa, which barely features in his oeuvre, would play an important role in his future; as he had left there buried the only peace he ever truly knew. To him, his father had been but a friendly ghost he barely ever saw. In that time, and never again, he had truly been mama's boy. Much like she had been a mother hen to him. In that different place, however, everything was bound to change. Instead of his aunts and maids, an intruder now always accompanies his mother. Lisbon is part of his past. For the child, it now truly was *Paradise lost,* in the words of Milton's most important book. "Every wharf is a nostalgia made of stone", the stones of the harbour he departed from. And thus begins the "creeping feeling" that is his African adventure.

Good-bye, good-bye everyone who didn't come to see me off,
Good-bye my abstract and impossible family!
(…)
To depart!
I'll never return.
I'll never return because there is no return.
The place one returns to is always different.
The station one returns to is never the same.
The people are different, the light is different, the philosophy is different.

To depart! My God, to depart! I'm afraid of departing!…

Là-bas, je ne sais où…, Álvaro de Campos

Terra incognita
(Unknown land) Term used in cartography for regions that have not been explored

WHITE AFRICA

Arms crossed, he stares beyond the sea (...)
The sea that may exist beyond the land.
Message (King João the Second), Fernando Pessoa

A new land

He spent 30 days at sea. "Thirty days travel, three days travel, three hours travel – oppression ever manages to sink deep into my heart"; even "when the ship approaches" and "a slope emerges with trees that from afar were invisible". That first sight of the continent, sparsely forested and looking like a hippopotamus from afar, was mount Bluff – the "wooded slope shimmered" and, at night, it shone "under the great African moon". At its tip, the place called The Point, where the mount sinks into the waters. After so many days, finally "the distant coastlines, flattened by the horizon (…) and sandy beaches" of Durban. "Ah, the distant beaches, the wharfs seen from afar, and then the beaches close up, the wharfs in plain view". On account of the river's sand, the harbour isn't prepared for large ships, which forces the visitors to use longboats. "The land opens in sounds and colours. And, once ashore, there are birds and flowers where just a far-off, abstract line had run". Far from his distant homeland, he had just arrived at a new world.

Ah, how fresh the mornings of arrivals are,
And how pallid the mornings of departures,
When our insides tighten into a ball
And a vague sensation akin to fear
–The ancestral fear of leaving what we know and going away,
The mysterious ancestral fear of Arrival and the New–
Makes us shrink in our skin with anxiety.

Maritime ode, Álvaro de Campos

Durban lies in the province of KwaZulu-Natal, Cape colony – today's South Africa. The story of that small city begins at the end of 1497 with Vasco da Gama, at a time in which the Portuguese were "essentially navigators and discoverers". The old sailor knows that, "beyond absolute distance", there lies the gloomy sea. But he fears it not, and picks a sea route which might take him to the Indies. "The one typically Portuguese thing that Portugal had were the discoveries. The Time of the Race had come at length with Vasco da Gama" – a man who already wore the Cross of the Order of Christ, and would eventually become viceroy of India. To him, he was "an Argonaut"[1]. Departing from Lisbon, he first travels to the edge of fear at Africa's western coast: Cape Bojador – which had been successfully navigated by Gil Eanes in 1434, after 12 years of tragic attempts which left numerous wrecks in its depths.

Whoever would go beyond the Cape
Must go beyond sorrow.
God placed danger and the abyss in the sea,
But he also made it heaven's mirror.

Message (Portuguese Sea), Fernando Pessoa

Carrying on with his voyage, on the course of the icy seas of Antarctica, he passes by Cabo Negro, traversed in 1484 by Diogo Cão; and eventually comes across another cape, which Bartolomeu Dias had dubbed Cape of Storms (lately rebaptised by John II as Cape of Good Hope. Dias had the right of it, considering he met his maker in those very waters in 1500.

Here lies, on the small strand of the furthest reach,
The Captain of the End. With Awe[2] now rounded,
The sea is the same: let no one fear it now!
Atlas[3] shows the world high on his shoulder.

Message (Dias' epitaph), Fernando Pessoa

1 Argonauts were Greek heroes who, according to legend, travelled in search of the Golden Fleece – the skin of a winged ram with golden wool.
2 "Awe" here being the Cape of Storms (of Good Hope), which Camões portrayed as the giant Adamastor.
3 The image evokes the titan of Greek myth, condemned by Zeus to hold up the sky.

Durban at the end of the 19th century

Having traversed the farthest reaches of Africa, he sailed from the Atlantic into the Indian ocean, "most mysterious of all", and then took a rest at a bay which he named Port of Natal in 1498. In 1835, the place was rebaptised in honour of sir Benjamin d'Urban – a British general who had fought in the Napoleonic Wars, and who subsequently became governor and commander in chief of the Cape colony. Races mixed there, at the end of the world, like so many spices – *cinnamon and curry, cumin and clove,* as Clara Ferreira Alves put it. Except not quite so. Therein lived around 2 thousand Indians and Zulus, *Shaka's people*[4], plus 31.870 Whites – according to the numbers provided by Albertino dos Santos Matias, former Portuguese consul at Durban. The province is the most important one in a land populated by 400 thousand natives, 80 thousand Indians and 40 thousand Whites. There, since 1899, the English had fought the Boers – South African settlers of Dutch origin, who struggled for independence and shared with the British a mutual hatred and desire to treat the black natives like slaves. The Africa that Pessoa knew at the time was very much white. Photos of the time show Durban as one of those cities meant for tourists, with white houses made of wood, zinc, stone and brick, all quite simple, and very different from

4 Thus named after Shaka Zulu, tribal chief who had bequeathed them an empire and whose death was ordered by his aunt and brothers.

cosmopolitan Lisbon. The streets are wide, packed with trundling carriages – all of them open, due to the heat – sweaty faces, the smell of the wild, dust sticking to hair and caking the corners of one's mouth.

I wish I was but road dirt
And that the feet of the poor trampled upon me…
(…)
I wish I was a miller's donkey
And that he hit me and care for me…
Rather than going through life[5]
Looking back and feeling sorrow…

The Keeper of Sheep, Alberto Caeiro

A young journalist of London's *The Morning Post,* one Winston (Leonard Spencer) Churchill (1874-1965) – who would eventually become a member of the House of Commons (1900), prime minister (1940) and Nobel prize winner in Literature (1953) – spent the night in the city on the 23rd of December 1899. A holiday is decreed in honour of the hero who had come to

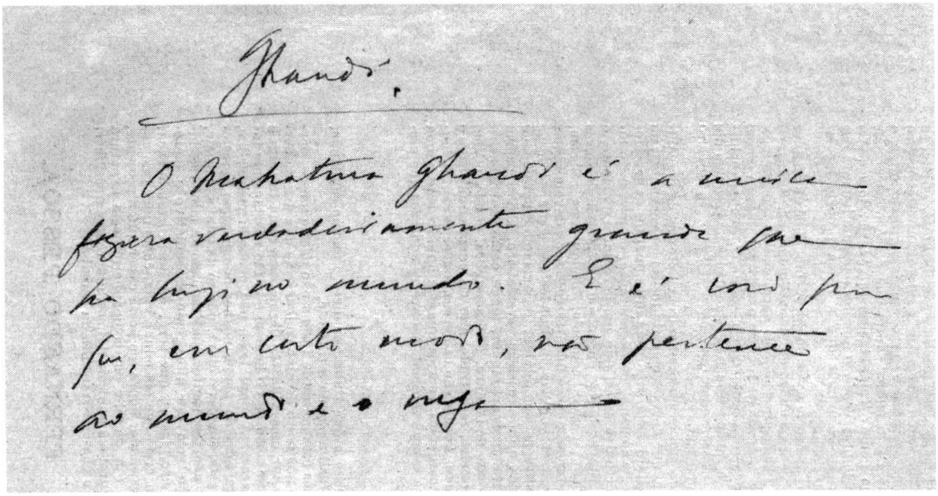
Ghandi.

O Mahatma Ghandi é a unica figura verdadeiramente grande que ha hoje no mundo. E é-o porque, em certo modo, não pertence ao mundo e o nega →

Pessoa's scribblings on Gandhi

organize the resistance in the war, after having escaped in spectacular fashion from the Transvaal prison and Krueger's troops in the Boer Wars. Churchill was one of two figures who greatly impressed Pessoa in South Africa. The other was Mohandas Karamchand Gandhi (1869-1948), a "weaponless hero",

5 In one of his "Odes", Ricardo Reis uses a similar construction: *Better this life than/ The lives lived by men,/ Covered with soot that/ Swirls up from the road.*

"the one truly great man alive today". Gandhi had a law firm in Johannesburg *(M.K. Gandhi Attorney),* and came to Durban in 1893 to represent an Indian customer. He got into trouble almost immediately upon arrival, refusing to take off his hat before a judge in court and getting kicked out of a train's first class carriage despite carrying a ticket, as it was meant for Whites only. He was eventually sent away. But, at the end of 1896, when Pessoa was already living in the city, he returned to protest against English colonialism. His ship was quarantined, off the harbour, as no one wanted him around, and, upon disembarking on the 13th of January 1897, he was met with 4 thousand Europeans and their Black servants, all with rage in their eyes. He was physically assaulted, and only the local police prevented his lynching, but, against all better judgement, he carried on with his pilgrimage. Pessoa was fascinated by such boldness and vindicates him when he criticizes colonial secretary Joseph Chamberlain (1836-1914), who would later become prime minister of George VI:

> Be thy name erased
> From the full mouth of men; nor be there traced
> To thee one glory to thy parent land;
> But'fore us, as'fore God e'er do thou stand
> In that thy deed forevermore disgraced.
> Where lie the sons and husbands, where those dear
> That thy curst craft hath lost? Their drops of blood,
> One by one fallen, and many a cadenced tear,
> With triple justice weighted trebly dread,
> Shall each, rolled onward in a burning flood,
> Crush thy dark soul. Their blood be on thy head!
>
> *Joseph Chamberlain*, Alexander Search

Slavery

The city is a piece of colonial England wedged into a black continent. But slavery, which was ever present there, doesn't seem to bother Pessoa all that much. Having been brought into a culture of apartheid, and still too young to comprehend the social dimension of prejudice, he wrote: "It just so happened that a guy threw a brick at a Negro's head, and it was the brick that broke". In George Goddard's *Racial supremacy,* he jots down several annotations with a similar tone. And, in "A opinião pública" ("The public opinion"), an article written in 1916, he defends "the slavery of olden times". In *Ultimatum* (1917), he expounds upon the matter and advocates for a rule of "supermen" and believes that workers should be "reduced to a condition of slavery even more intense and rigid than the one we call capitalist *slavery".*

And he goes even farther than that: "That old saying by Aristotle – who wasn't all that given to tyrannical solutions – that slavery is one of the foundations of social life, can be said to be standing still to this day. Considering there is no way to do away with it". "Slavery is logical and legitimate; a Zulu [a Bantu-speaking native of the south of Africa] and a Landim [Portuguese-speaking Mozambiquean native] are of no real use to the world. To civilize either, whether through religion or by any other means, is to want to give them that which they cannot have. What is legitimate is to force them to serve the ends of civilization, since they aren't even proper people. To enslave is thus the logical thing to do. The degenerate concept of egalitarianism, with which Christianity has poisoned our social concepts, has done great harm to this most logical attitude". "Slavery is the law of life, and there is no other, as this one must be carried out and must not be rebelled against. Some are born slaves, some are made. The cowardly love we all share for freedom is the true sign of the weight of our slavery". In an article penned for the *Revista de Comércio e Contabilidade,* issue number 2 (1926), the topic is further elaborated upon: "Someone has yet to prove that abolishing slavery would be a net social positive"; or "Who can say that slavery isn't a natural law of healthy societies?". On the other, contradictory hand, we have texts of his that rail against slavery, mainly in English, such as this sonnet critical of England:

Mother of slaves and fools, Thou who dost hold
Within Thine iron chains enslaved mankind,
Old in Thy yoke and in their slavery blind,
Harden'd to grief and woe, corrupt and cold,

But in the craven following, as of old,
Of those old ways, unwise, unfirm, unkind,
Bound ever in the animal bonds that bind
Fish, bird and beast in flock and herd and fold.

The light hath fallen of many a cherished name,
And many a land of love hath been the nurse,
But man's worn heart is evermore the same -

Unwilling ever to shake off the curse,
Once self-inflicted, and the time-grown shame
That loads the weary, lightless universe.

Convention, Alexander Search

His time at Convent School

As their official residence wasn't yet ready, commander Roza (with a 'z' instead of the usual 's') first brings his family to a hotel – the Bay View, at Musgrave Road. The couple issues the following protocolary card for their friends in Lisbon: *Maria Magdalena Nogueira Roza and João Miguel Roza wish to inform you of their marriage, and offer you their house, Durban, Natal.* That *house* they soon will move to is Tersillian House, the head office of the Portuguese chancellery, built in the 19th century's colonial style and surrounded by balconies, sedges, mango trees and palm trees, today it's nothing but a

The family at Tersillian House

machinery deposit. Located at 157 Ridge Road, West Street – Durban's main thoroughfare, leading to the Ocean Parade boardwalk and the beaches – it overlooks the city's downtown and its harbour. "West" doesn't refer to the cardinal point, but to the name of the colony's first governor, commander Martin West. At the time, the streets were almost all named after people: Thomas Street, Musgrave Road, with the four main ones intersecting: West Street, Smith Street, Broad Street, Grey Street.

On February 1896, the very month of his arrival, Pessoa begins his studies at Saint-Joseph Convent School, run by Irish nuns, at the very street he moves to. An austere, classic affair with a belfry, it also hosts the West Street Convent, where Pessoa will have his first communion (13/06/1896). Despite having many classmates, he doesn't (or doesn't want to) make any friends. According to his sister, Teca, *he was a child that preferred isolation, living in his own world, taking refuge in his imagination.* Other than his family, he also shares his new home with Paciência, a nanny that the children called Pá, and a black Mozambiquean servant, Saturnino. In Pessoa's own words, from one of the texts written during his time in Africa:

My heart is full of lazy pain
And an old English lullaby
Comes out of that mist of my brain.

Lullaby, Fernando Pessoa

His mother gives him more siblings. Henriqueta Madalena, born on the 27th of November 1896 – the same year in which his maternal mother died at Terceira. After uncle *Taco,* he now has a sister he calls *Teca.* She would be Pessoa's most constant company in the last 15 years of his life, and studies at Stella Maris, a women-only school. Two years later, on the 22nd of October 1898, Madalena Henriqueta is born (she would die in 25/06/1901 due to meningitis). Their inverted names were in honour of grandmothers Henriqueta Margarida Rodrigues (mother of commander Roza) and Madalena Xavier Pinheiro (Pessoa's maternal grandmother). A proper, twofold homage. After them came brothers Luís Miguel *(Lhi),* on the 11th of January 1900, and João Maria *(Mimi),* on the 17th of January 1902. According to Manuela Nogueira, Teca's daughter, João Maria *hated his nickname.* Perhaps owing to that, as well as his English upbringing, his brother only called him *John.* Finally, Maria Clara is born on the 16th of August 1904 (she would die of septicaemia in 1906). "From Durban, I brought but the distant sound of those things of my childhood that I can't forget, my mother's gentle voice as she sat at the table, the tears of my siblings' funerals". He is supposed to have written the following in honour of his sister Madalena Henriqueta:

"Christians! Here lies, in the dust of the second land
A young daughter of melancholy
Her life was rife with bitterness
Her laughter, sobbing, pain her joy.

As I sit by the window,
Staring through snow-fogged panes
It is her I think I see
No longer passing through… no longer…[6]

Epitaph, Fernando Pessoa

6 This last quatrain is almost identical to the first of *Quando ela passa,* by heteronym Dr. Pancrácio, written shortly before, and in which only the last verse is different.

Doubts linger concerning his intent, seeing as his sister died in June 1901, and the poem was written quite a bit later, on the 15th of April of the following year. The one that was indubitably dedicated to her, written in English and with the note of "DG"[7] next to it, begins as follows:

> Sing into sad tears our distress!
> Oh, let soft sorrow be thy strain!
> She's gone beyond our love's caress,
> Giving to life more loneliness
> And to mystery more pain.
>
> *On baby's death*, Alexander Search

Even though he now lived in a new world, Pessoa's heart remained in distant lands. For example, his favourite music was all foreign – Arabic *jácaras* or Portuguese folk songs such as "Era um Homem Muito Rico", "Donzela que Vai à Guerra", "Cego Andante", "Gerinaldo o Atrevido". In "Maritime ode", he even recalls an "old aunt" who "used to sing me to sleep", "sometimes she sang 'The Good Ship Catrineta'", known by common folk as "Nau Catarineta", "Catarineta", "Náo Caterineta", "Caterineta", or "Santa Caterina"[8]. The song has numerous versions and poems, such as "Prosopopeia", by Bento Teixeira[9], which is held as the very first Brazilian piece of literature. In "Maritime ode", Pessoa recalls its beginning:

> There goes the Catrineta,
> Over the waves of the sea…

These are the two first verses of one of the 12 variants gathered by historian (and Portuguese president) Teófilo Braga. This version is different from the better known one *(Versão do Algarve),* and goes as follows (excerpt):

> Lots they then drew,
> As to who was to die;
> As luck would have it
> It was to be the captain general.

---

7 Likely *Death of God.*

8 This *auto* tells the epic tale of Jorge de Albuquerque Coelho, son of Duarte Coelho Pereira, donee of the captaincy of Pernambuco. Having been summoned by Sebastian I, he departs from Recife to Lisbon in 1575. He faces mutinies and bloody battles with pirates, and miraculously arrives at Portuguese shores, after having sailed aimlessly for many days.

9 Teixeira (1560-1618) is alternately said to have been born in Porto (where his Christian convert parents had immigrated to) or at the captaincy of Pernambuco, Muribeca. Other than his literary skill, he was notable for having butchered his Christian wife Felipa Raposo, who had cheated on him. Not even the vicar of the parish of Santo Agostinho, considered a *thuggish cleric* at the time, could avail him, and he was executed at an *auto-de-fé* in 1599.

Up you go, then, matey,
Up the royal mast,
See if you sight the lands of Spain
Sands of Portugal.
I see three maidens
Under an orange grove:
One is sitting as she knits,
The other spins her distaff,
The fairest of them all
In the middle, crying.
All three are my daughters
Oh! To be able to hug them!

At "Maritime ode", Pessoa quotes another song:

And at other times it was "The Fair Princess",
With its wistful, Medieval melody…
(…)
Yes, the "Fair Princess "...
I'd close my eyes as she sang:
The Fair Princess
Sat in her garden

These are the first two verses of one of the (many) versions edited by Almeida Garrett. Two other verses from it are quoted at "Maritime ode":

Combing her hair
With her golden comb…

Still from that version (excerpt):

She cast her gaze over the sea
And saw a noble armada
The captain than led it
Did so most excellently.
Tell me, o captain
Of that most noble armada
Did you find my husbands
In the land that God tread?

Durban High School

On the 7th of April 1899, Pessoa enrols at Durban High School, a school meant at the time for White boys (nowadays, Blacks and Coloureds are also allowed). The old brick building at St. Thomas Street boasts archways on its façade, ample classrooms with mahogany-panelled walls and playing fields. Pessoa is the 48th among 673 candidates, and manages to enrol with the highest distinction of First Class. Today, there is a bust of him at the school (with his hat but sans glasses) close to the deanery, where the principal's office used to be, at the Dead Poets hall. The original school was rebuilt in 1973 and, on a black granite column, one can find the dates of his birth and death, as well as a verse from *Message* ("Portuguese sea"): "Oh, salty sea, how much of your salt/ Are tears of Portugal"[10]. The syllabus mandates English, Latin, Mathematics and one science subject. Pessoa chooses Physics. History and French are optional. He skips Form I and quickly transitions from Form II-B to Form II-A, by decision of headmaster Willfrid H. Nicholas.

Herbert D. Jennings has the following to say: *It beggars belief that mister Nicholas should subject the young foreigner to such a heavy burden. One would think he believed the lad to be endowed with gifts which would allow him to endure where others would have succumbed. And endure he did, but certainly paid the price for it.* He is awarded the Form Prize for General Excellence, reaches Form III and, in December, Form IV. On his first year, on account of being his class' top student, he is awarded Arthur Gilman's *The story of Rome from the earliest times to the end of the Republic.* The following year, the prize is Mary Macleod's *Stories from the faerie Queene,* for his written assignments in French. His school records invariably state *excellent, brilliant, very good,* always with top marks. In June 1901, he undergoes the School Higher Certificate Examination, which signals the end of his secondary education, and finishes the course in two out of the expected five years. At the age of 13, when his classmates are all 15 or older. Nowadays, we can read some of Pessoa's better known verses, translated into English on the school's walls.

Travelling to Portugal

In June 1901, his stepfather is named first-class consul, which entitled him to a sabbatical[11], and so he decides to spend a year away from Durban and the risks of the Boer War, which was now entering its critical stage (and would end later that year with an English victory). The decision to travel stemmed from his belief that the city wasn't a safe place for women and children; besides, it had already been too long since they'd last seen their friends and family in Lisbon. On the 13th of September 1901, *O Século* had the following news:

10 Almost ironic, considering those verses aren't actually Pessoa's, inspired as they were by a quatrain from *Cantigas* (1898) by António Correia de Oliveira: *O waves of the salty sea/ Wherefrom all your salt?/ It comes from the tears shed/ In the beaches of Portugal.*

11 A right reserved for some Portuguese civil servants every seven years. Thus named after the tradition of the Sabbath, the religious rest Jews must observe at the last day of every week.

Yesterday, the English attacked Vanderven's command near Driefontein, taking 37 Boers prisoner, among which the Red Cornet Duplessis, and killing two, among which lieutenant Vanderven. Four Englishmen were killed, and three wounded. The following day, on page four: *Consul Roza and three children arrived from Durban on the German ship* Koenig, namely Pessoa (13 at the time), his sister Teca (5) and brother Luís (2). Unmentioned were *dona* Maria, the nanny Paciência and the ashes of Madalena Henriqueta, which were to be buried in Portugal, according to Pessoa's biographers. Perhaps they weren't ashes, considering how rare (and expensive) it was to resort to cremation at the time. It might have been the body, or, more likely, the bones.

After having arrived in Lisbon, after a 43 day long journey, the family stays at a rented flat at Rua Pedrouços, 45, ground floor, close to the Quinta Duque de Cadaval – where resided grandmother Dionísia (fresh out of the asylum) and great-aunts Maria Xavier Pinheiro da Cunha and Rita Xavier Pinheiro. Maria, who had recently lost uncle Gualdino, is "the type of cultured woman of the 18th century, sceptical of religion, aristocratic and monarchical", but also endowed with a spirit that was "mannish, bereft of fear and any feminine tenderness". Rita, on the other hand, was the sweet spinster who became close with Pessoa. Their new home is at Pedrouços, a small fishing village near Lisbon, the most attractive beach of the region. Pessoa would evoke the place throughout his life. About the house: "From the upper floor, over our home, there often came the sounds of piano scales, the monotonous learning of a girl I never saw. I was a child, then, and no longer am; but the sound is the same in my memory"; and the yard: "Divided by a tall, flimsy fence of crossed wooden strips, my heart lies forgotten in vegetable garden and backyard". In October, the family travels to Tavira to visit Pessoa's paternal family members – among them dear aunt Lisbela. That trip would later be remembered in form of a poem:

> I finally arrived at the village of my childhood[12],
> Upon leaving the train, I remembered, looked, saw, compared,
> (all this in the time it took to cast a tired look)
> All is old where I was once young.
> (…)
> That village of my childhood is now a foreign city.
> I am a foreigner, a tourist, a passer-by,
> Of course: That is what I am.
> Even in myself, God, even in myself.
>
> *Notes on Tavira*, Álvaro de Campos

On the 2nd May 1902, in order to meet his maternal family and to resolve some issues with the inventory of *dona* Maria's mother, they travel to Angra do

12 Actually, his father's.

Heroísmo, Azores. Pessoa describes the landscape with a measure of longing: "The small beach, forming a tiny bay, hidden from the world by two miniature promontories, was my retreat of myself". They stay over at aunt Anica's house, at Rua da Palha (currently Rua Padre António Cordeiro), but, nine days later, there is an outbreak of meningitis, the same illness that had befallen sister Madalena Henriqueta in Durban. They return to Lisbon post-haste. On the 26th of June, stepfather, mother and siblings return to Durban on the *Kurfürst,* back towards the distant land Pessoa never really considered his own; he himself would only depart on the 19th September – *Herr F. Pessoa,* as it stands on the *Herzog's* first and second-class passenger log. "He remained in Lisbon from August [in truth, September] 1901 to September 1902; inevitably suffering the immoral, corrupting influence of urban sensuality".

> As a child I was different…
> To become what I am,
> I grew up and forgot.
> What I have today is a silence, a law.
> Have I won or lost?
>
> *Untitled* (undated), Fernando Pessoa

Durban Commercial School and University of the Cape of Good Hope

At the end of 1902 and the beginning of 1903, he attends night classes at a school of debatable concept, the Durban Commercial School. It probably wasn't his choice, but rather his stepfather's, who likely wished to steer him towards a profession that would allow him to remain in the closed local society. "It was a good thing, for myself and others, that my presence at home was constant until my 15th birthday, private as was my wont. But, at that age, I was sent to a school far away from home, and it was there that the new being I so feared sprang into action and took on a human life". That school away from home is the University of the Cape of Good Hope. He takes the Matriculation Examination on December 1903. Out of 899 candidates, 19 go to first class, 161 to second class, and 262 to third class, with Pessoa among them. The others either quit or failed. His mediocre grades are incompatible with his prior good results, and were likely due to the time sink that was the Commercial School, or the very tests' subject matter – which also involved Algebra and Geometry, which were both new to him. Augustine Ormond, a classmate he would hold correspondence with until the advent of World War I (when Ormond moved to Australia), defines him as *a shy, gentle boy, sweet-natured, extremely intelligent, who took care to write English in the most academic fashion he could, and whose good judgement belied his age.*

A lively, cheerful and positive boy with attractive character; I felt drawn to him as a piece of iron would to a magnet. Despite being British, Mr. Ormond confesses that *Pessoa spoke and wrote English better than I did,* and adds: *I recall something about him, something I just felt, and which I now realize was his genius.* In the words of Alexandrino Severino, *he was far beyond his peers at that age.*

Queen Victoria Memorial Prize

Despite his low performance at the university's admission exams, he would still win the prestigious Queen Victoria Memorial Prize in 1903, awarded by the Young Jewish Guild of South Africa, in honour of the then recently deceased (22/01/1901) Queen Victoria, queen of Great Britain and Ireland and empress of the Indies. The letter which communicates the best essay in English – on the topic of a) what it meant to be a cultured man; b) common superstitions; c) gardening in South Africa, to be written in 60 minutes – is dated the 20th of February 1904. The text is lost to us, and so it is unknown which topic Pessoa picked, although most assuredly not the latter one. Ángel Crespo and Fernando Cabral suggest that he likely would have chosen the second. Just a hunch. The award consisted of 7 pounds' worth of books, minus a pound for their cover's binding. He picks the works of Ben Johnson, Poe, Keats and Tennyson. That same year, he begins to write regularly for the *Natal Mercury.* His column published every Saturday (and repeated on next Friday's weekly edition), is peculiarly titled *Man on the moon,* signed by Charles Robert Anon. He writes charades, published between September 1903 and June 1904; or more serious texts, such as this one dated the 7th of June 1905:

> It has never occurred to us Englishmen, most selfish of men, that misery and pain are ennobling… A drunken woman, stumbling through the street, is a sight that evokes pity, or, perhaps, an amusing show. But that same woman, drunken and bumbling as she may be when she cries her son's death, is neither contemptible nor ridiculous, but rather a tragic figure, as great as Hamlet or King Lear.

Intermediate examinations

At the start of the academic year, Pessoa enrols in Arts. The university doesn't have any regular courses, nor does it demand attendance. The school system of English colonies of the time allows for the first year at university to be attended abroad. Pessoa studies alone, at home, and does well. At his intermediate examination on December 1904, he has the highest mark: 1.098 points. Headmaster Nicholas writes *excellent* as a side note. Still, the official laureate is another student (in a class of two), who had scored but 930 points, one Clifford E. Geerdts. He is the winner of the Natal Exhibition and goes on to study Law at Oxford's Lincoln College for four years, at the expense of the province's government. Legend has it that the choice was owed to the fact that *mister* Pessoa wasn't English. But the real reason is rather more simple, as the scholarship required the student to have studied at Natal's schools in the four years preceding it, and Pessoa had been in Portugal from 1901 to 1902. That same December, he writes for the *Durban High School Magazine* what which would be his first serious text, signed as F.A. Pessoa. It is an essay written in English about the oeuvre of historian and politician Thomas Babington Macaulay (1800-1859), author of *The History of England, from the accession of James the Second.* Comparing Macaulay to Carlyle, always favouring the latter, the 2 thousand words-long essay concludes thus:

> There is something about him, or rather his style, which might lead a cynic to ponder whether to consider him a genius or merely a man of tremendous talent. Whereas Macaulay appears to ever be merely sensible[13].
>
> *Macaulay*, Fernando Pessoa

The amazing African storms

One of the most enduring memories Pessoa kept from his time in Africa were the amazing storms, much stronger than the European ones. As a child, he used to lean his head against the glass panes of his room's window to watch "a limp lightning, the sound of rain, the rumbling of the thunderstorm" over Mount Bluff. His sister Teca recalls: *When he was very little, he watched a bolt of lightning cleave a tree asunder. From that day on, he'd always panic whenever there was a storm. He could even feel it approaching, and would slip into bed and cover his bed with a pillow. He would hide in the darkest place. Even if it were just a cubicle. As an adult, he still felt that fear.* Those "rains in the street risen from the abyss" are, to him, "a malaise of all", spilling "a murky restlessness all over the landscape". "I might be dead – who knows? – the day after tomorrow, in which case the storm that will strike the day after tomorrow will be a different storm than it would be if I hadn't died. I realize that the storm doesn't fall from my eyes, but if I'm no longer in this world, the world will be different – there will be one person less – and the storm, falling in a different

13 Pessoa's assessment would be vindicated, as Macaulay, then quite famous, eventually lost the regard of his countrymen and died an ordinary man.

world, won't be the same storm"; his permanent dread conjuring up the saint (Anthony) he was named after.

> I truly
> Know not whether I am sad or not.
> And the rain falls lightly
> (As consented by Verlaine)
> Inside my heart[14].
>
> *Untitled* (1935), Fernando Pessoa

His friend Almada Negreiros recalls an event which took place at the Martinho da Arcada restaurant: *Suddenly, a tremendous thunderstorm broke. It rained and rained, quite loudly, wind, lightning, thunder, unceasing. I went to the door and screamed outside – Hooray for lightning! Hooray for thunder! Hooray for the wind! Hooray for the rain! When I went back inside, he was nowhere to be seen. Until I spotted a foot under the table, and there he was. I pulled him out, pale as a transparent corpse, and helped him up, inert and all but dead.* And that wasn't the only time. Another, he was surprised at work, in a "horrendous night filled with truth". His description is precise: "Everything darkens.. I fall into an abyss made of time… Sweeps everything to the corner of the ceiling that stands behind me, and on the paper where I write, between it and the quill that writes, lies King Cheops' corpse, staring at me with wide open eyes". That fear is spelled out in an untitled poem dated the 1st of December 1914, in which he describes how "the sound of rain attracts my useless agony". In *The Book of Disquiet,* there are ten passages about rain and thirteen about storms. In a letter addressed to Gaspar Simões (01/12/1913), he confesses: "Only the lack of money (at the moment it is felt) or a storm (as long as it lasts) are capable of making me feel depressed". In another letter, this one to Mário Beirão (01/02/1913), he says: "The other day, the sky was threatening rain. There was no thunder, but the threat persisted, and it began to rain – those (large) droplets, warm and spread out. I headed back home as fast as I could without running, with the mental anguish you can imagine, very much distraught, uncomfortable to the core of my being. And it is in this state of mind that I am now composing a sonnet". That sonnet, published much later at issue 9 of *Ressurreição* (01/02/1920) begins thus:

---

14 Verses inspired by *Romance sans paroles,* by Paul Verlaine (1844-1896), a book in which the untitled poems are all numbered. Namely the third, under the epigraph of Arthur Rimbaud (1854-1891), a poem called *It rains gently upon the city,* which begins thus: *There is weeping in my heart/ As it rains upon the city./ What is this faintness (languor)/ Which penetrates my heart?*

O night eternal, call me your son
And take me into your arms. I'm a king
Who relinquished, willingly,
My throne of dreams and tedium.

Abdication, Fernando Pessoa

Goodbye, Africa

There are no significant references in Pessoa's oeuvre to his time in Africa; perhaps because, deep down, he never truly left Lisbon. In Africa, the Tagus was the Ungeni river, a name he never wrote down. It was a chapter in his life that could never have lasted long, as he himself had predicted before. "I shall strike Africa out of all my writings, my feelings, my heart. Africa and the memory of it oppress me", so says he in a letter to his *secret friend* – as Herbert D. Jenkins[15] described himself. Many specialists have attempted to give intimate explanations for his return to Portugal, which I will synthesize in the words of António Quadros: *To Pessoa, Lisbon was a quest of his father's, psychologically projected as a search for the homeland.* Personally, I believe there was a much simpler explanation. After all, everything pointed to Africa being but a hiatus, incompatible with his true aspirations. For instance, he could never be a public servant, as he wasn't an Englishman, nor could he become a university teacher, as he lacked the required higher education in England. The best of his limited options was a career in commerce, which was quite far from his thoughts. The different language, the provincial geography, the distance from the large cultural centres – mainly France and England – everything pointed to his place being one quite far from there. His definite return to Europe would happen on the 20th of August 1905, *under the care of an officer,* according to Teca, and aboard the same German steamship *Herzog,* in which he had returned on his own to Durban in 1901. History repeated itself. "How long, Portugal, how long have we lived apart", he says, mournfully, remarking that only there can be found all "which I like, and which I don't like – both equally missed". He would live there with the modest pension his stepfather gave him and what little he inherited from his mother's family. In his suitcase, but a few old clothes and the pile of letters his father wrote to *dona* Maria, in Telheiras. "I who lived here, and came back, and came back again". Forever "o, Lisbon, my home".

15 A letter made public by Clara Ferreira Alves in *Tabacaria* #11, Spring 2003), considered mere fiction by Lucília Nogueira. With no access to the source material, I'll just let it go on record.

Once more I see you–Lisbon, the Tagus and the rest–
A useless onlooker of you and of myself,
A foreigner here like everywhere else,
Incidental in life as in my soul,
A ghost wandering through halls of remembrances
To the sound of rats and creaking floorboards
In the accursed castle of having to live…

Once more I see you,
A shadow moving among shadows, gleaming

Lisbon revisited (1926)[16], Álvaro de Campos

16 Pessoa wrote two poems with the same title, *Lisbon revisited.* To tell them apart when he published them in *Contemporânea* magazine, be put their dates in parenthesis as part of the title: "Lisbon revisited (1923)" in #8, in 1923, the first poem dated by Campos; and "Lisbon revisited (1926)", in #2 of the second series, in 1926. Underneath the titles, penned in normal, dark handwriting, the dates are written in bright blue colour.

Hoc erat in votis
(This is what I wished for) Horatio

RETURN TO LISBON

Once more I see you,
City of my horrifyingly lost childhood...[1]
Lisbon revisited (1926), Álvaro de Campos

Familial troubles

Having been exempt from military service[2], there's nothing truly keeping him in Africa. His stepfather decides to remain there indefinitely, and moved to Pretoria – today's Tshwane, South Africa's administrative capital – in 1910. His stepson, *gently stubborn* as he was, had very different plans, however. And so began his many familial troubles. The scenario he paints in a draft of an undated letter to his mother is quite clear: "Papa[3] is an honest man, to whom I owe a great debt of gratitude and whom I greatly respect and cherish, but in this matter he has no word in, nor access to the Temple[4]. I forgive his not being capable of understanding me and sticking his nose in matters in which his good will isn't the driving force, nor his honesty the guide. There is one thing we can definitely agree on, which is out mutual affection. Beyond that, the moment what is *mine* is concerned, there begins the needling of my soul, and any compromise or relational well-being becomes an impossibility. For my part, I can respect all prejudice… and the honest incomprehension of his soul". A text penned by his heteronym Anon bookends this train of thought: "Familial affection – that of my family towards myself – has taken on a cold aspect, a

1 A variant Pessoa wrote went: "city of my horrifyingly *spent* childhood. Reflecting upon the true meaning of such words, Teresa Rita Lopes asks the following: *Is it the childhood, or the city he considers "horrifyingly lost"?*

2 The request of waiver was sent to the Recruitment and Reserve District on the 9th of September 1902.

3 He had first written and crossed out "stepfather".

4 A metaphor of an initiation bent, likely a generic reference to temples as a space of limited access to mere mortals. Such as King Solomon's, in Jerusalem, in which it was necessary to go through several stages before reaching the centre.

dolorous veneer". Little by little, without him even realizing it, he was growing out of being mama's boy.

His stepfather isn't the only one who doesn't understand him. Pessoa's relationship to *dona* Maria was no longer the same, as evidenced by this draft letter: "Mother cares for me, but doesn't empathise with me. We get along fine. As intolerant as you are, I am not. I understand that Mother can't understand and, even though that lack of understanding wounds and aggravates me, and your revolting lack of tact does exceedingly so, what I truly suffer with are the pangs of near-hate caused by it. I well know you will respond to this in a rather ironic tone, Mother. But that doesn't wound me. What nauseates me is the damned advice and *true* lack of understanding". The text ends thus: "From here on, I am alone, humanly abandoned and lonely, but hardened from the arrows of your unawareness and the spears of your uncomprehending affection. When it has happened, then maybe Mother will understand why she understands me not. But this, which might grow our souls closer, will not help you understand me, and I will be eternally alone". Celeste Malpique makes the unsourced claim that *this letter wasn't sent, as it showed suicidal intent.* The "it has happened" bit probably referred to his departure to Lisbon, however. Then, on a piece of paper, he writes: "A family isn't a group of relatives; it is more than blood relations, it should also be an affinity of temperament. Geniuses often don't have a family. They have relatives".

His lamentations continue in an annotation on the 25th of July 1907: "I am tired of shedding tears, feeling sorry for myself. My family has no understanding of my mental state – none. They laugh at me, mock me, do not believe me, say I wish to be someone extraordinary. They cannot understand that, between being extraordinary and wishing to be so lies but the awareness of that wish. I have no one I can confide in. My family doesn't understand. My family understands nothing. A man clad in silk can suffer as much as one who is covered with but a bag or a ragged blanket. Enough". There are no certainties as to who made the decision of his return to Portugal. Both his mother and stepfather already felt that would be the logical step to take. But the decisive factor was probably the fact that he had wished to tread new paths for the longest time. Not long after that (12/11/1907) he writes a poem in English, scribbling "AG" at the edge (likely indicating the title he would give to that particular volume: *Agony)* and pours his heart out:

> In family or social ease,
> In worldly, usual jollities
> Or children playing round,
> Happy were I but to have then
> The usual life of usual men.
> (...)

I, the eternally excluded
From socialness and mirth,
(...)
Ay me! and none to comprehend
This wish that doth all things transcend.

In the street, Alexander Search

Favourite readings

The decision to move back to Lisbon, a city far bigger than Durban, is also owed to his love of reading and writing. From an early age, and increasingly so. When he was 3, he pieced together letters he saw in newspapers and books. At the age of 4, he was already writing full sentences. Thanks to his mother's influence, he had "books that slept with me on my nightstand", especially "numerous mystery novels and horrible adventures". "My favourite readings are the repetition of banal books, which never leave me": Father "António Cardoso Borges de) Figueiredo's *A retórica (rhetoric); Reflexões sobre a língua portuguesa (Reflections on the Portuguese language),* by father (Francisco José) Freire; John Milton's *Paradise Lost,* a work that was superior "on account of its coherent scale of values", "a cold, colossal poem" that "overwhelms the imagination"; Jonathan Swift's *Gulliver's Travels,* "a play on accurateness written in an ironical book, or fantasy for the pleasure of superior beings"; and Charles Dickens' *The Pickwick Papers,* "which I read and reread to this day, as if I were but recalling it" and "which I always keep at my side". "Some poets and prose writers will endure, not due to their absolute value, but their absolute relativity. That is what will keep Dickens' oeuvre sweet and alive". Later, he even plans on publishing the book through his company, Íbis.

He will also constantly refer to the character throughout his life. "Mr. Pickwick belongs among the sacred figures of the world's history. Please, do not allege he never existed". He laments the fact there are "creatures that genuinely suffer for not having lived in the real life with Mr. Pickwick", and says that "if a mystic can claim personal knowledge and a clear vision of Christ, then a human creature can allege personal knowledge and a clear vision of Mr. Pickwick – even though he confesses that "having read *The Pickwick Papers* is one of the greatest tragedies of my life". Even so, not a single copy of the book is to be found on his bookshelf. Perhaps because, much like he did with a number of crime novels, he resold it[5]; either that, or the copy didn't survive so much leafing through. Alexandrino Eusébio Severino claims to have found

5 A curious fact of Pessoa was that, when reselling a book an author had signed for him, he tore off the signed page. And he kept doing it even after being warned by his friend Joaquim Palhares, that collectors would pay double for signed books.

Pessoa, aged 7, before travelling to Durban
(a type of photo most children took at the time)

a very perused copy with loose pages at an English books library in Durban. Who knows, it might just have been his – left there by his family when he returned to Portugal for good. At a young age, he read a book a day, and even once wrote in his diary (06/08/1903) that he hadn't read any book that day on account of "being too busy thinking". In his *reading diary* of that very same year, the list of authors was already quite respectable:

April, May – Jules Verne, Guerra Junqueiro, Byron, Harold, Keats, Forjaz de Sampaio, Lombroso, Chesterton.

June – Byron, Espronceda, Farnay, Hudson, Keats, Laing, Molière, Pigault Lebrun, Shelley, Silva Passos, Thomas Child, Tolstoy, Voltaire,[6] Weber.

August – Schopenhauer, Plato, Shakespeare, Fouillée.

November – Hamon, Zeno, Funck Brentano, Aristotle, Rimbaud.[7]

6 He would later say "organically, Voltaire is a corpse".

7 To whom he would dedicate the poem "The life of Arthur Rimbaud", which ends with the literal sentence: "Your life was your forgiveness". As Rimbaud (1854-1891) had a tempestuous love with Paul Verlaine (1844-1896). They even wrote together the *"Sonnet du trou du cul" ("Sonnet of the asshole"),* with Rimbaud writing the first two strophes and Rimbaud the last two, and which begins thus: *Dark and puckered like a purple floret/ It breathes; it hides humbly amid the moss/ still moist with love that trails the gentle floss...* Both lived together until the lover, after having abandoned wife and child for him, shot him in Brussels (1873). Rimbaud then went to

Later, that reading fever would only increase. In an annotation of May 1906, he says: "I shall read two books a day, one of poetry or literature, the other of science or philosophy". Other names he wrote in his diary were Campoamor, Lindholm, Zenão and, once again, "my comrade William Shakespeare, a man of certain standing among the gods", as he described him in a letter to Gaspar Simões (01/11/1931). Pessoa would constantly derive inspiration from him. The image of the lark, for one, so dear to Shakespeare, is present in many of his poems, such as *In articulo mortis:* "Maybe it isn't the robin singing… let us hope it is the lark". Or in "The Mad Fiddler" ("The master said"), where the "lark finds the air", almost reproducing *Romeo and Juliet's* Scene V (Capulet's Garden), in which the lark was the *Messenger of Dawn.* To his friend Côrtes-Rodrigues, he adds "other influences". Such as (Lord Alfred) Tennyson – he who "put the whole of paganism into a single verse, *self-knowledge, self-reverence, self-control,* which encapsulates the whole calendar of asceticism". Other names include António Correia de Oliveira, António Nobre, Baudelaire, Garrett, his uncle Henrique Rosa, José Duro, Maurice Rollinat, Poe, Wordsworth, the French symbolists and Goethe – the European he cherished above all save Shakespeare and Milton. Also Antero de Quental, "a complete poet, the likes of which speak loud and clear to Europe and civilization in general"; he to whom he writes a poem (26/07/1914), *À la manière de Camilo Pessanha;* and Gide, despite claiming he "never could read Gide". In a note from 1914, he completes his preferences, referring "the remains of the influence of Portuguese subpoets I read in my childhood" and "slight influences from Pope's school and the prose of Carlyle".

Oddly enough, some of the authors which did influence him are not part of that list. Such as Oscar Wilde, of whom he spoke thus: "This man, being a man of letters, devoted himself to the culture of conversation and all manner of complex futilities the act of socialization entails"; or that Wilde "had already belaboured that point, leaving, as was his wont, everything to be said about the matter"; or that "he uses the pure melody of words, and is singularly clumsy and primitive"; or, by way of a summary: "Wilde was no artist". Five of his books can be found on Pessoa's bookshelf, including those which have most impressed him: *Intentions, The Picture of Dorian Gray,* his only novel, and *De profundis* – a long letter written at Reading's prison, to his lover lord Alfred Douglas (Bosie). 50 of Pessoa's manuscripts directly mention Wilde. At "The Passing of the Hours", his Freddie even evokes the paleness of Wilde's Bosie, according to Mariana de Castro. Suzette Macedo, quoted by Zenith, suggests it is impossible that he didn't feel Wilde's strong presence, as evidenced by

live in Africa, in Aden (today's Yemen), where he made a living trading weapons, slaves, furs, ivory and coffee, never again writing a single line of poetry. Only at the final stages of his life did he return to the company of his sister Isabelle, at Charleville, the French city he had been born in, and died at the age of 37, having already lost a leg, in Marseille.

the Irishman's words: *Lying and poetry are arts,* or *The only real people are the people who never existed (The Decay of Lying); For in art there is no such thing as a universal truth,* or *A Truth in art is that whose contradictory is also true (The Truth of Masks);* and even admits that *Autopsychography* or *This* might be as unto *translations* of Wilde. Pessoa does Wilde's horoscope (in 1917), comparing it to his own; and Bernardo Soares, at *Disquiet,* claims that "Both fish and Oscar Wilde die because they can't keep their mouths shut". On the same 30th of November Pessoa would die in, 35 years later.

But none of those omissions is as difficult to understand as that of the object of the following words: "I salute you, Walt, salute you, my brother in the Universe", written in *Salute to Walt Whitman* – a typewritten poem with a pencilled title and the peculiar beginning verse of "Portugal the Infinite, June 11th, nineteen fifteen, Hé-lá-á-á-á-á-á-á!". Pessoa even said that Álvaro de Campos wrote "like Walt Whitman, with a Greek poet inside him". Walter Whitman Jr., as a reminder, wrote but a single book of poems in his entire life, *Leaves of Grass.* At each new edition, he would merely alter, add or delete poems. The first, from 1855, with 91 pages, contained 12; the second, 32, among which the famous "Salut au monde", which was initially titled "Poem of salutation"; the third had 130; the ninth and last, 293 – besides a posthumous *Death bed edition,* from 1892, which had minor changes. Pessoa had two copies of that book: One from 1895, with a red cover he scribbled on; the other from 1909, which can be found today at Casa Fernando Pessoa (among the 18 signed by heteronym Alexander Search), with verses underlined with common black pencil or purple crayon. Restless and averse to rigid rules, a 12 year-old Whitman dropped out of school to be a carpenter and a journalist. When Pessoa was born, he was already close to the end (and would die four years later), and it is an old man, white-bearded and crippled (since the age of 52) who writes the following, as if assessing his life: *I now expect to stop only with death;* or, referring to his oeuvre, *time will determine its worth.* In *To foreign lands,* it is as if he were addressing Pessoa: *I send you my poems that you behold in them what you wanted.* According to critic Harold Bloom, *Pessoa is Whitman reborn.*

Later, Pessoa is no longer dazzled by these authors which so influenced him. In a letter to journalist Boavida Portugal (undated, 1912), he acknowledges that "the greatest heights of poetry were achieved in *The Iliad* and with Shakespeare, and, below these, by the Greek playwrights and the two Supreme Epics of the Renaissance by Dante and Milton" – though he later believed the latter did not possess the talent of a true genius. He was but "workmanlike", but still "greater than Camões". At the end of 1931, he confesses: "Today I am awestruck – and horrified – with what I admired – sincerely and intelligently – until the age of 30, in the past and in the [then] present of international literature"; concluding that "literature is but a servile way to dream". Therefore, he "abandoned the habit of reading"; and, "if I must dream, why not dream my own dreams?". He then dreams, "more than Napoleon did", until, "tired of dreaming", he realizes he has no time left.

> Between sleep and dream
> Between me and that which is in me
> The Who I assume to be,
> An endless river flows.
> (…)
> And he whom I feel to be and he who dies
> In that which links me to myself
> Slumbers where the river flows
> That river without end.
>
> *Untitled* (11/09/1933), Fernando Pessoa

An announced poet

Still in Africa, and given the obvious quality of his poems, his destiny was clearly that of a writer. As evidenced by the following two examples of poetry, unpublished at the time. The first reveals the pain of living in that distant land, written in English at the age of 12:

> Somewhere where I shall never live
> A palace garden bowers
> Such beauty that dreams of it grieve.
>
> There, lining walks immemorial,
> Great antenatal flowers
> My lost life before God recall.
>
> There I was happy and the child
> That had cool shadows
> Wherein to feel sweetly exiled.
>
> They took all these true things away.
> O my lost meadows!
> My childhood before Night and Day!
>
> *Anamnesis*[8], Fernando Pessoa

8 The title is inspired by the theory espoused by Plato, according to which all knowledge stems from the memories of past situations.

Another, dedicated to his mother, written in Portuguese at age 13[9]:

Hail, Mary, so pure,
Virgin unsullied
Heareth the prayer which stems
From the bosom of my bitterness.

You, who are full of grace
Hear my prayer,
Guide me by the hand
Through this passing life.

The Lord, your son
May he always be with us,
As with you he doth
Shine forevermore.

Blessed are you, Mary,
Among the women of the world
You whose soul doth encase
A sweet image of joy.

More radiant than light itself
And blessed, o Holy Mother
Is the fruit that comes
From your womb, Jesus!

Blessed[10] Holy Mary,
You, Mother of God
Who lives in the heavens
Pray for us[11] each day.

Pray for us, sinners,
To your son, Jesus,
Who died for us on the cross
And who so greatly suffered.

Pray, now, o dear mother
And (as luck will have it)
At the time of our death
When life escapes us.

9 Two versions were written. The first, dated 12th of April 1902, and a second, little different, which consensus deems to have been written subsequently, but Pessoa claims to have written on the 7th of April 1902 in a list of poems he tallied as having written "until the age of sixteen".

10 *Glorious* in the second version.

11 *Watch over us* in the second version.

Hail, Mary, so pure,
Virgin unsullied
Heareth[12] the prayer which stems
From the bosom of my bitterness.

Ave Maria, Fernando Pessoa

His début as a poet

In spite of its schoolboy-like handwriting, his first real poem was *Separated from thee, treasure of my heart* (12/05/1901), which was later included in his *English poems* – as per Jennings, it was influenced by a poem written by Shelzeny at the age of 18, *To the queen of my heart.* But his first published work as a poet was at Lisbon's *O Imparcial* (18(07/1902), a daily that held itself as *the defender of the nation's economical and moral interests,* headed by a politician of the Regeneration, professor Carneiro de Moura. This is how he was introduced to the public (abridged):

A 13 years-old poet

Today, we present to our readers Mr. Fernando A. Pessoa Nogueira, a charming and restless child of 14 years with a bright and vivacious spirit, son of the departed Seabra Pessoa. His are the rhymes we publish below, and which show great promise of this aspiring poet's talent, as he elaborates upon Augusto Vicente's beautiful quatrain[13] with his own *glosa*[14]:

The motto of the poem is as follows:

Your eyes, dark beads,
Are two Hail Marys
Sorrows of a rosary
I pray with every day.

Pessoa's *glosa* follows, and each verse of Gil's quatrain is the final verse of each of the four stanzas:

When pain embitters me
When I feel hard grief,

12 *Hear* in the second version.

13 It would later on become clear that the quatrain was actually from another Augusto, Gil, director-general of Beaux-Arts of the Ministry of Illustration. It was published in his book, *Versos,* and he would later become one of Pessoa's favourite café companions.

14 *Translator's note:* Poetic scheme in which the topic or motto is reused or commented on.

My sole solace is
Your eyes, dark beads.

Naught but love sprouts from them
Not a shade of irony:
Those enticing eyes
Are two Hail Marys.

But if wrath were to cloud them
I suffer tortures most dire
As I pray with every bead
Of a rosary of bitterness

If they happen to be drowned in distress
I supplicate joys of you
In a fervent prayer
I pray every day!

Untitled (31/03/1902), Fernando Pessoa

Arco de Jesus School

Shortly after his return on the 2nd of October of 1905, he begins attending an advanced course in Portuguese at the Arco de Jesus School, which was created by Pedro V in 1858 at the Sé parish, "thus called because of the arch that remains there. The building was the headquarters of the Convent of Jesus". The school taught a general degree and four specific ones: librarian, teaching, and diplomatic. As he considers himself "a poet animated by philosophy, and not a philosopher with poetic faculties", he enrols as a paying student in the latter option, to the tune of 6 thousand réis at the beginning and a further 6 thousand at the end of the academic year. There are four regular students and 22 registered as volunteers. The course has five classes: French, Roman Philosophy, Geography, English and World History. According to the class records, he also attends classes as a voluntary student of Geography, and French, German and English Language and Literature. He also considers Greek and Philosophy, but these latter two are scratched out in his application. His shyness, the lack of girlfriends, the way he was smartly dressed, his English upbringing, it all sets him apart from his peers. "I hold no hope for any friendship here; I shall endeavour to leave as soon as possible". His only intimate friends at the time are colleagues Armando Teixeira Rebelo, who studied at Pretoria, and Beatriz Osório de Albuquerque, who addressed Pessoa as *mon cher mage rouge* (my dear red wizard). The three classmates always talked in English with each other. Later, when the two got married, Pessoa was the godfather of Signa, their daughter.

Contrary to what is commonly believed, he did not fail the year due to repeated absences (as did a third of students that year), but because he fell ill between May and August 1906, and couldn't take the July exams (called *normas).* He tries to take them in September, but his request is refused, on the 6th of October, because *the legal provisions of the deadline hadn't been fulfilled... nor the certificate of illness,* according to the university's administration. He enrols again, this time as a repeater, in "the diplomacy course, plus a course of Philosophy". He would not conclude it. On account of his temperament – in the words of heteronym Jean-Seul de Méluret, he "was an anarchist at the age of 17" – or perhaps because he knew that, even if he were to become a diplomat, he'd be serving a government in its death throes. It held no real appeal to anyone, especially young men driven by democratic dreams such as he, who considered that "in Portugal, at least, there is hope, that of the Republican Party". A while later, in *Carta Aberta,* he would position himself against the monarchy, which he considered "crowned by a sanctimonious, debauched court, sickeningly sanctimonious and sickeningly debauched", and "swimming in all manner of muck and attracting all sorts of rot".

In a draft of a letter meant for his mother, he admits to "lacking motivation for the degree". Still, at the beginning of the new term, he misses less classes, which indicates that his health had improved by then. But he is no longer interested in finishing his studies. In an annotation dated March 1907, referring to his studies, he describes them in plain English as "a dull and stupid day" – adding "tedious" and "boring", in Portuguese, at the margins. The country is living through difficult times, divided between several factions of monarchists and the insurgency of republican ideals. João Franco, leader of the Regeneration Party and a figure of considerable stature in the government, had decreed the closure of the University of Coimbra the previous year. The students' reaction would only come in April – in a strike that, initially, was merely protesting the flunking of doctoral candidate José Eugénio Ferreira, and would grow into a protest against the monarchy itself. The student movement had strong republican undertones, and spread out to other universities at Porto and Lisbon. As the legend goes, Pessoa was one of the men responsible for the strike. According to half-brother João Maria, *he was one of the instigators. But I suppose he wasn't expelled.* There are no records of it at the university. And it is highly unlikely that it happened like that. Not that he held any particular sympathy for the monarchy – quite the opposite, as we saw. But rather because his temperament would forego such boldness. Classes are suspended on that 15th of April, by order of the Kingdom's Ministry, and the Chamber of Deputies is dissolved on the 8th of May, also by its decree. Pessoa's family spend some vacation time in Lisbon, but return to Durban without him. It was to be the last time they'd all be together. At the end of the strike, on the 1st of June, all exams are postponed from July to September, the month in which his grandmother would die (on the 6th). By that time, Pessoa will already have left his studies, as he noted down in a loose note saying *"C.S.L.*[15] *and end thereof".*

Later (in 1908), as he so strongly disapproved of the authoritarianism that underpinned life in Portugal, he creates the *Order of the Blown Out Match (of the value, loyalty and merit of blunders),* in which the award is "a bronze-cast donkey's skull with a blown out match in its mouth", the purpose of which is "to duly honour the cultivators of of national blunders". But not only of the national kind, as "blunders have no motherland". Those who yearned for such honour could apply via an application in "common foolscap folio", and the first *Degree of Blunder* was awarded to Manuel II (The Patriot) – who, with the murder of his father, had just been proclaimed king. He also sketches out a "revolutionary treaty", *Pela República (For the Republic),* with an introduction in which he justifies said murder. His reasons for having dropped out aren't entirely clear; *It seems like he disagreed with how the university*[16] *was run, and just decided to quit,* according to João Maria. Or the idea of becoming a diplomat for a dying monarchy just didn't appeal to him. In my estimation, his grandmother's death also contributed to his decision, as Pessoa knew he was her sole heir and could eke out a living with what she would bequeath him, thus no longer needing to graduate or being dependent on others. Besides, he had already begun working in commercial enterprises. And so, naturally, he gave up on his studies and his career, as he gave up on almost everything he had ever wanted. "As great as tragedies may be, none is bigger than the tragedy of my own life".

> Our Lady of the Hours that Pass, Madonna of stagnant waters and dead algae, Tutelary Goddess of vast deserts and dark landscapes of barren rocks, free me from my youth.
>
> *The Book of Disquiet*, Bernardo Soares

Awaiting destiny's pleasure

"Whither goes my life, and who carries it"? After dropping out of university, he doesn't return to Durban. "I left the nebula of childhood and adolescence", with no idea of what fate had in store for him. His learning period was over. "Twenty one years lived in pure and useless undefined lassitude", feeling "useless in the rumbling frothing of life", "good, but only in a real description". His feeling of loneliness and obsessive fear of madness become more acute, with the latter only slightly alleviated in 1910. "Ah, how I wished to cast but a measure of poison, disquiet or restlessness into a soul". From then on, he

15 *Translator's note:* "Curso Superior de Letras", or Degree in Letters.
16 He misspoke here, as Lisbon's classic university was only founded in 1911.

starts to fully enjoy "the sweetness of having neither family nor company with… which we feel the pride of exile dim in uncertain voluptuousness the vague restlessness of being far away". In that city, in which he knows very few people, he feels "abandoned like a castaway in the middle of the sea", doomed to "this exile that is me". Nonetheless, he still placed an enormous trust in the future – which would then, little by little, fade away. Now, "my life follows a route and a scale", and in it "my own shadow guides me, as God made of me its altar". Later on, he would write the following note in English:

> Every year ending in 5 has been important in my life.
> 1895. My mother's second marriage; the result: Africa.
> 1905. Return to Lisbon.
> 1915. *Orpheu.*[17]
> 1925. The death of my mother.
> All were the beginnings of certain periods.

Missing was the year of 1935, in which he died.

17 A literary magazine he would serve as director in, as we will see later on.

Ecce homo
(Behold the man) Words uttered by Pilate as he pointed Jesus to the Romans

A KNIGHT OF SAD FIGURE

I am an immense desert
Not even I am in.
Untitled (undated), Fernando Pessoa

A spectator of life

At the presentation of *Anónimo transparente,* a book by Hermenegildo Sábat, José Saramago wondered: *What manner of portrait would Pessoa had painted of himself, had he been a painter instead of a poet?* Certainly not only one portrait, but many. Which was why he who sought to be "a spectator of life without mingling with it" had such varied ways with which to define himself: A *seafaring angel, one unknown to himself,* a *strange stranger,* a *stranger lucid of himself,* a *man who never existed,* a *sincere liar,* an *insincere truth-teller, a sphinx presenting the riddle, a black daffodil,* a *labyrinth, an infinite solar system, a galaxy, poet of depression, poet of the garret, poet of the absurd hour. Man from Hell,* as per Eduardo Lourenço's peculiar definition, *if one believes in Dante.* In every case, one acknowledges that the scope of his oeuvre greatly exceeds this "abandoned boat, unfaithful to fate" that is his life. António Mega Ferreira points out: *As a poet, he is above the mere human; as a man, he lives below normal.* Cleonice Bernardelli confided in me in a conversation that she felt *the closer one gets to Pessoa, the further he moves away.* Pessoa himself would conclude: "There is but one art, that of living". The problem was the fact that "living frightens and tortures me". Whatever the case, and despite feeling that "God knows who I am better than me", "it is now necessary for me to say what kind of a man I am".

I'm going through infinity, I'm coming out the other side!
Whether or not I make it there's not your problem, so let me go…
It's my problem, and God's – it's up to what I mean by the word Infinite…
(…)
I can be everything, I can be nothing, I can be anything,
Depending on what I crave… it's none of your business…

"Salutation to Walt Whitman", Álvaro de Campos

A blend of noblemen and Jews

Pessoa considers himself "Hebrew by fatherly descent and physiognomy"; on account of his facial features, inherited from his mother, which he characterizes as "a sheepish muzzle that offends mankind". "A proboscis akin to a gas meter", as per his words written to his unlikely beloved Ophelia Queiroz (16/02/1929). Drawings of several types of noses can be found in the Chest, with the margins scribbled with attempts at guessing the character traits of those who bore them: *Pride, self-esteem, confidence.* In an entry in his diary, dated the 27th of February 1913, he notes that one of his friends, the Jewish dentist "Israel [Abraham Cagi] Anahory, informed by myself that I had a dab of Semitic", concurred "yes, the nose, a bit".

It wasn't by chance that he expressed his descent in *Message*, according to Ioram Melcer, in poems such as "The field of the escutcheons", in which one finds a variation of *Shaddai, one of God's names in the Bible* – the letters of which can form *Asher dái bo* (sufficiency of self), and which conceivably inspired the verses "Let it be sufficient for whom there is sufficiency/ The sufficient to suffice him!". Or "Padrao", in which can be found *part of the Massechet Hagiga,* wherein one reads that *God* rebuked *the sea that wished to spread out and imposed bounds upon it,* "That the bounded sea may be Greek or Roman"; rather different from that of Sebastião I, which was much vaster, "The sea without bounds is Portuguese".

His Jewish features evoked his ancestors, the eldest among which being Filipe Rodrigues, son of baptised Jews (1497), a native of Castelo Branco. Or his six-times-great-grandfather Custódio da Cunha de Oliveira (1632-1669), who hailed from Alcaide and was a clerk at the *almotaçaria*[1] at the fiscal court of Montemor-o-Novo. He was married to Madalena Pessoa de Gouveia – a female name which would perpetuate itself among the family. The man who sired the Pessoas at Tomar and the Algarve was one Manuel da Cunha Pessoa (born in 1669), brother of Sancho Pessoa da Cunha (born in 1662), a psalmist and astrologer who, in 1706, like so many others in the Iberian Peninsula, was subjected to an *auto-de-fé.* The records of the process (#9.478 of the Inquisition of Coimbra) can still be found at the Torre do Tombo, albeit with its 183 pages severely deteriorated. Even so, the following remains readable: *The defendant is a Christian convert, a merchant, married to an unknown spouse, cousin of Brites, hailing from the town of Montemor-o-Velho, bishopric of Coimbra, and resident at Fundão, in the outskirts of the town of Covilhã, bishopric of Guarda.* The end of the process contains the following *Term of Abjuration in Form,* in which Sancho Pessoa da Cunha declares (abridged):

1 *Almotacé* was the title of clerks in charge of tributes, weights, measurements and the distribution of food.

I, before my Lords Inquisitor, swear by the faith in the Holy Gospels I place my hands on that I anathematize and cast out any and all Heresy and Apostasy that goes against out Holy Catholic and Apostolic Faith. And I shall ever be obedient to our Most Holy Pope, President of God's Church. And, should I ever again fall into the traps I now forswear, I wish to be considered a relapser and duly punished, with no recourse to this absolution, and to fully submit myself to the severity of the sacred canons.

After which he is provided with his Terms of Release and Secrecy (abridged):

The defendant was informed that he should keep secret of all he witnessed and heard in the Inquisition's gaols, and tell no-one of those he was locked in with, nor of those who remained, nor to carry any message from them. Should he go against these prohibitions, he shall be severely punished; all of which the defendant agreed to, under oath of the holy Gospels. And the Lords Inquisitor thus had him released.

His grandson Martinho da Cunha e Oliveiro wasn't as lucky. He was the brother of Diogo Nunes da Cunha Pessoa, a smelter and tinsmith, born on the 15th of January 1709 at Fundão, and Pessoa's fourth-great-grandfather. In 1747, he was first arrested by the Inquisition of Coimbra and granted the chance to abjure and benefit from the Terms of Release and Secrecy, but was later the object of *greater excommunication* by the Inquisition of Western Lisbon. He paid the sum of 188.070 cruzados – which amounted to the pay of the council's secretary, the prosecutor, the bailiff, and the mayor himself – and his brief life ended in the pyre. This process (#8.106, Inquisition of Lisbon) can also be found at the Torre do Tombo, clocking in at 238 pages, is borderline illegible. According to genealogists José António Severino da Costa Caldeira and Rui Miguel Faísca R. Pereira, the following were also ancestors of Pessoa subjected to the Inquisition: Beatriz and Rodrigo da Cunha (arrested 28/11/1621), Custódio da Cunha e Oliveira (13/05/1669), Diogo Dias Fernandes (process no. 5.289, Inquisition of Évora), Diogo Fernandes Bacalhau (process no. 9.478, Inquisition of Évora) and Diogo Fernandes (burnt at the pyre). At that time, when one such heretic was killed, all due and undue precautions were taken to prevent their souls from returning home. Thus, the souls of all those ancestors probably coalesced into Pessoa's tortured soul, after having wandered aimlessly across distant, indistinct skies.

Ergo, a "blend of noblemen and Jews"[2], as he described his family. "Noblemen" here being but two forefathers. From his mother's side, Gonçalo Anes da Fonseca (born in 1475) in Lagos, knight of Manuel I and one of the first inhabitants of the Azores. From his father's side, José António Pereira de Araújo e Sousa (1746-1799), captain of the Artillery Regiment of the Algarve

2 Proof of his Jewish descent can be found in an annotation in his diary (23/03/1906): "I must be operated on, circumcised"; and later on hopes to have "rectified that failing", although there is no proof that he was circumcised.

and true nobleman with a coat of arms, hailing from Fermedo (Arouca), whose letter of nobility was scribed the year he died in. A descendant of royal chief prosecutors, he was granted permission to coin his own coat of arms. As a child, Pessoa copied it many times, basing on an image he saw at the Genealogical-Heraldic Archive of Portugal, a quartered shield with the following arms in each quarter: the Pereiras' in the first, the Camisões' in the second, the Sousas' in the third and the Araújos' in the fourth. The same coat of arms that was engraved upon a ring he never parted from as an adult, as corroborated by friend Luís Pedro Moitinho de Almeida: *He had the affectations of a nobleman and wore with certain pride a silver ring with the crests of the Sousas, the Camisões and the Araújos* (he forgot to mention the Pereiras). Another illustrious ancestor was Daniel Pessoa e Cunha (1780/1822), doctor at Tavira's Royal Hospital, from Serpe (Salvador). Taking such ancestry into account, he truly is a walking contradiction: Converted Christian, from his father's side, and Catholic from his mother's, and racially classified by friend and poet Mário (Pais da Cunha) Saa as *Anglo-Lusitanian-Jewish.* According to Pessoa himself, he was but a "converted pagan".

A discreet man

"I visit no one, nor do I socialize – not in living rooms, nor in cafés", as doing so would entail "partaking in useless chatter and wasting time that could be better spent in cogitation and in my projects, or at least in my dreams, which will always be more beautiful than the conversation of others". The explanation he provides for such aversion to social practises is simple (and pretentious): "I owe myself to future mankind. If I waste myself, I waste the divine heritage men of the future could benefit from, I diminish the happiness I could give them". On the dimension of his thought, he says only that "I never held my physical presence in high regard. I have the look of a spent Jesuit. I am a deaf-mute who screams out his gestures". Those gestures are restrained, "extremely courteous", delicate, even. Polite, *he opened the door for the servants bringing groceries into his building, at Rua Coelho da Rocha,* according to Manuela Nogueira. "I am shy, and the thought of exhibiting my anxieties is abhorrent to me"; which is why he (almost) never hands out visiting cards – always claiming they remained undelivered at the printers'. "Calm and joyful before others", he is, "generally speaking, a creature others easily sympathize with". He seldom laughs and prefers listening to speaking – "one should not speak too much". Deep down, "for me, listening has ever been something to do in tandem with looking", since "unless you listen, you cannot truly see". His interest lies in having a dialogue, rather than debating. And he does not enjoy showing off. And even less hurting others. His heteronym, the Baron of Teive, whose life almost mirrored Pessoa's, says: "I always set myself apart from the world and life in general… No one ever treated me badly, in any way, shape or form. I was treated well by all, if distantly. I soon realized the distance emanated from me and was of me. Therefore, I can say with no self-delusion that I was always respected. But not loved or cherished".

The statements of those who consorted with him express similar sentiments. According to sister Teca, *he was very reserved, and often seemed oblivious to what surrounded him. That said, he was ever dedicated, easy to please, and I can't recall ever seeing him angry. He would never raise his voice and was polite to a fault. He had a kind word for anyone, and was what you would call a gentleman, that you would.* Ophelia Queiroz follows: *Fernando was extremely reserved. He spoke very little of his intimate life.* Carlos Queiroz, Ophelia's nephew, claims that *his gestures, nervous yet plastic and measured, had the rhythm of a monologue, as if trying to rhyme with every word. I never heard anyone complaining of having been accidentally hit by him.* For French writer Pierre Horcade, *he positively radiated an undefinable charm which consisted of extreme courtesy, good humour and a measure of feverish intensity, all of which bubbled under the façade of pleasant company.* António Cobreira declares he was *an affable creature, beyond reproach in how he treated others, utterly polite, incapable of disloyalty, immaculately honest, extremely delicate, sad and shy.* Jorge de Sena spoke of him as *a softly pleasant gentleman, very smartly dressed, whose upper lip hid a slightly ironical smile. His bald spot, his spent eyes, the way he sat with hands under his knees, and his soft voice made him look foreign, distant in time and space.* Casais Monteiro suggests that *no one has ever wanted to be less seen,* summing up his life as *a discreet modesty, a love of silence, and contemplation.* Friend Almada Negreiros remembers him as *a quiet person,* the most silent in the group. *He was of auditory nature, mine was visual.* In a conversation with António Quadros, he adds: *But none of us had any doubts, he was the master!* Luís de Oliveira Guimarães concludes: *As a person, Pessoa was an utter bore, mopy like you wouldn't believe. We talked often enough, or, rather, I did the talking, as he remained silent. In fact, no one actually knew who Fernando Pessoa was. His glory only came 20 or so years after his death.*

He speaks with his face resting on his arm and often, whenever intensely agitated, presses his head between both hands. "The mouth, the last thing one notices," has "a smile owed to existing, not of his talking to us". "Between myself and my voice, an abyss has opened", which has no scream in its voice, barely has a voice to speak of". Perhaps his own verses, written in 1914, are applicable to himself: "Imperfect, elect serene voice/ To speak to inert gods with". That voice is "spoken in a tone of one who seeks but to say that which he is saying – not high, not low, free of intent, of hesitation, of shyness". But his pitch changes at times, and then he speaks in a shrill monotone. Famous

Portuguese actor João (Henrique) Villaret (1913-1961) once heard him reading poems and whispered to poet António Botto, who had introduced both to each other: *Um, Botto, that friend of yours, with that voice, could never be an actor.* The same sentiment is expressed by others, even if the words are different.

> Who put[3] in my voice, dull sound that it is,
> The miracle of words and their shape
> And the greater miracle of their meaning?
> My voice, half noise as it is,
> Lights up from the inside...
>
> *Untitled* (11/09/1913), Fernando Pessoa

His father's frail body

"My body's the abyss between I and I". A frail body, much like his father's – disarticulated, sallow, with a flat, consumptive chest. A disaster for one like himself, who holds that "an artist should be born beautiful and elegant, for he who loves beauty cannot be bereft of it. And it is certainly a terrible pain for an artist not to be able to find in himself that which he so ardently seeks". Despite appreciating football, he partakes in no sporting activity, which comes as little surprise for a man with long legs with little muscle on them. *He was pale, skinny, and seemed physically underdeveloped. Hunched, his chest sunken, he had a peculiar gait* – according to Clifford Geerdts, his colleague at Durban. He walks with disjointed steps as he swings his flaccid arms. "Lo, my arm, the banner of God". His hands "are white, human hands, so human! Such mystery! How odd that there should be people and hands!". Also, "slender, a little pale, a little shadowed". When he sits, he hides both hands under his knees. "At times, when I look at my hands, I become fearful of God". As prescribed by Dr. Egas Moniz[4], from 1907 on, he starts doing physical exercise "for fitness purposes" – a frequent reference in his texts, even when he is simply discussing literary styles: "I lived under the atmosphere of Greek and German philosophers, as well as the decadent French, whose action was swept off my spirit by Swedish gymnastics". His

3 "Puts", in an earlier version.

4 Antonio (Caetano de Abreu Freire) Egas Moniz (1847-1955), professor of Neurology at the University of Lisbon, inventor of cerebral arteriography and the pre-frontal lobotomy technique. He was awarded the Nobel Prize in Medicine in 1949, sharing it with Swiss Walter Rudolf Hess (1881-1973), due to his research on the influence of the brain over other organs. Pessoa had the following to say about him in a text written in French: "He does not exaggerate when he articulates everything in pretty clear and precise terms – every man is naturally sexual, every woman is naturally a mother. All who stray from that are abnormal. It is very true". And, on the 13th of November 1914, he would dedicate an untitled sonnet to him, which goes: *There yet remains some of your blood in my veins./ And what little I am is yours, distant grandfather.*

trainer, Luís da Costa Leal Furtado Coelho, was also king Manuel's, and wrote a number of books on the subject, chief among which *Método do sistema sueco de educação física: Rendimentos de uma técnica pedagógica* (1935), dedicated to *My former disciple and good friend.* Pessoa wrote about him in *A Fama* (1933), in an article titled "What an American millionaire did in Portugal[5]". "In less than three months, at the rate of three lessons per week, Furtado Coelho elicited such transformation in me that, it should be modestly said, I persist to this day – to what degree of benefit for the European civilization is not up to me to say". Coelho was (probably) the one who instilled in him the habit of taking cold showers every morning, as soon as he woke up, with soap provided by his friend Francisco Peixoto Carvalho e Bourbon (originally from Angra do Heroísmo, a botanist and professor at the University of Coimbra), a particular brand which was advertised thus in Portugal: *No* cê-cê[6] *for me, I use Lifebuoy.*

The description made by doctor Taborda de Vasconcelos, a contemporary from Porto, is definitive: *Puny, slender legs, retracted thorax, long head with receding hairline, sinewy in build, sober in demeanour, withdrawn and distant, he had a sphinx-like air about himself – all in all, the quintessential spent, asthenic type.* In *Disquiet,* heteronym Vicente Guedes (afterwards converted to Bernardo Soares) sets an appointment with "an individual whose appearance at first did not interest me in the least, but which I gradually grew interested in". That anonymous individual, who was Pessoa himself, was described in the following terms: "A man who appeared to be in his thirties, thin, closer to tall than to short, exaggeratedly slumped when sitting, but less so when standing upright, dressed in not entirely slovenly fashion. In his plain, pale face, an air of suffering failed to make it in any way remarkable, and it was hard to ascertain just what sort of suffering it stemmed from – it seemed to belie vices, anguishes, and that peculiar suffering borne of indifference that arises from having suffered too much. His voice was dull and shaky, much like that of creatures who expect nothing, as to them it is perfectly useless to expect anything whatsoever". To say nothing of his "poor-ish hearing", which proved that his "hearing was poor". In conversation, Teresa Sobral Cunha defined him as *someone who didn't believe in his body.* Taking into account the veritable wreck of a body he had, he himself sheepishly declared that "someone in me hates being myself". To wit, "I am not a cadaver[7], only because I yet live".

5 Said millionaire was Bernarr Macfadden (1868-1955), owner of newspapers, magazines and hotels in New York. Having decided to use his fortune for the benefit of the common good, he founded numerous educational institutions for children all over the world, including one at São João do Estoril. The relationship between Coelho and the millionaire stemmed from the American having devised a way of life which consisted of a simple diet, fresh air and Swedish gymnastics. Pessoa wrote two letters to him, on the 15th and 19th of May 1933, commenting on what he had done in Portugal. There are no records of any replies.

6 Popular term for bromidrosis.

7 Not much stock is put into a popular belief that the word is a merging of the first three syllables of the Roman expression *caro data vermibus* (meat given to the worms). With his penchant for

My body weighs on the thought
That I can never quite attain my soul
And always linger in the moment
Here, eternal while it lasts…[8]

Untitled (10/01/1916), Fernando Pessoa

His health was ever the cause for complaints. His diary[9], in the annotations of a single month (November 1919), reads: "I woke up with a sore throat" (15th); "physically indisposed, flatulence" and "I experienced three spells of a peculiar form of dizziness" (16th); "a bout of the flu with fever at nightfall" and "a slightly final stage" (29th). Other notes spread about include "I felt myself fading away, almost passing out"; or "I feel rather anaemic and drained, albeit poetically excited"; or "ah, how I wish I could see the oasis in the desert of my fever". In letters to his friend Álvaro Pinto, he claims to have been "ill, feverish" (31/12/1912); or to having "spent five days in bed with the flu… my head is still out of sorts" (13/06/1913). To Ophelia, he confesses to having had "another angina" (18/03/1929). Her concern for his health is clear in her reply: *I was most concerned to know your condition worsened, and my not being able to visit* (18/03/1920); *I missed you greatly and it pained me to know you ill and not being able to tend to you* (19/03/1920); *Are you feeling better?* (20/03/1920); *How did you spend your night?* (30/03/1920); *God willing, it will never come to pass, but should you fall ill after we are married, you, my love, shall see how tender I will be* (20/07/1920). But Pessoa doesn't much care to speak of it. In the second stage of their relationship, he writes (29/09/1929): "It is bad enough that I am ill: There is no need to inquire upon my health as if it were within my control or I were under the obligation of reporting on it".

I have a great cold,
And all know how great colds
Alter the universe's system,
Make us angry at life,
And cause metaphysics itself to sneeze
(…)
Excusez un peu... such a physical cold!
I need both truth and aspirin.

Untitled (14/03/1931), Álvaro de Campos

---

the unconventional, Pessoa would certainly consider it a good definition.

8 This verse is reminiscent of Vinícius de Moraes' "Soneto da Fidelidade": *Be it not immortal, as it is but flame/ But let it be endless for as long as it lasts.* According to Alberto da Costa e Silva, the words were inspired by Henri de Régnier, French poet and novelist (1844-1936): *Love is eternal for as long as it lasts.*

9 Pessoa's diary, first written in English, begins on the 15th of March 1905 and is interrupted on the 2nd of June 1906. After a couple of pages written between 1912 and 1913, signed by C.R. Anon, he resumes his entries on October 1915, now in Portuguese, but starts using English again three days later, and would continue to do so almost until 1920.

His myopic eyes

He has "attentive eyes and ears", of one who "sees like a damned man", quite unlike what he described in an untitled poem of 1916: "Precise vision… a gaze from beyond". For him, it would always be his "short-sightedness". His ID describes his eyes as *brown.* And he's also myopic. "We are all myopic, except when looking inwards. None but dreams can truly see with the stare". He would patronize opticians his entire life. In an annotation listing his "obligations of the day", when he was already over 40 years old, next to "little ones' birthday", it reads: "Optician". At the age of 17, according to a prescription written by L. Xavier da Costa, he has *-3D* in each eye. Next to the prescription, it reads: *12 degrees, myopic,* and a complement for *being able to see from a distance.*

Taborda de Vasconcelos says he has *small, deep-set, almond-shaped eyes, his look distant from behind the thick, rimless lenses.* Luís Pedro Moitinho de Almeida recalls his glasses as *more akin to spectacles,* which, at the end of his life, *lent him a look of shyness, despite the aggressiveness of his American-style red moustache, contrasting with what little grey had sprouted from his hair.* Those glasses are round-shaped, indistinctly made of metal (at the beginning) or tortoise shell (later on), with often foggy lenses[10]. Pessoa saw everything blurred from a distance, even when wearing glasses, which was why he couldn't practise any sport requiring precision in locating balls or the like. But using glasses such as these is a minor inconvenience for those suffering from myopia, as they don't need them to read. It is even common for them to write in small letters and read without glasses.

> I know not with which eyes I see
> Or with which ears I hear
> Their faces and their voices
> Which I see not, yet see
>
> Which I hear not, yet hear
> Which I dream not, yet dream,
> Which is not me, nor another…
>
> *Untitled* (17/09/1916), Fernando Pessoa

10 This observation, made by many of those who knew Pessoa, is most strange in the eyes of Pernambucan optician Dr. Saulo Gorenstein, as *a short-sighted person can't cope with dirty glasses.* Proof of his slovenliness, perhaps.

Hair, moustache and beard

From the beginning, and until the day he died, Pessoa never once shaved himself, claims cousin Eduardo Freitas da Costa. Which was why he was such an avid frequenter of barbershops, and why so many of his texts take place in such establishments, such as this one from *Disquiet:* "I went into the barbershop as usual, with the pleasant sensation of entering a familiar place, easily and naturally. New things are distressing to my sensibility; I'm at ease only in places where I've already been. After I'd sat down on the chair, I happened to ask the young barber, occupied in fastening a clean, cool cloth around my neck, about his older colleague from the chair to the right, a spry fellow who had been sick. I didn't ask this because I felt obliged to ask something; it was the place and my memory that sparked the question. *He passed away yesterday,*[11] flatly answered the barber's voice behind me. The whole of my irrational good mood abruptly died, like the eternally missing barber from the adjacent chair. A chill swept over all my thoughts. I said nothing. Nostalgia!" One of his favourite games was to pretend his niece Manuela was his barber; an oft-repeated scene in which he'd sit on the couch with towel around his neck, and the girl would wield *a Bakelite-handle knife, pretending it was a razor.* After that, cologne and a coin for her trouble, which would then invariably be used to purchase chocolate. As he never walked around with his head exposed, he criticized the "merchant who uses his head for lesser purposes than wearing a hat". And he also had a moustache, which would lead Ophelia to confess the following in a letter written on the 22nd of November 1929: *Did you know that Íbis' moustache tickles Íbis' mouth?*

> But poor is the dream that wishes to have none!
> Poor is the hope that solely exists!
> As one runs his hand through his hair.
>
> *Untitled* (02/08/1933), Fernando Pessoa

As far as I could ascertain, his hair and beard were entrusted to the care of two barbers. Armando Ventura Teixeira, at Chiado, close to where he had once lived, and Manassés Ferreira de Seixas, at Mr. Celestino Rodrigues' barbershop at Rua Silva Carvalho 10, after he moved to Campo de Ourique (1920). He remained the latter's client when Manassés opened Barbearia Seixas at Rua Coelho Rocha 5C, almost in front of the apartment he spent his last years in. A simple man with a limp and a cane, he ends up Pessoa's friend and confidant. He is the "barber with the jokes" Bernardo Soares speaks of. It was Manassés who gave him his last shave, before he went to the hospital he would die in. In

---

11 That barbershop clearly isn't that of Manassés, the family of which maintains he never had an employee pass away.

his sickbed and near the end, it is Manassés who goes daily into his room to shave him. Very early in the day, before opening his shop, and almost always in the company of his son. Because, as he passed by the barbershop, Pessoa saw the child playing inside, and asked Manassés to "bring the child". He talks to the child more than he does with the father. Said child was António Manuel Rodrigues Seixas, who would later become an electrical engineer in a workshop that took the place of the old barbershop, and who, as a child, almost became part of that room, which he described as *depressing.*

> Lay your hand
> On my hair…
> All is illusion.
> To dream is to know it.
>
> *Untitled* (15/12/1912)

A smartly dressed man

He is most certainly an elegant man where his clothes are concerned. *His manner of being, of feeling, even of dressing, was special,* according to Ophelia. *He was skinny,* recalls friend and journalist Artur Portela, claiming he lived *as if huddled in his threadbare raincoat, his entire frame crowned by a ridiculous hat.* An unfair description, except perhaps for his final days. He always wore his hats tilting to the right, and they were invariably black or dark grey, "with hemmed, upturned brim" in *diplomat* style, in stark contrast to the straw ones he had used in Durban. But sometimes, and despite there being no photographic evidence, he also used the latter in Lisbon, as Ophelia attests (01/06/1920): *The straw hat looks so good on you, my love! It makes you seem joyful.* "At night, I was pleased to having heard two kind references to my being well dressed (Oh! Me?)". Said two references were made by friends Armando Côrtes-Rodrigues and José de Azeredo Perdigão. As a young man, he used his trousers tucked into his gaiters; later on, as per the fashion at the time, he starts wearing the type of short tight pants known as *papo seco.* His shoes were always impeccably shined – there are records of purchases made at the shoe store Sapataria Contente, at Avenida da Liberdade. His shirts, immaculately white and *very starched* (by the hands of Irene, the family's washerwoman, in his last 20 years), had *straight cuffs and tipped collar* – as opposed to the turned tips that were fashionable at the time. A note of his reads: "soft shirts, no collar, at the shirt shop at Rossio, middle of 1st block, side of the Rua do Ouro"[12].

12 The official name is Rua Áurea (golden), but everyone refers to it as Rua do Ouro (gold), including Pessoa himself who dreamt of "waking up at the Rua do Ouro".

The shop in question is Camisaria Pitta[13], one of Lisbon's most refined, where, according to the same note, "handkerchiefs and other things" are also to be found.

> My torn shirt
> (As I have no one to sew it for me)
> (...)
> But I know the shirt is nothing,
> That a tear is not a bad thing,
> And that the torn shirt
> Will not fool my soul
> In search of the Holy Grail[14].
>
> *Untitled* (31/10/1933), Fernando Pessoa

He wears a long, form-fitting jacket, and suits in Anglo-Saxon style – specially made by the masters at Casa Lourenço & Santos, the most expensive of its kind in Lisbon. Of the three addresses of the tailor shop, Eduardo Freitas da Costa and Jorge de Sena confirm the one he frequented was at the ground floor of the Avenida Palace hotel, at the corner of 1° de Dezembro with the Praça dos Restauradores[15], where one can find the monument honouring Portuguese battles – including the one at Guararapes, with the inscription *Pernambuco 27th of January 1654*[16]. But luxury is expensive, especially for one of modest means, and the store often had to resort to the services of Procuradoria Fénix or Procural, two companies specializing in getting money from customers that were slower and less concerned about paying things on time. Their collectors wore garish red tuxedos[17] in order to embarrass debtors. Pessoa's Chest has a receipt of a payment made at Fénix (at Rua do Crucifixo), on the 27th of January 1932, referring to *the remainder of his debt to the company Lourenço & Santos,* totalling 200 escudos, corresponding to an overcoat. Despite his financial limitations, he never sought out a cheaper tailor and grew accustomed to having debts. Such was also the case almost every month at the bookshop Livraria Inglesa at Rua do Arsenal, where he purchased books and where he met with Ophelia after work. Because, according to friend Augusto Ferreira Gomes, *Mr. Tabuada, the owner, was uncompromising when it came to accounting.*

---

13 It exists to this day, but in another address – Rua Augusta 195-197.

14 The Holy Grail is the platter, bowl, magic stone, or – according to its most famous version – chalice used by Jesus in the Last Supper, with which Joseph of Arimathea later collected the blood flowing down the Cross.

15 Nowadays, it can be found at Praça dos Restauradores 47. The former address now houses a Caledonia lingerie shop.

16 The day in which the Dutch West India Company was expelled from Pernambuco.

17 A tradition that endures to this day, as evidenced by a classified ad at *Diário de Notícias* (26/04/2010).

Pessoa at the age of 26

To complete his "civilized accoutrements", he wears dark or grey bow-ties, to match his dark suits. "Let me take off my tie, unbutton my collar. You can't let off steam with civilization looped around your neck". In a text titled simply *Prefácio* (Preface), he says: "I tear off my throat a hand that is choking me. On the hand with which I tore it off, I see a bow-tie which fell from my neck with the gesture. I put the bow-tie away carefully, and it is with my own hands that I almost strangle myself". To "Dear Mr. Wiesenthiel", in Vienna, he says the following in a letter on the 18th of August 1933: "You kindly asked me to give you the measurements of my neck – not to hang me, I should hope – and I hereby inform you that it corresponds to 39 centimetres".

Eternal insomnia

"I don't sleep, nor do I expect to. Not even in death do I expect to sleep". Ever since Africa, his are nights of horror, hovering "like bats over the passivity of the soul, vampires sucking the blood of submission, larvae of waste, nauseating worms, snakes from the absurd recesses of lost emotions". He lies down for hours, but can't sleep. "What I mostly feel is slumber. Not a slumber that latently brings – like all other slumbers, even those caused by sickness – the privilege of physical rest". He lies on his side over his left arm, "listening to the existence expressed by my heart". But his slumber is "sad, filled with dreams, physically painful", and "even in bed, that pain persists… I can't sleep, nanny". "Anyone wanting to make a catalogue of monsters would need only to photograph the things the night brings to somnolent souls who cannot sleep". His night is, therefore, comprised of a "slumber I cannot have". "Of half sleep". Besides, "I wake up during the night and write, I must write", as he confesses in a letter to Ophelia (05/04/1920). "Nighttime, in bed, hard to sleep due to mental excitement" (diary, 14/11/1905). He spends those nights on his feet, in front of the writing table in his room, and writes. "I sleep little, and with paper and a pen on my bedside". Thus, his would be "a nocturnal oeuvre". But he doesn't only sleep little and late. Quite often, he also gets up early, as "the city takes its time waking up". All of a sudden, "the cock crows, knowing not he is doing so for the second time" and "I await the dawn, of which I've seen so many".

> I've done nothing, nor shall I ever
> But from doing nothing I have learned
> That doing everything and nothing is the same
> Who I am is the spectre of what I will not be.
>
> We live at the whims of abandonment
> Truthless, doubtless, masterless
> Life is good, but better is the wine
> Love is good, but better is sleep.
>
> *Untitled* (1931), Fernando Pessoa

Smoking and freeing his thoughts

He smokes just about everywhere – in the street, in cafés, in the offices he works at, in the rooms he lives in. He smokes a lot. And he only *burns* his cigarettes (without inhaling), as one does with cigars. The tips of the two fingers (and respective fingernails) of the hand with which he holds the cigarettes are yellowish – although, at times, he also uses his left hand. Heteronym Abílio Quaresma is described thus by Pessoa (based on his own appearance): "The equally grimy look of the thumb and index finger in his right hand, as well as the left's (albeit not as much) was a sign of tobacco".

"It is the cigarettes' smoke that which, usually, can rebuild the moments of my past in most spiritual fashion". *80 per day,* according to cousin Eduardo Freitas da Costa, along with some cups of coffee, which, according to brother João Maria, *he liked to drink with a cup of cognac. That's what he usually drank his coffee with, and he drank plenty of coffee throughout the day.* Habitually. In a letter dated the 6th of March 1920, Ophelia mentions she had stowed away the box in which Pessoa stored the tobacco for his cigarettes. *Do you know where it is going to spend the night? Can you guess? Underneath my pillow, which is where it is best.* An (undated) note reads: "One of the volumes of one of those authors [Conan Doyle and Arthur Morrison], a 45 pack cigarette[18], the idea of a cup of coffee… encapsulated my idea of happiness". That image is conjured up in *Disquiet:* "A cup of coffee, a cigarette, the penetrating aroma of its smoke, myself sitting in a shadowy room with eyes half-closed – I want no more from life than my dreams and this", since "my dreams can substitute quite well for the universe and its stars".

"I have never done anything but smoke life". According to sister Teca, he would sometimes *make his own cigarettes, like many people at the time, but he didn't inhale.* In order to taste those cigarettes, the smoker would have to patiently fill a wrapper of paper (or straw) with ground tobacco, and then moisten the glue-soaked edge of the wrapper with the tip of his tongue, and then seal it. General Oscar Carmona, who was elected president on the 16th of December 1926, was a known enthusiast. But it wasn't proper for a president to use his tongue in public, to say nothing of the fact that the production of cigarettes, which had been the exclusive purview of the Companhia de Tabacos de Portugal[19] since 1891, ceased to be a private monopoly on the 30th of April 1926. In that same year, the state factory Tabaqueira, headed by public servants, started making cigarettes on an industrial scale, provisionally calling them *Provisórios, french tobacco* (despite being made in Portugal). Later, the more definitive *Definitivos* would replace them. The brands remained in the market until the 40s. But, at the end of his life, Pessoa would prefer the brand *Bons.*

"I lit a cigarette that I smoked without thinking, and only when I saw that ash had fallen on the pillow did I realize that my consciousness had become fused with the void". Nothing bad ever happened to him on those nights he smoked in bed. He was luckier than Brazilian poet Clarice (Chaya) Lispector (1925-1977), who suffered severe burns when her bed caught fire due to a cigarette that remained lit on her fingers as she slept. And he didn't just smoke cigarettes, but also pipes. And "expensive cigars". Pessoa's *Anarchist banker,* "a well-known capitalist and tycoon, absent-mindedly smoking a cigar". A preface of Abílio Quaresma's novels includes one such brand: "One can love a brand of cigars. Some fight and die for abstract ideas that don't even have a brand; Peraltas had it". In *O caso Vargas* (The Vargas Affair), perhaps mirroring what was happening with himself, one of the chapters ends with "Quaresma dropped his cigar's ash on the front of his shirt". He often spends his afternoons writing at Casa Moitinho de Almeida, as his boss' typewriter is available to him there. And *the tips of cigars marked his passage there,* according to lawyer Carlos Moitinho, son of Luís Pedro Moitinho de Almeida.

18 A special type sold in Portugal, in packs of 45.

19 70% of the company's capital was foreign, mainly French. The so-called *tobacco matter* was broached at length by Pessoa in the text *"Régie, Monolólio, Liberdade"* (Governance, Monopoly, Freedom), published on issues #2 and #3 of *Revista de Comércio e Contabilidade* (1926).

"Through the light taste of smoke, the entire past revives me". When Sá-Carneiro is in Lisbon, he accompanies him in his forays to Tabacaria Mónaco[20], where his friend buys newspapers, magazines, and new books from Paris. But Pessoa doesn't have a particular place he goes to buy tobacco: He also frequents the creamery where old friend Júlio Trindade works at, at Rua Coelho da Rocha; Tabacaria Costa, at Rua Áurea; Tabacaria Inglesa, at Cais do Sodré; Habaneza, next to Brasileira do Chiado; or Habaneza dos Retroseiros, in front of the offices of Casa Moitinho de Almeida. In a letter to Gaspar Simões (11/12/1931), he exercises his renowned irony: "For example it had never occurred to me that tobacco (and alcohol, I should add) was a metaphor for onanism. After what I read on this subject, in a brief study penned by a psychoanalyst, I promptly realized that, of the five perfect onanistic specimens I know of, four of them partake in neither smoke[21] nor alcohol, and the one who smokes hates wine". At the end of his life, he is racked by a strong cough and the tell-tale dry throat parched by addiction. But he never once considered the notion of ceasing to smoke.

> I light a cigarette…
> And I taste in the cigarette the liberation of all thoughts.
> I follow the smoke as a route in itself,
> (…)
> Then I lay back on my chair
> And I keep smoking.
> While Destiny allows it, I'll keep on smoking.
>
> *Tobacco shop*, Álvaro de Campos

Stamps

Pessoa has small habits, typical of the time, such as collecting postcards and stamps. He even writes about it in the short story *"The philatelist"*. He bequeathed his collection to sister Teca, *a huge album, very heavy and valuable,* as she herself puts it. Leather-bound and with a title with golden letters, its 844 pages weigh at 12 pounds. It was a gift from his parents on his 14th birthday. On the cover page, next to his signature, is the date he started collecting stamps, the 13th of June 1902. The album contained at a time 605 stamps affixed with *charneira*[22] or glued with gum arabic, as opposed to today's modern Hawid glue pens. But not all of them remained inside their pages. Today, the collection

20 Still open to this day, at Praça D. Pedro IV, at Rossio.

21 Churchill smoked 125 cigars a day, whereas Hitler was the first ruler to forbid smoking in front of him. According to Carlos Heitor Cony, *he is the patron saint of today's anti-smoking advocates.* For the record, Mussolini also didn't smoke. Neither did Salazar, nor Gaddafi.

22 A small strip of paper used by philatelists to stick stamps to albums.

lacks all stamps of the Azores (26), Lourenço Marques (12), Mozambique (16) and Portugal (41).

> Basin number TEN
> For he who sticks stamps to his fingernails.
> And, as the hands are cold already,
> Put a lid on the basins!
>
> *Casa branca*, Fernando Pessoa

The music from his youth

After dinner, he listens to music, at a time in which there was no radio or television inside the household. "I am only well when I listen to music". It's one of the few things he actually likes. Mainly classical – Beethoven, Chopin, Liszt, Mozart, Rimsky-Korsakov[23], Verdi, Wagner. According to Teca, *Fernando loved to listen to them, he'd be sitting in total silence and just stayed there.* Even in his final years, he still attended concerts at the São Carlos. He also enjoys fado, of course, and writes: "All poetry – and song is poetry with aids – reflects that which the soul does not possess. Which is why the singing of sad people is joyful, and the singing of joyful people is sad. Fado, however, is neither sad nor joyful. It is an interval of sorts. The Portuguese soul formed it when it did not yet exist and yearned for everything without the strength to yearn for it. Strong souls attribute everything to Fate; only the weak believe in free will, as it doesn't even exist. Fado is the weariness of the strong soul, the look of contempt Portugal casts towards the God it believed in and who abandoned it. In fado, the gods return, legitimate and distant".

In a note reminiscing about his time in Durban, he recalls "music playing in a calm, wild soirée". Those are his "tunes of peace and hearth". At night, his family plays dominoes, keno[24], chess[25], or derby, a dice-powered horse racing game[26]. In games, much as in life, *alea jacta est* (the die is cast); even knowing, as per Mallarmé's poem, that "a throw of the dice will never abolish chance". During those soirées of past times, his stepfather's flute accompanied his mother's piano, and "soft seem the chimes of boyhood sweet". One in particular, by Felix Godefroid, the sheet music of which his family retains to this day – "Un soir à Lima". He will write over 300 verses about that piece, in

23 He dedicates a poem to him, "Scherazad", in which he says: "Better to dream of hearing you than to hear you".

24 A habit he brought to Portugal. An entry in his diary (16/03/1906) says that he "played keno until tea time".

25 Pessoa's bookshelf has Edward Ernest Cunnington's *The British Chess Code.*

26 Pessoa recalls those dice in *Inscriptions (V): I conquered. Far barbarians hear my name./ Men were dice in my game,/ But to my throw myself did lesser come:/ I threw dice, Fate the sum.*

the only text in which he evokes his stepfather and that time he spent in Africa. Two months before his death, he listens to it on the radio[27], and is haunted by the memories. He misses his father, with whom he barely shared any time; his mother, who had all but traded him for a new husband; of all "that might have been"; and then, pale, is "overcome by a longing for a mysterious past of mine", like an ominous sign that his hour was nigh.

> I stop smiling
> My heart stops beating
> And from the unconscious receiver
> That sweet and accursed melody
> Breaks forth
> My soul loses itself
> In a suddenly resurrected memory
>
> *Un soir à Lima*, Fernando Pessoa

A thing against photos

Pessoa most certainly dislikes them. "I am an abundantly impressionable photographic plate". Ophelia herself states: *You always had a thing against photos... you should have put it aside and indulged me the minute I asked one of you* (letter from 30/04/1920). She, his greatest love – if it can even be said that he had one during his life – begged him for a photo in numerous letters at the beginning of their relationship: *Don't forget the photo, Nininho* (24/03/1920); *When will you take a photo and give it to me?* (23/03/1920); *Take a picture, Nandinho, humour me* (24/04/1920); *Don't forget to take a photo, I don't even mind if it is small, provided it is well taken and I can see your ugly face!* (25/04/1920). Almost ten years would pass since her first request, until, in the beginning of September 1929, he sent her a photo in which he can be seen sipping wine in front of a barrel of claret, which contains the famous dedication like in the original, the line should break here, followed by "Caught red-handed" (in bold or italic) and the photo (that is on the following page) underneath it. The photographer got a different dedication altogether: "Sojourning at Villa Abel. Thank you, Manuel [Martins] da Hora". The photo was taken at "a branch of the liquor business" of the Abel Pereira da Fonseca company, called Val do Rio at the time. Nowadays, the building the photo was taken in (Rua dos Fanqueiros, 123) is part of the numbering of

27 Pessoa usually listened to a famous program called Rádio Lisboa.

Caught red-handed

Rua São Nicolau 8, and on its walls one can still see the bas-relief of a frigate sailing across the Tagus engraved upon the stone, its sails billowing as it carries barrels of wine[28]. He would send another photo at the end of 1929, with "a kiss", to "prove he (1) is 8 months old, (2) handsome, (3) exists". A photo of his brother Jorge, dead before he had completed his first year of life. And the switch was probably intentional, as that photo showed Pessoa at the age of 2. In another one, dedicated to his aunt Anica, he calls it "the provisional visual representation of myself"; sends "a hug as sizeable as his lack of consideration"; and signs as "your nephew and friend, brilliant and thankful", with the additional explanation: "Photo taken in January 1914, as it was bound to happen someday".

At a noon of an ending spring
I had a dream like a photograph.
I saw Jesus Christ coming down to earth.

The keeper of sheep, Alberto Caeiro

28 Besides this one, Val do Rio had 34 other trading houses in Lisbon, catering exclusively to buyers of vinegar, liquors, retail wine and its by-products. This house closed in the 1960s. Its successor, Empresa Val do Rio Júnior, has its headquarters at Rua dos Douradores, 69, first floor, in front of a monument in homage of Lisbon's sett pavers.

Mirror, mirror

It was another one of his pet peeves; "the creator of the mirror poisoned the human soul". Perhaps because "the image of myself I saw in mirrors is the same one I hold against the bosom of my soul". That distaste grew gradually, however, as "when I was young, I kissed myself on mirrors". But never again. "The adult aversion to my physical appearance made me automatically turn my back to whatever mirror I found". One might even say, in the words of Jorge Luis Borges, that both mirrors and copulation are abhorrent, as both multiply men. "A mirror reflects right; it doesn't make mistakes because it doesn't think; to think is essentially to be wrong". And "were I asked to discuss the social causes responsible for my soul's condition, I would speechlessly point to a mirror, a clothes hanger, and a pen". In a letter to Ophelia (28/05/1920), he says he sees himself in the mirror as "a general expression of not being there", but rather "in the toilet of the house next door". The same toilet his heteronym Álvaro de Campos asks him to chuck into "the mental image that he might have shaped" of his "intimate and sincere friend" – Pessoa himself. In another letter, this one addressed to aunt Anica (24/06/1916), he claims that "often, when I look into the mirror, my face disappears". Except, in that particular case, it might not have been the mirrors' fault, but rather the *glasses of aguardiente* which were is faithful companions throughout his life.

> The magic mirror where I always looked the same has shattered,
> And in each fateful fragment I see only a piece of me –
> A piece of you and me…!
>
> *Lisbon revisited (1926)*, Álvaro de Campos

His dislike of dogs and gramophones

He can hardly suffer "whining dogs and telephones". Ophelia herself says: *Fernando was very superstitious, especially with whimpering dogs. He said that, whenever he went home, dogs would whine at his passage, and that meant there was something about him which made them whine"*[29]. That dislike was later extended to machines in general, which he accepted "much as one does trees". He also could "do without vehicles, have no need for and detest the products of science – telephones, telegraphs – which make life easy, or the by-products of fantasy – gramophones, Hertzian antennae. I care for none of that". Radio simply hadn't been part of his childhood, but he had often listened

29 What the dogs could smell from afar was likely the adrenaline produced by his fear.

to music with his family at Rua Coelho da Rocha: The musical hits of London, Madrid, New York, Paris and Rome, played by the gramophone set up at the apartment's drawing room.

> Any music, ah, any music at all,
> That soon purges my soul
> Of this uncertainty that desires
> Any impossible calm.
> (…)
> Anything that isn't life
> Bolero, fado, the whirl
> Of the living dance […]
> Just so I don't feel my heart!
>
> *Any music*, Fernando Pessoa

Typewriters

"I wish to rule the world through a pencil". When writing, he likes to use the many pencils he always carries with him in his jacket's outer pockets, along with handkerchiefs and coins. According to friend Luís Pedro Moitinho de Almeida, they were *always used, never new, well sharpened on both ends;* and would use all brands except for Ko-hi-noor-bh – at the time used by students – which, according to him, were "no good. Hard and rough-tipped". Either that, or he used a quill, which is why he mentioned "the diminutive form of my inkstand under the vast indifference of the stars". Later, he would also use pens – such as "my Waterman (bought with money I didn't have to borrow)!". But he also makes plenty use of typewriters. "With the advent of the typewriter and its companion carbon paper, the hoary copyist was replaced with a surplus of time, perfection and efficiency". He learned how to use it at the Commercial School of Durban. "Whenever I use the typewriter to write my letters, which I always do when they are long, or when clarity is important, it is as if I were effortlessly copying it via carbon paper" he explains to Gaspar Simões in a letter (14/12/1931). At the beginning, he wasn't particularly fond of typewriters, as they "made poetry less poetic"; but would then make ample use of them, mainly for practical reasons. "To me, writing on a typewriter is much like talking". In a study carried out by Luiz de Miranda Rocha, quoted by João Rui de Sousa, it is made plain that the advent of the typewriter had, at the time, *an impact almost comparable to that of computers today.* It should be pointed out that Pessoa was one of the first Portuguese authors to make frequent use of it.

"I write fast, and when I write fast I'm not particularly lucid". His handwriting was almost illegible, and typewriting was "faster and clearer to read". In another letter to Gaspar Simões (30/09/1929), he says "this one was typewritten, as the letters are clear and the answer is unrestrained by the hurdles of handwriting". In another (28/06/1930), "I wrote this on the typewriter, as at least this way you'll be able to read it". At first, he only used those that were available in his workplace, describing to Olavo Pinto (01/05/1912) "the office in which my articles are typewritten" – Casa Moitinho de Almeida, in which he shared a *Royal* with the owner. He even refers to those texts in a special way, as one can see in the letter addressed to Luís Pedro Moitinho de Almeida (09/11/1931), in which he thanks "as the British would say, the written guy[30]". According to brother João Maria, he would be typing poetry, when suddenly work would arrive. He would then *rip the paper out of the machine, write his correspondence, and then continue working on his poem.* Eventually, it became a habit. "I am aware that my manuscript should have been typewritten, but the means I have do not allow for it". Only at the end of his life would he have one of his own at his apartment[31].

> Beside me, creepily banal accompaniment,
> The cracking tic-tac of the typewriters.
> (...)
> Back then, when I was someone else, there were castles and cavalries
> (Illustrations, perhaps, from any children's book),
> Back then, when I was true to my dream,
> Back then...
>
> *Typing*, Álvaro de Campos

Playing with the little ones

When his family returns to Lisbon, on yet another of his stepfather's sabbaticals (October 1906), Pessoa tells his brothers a fun, endless story in daily chapters for the entirety of their stay. Later, at Rua Coelho da Rocha, he finds other ways to amuse himself and others, such as, pretending to have lost his money upon returning home from work and inviting passers-by to search for it. *People could be forgiven for thinking you're mad,* his sister says. "That's what I'd like", he replies. He enjoys it, naturally. But he takes special pleasure in entertaining his nephews and other children around the house, such as the *five or six children aunt Anica had,* as niece Manuela Nogueira told me, admitting to not recalling the exact number. There were seven of them, two from Maria and five from Mário. Among those five, little Madalena, who was

30 *Translator's note:* A bit of wordplay by Pessoa, who made a literal translation of "typewritten" to Portuguese, in which *tipo* can mean "type" or "guy".

31 This according to barber Manassés' son, who often saw it. That typewriter was donated to the Casa Fernando Pessoa, and, despite all the rust, one can still decipher that it was produced by *Lower.*

Pessoa's goddaughter, would die of tuberculosis in her teens. A fate shared by her father, Mário. Brother João Maria corroborates: *He was great with small children. He got into their world as if it were his.* As if he were their age. One of his favourite bits of play-acting was to play the parts of characters in a poem. *With gestures, and all,* according to Maria Nogueira. Such as this one, which he recited while pretending to limp:

Hoot, hoot, hoot
Cried the owl
Which belonged to a gimp.
One day

The gimp got mad
And threw the owl away
What a hoot, hoot, hoot.

Poems for Lili[32], Fernando Pessoa

But his favourite bit of play-acting is to pretend to be an African sacred ibis represented by a human figure with the bird's head, in the likeness of Thot, the Egyptian god of the moon, patron of astrologers, enchanters and mages. In Greek mythology, he ended up converted into Hermes, son of Zeus and Maya, god of trade and theft; although, as Hermes, the bird's head gave way to a wide-brimmed hat, the petasus. That same bird would also be a heteronym of his, as well as a nickname for Ophelia ("Ibis' Ibis") and other people close to him, such as cousin Mário ("other Ibis"), aunt Palmira ("Jesuit Ibis"), and Maria Madalena, the daughter of aunt Anica ("combative Ibis"). When play-acting as the bird, he'd pull up a leg, crane his neck, open his arms like wings, and recite the following verses, which he composed for such occasions:

The ibis, an Egyptian bird,
Always stands on one foot
(Which is quite absurd).

This bird stands ever still
Pecking at things with its bill.
Like a stork it seems
Perchance a stork with regrets
  It dreams
  And forgets –

32 *Lili* was a porcelain doll his sister Teca used to play with. It was one of the few belongings that survived the trip back from Africa, when the family returned to Lisbon for good, with his mother again a widow. This small poem is one of three written under the same title.

It stands undeterred
As would any such bird.
When I see Lisbon most dear
I always say how I wish
  (Funny it is to hear)
I were an ibis without hands
Or, at least, standing on Egypt's sands.

Untitled (undated), Fernando Pessoa

The Chest

During a visit to one of the offices Pessoa worked at, friend Luís de Montalvor said: *For you to remain unknown is a crime.* "Never you mind. When I die, I'll leave plenty of full chests behind", he replies. "My soul is in such an intensely seething creative process, that my focus needs to be a notebook; even so, I have so many sheets to fill, that some invariably get lost". It's such an expressive number that "I must have roughly a virtual library of unpublished works". Such hyperbole can be justified by the fact that, as a rule, he made copies of everything he wrote, which is why we have access to his entire correspondence, with the unfortunate absence of the letters he wrote to Sá-Carneiro. All duly separated inside paper bags tied with string, with the recipients scribbled by hand. "At times, in the vulgar mess of my literary drawers, I find things I've written ten, 15 years ago, or perhaps even more". "Other times, I find excerpts I don't even remember having written – which isn't that surprising, really – but which I can't even conceive of having written – which frightens me". To say almost all of it would have been more precise. In 1968, his writings began to be catalogued – after having been handled by far too many people with far too many different intentions, and have been stored on the third floor of Lisbon's National Library since 1973. At home, they remained in a trunk which was a faithful companion throughout his life. *Messy drawers,* according to Teresa Rita Lopes. *A bag full of people,* as Tabucchi prefers. "My big box", in his own words.

He also stores his papers in a *common wooden* briefcase, *with metal stripes, which stayed with his brother Luís Miguel,* as Manuela Nogueira assured me; as did a large sack, a cardboard briefcase and a package. Everything else was unclassified: 28 notebooks identified as *ongoing tales,* in which one can find projects and texts by Search – the latter of these was acquired by Lisbon's National Library in November 2007; around 2 thousand documents in the possession of his nephews, among which the letters to Gaspar Simões; a typewritten version of *The mad fiddler;* the Crowley dossier – both of which later sold in an auction. The Chest, a reddish-brown wooden chest with a discreet lock and delicate legs, was sold in an auction in 2008 by Teca's heirs, and decorated the family's living room for decades, with a flower vase and a medal dedicated to the poet on top of it. The house is in a quiet area of São João do Estoril, at Rua de Santa Rita, 331 (formerly 5), right in front of Rua Fernando Pessoa. According to Manuela Nogueira, *he came by train from Estoril and walked all the way to our home from the S. João stop.* On the rose-coloured wall, one can see a plaque which indicates that the poet lived there. "I reread? A lie! I don't dare reread. I can't reread. What good would it do me to reread? The person in the writing is someone else. I no longer understand a thing… I weep over my imperfect pages, but if future generations read them, they will be more touched by my weeping than by any perfection I might have achieved". He uses papers of varied colours: Light blue, white, pink, sepia. Some written by hand, others typewritten (in blue, black, purple, green and red). But that wasn't all. When he had "no decent paper" left, he used newspaper pages, bills, letterhead or "copy paper" of the companies he worked for, calendar sheets, the backs of previously used envelopes, "the back of a letter", the empty spaces of other texts, sometimes unsigned or incomplete; and got rid of all excess ink with "a dirty, white blotter" that rested "on top of the ancient inclined desk". That small and simple piece of furniture stood to the right of the door of his room at Rua Coelho da Rocha, as confirmed by António Manassés, who went there almost daily during his last years, and can be found today at Casa Fernando Pessoa, next to a window.

His papers have been archived at Lisbon's National Library since 1985, disposed in 105 boxes which scholars can read only via microfilm. Having been granted special privilege by the board, I was allowed to examine some originals. Papers so thin, that frequent perusal would doubtlessly reduce them to dust. At the *Inventário Topográfico (Topographical Inventory),* titled *Espólio de F.P. (Estate of F.P.),* the following envelopes are ordered by author: Anon, two; Baron of Teive; one; Caeiro, two; Campos, three; Mora, four (and seven others of *Prolegómenos);* Search, nine. *Disquiet* tops the list at seven, each of them with its own annex, and two others (eight and nine) without any annexes. Others still were archived according to topics: Prefaces, one; Freemasonry, four; Signs, seven; Religion, twenty-six. According to the library's archives[33], the totals are as follows:

Archives:

Images	45.000
Documents	27.543
Envelopes	343

33 The apparently mismatched numbers are owed to the different criteria applied when classifying the documents.

Pessoa's originals	
Autographs	18.816
Typewritten	3.948
Mixed	2.662
Notebooks	29
Copies of originals	893
Third-party originals	
Third-party autographs	267
Handwritten copies by Fernando Pessoa	291
Printed fragments	893
Leaflets and other publications	34
Press clippings	289

In a letter written to Gaspar Simões (28/09/1932), he says: "I am beginning – slowly, as it's no matter to rush – to label and review my papers". In *Plano de vida* (Life plan), an undated draft, he describes how he aims to organize his oeuvre, with the certainty that he'd be living "in an ample home, so I can sort all my papers and books in their proper order, replace by big box with smaller boxes in which I can store my papers by order of importance". But that dream, like so many others, would never come true. In a letter to his brother Luís Rosa (10/10/1935), he belabours the anguish that disorganization caused him: "I can say I have concluded the preliminary storage of three fifths of my most numerous (oh, how numerous they are!) papers; and so, it shouldn't be long until I'm finished". Except he would die a month after that particular letter.

Rules to live by

"My name matters not, nor does any outer detail of my person. It is my character I should speak of". In that regard, with no apparent unease, he admits "I never had convictions in myself. Only impressions". "This is a fundamental character of my mind". At the *Revista de Comércio e Contabilidade,* he states that "bookshops all over the world are filled with books that *teach one how to win".* In spite of the ironic fashion with which he alludes to such books, he writes his own "rules to live by" in a number of papers – copying religious texts that profess the righteous path to proceed, or anticipating the self-help manuals which would eventually become so successful. In an undated note, he suggests the following rules: To "work nobly, wait honestly, feel people tenderly, this is true philosophy", after which he offers further advice:

1 – Have no firm opinion, and do not put too much stock in the value of your opinions.
2 – Be tolerant, as you can be sure of nothing.
3 – Judge no one, as you cannot see motivations, only the acts.
4 – Expect the best and prepare for the worst.
5 – Do not kill or spoil, as you know nothing of life, other than it is a mystery.
6 – Seek not to reform anything, as you know not which laws things abide by.
7 – Strive to act like others, but to think differently than them.

In *Disquiet,* for example, we can read: "For a man to be utterly and absolutely moral, he has to be a bit stupid. For a man to be absolutely intellectual, he has to be a bit immoral". As such, it was good to "reduce your necessities to a minimum, so as not to depend on anyone for anything". Perhaps because "scruples are the death of action". His great-niece Isabel Murteira França says: *That's just how Fernando was. He always had a thousand plans, a thousand ideas, sketches, and never followed through with many of them. His spirit, almost fragile as it was at times, lost itself in the bitterness of his inner disquiet.* Pessoa also claims to "belong to the sect of the procrastinators, as well as a true futurist, in the sense that I put everything off till tomorrow". And, in a text that was only published in 1979 (at *O Jornal*'s *História* magazine), he suggests further rules of life (abridged):

1 – The less you confide in others, the better. It's best not to do it at all, but, if you must, be either false or vague about it.
2 – Dream as little as possible, except when the dream's direct goal is a poem or literary product. One should rather study and work.
3 – Endeavour to be as sober as possible, anticipating the body's sobriety with that of the spirit.
4 – Be pleasant only to please, and not to open your mind or openly discuss with those who are stuck to the spirit's inner life.
5 – Foster concentration, temper your will, become a force by thinking in as personal terms as possible that you are indeed one.
6 – Consider how few friends you truly have, as not many people are able to truly be someone's friend. Try to seduce with the content of your smile.
7 – Learn to be expeditious in small things, in the everyday things of mundane life, of your home, so they won't keep you away from yourself.
8 – Organize your life like a literary work, making it as unique as possible.
9 – Kill the murderer[34].

34 Here, he refers to a quote of a book he translated: Helena Blavatsky's *The Voice of the Silence.* According to madame Blavatsky, the mind is the "killer of reality", which is why she preaches that the "disciple should kill the murderer".

Little by little, he comes to terms with his fate. “I’ve never done anything but dream. This, and this alone, has been the meaning of my life”; and thus “I envy all people, because I’m not them”. Deep down he is “all those things, though I want it not”, comfortable in “the series of disasters which have defined my life”. “This, perhaps, is what constitutes my tragedy, and what makes it comical”. To wit, “I was nothing, I dared nothing, and did nothing”.

His final portrait

“Each of us, alone in the silence of being a being, has an inexpressible personality that no words can convey, that the most expressive of looks cannot interpret”; and so “I’ve always rejected being understood. To be understood is to prostitute oneself. I prefer being taken seriously for what I’m not”. Still, it is possible to draw the profile of a discreet, self-restrained man, who doesn’t care much for mirrors or taking pictures of himself. Someone who is hard of hearing, soft-spoken, who sleeps little and smokes a lot, despite the fragile body he inherited from his father. A description which fits the crowd of anonymous men no one paid any real heed to. This, in spite of him being an extremely vain man. One who buys shoes and shirts in shops meant for the wealthy, and orders custom-made clothes at Lisbon’s most expensive house, despite not always being able to afford it. A man who wouldn’t be parted from a silver signet bearing his family’s coat of arms. But only up until the end approached. By that time, vanity ceased to make any sense.

Thus was Pessoa. In the words of Saramago, *the portrait is drawn. It’s a devout genuflection, a mocking titter, it matters not, as each of those traits, when superimposed, gets one closer to the moment... in which it reflects no light, not even the sun’s fulgent radiance.* In conclusion, *between reverence and irreverence, somewhere in an indeterminable point, there lies perhaps the man that Fernando Pessoa was.* A complex, contradictory character. Eduardo Lourenço recommends: *Perhaps, before “questioning” Fernando Pessoa, one ought to accept him in his strangeness, be it real or apparent.* To accept him as one who chose to live a life like that of so many others, yet distant from them all, especially when it came to the scope of his dreams. “What do I mean to say with my life?”. The answers, surprising and majestic, are to be found in his oeuvre.

> I am the ghost of a king
> Who walks unceasingly
> In the halls of an abandoned palace
> I know not my story
> Far from me, in the smoke of my thinking of it
> Dies the idea that it ever had a past.

I know not what I am
Whether or not I am the dream
That someone in the outside world might be having…
I do believe I am
Being the casual portrait of a sad little king[35]
Of[36]a story being read by some god…

Untitled (19/10/1913), Fernando Pessoa

35 A variant was *I am perhaps a laughing paragraph.*
36 A variant was *In a*

Amantes amentes
(Lovers are lunatics) Terence

FEMININE TEMPERAMENT, MASCULINE INTELLIGENCE

Every pleasure is a vice.[1]
The Passage of the Hours, Álvaro de Campos

The joys of love

"I wasn't born for joy or love". Or, perhaps, for him to love was just "to tire of being alone". In an attempt at understanding what he truly was, he says in a draft to *Answers* magazine: "I find it not the least bit hard to define myself: I am feminine temperament with masculine intelligence. My sensitivity and the movements stemming thereof, namely temperament and its expression, are a woman's. My faculties of relations – the intelligence of impulse – are a man's". That theme would pursue him, like an obsession. Looking at other writers, he tells apart Shakespeare ("who turned out to be a pederast") from Rousseau (in which this impulse turned out to be "passive"), and fears what others might think of him. In a letter to Gaspar Simões (11/12/1931), he confesses: "Robert Browning[2] – who, more than a great poet, was an intellectual and subtle poet – was once told about Shakespeare's pederasty, as evidenced in his *Sonnets*. Do you know what Browning said in response? If so, the less Shakespeare he!". Therefore, it hardly comes as a surprise that Pessoa would write poems about his fear of assuming what he was. Verses such as:

> What do I know! What do I know! So many people in me!
> So much lost and contradicted impetus!
> I fail so much at being my own person
> That the greatest torture might, perchance be

---

1 He repeats the thought in *Disquiet:* "All pleasure is a vice because seeking pleasure is what everyone does in life, and the worst vice of all is to do what everyone else does".

2 He would later say that Browning (1812-1889) – married to Elizabeth Barrett Browning, author of *Sonnets from the Portuguese* – much like Byron, "would leave no trace behind, not even their own names".

To accept and see myself tied up, distressed,
Incapable of the final act.

Untitled (1919), Fernando Pessoa

Perhaps for those reasons he sees "sexual desire" as "a hindrance to superior mental processes", as love as but "the most carnal of illusions". "I well know that no one is forced to requite love, and that great poets want nothing with being loved. But there is a transcendental rancour". To him, "a strong artist not only kills whatever love or mercy he might have, but also the very seeds of love and mercy. Genius is the biggest curse God can bless a man with", since "there is in each of us an element of such order, regardless of how little one instinctively specializes its obscenity". Still, deep down, he considers love important, even when it doesn't abide by the standards of the strict society of his time. "The influence that pure love can have in perfecting a being, whether that of a woman or a boy, is one of the charms of existence". Which should come as no surprise from someone who would always display a dual nature in his writings and in his life. "I am tired of being everything but myself". Little by little, he came to realize that such art was beyond his capabilities. In an epitaph he wrote in French (04/09/1907), when he wasn't even 20 years old, it says: "He may die; he never loved". And so, he who "never knew how to love", ended up renouncing love in favour of the greatness he felt his oeuvre would attain.

Poems of the love phenomenon

In a letter to Gaspar Simões (18/11/1930), he says he's planning a book that might "cover the circle of the love phenomenon", translating "the feeling appropriate for the Fifth Empire". The first draft of that book had the following outline: "Antinus: Divineness; Ephitalamium; Prayer to a Fair Body, Spring 1917". Followed by: "(1) Greece, Antinous; (2) Rome, Ephitalamium; (3) Christianity, Prayer to a Woman's Body; (4) Roman Empire, Pan-Eros; (5) Fifth Empire, Anteros". Two of them, "Antinous" and "Ephitalamium", are the only poems (or even compositions) that I wrote than can truly be called obscene". The "three last poems are unprecedented". "Anteros" might have been the "visual lover" – briefly alluded to by Bernardo Soares as he "who loved with his stare, with no desire or preference for sex". Nothing was found of the last two, perhaps because he never even began writing them. He wrote "Ephitalamium" at the age of 25 and "Antinous" when he was almost 27; two poems suggestive of the past, when his dreams were all in the future. In archaic English, at a time in which his language already was Portuguese. So that they would reach more readers in other countries. All things considered, with the passage of time and lacking the repercussions he had expected, he seems to have regretted it. "I don't know why I wrote any of those poems in English".

"Ephitalamium"

"The first poem 'Ephitalamium'", written in August 1913 (377 verses), "represents the Roman concept of the sexual world. It is brutal, as are all colonial emotions; beastly, as are all natural things, when they're secondary, as they were for men such as the Romans, veritable animals running a state". "Direct and awesome", as he would sum it up in 1930. "Seven or eight" of its stanzas were written "at Mayer's office" (Lima, Mayer & Prefeito de Magalhães, Lda.). *Thalamos,* in Greek, means 'nuptial chamber'; 'ephitalamium' is the song sung by couples at the door of the room where they will be spending their wedding night. It's a recurring theme in literature. Rome gave us 17 ephitalamia, with Catullus' being the most renowned. In Portugal, those written by Sá de Miranda (1481-1558) and António Ferreira (1528-1569) were the best known, even if they restricted themselves to celebrating the weddings of noblemen at the time. That realistic poem describes the bride's awakening on the day she is to marry, the opulence of the celebration, the desires of her groom-to-be, the sexual act that consummates the union, mainly from her point of view – with fears, fantasies, "her beloved's hand caressing her breasts", caresses Pessoa could scarcely conceive of:

Chant I
Set open all shutters, that the day come in
Like a sea or a din!
Let not a nook of useless shade compel
Thoughts of the night, or tell
The mind's comparing that some things are sad,
For this day all are glad!

Chant V
Now will her grave of untorn maidenhood
Be dug in her small blood.
Assemble ye at that glad funeral
And weave her scarlet pall,
O pinings for the flesh of man that often
Did her secret hours soften
And take her willing and unwilling hand
Where pleasure starteth up.

Chant XIX
Half late, too near the gush.

And even now doth an elder guest enmesh
A flushed young girl in a dark nook apart,
And leads her slow to move his produced flesh.
Look how she likes with something in her heart
To feel her hand work the protruded dart!

Chant XXI
Till their contacted flesh, in heat o'erblent
With joy, sleep sick, while, spent
The stars, the sky pale in the East and shiver
Where light the night doth sever,
And with clamour of joy and life's young din
The warm new day come in.

Ephitalamium, Fernando Pessoa

"Antinous"

"The second, 'Antinous'", written in January 1915 (with 361 verses), "represents the Greek concept of the sexual world". "It is Greek as far as feelings are concerned", "but Roman with regards to historic setting". Pessoa wrote another reference to the theme in his poem "Livro de outro amor" (Book of another love) (1913) – in which we see "Antinous awaiting me in the sky". He'd confess to Gaspar Simões (18/11/1930) to not being satisfied with the published version (having already made changes to a previous version, from 1914) and recalls that "the poem was rebuilt and perfected" afterwards (in 1921). Contrary to "Ephitalamium", and even though it was written subsequently, "Antinous" was published as an autonomous book, likely owing to the higher quality of its writing. Still, both feature in his "English poems". First, a heterosexual poem; now a homosexual one. And it is curious indeed that Pessoa signed both with his own name, considering he'd previously told *Punch* magazine in a letter (21/02/1906) that "I signed my manuscript with a pseudonym; when a stranger writes something, especially a poem, it is best not to directly attribute it one's authorship". Many authors had previously written about Antinous, chief among them Balzac, Baudelaire, Jean Lorrain, the Marquis de Sade, Proust, Ronsard and Oscar Wilde, who quotes him in *The Picture of Dorian Gray.* That poem, "much like all other primitive concepts, is substantially perverse; like all other innocent concepts, the manifested emotion is purposefully disallowed". Antinous, in Latin, is Antonius. The same letters. Perhaps he who Fernando António always wished to be.

It retells the story of the Hispanian Publius Aelius Adrianus, born in what is today Seville (in 76 a.D.), Roman emperor between 117 a.D. and 138 a.D., the year of his death – a protector of the arts, letters and his people. A descendant of an Andalucian family from the shores of the river Guadalquivir, he was the successor of Trajan – a cousin, also a Hispanian, who adopted him. The verses emphasize the importance of his relationship with the Bythinian Antinous – young, athletic and "blond-haired"[3], which he came to know in 123 a.D. Knowing through an oracle that the emperor would die because of him, he drowns himself in the Nile to prolong the life of his lover. Adrian declares it an accident and builds the city of Antinopolis over the place of his death, a place which would become the administrative capital of the region. Eight years later, feeling his final hour approaching, he writes the famous poem "Animula vagula blandula"[4], lamenting the death of his beloved. The poem was inscribed on Castel Sant'Angelo, which he built and where he was buried at.

The rain outside was cold in Hadrian's soul.
The boy lay dead
On the low couch, on whose denuded whole,
To Hadrian's eyes, whose sorrow was a dread,
The shadowy light of Death's eclipse was shed.
Antinous is dead, is dead for ever,
Is dead for ever and all loves lament.
Venus herself, that was Adonis'[5] lover,
Seeing him, that newly lived, now dead again,
Lends her old grief's renewal to be blent
With Hadrian's pain.
Thy vague hands grope, as if they had dropped joy.
To hear that the rain ceases lift thy head,
And thy raised glance take to the lovely boy.

Ah, there the wanting breath reminds his lips
That from beyond the gods hath moved a mist
Between him and this boy. His finger-tips,
Still idly searching o'er the body, list
For some flesh-response to their waking mood.
But their love-question is not understood:
The god is dead whose cult was to be kissed!

---

3 Bythinia was a region in Asia Minor (currently Turkey), which is why he could hardly be the *blond* slave Pessoa described. He would probably look like Adrian himself, *the olive-skinned one.*

4 "Gentle wandering little soul" would eventually become the inspiration for Petrarch's sonnet 37, dedicated to his platonic love, Laura, which begins with the verse *Beautiful soul, freed from the knot that was;* and also for the renowned sonnet 48 of Camões, which was allegedly inspired by one of his loves, a Chinese girl called Dinamene, who supposedly died at his side at the Mekong river. Nothing but a legend, as Camões' real love was Violante, wife of the Count of Linhares, who he served as a personal servant. At length, he realized Violante was an impossible love and then fell in love with her daughter, Joana, but his love of both was unrequited.

5 Adonis died in a hunt, wounded by a boar, a victim of Ares' envy due to his personal beauty, according to the Greek legend.

My love that found thee, when it found thee did
But find its own true body and exact look.

The gods came now
And bore something away, no sense knows how,
On unseen arms of power and repose.

Antinous, Fernando Pessoa

Sex and heteronyms

In some of Pessoa's texts, women play a clearly secondary role[6]. "All Christian literature is a litany for the Virgin Mary, as personified by several ladies who, as a rule, rather bring to mind a Mary Magdalene in her early stages. All Christian literature is female-driven; worse, it is female"; and "not as absurd as the discussion seems to be… whether or not women have souls. When compared to men, the female spirit is mutilated and inferior"; also "the true original sin, innate in men, is being borne by woman!". The heteronyms follow suit in that veritable dance of prejudice. Quaresma Decifrador claims "women detest absolutely strong men, the men they feel might do without them emotionally". For Thomas Crosse, "the abusive liberation of the spirit that is naturally subservient to women and plebeians will inevitably result in disaster for morals and societal order". According to António Mora, "the three classes which are most profoundly debased in their social mission, on account of the influx of modern ideas, are women, the unwashed masses and politicians. In our age, the woman presumes to have the right to a personality; which might sound *fair and logical* and such; but which has unfortunately been otherwise ordained by nature".

In other texts, Pessoa also reveals hints of homosexuality. Same with his heteronyms. "I know not who the woman was who Caeiro loved. Nor did I seek to know it, not even as a matter of curiosity. There are some things that the soul refuses not to ignore". On the sexuality of Ricardo Reis, he implies: "The fortunate thing about Reis is that he writes in such compressed fashion, that it becomes almost impossible to follow with any type of precision – if precision is needed – the complete and exact sense of what he says. That is what makes him write the Ode [21/10/1923] which begins thus: *The flower you are, not the one you give, is what I want* (behold, the I before the want, going against the core of Ricardo Reis' linguistic nature!). Bernardo Soares, despite having claimed to love a woman, writes: "Our distaste for action can't help but feminize us. We missed our true calling as housewives and idle chatelaines"; confesses that "my

6 One of the books on Pessoa's shelf was *La indulgencia espiritual del sexo feminino* (The spiritual indulgence of the feminine sex), by Dr. Roberto Novoa.

horror of real women endowed with sex is the road that brought me to you"; says that "I wouldn't know how to bring my body to possess hers"; and, lastly, laments "not having been the madam of a harem! Such a shame that never came to pass". Ángel Crespo completes the thought, considering it's a shame that *it never happened to him, Fernando Pessoa.* In 1910, Álvaro de Campos is an out-of-the-closet homosexual, to the point he feels comfortable enough to write the following in 1916:

> Furious madness! I want to bark, jump,
> Bellow, bray, do cartwheels and somersaults, my whole body howling,
> (...)
> Throw myself in front of the slashing whip about to strike,
> Be every dog's bitch and them not enough for me,
>
> *Salute to Walt Whitman*, Álvaro de Campos

And yet, he who initially claimed not to want to be "married, futile, predictable and taxable", bore no traces of his homosexuality in the end – in a transition which reproduces the trajectory of Pessoa himself, starting from the presence of Ophelia in his life.

A possible diagnosis

Most children are asexual up until the age of 5 – when Pessoa lost his father. The same father he had already lost long ago, having lived only with his mother since he was 2, with only the occasional visit to Telheiras. With no friends to play with, he was surrounded by women at all times – his mother, grandma Dionísia, two nannies and some aunts. The stepfather he would eventually get could never quite fill the role of a paternal figure, and that incomplete substitution may well have caused behavioural disturbances. The libido he lacks is spread out among several characters created by him, the canvas on which he projects his sexuality. According to a study conducted by Nancy J. Andresen, Ph.D. at the University of Iowa, Freudian psychology holds that *creativity is the sublimation of aggression and sexual impulses, or a response to emotional pain;* and concludes saying that *writers are a different kind of people.* At the beginning of a tale, Pessoa articulates his lot in life: "Once upon a time, there was an elf (which is a male fairy) who was in love with a princess that didn't exist".

> Legend says there once slept
> A princess, charmed
> Who could be awakened but

By an Infant who'd come[7]
From beyond the road's wall.
(...)
But each fulfils their own destiny –
She, sleeping, charmed,
He, seeking her senselessly
By divine process
Which brings the road into being.
(...)
And, still dizzy by what had been,
His head, in a sea of giddiness,
He raises his hand, and finds ivy
And sees that he himself was
The princess who slept.

Eros and Psyche,[8] Fernando Pessoa

In an interview he gave to *A Informação* magazine (17/09/1926), Álvaro de Campos recalls an episode which took place in Barrow-on-Furness, at lake County, in the south of Scotland. According to him, he'd "just finished writing a sonnet" when "a girl, so to speak, approached – a student at the local school, as I later came to know – and struck up a conversation with me... The afternoon, as it was traditionally wont to do, fell slowly and smoothly". Much has been said about this text, with the gender of student often being changed to accommodate the "a girl, so to speak" bit[9]. Except this wasn't an oversight. Carlos Queiroz recalls that Pessoa himself brought "that voluntary error" to his attention, thus highlighting Campos' sexuality. But Campos wasn't Fernando. Or, rather, he would cease to be, after Ophelia. And so, far from a writing mistake, this was very much a deliberate choice. Pessoa would even repeat that *error* with heteronym Maria José, who says: "I won't even try to ascertain it"; or, in *Disquiet,* "my best girlfriend, a ravishing young man I invented". To wit, and in his own

7 In a first version, "By a prince (Infant) who'd come". In this case, it isn't a new redaction per se, as Pessoa had a habit of writing variants between parenthesis, so he could later pick the one he liked best. The fourth verse says "Prince (Infant)"; he'd pick *Infant.* The tenth, "by (through); he'd stick with *by.* The seventeenth verse, "Intention (intent)"; he'd stick with *intent*. Only the twenty-ninth verse would have a wholly new redaction, in which *returning* was replaced by *winning.*

8 When the poem was published in *Presença* magazine (numbers 41 and 42, May 1934), there was the following epigraph under the title: "From the Grand Master's ritual, at the Hall of Portugal's Templar Order: *And so you see, my brother, that the truths that have been given to you... are opposed to our truth"*. Later, in a letter to Casais Monteiro (13/01/1935), he denies having written any such thing: "I would not quote the ritual, as the order is no more... for one should not quote passages of rituals which are ongoing". And so, far from an adaptation of the story of Sleeping Beauty, the poem was mainly a compromise of an initiation.

9 *Translator's note:* In Portuguese, *aluno* is a male student, and *aluna* is feminine. Álvaro de Campos' original text said *aluno.*

words, "a normal man aspires to three things in life: Peace (or happiness), power (power includes fame)" and "pleasure". Pleasure which could come from both genders.

Homosexual Pessoa?

Close to the age of 30, Pessoa wrote two letters to the *British Journal of Astrology* (8 and 11/02/1918), asking them for his horoscope, and got the following reply from editor E.H. Bailey (06/03/1918): *It is impossible to ascertain Aquarius Rising for the pre-holiday season, as it would result in a female ascendant area, and, with the moon being negative, the pre-holiday season would forcefully have to be that of a woman's.* He was wrong... or, perhaps, not that wrong. But a mature understanding of Pessoa's life vehemently denies any and all hints of homosexual practices, which also happens to be the opinion of Teresa Rita Lopes, with whom I had a long conversation on the subject. In a letter written on the 2nd of December 1930, Ophelia writes: *Goodbye, my doll – for Nininho is also a girl – kisses, many kisses of this devotedly yours Ophelia.* But she meant it solely in jest, considering there is no photo with him in a suspicious pose, nor did he ever write a single intimate sentence of such nature. Quite the opposite, in fact. In the aforementioned draft to *Answers* magazine, for example, he confesses: "I have no illusions when acknowledging the nature of the phenomenon. It is a coarse sexual inversion". And "it has ever perturbed me in those moments of meditation, the fact that I've never been sure, and still can't claim to be, that this temperament of mine wouldn't one day manifest itself in my body". It certainly wasn't for a lack of willingness that it didn't come to pass, considering his words in *Disquiet:* "Those of us who aren't pederasts only wished they had the courage to be so". Whatever the case, after Ophelia, even the possibility ceases to make any sense.

Nor did any of his friends and acquaintances ever as much as implied it. Well, actually, there was one statement from António Botto, who suggested to Jorge de Sena that he *looked at little boys in a peculiar way.* But Botto's words are suspect, as he was an out-and-proud, almost delirious homosexual. To José Blanco, *Botto was a faggot, mad and a megalomaniac,* and everything he said *should be taken with a substantial grain of salt.* He even said to his friends that *António Botto has a thing for sailors, that he does.* Blanco shared with me a story that Pessoa had allegedly told him, of an event that transpired at the Coliseu dos Recreios. Botto was staring intently at a couple, and the husband came to confront him. *Pray tell, sir, why are you staring at my wife?* Botto's reply: *I wasn't staring at your wife, but at you.* According to Álvaro Moura, Botto *was a lech,* with a *monstrous urge to satisfy his carnality.*

Whatever the case, life wasn't kind to him. He ended up fired from his well-paying job as a clerk, in 1942, for harassing a colleague. And, in time, he increasingly felt wronged due to the glory Pessoa had attained and which had been denied him. Upon perusing his papers at the National Library, Teresa Rita Lopes confessed to having become *unpleasantly surprised by the role of detractor he seems to have taken upon himself.* There was a hint of envy in his every word. Perhaps on account of certain criticisms levied against him by Pessoa. Such as the one claiming that his books, among which *Motivos de Beleza* (1923), were "good for nothing and worth nothing but pity. This much I told the author – albeit with a more moderate wording", as he says in his letter to Adriano del Valle (23/04/1924). Or his review in *Diário de Lisboa* (01/03/1935) of another book, *Ciúme,* in which he called the author "versed in superficiality". Later on, already suffering from syphilis, he made up wild tales, such as being the lord of São Paulo (where he lived). In 1951, he moved to Rio de Janeiro, where he fawned over sailors under the understanding gaze of his wife, Carminda Rodrigues. He died run over by a car at Rua Santa Luzia, in front of the Monroe Palace, a final touching scene in which his wife cradled his face in her hands, huddling over him and sobbing uncontrollably.

But, as untrustworthy as source as Botto was, one sentence of his provides food for thought, when he suggests that *his manhood, small as it was, explained his shamed abstinence.* Coincidentally, we see the following in one of Pessoa's psychic readings: *Man with no manhood! Born without a man's penis! Man with a clitoris instead of a penis!* Considering that those readings consist of Pessoa writing his spirits' words, one might speculate that, if it were indeed true that he had such a small manhood, to the point he'd equate it to a *clitoris,* his sexual abstinence may well have owed itself to shame. The physical shame of exposing himself and his small penis to a partner during a sexual act. That's all we have to base our conjecture on. Whatever the case, little by little, he lost his interest in love: "It horrifies me; it is abandonment, intimacy". He's well aware of the mission the gods had entrusted him with; privilege or curse, he devotes himself fully to it. Could he have regretted it at the end of his life? It is hard to tell.

> Love is what is fundamental.
> Sex is but an accident.
> It can be the same
> Or different.
> Man is more than an animal:
> He is an intelligent meat.
> Though, at times, sick.
>
> *Untitled* (05/04/1935), Fernando Pessoa

Lusting for women

"I have no lovers or girlfriends, and it is another of my ideals; even though, as much as I search, I can only ever find emptiness in that ideal, and nothing else. Impossible, the way I dream of it! Alas!". Still, his texts have a number of passages in which his carnal cravings are plain to see. Such as his impressions of one Maria, who had "a mouth like a purple carnation". Or an annotation in his diary (29/11/1916) on his visits to Hotel Avenida Palace[10] – where his aunt Lisbela was staying at. "A most unpleasant day, as it rained a lot; my suit got wrinkled, I had to wait half an hour in the street, and also because there was scant progress in the translation [he did for London editor Warren F. Kellog]. But I did enjoy a brief visit to the hotel", where he was "making eyes" with "a lassie" – the "lassie (aged 17, excellent)", her sister and her deaf mother. He would then return to the hotel: "It wasn't a chore, and the lassie's sweetness was still there, even though I had been gone for three days". Later, in a letter to Ophelia Queiroz (31/02/1920), he claims to have gone there "to drop off my sister". Pessoa's papers at the National Library also have the following annotation: "I loved a woman; it was a story of sex, an emotional novelty. Those were sexual relations, nothing more". And it was spoken of no more, meaning it could have been a fact of life or just another dream.

Outside of his oeuvre and in real life, it is rumoured that he patronized a brothel at Rua do Ferragial de Baixo – at Bairro Alto, between the São Carlos Theatre and Cais do Sodré. It belonged to madame Carriço, who supervised her licentious pupils personally. In the same building, there was another house of ill repute, belonging to madame Blanche. Victor Eleutério describes it so: *It was a building like any other. The entrance was a dark door, which was always open, come sun or rain, with more urine puddled at its doorstep than the rest of the street. The stairway was ample, in rich Pombaline style with sharp stone corners. It was rather strenuous to climb, and demanded frequent stoppages to light another match, as the light was dim and shed precious little illumination on anything. One could, however, follow the smell and the loud noises heard from the first floor. There wasn't the faintest doubt. A gated door reinforcing another one with a wicket.* It was there that, according to his friend Peixoto Bourbon, lived a flame of his, who, according to those who studied Pessoa, is nothing but a legend. With Ophelia Queiroz, the relationship was extremely discreet. "May she remain anonymous, even for God!". Pessoa proposed to her as a lark, to which Ophelia replied in a letter (20/07/1920): *You asked me in the car if I wanted to marry Ibis, which surely you meant in jest (that is how I took it, at least). Do I want that engagement? It is my greatest concern, my greatest desire and the biggest joy in my entire life.* But she would have no such joy. Between the two stages of his relationship with Ophelia, Pessoa would

10 This luxury hotel still stands at Rua 1º de Dezembro 123, Lisbon.

fall in love with another woman – the daughter of his washerwoman Irene, called Guiomar, as we can verify in "Tobacco shop". "You won't be where I see you… you won't be anywhere". And let us not forget that, even before Ophelia, he is to have had an unknown love – to whom he wrote "Adeus" (Goodbye), whining as one is wont to do at the age of 19. With verses which, truth be told, could be appropriate for either a man or a woman:

Goodbye, goodbye forevermore
As love would not consent
Friendship nor desire
Nor anything to repent

It is best to just leave and vent
When there is nothing to lament.

Adeus, Fernando Pessoa

He had a mysterious relationship with Madge Anderson, sister of sister-in-law Eileen, married to John Rosa. When recently divorced, she visited Lisbon a number of times and met up with Pessoa. Upon returning to London, she wrote back to *Fernando my dear* and thanks him for sending her a *little poem.* In a postcard, she considers herself a *poor little fool* and asks him to send her *another poem and teach me how to regain my spirit.* He apologizes for not having been warmer when they were together. Luís Miguel Rosa, Pessoa's nephew, confirms: *Apparently, there was some sort of reciprocal affection. She was a very intelligent woman, and supposedly worked to decipher German coded messages during World War I. She was very cultured, but possessed something of a temper. Which is probably why she was interested in uncle Fernando.* According to brother Luís Miguel (Lhi), Teca even gave him some grief *for not having met Madge the last time she came to Portugal, but he probably was holed up at home during one of those "psychodepressive" crises he would occasionally suffer from.* Ophelia reacts: *Surely, that Englishwoman is single and does not intend to marry, and, if she is married, she clearly doesn't much care for her husband* (25/11/1929). No further records of the importance of Madge in Pessoa's life exist. Nor did he harbour any hurt feelings, as "a home, rest, children and a wife – none of those things are the lot of those who aspire to something beyond this life". He did write the following with her in mind the next year, however:

That English girl, so blonde, so young, so nice
Who wanted to marry me…
Such a pity I did not marry her
I would have been happy.
But how do I know I would have been happy?

Untitled (29/06/1930), Fernando Pessoa

And, later:

> In exile from you, I look at your white hands
> Resting (good English manners) on the tablecloth,
> (…)
> I'm tired of thinking…
> I finally raise my eyes to your eyes as they eye me.
> You smile, knowing full well what I was thinking about…
> (…)
> That's the bad thing about symbols, you know.
> Yes, I know.
>
> *Psychotype*, Álvaro de Campos

The mysterious blonde

All that's missing is the last love of his life. In a conversation I had with José Blanco, he said that Ángel Crespo had told him about that elusive final love I was chasing after – *a blonde lady who lived in Estoril, unfortunately married to a friend of his.* Pessoa has several accounts of supposed intimate relationships with married women, without ever identifying them. "Possess you? I don't know how that might be done. And even if I had the human stain of knowing how, what a disgrace I would be to myself, what a flagrant insult to my own greatness were I even to think of putting myself on a par with your husband… I don't dream of possessing you. Why should I? It would only debase my dream life. To possess a body is to be banal". Perhaps he was thinking of her when he wrote "when circumstances mischievously led me to suppose that I loved and to verify that the other person truly loved me, my first reaction was of bewildered confusion, as if I'd won a grand prize in an inconvertible currency. And then, because no human can avoid being human, I felt a certain vanity; this emotion, however, which would seem to be the most natural one, quickly vanished. It was followed by an uncomfortable feeling that's hard to define but that was composed of tedium, of humiliation, and of weariness". In *Anteros,* one of Abílio Quaresma's crime novels, these were the "elements for the plot: (1) the husband, a hale man, kind, hard-working and hearty, (2) the wife, an elegant creature, with an artistic temperament and sudden whims, (3) a shy man, personally faded, highly intellectual and with psychologism". "Personally faded"; perhaps these words were code, as if Pessoa himself was a part of that love story. There's also the following letter he wrote to a woman we know nothing of.

> Dear lady: I haven't seen you that often, but once would be enough to convince me that I need search in none other, if not my happiness – for that would be dependent on your answer to this letter – then at least the hope for said happiness. I know not if you'll

think this letter too bold, but he who feels strongly dares with equal intensity, even if he is not of bold bent. I would like you to tell me if I can aspire to one day have your sympathy and your sincere affection, which is all I could wish for my intimate life. Tell me if there is any hope to be had.

Back to Crespo's research, his suspicions first fell on author Fernanda de Castro, who had been married to Pessoa's friend António Ferro since 1922. Ferro was in Brazil at the time, having been invited by a theatre company, so they had a proxy wedding. A temptation that, perhaps, hearkened back to his own past, as if Fernanda reminded him of his own mother, who had married under similar circumstances. Luís de Oliveira Guimarães defines her as *an energetic woman, kind, talented,* and adds that *Pessoa really liked her.* Manuela Nogueira confirms, recalling that Pessoa always felt a *great admiration* for her. She was a poet, the founder of the Sociedade Portuguesa de Autores (Portuguese Authors' Society). "With an artistic temperament", indeed, as per Quaresma's novel. According to Fernanda's granddaughter, renowned journalist Rita Ferro, her grandmother found Pessoa *extremely shy and rather dull.* It was perhaps with her in mind that he wrote the following drafts of verses in French, dwelling upon an impossible love with "another man's woman" (19/08/1933):

Why suffer
And, above all,
Why even tell her?

And another one, also in French, written on the 28th of April 1935:

Oh, she
She who is so beautiful
Is invariably another man's woman.

As *dona* Fernanda was a brunette, she was off the suspects' list. Time passed, and, after Crespo's death, José Blanco continued the search. He considered the wife of lawyer José de Andrade Neves, son of Dr. Jayme de Andrade Neves, Pessoa's cousin and doctor – a woman known as *Titita* among her loved ones. Blanco's research only unearthed the fact that Pessoa didn't attend their wedding, despite having been invited – which proves nothing, really, since Pessoa wasn't much for weddings. *Jealousy, perhaps,* he speculates. He also found out that, when they were introduced, Pessoa told Titita he was "the family's resident drunken cousin" – though he wasn't at the time. According to Titita, *he had plenty of faults, but we never saw him drunk, or even with a bottle in his pocket.* According to cousin Jaime, *after we married, he'd often come over for dinner, and he really loved the aguardiente from my in-law's farm.* In time, they grew close; so much so that, when she was ill, *cousin Fernando* would sit by her bedside and read to her. When Blanco met her, she was already white-haired, and asked her if she had been blonde. No. Much like that of her in-law Georgina Cardoso, Titita's hair had been dark.

> I know, how well I know… the cuckold's pain
> Though I wasn't the one to call it such
> Loving you upsets me greatly,
> Though I know not what manner of upset.
>
> *Untitled* (03/04/1929), Fernando Pessoa

I took up that search for Pessoa's late love. And the first impression I got is that it might not have been that late at all. Ophelia herself mentions in a letter written on the 27th of March 1920: *You won't be seeing the blue-eyed blonde?* Said blonde is mentioned in several other letters by Ophelia. What one gathers from reading one of them is that it was a lady who once sat in front of Pessoa in a tram and stared at him intently. However, in others, she mentions someone with whom he was physically intimate. Such as this one, dated the 3rd of June 1920: *Today you were seen with a blue-eyed blonde woman, fair-skinned, tall, dressed in red... Is it true or not, that you were in such company at that time?* Later, in "Chance" (Álvaro de Campos, 27/03/1929), one reads: "By chance, in the street, the blonde girl, by chance". Then, in an annotation between 1929 and 1930, he recalls a woman with blond hair and teeth "as clean as river pebbles". Perhaps it was Madge – who, according to Luís Miguel Nogueira Rosa Dias, Pessoa's nephew, had *light brown hair.* Or perhaps it was the one in whose honour he wrote the following in French, between the 26th and 28th of April of his final year:

> I found her
> I found her again.
> Because I so often dreamt of her
> For so long
>
> And I loved her
> And would always love her.
>
> No, I know not
> If you truly exist…
> (…)
>
> Are you a queen?
> Are you a mermaid?
> What does it matter to that love
> Which makes you a sovereign?
>
> *Untitled* (1935), Fernando Pessoa

Perhaps he was also thinking of her when, on the 22nd of November 1935, eight days before he died, he wrote his final poem, also in French:

> My blonde
> Perhaps, in another time
> Or in some corner
> You[11] will love me, one day only,
>
> The light, its golden glow
> Which floods me,
> Serves but to make me as one
> With the golden sheen of your shining hair
> My blonde.
>
> *Untitled* (1935), Fernando Pessoa

The fact that he wrote those verses in French – which he spoke at home, with his mother – suggests he was broaching something intimate and real, as they would almost certainly have been written in Portuguese or English if the feeling had been *feigned.* Regardless, we still don't know who the *blonde* was, and the mystery remains.

> One day, you will notice you loved me
> And that, perhaps, you loved me and me alone
> Happily married, you tread
> The road that is said to have no end.
>
> *Untitled* (30/11/1914), Fernando Pessoa

Sex and psychic readings

During his psychic readings, mainly from 1916 to 1918, the recurrent topic is sex. Including his virginity at the age of 30! As if following "that Rosicrucian demand, not only of mere chastity, which is but a temporary or conditional *retreat,* and therefore relative, but that of virginity, which is the absolute *retreat".* At the end of that reflection, he adds that "male chastity, when properly thorough, compels the semen to be reintegrated into the body, percolating into the bloodstream. This way, the individual impregnates himself, as it were, being as unto his own woman". Spiritualist Wardour claims that it is *a virtue reserved for monks* – which isn't Pessoa's case. That is perhaps why "the unfolding of the self is a phenomenon which occurs in many cases of masturbation". Those

11 In French, the use of *tu* denotes greater familiarity than the formal *vous.* One might thus assume that it was someone close to Pessoa.

are sentences that his hand writes freely and somewhat carelessly, as if they were being dictated to him from the beyond. Several passages are struck out, which wouldn't happen in true spiritual communication; rather, it would appear that Pessoa wasn't pleased with his texts and would cancel or correct them.

– You should not strive to keep your chastity.[12]
– It certainly makes you happy, as it makes you a man.
– Like you, she is a virgin, and a nomad in life, just like you. She isn't a woman one marries.
– She is very much like you, except she's strong and you're weak.
– She is your future lover, not your future wife.
– She never had sex with a man.
– You are about to meet the girl who will possess you, the girl who will make a man of you (annotated on 01/07/1916).

Deep down, he puts little stock and hope in those readings. The meeting would take place *during a soirée, and any and all manner of resistance from your part will be futile.* Perhaps it might be an *actress,* or a *governess,* or a *farmer's daughter.* Henry More's spirit first tells him: *A man who masturbates isn't a strong man;* and then recommends the following: *You must not keep your chastity. You are so misogynistic that you will find yourself naturally impotent, and thus will be unable to produce a complete oeuvre in literature.* Little by little, more details emerged:

– The woman who will initiate you in sex is a girl you have yet to meet.
– She is a poet, a devoted amateur.
– She is a poet in the sense that she writes poetry.
– She got her education in France and England.
– You will meet her in a place you shall never again visit.
– None of your male acquaintances knows her.

All those point to Ophelia Queiroz – who Pessoa hadn't yet met at the time; she wrote poetry, spoke English and French; met him at a company which would shortly go bankrupt; and almost none of those closest to him knew her. At the end of one of those readings, the following was relayed to him: *Pregnant. She will ask you to marry her, you won't help her, so she commits suicide.* They would meet in 1917. As he expected it, he wrote that same year:

Hours and hours become months at length
Awaiting the yearned-for joy

12 This in spite of him claiming in *Disquiet* that "there are but three distinct things – one is tedium, the other, reasoning, and the other, chastity".

I think of you with every breath
And you, so coy.

Canção triste, Fernando Pessoa

Gradually, a name begins to take shape via the spirit of Henry More:

– She is a lithe, agile girl, but busty. Wait for her lips. They will drive you mad. She is the wine you need to drink.
– No. A woman now stands in your way. Her name is Olga. You will find her on the 12th of June.

"Her name is Olga", the spirits say. He laughs, recalling a jest he had written in 1914: "If one were to remove the *l* from Olga and add an *s,* one would get *osga* [gecko]". Except this Olga would be far more than a mere jest.

– The woman's name is Olga de Medeiros. She is the niece of a man with an office at Rua Augusta, who is an acquaintance of José Garcia Moraes[13], the managing partner.
– Olga Maria Tavares de Medeiros, born in São Miguel, on the 10th of October 1898 at 05h38 local time.[14]

And so, here was the name, Olga. With an O, just like Ophelia.

13 A shopkeeper who had a store at Rua Augusta.
14 What is most peculiar is that there was indeed a woman with this name was indeed born in São Miguel – four years before the stated birth, on the 25th of September 1894.

Dimidium meæ
(Half of my soul) Latin phrase with which one designates partners

OPHELIA QUEIROZ

Let us remain in front of each other,
like two childhood acquaintances,
who loved each other a little when they were children.
Last letter to Ophelia, in their relationship's
first stage (29/11/1920), Fernando Pessoa

How they met

Ophelia Maria Queiroz is called *Ofelia* because her sister and godmother Joaquina Paula de Queiroz (Nunes de Ribeiro after her marriage), 20 years older and her most loyal companion throughout life, was reading *Hamlet* on the day of her birth – 14th of June[1] 1900. Her name is written as Ophelia in her birth and baptism certificates, although her marriage and death certificates say Ofelia – on account of the orthographic reform, which replaced *ph* with *f.* According to the baptism certificate (number 405) of the Santos-o-Velho church, she is the *legitimate daughter* of Francisco dos Santos Queiroz and Maria de Jesus Queiroz – Catholic, as befits the daughter of *dos Santos* (of the Saints) and *de Jesus* (of Jesus). Her parents had Algarvean roots, much like Pessoa's paternal lineage. According to the social structure of the time, her family was lower middle class, as her father had an export business of Algarve products, her grandfather was a barber, her great-grandfather was a tinsmith, and all women in her family were or had been housemaids. In contrast to Shakespeare's, however, this Ophelia was cultured, spoke fluent French, good English, and could use a typewriter. Physically, she was like so many other lasses of the time, thin, short, big-eared, dark eyes and hair, and *chubby arms and legs,* according to her own words. She wears no make-up. Judging by the photos from her youth, she has a beautiful face. Even those taken later, in which she looks the part of a matron from the inner country, still show a dignified figure. In a statement to her great-niece Maria da Graça (Borges) Queiroz (Ribeiro), she says: *I was 19, was of good cheer, smart, independent, and, against the*

1 A day after Pessoa's birthday, although her birth certificate erroneously says 17th of June.

will of my parents and family, decided I wanted a job. Not because I needed one, as, being the youngest of eight siblings [four men and four women, of which five died of pneumonia] *and the only one who remained single, I was very pampered and could have anything I wanted.* Pessoa had once written a few verses on Shakespeare's Ophelia, which almost read like a premonition of sorts:

I thought my heart dead
(…)
Ophelia going with the current
I know not which of my uncertain emotions[2].
Whomever you wish to want you…
Sad heart, lives with you.
(…)
May it be the sole grand gesture
In the cold nothingness of your suffering

Without wanting your one dream to abate
Your…[3]
Relinquish it and live off not living.

Untitled (26/07/1917), Fernando Pessoa

The year was 1919. In the beginning of November, according to Ophelia, *Diário de Notícias* published an ad for a job opening at Félix, Valladas e Freitas Lda[4]. It was an office of *commissions and consignments,* which had opened for business on the 1st of October that year and would go bankrupt three months later, owned by José Damião *Félix* (capitalist and controller of the company), Fernando *Valladas* Vieira (of the Republican National Guard, "somewhat rude", didn't get along with Pessoa), and cousin Mário Nogueira de *Freitas.* Ophelia writes to the ad agency and soon gets her answer, which gives her the address for the interview, at Rua da Assunção, 42, second floor. She goes there, chaperoned by her sister's housemaid, who said that *girls from good families shouldn't go around by themselves.* The door is closed, so they wait for someone

2 In the original, he had a number of variants, such as *variations* and *suppositions.*

3 The original would later be completed, and was composed of this one word.

4 Not quite so, from what I could gather. Among the 1500 job ads published during that month in that newspaper, I couldn't find a single one from this company. But she was likely referring to the agency that *put up* said ads. Candidates would thus have to contact that agency, which would then give them the day and time they were to go to the job interview. For the record, these were the ones operating at the time: *A Mensagem* – Agência de Publicidade, Rua das Gávias, 54 (Bairro Alto); *Agência Anunciadora* – Travessa do Convento a Jesus, 37; *Agência Rádio* – Rua Áurea, 146; *Agência Universal de Anúncios* – Calçada do Garcia, 4; *Bastos & Gonçalves, Sucessor* – Rua da Conceição, 147; *D. Anahory* – Rua do Alecrim, 169; *Empresa Geral do Trabalho* – Rua Nova do Almada, 18; *Agência Havas* – Rua Áurea, 30 and Rua Augusta, 270, 1º.

Ophelia Queiroz, age 20

to arrive, and the first one to do so is Pessoa, who is heading for work. We saw *a gentleman coming up the stairs, clad all in black (later, I found out he was mourning his godfather*[5]*), wearing glasses and a bow-tie. As he walked, he seemed to scarcely touch the ground. And his trousers were tucked into his gaiters. For some reason, it made me feel like laughing. He was very considerate and told us to wait a little, as he wasn't the office's owner.* Ophelia thus began to enter his life like a Spring breeze, and caused a deep impression. "When I saw you, I loved you long before, I was born for you before there even was a world". It would be a complicated love for both.

> When I wasn't with you
> I loved Nature like a monk contemplating Christ…
> Now I love Nature
> Like a monk contemplating the Virgin Mary,
> (…)
> You changed Nature…
> You brought Nature to my feet,
> Because you exist I see it better, but the same,
> Because you love me, I love it the same, but more,
> Because you chose me to be with you and love you.
>
> *The amorous shepherd*, Alberto Caeiro

5 Commander Rosa had died shortly before, on the 5th of October 1919.

The beginning of the courtship

Three days later, she was hired as a typist, *with a salary of 18 mil-réis,* as per her own words. And thanks to his intervention, as they only wanted to pay her 15. She would be the company's only female employee. Ophelia would later recall that, right off the bat, *he looked at me a certain way.* Their esteem was mutual, but, at the time, she was dating painter Eduardo Cunha – who had prevailed over his sculptor brother in the fight for her affection. And they would date until Christmas 1919, when Eduardo's father died. Although he knew she wasn't single, on the 28th of November, Pessoa worked up enough courage (which he didn't even know he had) to send her a cheeky little poem:

Baby isn't bad
She's quite good, actually
So tell me, then
And be truthful, now)
Who can it be…?!
I know who it is.

Earlier (1910), he had already written about amorous babies in almost premonitory fashion, as if he knew that a bigger baby called Ophelia would become as unto a trail of promises and remorse in his life.

Babies, at this rate,
Shall no longer belay
The time to enunciate
"Mama" won't be the word they say
But, rather, "love, such is fate.

One I have already dated, Fernando Pessoa

On the 22nd of January 1920, the impossible happens at length. Osório, who had worked for the firm on occasion, had already left. The two were alone, and Pessoa decides to pour out his heart on a whim. According to Ophelia: *A little before closing time, he sent me a small note which said "I'm asking you to stay…".* It was dark inside, because *the lights had gone out in the office.* And then, as if he had spent his entire life preparing for it, *Fernando sat on my chair, put down the lamp he carried and, turning towards me, began to declare: Oh, dear Ophelia! My verses are ill-measured; I lack the art to measure my sighs; but my love for you is of extreme intensity, believe me!,* he said, channelling his inner Hamlet. And Pessoa likely said them with the intonation of one who recites sentences he memorized, unaccustomed as he was to romance and thus resorting to what he knew best – literature. She confirms it in a letter written on the 22nd of March 1920 (mistakenly dated as 1919): *It is three months today since you made a representation of Hamlet.* She is on her feet, putting on her coat, and seems not to quite understand what is going on. *Then, suddenly, unexpectedly, he grabbed me by the waist, hugged me and kissed me wordlessly, passionately, like a madman.* She kisses him back, as if it were something natural. He then becomes hesitant, surprised at having done something he did not believe himself capable of. Ophelia confesses to having been *most distraught,* gathers her belongings and leaves in a hurry. She returns home on her own, recalling their mutual boldness, still undecided as to whether or not she wished to live such a love. He remains in the office, alone, paralysed, incapable of imagining what would follow. The following day, Ophelia receives a poem, the first verses of which she commits to memory:

> I was maddened, I was dizzy
> Kisses sending me into a tizzy.
> I held her tight
> Cradled her in my arms
> I was maddened, that is right.

What she forgot was the second to last verse "Succumbed to her charms". It only became known because the poem (composed of six stanzas, with six verses each) was dutifully kept by Pessoa in his Chest, in spite of the text's questionable quality. But the fear of loving soon makes itself felt again, and he carries on as if nothing had happened. A month earlier, as if foretelling what was about to happen, he wrote a poem which ended thus:

> I do not quite believe
> Could it truly happen to me
> You, your kisses and joy, such reprieve?
> That it is, and yet can never be.

But it did happen, and now he knew it. Upon recalling the night of that first kiss, Ophelia says: *I went home, impaired and confused. Days passed and, as Fernando seemed to be ignoring what had happened between us, I took it upon myself to write him a letter* [28/02/1920], *asking him for an explanation. That was what prompted his first letter-answer, dated March the 1st* – the one in which he says: "I fully acknowledge how comical this may appear, and that I am the most comical element of it. I would find it funny myself, if I did not love you so much". *And so we began our courtship,* Ophelia says. In that very letter, she affirms he was the one she chose: *I have just spoken with the boy who makes me think so much about my Fernandinho. I am scorning a boy who loves me dearly, who would make me happy, and whose ideas about me I well know, as I know what he pretends from me* (28/02/1920). Said boyfriend, Eduardo da

Cunha, still insists on meeting her. *Ex-boyfriend,* she clarifies (19/03/1920). In another letter, this one from the 25th of March 1920, she says: *You have no idea how much the boy has vexed me today, as he just won't leave me alone... At night, by 10 o'clock, he paces around my street, a nuisance you would not believe, to the point my brother had to confront him.*

On the 26th of May, she writes again about that former flame: *He knew through others that I was being courted, and wanted to see it with his own eyes to take revenge in his own way.* Eduardo tells Ophelia's father about her relationship, and threatens her mother: *From yesterday on, I had an enemy capable of anything.* Tormented by the memories of that former love, Eduardo would harass her for years to come. Ophelia doesn't just change boyfriend, she changes job as well. On the 20th of March 1920, she is already working as a translator at C. Dupin & Cia. Comissões, a company specializing in *firewood, doors, mechanical carpentry and economical furniture.* It was located at Cais do Sodré, 52, third floor (telephone 5151), bairro dos Remolares[6]. Close by, at Praça Duque de Terceira, there was the Taverna Inglesa of which Eça de Queiroz spoke in *Primo Basílio,* and the famous Hotel Central, of *The Maias* fame, which hosted kings, princes and assorted wealthy individuals. She gives notice of her new address in a letter a day before. And it wouldn't be her last, as she soon after starts working for the Olímpio Chaves[7] company, in Belém. Pessoa gives us evidence that she worked there, by timing the train ride from Belém to Cais do Sodré – 37 minutes, at the time. She would subsequently work for Metalúrgica Portugal Braz, an affiliate of Henrique & Cia. Lda., at Rua Moraes Soares, 166 (telephone 3129). Those were all temporary arrangements, which is why she later confesses that, *after leaving C. Dupin, I never worked again.* Considering the physical distance between them, the two start writing letters more often. And so began their long correspondence.

The first stage of the relationship

Above all, Ophelia was a surprise for him, as she didn't quite fit into his life. "The greatest love is not that which words softly express. Nor is it the one a look conveys, or the one a hand communicates by touching another hand. It is that which envelops two beings who neither look at nor touch each other when they are together. That love must remain unsaid and unrevealed. It must not be spoken of". And so it would be with their suburban, secret romance. Even without fully understanding this new state of mind, Pessoa decides to carry on with it and, as expected of boyfriends, he buys her gifts almost every day. Some

6 *Remolares* were the craftsmen who made the oars of vessels during the time of the discoveries.

7 Despite the reference, written by Ophelia herself, I could find no trace of that company at Lisbon's Commercial Registry.

of them even of value, as an enamelled medallion with kittens. Ophelia proudly shows it off to her family – *my mother was most appreciative of the medallion, she thought it most fine* (letter dated 14/06/1920) – and would keep it until the day she died[8]. Others were merely exotic, such as a small red straw chair for her doll house, or matchboxes filled with *meiguinhos* – little wire figures that were collectibles at the time in Lisbon (Ophelia mentions a *meiguinho-chinês* in a letter dated (23/03/1920). To say nothing of treats such as *rebuçados*[9]. The following verses also came in a box:

A bonbon is a sweet
Or so I've heard
Not that it were
Useful for me to know
Considering the sweet
Is not meant for me.

At the end of each day's work, and in spite of the distance, they usually go together to the house of her sister Joaquina, where she lived at the time. Their route takes them through Rua Áurea, Largo do Pelourinho, Rua do Arsenal (where Pessoa had his post office box), occasionally passing by the bookshop Livraria Inglesa. Whenever Ophelia wishes to see him away from indiscreet stares, she mentions wanting *to take a walk to India* – it says as much in several letters, the first of which on the 23rd of March 1920. Those dates weren't proper, according to the rigid mores of the time, as Ophelia was only 19 years old and the two should be seeing each other under the watchful gaze of her family. Coincidentally, in a letter on the 23rd of May 1920, she claims to have gone *to that lady's house at Rua Saraiva Carvalho, which is hosting a stag party for her son, who is departing for India.* Pessoa is of the jealous type, and doesn't like it when she wears dresses with cleavage or speaks to other men. During one of their walks, he actually makes a scene, claiming she *was giving the looks to Pantoja*[10]. Her beloved's accomplice, Ophelia occasionally signs her letters as one of Pessoa's heteronyms, Ibis. To him, she would be "Ibis' Ibis", or "hopeless and tastefully oblivious Ibis"; or, later, "Ex-Ibis" or "Extinctibis". To his letters, she always replies with *sweet kisses from she who is most yours,*

---

8 Her grandniece Maria da Graça showed us the keepsake, which could be opened to keep a portrait inside. It contained one of her nephew Carlos Queiroz, as the only photo Ophelia had of Pessoa was far too large to fit in.

9 A speciality of Portuguese confectionery, made of sugar, butter and egg yolk, covered with a thin and transparent layer of syrup and wrapped in cellophane paper.

10 Joaquin Pantoja was a Spanish friend of his. Apparently, he worked at an office that Pessoa provided some services for. In a letter to Ophelia (29/03/1920), he lays out his intentions to "let Pantoja replace me up there". Pessoa once wrote him a letter, on the 7th of August 1923, telling him: "We all feel. We all think. But not everyone can feel with their thoughts, or think with their feelings. That is why there are many people, but few artists".

to my dearest little Ibis. She writes him every day and explains why it is so in a letter dated the 23rd of March 1920: *I'm writing you a little something because I can no longer do without writing you little somethings.*

Love letters

Pessoa bequeathed us 51 letters: 38 from the first stage of the relationship, from the 1st of March to the 29th of November 1920 – two of which undated, another one that didn't specify Ophelia as the recipient (18/03/1920), and 12 from the second and final, penned between the 11th of September 1929 and the 11th of January 1930. Invariably addressed to "little baby" or its variants – "angel baby", "fierce baby", "terrible baby", "littlest baby", "little bad baby", "bad, beautiful baby", "my little grumpy baby", in 27 of the first stage letters and five more of the second; with the occasional and almost protocolar "little Ophelia". Letters from an *orphelin* (orphan) to his *Ophelina,* the words of which were somewhat evocative of an escape of sorts, according to António Quadros. She wrote 230 of them, 110 of which have been published, along with 46 postcards, two telegrams and several notes, to her *Pretty Ibis, My Black One, My Fair Master, Mr. Pessoa* or *Mr. Venomous Beetle,* which she signed as *your waspish enemy* – but often she would stick to *Nininho, beloved Nininho, Nininho of my sins.* The Queiroz family vetted the publication of two letters, along with some paragraphs of a couple of others. Grandniece Maria da Graça told me that they were but family references, of no interest to the audience. And so it was, as I ascertained upon perusing said letters (nowadays in possession of Brazilian collector Pedro Corrêa do Lago) and found two topics that were the cause of such reservations. On the one hand, it was the dire financial straits of Ophelia's family. On the other, it was the almost naive accounts of female maladies: *You have no idea how terrible my night was, oh!, such pain, and without ever calling for mother* (02/07/1920); or *Mysterious illness? No, Nininho, there is nothing mysterious about my illness... it is the most natural thing... It is the most natural thing a woman can have, you do understand, do you not?* (03/07/1920).

Their correspondence was handled by a delivery boy, the aforementioned Osório from the previous job, who subsequently also worked for C. Dupin. His existence is confirmed in Ophelia's second letter, and in many others which followed. Pessoa also writes her small notes saying "kiss me" (in English) or "won't you give us a little kiss?". She replies with romantic postcards. One in which lovers are embracing under a silver moon; another in which a woman is walking by a river, with the inscription *I trust none but you* – and, underneath, by her own hand, *I live in hope, my happy love;* and another with a couple between a flower, with the inscription *your pretty eyes are the stars of my life*

– at the side, once again by her own hand, it says *oh, how I miss he to whom I belong and who I am so far away from.*

> I can't quite yet fathom what I feel –
> Your kisses, my dear,
> Are the dawn that doth anneal
> The deepest recesses of my heart drear.
>
> *To Ophelia-I*[11], Fernando Pessoa

Some letters are addressed to the *honourable Mr. Álvaro de Campos* – even though Ophelia doesn't much care for his interference in the romance. *Does Álvaro de Campos like little Baby very much, then? I don't believe so, Nininho. If he did, he wouldn't be as mean and unfair as he's been… I just don't like him, Nininho, he is mean* (letter dated 12/06/1920); she even warns him that, when she is married, she doesn't want him *in our little house.* Either that, or they were meant for heteronym A.A. Crosse, on whom she placed her hopes that he might make enough money in a *Times* quiz competition so they could marry. At times, Pessoa replies to Ophelia in kind, writing as if he were a child in letters of rather questionable taste.

> Nininho-ninho's little baby
> Oh! Just witing to tew yuw that I wiked Little Baby's wetter wewy much. Oh! And I was tewibly sowy for not being with Baby to give her kissy-kisses. Oh! Nininho is so widdle!
> Today Nininho won't be going to Bewém, because he didn't know if there wewe any caws, so I said I would be hewe untiw six o'cwock. Tomowwow, unless Nininho weally can't, he wiww be weaving here at five o'cwock [drawing of a sock], this is the sock of five and a half[12]. Baby will be waiting for widdle Nininho tomowwow, yes? In Bewém, yes? Yes?
> Kissies, kissies and mowe kissies
>
> Fernando, 31/05/1920

In the first issue of *Revista de Comércio e Contabilidade* (1926), Pessoa says that "at the end of any letter in which one treats the other party with deference, one should never make use of the word *esteem.* Those we defer to deserve *regards* or *respect. Esteem* is reserved for those one worships[13]. Generally speaking, one should stick to *affection, admiration, friendship,*

11 Pessoa wrote five poems for Ophelia, four of them thus titled, with the first one dated the 2nd of February 1920, and a fifth one titled "Love as an exercise in style".

12 *Translator's note:* "Five and a half" is "cinco e meia" in Portuguese, and "meia" also means "sock".

13 This didn't stop him from using that so-decried *esteem* in letters to two friends he most certainly did not worship: João de Freitas Martins (07/10/1921) and Adriano del Valle (31/08/1923).

appreciation, camaraderie, consideration, dedication, acknowledgement, respect, longing, sympathy". He uses none of those with Ophelia, invariably using "yours, always" or "ever yours indeed". But only during the first stage of their relationship; the second had far more formal letters. In one of them, Pessoa begs: "Do endeavour to actually care for me… at, least, endeavour to pretend to" (March 1920)[14]. *Those are love letters between Fernando Pessoa and Fernando Pessoa,* suggests Janice de Souza Paiva; her inspiration for such a comment was likely Pessoa himself, for whom "all letters should be from one to oneself, at least for the superior man". It is with such correspondence in mind that, a month before his death, he writes (ending each stanza with the same word, *ridiculous):*

All love letters are
Ridiculous.

They wouldn't be love letters if they weren't
Ridiculous

In my time, I also wrote love letters,[15]
Like all others,
Ridiculous.

Love letters, provided there is love,
Must perforce be
Ridiculous.

But, actually,
Only those who never wrote
Love letters
They're the one's who're
Ridiculous.

Would that it were so when I wrote
Unaware I was doing so
Love letters, which were
Ridiculous.

Truth is, today
My memories
Of those love letters

---

14 The original didn't specify the day. Comparing it with Ophelia's letters, it was probably written on the 20th or thereabouts.

15 This is a peculiar verse, even taking into account that it was signed by Álvaro de Campos, considering that Pessoa never admitted to having written love letters. There was no reason for him to confess now, except maybe the certainty of impending death and that keeping secrets no longer made any real sense.

They are the ones which are
Ridiculous.

(All outlandish words,
As all outlandish feelings
Are, naturally,
Ridiculous.)

Untitled (21/10/1935), Álvaro de Campos

Though loving be a thing to fear

Their relationship is mainly spiritual. Nonetheless, there are plenty of hugs, kisses and even greater intimacies short of an actual sex act. At most, some touching of breasts, according to Ophelia's family. Pessoa all but admits it in the verses that refer to said breasts as *little doves:*

My little doves would fly away.
They flew off to someone else.
All I know is they were taken from me.
I know not to whom they might be given.

My little doves, my little doves,
That no longer nest
Close to me.
Such is the lot of all my cuddles
They kill them all!

Ophelia reminisces: *One day, as we were walking by Calçada da Estrela, he told me: "Your love for me is as great as that tree". I pretended not to understand. But there is no tree over there... "Precisely", he replied. Again, he said: "It's almost Christian charity that you would like me. You are so young and pretty, and I so old and ugly".* He is 32 at the time; she is 19. In a letter on the 24th of September 1929, at the second stage of their relationship, he actually asks: "Does my little wasp truly care for me? Why should you care so for the elderly?". Physically, Ophelia does indeed look younger than she is, which is why Pessoa sends her notes such as this one (28/02/1920), written on the back of his business card:

Baby begins with a B
And B is the first letter of kiss [beijo]
Come kiss me, Baby
Come quickly, o kiss.

When we get married, and when I get home, come in and ask – did anyone happen to see my wife? Then you show up and I say – Oh! There you were! You're so tiny, I could barely see you, Ophelia recalls. Not only young, she was also quite petite, whereas he, from the heights of his 1m73, was actually tall for the time. Other than these jests, the letters also contained something akin to promises. Such as this one, on the 13th of June 1920: "Wouldn't it be funny if, come next year, I could tell you these words before getting up from bed, do you see what I'm getting at, Nininha?". But, deep down, he never truly entertained the possibility. In a letter to Gaspar Simões (17/10/1929), he confesses: "I'd rather follow Punch's[16] famous advice to those who are about to marry – *Don't*". Which was to be expected from one who railed against marriage in his texts, such as *On the Institution of Marriage* and *Dissertation Against Marriage.* Optimistic (or just plain naive), Ophelia really does believe she will marry him and begins preparing her bridal trousseau. He feeds that hope of hers in letters, such as this one from the 5th of April 1920: "My baby to sit on my lap! My baby to nibble at! My baby to… (and then baby is bad and hits me…)." He even writes an acrostic for her (undated):

O where doth evil reside?
Paltry few would know.
How to tell?
Ere one cries, one drives one to
Laugh and to respond
Inciting cruelty such that one can
Ascribe no understandable meaning.

Ophelia replies on the birthday of Teca, Pessoa's sister, with another acrostic (27/11/1920):

Fair would it be for you,
Egregiously so, to tell me the
Reason why you said that I am
Not the bonbon for you…
And, lest the bakery cares
Not to give you one
Do tell me how you came to such an
Idea, for I haven't the faintest,

16 There remains doubt as to what he meant with this reference. Some claim it was an allusion to British publishing house Punch, of Bonverie Street (London), with which he corresponded in 1906. Manuela Parreira da Silva agrees. But, taking into account the comment's nature and when it was written, he may well have been alluding to Mr. Punch, the traditional British puppet character who always fought with his wife, Judy, a reminiscence of the Italian *Commedia dell'Arte,* which had its equivalents in: Germany (Kasper), Denmark (Mester Jacker), France (Polichinelle), Netherlands (Jan Klaasen), Italy (Pulichinelle), Romania (Vasilache), Russia (Petruschka), and Portugal (Dom Roberto).

None whatsoever
Have you no will to eat it?
Or not enough dough to buy it?

Pray, pay no heed
Excuse this inappropriate poem
Sooth to say, you're kind
Stupid am I, and ashamed
Of how good you have to be
At putting up with little old me.

Other times, she does away with any and all subtlety and prefers to be direct about her positions: *I look forward to being your bride; for no reason other than to see if I like seeing myself thus clothed. To lock down my Fernandinho and make sure he is all mine and live out the rest of my days with him* (08/04/1920). Then, in time, Pessoa's letters change their tune, when he says that "Baby has died" and that desire of laying down with a woman, if he ever truly had it, simply disappears.

I've lost you. Never had you. The hour
Soothes my anguish so as to leave,
In my remembering being, the power
To feel love.

Though loving be a thing to fear
A delusory and vain haunting
And the night of this vague desire
Has no morning.

Untitled (undated), Fernando Pessoa

Ophelia is a woman of her time, torn between the limitations imposed on women by the rigid local society and the yearning to carve out an independent life for herself. For many, like her, marrying is an emancipation of sorts – from her family or financial limitations. She goes as far as admitting to feeling *distressed at the thought of you bidding* [Luís de] *Montalvor goodbye and coming to meet me afterwards, and him seeing you; do bear in mind, I'm not afraid of him seeing me with you, but that he'd take revenge by telling my father* (letter from 26/05/1920). This because Pessoa, utterly oblivious to such concerns, didn't even consider being introduced to her father and demanded their romance remain secret, and so never made it known to his own family, as sister Teca declared to *Jornal de Letras* (#177, 1985)[17]. Nor did he accept the

17 It wasn't quite like this. As we will see, Ophelia herself confesses that his family knew (and did not approve) of their relationship.

premise, as Ophelia put it, of a "fling" or "simple courtship". "Just say we love each other". Not for much longer, they wouldn't.

> I wish to cast off having you
> To die of loving you
> Your presence commutes
> My forgetting into hating you.
>
> *Setting*, Fernando Pessoa

Mismatch

On the 30th of June 1920, Ophelia goes *to consult madam something or other, at Calçada dos Cavaleiros. Let's see what she has to say about our future. I hope she says that which I truly wish to hear.* And she speaks no more of that, probably because said madame didn't quite predict the future she longed for. Indeed, their relationship is called off shortly thereafter, as Ophelia writes (27/10): *I am not your ideal, I fully understand that; the one thing I am sorry for is that you only realized that after almost a year. If you truly cared for me, sir, you would not proceed in such fashion, as you wouldn't be able to bring yourself to do it. Our natures are contrary to each other. What is more important is to care for one another. Your will be done, then. All the best.* Pessoa replies with a short note (29/11/1920): "Love has moved on. Remember me fondly, as I shall cherish your memory, unchanged", and asks to keep her letters. She replies (01/11/1920): *Concerning my letters, you may do with them as you like, though they are surely too simple for you. All the best.* Pessoa says no more. He doesn't even send her the following sonnet (written in English), which was later found among his papers:

> So often did I wish this mockery of a love
> Between us would end right now.
> But not even to myself can I pretend
> That, with that end, I would be truly happy.
>
> All is a departure
> Our happiest day also makes us a day older.
> To reach the stars, we must also have darkness[18].
> The crispest hour is also the coldest.
>
> I dare not hesitate to accept
> Her letter of goodbye, and yet I yearn
> With a vague feeling of jealousy I can scarcely reject

18 This notion is later reiterated in *Message* ("Portuguese sea"): *God placed danger and the abyss in the sea,/ But he also made it heaven's mirror*

That ours might have been a different path.
Goodbye! Should I smile at that, or not?
The feeling is now lost in thought.

Untitled (Undated), Alexander Search

And dona *Maria returns from Africa*

Pessoa doesn't write his mother often. As he explained to Ophelia: "Letters are for people you no longer wish to speak to. I never willingly wrote letters to my mother, because of how much I care about her". To assuage his guilt for his late replies, he uses the same ploy he used with his friends: Putting previous dates on his letters. *Dona* Maria addresses him as *my dearest son* or *my dear Fernando;* always sends him *hugs from your father who misses you,* and reprimands him, saying she *wishes you would be more expansive with us. No one loves you more than I do, and no one ever shall, believe me.* One of those letters (22/11/1915) makes Pessoa particularly happy, as his mother thanks him for a photo and mentions one Mrs. Birne described him as having as *the head of a poet.* The difference between mother and son would become more evident later. *Dona* Maria's letters were all religiously kept by Pessoa, but his were lost. Shortly after meeting Ophelia, he writes *dona* Maria a poem which begins thus:

Others might deserve
A home, who knows, love, peace, a friend.
While dark and cold loneliness I conserve
Within me penned.

Untitled (13/01/1920), Fernando Pessoa

That "home" with the "love" and "peace" he so yearned for, is the one *dona* Maria would reside in upon her permanent return to Lisbon, after 25 years in Africa. Bringing her three children but not her husband, who she had lost shortly before, while she herself was suffering from a severe case of uraemia – this at the same hospital in Pretoria in which Teca was hospitalized due to pneumonia. That photo in the room, dedicated to the Commander with an *Always yours, Maria* is now but a memory of the past. Once again a widow, *dona* Maria bids him goodbye with yet another poem (in which she displays a lack of familiarity with her language):

I shall never see you, beloved husband
Where you are, I cannot reach you
Would that I could depart
But a mother's duty commands me to stay.

Due to a strike at the postal service, Pessoa wouldn't get the letter announcing the date of her arrival, but postcards meant for her and his brothers arrive at the apartment he resided in. Judging by the dates on the stamps, he concludes they will be arriving on the *Lourenço Marques,* with expected arrival in the morning of the 4th of April 1920 (Ophelia confirms as much, in a letter of 26/03). But there was a strike at the harbour, and no ship arrived at the Tagus docks that morning. Later on in the afternoon, cousin Mário de Freitas (who worked in the shipping industry) informs him of their arrival, and both go to the harbour. All other passengers had already departed, and only the family remained, bringing with them the remains of commander Rosa and what little belongings they could – everything else was left behind in Africa. Sister Teca provides an account of their encounter, excusing the fact that Pessoa came so late: *When the ship dropped anchor, the passengers began to come out and, to our great astonishment and sadness, we realized there was no one waiting for us in the docks... It was then that, in the middle of the crowd, we made out Fernando and Mário. Fernando looked very crestfallen, he'd just had a bout of the flu and was feeling very under the weather.*

At last, after so long, he finally sees his "one true love" again. But his mother, although she was only 58, returned from Pretoria a drained woman. Her face looks invariably sad in photos. He told Sá-Carneiro (26/04/1916) that she had suffered "from what is colloquially called a *bout of apoplexy"*. He had received the news from his father, to whom she was a *beloved wife and your mother.* That stroke she suffered in November 1915 left terrible marks – the corner of her mouth was pulled, the entire left side was compromised, with an inert arm and leg with limited range of motion, to the point she had to use crutches. But she wasn't the only one who had changed. Her son was no longer her little boy, either. With his anaemic body ravaged by the flu, he reminds her of the husband she lost to tuberculosis. Everyone stays at the home of cousin António Maria Silvano at Avenida Casal Ribeiro 35 for a couple of days; on the 29th of March 1920, they move to Rua Coelho da Rocha 16 (Ophelia writes Coelho da Roxa). In May 1920, his two brothers move to England, as they didn't know nearly enough Portuguese to study in Lisbon. Luís Miguel graduates in chemical engineering, João Maria in economy and finance, both through the University of London. Having been born in Durban, they were British citizens according to English law. Only his mother and Teca remain with Pessoa, who writes the following poem to the latter in 1920:

And if one were to think she is fairer
At night, when she is at her most soulful,
Pay attention to her eyes
The colour of still night.

And so, lively in the morning
And evoking night with their colour
If there be eyes of equal beauty
They have yet to make themselves known

Teca, Íbis

The following year, the eyes of this poem's muse enthralled captain Francisco José Caetano Dias, 28 at the time to Teca's 25. They get married on the 21st of June 1923. After their honeymoon, and due to her need for constant medical care, *dona* Maria goes to live with her daughter at Quinta dos Marechais, at Buraca, Amadora (formerly Porcalhota), municipality of Oeiras. Niece Manuela Nogueira described me the farm as *a place the military reserved as a residence for army men,* a purpose its own name (Marshal's Grange) gives away. With them also goes the (quite ill) general Henrique Rosa, brother of *dona* Maria's second dead husband. But not for long. Two years later, in 1925, the general dies on the 8th of February, and Pessoa's mother suffers her final stroke on the 5th of March. Pessoa wanders around the grange, speaking to no one, and doesn't enter her room during any of her last 12 days. Finally, on the 17th of March, her suffering ends.

> The death of my mother broke off the last of the external bonds that still connected me to the sensibility of life. At first, I was dizzy. Then, the tedium that had evolved into anguish was numbed into sheer ennui. Her love, which had never been clear to me in her life, became so in death. It was upon missing it – as tends to be the case whenever one ascertains the worth of anything – that I realized how much I needed her affection, which, much like air, is breathed in without actually being felt.[19]
>
> Annotation, Baron of Teive

Around September, his sister and her husband move to live with him, according to Manuela Nogueira, *due to all the grief experienced at the grange,* as other than Henrique Rosa and *dona* Maria, that year had also seen the death of Veríssimo Dias (the brother-in-law's father)[20]. Back at Rua Coelho da Rocha, there was to be a brief and joyful respite with the birth of his niece Manuela Nogueira on the 16th of November of 1925. The midwife was Ms. Price – who, according to Manuela, was something of a high-end accoucheuse. The baby,

19 The image evokes an allegory of (Immanuel) Kant's (1724-1804) in his *Critique of Pure Reason* (1781): *The light dove, cleaving the air in her free flight, and feeling its resistance, might imagine that its flight would be still easier in empty space.*

20 The man had lived a modest life, despite coming from a wealthy family, because, at the time, the entirety of the parents' inheritance went to the eldest brother. For that reason, it wasn't uncommon to see a wealthy brother and another desperately trying to make ends meet.

Maria Leonor, would die of an intestinal infection before the end of the year. Pessoa wrote the following for her:

> The wooden cart
> The baby left behind…
> Baby is dead
> The cart stowed away
> Baby's memory fading away
> Life is for those
> Who carry on living…
>
> *Untitled* (undated), Fernando Pessoa

In the last months of 1927, his sister moves with her military husband to Évora. Pessoa visits them occasionally and describes his visits in *Disquiet.* He meets with Ophelia *by chance a couple of times,* in her own words, but they aren't on speaking terms. He would later confess to having seen her "with a lad I assumed was her fiancé or boyfriend" – perhaps her ex, Eduardo, struck by the pain of a lost love. But, in the beginning of 1929, she is single and available again.

The second stage of their relationship

On the 2nd of September 1929, Pessoa hands poet Carlos Queiroz a photo with a note – "This is me at Abel's, which is to say close to earthly paradise, lost". As we previously saw, this Abel is the merchant Abel Pereira da Fonseca of the Val do Rio wine cellar. The young poet's aunt no longer does any office work, having lived at her sister Joaquina's ever since her parents' death, and would craft hats to make ends meet, according to some. She would only hold another steady job in 1936 at the SPN, in deference to António Ferro. Ophelia sees the photo and asks her nephew for another one just like it – only he mustn't reveal for whom it was. That second photo also gets its own dedication, the "caught red-handed" one we've previously seen. She thanks him for it on the 9th of September, closing of her letter with a sniping *Have you no shame?* Two days later, he replies, saying he couldn't see how "a photo of some random miscreant, even if it were the twin brother I do not have, could possibly be reason for thanking me. Does a drunken shade have place in your memories?", concluding "To my exile, which is as unto myself, your letter arrived as a joy at home, and I am the one who should be thanking little old you. Another thing… No, it is nothing, sweet mouth". She replies three days later. *But tell me, Fernandinho, what was that "another thing" you were going to write? Do tell. I would so much like to know it! Don't be mean... Goodbye, dear*

Fernandinho; Ophelia never forgets you. They schedule a meeting at *the tram stop at Estrela, at around 18 ¼,* and, according to her own words, the *courtship* then truly begins.

Were the two of us dead,
In another river without a place
In another boat, once again alone
That we might begin anew
That you might just be
The Other.

A outra,[21] Fernando Pessoa

Their relationship is unlike those she had with previous boyfriends. He had never gone to her parents' house (at the corner of Rua Poiais de São Bento), and would even now seldom go to her sister's (at Praça D. João da Câmara, 4, second floor, in front of Café Martinho do Rossio). On those occasions, according to her, he presents himself as *a friend of my nephew* [Carlos Queiroz], *with whom he got along nicely. He would come in, shyly say hello to whomever was present, and the three of us would stand in the room, chatting. He spoke of poetry, books and friends.* And also about matters concerning Ophelia's family: Her brother's politically motivated incarceration, the unhappy marriage of her sister Joaquina, or her other sister's unemployed husband. In his own way, Pessoa does like her, and confesses in a letter on the 29th of September 1929 that "if I should marry, then only with you". But he's not easy to be with. He misses scheduled dates, goes days without saying a word, and has incomprehensible attitudes towards Ophelia. *He'd often tell me he was afraid he couldn't make me happy, due to the time he had to put into his writing.* His mood too was mercurial. *Fernando had these bouts of passion which frightened me. In one of those sudden attacks, we were both at the tram stop of the Rua de São Bento, when he pushed me behind a staircase, grabbed me tightly and gave me a huge kiss. Or we'd be talking and, all of a sudden, he'd say his name was sulphuric acid.* In a letter written on the 3rd of October 1929, she even complains: *Have you recovered from your bout of madness?* To say nothing of Álvaro de Campos' constant interference in their relationship – which might explain one of Pessoa's letters to Gaspar Simões (30/09/1929), in which he says his existence has been "reduced to a miserable contemplation of Álvaro de Campos' folly". And he wasn't the only one who took to disliking Ophelia, as evidenced by the words of another heteronym:

Ophelia of the grey gaze
And soul dripping with longing

21 These verses were written on the 28th of July 1935.

> Get thee to a nunnery…
> Or, better yet, a priory.
>
> *Untitled* (undated), Pero Botelho

During the final months of 1930, his sister, brother-in-law and niece move back to live with him at Rua Coelho da Rocha. That same year, they buy a plot of land at Estoril. Then, on the 1st of January 1931, Luís Miguel, his second and last nephew, is born. At that point, Pessoa is no longer the man Ophelia loved. *Pessoa looked different. Not just physically, as he had gained quite a bit of weight, but especially in his way of being. He was ever nervous, and lived obsessed with his oeuvre.* On the 9th of October 1929, she says an aunt asked her: *And just when will you be marrying, missy? My answer: Would that I knew. When the cows come home.* Ophelia was right. His last letter, on the 11th of January1930, included a poem "to be read at night in a dark room", was trite like all others. The letter with which he was to say a proper goodbye was never written. On the 11th of April 1930, she laments: *As was to be expected, that which I didn't wish to happen, happened... Ever since we split, I've been so sad that I have yet to salvage a bit of a good mood.* Pessoa gives her a call on the 7th of October, but she isn't home and so misses the chance to know what he wished to tell her.

> I loved you, and because I loved you
> I saw everything but you.
> You were the sky and the sea,
> You were night and day…
> Only when I lost you
> Did I truly get to know you
>
> *Eros universo*, Fernando Pessoa

Pessoa's letters are all cold, while Ophelia makes no secret of how in love she is. It is impossible for one not to be touched by her devotion and how she utterly gives herself to him, which is plain to see even in the simplest of sentences: *My future little husband* (23/05); *O lie of my life, when will I be happy? Or let my martyrdom end... or my life* (26/05); *I know how to love you, I do, I am quite convinced of that* (30/05); *I am and always will be yours and very much yours* (31/05); *Oh, would that I were already living with you! That I were yours!* (06/06, all from 1920). What she didn't count on is that there would never be a place for her alongside one who only wanted to write. "My life is about my literary work. Everything else is of secondary interest to me – good or bad as it is or might be". "What remains to be seen is if marriage, hearth (or whatever you might call it) are things that can align themselves with my life of thought. Time will tell". And so time did. "So often did I wish that this love might end up derisory between us! And now it has". Leaving nothing behind. "All temporal love ever did for me was to remind me of what I had lost". On the 10th of January 1908, he all but predicts what was bound to happen:

> "Tell me", one day to a poet said
> A deep, brutal man,
> "If you had to choose between seeing dead
> Your wife whom you do love so well
> And the loss complete, irreparable,
> Of your verses[22] all, instead –
> Which loss would you rather feel?"
> (…)
> And he did not answer; and the other
> Smiled, as elder to younger brother.
>
> *A question*, Alexander Search

Ophelia still writes him a letter on the 29th of March 1931: *If Nininho can afford to rent a house... the most modest he can get, furnish it with but the most essential objects one needs to live, with nary a shade of luxury... why won't you bring me with you, so I can realize my one true ambition?... I shall suffer no disappointment, for I shall be happy to have your constant company – as much as possible – your friendship and tenderness... Oh, my love, take me with you as soon as possible, for I can no longer resist the urge to kiss you... to be part of your life.* Only problem was that, by then, Pessoa had already gotten away – "with rancour, humiliation, but a healthy measure of relief". To him, all that remains is "gratitude for those who loved me". *We wrote and saw each other until January 1930,* she recalls. *Fernando told me that he was crazy. I did not reply to the last letters, as they didn't look like they were meant to be replied to. It wasn't worth it. I felt there was no answer to give.* It wasn't to be, and perhaps because she felt *you still cared for me,* she'd write an additional 21 letters, the last one on Christmas 1932. Pessoa never replied to any of them. "My fate is in the hands of another Law, the existence of which little Ophelia is scarcely aware of, and is subordinate to Masters who neither relent nor forgive". Deep down, it's his "fear of love". Lost in his Chest, dated the 26th of August 1930, the following quatrain would eventually be found:

> Be there a grave
> Or dust-filled attic
> Baby is gone
> My soul is forlorn.

22 A reference to the legend of Camões, who preferred to save his *Lusiads* in a shipwreck, leaving his beloved Dinamene to die.

Longing for the times of love

"Should I ever choose a wife from among the women of Earth", he said as Bernardo Soares, it would be Ophelia. Only he never truly considered it in earnest. Paulo Ferreira, friend of António Ferro, says it was simply a case of *Pessoa not having enough money to marry.* According to Teresa Rita Lopes, had he been able to get the job of curator in Cascais he had applied for in 1932, *he would probably have married Ophelia, they might have been happy, and while he was unlikely to have many children, he would probably have lived longer and written more books.* Having said that, she confided in me that she didn't really believe they would have married anyway. Cleonice Berardinelli, Teresa Sobral Cunha and Yvette Centeno were all of a like mind. "When will you be but a longing of mine?". After that final separation, Pessoa visited her before Christmas 1934. In Ophelia's words: *One day, there was a knock at the door, and the maid brought me a book. When I opened it, I saw it was* The Message, *with a dedication of Fernando's* ["To Ophelia, affectionately, Fernando 10-12-1934"]. *When I asked who had brought it, I realized by the description that he himself had done so. I ran to the door, but couldn't catch sight of him.* In avoiding her, Pessoa missed the chance of getting back his dark smoking pipe of the EP brand, which Ophelia had taken from him on account of his excessive smoking. "I cry not for the time in which I loved you, I cry for not longing for the time in which I loved you". He likely recalled the sonnet he had written in English on the 5th of November 1920, at the end of the first stage of their relationship.

Farewell, farewell for ever,
Since love left not behind
Nor even friendship nor endeavour
Nor sorrow mad or kind.
'Tis fit indeed those souls be parted
That cannot e'er be broken-hearted.

Farewell, farewell for ever;
'Tis time this thing were done,
When love is cold which was a fever
And vulgar as a stone,
When life from woe to woe doth flee
And change itself is misery.

Farewell, Alexander Search

"Each of us was as unto a dream for the other". From that point on, their relationship boils down to annual letters or telegrams, in which Ophelia claims to be his *devoted friend.* He sends her his last one on the 2nd of June

1935, shortly before her birthday (14/06). Hers, on the 13th of June, says only *Congratulations from your Ophelia, who misses you.* A phrase Pessoa would scarcely dream of using, he who "never missed anything. There are no periods in my life which are pleasant to recall. In all of them, I have ever been the same – the one who lost the game". Once they split, Ophelia was nothing more than a dream of the past to him – as we can see in these verses written in Christmas 1930, in which he remembers the times they were still seeing each other and when he tried to get her attention, walking by her window:

Once I loved the Queen
And in my soul there has ever been
A throne to fill
Whenever I can dream
Whenever I cannot see, I place
The throne on that place;
Beyond the curtain, the hearth[23],
Beyond the window[24], the dream.

Untitled (1930), Fernando Pessoa

Ophelia, post-Pessoa

Ophelia was faithful to him until his death, despite them no longer being in a relationship; and, other than two statements to her grandniece Maria das Graças Queiroz, she always refused to do interviews. The first one she gave was "Fernando e eu" (Fernando and I), which came with the edition of "Cartas de amor de Fernando Pessoa" (Fernando Pessoa's love letters), published by Ática in 1978; the second and last one was published at *Jornal de Letras* on the 12th of November 1985. In a letter to journalist Ronald de Carvalho, then working at TV Globo, she says: *I have always refused to do interviews or presentations, no matter with or to whom... because I was certain that Fernando, reserved and simple as he was, wouldn't have liked it. He never confided about our love to anyone* (17/11/1985). The romance was known only by her own family, and by his sister and brother-in-law, who didn't

23 Shortly before (07/10/1930), he recalls that hearth in an untitled poem: *When I was a pilgrim/ Of my own destiny!/ How often did I scorn/ The hearth I've always loved!/ How many times did I reject/ That which I wished to have,/ I made of my verses a mild/ Haven of not-being.*

24 A reference to one of Ophelia's letters (20/03/1920), in which she says: *When you pass by in your car on your way to Benfica* (where Pessoa lived at the time, at Avenida Gomes Pereira), *always look at the window, won't you? (If you can, of course). Because, at times, I might be at the window, and when I'm at the window I always look at cars going to Benfica, so it is entirely possible that I might see you... Won't hurt to try.* Pessoa replies (18/08/1920): "I will be passing by Largo de Camões right now: I hope I can see you at your sister's window.

approve of it on account of Ophelia's humble origins[25] – this according to her own words to the journalist to whom she gave a last interview, shortly before her death. Other than some of Pessoa's friends, such as Almada Negreiros, most hadn't an inkling of his relationship, which was only made public when (José) Carlos Queiroz (Nunes Ribeiro), 1907-1949, son of sister Joaquina, gave a radio conference at Rádio Emissora Nacional days after Pessoa's death. That text, along with six letters and a drawing by Almada Negreiros, was published in *Presença* #48 (July 1936), and then converted into a 47 page pamphlet, *Homenagem a Fernando Pessoa* (Homage to Fernando Pessoa) in August of that same year, by Editorial Presença. It begins thus: *My dear Fernando: – After a long and almost unsound hesitation,* and without *knowing how to avoid the lacrymatory effect of funereal euologies*... The reference to Ophelia contained therein is in the following passage: *Because you loved, Fernando, let me tell everyone about it. You loved and – which is all the more extraordinary – did so as if you weren't a poet.* Still remembering those letters *Fernando wrote to the one you addressed the following words to: "If I should marry, then only with you"*. But, even though the text reveals the relationship, Ophelia's name is replaced by three asterisks, and the text was dedicated *to Ophelia, Pierre Hourcade and my friends at Presença.* It was a revelation, considering Pessoa himself had told Ophelia: "None know whether or not I care about you, as I have confided in no one about the matter". The name would only be revealed in 1950, with João Gaspar Simões' biography – *Vida e obra de Fernando Pessoa, história de uma geração* (Life and oeuvre of Fernando Pessoa, story of a generation) – in which Ophelia was revealed as the anonymous woman of the love letters, the content of which was only made public (save for the two censored ones) in 1978, when Ophelia was 78 years old and a widow.

Despondent after Pessoa's death, Ophelia declares: *Let us pretend I also died.* But it wasn't so. In 1936, on occasion of *A severa,* the first Portuguese non-silent film, she met Augusto Eduardo Soares, the administrator of Tobis Portuguesa, who also dabbled in theatre. Born on the 4th of August 1886, he had his acting debut at *O guarda* (1906). Soares would later perform on Lisbon's theatres such as Apolo, Avenida, Maria Vitória I, São Luís, Trindade, Variedades, and also Porto's, such as Águia d'Ouro, Carlos Alberto and Sá da Bandeira. He also conducted operas at the São Carlos. Between 1938 and 1939, he organized Portuguese folkloric bands for the international congresses of Hamburg and Berlin, at the invitation of Kraft durch Freude[26] – which was a sign of his future sympathies towards Germany during World War II. When he

25 Pessoa's family disagrees with this version. According to Manuela Nogueira, *Fernando simply did not wish to marry, and that caused some discomfort.*

26 German for *Strength through Joy,* a Nazi foundation which controlled German leisure so as to increase workers' productivity.

married Ophelia on the 28th of July 1938, he was at the peak of his career. He was 51 to her 38. For the standards of their time, it was an age difference more appropriate for relationships of expediency. Soares had already been married previously through the Church, so this second marriage was civil – record #261 at book 79, sheet 61 at Lisbon's Sixth Registry Office. The godparents were José Alvelos and filmmaker António Filipe Lopes Ribeiro – who Ophelia had collaborated with when filming *28 de Maio*[27].

> I know you got married in one of life's
> Awe-inspiring somewheres. I believe you're a mother. You must be happy.
> Why wouldn't you be?
>
> Only because of unfairness…
> Yes, it'd be unfair…
> Unfair?
> (…)
> Life…
>
> *Holiday in the country*, Álvaro de Campos

From that point on, she begins to sign her name as Ofélia Maria Queirós Soares[28]; the two were happy, in their own way. *I always tried to give him the happiness he deserved,* she confesses. Before getting married, Ophelia destroyed all the love letters she had. Except for Pessoa's – a decision even her husband agreed on, as he was an old fan of his. So much so that, whenever he read news speaking about *her friend,* he would bring them to his wife's attention. He would die of cancer at the age of 68, on the 6th of February 1955. The following day, *Diário de Notícias* reported on his passing in the obituary section.

> Ofélia Maria Queirós Soares, Deolinda Soares Alonso[29] and her husband, Júlio Eduardo Soares,[30] wife, children, grandchildren and family[31] do their painful duty of informing that God found it fit to bring to His divine presence their beloved husband, brother, brother-in-law, uncle and relative, whose funeral shall take place today, at 11:30, at the chapel of the Portuguese Oncology Institute, to a cemetery to be determined. Agência Salgado.

Towards the end of her life, Ophelia lived at Largo do Jerónimo 38, parish of Camarate, Loures, and died a tranquil death on the 18th of June 1991, after

27 The 28th of May was when the coup that brought Salazar to power was carried out.
28 Ofélia now, instead of Ophelia, and Queirós instead of Queiroz.
29 Sister of the deceased.
30 His second and last brother, head of Montepio Comercial e Industrial's treasury.
31 Only that of the deceased. There is no mention of Ophelia's.

which she is buried at the Alto São João graveyard, in Lisbon. Having bid life goodbye at the burdened age of 91, and not like Shakespeare's maddened Ophelia, drowned in the river amidst flowers.

> And to you, o Death, go our souls and our beliefs, our hopes and our salutations! Virgin Mother of the absurd World, shape of misunderstood Chaos, spread out and extend your demesne over all things, between the error and the illusion of life!
>
> *Book of Disquiet (Grandes trechos)*, Bernardo Soares

Amicus usque ad aras
(Friends to the death) Plutarch

THE DRUNKEN GENERAL, THE EGYPTIAN NARCISSUS, THE LATIN SOOTHSAYER AND OTHER FRIENDS

I am the face of all fatigue
The pain of all anguish.
Untitled (21/12/1913), Fernando Pessoa

Friends from the streets

In Lisbon, Pessoa socializes with "curious individuals, faces bereft of interest, a series of side notes of life". Among them, it is safe to assume, Chico Aú, plump and with a drunkard's red nose, who replies to his friend's insults at the bar with verses. Flowers Tlim, who, in exchange for alms, hands out flowers and salutes those who pass him by with songs. Monkey-Man, an exceedingly polite bohemian, is known by this sobriquet on account of his clutching at balconies during his seizures. Crazy Pine, utterly witless, lives giving out moralistic speeches at Chiado, insults female passersby, calling them *sows* and tells them to *go sew socks.* Pirilan enjoys drinking in general (except water, of course) and to play the fife. Five Réis, a Galician delivery boy, doesn't much care for spending what little money he has; when people present him something to buy, he invariably says *I wouldn't even give five réis for that.* Costa Swallowbullet is a switchblade-wielding tough who kicks out misbehaving patrons from taverns.

"I've always had a measure of talent for friendship, but I never had friends. I always lived isolated, and ever more isolated the more I became aware of it". Ever since Africa, where he felt like a pariah. Upon his return to Lisbon, he lived on his own and felt like "an intruder to all". "A stranger here just as everywhere else" – to others, to his homeland, to the world. More than that, he's a "perpetual stranger" to himself. According to Ophelia, *he didn't even have what one calls an intimate friend* – at the time of that comment, Sá-Carneiro had already died. "Does this mean I have no true friends? I do have some, but they aren't true friends". He mentions this in a number of texts (which I gather here in a unified sample):

We all have two lives; the true one, which is the one we dream about during childhood; the false one, which we share with others. Living with others is torture. Even those who are dear to me aren't truly dear to me; I am surrounded by friends who aren't really friends of mine and acquaintances who don't really know me. I am everyone's brother, without actually belonging to the family. There isn't a single character in this world which even comes close to what I hold to be a close friend. The presence of others derails my thoughts. No temperament matches mine. I am my best friends and my true enemies. I am surrounded by an absolute void of fraternity and affection. While the average man finds contact with others to be stimulating for expression, to me, that same contact is a counterstimulus. My way is that of solitude, and not that of men; I don't know if it was Rousseau or Senancour[1] who said as much. I have in me a world of friends, with lives of their own, real, defined, imperfect. They are spectral, imagined friends, stupid as Mary Pickford or Rodolfo Valentino.[2]

The friends at Orpheu

But he does have friends, and plenty of them – though perhaps 'acquaintances' might be the most appropriate term for most of them. The entries in his diary between February and April 1913 mention [Israel] Anahory, António Arroio, António Cobeira, [José Manuel] Boavida Portugal, [Alberto da] Cunha Dias, Idílio Perfeito, João Correia de Oliveira, Jorge Barradas, Rui Coelho, (cousin) Vitoriano Braga. And also those who work at *Orpheu* with him, such as Ângelo de Lima, António Ferro, Armando Côrtes-Rodrigues, José Pacheco, Luís de Montalvor, Mário Beirão, Ponce de León, Raul Leal, Sá-Carneiro, and the Brazilians Eduardo Guimarães and Ronald de Carvalho. "I fondly recall our time at *Orpheu,* the old camaraderie". The *boys from Orpheu,* as aunt Anica affectionately put it. Some, like Alfredo Pedro Guisado, were even close to what one might call an intimate friend. Poet, journalist and holder of a law degree, his father was the owner of the Irmãos Unidos restaurant (at Praça D. Pedro, in Rossio), and he was a member of the Portuguese Republican Party, eventually becoming the civil governor of Lisbon. He wrote *Treze sonetos* for *Orpheu 3,* and occasionally signed his works with the pseudonym of *Pedro de*

1 Étienne Privert de Senancour (1770-1846), author of the novel *Obermann,* was a French friend of Jean-Jacques Rousseau (1712-1778), Swiss jurist, author of *The social contract.* According to Pessoa, "we are all children of Christ through His grandson, Rousseau". Ironical, considering Rousseau put all of his children in orphanages. Perhaps for that very reason, Rousseau himself said during the presentation of his autobiography: *I wish to show my peers a man in the unvarnished truth of nature; and that man shall be myself – Myself alone.*

2 Gladys Marie Smith starred in over 200 silent films and a single sound-film, *Coquette,* which earned her an Oscar. She was married to fellow actor Douglas Fairbanks. And Rodolfo Alfonso Raffaello Piero Filiberti Gulglielmi, later Valentino, was an Italian immigrant who started life in the USA as a gardener and dishwasher, but ended up becoming one of the most legendary actors in the 20s.

Meneses, such as when writing the dedications for the books he gave Pessoa (*Ânfora* and *As treze badaladas de mãos frias).*

Augusto Ferreira (de Oliveira Bogalho) Gomes, director of the mines of Porto de Mós[3], was another. Journalist, specialist in graphic design and a poet who also wrote for *Orpheu 3,* his *Quinto império* (Fifth empire) had a preface written by Pessoa. They became close due to their mutual interest in mysticism, and remained friends even when Gomes associated himself with Salazar, president of the Council of Ministers. Luís Pedro Moitinho de Almeida says: *Augusto Ferreira Gomes gave me the impression that he was Pessoa's best friend – or at least the one Pessoa most often confided in.* Luís Pedro was the son of Carlos Eugénio Moitinho de Almeida, owner of Casa Moitinho de

Book with a preface by Pessoa

Almeida, where Pessoa worked at. He was quite a bit younger than Pessoa, who was rather frank with him, such as when Luís Pedro asked him for his opinion on a bunch of verses he had written in French. The answer was: "A friend of mine [Pessoa himself, naturally], who has a deep knowledge of French, asked me not to repeat those verses". He worked as a lawyer in Setúbal and Lisbon, and José Blanco told me he could always be seen *robe in arm, walking towards Boa Hora* [Lisbon's criminal court] *to the day he died.* Pessoa encourages him to pursue poetry and even writes a preface for a book of his,

3 Despite its name ('*Porto*' meaning 'port'), Porto de Mós lies 15km away from the sea. Its name is owed to the fact that the river Lena was navigable during Roman times.

Acrónios[4]. Adolfo Casais Monteiro had the following to say in *Presença* #35: *In this preface, we have today's biggest Portuguese poet showing us how he isn't that much of a poetry critic.*

João Gaspar Simões was also important in his life. Born in Figueira da Foz, lawyer at Coimbra, critic, essayist and one of the founders of *Presença* magazine, he was responsible for the first studies on Pessoa: "Fernando Pessoa" in *Temas* (1929), and "Fernando Pessoa ou Vozes da inocência" in *O Mistério da poesia* (1931). Later, he was also his first biographer – in *Vida e obra de Fernando Pessoa* (1950). A resident of Porto, he only began to live in Lisbon in 1935. Due to that distance between them, their friendship was manifested via letters, but they became intimate to the point that Pessoa felt comfortable giving him the following advice (03/12/1931): "My dear Gaspar Simões, never apologize for anything, especially to the public". Simões dedicated his novel, *Elói,* to *the most admirable spirit I have the pleasure of consorting with.* And there was also Mário da Cunha e Silva, author of several books that he gave his friend Pessoa with amusing dedications: *To Fernando Pessoa and to Fernando Someone, to us Fernando Pessoa this book of ours,* or *To your admirable courage* – after which he signed *Mário, the godless.* The same man who, when Pessoa's mother died, wrote him a letter in which he showed how close the two were: *Cry, flagellate yourself in memory and longing of She whom you've lost, the sweetest and most affectionate affection on Earth.* Other than these, there was also a considerable amount of intellectuals with whom he also worked in other literary magazines. But those *friends,* for conciseness' sake (some of which we will mention shortly), share but one thing in common: The fact that (almost all) could scarcely be considered *normal,* according to the patterns of the social conventions at the time. That all wouldn't conform to the nostalgia that permeated Portuguese literature. That, borrowing from Almada's words, they *drank of the delirious poison of belonging to nothing.* That they yearned for that which was new, at any cost. That they wished live life to its fullest, and were willing to relinquish it.

> Ah, to have the peace of mind
> Of there being one to understand and be with me!
> He who is my closest[5] friend
> Is as distant from me as the soul is[6] infinite.
>
> *Untitled* (undated), Fernando Pessoa

---

4 Yvette Centeno told me she admitted the possibility that Pessoa might have *made a few suggestions* (which is to say, rewritten a few poems) for that book.

5 A variant was *most intimate.*

6 A variant was *two souls.*

General Henrique Rosa

Henrique Rosa

Henrique dos Santos Rosa (1850-1925), the brother of his stepfather, was born on a 1st of December, the same day of Guerra Junqueiro. A Knight of the Order of Saint Benedict of Aviz, he became a brigade general in 1903. He had medals of honour and a long, carefully groomed dark moustache of the type that seems made to be twirled. His eyes bulged considerably, as was typical of those suffering from hyperthyroidism, and so blue that his niece Manuela Nogueira said they looked like *marbles.* According to Pessoa, he was "a tremendous, wonderful spirit, a philosophical pessimist of considerable category" with "immense scientific knowledge". Even though he kept all his manuscripts bound, he never published a single book. Knowing numerous writers, he slowly introduced his nephew to his circle of literary acquaintances. His house at Praça Príncipe Real (formerly Praça Rio de Janeiro) 33 is often frequented by intellectuals of all stripes. Pessoa mingles with them, even at a young age, owing to his already considerable knowledge of classic authors, mainly English ones. And he frequently discussed literature with his uncle, who once pointed at a magazine to him and said: *Just look at what this gentleman is saying* – it was a critical review of Ricardo Reis, at which his nephew vigorously defended his heteronym, and the discussion went on through the night. And the general never got to know that Reis and Pessoa were the same person. A man of "peculiar culture" and a compulsive reader, he was also the author of abject poetic verses. Still, out of gratitude (rather than literary merit), Pessoa considers getting his uncle's poems published by Olisipo, and afterwards in *Athena* magazine, when the general was already near death. And in his list of *Sonnets to be translated* into English there is a poem of his uncle, "Ponto final" (Period), which begins thus:

> Now that I'm ready to bid life adieu
> Not one of longing, it could not be
> 'tis a long goodbye I eschew
> As life was but suffering for me.

Rosa would spend years without getting out of bed, surrounded by books and bottles. Manuela Nogueira told me he had *a phobia of crossing the street.* According to João Maria, Pessoa's brother, *on account of being a general, he was a wrathful and grumpy person (sort of), as it is the type of role that leads one to becoming wrathful and grumpy. Back in Africa, he caught a virus that made him all but paralytic during his final years.* That unknown disease prevented him from moving, and he caught it while working as an engineer building bridges for Angola's Public Works Company, between the 1st of August of 1876 and the 8th of September 1881. Not even the great Egas Moniz could come up with a diagnosis. His family believed him. Or pretended to do so, considering he wasn't quite invalid, as they one day witnessed when a baker was arguing with the housemaid on the ground floor: He came down from the first floor, kicked the man out and then went right back up as if nothing had happened, spending then a couple more months in bed. To say nothing of the fact that he'd often go out at night with his hard-drinking friends. His behaviour was typical of a patient with *anxious phobic discourse,* likely *agoraphobia* – a fear of open spaces, which makes the patient feel vulnerable. Whatever ailed him, he declared himself *unable to leave* [his house] *since February 1917,* and names Pessoa as his proxy. From 1905 on, Pessoa learns from him how to appreciate Republican ideals and the joys of drinking. A childless widower, his uncle always had lunch with him in restaurants or greasy spoons, meals which could last for hours and dutifully drenched in wine. The general would pass away at Quinta dos Marechais in 1925. Pessoa would outlive him by 10 years, drinking for himself, his uncle and every other poet in the world.

Almada Negreiros

José Sobral de Almada-Negreiros (1893-1970) was born in São Tomé and Príncipe, at Roça Saudade. Son of a Portuguese father and a Guinean mother (dead at the age of 24), he is a "quick, spontaneous" mulatto, "ever exaggeratedly boyish" – the words Pessoa used to describe his friend, who was five years his junior. "That Almada Negreiros isn't a genius is manifested in the fact that it doesn't manifest itself. But what this artist does have is brilliance and intelligence, much of it – this is what one cannot deny. One need but notice the smile of his pencils, allied to the polymorphism of his art, to turn our backs to the notion of considering him merely intelligent". Among other quirks, his friend proposes the *1 + 1 = 1* formula, characterized by an eternal return to the beginning of it all – represented in the form of the serpent eating its own tail, the symbol of knowledge. Almada uses his artistic name unhyphenated, and becomes notorious after his *Manifesto anti-Dantas,* released shortly after *Manifesto futurista de Marinetti,* works which led Michael Armand to call him a *lyrical spitfire.*

The target of Almada's sharp tongue was Júlio Dantas (1876-1962) – doctor, writer, a man of the theatre, state minister (in several cabinets), president of the Portuguese Science and Arts Academy (from 1922 onwards), and nominated for the Nobel prize multiple times. He was chosen as a victim on account of being (extremely) conservative, but mainly for rudely criticizing *Orpheu* magazine. In *A Capital* (30/03/1915), Dantas was behind statements such as *a mange of words and syllabic detritus jumbled together with consolidations and consonances, deathly wounded by disastrous incoherence;* and declared in an article for *Ilustração Portuguesa* (19/04/1915) that the magazine's members were *people bereft of sense* or *paranoid.* The first reaction came at the début of *Sóror Mariana,* a play of Dantas', which wasn't only criticized by Almada, but also by Sá-Carneiro in his poem "Serradura" – in which he refers to him as *genial mr. captain doctor Dantas* – and Pessoa himself, who prophesied that the Portuguese "would have in Júlio Dantas their own Shakespeare". Written on the 21st of October 1915, the poem would be published in the very same *Ilustração Portuguesa* in April 1916, signed by *José de Almada Negreiros, poet at Orpheu, Futurist and All That.* Sold at Livraria Portugal-Brasil, almost every copy of the issue was purchased by the person concerned, Dantas himself, who then burned them all to ash. Here, a sample of the manifesto:

> Enough, bing, enough!!!
> A generation that acquiesces to being represented by one such as Dantas is a band
> Of vagrants and blind dolts! It is a coterie of charlatans and sell-outs.
> A generation with a Dantas astride a horse is an impotent donkey!
> A generation with a Dantas at the helm is a dry-docked canoe!

Dantas wears mesh britches!
Dantas looks awful when naked!
Dantas is the scorn of conscience!
If Dantas is Portuguese, I'd rather be Spanish!
Camões' Plaza should be changed to Dantas' Plaza, and soaps' brand should be "Júlio Dantas", and Dantas toothpaste for the teeth, and Dantas shoe polish, and Dantas margarine, and Dantas pills, and Dantas flushes, and Dantas, Dantas, Dantas, Dantas… and Dantas-Magnésia lemonade. And know, Dantas, that, if justice were to be made one day in Portugal, the whole world will know that the author of *The Lusiads* was Dantas, who, in a memorable bout of modesty, allowed his pseudonym Camões to take credit and glory.
Death to Dantas, death to him! Bing![7]

Almada was responsible for most of the best portraits and paintings we have of Pessoa. The one that is perhaps the most famous one, in shades of red and black, was commissioned by the restaurant Irmãos Unidos and painted in 1954, almost 20 years after his friend's death. In it, we see Pessoa sitting at a bar table, with blank paper and a pen over it, a cigar on his left hand – which, as we have previously ascertained, certainly was the case at times. In front of him, a white cup of coffee, a sugar bowl and *Orpheu* #2 – all in black, with but the title and a large silvery '2' occupying the entire page. Underneath it is what is assumed to be the magazine's first issue. The painting was ceded by the City Museum (of Lisbon's City Hall) and can today be found at Casa Fernando Pessoa, decorating the stairway which connects the library's two floors. Later, in 1964, he painted a similar one for the Calouste Gulbenkian Foundation and simply switched the hand the cigarette was in, moved *Orpheu* to the left, and changed the cup's colour from white to brown. According to António Telmo, it was a collection of Freemason symbols: Brimmed hat, the infinity symbol; a staff, represented by an unlit cigarette; a tray, by the blank sheet of paper; a sword, by the pen; the sugar bowl and the cup, suggestive of the two main elements of creation, sweet and sour; and crossed feet underneath the table, *over an irregular Masonic floor.*

7 This *bing* was preceded by a black hand with an outstretched finger, as if ready to ring a bell at a hotel's desk. But, sometimes, when it is recited (such as by the late Carlos Wallenstein), it represented the sound of a gunshot.

Pessoa, by Almada Negreiros

Mural with a drawing by Almada Negreiros

Another drawing of his can be found at the lobby of Lisbon's Faculty of Letters, to the right of those who enter the building. The canvas appeared to me as washed out marble, on which were sculpted in bas-relief the figures of Caeiro, Reis and Campos, all of them wearing suits, their names inscribed into the lines, and a prone body with a uniform and boots, representing a dead soldier. It is *Mother's little boy:* Pessoa himself. Of that there is no doubt, since there is even a cigarette box close to his body – "Felled from his pocket, a small cigarette box", as per the poem in which he describes a soldier fallen on the battlefield..

Almada always used sharp suits and bowties, and was known as *Egypt's Narcissus.* In a futurist conference which took place at Teatro República (14/04/1917), he makes a *Ultimatum futurista às gerações portuguesas do Séc. XX* (futurist ultimatum to the Portuguese generation of the 20th century), in which he voiced some highly critical opinions on his country and the time he lived in (excerpt):

> Through no fault of my own, I am Portuguese, yet I feel the strength not to let my homeland rot, unlike the lot of you
> (…)
> Because, when Portugal isn't a country of vagrants, it is a country of amateurs.
> (…)
> One must create an adventurous spirit in order to oppose the literary sentimentalism of those who yearn for the past.
> (…)
> Ye Portuguese,
> You insult danger.
> (…)
> You bear the arrogance of those who are whole and sound.
> (…)
> Take heart, Portuguese, all you lack are the qualities.

As an aside, there was a note Pessoa wrote to him: "Almada Negreiros, you cannot fathom how thankful I am for your existence". Almada will later fondly remember his friend: *Poet Américo Durão recalls that I was the only one at* Orpheu *who hobnobbed with Fernando Pessoa.* In 1920, he leaves Lisbon to live in Madrid and Paris, as, according to his own words, *it is impossible to live in Portugal.* He would only return in 1935 to found *Sudoeste* magazine, a blend of those which were the most important literary adventures of his day and age, *Orpheu* and *Presença.* Pessoa would write his last typewritten text for it – "Nós os de *Orpheu".* In that very same #3 (November 1935), Gaspar Simões published by way of reply "Nós, a *Presença";* explaining to readers that, *in order to maintain individuality with a measure of common ground... one cannot in good propriety write "Nós, os da* Presença" (We of *Presença), but only "Nós, a* Presença" (We, *Presença).* On the 6th of December 1935, he writes for *Diário de Lisboa: I have no letters from Fernando Pessoa. Our coexistence was exclusively through art.* Almada would pass away in 1970, in the same room at São Luís dos Franceses hospital, where Pessoa had died 35 years prior. Close to his final hour, the man who considered himself *the seven plagues of the Nile,* or *the soul of suffering liars,* had a bout of modesty and claimed that *the most memorable date of my individuality shall be in 1993, when the centennial of my birthday will be celebrated.* Unlike his predictions, the celebration was on the modest side, but Almada, already in Heaven's embrace, did not protest.

Santa-Rita Pintor

Guilherme de Santa-Rita (1889-1918) is the most eminent figure of Portuguese futurism, but also "imaginative, mystifying, contradictory, friend of buffoonery and scandal, the prototype of a bona fide charlatan", "an interesting, yet lamentable and despicable character". His qualities were "hypocrisy, selfishness and calculation". To Pessoa, he was "a professional of intrigue". He always writes to him from Paris, his place of residence, relaying the things he saw there, such as *the pederasty of the Apollinaire at the Semaine de Paris*[8]. Santa-Rita Pintor (his pseudonym) had a painting course at the Académie des Beaux-Arts in Paris thanks to a scholarship paid for by the Portuguese state. Journalist Rabelo de Bettencourt wrote about him in the first and only issue of *Portugal futurista* magazine, calling him *the artist that the genius of our times brought about.* His work is characterized by an *intuitive abstraction,* according to Dr. Manuel Leal; but he is also clearly unhinged. Sá-Carneiro had the following to say about him: *I expect pretty much anything out of Santa-Rita,* and sarcastically recalls his paintings: One represented *noise in a room bereft of furniture,* and the other one *a bathroom.* Which is hardly surprising, considering that, at the time, Russolo painted his *Music and perfume;* Boccioni, *Laughter;* Balla, *Girl running on a balcony;* and Duchamp, *Nude descending a staircase.* Anything goes in futurism. A poem dedicated to him by Sá-Carneiro encapsulates the folly that reigned at the time (excerpt):

> Ha, ha, ha! I am polishing my nails
> Pie, poe, poe! diddly diddly! diddly doo!
> Such fancy burlap it is!
> Cubic eyes, futurist ears, horizontal head
> Life is moonlight.

Santa-Rita tells Sá-Carneiro *a terrible secret,* as if it were really so – the story of his life. His father, responsible for his *manly and uncouth upbringing,* had tasked a nanny with raising him. *The nanny had a son, and one of the family's children had died.* The nanny's husband, a potter by trade, then said the dead child *was his son,* and, upon his return home, the child was treated as if it no longer were its parents'. In 1906, the nanny passed away, leaving behind *a letter for my mother, in which she confessed that the dead child had been hers.* The one belonging to the Santa-Rita family. As Santa-Rita established at length, *I wasn't my mother's son, but my nanny's. This is the lamentable secret, the tragedy of my life. I am an intruder.* Sá-Carneiro finished the letter in which he told the above story with the following question: *You tell me, Pessoa, if this*

8 He was alluding to *Les soirées de Paris,* in which art critic and poet Wilhelm (Albert Wladimir Alexander) Apollinaris de Kostrovitsky (1880-1918) published, in 1918, a series of poems called *Calligrams* which he had begun writing six years before.

is true. The account wasn't totally devoid of use, however, as it did at least explain why Santa-Rita occasionally signed his correspondence to his brother Augusto as *Guilherme Pobre*. Guilherme, as himself, or Guillaume Apollinaire, who he held as *an example of futurism;* and Pobre (Poor), because he was the son of a nanny.

Sá-Carneiro considers his fellow Paris townspeople [Santa]-*Rita* [Pintor], *MontalvAr*[9] *& Cia.* a bunch of *scoundrels;* urges his friend to *send Santa-Rita to the devil* (02/10/1915); and even says that *he doesn't strike me as a clinical case, but rather – and this might surprise you – bound for Limoeiro*[10] (31/12/12). Another letter said: *Master Rita, the boss of us? Oof!* – as he often was the butt of his friend's jokes and pranks. Such as the one episode involving a prostitute, which he snarlingly reported to Pessoa (abridged): *This one time, he* [Santa-Rita] *introduced me to a hideously ugly Pole and told her I was a homosexual! To which the Pole said she had a soft spot for degenerates!!! And, last night, at 11 ½, he comes up to my room, when I was already in bed, bringing a Frenchman whom he told I was a Portuguese Jesuit émigré!!!...* (16/11/1912).

One particular story of his at the Teatro da República (currently São Luís) became renowned. The affair took place on the 4th of April 1917, at Almada Negreiros' first futuristic conference, which was closed with a reading of Marinetti's "Matemos o luar" (Let us kill moonlight). Santa-Rita went there wearing coveralls and began to insult one Correia António de Oliveira; and was promptly corrected by João Correia de Oliveira, the accused's brother – *Not Correia António de Oliveira, it's António Correia de Oliveira!* – a proponent of nostalgia (1879-1960), author of *Dizeres do povo* (1911), connected to *Renascença Portuguesa* and *Águia* magazine. To that, Santa-Rita went up on a box and shouted to the delight of those in attendance: *For you, maybe, as you're standing over there and read from there to here.* In the audience, Pessoa, who never appeared in public with a woman, was chaperoning a local star called *Preta Fernanda*, and doesn't take sides. Santa-Rita was just being himself, as he had done with so many other people, such as Júlio Dantas, the target of Almada's ire. *Good morning, mister Dantas Júlio,* he said. *Beg pardon,* the other replied, *it's Júlio Dantas.* To which Santa-Rita concluded: *So say you, sir, as you are coming out, but I am coming in...*

9 A disparaging and intentional misspelling of Luiz de Montalvor's surname; "alvar" means "uncouth".

10 A correctional facility described by historian Francisco de Melo e Noronha as *a repugnant school of all vices and a stain on our capital.* Former *tenants* were Bocage (1797), Almeida Garrett (1827) and Hipólito da Costa, the founder of *Correio Braziliense,* Brazil's very first newspaper.

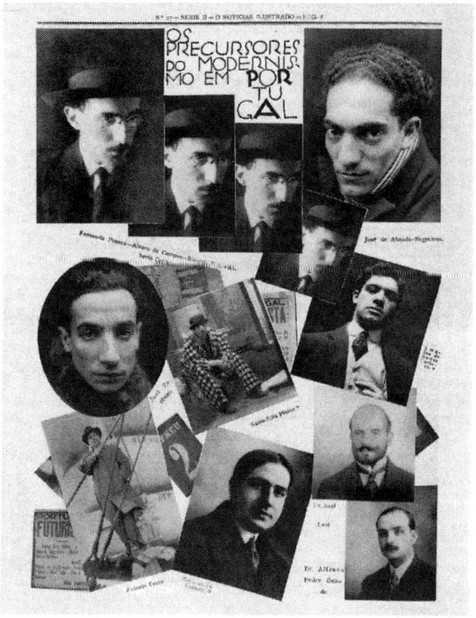

Almada, upper right, and Santa-Rita, middle

Santa-Rita Pintor's features are indicative of an unhinged personality. He wears a suit in almost every photo, with a string tie and a smoking pipe in hand, but occasionally goes to A Brasileira café wearing all black and with an inmate's hoodie. On the 29th of April 1918, dying from septicaemia brought about by the Spanish flu and believing that his oeuvre was inferior to his genius, he still managed to find the strength to ask for everything he painted and wrote to be burnt. He was far from the only one to have done so in history. Virgil (70-19 BC) had an ailing liver and was as much of a perfectionist as Pessoa, and begged emperor Augustus to burn his monumental *Aeneid.* His request went unheeded and the poem was published as the author left it, lacking verses and all. Franz Kafka (1883-1924) asked the same of Prague-born German writer Max Brod, and the fact that the latter didn't comply with his wishes is why masterworks such as *The Trial* and *The Castle* were saved. Mallarmé (1842-1898) too was denied by his wife Marie and his daughter Geneviève, who subsequently published *Le Livre* with the drafts he had disowned. Time goes by and life repeats itself. Pope John Paul II made a similar request, having expressly written in his *Spiritual Testament* that *My personal annotations are to be burned.* His successor Benedict XVI did honour the request, though, as did Santa-Rita's brother, the poet Augusto de Santa-Rita – his sole surviving paintings were *Cabeça* and *Orpheu dos Infernos* (both from 1913). The day following his request, on the 30th of

April, he was buried at Prazeres[11] graveyard. With Santa-Rita's death, so too did Portuguese futurism die.

Miguel Torga

Miguel Torga (1907-1995), hailing from Sabrosa, São Martinho de Anta (Vila Real), is rude-featured peasant who, after a brief period at the Lamego seminar, lived from age 12 to 18 as a coffee picker and snake catcher in a plantation at Minas Gerais, Brazil, which inspired him to write the eponymous "Brazil":

> Brazil, where I lived
> Brazil, where I suffered
> Brazil, land of my childish awe
> Long ago have I left you
> Dock on the other side of my destiny.

Upon his return to Portugal, he became a doctor and would spend the entirety of his adult life in Coimbra, which is why their friendship was mainly through letters. Pessoa had long and heated arguments with him, always calling him by his true name of Adolfo (Correia da) Rocha, under which his first books were actually published – a process which he paid for with his own money, so they wouldn't be subject to censorship. Only later (1934), with the release of *A terceira voz,* would he adopt the pseudonym of *Miguel,* in the mould of Cervantes and Unamuno, two authors he greatly admired; and *Torga,* the name of a plant which grows in the North of Portugal, where he was born. "I am never dogmatic, for one who changed his opinion daily cannot be so and is, by temperament, unstable and floating", said Pessoa. In an undated letter from 1930, he advises Torga to "focus on a clear point" and have a "more balanced distribution of intellectualization amidst the prevailing feelings". In another (06/06/1930), he claims he still needs "to perfect the way you make use of sensitivity", to which Torga replies: *How often can a "master" speak in such definitive terms... But let none claim to hold the one truth in his hand.* Pessoa explained one of their arguments to Gaspar Simões (28/06/1930):

11 In Pessoa's time, Lisbon was said to have three things which were difficult to understand: The palace in which kings had lived, which was called *Necessidades* (Needs); its main avenue, *da Liberdade* (of Freedom), which was somewhat incompatible with Salazar, and this graveyard which was called *dos Prazeres* (of Joys). In spite of the names' apparent strangeness, all of them have their reasons: The graveyard was a homage to the Seven Joys of the Virgin Mary; the palace was an homage to another one of the Virgin Mary's sobriquets in Portugal; and the avenue was so named because the troops which overthrew the monarchy and proclaimed the republic in 1910 had camped there.

> I received a letter from Adolfo Rocha. The letter was written by someone who took offence in the fourth dimension. It isn't quite bitter, nor is it insolent, but a) it all but subpoenas me to justify my previous letter, b) says my opinion is the most uninteresting he's heard on his book, c) expounds in rather obtuse fashion upon how ridiculous intellectuals are, and that the age of Masters is long past. Thus, I thought it better not to reply. What the devil could I have said in reply? Firstly, it is indecent to accept subpoenas in non-judicial matters. Secondly, it hadn't been my intention to enter a competition of interesting opinions. And thirdly, I could only have rationalized the images that, in my haste, Dr. Álvaro de Campos had conjured in my name. And so I gave up.

In a minute of another letter to Gaspar Simões, in which he also spoke of Torga, Pessoa asked the following: "You would do me a great favour if you would indicate me the extra-intellectual formula one should base oneself on when dealing with these rising authors[12]. Do they categorically demand to be called geniuses?". There are no records of that letter ever having been sent, or that Simões replied to it. As if confirming Pessoa's words, Torga (almost) never gave autographs to anyone. In his diary (December 1935), he writes about his friend's death, acknowledging him as *our greatest poet today.* The big irony in both friends' lives is the fact that Torga was a candidate for the 1960 Nobel Prize in Literature, along with Aquilino Ribeiro, whereas Pessoa, who had always dreamed of it, didn't even get that.

Café acquaintances

It is astounding that Pessoa's circle of friends didn't include a single genuinely important name: Someone rich, some remnant of the dying monarchy, an emerging republican politician, someone who was part of one of the many academies flourishing in Portugal at the time. Nothing of the sort. Quite the opposite, he seemed to mingle mainly with pariahs, people with scant academic bona fides, known only in the literary circles he hobnobbed with. All the more unusual, when one takes into account that the society of Pessoa's time was far smaller and less literate than today, and that it was all but impossible for him not to meet those people in the bookstores, cafés and clothes shops he frequented. And how did he manage to work for his brother-in-law in an economics magazine for six issues without meeting a single renowned businessman, even though he mainly worked for merchants of little or middling wealth? The only possible explanation is that he took no real interest in such networking; and the fact he corresponded only with those he did relate to was a choice of his – a conscious choice of being apart from the social scene, little more than a cipher.

12 Pessoa was almost 20 years Torga's senior, and his impatience wasn't only directed at the latter. On Alexandre Seabra, the author of *Nadas,* he had the following to say: "Whatever his age, his brain is far too juvenile; and his art – despite what others might say – is the work of an old or aged man".

"Some are quaint, some are just quaint, others don't even exist yet. The quaintness of cafés is measured by bon mots directed at those who are absent and the insolence directed at those who are present". "The extraordinary thing about all those was the lack of importance of them all. Some were editors at important newspapers, and managed not to exist, others were established poets". "Some were heroes, others were seducers", "some are completely unhinged, others are big pederasts", "poor demigods", "my poor companions with big dreams", "dear vegetables". Such was his life amidst those he considered his friends, "taking nothing too seriously", and "knowing not where it would lead me, as, in truth, I know nothing". Divided between "the dream hated by my intelligence and the action my sensibility abhors". Even when in the company of the acquaintances the shared his days with, he had no real desire to become true friends with any of them. "Friends of fashion", with which he delighted in "endless" conversations "in imaginary cafés", in the strange world that was his world.

Where doth my life lead to, and who leads it?
Why is it I always do that which I don't want to?
What manner of continuous fate passes me by in the dark?
Which part of me I know not of truly guides me?
(…)
Who am I, Lord, in your darkness and your smoke?
Other than my soul, which other soul resides in mine?

Untitled (05/06/1917), Fernando Pessoa

The only one missing from this list is the one who he described in a letter to José Régio (17/01/1930) as "the one true friend I ever had".

Atque in perpetuum, frater, ave et vale!
(And forever, brother, be happy![1]) Catulus

SÁ-CARNEIRO

We were as one!
Sá-Carneiro, Fernando Pessoa

His best friend

Mário de Sá Carneiro was born shortly after Pessoa, on the 19th of May 1890. Like him, also in Lisbon – at Rua da Conceição, 93. Theirs was Pessoa's longest and truest friendship, the one he truly devoted himself to. Sá-Carneiro[2] himself said: *You are my best, most intimate friend.* Both lived similar lives, and they even have identical photos taken when both were one year olds, both in a format known at the time as *carte de visite,* sitting in the same baby chair at Foto Camacho – Lisbon's most famous photo studio at the time (Rua do Almada, 166, first floor), belonging to the Royal House's very own official photographer, João Francisco Camacho. His friend lost his mother, Águeda Maria Murinello de Sá Carneiro, at a very young age, and was raised by his grandparents at Quinta da Vitória, in Camarate (Loures). At the age of eight, he also lost his grandmother, and his father, colonel Carlos de Sá Carneiro, took another wife in *dona* Mimi (Maria Cardoso) in November 1915 – also by proxy, as he was overseas in Lourenço Marques at the time. It almost mirrored Pessoa's own story, with only the parents' roles reversed. "Sá-Carneiro's oeuvre is characterized by inhumanity; it is bereft of human warmth or human tenderness, except that of the introverted kind. Do you know why? Because he lost his mother when he was two and never experienced maternal tenderness. It has been my experience that those who life has deprived of mothers are lacking in tenderness, be they simple artists or simple men" (letter to Gaspar Simões, 11/12/1931). As Sá-Carneiro himself would later say, *I pity myself, poor ideal boy that I am.*

1 Pessoa included this inscription in his poem "Sá-Carneiro".
2 His literary name gained a hyphen after his first writing in 1910.

A victim of his family's overzealous care, he could barely dress himself at the age of 14. At the age of 17, at school, he edited the newspaper *O Chinó* – an early indication of his literary proclivities. Five years later, at the beginning of the year in which he knew Pessoa (1912), he published a book dedicated to his father, *Princípio;* and also a theatre play in three acts, *Amizade,* which he had written with Thomaz Cabreira Júnior, one year his junior. The same poor Thomaz who, on the 8th of January 1911, looked Sá-Carneiro in the eye at the steps of their school before putting a bullet in his own head[3]. Sá-Carneiro would later dedicate his poem "A um suicida" (To a suicidee) – published in António Ferro's *Alma Nova* magazine. In 1913, he published another novel, *A confissão de Lúcio,* and, six months after moving to Paris, *Dispersão* (1914). The surrealist cover was drawn by José Pacheco (1885-1934), a friend he met in Paris, an architecture student, three years his senior, who claimed to be *an architect by the grace of God.* The very same who later would found *Contemporânea* magazine, and who Pessoa sometimes referred to by his artistic name, Paxeko. Finally, in 1915, he gathered 12 novellas in *Céu em fogo* – a book in which his anguish was anything but subtle. So much so, that in one of *Dispersão*'s 12 poems, on the 15th quatrain, he all but foretells his own fate.

> And I feel that my death
> My utter dispersion
> Awaits me there, in the north
> In a large capital.

Paris

Said *large capital* is none other than Paris. In his letters, he always refers to it in affectionate terms, such as *my tender Paris, Paris where War was Waged, Astonishing Capital, Capital of Dancing, The Grand Capital, The Grand City, My City, Magnificent City, Paris;* and, in his verses, as *My City-Figure, My City with a Face; My Barely Ripened Fruit, Paris my Wolf and Friend, Paris of the Beautiful Secret, Paris My Child, Paris the Ultimate Shield, Silence of my Folly.* According to him, *today's Paris is also missing, as am I. And that is the truth: I believe I have utterly disappeared from myself.* During that period (the letter dates from the 29th of August 1914), as if having a vision, he *imagined the end of me, blowing my own trumpet.* He visited the city for the first time with his father in August 1904, staying at the

3 The play's manuscripts, which ordinarily were always kept by Thomaz, were with Sá-Carneiro for some reason. Luckily for him, as his friend destroyed everything he had written before killing himself.

Grand Hotel, the best in the city, right in front of the Opéra Garnier[4], at the time the only one in Paris. Right in that corner, one can also find the famous Café de la Paix. Following that, he visited the city again with his father (in 1907) and then on his own (1912), when he stayed at Hotel Richemond – 11, Rue do Helder – still open to this day, only five minutes away from Opéra Garnier. Not for long, though, as on the 28th of October he moved to a more affordable place, the Grand Hotel du Globe 50, Rue des Écoles, at the heart of the Quartier Latin, between the Sorbonne and the Collège de France – and would later move to a number of private apartments. Sá-Carneiro's departure to Paris would be the beginning of a series of losses for Pessoa: His family remained in Africa; Alfredo Guisado, a close friend, moves to Galicia; his lawyer Alberto da Cunha Dias is institutionalized a number of times, writing to Pessoa on the 2nd and 21st of September 1916 to say he felt as if he were *in jail*; aunt Anica, with whom he had lived with for so long, moves with her daughter and son-in-law – "what family I had here moved to Switzerland". Pessoa, much like Sá-Carneiro, feels abandoned and lonely.

On the 23rd of June 1913, on account of the start of the war between Serbia and Austria-Hungary, he returns to Lisbon and to the old routines with his companions; but, as Sá-Carneiro felt (letter from 29/08/1914), *I cannot live without Paris;* which was why, on the 16th of June 1915, and despite the risks of World War I, he leaves once again, this time forever. After a first temporary address, he would settle at the Hotel de Nice, which rented rooms for the month – a few metres away from the Place Pigalle, at Butte Montmartre, ninth *arrondissement,* a place of musicians, dancers, painters and artists of all stripes and sizes. He would remain there until the day he died, one year later, owing months of rent. Around Hotel Nice, everything suggests art. It is situated at 29, Rue Victor Massé, a known French composer (1822-1884). Not more than 30 metres away, there is Rue Henri Monnier – artist, caricaturist, sculptor and comedian (1799-1877). In front of it, the Rue Frochot – *premier préfet de La Seine* (1757-1828). A lively place, as well as much cheaper than his previous addresses. Today, it stands between the Pharmacie des Arts and Oldies Guitars, a store which sells second-hand guitars, right in front of Pub Frochot. In 1981, it changed its name to Hotel Ninon, and, in 1993, to Hotel des Artistes. Its pleasant owner, the elderly Moroccan madame Fatima Hannouf, proudly displays a plaque at the entrance which says, in French: *Portuguese poet Mário de Sá-Carneiro, 1890-1916, lived in this house and here he passed away on the 26th of April 1916.* The last time I saw the hotel, in 2007, it was undergoing a large-scale makeover, with labourers and painters milling about inside, and nothing in it hearkened back to the past; its walls, now repainted, only held the memories of an almost-boy who fulfilled his fate between them.

4 An homage to Charles Garnier (1825-1898), its architect.

The letters

The friendship between the two men lived on through their letters, in which Sá-Carneiro defined himself as *Daddy's Boy;* or, alluding to his future obesity (and latent homosexuality), *Fat Sphinx.* 216 letters of Sá-Carneiro were saved by Pessoa, but only four of his remain, and only because Pessoa made copies of them – from December 1913 (undated, perhaps just a draft), the 28th of July 1914 (likely another draft), the 6th of December 1915 and the 14th of March 1916; also a fifth, which was never sent, written on the 26th of April 1916, the day his friend committed suicide. Poet Ponce de León, with whom Sá-Carneiro wrote the play *Alma,* later told Pessoa that *Sá-Carneiro read to me or asked me to read pained and concise letters of his.* Those letters are addressed to *My Dear Friend, Saintly Friend, Saint Fernando, Martyr St. Fernando* [Pessoa] *of Tribulations, St. Fernando (person*[5] *who proofreads),* a rather peculiar *H'!'.·.,X,14-xv321b~(H)W,* or even, evoking his stay at Barcelona's Palace Hotel, *Al Señor Don Fernando Pessoa.* From there, in letterhead from the Café de France and Bar-Café El D'Lúvio, he recalls (01/09/1914) that *Unamono was kicked out of the University of Salamanca and is no longer its dean*[6]. The information is relevant, as Pessoa had written Unamuno a letter (26/03/1915) asking him for an article to be published in *Orpheu,* to "expand our influence as much as possible and, through our movement... to attain a spiritual rapprochement with Spain, something seldom attempted". All in vain, as, two months later, *Orpheu* would cease publication.

In those letters, Sá-Carneiro displays a chaotic way of writing, making ample use of French expressions, abbreviated or random words, a profusion of colons and dashes, he is simple incapable of respecting the conventions of punctuation: *As for my spelling, it is likely that a number of mistakes will slip through – an O instead of an U, or a C instead of an SS. Should that be the case, kindly correct them for me. And you be the arbiter of punctuation.* In *Disquiet,* as if referring to that, he says: "Life is the hesitation between an exclamation and a question. Doubt is resolved by a period"[7]. Pessoa brings up "Sigismund, King of Rome", who also thought himself "above grammar" – which was why "he became known as Sigismund *super-grammaticam"* and rebukes his friend

5 *Translator's note:* Wordplay with Pessoa's surname.

6 Miguel de Unamuno (1864-1836) would later regain his role as dean, only to lose it again during the Spanish Civil War, on account of an incident (12/12/1936) in which general Millán Astray interrupted his speech, shouting *Long live death, down with intelligence.* All under the complacent gaze of Cármen Polo, wife of general Franco. Unamuno replied to that *necrophiliac, mindless shout,* sentencing that it'd be *useless to urge you to think of Spain.* He died shortly after of heartbreak in that same year. But, by then, both Pessoa and Sá-Carneiro were already in the company of the gods, and thus unable to comment.

7 The phrase is reminiscent of another of Pessoa's texts, which was published posthumously in *Colóquio* magazine. "This deficiency reminded me of Mallarmé's extravagance, as some of his poems lack any and all punctuation, with nary a period at the end".

for acting as if he were the Roman emperor, both in prose, "I certainly make abundant use of the old spelling… whereas Sá-Carneiro makes use of modern spelling" and in verse, "Having touched Christ's feet,/ Is no excuse for errors of punctuation". All due to the orthographic reform implemented in 1911, right after the Republic[8]. Pessoa refused to part with the spelling he had been taught, and never paid much heed to said agreements – to him, "the written word" is "a product of culture, every man has the right to write according to whichever orthography he pleases". And "the only presumably preferential effect these spelling divergences might have is that the public could be confused". In "A chamada reforma ortográfica" (The so-called orthographic reform), he says that "orthography is a cultural phenomenon and, therefore, a spiritual phenomenon. The State has no business interfering in spiritual matters. The State has no right to compel me, on a matter in which it has no jurisdiction, to write according to an orthography that is repugnant to me, much like it has no right to impose upon me a religion I do not accept". In a letter to Gaspar Simões (03/11/1931), he called that new way of writing "Republican orthography".

According to Manuela Parreira da Silva, Pessoa had a code all of his own to define the intensity of his relationships in the letters he wrote. To those he felt a close bond with, he showed affection mainly when saying goodbye – as can be seen in those directed at Sá-Carneiro: "My brother from beyond", "a big, fraternal hug", "yours, always". To which his friend initially replied with *a big hug* or *a big, big hug;* and later with *pity me;* and, closer to the end, *goodbye, my dear Fernando Pessoa, goodbye from your poor Mário de Sá-Carneiro,* or just *goodbye.* "It is in these times of an abyss felt within the soul that the slightest detail oppresses me as would a goodbye letter".

> The commercial formality at the beginning and end of letters:
> Dear Sirs–Messieurs–Amigos e Senhores,
> Yours faithfully–Nos salutations empressées…
> All of this isn't only human and tidy but also beautiful.
>
> *Maritime Ode*, Álvaro de Campos

A higher, rare and expensive destiny

Sá-Carneiro has no real vices to speak of. *I abhor alcohol, don't smoke, don't gamble, and do not partake of cocaine or morphine.* The grapevine claims he

8 This unilateral reform, which was revoked by the Brazilian Academy of Letters in 1919, would be replaced in 1931 by a more thorough orthographic agreement between Portugal and Brazil, which was complemented by two others in 1943 and 2008.

likes boys, though. He enrolled in Paris' School of Law[9] and only attends a small number of classes, much like Pessoa, who barely attended his. Months before his death, he would send his friend his *carte d'étudiant* which has his name, *M. de Sá Carneiro;* number, *1.250;* and a photo taken in the year he first arrived in Paris – *the good old days,* when he wrote *even the* folie [revelry] *I love to death – it is a thing of beauty.* The photo no longer corresponds to his ravaged features. In a letter to Gaspar Simões (30/09/1929), well after his

Mário de Sá-Carneiro

friend's death, Pessoa described him as "racked Sá-Carneiro (his own stare said as much), emaciated and finished". He hold Pessoa in great devotion. *You are a saint. The most beautiful day in my life was the one in which I made your acquaintance. If we were in 1830 and I were H. de Balzac*[10], *I would dedicate to you a book of my Human Comedy, wherein you would feature as the Man-*

9 A good many of Pessoa's biographies mention that Sá-Carneiro studied at the Sorbonne, which is incorrect, as that simply refers to the university's Faculty of Philosophy, Science and Letters.

10 Honoré de Balzac (1799-1850) wrote numerous novels, with over two thousand characters, which compose the monumental *Human Comedy,* a gigantic fresco of the French society he lived in. The same Balzac who said (in *Ode à une jeune fille),* as if he were talking about Pessoa: *It comes in the night, you shall see it amidst shadowy sails, like a tip of dawn reaching the stars in its fraternal flight.*

Nation – as Prometheus[11] *who would carry an entire nationality, a race and a civilization, within the inner world of his genius.*

Sá-Carneiro's biggest problem was that he had no job. *To earn one's bread with the sweat from one's brow – there is no greater sorrow. Nor greater villainy.* In their letters, the topic almost always centres around money. One of them ends with a synthesis of his tragedy: *I do not have it in me to live with less than 350-400 francs* (22/02/1916). He lives off that allowance, as *daddy is good to me* (13/09/1915). But *my destiny is another, higher and rare. It just happens to be rather expensive.* On the 5th of March 1916, he needs Pessoa to pawn off the gold cord he had left at a nanny's house. On the 15th of March, his friend sends him 160 francs. It wouldn't be enough. *I asked my father for a further 250 francs per month. Currently, I get 280. I wonder what he cannot afford in order to enable my present situation. It is for the soul... and my scholarship* (22/02/1916)! His father came from a bourgeois family and had been well-off, but, at the end of 1915, old and broke, he lived in Africa and worked a menial job at the Mozambiquean railway. And he can no longer afford to support his son, who lives in the world's most expensive city and refuses to work. Tragedy thus begins to unfold.

The beginning of the end

Sá-Carneiro slowly crumbles with an air of inevitability. In a letter to Côrtes-Rodrigues (02/09/1914), Pessoa already proclaims "his very likely final defeat". *Be that as it may, I must live out the last colourful days of my life.* Tant pis [Oh well]. His inspiration might well have been Raul Leal, a homosexual who abandoned a career in Law to live out his spiritual life, in which he inherited a small fortune, which he quickly burned in Parisian orgies, and attempted suicide in Madrid, hurling himself under an automobile[12]. Pessoa confides the following in another letter to Côrtes-Rodrigues (04/09/1916): "Leal is in Madrid in a sorry state of mind. He now intends to enlist as a volunteer in the French army"; and, in "Salute to Walt Whitman", it almost feels as if he were referring to him, when he mentions "my whole body howling, clamp myself onto a car's wheels and go under".

11 Sá-Carneiro likely thought that, much like Prometheus sculpted Man from clay and gave it life with the fire from the skies, so too did Pessoa possess the gift of creating human beings – his heteronyms, perhaps.

12 In a letter to Pessoa, Leal summarized his circumstances: *Soon, the wife will kick me out and, other than hunger, I shall have to suffer through the cold. I have no other shelter. I am forced to change my clothes only every other eighth day, as I own but two of each piece, and take them off every Sunday in a filthy state, as my body is constantly beset by boils and syphilitic sores, which taint everything with blood and pus. The spirit shines ever brighter through the growing rot of matter and life.*

Leal escapes death, as the driver managed to swerve away in time, and he returns to Lisbon to carry on living his life, as if nothing had happened. Sá-Carneiro wouldn't be so lucky. *I am very sad. Dismally and impassionately sad. It is a silent sadness. Had I not told you I had grown mad? I have been living through a nameless hell for weeks. I am getting myself into a decidedly uninteresting pickle. The tombola rolls fast, I know not where it will stop – it matters little where, as long as it simply stops.* In that letter, he hearkens back to verses he had written long ago:

Roll, drums, let the posters be glued!
Roll the tombola, let the carousel begin!
I shall venture into the carnival once again:
– Mountebank! burn down the whole fair!...

On the 16th of February 1916, Sá-Carneiro sends Pessoa "Feminina", a *most aggravating* poem, in which he says: *Would that I were a woman, to arouse those who set eyes on me, would that I were a woman so I could turn myself down.* Soon after, on the 4th of April, he lets him know that he intends *to let the female character of this entire mess sleep* – the "female" was inspired by Helena, a Portuguese, and the only known mistress of his. The next day, she alerts the Portuguese consul to what she believed to be an imminent suicide. The consul allayed her worries; after all, it was just another one of *Orpheu's madmen.* He is correct in his assessment of Sá-Carneiro's mental state[13], but wrong about the suicide. In letters to his friend, Sá-Carneiro confesses: *Recently, I have begun to question whether or not I have gone mad* (07/08/1915); *In truth, I believe that I have been scientifically mad for a year* (30/08/1915); and often ends his letters with *Oh, well... oh, well... madness... madness...* (24/07/1914). When he feels this way, he writes poems such as "Manicure" (May 1915), which was published in *Orpheu* #2:

I run to the street, hopping and wailing:
– Hee-lah! Hee-lah! Heela-ho! Eh! Eh!...
Dun... dun... dun... dun dun dun dun...
Wheeeewheeee...
Dudum... dudum... dudum...
Whootsh! Whootsh!...
Zing-tang... Zing-tang...
  Tang... Tang... Tang...
To the KK!...

13 Artist Rodrigues Pereira, who also worked as a journalist at *A Capital,* included the group *in the category of those individuals that science has defined and classified as fit for mental institutions, but who can safely live outside them* (30/07/1915).

Preparing to commit suicide

Little by little, as if it were the logical thing to do, Sá-Carneiro begins to seriously consider putting an end to all his anguish. He first mentions suicide in a letter to Pessoa, in the very year they first met. *I have no faith in myself, nor in my degree, nor in my future... one day, I proudly felt that I had finally gathered the strength to disappear* (16/11/1912). Then, he mentions *there are two ways of disappearing: one easy and brutal – deep water, the bang of a gun; another soft and difficult.* And concluding the line of thought with: *Ah! how I often violently yearn to achieve that disappearance* (02/12/1912). Still, he reassures his friend: *I won't do it.* On the 4th of May 1916, Pessoa tells Côrtes-Rodrigues that his friend's temperament would "fatally lead him to that": But, in spite of all the hints, deep down, he'd lament not having had the strength to prevent that presaged future, even with the knowledge that the story had already been written; that Sá-Carneiro's obsession with suicide had steadily progressed, as one can see in the letters he wrote Pessoa in 1916, the year he died (summarized):

13th of January: Sá-Carneiro has gone mad. There's no words, I let the napkin fall. It is horrible.

16th of January: Sá-Carneiro, the Mário of 1913, was happier, for he still believed in his own desolation... Whereas, today... it is a gooey, sugary thing, and most pitiful.

19th of February: A little calmer today, but the winds keep howling. Whatever might have been interesting in me is now nothing but torn paper. I've had it! Had it! Had it!

22nd of February: My sadness is limitless, the sad child cries in me – lighting up my longing for tenderness. Pity me, if you would. It's a matter of time, now. To wit, I know nothing.

15th of March: Do not be frightened, nor cease to be frightened. It's bound to happen. I have no fear, I assure you. But I know nothing. Soon, I shall certainly be in Lisbon – or wherever the hell I might be.

24th of March: Unfortunately, my disturbance hisses with increasing intensity, ever more dangerous. I know not where this shall lead. Could it be that the gears might not crush me? But it is so beautiful to mess up.

31st of March: I find it difficult to write this letter, as I've always found goodbye letters to be ridiculous. I could be happier for a little longer, psychologically, everything is going swimmingly for me: But I have no money. Were it not for the material matter, I could be so happy – everything could be so easy. Today, I shall live out my last day of happiness. I am most pleased. A thousand years separate me from tomorrow.

3rd of April: Kindly tell my grandfather [José Paulino de Sá Carneiro] the news of my death – and please go to my nanny at Praça dos Restauradores. Tell her I remember her fondly in these final moments and that I send her a big, big kiss. Tell my grandfather I give him a strong hug [the letter is tear-stained].

6th of April: [Only says] *Bien* – Carneiro.

17th of April: Not even my admirable selfishness can save me this time.

18th of April: Pity me greatly.

The death of Sá-Carneiro

On that 18th of April in which he wrote his final letter, he still asks his friend for the following: *See my horoscope. Now, more than ever, is the time for it. Tell it to me. I fear naught.* Pessoa writes the draft of a reply, on the 26th of April acknowledging the following: "I know not if you have correctly ascertained how much of a friend I am to you, the point to which I am devoted and attached to you. The fact of the matter is that this crisis of yours was a crisis for me, too"; and finishes with the following: "It could have been no other way". He even writes down his name and address on the envelope, but the letter would never be sent – as, in Sá-Carneiro's own words, *The big golden bird/ Flapped its wings towards the sky.* On that very 26th of April, in Paris, he met with painter and ceramicist Jorge (Nicholson Moore) Barradas (1894-1971), and nothing in that encounter as much as hinted at what would follow shortly thereafter. Sá-Carneiro had already all but predicted what was about to happen in "A grande Sombra", describing the future corpse with almost the same clothes he'd wear for the occasion: *Impeccable and smiling, wearing a suit with a new flower in the lapel, a big red rose.* Another writing of his, "Página dum suicida" (Page of a suicidee), reads: *After all, I am but a victim of my time, nothing more... now, what else is left to me?... as of now, the sole interesting thing in life is death!* In a loose note, he also wrote: *It could have been no other way. I have taken leave of myself. I have broken the crystal bowl of amazement. I am undone.* He was only 26. It is 8:30 in the evening – approximately the same time of Pessoa's death, almost 20 years later. He dresses up, as if for a party, quaffs five flasks of strychnine and, in less than

20 minutes, it is over. In the words of Almada, *He kills himself out of an inability to wait.* As Sá-Carneiro himself had once written (10/05/1913), *It is time to sleep.*

Goethe caused a number of suicides in Europe in 18th century Europe with his *The Sorrows of Young Werther*[14], in which the main character kills himself because he can't have his best friend's bride. Later, while commenting on the sentimental adventures and the suicides brought about by the novel, Goethe admitted that he had written it so he wouldn't kill himself. With Sá-Carneiro, it would be different, "a logical and unexpected development (unexpected as are all sad, logical developments)". It had been "an awful death", as Pessoa said in a letter to Côrtes-Rodrigues (04/05/1916). The news is broken by his friend Carlos Alberto Ferreira, who wrote a telegram of questionable lyricism: *Dearest Fernando Pessoa. You must be brave, as was our now mourned Mário. Yes, mourned! Be patient and strive to keep the tears from glazing your eyes. Mário took his own life yesterday.* With it, an envelope with a short last note for Pessoa: *A big, big goodbye from your poor Mário de Sá-Carneiro.*

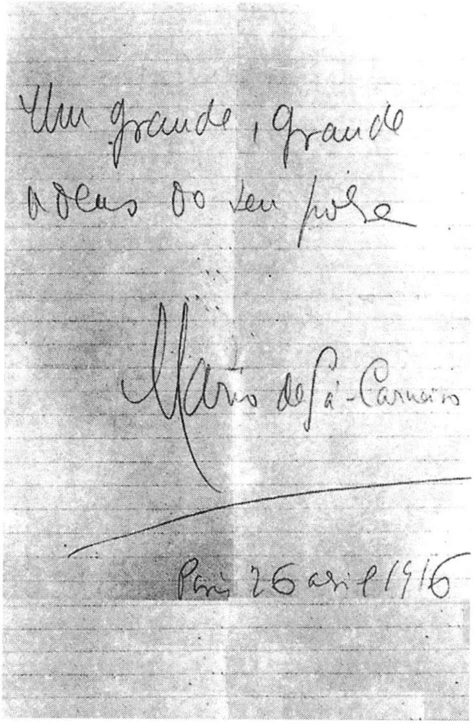
Um grande, grande
adeus do seu pobre
Mário de Sá-Carneiro
Paris 26 abril 1916

Sá-Carneiro's final note to Pessoa

14 Pessoa's bookshelf had a copy of *Werther-Faust.*

Almost echoing the words he had written two years prior, on the 13th of July 1914: *Goodbye, my dear Fernando Pessoa. Forgive me everything, everything. And a big, big hug from your poor Mário de Sá-Carneiro.* Folded four times and written in the same notation paper of his previous letters, Ferreira had no reason to think it was anything other than just another letter. José de Araújo, a merchant residing in Paris who had met him only six months prior, was the last friend he made, as he himself would later tell Pessoa. Apparently, Sá-Carneiro had even invited Araújo to witness his death, but the invitation wasn't taken seriously. Had it been otherwise, things might have played out quite differently. His goodbye letters were left on top of the oven, one for Araújo, one for his father, one for his mistress Helena, one to friend Carlos Ferreira and the note for Fernando Pessoa. As if envisioning this end of his, Sá-Carneiro once wrote:

When I die, bang the cans,
Start screaming and cavorting,
Crack the whips,
Call for clowns and acrobats!

Let my coffin be carried by a donkey
Of Andalucian breed:
A dead man shall not be denied,
And I must needs be carried by a donkey!

He is buried at midday of the 29th of April, at the famous cemetery of Pantin, the largest in Paris. His grave lies right next to *La gougle,* Louise-Josephine Weber, the most famous can-can dancer of the Moulin Rouge, who had been immortalized at the end of the 19th century by the drawings of Toulouse-Latrec. There was no donkey – Andalucian or otherwise – and the dead man was indeed denied. After five years, his remains were transferred to an ossuary, and subsequently cremated, as, according to what I've been told by a worker at the Service Administratif que Conserve la Mémoire des Défunts Enterrés, no one came to pay the cemetery's *droits de résidence.* José Araújo takes care of all arrangements, including placing the books Sá-Carneiro had written on top of his coffin. Carlos Ferreira would later confess in a letter to Pessoa that: *It was impossible to dress him up any better, as he had spruced himself up for death.* But that elegance wouldn't endure, as the corpse bloated up during the night, his clothes' buttons popped out and he needed the mortuary's largest coffin. At that moment, one he couldn't possibly have predicted, he did his nickname justice – there, lying motionless in the irreversible darkness of the coffin, now definitely lay a *fat sphinx.*

After his death

"He did not die prematurely, as nothing happens prematurely, but always at its proper time and place, as per the attentive wisdom the Gods employ in the world ruled by Fate". In *Athena* #2 (November 1924), Pessoa writes the article "Mário de Sá-Carneiro", which begins with the following: "Those whom the gods love die young"[15]. It is a reference to Antinous, who also committed suicide – although Pessoa's "Antinous" was only written in January 1915, before his friend's untimely death. In his text, Pessoa wrote: "Sá-Carneiro had no biography, only his genius"; and that "even if it were another Earth, his fate would be the same". He entrusts his *Book of verses* to his friend, with the indication that he was to make use of it *as if it were your own* – the very same that, in 1937, would be edited by *Presença* magazine under the title of *Indícios de oiro* (Signs of gold). For his grave, Pessoa suggests "a crest"[16], which would read: "Misunderstood and unclaimed by any homeland, he was one of the most prominent intellectual figures of a nation". In 1934, almost 20 years after that final day, Pessoa would write another poem in his honour, "Sá-Carneiro". It probably wasn't its final title, as it has been scribbled at the edges of the sheet, with a pencil, almost like a note. The title is followed by Catulus' inscription in Latin, *And, forever, brother, be happy.* The poem is usually published with a small commentary underneath the title: "In that issue of *Orpheu,* which shall be made of roses and stars in a new world".

> Oh, how we were as one, speaking! We
> Were as unto a dialogue in a soul.
> I know not if you sleep (…) easy,
> I know that, without you, I am missing one
> (…)
> Ah!, my greatest friend, never again
> In the buried landscape of this life
> Shall I find a soul so dear to me
> The things that, in my being, are real.
> (…)
> No more, no more, ever since you departed
> This shuttered prison that is the world
> My heart is inert and infecund
> And what I am is a saddened dream.
>
> *Sá-Carneiro*, Fernando Pessoa

15 A literal translation of *Quem dii diligunt, adolescens moritur,* which Pessoa described as "a precept of ancient wisdom". It hearkens back to Greek poet Menander (342-291 BC), the most important author of the so-called *New Greek Comedy.* It would also feature in Plautus' (254-184 BC) *Bacchides* and in Terence (190-159 BC), and even in the 19th century, by way of David Gray's "I die being young", Lord Byron's *Don Juan,* and D.H. Lawrence's *Pansies.* The saying also inspired Aleister Crowley, a strange mage Pessoa once met (more on that later), in his play *Hermes: 'twas a wise man who sang:/ Those whom the gods love, they love lobsters/ They die young./ Meanwhile, a greater sage said in a sublime way/ Look ye not upon the lobster while it is red.*

16 In truth, he should have written *epitaph.* But he might have opted against that word in his text, as in Greece it isn't an inscription on a gravestone, but rather a funereal prayer uttered in honour of those slain in combat. Pessoa would use the expression in numerous poems written in English.

ACT II

IN WHICH THE ART OF FAKING AND HIS HETERONYMS ARE RETOLD

Ars est celare artem
(Art consists of hiding art) Latin proverb

THE POET IS A FAKER

After dealing with dreams, I have become
as unto a dream myself. The dream of myself.
The Book of Disquiet, Bernardo Soares

The precision of language

Pessoa had an early understanding of the multiple dimensions that an image, a gesture or a feeling might have, that "everything in this world is, perhaps, but the shadow and the symbol of something else". "We are born without knowing how to talk, and die without having ever known how to say… and, around it all, like a bee buzzing over a place where there are no flowers, hovers a useless, unknown destiny". According to his law, language "is the very water in which I float, a fallen leaf, a dead lake"; and the word is "the supreme abstraction", "three distinct things in a sole unit – its rhythm, the feelings it evokes, and the rhythm that envelops said rhythm and feelings". And so, "I often write without thinking, in an external reverie, letting the words caress me, as if I were a young child on their lap". Deep down, he wishes for "an absolute grasp of expression, the power of going beyond oneself, of splitting oneself in two, in search of the *translated sincerity"* which makes literature "the most pleasant way of ignoring life". To him, writing is mainly the act of choosing between ideas which "pass me by in loud parades of faded silks", since "between two ideas, there is always a path". That relationship between content and form is reflected in his entire oeuvre. Thus, to understand the author, one must first consider the essence of his discourse, which is marked by the apparent hesitation between what is real and what is imagined, from the standpoint of two specific elements.

The first element is the precision of language. "I hate with a passion, the one true hate I feel… the badly written page, the wrong syntax… the spelling bereft of an upsilon, much like the direct gob of spit which disgusts me, regardless of who spat it. Yes, for spelling is much like people". The papers in the Chest reveal how often he hesitates before writing some words. Or how he scribbles a number of variants over them, to then pick the one best suited to what he had imagined. Or how he leaves blank spaces to be filled later. In December 1912, he already says his method is to "make, unmake and remake". "Why do I write this book? Because I know it to be imperfect". Sometimes, he maps out his text, drawing small lines on blank sheets, imperceptible to the unsuspecting eye. In his search for perfection, "none of my writings has ever truly been finished; there were always new thoughts popping up, associations between extraordinary ideas I couldn't possibly exclude, with infinity as the limit. I cannot avoid the aversion I have to the act of finishing something". And "my instinct… should refrain from ever beginning".

That concern of his with precision can be seen when, for example, he sought to define the word *spiral:* "There is nothing more difficult than defining a spiral in words: Some say one needs to wordlessly draw it in the air with gestures; a spiral is a circle that goes up without ever coming together. Or, better said: A spiral is a virtual circle that unfolds upwards without ever going full circle. No, the definition remains abstract. I shall endeavour to be concrete: A spiral is a snake that is not a snake, that coils vertically on nothing". "Once, I heard a child on the verge of tears say, not *I feel like crying,* as an adult would put it, but *I feel like tears.* That small child defined its spiral perfectly". In another passage, he recalls "once having heard from a little one – do you know what a box is? I asked him, I'm not sure why – yes, sir, I do, the child said, it's something to put things in it". He uses a similar lack of sophistication to define a well as "a deep, narrow thing". In broader terms, that search for perfection, which is ever present in his writings, goes beyond the very meaning of words. Like he says in *Disquiet,* "a ship may seem to be an object whose purpose is to sail, but no, its purpose is to reach a port".

The rigour of form

The second element is the rigour of form. "Form is essential to art"; by "form" he means "not the mere rhythm or structure, but the set of factors whose product is expression". Therefore, "whenever I reflect upon a work of written art which is visibly imperfect, I experience tedium, nausea". Which might explain why his publishing output was so scarce during his lifetime, as he always strived for better. But that rigour only extended to his oeuvre; in life, he was ever "two abysses". "A shelf of empty flasks". "The interval between that which I am and that which I am not". To be and not to be, all mixed up, "both in the distance – conjoined twins stuck to each other". Deep down, he might have been but "a humble clipper of paradoxes", seeing "reality as a form of illusion and illusion as a form of reality". "A cardiac slave of the stars", he understands well that "much like words fail whenever they seek to express any given thought, so too do thoughts fail whenever they seek to express any given reality". And he yearns for spaciousness.

To feel everything in every way
To hold all opinions.
To be honest, contradicting oneself at every minute,
To displease oneself through sheer liberality of spirit,
And to love all things as God.

The Passage of the Hours, Álvaro de Campos

To him, a poem is but "a meat of emotion opening up the skeletons of reason"; and "given that, maybe, not everything is false, nothing will ever cure of the pleasure of lying. The absurd lie has all the charm of that which is perverted, and the greatest charm of innocence". To wit, "excessive sincerity allows for no illusion of happiness". In 1903, at the age of 15, he wrote a play in English *(Marino),* which ends with a precise diagnosis of such voluptuousness: "I lie in order to amuse myself, I lie like hell, for I know I am sick and, besides, lying is what gives me the most pleasure".

Such is his fate. When he isn't lying, others lie for him, such as when Ulysses Guimarães wrongly attributed to him the quote *It isn't necessary to live, only to sail,* in 1973, in the beginning of his speech as *an anticandidate to the presidency*[1]. In *Disquiet,* a similar idea is articulated: "The Argonauts say that it wasn't necessary to live, only to sail. We, Argonauts of our pathological sensibility, say that it's not necessary to live, only to feel". Except *Navigare necesse, vivere non necesse est* is even older than that, and was uttered by Roman general and consul Pompey (106-48 BC), who formed Rome's first triumvirate with Caesar and Crassus. Amidst a storm, and needing to bring a load of wheat to Rome, Pompey used those words to encourage his sailors to take on the perilous trek. The same words which would be used for the motto of poet Gabriele D'Annunzio (of the Hanseatic League) and the School of Sagres – for those who believed there to have been a School of Sagres, naturally[2]. However, there might have been an added layer of meaning, as the Portuguese word for necessary, *preciso,* also means 'precise'. Thus, sailing was a thing of certainty, unlike the intermittence of life.

1 The error likely stemmed to the fact that the line did indeed appear on the first page of Pessoa's *Obra poética,* published by Nova Aguilar – a very prestigious edition in Brazil. Pessoa's words were as follows: "Ancient sailors held a glorious phrase: *To sail is a necessity, to live isn't".* Pessoa probably took inspiration from Plutarch's "Parallel Lives", in which he compares the trajectories of Agesislaus and Pompey, which was a popular book in Lisbon at the time. Francisco de Almeida Sales, the friend Ulysses charged with writing his speech, likely didn't realize the sentence referred to an old saying.

2 The city of Sagres lies at the southwest tip of Portugal, and was built in 1416 by John I. It grew to become a centre for nautical technology development, boasting a naval arsenal, an observatory, and, according to undocumented belief, a school for the study of geography and sailing, the *School of Sagres.*

Irony

For Pessoa, that was the highest moment in his search for perfection in writing. In *Disquiet,* he sheds light on the matter: "Irony is the first sign that our consciousness has become conscious, and it passes through two stages: The one represented by Socrates, when he says *All I know is that I know nothing,* and the other represented by (Portuguese Francisco) Sanches, when he says, *I don't even know if I know nothing.* To know oneself is to err, and the oracle that said 'Know thyself' proposed a task more difficult than the labours of Hercules and a riddle murkier than the Sphinx's. To consciously not know ourselves – that's the way! And to conscientiously not know ourselves is the active task of irony". This because "in order for there to be irony, an absolute mastery of expression is necessary, the byproduct of an intense culture; that which the English call detachment – the power to stand apart from oneself, to split oneself in two". More explicitly, "it is in the incapability of irony that lies the deepest trait of mental provinciality, irony here being not the telling of jokes, as seems to be the belief in cafés and newsrooms, but the saying of something which means its opposite". That trait is present in nearly all of his writings, such as in the following examples, like this first one, published at *O Jornal* (1915):

Only artificial creatures hold deep convictions.

Or in this letter to Austrian company Hofher-Schrants-Clayton-Shuttleworth (18/08/1926):

> Should we not reply [to your letter] on the very day in which we receive it, it is because we were otherwise preoccupied in procuring that reserve of patience and that natural kindness of humans which were absolutely required for us to respond to your allegations on a humanitarian basis, as it were. It is difficult to negotiate with you gentlemen in earnest, but we feel unable to engender that mix of Mark Twain and comical clippings that the situation would require...[3] Your objection... is unworthy of a village idiot in a terminal stage of intoxication. As for your threats... we might bring ourselves to forgive them, if only the gentleman were able to write better in English... There is a limit for tolerance, as I'm sure even the gentlemen will acknowledge.

3 Mark Twain (1835-1910) was renowned for his humorous texts, for being a compulsive liar, and for his uncanny ability to make enemies. When he travelled to London in 1897, the New York press thought it was the perfect moment to take revenge and reported on his death with rather complimentary obituaries. Twain's reaction became famous, when he assured the public that *the reports of my death are greatly exaggerated.*

Or in another letter, this one for *Daily Express* (14/02/1927):

> As I am presently undertaking a rigorous scientific study on microcephaly, I would be extremely grateful if you could provide me with the cranial measurements of your London collaborator who, in his utter obliviousness, gave birth to such news.

Or in a random note written on a sheet of A. Xavier Pinto e Cia. paper, commenting on a sensationalist manifesto:

> Reading that manifesto requires a metaphysical and dialectical culture which one cannot expect but of those who are utterly ignorant.

Or, in *Disquiet:*

A friend of mine who committed suicide – whenever I have a longer conversation, I suicide a friend – had made it his life's mission to destroy all verbs.

Or, in "Coisas estilísticas que aconteceram a um gomil cinzelado, que se dizia ter sido batido no céu, em tempos da velha fábula, por um deus amoroso" (Stylistic things that occurred to an engraved pitcher, which is to have been hammered out in heaven, in the times of olden fables, by an amorous god):

> Take a horn, call it prose, and you get the style of Mr. Manuel de Souza Filho. This pitcher balderdash is impossible to like. It's horny mush, a maudlin spiral, a cross-eyed artificiality. Just stop, Souza Pinto. Go back to writing chronicles; write what you know and are capable of, and leave novels to novelists. This is the translation of the interjection I wrote on the last page of your book, between the word END and the blessed definitive disappearance of your damned pitcher. Whoever told you to play the bull fiddle? You know nothing of music…

Or the commentary Álvaro de Campos wrote on Pessoa's own text, published at Solução Editora's *Revista* #4:

TO FERNANDO PESSOA
AFTER HAVING READ YOUR STATIC DRAMA
"THE SAILOR" IN *ORPHEU 1*

> After twelve minutes
> Of reading your drama "The Sailor",
> In which the quickest and most cunning
> Feel sleepy-headed and brutish,
> With nary a sign of sense,
> One of the mourners says
> With languorous magic:

Eternal and fair, there is but the dream. Why do we speak still?

The very same question
I meant to pose them.

A discourse of contradictions – the oxymoron

A telling trait of his poetry is the use of the oxymoron. That rhetorical device, which entails the usage of words (or sentences) with opposed meanings, can be seen in pretty much every heteronym of his, sometimes revealing themselves as true paradoxes – which goes beyond mere opposition. He states something and, immediately thereafter, its exact opposite. Such as sequential syllogisms, in which truths are revealed in the opposition between theses and antitheses. *A Morse transmitting no from yes,* as Antonio Tabucchi said. Specialists call this the *pessoan oxymoron.* They are *Fernando Pessoa's Dialectic Oxymorons,* as per the book written by Roman Jakobson (1896-1982). A style very much his own, different from everything else being written at the time. Let us take, for instance, these opposing verses from "Tobacco shop":

All or nothing:

– With Destiny driving the wagon of everything down the road of nothing.

or

– Since I had no aims, maybe everything was indeed nothing.

or

– Because it is possible to construct the reality of it all without actually doing any of that.

Being and not being:

– What do I know of what I shall be, I who do not know what I am?

or

– I made of myself what I did not know how,
And what I could have made of myself I failed to do.

Inward and outward:

– To the outward reality of the Tobacco Shop across the street
And to the inward reality of my feeling that everything is but a dream.

What is certain and what is less certain:

– I, who do not have any certainties, am more or less right?

To come and not to come:

– And the rest that may come if it comes, or if it has to come, or if it has not.

Sometimes, those contrasts are affirmed in a sequence, much like waves:

– Always one thing as useless as the other,
Always the impossible as stupid as reality,
Always the mystery of the bottom as true as the shadow of mystery of the top.
Always this thing or always some other, or neither one nor the other.

Blank verses

With Walt Whitman, he learns the art of free verses, bereft of metric or rhyme. Campos, who made abundant use of them, claims they have a "paragraphic rhythm"; and, as a critique of classical poetry with its rigid schemes, declares: "How can one feel when caged like that?". In *The Keeper of Sheep,* Caeiro adds: "I don't care about rhymes. Few times two trees are alike, one beside the other". In Pessoa's registry, he says that "rhythm isn't inherently needed for poetry", which was why "the absence of rhyme represents liberation". Still, he advises caution in its use, as "the blank verse is an extremely monotonous vessel of expression". Heteronym Dr. Pancrácio, in *Carta a um jovem poeta* (Letter to a young poet)[4], teaches that very art in rather candid fashion: "The first thing to do is to procure yourself ink, paper and pen; then write down, in the ordinary commonplace language that you speak (technically called prose),

4 Almost the same title of Rainer Maria Rilke's (1875-1926) posthumous book *Letters to a Young Poet,* which compiled his correspondence from 1903 to 1908. In spite of Rilke's influence on Pessoa, with his *The Notebooks of Malte Laurids Brigge* having allegedly inspired *The Book of Disquiet,* this particular case was but a coincidence, as Rilke's book was first published in Germany in 1929 (and, in England, only in 1934), whereas Dr. Pancrácio, the heteronym created during his time in Durban, was abandoned by Pessoa in 1905. Which is why the text could never have been written by Pessoa that much later. For the record, Peruvian author Mario Vargas Llosa, winner of the Nobel Prize in Literature in 2010, wrote *Letters to a young writer* (2009), in which he suggests that a true novel should be *life itself manifesting through characters, sceneries and happenings which are reality incarnate, the read life.*

what you wish to say, or if you be clever, what you think. The next step is to lay your hands upon a ruler graduated in inches or in centimetres, and mark off, from your prose's effusion, bits about four inches or ten centimetres long: these are the lines of your blank verse composition. In case the four-inch line does not separate the fragments of your prose efforts, then either the addition of a few Alases or Ohs or Ahs, or the introduction of an invocation to the Muses will fill in the required space". Then, he further elaborates in a note: "Verse differs from prose, not just materially, but also mentally. If it didn't, there would be neither one nor the other, or but one which were akin to a combination of both. The outer difference between prose and verse is rhythm. There is rhythm in prose, and there is rhythm in verse, but rhythm isn't necessary in prose, merely accessory – an advantage, but not a requirement".

Faking as an aesthetic

To him, faking has an aesthetic dimension: "Deep down, I am a dramatic poet. As a poet, I feel. As a dramatic poet, I feel by detaching myself from myself. As a dramatic (sans the poet bit), I automatically transmute whatever I feel into something unconnected to what I felt, constructing a non-existing person to truly feel that emotion and, in so doing, feel other derived emotions that I, and merely I, had forgotten to feel". "The core point of my personality as an artist is that I am a dramatic poet; in everything I write, I seek the intimate exaltation of the poet and the depersonalization of the dramatist". In another writing, while distinguishing the character from its creator, he says: "That is felt in *another's person;* it is written *dramatically,* but Lear is nevertheless sincere, even though he isn't Shakespeare, but only his creation"[5]. Álvaro de Campos asks José Pacheco in a letter (17/10/1922) supposedly penned in Newcastle upon Tyne: "Tell Fernando Pessoa I am wrong". Another letter, this one to João Gaspar Simões (11/12/1931), reads: "the study on me [conducted by Simões himself, later included in his *Mistério da poesia]* has the flaw of being based upon false facts which are held as true, given that I, artistically, can but lie", and that "I always held toying with ideas and feelings to be the most supremely beautiful fate".

But faking is also indicative of a psychological trait of his. "That this quality in authors is a form of hysteria, of the so-called dissociative identity disorder,

5 In *Disquiet,* he wrote: " If I had written *King Lear,* I would be plagued by remorse for the rest of my life". That said, Shakespeare didn't always create his own characters, as was the case with Othello – created after Giovanni Battista Giraldi's *The Moorish Captain;* or *Romeo and Juliet* – which was mainly inspired by two contemporary versions: Luigi Groto's *La Hadriana,* down to the character's names; and Arthur Brooke's *The Tragical History of Romeus and Juliet,* which, in turn, had copied Pierre de Boisteau (de Lunay), who had copied from Bandello, who had done likewise with Luigi da Porto.

is something the author of these books shall neither confirm nor deny". In April 1906, for example, he wrote his essay *Against the death penalty,* only to follow up with its polar opposite, *Defence of the death penalty.* Almost mirroring Uruguayan-born Frenchman Isidore Ducasse (1846-1870), the Count of Lautréamont (his pen name), who, in his short 24 years-long life, wrote but two books. First, *Cantos de Maldoror* (paid for by his father), in which he expressed a tragic view of reality; and then *Poesias,* where he did away with his former pessimism to indulge in visions of redemption. According to Michael Foucault, in order for one to truly comprehend history, one must group together what has been (being) with what hasn't been (non-being), but might have. Gilberto Freyre expressed similar thoughts when teaching that the *scientific* method used by him didn't seek to *explain* Brazil, but to *understand* it. Similar sentiments to those of Pessoa, for whom "to interpret is to not know how to explain", revealing an aesthetic duality which is transversal to his entire oeuvre:

I have a quill which pens
That which I feel.
When it is a lie, it flows freely.
When it is true, it has no ink.

Quadras ao gosto popular, Fernando Pessoa

In *Disquiet* ("Sentimental Education"), he expounds upon the methods which a dreamer should follow in the process of "incarnating the pain in an ideal figure". One of them entailed creating "another I, charged with suffering – in and for us – everything we suffer. Next we need to create an inner sadism, completely masochistic, that enjoys its suffering as if it were someone else's"; for "the excessive employ of intelligence, the abuse of sincerity, the example of justice, are qualities which do not allow for the illusion of happiness". To him, "sincerity is the greatest obstacle an artist has to overcome. Only a prolonged discipline, an apprenticeship of feeling everything but literally, can raise the spirit to such heights". "Were I writing to you, I'd have to swear that this letter is sincere", as he told Sá-Carneiro (14/03/1916). As summarized by Caeiro, "I seek to tell that which I feel, without thinking that I am feeling it"; not for nothing did Pessoa hold up "master Caeiro" as "the one truly sincere poet in the entire world".

Say nothing!
No, not even the truth!
There is so much softness
In saying nothing
And comprehending all –
Half of all
Of feeling and seeing

Say nothing!
Let it be forgotten.

Untitled (23/08/1934), Fernando Pessoa

In an article for *Sudoeste* magazine, he further elaborates upon the matter: "The superior poet says what he really feels. The average poet says what he decides to feel. The lesser poet says what he thinks he ought to feel", and "none of that has anything to do with sincerity. Firstly, no one truly knows what they feel. It is possible to feel relief at the death of a loved one and to believe we are grieving, as that is what one should feel on such occasions". In an ambiguous speech, he acknowledges that "most people feel in conventional fashion, albeit with greater human sincerity; to not feel with any degree or kind of intellectual sincerity, that is which matters to the poet". To wit, "it is hard to be sincere when one is intelligent. Much like being honest when one is ambitious". In him, this process slowly coalesced. "To express oneself is to say what one does not feel". A good example is an untitled poem of his from *Cancioneiro,* which begins with the verse "She sings, the poor reaper,", which Pessoa refers to as "the one with the female reaper" at the end of his life, to tell it apart from one which he wrote in 1932, titled "Reaper". Pessoa scholars draw the obvious parallels between her and the figurative Grim Reaper, she who is described thus in the first stanza's verses: "Singing, reaping, her voice rich/ Of joyful and anonymous widowhood". A comparison made all the more plausible by the latter verses, all of which with exclamation marks[6]:

…science

Weighs so, and life is so short!
Come into me, then! Make of
My soul your light shadow!
Then, taking me, pass through!

Untitled (1914), Fernando Pessoa

Faking as a feeling

Another layer of faking is his peculiar way of being. It is imprinted upon his very soul. "Feelings, which percolate into others' will like the hand on the glove or the hand on the sword's hilt, have always been but another way of

6 He wasn't the only one fond of exclamation marks. Portuguese poet Alexandre O'Neil lauds them in *Poemas gráficos;* Tom Wolfe wrote over a thousand of them in *The Bonfire of the Vanities;* and Queen Victoria liberally sprinkled her sentences with them.

thinking to me". "I wear my feelings on my imagination's sleeve, and it almost makes me cry, which makes me revert into the happy child I never was". It is as if a biological necessity were responding to the uncertainties of pretty much everything which concerns his life. At work, torn between the comprehension of economic laws (as one can see in his texts written for *Revista de Comércio e Contabilidade* magazine) and his utter inability to follow up on them; much like in romantic relationships, in which he always set himself apart; all of it revealing that, deep down, he feels "an insatiable, numberless yearning to be always the same and another". In May 1930, he summarizes: "To live is to be another. It isn't even possible to feel, if one feels as he felt the day prior: To feel the same one felt the previous day is the same thing as not feeling at all. It is to merely recall what one felt before, to be the corpse today of what was a lost life yesterday". Therefore, "I seek to say what I feel without thinking that I'm feeling it" and "I simply feel with my imagination. I don't use my heart". He says the same in verse, such as in this poem:

I have so many feelings
That often manage to persuade myself
That I am actually sentimental,
But, as I take my measure, I acknowledge,
That everything is but thoughts,
That I did not actually feel.

All those who live have
A life which is lived
And another which is thought,
And the only life we have
Is the one which can be found
Between the real and the wrong one.

However, none can truly say
Which one is real
And which one is false;
And we live in such a manner
That the life we have
Is the one we must think of.

Untitled (18/09/1933), Fernando Pessoa

"In me all affections take place on the surface, but sincerely. I've always been an actor, and in earnest". In that vein, "dreaming, however, substitutes for everything. I can enter battles without the risk of getting scared or being wounded. I can reason without aiming to arrive at some truth. I can love without worrying about being rejected or cheated on, and without getting bored. I can change my sweetheart and she'll always be the same. In dreams I can experience the worst anxieties, the harshest torments, the greatest victories". That faking contaminates his very existence. For example, as he once took a walk through the beach of Cascais' boardwalk, he looked at the houses and felt that he was living "the daily lives of all their inhabitants, living them all at the same time. I'm the father, mother, sons, cousins, the maid and the maid's cousin, all together and all at once, thanks to my special talent for simultaneously living the lives of various people". "Perhaps on account of my thinking too much or dreaming too much, I can no longer tell apart the extant reality from the dream, which is the reality that doesn't exist". And the price of that conscious duality of his is high indeed. "To create, I've destroyed myself. I've so externalized myself on the inside that I don't exist there except externally. I'm the empty stage where various actors act out various plays". That's the way it always was with him. "When I speak truthfully, I know not what truthfulness I speak with". To sum it up, and in his own words in one of the prefaces he drafted for his works: "Do I fake it? Do I not fake it? If I wanted to fake it, why would I write this?".

> Yes, I know...
> There is a law
> Which says that, in feeling
> One should adhere to
> A certain road
> Which leads nowhere.
> (...)
> I follow the path
> Which ever abuts on me
> For I am not
> Who I here am.
>
> *Untitled* (11/10/1934), Fernando Pessoa

Autopsychography

The most renowned example of his art of faking is the poem "Autopsychography" – written on the 1st of April 1931 and stored in his Chest in a bundle titled *Itinerário* (Itinerary). He sent a copy to his friend Gaspar Simões and, two days later, scribbles in an old sheet of paper "am I mad for being more of a poet than a person?". It was published in *Presença* #36, in November 1932. Irene Ramalho Santos says it is *Pessoa's most quoted and analysed poem,* and that *unlike the vast majority of poems of any of his heteronyms, it isn't written in the first person singular.* It was far from an original idea. In 700 BC, the Greek Archilochus (712-664 BC), the creator of the iambic verse (two syllables, one short, the other long), had written *dry of inspiration, but not of sentiment;* and the Spanish military man and priest (Pedro) Calderón de La Barca (1600-1681), in his *La via es sueño y los sueños sueños son* (1635), said: *The poet who was unlucky in great pain/ Fakely cries and deeply touches us.* The duality, in this case, begins in the very title, as psychography is a psychological description of a person, as well as a writing guided by an incorporeal spirit.

The poet is a faker[7]
Who's so good at his act
He even fakes the pain
Of pain he feels in fact.

And those who read his words
Will feel in his writing
Neither of the pains he has[8]
But just the one they're missing.

And so around its track
This thing called the heart winds,[9]
A little clockwork train
To entertain our minds.

The interpretations of those verses are manifold. Most of them hold that faking the quality of a pain that is being felt is the highest one can aspire to when faking, as Manuel Gusmão put it. Or the suggestion that it's not about faking, but rather sublimating, as the reader knows nothing of what the poet is feeling, as August Willemsen put it. Or that acknowledging the pain is the essential basis of poetic creation, and that the faking is incorporated into his very style, as per Gaspar Simões. Being a "faker", the poet isn't necessarily faking the pain he didn't feel, but rather the pain he directly experienced. Real pain remained in the flesh, it never reached poetry. The pain expressed by poetry is the one readers have not experienced. Simões brushes off the author's unstable character to focus on the aesthetic facet of his art. To whomever might read the poem according to that perception, they would do well to heed Pessoa's own warning: "The essence of irony lies in being unable to discern a text's second meaning through its words, but in being aware of said second meaning on

7 In *The Year of the Death of Ricardo Reis,* Saramago imagines Ricardo Reis returning to Lisbon and asking Pessoa the following: *You said the poet is a faker?* To which Pessoa replies: *I must confess, those are but guessings that we blurt out, leaving us wondering what path we took to get to them.*

8 One thought, the other felt – different from those they (the readers) experience. As he said in a note: "The one pain the poet truly feels is the pain of his poetry". After his death, an untitled poem of his was published on the 10th of April 1939, which contained the following verses: *Ample is the pain that hurts me/ Two pains did I have.*

9 According to Jean Lauand, the Arabic word for 'heart' is *qalb* – from *qalaba* (spinning). And, according to the Koran, *hearts are meant to be spun (tataqallab).* And so, the verse respects the Muslim tradition, according to which God is *a spinner of hearts (muqallibu al-qalib).*

account of if being impossible for the text to actually be saying what it reads". I followed the trail. And began to note that, in the poem, there isn't a single line of interpretation. Júlio Pomar, for example, suggests that 'faker' is a technical term to describe a painter who specializes in *trompe l'oeil.* But that's just a little too far-fetched. I believe there to be another, far simpler explanation.

The problem with that apparent misunderstanding, which can be felt just by reading the text, lies in the very first stanza. If a poet is faking pain, it is because he doesn't feel it "in fact"; or, conversely, if he does in fact feel it, then it means he isn't faking it (in that moment, at least). It's of little consequence if a pain is faked at first but then ends up being felt physically; after all, the moment it becomes real, in which it is physically felt, then it can no longer be faked. The fragile human condition cannot possibly fake and, at the same time, not fake the very same pain[10]. Thus, the explanation lies not in the senses and feelings of the poet, but rather on the fact that he often writes in code. Playing with the precise and imprecise meaning of words. Often just for the sheer joy of using them as tools which dance in his hands. Or for operating at a higher stage of language, as if it were beneath him. Building models which only superior intellects (such as his, as he believes) could fully comprehend. And so he says: "I never give explanations that can be predicted; if it were so, what would be the use in giving them?".

The poem's core word is 'faking', which didn't always hold the meaning it does today; its archaic definition was actually 'to build'. Cleonice Berardinelli, Mário Sacramento and Richard Zenith were of the same opinion. In Portuguese, 'faking' *(fingir),* comes from the Latin *fingere,* to sculpt in clay, give shape to, build. It figures with this very meaning in the proverb *Humus de qua finguntur pocula* (the soil which venoms are made from). Or in the Brazilian expression 'fake sand' *(areia de fingir),* which is used to make cement. Ergo, building sand. Deep down, what else is faking, if not the building of a new reality? According to Pessoa himself, "the only true art is that of construction". In this case, his "three principles of art" are all checked: 1) feeling, 2) suggestion, 3) construction". He defines said construction as "the organic structure of a poem, that which makes us feel it is a living thing when reading it, a whole composed of parts, and not merely a sum of parts", as "poetic constructivity" is formed of an "heroic urge", a "religious urge", and a "pure constructive urge".

Professor António de Abreu Freire, from the University of Lisbon was the one who cleared up that explanation for me. From the end of the 19th century until the 40s, the *belle époque* was at its peak across all of Europe, with houses decorated in the *art nouveau* style. Inside walls were hand painted, picturing natural or hunting scenes, and ceilings were decked in plaster

10 As Marcello Navarro puts it in *Especulações em torno do poeta* (Speculations concerning the poet): *The poet is emotion's bawd/ he puts on a façade/ He fakes pain so utterly/ he feels nothing, really.*

arabesques. Outside, the façades were elaborately decorated with imitations of stone sculptures, but plaster couldn't be used for that effect, as it was far too vulnerable to harsh weather. Instead, a paste composed of mortar, the above-mentioned 'fake' sand and lime was used. Those stone façades were sculpted with instruments known as 'fake spoons' *(colheres de fingir),* some but five to seven centimetres long. The artists which specialized in those types of ornaments were already used to restoring wooden baroque altars (using a mix of sawdust and glue), and mostly came from the north of Portugal (Porto, Gondomar, Rio Tinto, Fafe). They came to be known as 'fakers' *(fingidores).* It couldn't possibly have lasted very long, as the upkeep of so much luxury was expensive, and these props gradually disappeared, as did those who restored them, as well as the memory of the people who stopped seeing them in the streets. But Pessoa knew of them, which is why he used that metaphor, that the poet is but a *faker.* Much like those craftsmen.

'Fake spoons'

House decorated by 'fakers'

In a letter to Francisco Costa (10/08/1925), he sums up the whole matter: "Art is expressing a thought through an emotion. It matters little whether or not we feel what we convey; it suffices to, having thought it, we're able to fake it [here the word is clearly used in its most widely accepted sense] without having felt it". Something which came quite naturally to one who proclaimed that "all sincerity is a form of intolerance" and amused himself coming up with "new ways of faking". As he was "a creature of varied and fictitious feelings", the sadnesses of the world no longer suffice him. Or they do not possess the delicateness, generosity and breadth his incandescent heart yearns for. The poet, if he truly is such, fakes nothing (in its most common sense), he merely constructs the pains he then truly feels. Let the reader decide which is the correct version for the poem: To accept the sophisticated interpretation of men of letters; to guess the poet's word games; or to *fake* your own. In any event, for that choice, one would do well to heed Pessoa's warning:

They say I fake or lie
All that I write. No.
I merely feel
With my imagination.
I do not use my heart.
All that I dream or live through
Whatever I lack or am deprived of,

Is much like a terrace
Over something else.
A most beautiful thing.[11]

And so, I write amidst
That which isn't close to me
Free from my grasp,
Serious about what it is not.
Feeling? Let those who read feel![12]

The art of faking

"I wanted to understand all, to know all, to accomplish all, to enjoy all, to suffer all, yes, to suffer it all. Yet I do nothing of it. My life is an immense dream. Let me weep", as he wrote in his diary (30/10/1908). That very same idea is expressed by two authors who he held up as references: Edgar Allan Poe (1809-1849), who suggested a number of times in his work that the world of dreams was far better than the real one; and Beaudelaire[13], who held Poe as his greatest literary idol. "Between a soul and a soul there lies an abyss". Or, in an even broader brush, "the [very] human soul is an abyss". Little by little, travelling companions are born, and he tasks them with faking, dreaming or living in his stead. "I am like a room with numberless fantastical mirrors which bend into fake reflections a single previous reality, which can be found in none and all of them". "Refiner of fake refinements that I am", he gradually complements himself "through intelligence, the abdication of life, analysis and pain itself". And so "I multiplied myself to feel myself", as "each of us is manifold". To wit, "my art is to be myself. I am many". He is ready to live the lives of others – those of his heteronyms, as it were. And, through them, he chooses to give "the unattainable an eternal pedestal" – so he may, in the end, "be crowned Emperor inside myself".

11 Carlos Drummond de Andrade would later write rather similar verses: *But the things I followed through on/ So much fairer/ Those will endure.* Likely not by accident, as "Memória", the poem containing these verses, was published in 1951 (much after Pessoa's, which was published in 1933), and came right after "Sonetilho do falso Fernando Pessoa" (Short sonnets of the false Fernando Pessoa), which will be transcribed farther up ahead, and which is part of the book *Claro enigma,* which ends with the word that gives title to Pessoa's poem – *isto* (This). All of this suggests Drummond was quite familiar with his work.

12 According to Manuel Gusmão, this last verse is inspired by Valéry (1871-1945), according to whom *The poet's function is not to feel the poetic state: this is a private matter. His function is to create it in others* (from his *Poésie et pensée abstraite).*

13 In "The Eyes of the Poor", Beaudelaire (1821-1867) said: *We had each sworn that all our thoughts would be common to the both of us, and that our two souls would nevermore do anything, but as one; a dream that has nothing original in it, after all, except that, dreamt by all men, it has been realized by none.*

They say?
They forget.
They don't say?
They've said.

They do?
Lethal.
They don't?
The same.

Why
Wait?
All is
Dreaming.

Untitled (1926),[14] Fernando Pessoa

14 The poem was born during a tram ride, as he told poet Carlos Queiroz. "This poem just *happened* to me during the ride, on the platform. Would you like to hear it?"

Una dies aperit, conficit una dies
(In one day it opens its blossoms, in one day it decays) Ausonius

THE ORIGIN OF HIS HETERONYMS

I have nowhere to run, unless it is from myself.
The Book of Disquiet, Bernardo Soares

The most important day

8th of March 1914. It was "the triumphant day of my life", so says Pessoa on the 13th of January in his famous letter to "dear comrade" Adolfo Casais Monteiro. Written "on copy paper", as "we have no more decent one; it's Sunday, and I can't get more". That letter would soon be followed by two others which complemented it. One on the very next day, the 14th of January, reminding his friend that "the paragraph on occultism, on page 7, must not be reproduced". Another on the 20th, in which he confesses to be a "dramatist" and says that his "previous letter… naturally leads to that definition. Thus, I do not evolve, I TRAVEL (I accidentally pressed the upper-case key and the word came out in capitals. It is nevertheless correct, so I shall leave it as it is)". That letter answers a question made by his friend about the origins of his heteronyms. And the choice of addressee was no accident, as Casais Monteiro loathed Salazar like he did, and had even scolded him for accepting his award for *Message.* Monteiro's book *Confusão* was dedicated to *Fernando Pessoa, with the highest esteem for the one who stands far above all others in the Portuguese poetry of our time,* evidencing the strength of their bond. A draft of the letter, which remained in his Chest, initially claimed that the *official* date was the 13th of March 1914; this estimate would later change because, on the 8th of March, there was a rare conjunction of planets, according to astrologer Nuno Michaelis at the behest of Nuno Hipólito. Astrologer Paulo Cardoso reached the very same conclusion. Apparently, it all took place in 1914 at Aunt Anica's house, where he lived at the time (abridged):

> One day, I remembered to play a prank on Sá-Carneiro – I'd invent a bucolic poet of a complicated sort and introduce him in some manner of reality, I know not quite which…

> On a day in which I had finally given up… I approached a tall dresser,[1] took a piece of paper and began writing. I wrote thirty or so poems in a row, in a rapture of sorts I cannot quite define. It was the triumphant day of my life, and I can never experience another quite like this. I began with a title, "The Keeper of Sheep"… After having written said thirty or so poems, I immediately picked up another piece of paper and then wrote the six poems which comprise Fernando Pessoa's "Oblique Rain". I then created a non-existent coterie. It would appear everything happened outside of my control.

That reference to "Oblique Rain" helps us understand the farce. According to his list of projects, the poem's first addressee was Caeiro, but the author kept changing. An undated note mentions "Bernardo Soares, Rua dos Douradores. Ultrasensory Experiences: *Oblique Rain"*. But the style is distinctly Álvaro de Campos', and should have been signed by him. In a letter to Côrtes-Rodrigues (04/10/1914), he even mentions the project of an *Anthology of Intersectionism,* which would contain "six poetries by Álvaro de Campos" – "Oblique Rain" among them. Finally, long after his "most important day", the author changes for the last time and the poem is signed in *Orpheu 2* by Pessoa himself.

> The church is illuminated from within the rain of this day,
> And each candle that is lit is more rain beating on the window pane…
>
> I am joyous to hear the rain because it is the temple being lit,
> And the glass panes of the church seen from outside are the sound of the rain heard from inside…
>
> *Oblique Rain*, Fernando Pessoa

It is also very unlikely that he wrote all those poems in one night. Certainly not "thirty or so". Out of the manuscripts for "The Keeper of Sheep", only two have that particular date – numbers I and II. Ten came before and the twenty-fifth is from the 13th of March. Not even the drafts' dates coincide. When he smoothed off their rough edges, he first wrote down a general date "1911-1912"; and a later one, with different ink, "from May to March 1914" – the reason for the inversion of the months' sequence is unclear. Ivo Castro, one of the organizers of the Chest's papers, mentions that five pens and two pencils were used to write the poems, *with variations in handwriting (each instrument had its own, with a number of variants),* as well as many corrections, all in even-handed handwriting which just didn't jibe with the quick longhand one would expect from inspired writing – they looked more like copies made in a moment of calm. And all in expensive

1 Pessoa always wrote on his feet. In his diary, he remarked (22/03/1906): "I remained standing until 02h30 with this blasted thing" – a dissertation on Alceste, Philinte and Célimène (characters of Molière's *Misanthrope),* for his diplomacy degree. Such was also the case of other writers, such as Goethe or Hemingway, who once said: *Writing and travel broaden your ass if not your mind, and I like to write standing up.*

foolscap, unlike the notes he usually took in his office. Still, even though Pessoa dated them earlier than when they were written, the poems are consensually believed to have been written between 1915 and 1919. Or even later. Such is also the case with many other of Caeiro's poems, which can be explained by the fact that Pessoa declared him *dead* at the end of 1915. Back to the date, Sá-Carneiro told him in a letter (15th of June 1914) he *missed our Alberto Caeiro,* as if he were speaking of a much older creation. Still (and as a sign of respect for the poet), we shall let him have the date he wished, the 8th of March 1914.

The notion of creating a "most important day" came, perhaps, from (Samuel Taylor) Coleridge's "Kubla Khan", which, in Pessoa's estimation, was "one of the most extraordinary poems in the English language – foremost of all literatures, except the Greek". That poem from 1816 was inspired by Marco Polo's "Book of the Marvels of the World", which praised Xanadu, the Mongol capital of Kublai Khan, the grandson of Genghis Khan, where all was *milk and honey;* a book which was scribbled piecemeal and under the effect of opium – so much so, that its complete title is "Kubla Khan; or, A Vision in a Dream: A Fragment". Pessoa wrote about it in "The man from Porlock" – published in *Fradique* #2, in 1934, and thus, before the letter in which he'd announce his "day". In that tale, one can see that Coleridge had an extraordinary dream, which he promptly woke up from. He then began to write compulsively about it, in which words flowed naturally from his spirit. Until the visit of a *man from Porlock* – a village near his residence – was announced to him. That visit lasted over an hour, and when Coleridge resumed his writing, he realized he had forgotten almost everything from the dream, except for the last 24 verses of the poem. The idea of texts which budded from the English poet was then appropriated by the Portuguese poet – in a process of *inspiration* which would frequently repeat itself across his entire oeuvre. The origin of the "prank on Sá-Carneiro" mentioned in the letter to Casais Monteiro dates back to the latter part of 1913, when his friend wrote in the originals of *Dispersão* verses such as *I was lost within myself/ For I was labyrinth.* Later, in his short story "Eu próprio, o outro" (Myself, the other), from his book *Céu em fogo,* a character of Sá-Carneiro's thinks about the *other* who lived in him and wonders: *Am I a nation? Had I become a country?* And, in his famous poem *7* (February 1914), he wrote:

> I am not myself, nor the other
> I am something in between
> The pillar of the bridge of tedium
> Transferred from me to another.

Pessoa responds to Sá-Carneiro with his multitude of heteronyms, among which he then began to live in chaos. "The author of these lines never conceived, nor did he feel, except dramatically, a person, the supposed personality which might more appropriately have experienced those feelings". Perhaps on account of the psychic experiences which led him to write through spirits, he confessed:

"I sometimes think my body is inhabited by the soul of some dead poet". Whether or not that was the case, "to each personality which the author of these books managed to live within himself, he gave a temperament, and made of that personality an author of books filled with their ideas and emotions". In his words, "I am the empty scene, in which several actors play a number of plays", and "my imaginary world has always been the only true world for me. I've never had loves so real and so full of verve and blood and life as the ones I've had with characters I myself created"; to say nothing of "the friends of my dreams – with whom I've shared so much in a make-believe life and with whom I've had so many stimulating conversations in imaginary cafés". Little by little, these *friends* of his are born, as decreed by fate. "Naturally, I cannot say if they truly did not exist, or if I am the one who doesn't. In these matters, like in all others, we must not be dogmatic". He is all of them. And he pays a high price for being so many. Perhaps because "to write is to forget, to ignore life".

Deep down, as pessoan scholars hold, his entire oeuvre is a search for a lost identity. *Paternal metaphors,* suggests Márcia Maria Rosa Vieira. "Some authors write dramas and novels, and in those dramas and those novels they attribute feelings and ideas to the characters which populate them. Here, the substance is the same, even though the form may be diverse. "Whatever is human in me, I split it between the several authors whose works I have carried out". "These aren't thoughts of mine, but thoughts that run through me. I do not feel inspired, I rave"; and, in some way, he lived his own life through those characters. "This fancy of mine to create a false world remains with me, and will only abandon me in death". Inspired by him, Carlos Drummond de Andrade wrote "Sonetilho do falso Fernando Pessoa" (Short sonnet of the false Fernando Pessoa), in which he says:

> Where I was born, I died.
> Where I was born, I exist.
> And of the skins I wear
> There are many I did not see.
>
> Without me, as without you,
> I can endure. I give up
> On all that is mixed
> And which I hated or felt.
>
> Neither Faust, nor Mephisto,
> To the goddess who laughs
> At this fond discourse of ours.
>
> Here I say: I witness
> Beyond, none, here,
> But I am not myself, nor this.

Writing through heteronyms

The practice of writing under false names, as if one truly were someone else, is usually attributed to poet and philosopher Søren Kierkegaard (1813-1855), the father of Existentialism and writer of the Danish *golden age* of the first half of the 19th century. To Albert Camus, he was *the Don Juan of knowledge.* Kierkegaard used seven heteronyms, which, according to him, were *pseudonyms, possibilities created by the imagination.* It all began in 1843, when he published *Either/Or: A Fragment of Life* – in Copenhagen. The manuscript, which was supposedly found in the drawers of a second-hand piece of furniture, was signed by Victor Eremita, the only of those heteronyms which deserved a biography. Still in 1843, two other *individuals* were born: Constantin Constantinius (author of *Repetition)* and Johannes de Silentio *(Fear and Trembling).* One year later, Johannes Climacus *(Philosophical Fragments),* Nicolaus Notabene *(Prefaces)* and Virgilius Hafniensis *(The Concept of Anxiety).* In 1845, there came the seventh and last, Hilarius Bogbinder *(Stages on Life's Way).* The following year, Johannes Climacus wrote *Concluding Unscientific Postscript to Philosophical Fragments,* and the fact that he was repeating a heteronym suggests he no longer thought it necessary to write through others – so much so that, in his final ten years, he did away with his creations entirely. An important thing to bear in mind about Kierkegaard is that he truly wrote as if he were his creations, which earned him the hallmark of true originality. Something which came naturally to one who, in his *The Sickness Unto Death*[2] (written under the name of anti-Climacus), claimed that *He who is willing to work gives birth to his own father;* or *the self is a synthesis in which the finite is the limiting factor, and the infinite the expanding factor.* Pessoa would later replicate this path, feeling entitled to set rules about the use of heteronyms:

> It is essential that the names be Portuguese. In the case of pseudonyms, a system should be used to attribute a series of constant traits to each pseudopersonality, so as not to compromise the aesthetics of pseudonymity. And, if the pseudonyms are Portuguese names, then they should sound like real names, for the sake of any given work's dramatic character.
>
> Letter to Francisco Fernandes Lopes (26/04/1919), Fernando Pessoa

It is a recurring idea among writers. (John) Keats (1795-1821) told apart *poetical identity from civil identity.* To him, the poet was *the least poetic thing in existence,* for *he has no identity.* Edgar Allan Poe (1809-1849) claimed that *for brevity's sake, every thought is felt by everyone as an affront to the very self.* Walt Whitman (1819-1892) said *I contain multitudes.* (Friedrich) Nietzsche

2 Despair, which is the twin brother of disquiet.

(1844-1900) said *a lone man with his ideas comes across as mad; and my heart... forces me to speak as if there were two of me.* (Jean Nicholas Arthur) Rimbaud (1854-1891) said *I is another.* And (Jean) Cocteau (1889-1963) held that *Victor Hugo was a madman who believed he was Victor Hugo* – the same Hugo who, for Pessoa, was "a great poet... but lesser than I thought". (Gustave) Flaubert (1821-1880) said: *Madame Bovary is me.* According to (Charles) Beaudelaire (1821-1867), *the man who is unable to people his solitude is equally unable to be alone in a bustling crowd. The poet enjoys the incomparable privilege of being able to be himself of someone else, as he chooses. Like those wandering souls who go looking for a body, he enters as he likes into each man's personality.* Also worth remembering his aphorism often recalled by Albert Camus (1913-1960), that *the right of contradicting ourselves* had *been forgotten* amongst the *Rights of Man.* Lastly, as Vergílio Ferreira (1916-1996) nicely summed it up, *total coherence is that of stones and, perhaps, the fools.* But the habit of writing under different names pre-dated Kierkegaard, albeit by the pen of writers less eminent than he.

(François) Rabelais (1494-1553), for one, signed some of his books as Alcofribas Nasier – an anagram of his own name. Jean-Baptiste Poquelin (1622-1673) was Molière. François-Marie Arouet (1694-1778), Voltaire. English poet Thomas Chatterton (1752-1770) wrote part of his poems as if he were Thomas Rawley, a 15th century monk, and one of his books, *The poetical works of Thomas Chatterton,* was in Pessoa's bookshelf – Chatterton committed suicide via poisoning before the age of 18. (Manoel Maria Barbosa du) Bocage (1765-1801) was Novalis. Henry Marie Beyle (1783-1842), Stendhal. George Gordon (1788-1842) was Lord Byron, who, in turn, was Childe Harold. Amandine-Aurore Lugile Dupin (1804-1876), the baroness of Dudevant, was George Sand. The Brontë sisters created three distinct imaginary beings: Charlotte (18156-1855), of *Le Professeur, Villette* and *Jane Eyre,* published under the name of Currer Bell; Anne (1820-1849) of *Agnes Grey* and *The Tenant of Wildfell Hall,* published under the name of Acton Bell; and Emily Jane (1818-1848), the most famous, of *Wuthering Heights,* published under the name of Ellis Bell. All of them retained only the initials of their first names. (Fyodor) Dostoyevsky (1821-1881) considered himself *the pure Alyosha and the miserable Smerdiakov*[3]. Jacques-Anatole François Thibault (1844-1924) was Anatole France. Walter Gorn Old (1864-1925) was Sepharial. And (Luigi) Pirandello (1867-1936), who won the Nobel Prize in Literature in 1934, wrote in 1921 *Six Characters in Search of an Author* – all of which, according to him, were *born with life;* as *the poet capable of lying in conscious, voluntary fashion, only he might tell the truth.*

The great Spanish poet Antonio Machado (1875-1939) wrote as Abel Martín and his disciple, Juan de Mairena; as well as 15 independent poets compiled

3 Two of the four Karamazov brothers: Ivan, an intellectual who went mad; Dmitri, a passive atheist; the mystic Alyosha and Smerdiakov, who killed his father and then committed suicide.

in a single book, *Los complementarios* – one of which Jorge Menezes, the heteronym's (Mairena) heteronym. Machado's heteronyms were only born after Pessoa's, true, but their inspiration was the same. All of them, to use Machado's words, pursued *the sweet and painful craft of living;* dreaming of *the loneliness of a darkened heart, of the boat with no shipwreck and no star;* knowing full well that *there are no paths to the wanderer, paths are made by walking.* Martín (in *Poesía y prosa),* as if speaking for Pessoa, says that *no one can be what he is not, if he cannot conceive of himself as he is.* Charles Lutwidge Dodgson (1832-1898), a famous English Oxford teacher and mathematician signed his works merely as Dodgson – books such as *An Elementary Treatise on Determinants, Pillow Problems,* or *Euclid and his Modern Rivals* – but, in literature, he became known as Lewis Carroll from 1856 onwards. The initials of his pseudonym (LC) were an imperfect, inverted anagram of his real name's CL. 'LC' also phonetically hints to 'Alice', which happened to be the name of a young friend of his, who inspired the heroine of *Wonderland*[4], born to be a conscious polar opposite of her creator: He is a man, she is a woman; he is old, she is young; he is worldly, she is naive; he is a reverend of the Anglican Church, she is very much a laywoman; point and counterpoint. The title of the book evidences it clearly, as the character is the author himself *through the looking glass.* Deep down, Dodgson was Alice. Much like Charles Dickens (1812-1870) did the same initials' anagram in the form of David Copperfield. Far more modest was the Belgian Georges Remi (1907-1983), the creator of Tintin, who contented himself with reproducing the sound of his inverted initials (RG) with a French accent; ergo, Hergé.

As a curiosity, a short story of Jorge Luis Borges (1899-1986) should be mentioned – he who was Herbert Quain in his novels. Borges famously wrote a letter to Pessoa on the 2nd of January 1985, in which he said: *The blood of the Borges of Moncorvo and of the geography-less Acevedos may help me understand you;* finishing the letter with a request: *Allow me to be your friend.* Even living so far away, both in space and time, he considered himself a close friend of Pessoa's; so much so, that Saramago even put a copy of Borges' *The God of the Labyrinth* in Ricardo Reis' hand in *The Year of the Death of Ricardo Reis.* The above-mentioned short story ("Ficciones") is the account of the tall tales of Pierre Menard, a 20th century French writer, who intended to make history by writing *Don Quixote.* Not another *Don Quixote,* but the very *ingenioso hidalgo Don Quijote de la Mancha.* And he intended to do so without living through the experiences of Miguel de Cervantes Saavedra: a sinewy, gaunt-faced vagabond who took part in a number of battles while

4 Pessoa may have read that book, as one of his notes ("any path might lead anywhere") almost reproduces Alice's meeting with the Cheshire Cat: *Would you tell me, please, which way I ought to go from here?,* to which the cat replies *it doesn't much matter which way you go,* only for Alice to conclude…*So long as I get somewhere.*

serving the Holy League, such as the one at Lepanto, where he lost the use of his left hand due an arquebus shot; and who served for years as a slave to the king of Algiers; and who indulged in freehand accounting of olive oil and grain, which often led him to prison. And it was in a prison in Seville (1605) where, at the age of 58, he began to write the first part of what is (arguably) the greatest novel of all. In the real world, one Alonso Fernández Avellaneda tried to ride his coattails and published a second part, signing it as Avellabeda, which prompted Cervantes to complete the work himself in 1615, a year before his death – unrecognised among his peers, cheated on by his wife, and having taken a vow of poverty at the Third Order of Saint Francis. Yet, he was fully aware of the true greatness of his work, going so far as to say: *Don Quixote was born only to me, and I to him; he to carry out actions, and me to write them down. We are as one.*

> And suddenly, more suddenly than before, from farther away
> and deeper down,
> Suddenly–oh the terror coursing through my veins!
>
> Oh the sudden cold from the door to Mystery which opened
> in me and let in a draft!–
> I remember God...
>
> *Maritime Ode*, Álvaro de Campos

Brazilian Heteronyms

Brazil too shows this tendency to change names, albeit little more than pseudonyms – with the sole exception of Franz Paul Tranim Heilborn, witty in polite company but utterly histrionic when taking on his Paul Francis persona. Other names include Olavo (Brás Monteiro de Guimarães) Bilac (1865-1918), who went by Arlequim Belial in newspapers and leaflets, Brás Patife, O Diabo Coxo, Pierrô, Pif-Paf, Tartarin lê Songer, Fantásio, Puck, Flamínio, Otávio Vilar. Aluísio de Azevedo (1857-1913), was Semicúpio dos Lampiões in newspapers and minor books, Acropólio, Victor Leal, Aliz-Alaz, Asmodeu. Mário (Raul) de (Morais) Andrade (1863-1945) was Florestan in *Ariel* magazine; and, much like Mário Sobral, wrote his first poetry book – *Há uma gota de sangue em cada poema* – which Manoel Bandeira thought was *bad, but in an odd way*. Carlos Drummond de Andrade (1902-1983) was António Crispim; or, in his film reviews, Mickey and Félix. Alceu Amoroso Lima (1898-1983) was Tristão de Ataíde. Cândido (Torquato) Portinari (1903-1962) was Brodosquinho. Alcides Caminha (1921-1992) was Carlos Zéfiro, although he never revealed his identity in life; it only became known six months before his death, thanks to jornalist Juca Kfouri. Patrícia Galvão (1910-1962) was Pagu. Augusto Frederico Schimidt (1906-1965) never signed his name, and was known as O Gordinho Sinistro. Júlio César de Melo e Souza (1895-1974), professor of mathematics at Colégio Pedro II do Rio was (Ali lezid Izz-Edin Ibn Salim Hank) Malba Tahan, who was to have been born in Mecca, at the village of Muzalit. And so it was for ten years, in secret, until he officially assumed his heteronym as his own civil identity. Hector Julio Páride Bernabò (1911-1997) signed his works as Carybé. (Alfredo de Freitas) Dias Gomes – (1922-1999), in his first *telenovela,* was Stela Calderón. Sérgio Porto (1923-1968) was Stanislaw Ponte Preta. Bastos Tigre (1882-1957) was Dom Xicote. One of the members of the military *junta* of 1969 (after AI 5), later ambassador in Paris, entered the Brazilian Academy of Letters thanks to deplorable sonnets which he signed as 'Adelita', as per the initials of his name – A for Aurélio, De for de, Li for Lira and Ta for Tavares (1905-1998). And João do Rio (1881-1921) was simply do Rio, just because he got tired of saying his whole name –João Paulo Emílio Cristóvão dos Santos Coelho Barreto.

Milton Fernandes (1924) was Notlim (his name backwards) in *O Cruzeiro,* Adão Júnior was Patrícia Queiroz and Emanuel Vão Gogo – a blend of Kant (Emanuel), Vão ('vain' in Portuguese), and Gogo (a poultry ailment), a veritable mix of German philosopher and Dutch painter – with which he signed his weekly comedy pages in *Pif Paf.* He later found an error in his birth certificate, in which apparently the clerk had transformed the line crossing the top of his 't' into a perfect caret for his 'o' and his 'n' into an 'r'; and so Milton became Millôr Fernandes, which he adapted into Volksmillor for his writings at *Pasquim.* True genius must be humoured, after all. Heteronyms were also used in music: Alfredo da Rocha Viana Filho (1897-1973) was Pixinguinha, José Barbosa da Silva (1888-1930) was Sinhô. João de Rubinato (1910-1982) was Adoniram Barbosa. Jorge Ben (or Benjor, 1942) was born Jorge Dúbio Lima Menezes. And many more.

Portuguese heteronyms

The act of writing as if one were someone else was recurring in Portuguese literature of that time. According to Jorge de Sena, *it culminated in a heteronymic tendency which manifested in European literatures ever since the Romantic Era (which, in turn, came about due to the desire for a realistic mystification of 18th century fiction, when books were presented in the picaresque moulds of the 17th century, as written by its heroes and narrators)*. It is true that, in some cases, writing as if one were someone else was but a ruse to escape reality. Or censorship, exercising what (Baltasar) Gracián y Morales (1601-1658) called the *Art of prudence*[5]. In any case, none did it at Pessoa's level. In that context, it makes little sense to speak of an author's *sincerity*. The irony of heteronymy is that some, like Pessoa, ended up being more *authentic* in the words of their heteronyms than their own; he even confessed as much in a letter to Côrtes-Rodrigues (02/09/1914): "I believe I am being honest". "Yes, I probably am being honest".

From the 19th century onward, a considerable number of Portuguese authors began writing under pseudonyms, contributing to a certain extent to Pessoa's speaking through heteronyms. Before him, there was Father Francisco José Freire, the main theoretician of Arcádia Lusitana, a literary academy in Lisbon, who signed his writings as Cândido Lusitano. Caldas Barbosa was Lereno Selinuntino. Francisco Manuel do Nascimento, later exiled to Paris due to the Inquisition, was Filinto Elísio – a name given to him by the Marquess of Alorna. Cesário Verde was Cláudio or Margarida. Joaquim Pereira Teixeira de Vasconcelos was Teixeira de Pascoaes. Eça de Queirós, Antero de Quental and Batalha Reis went even farther, inventing a satanic poet who criticized society, baptised as Carlos Fradique Mendes – a heteronym of sorts which all three made use of; to be later joined by Ramalho Ortigão and, more recently, by José Eduardo Agualusa (in *Nação Crioula*). According to Jorge de Lemos, Álvaro de Campos inherited some of Fradique's traits. Camilo Castelo Branco made use of 41 pseudonyms, among which Voz da Verdade. Alexandre Herculano was Um Moribundo and seven other. (Abílio Manuel) Guerra Junqueiro had six, among which Gil Vaz Comendador – along with Guilherme de Azevedo and Manuel Mendes Pinheiro. (João Baptista da Silva Leitão de) Almeida Garrett, held as the father of literary modernity in Portugal, had nine. So too had Antero de Quental. Tomás António Gonzaga was Critilo and Dirceu– Dirceu de Marília, naturally, as that was the name of his beloved, Maria Doroteia Joaquina de Seixas Brandão. He then forgot that Marília and married a wealthy black woman in exile, but that is another story altogether.

Pessoa's group of friends also made use of pseudonyms. Mário de Sá-Carneiro was Petrus Ivanovitch Zagoriansky, Esfinge Gorda or Sircoanera – an anagram of his own surname. António Ferro was Cardial Diabo. Luiz da Silva Ramos was Luiz de Montalvor. Alfredo (Pedro) Guisado was Alfredo Abril. João da Lobeira was Filomeno Dias (in the poems he published at *República* newspaper); and also, Albino de Menezes, Pedro Menezes or simply Menezes – such as in *Elogio da paisagem* and *Xente da aldeia*. Amadeu da Silva Cardoso was José Pacheco. (Armando Cesar) Cortês-Rodrigues, Um Anônimo Engenheiro Doente and Violante de Cysneiros. Francisco Alberto Alves de Azevedo, in his poems written in French, was

5 He did not, however, follow his own advice. Due to a distinct lack of prudence, this Jesuit – author of *Sigilo de Oro* – died in exile in Tarazona, province of Zaragoza.

Jean de L'Orme. Playwright Francisco Valério was Valério de Rajanto. The actress Ester Leão, pressured by her family (her father, Lisbon's first councilman after the Republic, did not approve of her profession), was Ester Durval. The one who left a legion of besotted men behind (such as Santa-Rita Pintor) when she moved to Rio de Janeiro, where she taught congressmen, ministers and presidents, where she went back to her real name. Francisco Mendes de Brito was José Galeno – of *Lira da Cidade* fame, which was dedicated *to young Fernando Pessoa, my futured futuristic brother from the future.*

Guilherme de Santa-Rita was Santa-Rita Pintor. Raul (de Oliveira de Souza) Leal was Henock[6]. José Rebelo was Rebelo de Bettencourt. Alberto de Hutra was Teles Machado. José Pereira Sampaio was Sampaio Bruno; the same who, in letters written to Pessoa, described himself as *old and fatigued, ravaged by physical and moral ailments and depressing heartache.* Luís Pedro Moitinho de Almeida was Fernando Trigueiro. Mário Paes da Cunha e Sá was Mário Saa; but, at times, only Mário, o Ímpio. So it was in a dedication written in 1915, in his *A invasão dos judeus,* where he lauded, *Pessoa's admirable courage.* Júlio Maria dos Reis Pereira, painter and poet, was Saul Dias – the name he used when dedicating his book, *Tanto,* to Fernando Pessoa, Álvaro de Campos, Alberto Caeiro and Ricardo Reis. A brother of his, José Maria dos Reis Pereira, was José Régio – playwright, fiction writer and poet who published, among others, *Poemas de Deus e do Diabo.* In a book dedicated to Pessoa, he confesses the *admiration we all owe you;* and finishes his renowned (and censored) *Cântico negro,* with what can be seen as a reference to the one he looked up to as his master: *I know not where I'm going by/ I know not where I'm going to/ All I know is I'm not going there!* More recently, Augustina Bessa-Luis, who wrote her first two novels under the name of Maria Ordoñes.

Occasionally, writing like this caused Pessoa a measure of distress. "I have reflected upon the case of a man who immortalized himself under a pseudonym, his true name hidden and unknown. Upon consideration, I realized said man would not consider himself immortal, but that the true immortal was some stranger. And yet, what is a name[7]?, he thinks; absolutely nothing. What is then the self, to myself, the immortality in art, in poetry, wherever?". Or, more simply, "the mental origin of my heteronyms lies in my organic tendency to depersonalization and simulation". According to Richard Zenith, *the fragmentation and de*pessoa*lization wasn't a voluntary phenomenon; it was*

6 Enoch. In an article published in *Presença* #48 (1936), Leal admits to having thought of writing *a letter-will to Fernando Pessoa, my greatest friend, companion in glory and misfortune,* which was to end with: *May God will it that, from the Astral plane, the prophet Enoch command the world!*

7 Reminiscent of Shakespeare's *What's in a name? That which we call a rose by any other name would smell as sweet.*

a fate he accepted. For Eduardo Lourenço, who held a similar opinion, it wasn't Pessoa the man who was *multiple* or *plural,* but rather his inspiration. According to him, Caeiro, Reis and Campos weren't the ones who created their poems; rather, it was the poems which necessitated their creation – much like Casais Monteiro said: *Pessoa invented the biographies for his works, and not his works for the biographies.*

> There are many living in us;
> I know not whether I think or feel
> Who, indeed, thinks and feels.
> I am merely the place
> Where one thinks and feels.
>
> I have more than one soul.
> There are more of me than myself…
>
> *Odes* (13/11/1935), Ricardo Reis

Amicitias immortales esse oportet
(Friendships should be immortal) Livius Andronicus

THE HETERONYMS

All that I think,
All that I am
Is an immense desert
I don't even find myself in.
Untitled (18/03/1935), Fernando Pessoa

Preparing the heteronyms

In Pessoa, the art of writing through heteronyms reaches new heights. "Some figures I insert into short stories, or in books' subtitles, and sign what they say with my name; others I merely project and simply say that I made them. The types of figures can be told apart in the following fashion: Those who stand out have a style different than mine, and, if the figure requires it, theirs can even be a wholly different style; the figures I concur with have a style identical to mine, barring some inevitable details, without which they couldn't be told apart from each other". Philéas Lebesque might have been the first to notice such (according to Nuno Júdice) in an article for the *Mercure de France* (January-February 1913), where he referred to Pessoa in the following terms: *He has his ideas, his feelings, his distinct modes of expression.* The identities of those heteronyms slowly cropped up: "There are moments in which I do it suddenly, with a perfection which astounds me; and I am astounded with no modesty at all, as I do not believe in any fragment of human freedom; as such, I am amazed with what happens with me, much like I'd be amazed with what happened to others – to strangers". Because, according to him, "a book written under a pseudonym is the author's as himself, except for the name he signs it with; the book written by a heteronym is the author's beyond himself, it belongs to an individuality entirely fabricated by him, as would be the case of whatever any given fictional character might say". Thus, Pessoa is a "human actor" waiting for his "other selves".

The three main heteronyms

Heteronyms are imaginary people to whom a literary work is attributed, boasting a style different than that of the author or being delegated to a specific task. More broadly, every heteronym (far more than a mere pseudonym) thinks and feels differently than the author. And writes with their own style, as if he truly were another person. Among scholars of Pessoa, there are many definitions that, however different they might be among themselves, mostly maintain the above-mentioned points (or little else). According to this strict definition, only Alberto Caeiro, Ricardo Reis and Álvaro de Campos would qualify. *No more than dreams,* said Eduardo Lourenço, *although having dreamt those dreams didn't release Pessoa from his loneliness.* "My God, My God, who is this I see? How many am I? Who is I?". It is him and three others, the perfect number of unity. Prof. Dr. Luís Felipe B. Teixeira explains the importance of that number for mystics like Pessoa, quoting the axiom of Mary, the prophetess: *One becomes Two, Two becomes Three, and from the third is One born as Four.* That fourth character would be himself. For Teixeira, *as an esoteric process, this heteronymic architecture should be understood as... an abstraction and evolution of consciousness".* "A junction point of a humanity mine and mine alone". With Pessoa being an astrologer, an explanation should also be sought on that level. According to Paulo Cardoso, *astrology allowed him to describe the life, personality and the physical traits of his every heteronym. The pyramid is a symbolic expression that bridges the four fundamental elements – the four sides of the square of the base, unity.* Thus, *through complex astrological calculi, Fernando Pessoa established the place, time and date of birth of each of his heteronyms: Ricardo Reis, Alberto Caeiro and Álvaro de Campos.* And *if we add the name of the poet himself to these horoscopes, examining the ascendants of these astral maps, we see that Pessoa belongs to the element of Water, Alberto Caeiro to Fire, Ricardo Reis, Air, and Álvaro de Campos, Earth.*

> Some act on men like the air, enveloping them and hiding them from one another, and these are the mandates of the world beyond. Some act on men like water, drenching and converting them into its own substance, and those are the ideologues and the philosophers that scatter among others the energies of their own soul. Some act on men like fire that burns out all accidental in them, and leaves them naked and real, and those are the liberators.
>
> *Preface to the Fictions of the Interlude*, Fernando Pessoa

Heteronym Thomas Crosse told them apart: "Caeiro has discipline: Things must be felt the way they are. Ricardo Reis has another kind of discipline: Things must be felt, not just the way they are, but also in a way that they fit a certain ideal of classical measure and rule. For Álvaro de Campos, things must simply be felt". The attribution of those specific elements is far from pure chance. "One needn't look for ideas or feelings of mine among them [the heteronyms], for many express ideas I do not accept, feelings I never experienced. One should simply read them as they are, which is how one should always read, in any event". "I endowed each of them with a deep concept of life, divine in all three, but always mindful of the mysterious importance of existence". In a letter to Casais Monteiro (13/01/1935), on the origins of his heteronyms, he clears up the differences in their writing styles: "Caeiro, out of sheer and unexpected inspiration, knowing and conceiving not that I was even going to write. Ricardo Reis, after deliberate abstraction, which suddenly took the shape of an ode. Campos, whenever I feel a sudden urge to write, but not what to write about". Pessoa also said that "the works of these three poets form a dramatic set; and the dramatic interaction of their personalities, as well as their interpersonal relationships, is well documented. It will all be included in future biographies, accompanied by horoscopes and, perhaps, even photos. Drama in the form of people, as opposed to acts". The traits of those main heteronyms can be defined as follows in the following chart, in which Pessoa is also included for comparison's sake.

Traits	CAEIRO	REIS	CAMPOS	PESSOA
Hails from	Lisbon (or thereabouts)	Porto	Tavira	Lisbon
Lives in	Centre (Ribatejo)	North (Porto)	South (Algarve)	Centre (Lisbon)
Day of birth	16/04	19/09	15/10	13/06
Year of birth	1889	1887	1890	1888
Sign	Aries	Virgo	Libra	Gemini
Death	November 1915	Self-imposed exile in Brazil	No recorded end	30/11/1935
Height	Medium height	A little shorter than Caeiro	1,75m	1,73
Skin	White, pale	Swarthy	Tanned	White
Hair	Blond	Brown	Black, straight	Brown
Eyes	Blue	Undefined (wore glasses)	Undefined (no glasses)	Brown (with glasses)
Occupation	Lives off rents	Doctor	Naval engineer	Business clerk
Religion	Pagan	Jewish	Pagan	Atheist
Education	Primary school	Jesuit school	High school	Unfinished diplomacy degree
Style	Primitive poet	Classical poet	Sensationalist poet	Many (all)
Favourite theme	Nature	Disillusionment	Solitude	Man
Main poem	"The Keeper of Sheep"	"Odes"	"Tobacco Shop"	Those from "The Message"

The art of being many

Who, then, truly is Pessoa? A conversation between Marino and his master Vicenzo goes as follows: "Who am I? Good question, but I don't know the answer". He repeats that question throughout his life: "Do you know who I am? I don't. I don't know who I am". And also through his heteronyms. As Caeiro: "I am born, I live, I die for a fate I have no command over. Who am I, then?". As Reis: "Who I am and was are different dreams". As Campos: "What do I know of what I am to be, if I don't know what I am?". As Search: *"Who am I?"*. As Soares: "I don't know who or what I am". The same Soares who, in *Disquiet,* wonders: "How many am I?", and then replies: "I am many". Yet, "amidst many, I am but one, alone, like the grave among the flowers". As he spoke of Pessoa's heteronyms, Jorge de Sena declared that *the only one who never existed was that peaceful citizen given to astrology... who split his time between a job which demanded little of him, socializing with some friends, his family, and solitude – and who might have been considered mad, were it not for the fact that it was everyone else who was mad.* To wit, "the universe isn't mine. It is me". And therein lies his biggest mystery. Thousands of books have been written, examining those differences, trying to ascertain which of them were heteronyms and which weren't, all with complex interpretations. But, perhaps, that isn't even a real problem. At the end of his life, Kierkegaard renounced all of his heteronyms to write as himself. Pessoa almost did the same in 1935, when he decided to publish the works of his heteronyms as his own. He simply didn't have the time to do it.

Álvaro de Campos, for example, has a biography with references that allude to Pessoa. He was born in his paternal grandfather's land; on Virgil and Nietzsche's birthday; is a little younger than Pessoa and has the same profession of one of aunt Anica's sons-in-law; he lost both mother and father, lives with two great-aunts, much like Pessoa; he travels to the city where Eça de Queiroz was a consul; mentions random happenings of his creator's life, such as having found a Bible in his hotel during a trip to Portalegre; "Opiary" is a retelling of sorts of another trip, half made by Pessoa, the other half by Rimbaud; his very surname stems from an acquaintance who had a nose much like Pessoa's; and he writes like the homosexual Pessoa never had the courage to be. But only up until the point Pessoa meets Ophelia; from that point on, he adopts Pessoa's identity and style. It's not a coincidence that "Tobacco Shop", Campos' most important work, is not comparable in the least to his initial output. It was no longer Campos writing. Had it been him, he never would have admitted to being happy at marrying the washerwoman's daughter; he'd been much happier at ending up with some lad. What remained then of the heteronym? Almost nothing, I believe, except for a few minor differences in style. In any case, the value lies in the work, and it matters little which name it was signed under. "Let us do away with distinctions, subtlety, interstices, what lies in between". It is best to evade that problem, even knowing full well the limitations of the choice, and just treat them all as heteronyms[1]. Especially given that *heteronym* (other name), *semi-heteronym, pseudonym, orthonym* (proper name), *autonym* (name used by a person to refer to themselves), *alonym* (another person's name) and *anonym* stem from the same Greek root, *ónmos* (name).

In *Tábua Bibliográfica,* written for *Presença* #17 (1928), it reads: "What Fernando Pessoa writes belongs to two categories of works which we may call orthonym and heteronym... If these three individualities [Caeiro, Reis and Campos] are more or less real than Fernando Pessoa himself – it is a metaphysical issue that he, unaware of the secret of the gods, shall never be able to solve". Those who qualified as heteronyms in a first sense, "the crossing of my vast being", are part of a restricted lot which consists of Caeiro, Reis and Campos, as has already been established. Alexander Search is all but an identical twin of his creator. Bernardo Soares, a *semi-heteronym,* was a "mutilation" of his own personality. Pessoa, himself, was an *orthonym* – and his name is included here among the heteronyms because scholars (more on them later) tend to place it in this category. Others also stood out from among the rest, such as António Mora, Barão de Teive, Raphael Baldaia. Thomas Crosse was but "a literary personality". He consorted with some of them, travelling companions that they were. Others left texts or signed jokes in little poems. "Some have to endure hardships, others have bohemian, picturesque or humble lifestyles. Others still are travelling salesmen. Others live in villages and towns at the edges of the Portugal that lies within me; they come to the city, where I chance upon them and recognize them, and receive them with open arms". For example, only four *physically* meet Pessoa: Álvaro de Campos, Alexander Search, Vicente Guedes and Abílio Quaresma. And so, the best way of summing up this phenomenon would be Bréchon's recommendation: *Let us do without explaining heteronymy, to seek its whys and wherefores, to turn it around... And the opposite of being nothing or nobody is not to be someone... it is to be several, many, everyone.* After all, "when I dream this, walking around my room, talking out loud, gesturing... when I dream this, and visualize myself finding them all, I feel happy and fulfilled, I jump with joy, my eyes shine, my arms open and I experience an immense, real happiness".

> The moment I was born
> I was an escapee.
> They closed me within myself,
> Ah, but I ran away.

---

1 Adriano da Guerra Andrade did something similar, opting for a generic classification and listing over 5 thousand names in his *Dicionário de pseudónimos e iniciais de escritores portugueses* (Dictionary of pseudonyms and initials of Portuguese writers), published under the distinguished seal of Lisbon's National Library.

To be one is to be in prison.
To be myself is not to be.
I shall live, fleeing
But I shall truly live.

Untitled, (05/04/1931)

Heteronyms and the like

There were so many of them. Campos even says "Pessoa are" instead of 'Pessoa is'. "Some I can no longer recall – those who lie lost in the remote past of my nearly forgotten childhood". Such is the case because "I made, and propagated, several friends who never existed, but who, to this day, almost thirty years away, I can still hear, feel, see". To say nothing of "others I've already forgotten, the forgetting of whom, much like the imperfect remembrance of others, is one of the great longings of my life". The following list refers the names I gathered following years of research, in which I perused the admirable works of Cleonice Berardinelli, Michaël Stoker, Richard Zenith, Teresa Rita Lopes, Teresa Sobral Cunha and Victor Eleutério. Knowing full well that no such list can hope to be considered complete for quite a while yet, as there are still ongoing studies being undertaken on the papers Pessoa left behind. In 1925, in one of the first critical texts on those heteronyms, Mateus de Prata and Julião Farnel published the following verses in *Cadastro (um tanto falso) impresso em Lisboa sem licença dos usuários de Martinho e da Brasileira:*

Fernandinho is a person [Pessoa]
With so many names
That one would be hard-pressed
To find more in the city of Lisbon.

The criteria for the definition of heteronyms is as follows: a) the heteronyms as such; b) the semi-heteronym; c) the orthonym; d) the almost-heteronym; e) the literary personality; f) all the names he signed texts with; g) characters from his imagination that, even without signing texts with their names, had roles of some importance in his life; h) those for which he assigned specific tasks in his oeuvre – even with no texts to their name. Conversely, it doesn't include the following: a) heteronyms' heteronyms; b) other names used by the same heteronym; c) characters from texts – even when specified as heteronyms by some specialists; d) names he only left in notes, without signing any texts with them, or for which he had no specific task. According to Teresa Rita Lopes, the first scholar to make a list of heteronyms was António Pina Coelho – who, in 1966, made a quick list of 18 names. Coelho would later include three others, making it 21. Subsequently, Teresa Rita Lopes made a far more detailed list of 72 names – *interestingly, the number of Christ's disciples,* according to her. And, more recently (2009), Dutch Michaël Stoker got to 83. What is certain is that such a number, depending on the criteria used, will always vary. According to the criteria used by specialists, I believe there are 127 true heteronyms, or personalities, or masks, or whatever one might wish to call them. Heteronyms in the broader sense, if you will.

Fidus Achates
(Loyal Achates[1]) Virgil

ALBERTO CAEIRO

My master, my master, who died so young! I see him again in this mere shadow that's me, in the memory that my dead self retains...
Notes for the Memory of My Master Caeiro, Álvaro de Campos

Who is Caeiro?

Alberto Caeiro[2] da Silva was born "on the 16th of April[3] 1889 at 1¾ in the afternoon, in Lisbon" (or "close to Lisbon") – thus he wrote, adding a side note of "Bravo!". The horoscope date is the same, except the hour is written differently: "1:45pm". He dies "in November" 1915, with no mention of a specific day. Before that, in a presentation he signed as Ricardo Reis, he claimed he was "born in Lisbon, on the (…) of April 1889, and died of tuberculosis in that very city on the (…) of (…) 1915"; and, in his famous letter to Casais Monteiro (13/01/1935), he was even more succinct: "Born in 1889 and died in 1915". In a preface to his oeuvre, written by heteronym Thomas Crosse (in 1916), it says: "Alberto Caeiro – not his full name, as two of them[4] are redacted here – was born in Lisbon in August 1889. He died in Lisbon this past June", not bothering to provide the days of his birth and death, or to explain why he was contradicting the previous ones. He had two brothers, António Caeiro da Silva and Júlio Manuel Caeiro. He was of medium height, had broad "albeit fragile" shoulders, pale skin and slightly salient cheekbones, his hair "a washed-up blond" and "a smile that was there without speaking to you", and holds the distinction of being the only heteronym with defined eye colour – blue "as the eyes of a fearless child". "My stare is blue as the sky and calm as the water under the sun". He has slender hands, much like Pessoa's, but

1 The most loyal companion of Trojan prince Aeneas in the *Aeneid.*
2 A fairly common surname in Portugal, like the historian José Caeiro (1712-1792), or Ballon d'Or winner Figo – Luís Filipe Madeira Caeiro Figo.
3 Perhaps a jab at Anatole France, who he wasn't particularly fond of, and who had been born on the 16th of April 1844.
4 Da Silva. The habit of constructing heteronyms with several names and then using only two was reflective of his own nomenclature, Fernando (António Nogueira) Pessoa.

with large palms. His countenance bespeaks "a peculiar Greek air about him, as if radiating from the inside"; which is why "in his total objectivity, he is frequently more Greek than the Greeks themselves". To him, "mystical poets are diseased philosophers… and philosophers are insane men. I doubt that any Greek would write that culminating sentence, *Nature is parts without a whole*."

> Nature is parts without a whole.
> This is perhaps the mystery they speak of.
>
> This is what, without thinking or pausing,
> I realized must be the truth
> That everyone tries to find but doesn't find
> And that I alone found, because I didn't try to find it.
>
> *The Keeper of Sheep*, Alberto Caeiro

Orphaned from a young age, he "lived off small earnings" at the house of his great-aunt – likely inspired in the maternal aunt of Pessoa's mother, Maria Xavier Pinheiro. That house is mentioned four times in "The Keeper of Sheep"[5]: In poem I ("the top of my hill"), VII ("on top of this hill"), VIII ("the side of a hill") and XLV ("on the hillside"). Other variants can be found in drafts, such as "almost at the top of a hill" or "at the slope of the hill". The reference of poem VIII is, out of all others, the most natural one, as the Largo de São Carlos, where Pessoa was born, stands right atop of a hill. The confusion with the address might have been caused by the first version of the poem, published in *Athena* magazine (1925); in it, the house is described as being "in the middle of the hill", and only later fixed "atop" of it – as if Pessoa were trying to disabuse his readers of the notion that he himself was Caeiro. His education consisted merely of primary instruction, and he was "ignorant in life, and almost the same in letters". Caeiro himself says: "Blessed be I for all I do not know". Perhaps on account of that, his life is pretty banal. "The tea comes, and the old deck piles up straightly at the table's corner. The huge cupboard darkens the shadow. And, unwittingly, I ponder the state of mind of those who play solitaire". Such is his life, playing cards with his "great-aunt", in a whitewashed little "country" house with "fields in front of it" and from which "the universe can be seen". Close to a river, close to his village.

> The Tagus is more beautiful than the river that runs by my village,
> But the Tagus is not more beautiful than the river that runs by my village
> Because the Tagus is not the river than runs by my village.

---

5 And not just there. It is also in "Inscriptions" (III), from "English Poems": *From my villa on the hill I long looked down/ Upon the muttering town.*

The Tagus has huge boats
And in it sails still,
For those who see in everything what's not there,
The memory of the ancient ships.

The Tagus runs down from Spain
And the Tagus enters the sea in Portugal.
All know this.
But few know what is the river in my village
And where he goes to
And where it comes from.
And for that, because it belongs to fewer people,
My village's river is freer and bigger

By the Tagus you go to the World.
Beyond the Tagus there's America
And the fortune of those who found it.
Nobody ever thought about what is beyond
My village's river.

The river in my village does not move thought.
Who's beside it is just beside it.

The Keeper of Sheep, Alberto Caeiro

Said river is the Tagus, naturally. But not "fairest" Tagus, the one which belongs to everyone and "enters the sea in Portugal". Born in Lisbon, Caeiro spends almost his entire life at Ribatejo, in the centre of Portugal, which is also crossed by the Tagus, which then disgorges at Extremadura, where Lisbon is located, to fulfil its fate of entering the sea. But the poem's river is another one, more intimate, the one Pessoa gazes at from his room's window at Largo de São Carlos; a river that "belongs to fewer people", that belongs only to a lone, sad child. To this day, from his room's window, the Tagus can still be seen shimmering under the sun; and only those who see it like this, as he did, can fully understand his words when he said "in which the sky is mirrored". From there, "one can see more than from the city, and therefore the village is bigger than the city". And so it was, as in poem VII from "The Keeper of Sheep": "Because I am the same size of what I see/ And not the size of my height..."[6]

6 A reference to the famous quote *Pigmei Gigantum humeris impositi plusquam ipsi Gigantes vident,* which, according to Robert K. Merton, was Bernard de Chartres' (date of birth and death unknown), the chancellor of the school of the Cathedral of Chartres between 1115 and 1124. Its meaning, *The dwarf, when upon the back of a giant, can see more than the giant,* was later quoted by numerous authors, such as Montaigne, Newton, Coleridge and Freud.

Caeiro and the world

In a letter to Côrtes-Rodrigues, Pessoa explains the prank: "As the only person who could ever suspect the truth was [António] Ferro, I asked Alfredo [Pedro] Guisado to casually mention that he'd met in Galicia *one Caeiro who was introduced to me as a poet.* Guisado met Ferro with a friend who was a travelling salesman and began talking about Caeiro. *It could just be a genus of* Lepidopera[7]. *I've never heard of him.* And, suddenly, the travelling salesman interjects: *I have heard of that poet, and have read some verses of his.* Eh? Guisado almost burst with barely restrained laughter". And Ferro buys it. And Pessoa writes with satisfaction that: "After this, who will wonder whether or not Caeiro existed?". Now that his heteronym was born, all he needed was character, so Pessoa said that "[Teixeira de] Pascoais, when turned inside out… equals Alberto". By "turned inside out", he was alluding to the fact that Pascoais was the founder of the literary movement of *Saudosismo,* which exalted the longing for the past that Pascoais held as *the defining trait of the Portuguese soul.* A nature very much in opposition to that of the nascent Caeiro. For Pessoa, more than a poet, his role would be that of a reference. "I never had anyone I could call Master", he says. But, the one "who rid me of dreams and tatters, inspired my inspiration and renovated my soul" was "born within me". "Master Caeiro taught me to be sure, to have balance, order in delirium and in derangement, and also taught me not to endeavour to have any sort of philosophy, but to do so soulfully". Other times, he calls him "my ghost" and claims: "I see him before me, and perhaps shall see him eternally".

> Master, dear master!
> Heart of my whole, intellectual body!
> (…)
> Refuge of the longing of all ancient gods,
> Human spirit of mother earth,
> Flower above the deluge of subjective intelligence…
> (…)
> I, slave to all like the dust of every wind,
> Raise my hands towards you, who are so, so far away from me!
> (…)
> You have freed me, but human fate is to be a slave.
> You have awakened me, but to be human is to sleep.
> (…)[8]
>
> *Untitled* (15/04/1928), Álvaro de Campos

7 The correct term is, of course, *Lepidoptera.* Here used in the sense of 'flighty' or 'irresponsible', as he did when calling people "butterfly", like in a letter to Côrtes-Rodrigues on the 4th of October 1914. I wasn't able to ascertain whether it was a genuine error or a mistake in the originals' transcription.

8 The poem was left unfinished.

The disciples

Caeiro is the sun around which Reis, Campos and Pessoa himself still orbit, says Octavio Paz; *and is without a doubt Pessoa's most intimate double,* this according to Gilbert Durrand. Eduardo Lourenço, however, holds it to be *the most uncanny and pathetic spiritual adventure of our literature;* and his work, writes heteronym Crosse, "has something luminous and elevated to it, much like the sun above the clouds on unreachable peaks". It thus naturally follows that he would have followers. "A philosophic continuator", according to António Mora, "who will conclusively prove the metaphysical and practical truth of paganism". "And two disciples, Ricardo Reis and Álvaro de Campos", who "followed different paths; the former intensified and made Caeiro's paganism artistically orthodox, whereas the latter's work was based on a different part of Caeiro's oeuvre and developed a wholly different system, based entirely on sensations". It was Campos who wrote the famous "Notas para a recordação do meu mestre Caeiro" (Notes in Remembrance of my Master Caeiro) – which, in a letter to Gaspar Simões (01/12/1930), he claims to be "in my estimation, the finest pages of my engineer". In them, he even compares him to other heteronyms: "My Master Caeiro wasn't a pagan: He was paganism. Ricardo Reis is a pagan, António Mora is a pagan, I am a pagan, Fernando Pessoa himself would be a pagan, were he not an inwards-wound ball of twine". Time passes, and a late disciple of Caeiro would eventually appear. It all began with Chant X of "The Keeper of Sheep":

> What does the blowing wind say to you?
> That it's the wind, that it blows,
> That it's blown before
> And will blow again.

During the resistance against Salazar's dictatorship, those verses inspired Manuel Alegre's "Trova do vento que passa" – parts of which were sung by António Portugal in fado (1963), in what would become Portugal's most famous protest song until "Grândola vila morena":

> I ask the passing wind
> For news of my country
> And the wind remains mum to woe
> And tells me nothing.
>
> But there is always a candle
> That woe itself seems to carry
> There is always one who will
> Sow songs in the passing wind.

Even in the saddest night
In times of servitude
There is always one who resists
There is always one who says no.

Caeiro's style

Caeiro is introduced to the public in February 1925 – when 23 out of the 49 poems of "The Keeper of Sheep" are published in *Athena* #4. He would then publish 16 more in that very magazine. Pessoa paved the way for his international début with an article written in French for *Mercure de France,* and translates some of those poems into English. In a preface to a book which would compile all of his writings, signed by Thomas Crosse, it reads: "There is nothing less poetic, less lyrical, that C[aeiro]'s philosophical attitude". Alexandrino Severino maintains there are great affinities between the works of Caeiro and Samuel Taylor Coleridge[9], to whom poetry is but *the best words in the best order.* The heteronym, with a style all his own, held a rather critical view on everything that reached his hands. "Someone read to me today Saint Francis of Assisi, they read it to me and I was amazed", for he could not conceive that a nature lover would call water "my sister. Why should I call water my sister, if she isn't my sister?". He goes further, still. In an article published in *Sudoeste* #3 (1935), "Nós, os de Orpheu", he also mentions "the time-worn, Asian maudlin nature of Saint Francis of Assisi, one of the most poisonous and treacherous enemies of Western mentality[10]". Pessoa himself clarified that "as I conceived him, Alberto Caeiro is the way he is; and so must he write, whether I like it or not. To deny that right would be akin to denying Shakespeare the right

9 Coleridge (1772-1834) authored *Lyrical Ballads* alongside William Wordsworth (1770-1859).

10 In order to properly understand the text, it bears remembering that the saint never celebrated mass. Born Giovanni di Pietro (his father's name) di Bernardone (his grandfather's surname), his father was an important member of Assisi's textile merchant guild. Upon returning from a journey to France, and charmed by the culture he had witnessed there, he decided to ignore the name the mother had given their child and simply called him *french (francese,* in Italian) – Franscesco (Francis). A child who so enjoyed heraldic adornments, that his mother said *he looks more like a prince than our son.* The same Francis who, according to Chesterton, *had a human horror towards leprosy and was far too practical to be prudent.* After experiencing a vision, he renounced all manner of luxury and began to wander the streets like the humblest of beggars. Later, he revolts against the Roman Curia for having reviewed almost all the rules imposed upon the order he had founded – such as preaching the right to disobey ecclesiastical superiors, or that friars should not carry pouch, money or staff. In the end, already cast out of his own order, and so very different from Pessoa, he always voiced the same prayer: *Who art Thou, my beloved God, and who am I if not Your servant?* Until finally, on the 3rd of December 1226, he died naked – *naked like Christ,* according to him. Lying on the ground on which he'd always slept (as Saint Anthony later also would) in a modest chamber at the Porziuncola in the valley of Assisi (Italy). His love for nature, filled with affectations and of a "time-worn maudlin nature", was thus very different from the one Caeiro's very soul bore.

to give Lady MacBeth's soul to express itself[11]". And "even if I were to write another *Iliad*[12], I could never in an intimate sense hope to equal it". Finally, he concludes: "It was like I had been born blind[13], but there yet remained the hope that I might see; and my knowledge with 'The Keeper of Sheep' was the hand of the surgeon who gave me sight with his eyes. In that moment, the Earth was transformed to my eyes, and the world acquired the meaning I had heretofore instinctively discerned".

Ricardo Reis claims that "Alberto Caeiro is the 20th century's greatest poet", and that his work represents "the integral rebuilding of paganism in its absolute essence"; he suggests that "Alberto Caeiro is more pagan than paganism, because he is more aware of the essence of paganism than any other pagan writer"; and laments that he "lived and died in obscurity, unknown. Such is the badge of the masters". A perfectionist in all aspects, Reis cannot forgive his style for lacking "in his poems something which should complement them: External discipline and the order which reigns at any work's core... If I find flaws, then I must call them as such, even if I do excuse them. *Magis amica veritas*[14]. Still, in Pessoa's estimation, "it's some of the best work I've done"; and his philosophical vision "is unequalled among poets". "Filled with thoughts, it frees us from the pain of thinking. Filled with emotion, it frees us from the useless weight of feeling. Filled with life, it sets us apart from the hopeless weight of the life we must needs live". To him, Caeiro's poems will be "the greatest the 20th century has produced", "luminous and elevated, much like the sun over the snow of unreachable summits". "If nothing else is to be extracted from Caeiro's work, we can always get Nature out of it". To understand just how powerful the idea is for the heteronym, "The Keeper of Sheep" alone mentions the word 'nature' 25 times. Always with a capital 'N', regardless of where it appears in the verses. "Caeiro's work is grander still because, not only is it deeply and revealingly original, it is a natural thing which charms and liberates".

> In the evening, leaning out my window,
> Watching the fields out front in the corner of my eye,
> I read Cesário Verde's Book
> Until my eyes were burning.

---

11 A complex character which always fascinated Pessoa, after inciting her husband MacBeth to kill king Duncan, being tormented by ghosts, and finally committing suicide.

12 Both the *Iliad* and the *Odyssey* were, according to Jared Diamond *(War, Germs and Steel),* composed and recited by illiterate bards for illiterate listeners, and were only transcribed hundreds of years later, after the Greek alphabet was developed. For Pessoa, "there must be, even in a poet's smallest poem, something which points to Homer having existed".

13 The reference can be explained by the fact that Homer was born blind.

14 A reference to Aristotle's quote *Amicus Plato, (sed) magis amica veritas* – Plato is a friend, yet truth is an even truer friend.

I felt so sorry for him! He was like a man from the country
And he walked through the city like he was out on bail[15].

The Keeper of Sheep, Alberto Caeiro

The Keeper of Sheep

It is his biggest and most famous poem. He would later tell Gaspar Simões that he could never "equal it, as it proceeds from a degree and type of inspiration… that exceeds that which I could rationally generate within me". Deeply familiar with mythology, Pessoa likely got the inspiration for that title from the recurring image of shepherds in legends, such as Anchises, Aristaeus, Augeas, Autolycus, Diomedes, Phylacus, Hephaestus, Heracles, Minos, Pales, Paris, Poseidon, Proeto, Theseus and so many others. And there was Ibis as well, the Egyptian god, a definite presence in his life, who led flocks with the sound of a lyre. Flocks of sheep, to be precise, much like Antagoras or Psyche.

A flock of ewes is a sad thing
Because we shouldn't be able to associate it with other ideas that are not sad
And because it is so and only because it is so because it is the truth
That we should associate sad ideas with a flock of ewes
It is for this reason and only for this reason that ewes are sad in fact.

Beyond Another Ocean, C. Pacheco

In his poem "Pérsio e Fauno", Bernardim Ribeiro says: *In the jungles close to the sea/ Persius, the shepherd, did/ Tend to his flock.* Pessoa too spoke of other shepherds, such as "Virgil's", who "played their pipes and other things". That evocation stems from the fact that Publius Virgilius Maronis (70-19 BC), the author of the *Aeneid,* held as much appreciation for nature, animals and the smell of dirt as did Caeiro. In his texts, Virgil, the son of a farmer in Mantua, replaces the rural universe he hails from with the imaginary Arcadia – a region of Greece inhabited by the Arcadians, a people of shepherds. For poets, it was the land of innocence and happiness. "Virgil's shepherds, poor guys, are Virgil; and

15 In a long text titled "Cesário Verde", written partly in Portuguese and partly in English, Pessoa clarifies: "A superficial spirit will think it a curious detail of Cesário's oeuvre that the author sang of the city just as he did the countryside. The most intriguing part of that detail is that it is false. Cesário sang about neither the city nor the fields. He sang of *human life in cities and in the countryside".* According to Álvaro de Campos, he was something akin to a literary ancestor of Pessoa himself, their lives sharing many common points. Cesário Verde, *Lisbon's poet,* as he was known, lost two brothers to tuberculosis, also studied languages and died at the age of 31, two years before Pessoa's birth. His oeuvre was only published a year after his death, and, as fate would have it, Pessoa would be buried right next to him at Prazeres Cemetery (before being moved to Jerónimos, 50 years later).

Nature is beautiful and ancient" ("The Keeper of Sheep", Chant XII) – he said, telling the author apart from its characters. In Caeiro's verses, "the flock is my thoughts" (Chant IX). The notion of a keeper of sheep in poetry is thus clearly not original. Jorge de Sena recalls the Englishman Sir Philip Sidney (1554-1586) – who, in his pastoral poem "Arcadia", as if referring to Virgil, says:

> My sheep are thoughts, which I both guide and serve.
> Their pasture is fair hills of fruitless Love.

And Jacinto Almeida do Prado Coelho suggests he had gotten his inspiration from another poem about an English shepherdess (of thoughts), character of Alice Maylene (1847-1922):

> She walks – the lady of my delight
> A shepherdess of sheep
> Her flocks are thoughts.

And those aren't the only two which might have inspired him. Pessoa translated and meant to publish – first in his publisher Olisipo (1919-1920), and then in *Athena* magazine (1924-1925), which he directed – the tales of O. Henry (William Sydney Porter, 1862-1910), an author with a life which was extraordinarily similar to his own. Orphaned at a young age, he was raised by an aunt; had fragile lung health; founded a newspaper in 1894 (the weekly humour newspaper *Rolling Stones);* and lived in a sheep ranch. In an undated note, referring to him, Pessoa spoke of a "poor man who had no one" and "found Our Lady on the road, dressed as a shepherdess, who led him by the hand towards heaven". Likely images which would later superimpose themselves. In *The Mad Fiddler,* Pessoa had already observed: "She leads his flocks beyond the hills"; and shortly thereafter, between 1914 and 1915, he wrote "Passos da cruz" (published for the first time in *Centauro* magazine, Lisbon, in 1916), in which there is an image Caeiro would never make use of, that of a "tranquil little shepherdess" tending to "her flock, a longing of mine". "The Keeper of Sheep" evinces Caeiro's thoughts and his special relationship with nature; radically different in both style and substance than everything else being written in Portugal at the time.

The death of Caeiro

"It was only in [Caeiro's] final months that he spent time in Lisbon, his home town". He died there of tuberculosis – much like António Nobre, Cesário Verde, José Duro, Manuel Laranjeira, Pessoa's father, his father's brother (José), cousin Mário and a daughter of that cousin (Madalena). An early death – in homage to his friend Sá-Carneiro, who committed suicide at 26, the same age Caeiro then had. The choice of the year of his death (1915), according to astrologer Paulo Cardoso, was based on the fact that in it *Jupiter, regent of the house of death in his horoscope, challenges the sun, which is the bringer of life and regent of the ascendant of this very horoscope, which is Leo.* He would be one of the few heteronyms who died – other than him, there was only Abílio Quaresma, António Mora and Vicente Guedes, all of natural causes – not counting those who committed suicide – Barão de Teive, Marcos Alves and Marino. The homage to his friend Sá-Carneiro lay in the heteronym's very name, according to Richard Zenith, as *Caeiro is Carneiro without meat*[16], pointing out that *his sign was, evidently, Aries.* Except he didn't actually perish in that year of 1915, as a number of posthumous texts were attributed to him, such as "Detached Poems"[17], written between 1911 and 1930 – even though all were ostensibly dated between 1913 and 1915; or "The Amorous Shepherd", from 1929-1930, which was retroactively dated from 1914. The dates were switched in order to make them compatible with the time in which the heteronym was still *alive.* Caeiro wrote his "Last poem" with the note that it had been "dictated on the day of his death", which reads:

> It may be the last day of my life.
> I saluted the sun by raising my right hand,
> But I didn't really salute it or even say good-bye[18] to it.
> I showed it that I've liked seeing it before. Nothing else.
>
> *Detached Poems* (Last Poem), Alberto Caeiro

Caeiro had some doubts as to the fate of his poems. "Who knows who shall read them? Who knows which hands shall peruse them?". But he faces death in peace. "I feel tremendous joy at the thought that my death matters not in the least". "You may pray in Latin over my coffin, if you so wish. If you want, you may even sing and dance around it" – a (likely) reference to the verses in which Sá-Carneiro spoke of his own death: *Roll, drums, let the posters be glued!/ Roll the tombola, let the carousel begin!* "I have no preferences for when I will no longer have preferences". And so it was that "the amorous shepherd (...) lost his staff". Álvaro de Campos bears witness: "I never saw my master Caeiro in a state of sadness. I know not if he was sad on the day he died, or the days prior. I never dared ask those who witnessed his death about his death or how it came to pass. It was one of my life's anguishes –

16 *Translator's note:* 'Carneiro' is Portuguese for 'Aries', as is 'carne' for 'meat'.

17 In a letter to Gaspar Simões (25/02/1933), he said: "As it just so happens, I have yet to compile all 'Detached Poems', and I know not when I will; and they also require another sort of revision, not only verbal, but also psychological".

18 A first draft said *so he might say goodbye*

that Caeiro died without me at his side. It is stupid, but it is human, and so it is". He then concludes: "Nothing serves as consolation for not having been in Lisbon on that day". Campos, according to himself, was living in England at the time. And Ricardo Reis' whereabouts were unknown. The only one who was present was Fernando Pessoa, "but it was as if he weren't even there". Caeiro wrote his own epitaph:

> Let my grave say
> Here lies without a cross
> Alberto Caeiro,
> Who went looking for the gods…

Selected texts

I

I've never kept flocks,
But it's like I've kept them.
My soul is like a shepherd,
It knows the wind and the sun
And it walks hand in hand with the Seasons,
Following and seeing.
All the peace of Nature without people
Comes and sits at my side.
But I get sad
As the sunset is in our imagination
When it gets cold down in the plain
And you feel night coming in
Like a butterfly through the window.

But my sadness is quiet
Because it's natural and it's just
And it's what should be in my soul
When it already thinks it exists
And my hands pick flowers
And my soul doesn't know it.

Like the sound of cowbells
Beyond the curve of the road,
All my thoughts are peaceful.
I'm just sorry about knowing they're peaceful,
Because if I didn't know it,
Instead of them being peaceful and sad,
They'd be happy and peaceful.
Thinking makes you uncomfortable like walking in the rain
When the wind gets stronger and it seems to rain more.

I don't have ambitions or desires.
Being a poet isn't my ambition,
It's my way of being alone.
(…)
I greet everyone who reads me,
I tip my wide hat to them
When they see me at my door
Just as the stagecoach comes to the top of my hill.
I greet them and wish them sunshine,
Or rain, when rain is needed,
And that their houses have
A favourite chair
Where they sit reading my poems
By an open window.
And when they read my poems, I hope they think
I'm something natural –
An ancient tree[19], for instance,
Where they sat down with a thump
In the shade when they were kids
Tired from playing, and wiped the sweat
From their hot brows
With the sleeve of their striped cotton smock.

VIII[20]

One noonday near the end of spring
I had a dream like a photograph.
I saw Jesus Christ come down to earth[21].
He came down the side of a hill
And turned into a boy again,

---

19 A reference to the trees on which he played until the age of five, in front of his apartment at the Largo de São Carlos.

20 In another letter to Gaspar Simões (03/12/1930), he describes it as "the poem about Christ coming to Earth" and explained it hadn't been published in *Athena* because Rui Vaz, the magazine's co-director and owner, was a devout Catholic. He then confessed to having written it "in starts and with repugnance at its infantile blasphemy and absolute anti-spirituality", making it clear than "in my poetry, I make use of neither blasphemy nor anti-spirituality". His anticlerical attitude was shared by other famous poets, such as Eça de Queiroz and Gomes Leal. Despite being dedicated to the memory of Cesário Verde, it was inspired by *A velhice do Padre Eterno* of winemaker, Republican and poet (Abílio Manuel) Guerra Junqueiro (1850-1923), the same who had adapted the *tragic and cadaveric* Spanish Christ, as Unamuno alludes to in his *The Christ of Velázquez.* Heteronym Frederico Reis acknowledges that that Baby Jesus was "the god which the pagan pantheon lacked". Unlike most of those that "The Keeper of Sheep" is composed of, the poem is written according to the new Portuguese orthography that had been approved in 1911, and was published in *Presença* (January-February 1931).

21 To Luís de Sousa Rebelo, that *descending movement* is inspired by *the intervention of Apollo in Orestes' trial,* which is described in Aeschylus' *Eumenides.* Orestes had killed his mother to avenge his father and ended up mad.

Running and rolling in the grass
And pulling up flowers just to throw them away,
And laughing so you could hear it far away.
He had run away from heaven.
He was like us too much to pretend
He was the second person of the Trinity.
In heaven everything was false, everything out of step
With flowers and trees and stones.
In heaven he always had to be serious
And from time to time become human again
And climb onto the cross, and start dying
With a crown of thorns all around,
And his feet skewered with a spike
And even with a rag around his waist
Like the black men in engravings.
They wouldn't even let him have a father and mother
Like other children.
His father was two people–
An old man named Joseph, who was a carpenter,
And who wasn't his father,
And the other father was a stupid dove,
The only ugly dove in the world
Because it was neither a dove nor of the world.
His mother didn't love a man before she had him.
She wasn't even a woman: she was the handbag
He came down from the sky in.
And they wanted him, who was born only of a mother,
And never had a father to love with respect,
To preach goodness and justice!

One day when God fell asleep
And the Holy Ghost went off flying,
He got into a box of miracles and stole three.
With the first he made it so that no one would know he had run away.
With the second he made himself a human boy forever.
With the third he created a Christ eternally crucified
And left him nailed to the cross that there is in Heaven
Where he's used as a model for other crosses.
Then he ran away to the sun
And came down on the first ray he caught.

Today he lives in my village with me.
He is a lovely, natural, smiling child.
He wipes his nose on his right arm,
Sloshes around in puddles,
Collects flowers and loves them and forgets about them.
He throws stones at donkeys,
Steals fruit from the orchards

And runs away yelling and crying from dogs.
And, because he knows they don't like it
And everybody else thinks it's funny,
He runs around the girls
Who walk in groups along the roads
With jugs on their heads
And he lifts up their skirts.
(…)
When I die, little boy,
Let me be a child, the littlest one.
Clasp me to your breast
And carry me inside your house.
Undress my tired and human being
And lay me down in your bed.
And tell me stories, in case I wake up,
To make me go to sleep again.
And give me your dreams to play with
Until the day comes
You know which day I mean.

XXXII

Yesterday evening a man of the cities
Talked at the door of the inn.
He talked to me, too.

He talked about justice and the fight for justice
And the workers who suffer,
And constant work, and those who are hungry,
And the rich, who only turn their back to it.

And, looking at me, he saw tears in my eyes
And smiled with sympathy, believing I felt
The hatred he felt, and the compassion
He said he felt.

(But I wasn't even really listening to him.
What do I care about men
And what they suffer or think they suffer?
Let them be like me–then they wouldn't suffer.
All the evil in the world comes from us bothering with each other,
Wanting to do good, wanting to do evil.
Our soul and the sky and the earth are enough for us.
To want more is to lose this, and be unhappy.)

What I was thinking about
When the friend of the people talked
(And what moved me to tears),
Was that the distant murmuring of cowbells
That evening didn't seem like bells of a tiny chapel
Where flowers and brooks were at mass
With simple souls like mine.

(Praise be to God I'm not good,
And have the natural egotism of flowers
And rivers following their bed
Preoccupied without knowing it
Only with blooming and flowing.
This is the only mission in the World,
This – to exist clearly,
And to know how to do it without thinking about it.)

The man stopped talking and was looking at the sunset.
But what does someone who hates and loves want with a sunset?

DETACHED POEMS

It's not enough to open the window
To see the fields and the river.
It's also not enough to not be blind
To see the trees and the flowers.
It's also necessary to not have any philosophy at all.
With philosophy there are no trees, there are only ideas.
There's only each of us, like a wine-cellar.
There's only a shut window and the world outside it;
And a dream of what you could see if you opened the window,
Which is never what you see when you open the window.

Maiorum gloria posteris lumen est
(The glory of the ancestors is a light for their descendants) Sallust

RICARDO REIS

Ricardo Reis... is a great poet – I admit it here –,
if there be great poets in this world
Outside the silence of their own hearts.
Loose note (undated), Álvaro de Campos

Who is Reis?

Ricardo Sequeira Reis was born on the 19th of September[1] 1887: "At around 11pm in Porto", Pessoa said in his famous letter to Casais Monteiro (13/01/1935); or "at 4:05 in the afternoon, in Lisbon", and has a brother, Frederico Reis. A doctor, it doesn't appear as if he was able to live off his profession. Reis is "one of those Portuguese Jews", a physical affinity after Pessoa's own descent. A little shorter than Caeiro, he is conversely "more robust and sinewy", his skin a shade between white and "a vague, matte swarthiness". His physical appearance was (likely) inspired by the director of Durban High School, Wilfrid Nicholas, who admired classical culture. Much like him, "Dr. Ricardo Reis teaches Latin in an eminent American college". Nicholas wasn't mentioned in any writing, but held a great influence over Pessoa, such as in his proclivity for quotes in Latin in his texts. Raised in a Jesuit school, Reis was "a Latinist by education and a semi-Hellenist of his own accord". If Caeiro is Greek, Reis is Roman. With him, "a Greek Horace who wrote in Portuguese" was born[2].

1 The text is unsigned, but, judging by its style, it is consensually attributed to Campos.
2 The sentence makes sense even when one can't find any traces of Horace in Pessoa, as Quintus Horatius Flaccus (65-8 BC) studied in Athens, despite being Roman, and the upper Roman classes tended to speak Greek at home. Marcus Aurelius wrote his diary in Greek, and the final words of Julius Caesar upon being pierced by Brutus' dagger were *Kai su teknon?* (You too, my son?). Horace was the author of satires and epistles, and also left numerous odes in four verse structure, some of which were quoted by Reis in Latin. The image suggests that Reis is a mix of Rome, Greece and, of course, Portugal.

Yes, I know full well
I shall never be anyone.
I am quite aware
I shall never have an oeuvre.
I do know
That I shall never know myself.
Yes, but now,
While this hour lasts
These moonlit branches
This peace we find ourselves in
Let me believe[3]
That which I can never be.

Odes (08/07/1931), Ricardo Reis[4]

Having given master Caeiro to the world, Pessoa proceeded "to discover – instinctively and subconsciously – some disciples". Then "I tore off his false paganism a latent Ricardo Reis, gave him a name and adjusted him to himself, as by then I could already see him". But, deep down, it is Caeiro who is born "a year and a half after" Reis; and both of them only after Campos already existed. "Dr. Ricardo Reis was born in my soul on the 29th of January 1914, around 11pm", he later wrote. Except it wasn't quite like that. In a letter to Casais Monteiro (13/01/1935), it reads: "Around 1912, unless I am mistaken (though certainly never by much), it occurred to me to write some poems of a pagan bent. I outlined some of them in irregular verse (not in Campos' style, but in half-regular fashion) and left it at that. However, the thinly outlined silhouette of the man who had written them had taken shape. (Without my realizing it, Ricardo Reis had been born)". From Paris, at the end of 1912, Sá-Carneiro sent him *sincere felicitations for the birth of Mr. Ricardo Reis.* The explanation for the birth was simple: "The day prior, I had been listening to an extensive discussion on the excesses of modern art. It occurred to me that one might react against both schools – both modern Romanticism and Maurras'[5] neoclassicism". Whichever the date he was conceived, it was well before 1914.

3 A first draft read "Let me believe *until I see"*.

4 The poem is unsigned and was attributed to Reis only because Pessoa archived it in his envelope in the Chest. Still, the fact that the original rhymes – and the content itself – is more reminiscent of Pessoa himself, an opinion held by specialists such as Maria Aliete Galhoz and Silva Belkior, who believe the poem ended up in Reis' envelope by mistake.

5 Charles Maurras (1868-1952) was director of *Action Française,* a writer who took pleasure in attacking whatever seemed wrong to him, both in life and in politics. Due to his excesses, he was expelled from the French Academy and sentenced to life for betraying France. Reis' character was of like mould – "Pagan ethics, half epicurean, half stoic" – and ended up exiled in Brazil.

Time passes
It tells us nothing
We grow old
Let's learn., almost
Maliciously,
To feel ourselves going.

It is not worthwhile
To make a gesture.
There is no resistance
To the cruel god[6]
Who devours always
His own sons.
(…)

Sunflowers ever
Stare at the sun,
Let us go from life
Tranquilly, with
No remorse
Of having lived.

Odes[7] (12/06/1914), Ricardo Reis

Odes

Reis only ever wrote odes. This form of lyrical verse was born in Greece, where it means *song,* and then migrated to Rome. Unlike Campos' grandiose odes, Reis' smaller ones often have stanzas with two verses with ten syllables and two more with six, almost all without rhyme. As they are untitled, Reis' Odes were catalogued according to their date (or their first verses). Philosophers, heroes, nymphs and pagan gods are mentioned in 31% of them – the most frequent names are Apollo (12 times) and Pan (7), according to Jaime Fernandes. Also mentioned are Ceres, Aeolus, Jupiter, Neptune, Pluto, Saturn, Uranus and Venus. According to another accounting, this one by Victor Jabouille, there are *33 mythical references.* In life, he published 28 of them – 20 in *Athena* (1924) and eight in *Presença* (1927 to 1933), with all others stashed in the Chest. Álvaro de Campos says in "Nota preliminar" (Preliminary note) that Reis "had a fortunate inspiration, if he even makes

6 Chronos, the youngest son of Uranus and Gaea, who cut off his father's testicles with a sickle provided by his mother and took his own sister, Rhea, as wife. His parents had foreseen he would be dethroned by one of his sons, so he began eating them as soon as they were born, before his foretold demise.

7 Likely the first of the "Odes" written by Reis.

use of it... I cannot, however, conceive that emotions, even Reis', are universally obliged to sapphic or archaic odes... I do not blame Reis any more than I do other poets. I have sincere appreciation for him". Even so, he declares that "while Reis' poetry is rigorously classic in form, it is utterly destitute of vibration".

Reis' muses

Three nymphs are mentioned in his "Odes", the same mentioned by Horace. "At this hour, Lydia or Neera or Chloe/ Either of you is a stranger to me". Neera, who is mentioned in four of them, was one the many ladyloves of Helios, brother of Eos and Selene, whom she had already borne two children. She is often associated with youth.

Let us not hide today, Neera,
We lack nothing, for we are nothing.
We expect nothing
And get cold at the sun.

But let us enjoy the moment, such as it is,
Lightly and solemnly in joy
And awaiting death
As those who know it.

Odes (16/06/1914), Ricardo Reis

Then came Chloe, also mentioned four times. The first one to write about her was Longus (3rd or 3rd century BC), a Greek from Lesbos, in "Dafnis and Chloe", a poem describing a bucolic scenery in which young lovers live.

How brief a time is the longest of lives
And Youth within it! O Chloe, Chloe,
Should I not love, nor drink,
Nor catch myself distraught.

Odes (24/10/1923), Ricardo Reis

The most important and often mentioned is Lydia, who appears in 16 odes – a biblical name, that of the first documented convert to Christianity in Europe, by the hand of St. Paul. Other than Pessoa, there were other Portuguese authors who mentioned her, such as Almeida Garrett, Filinto Elísio, Sophia de Mello

Breyner Andresen[8] and Saramago, for whom she was *a grown, well-shaped woman, a brunette of Portuguese persuasion, rather on the shorter size.* Unlike the others, which were episodic, Lydia follows Reis his whole life.

> Let us then live our lives as just one day,
> Willingly unaware, Lydia, that
> There's night ere and after
> What little our lives last.
>
> *Odes* (11/07/1914), Ricardo Reis

Plans for Reis

Reis meets Caeiro on a trip to Ribatejo and admits: "When had 'The Keeper of Sheep' read to me the first time, during a visit to Portugal, I experienced the biggest and most perfect sensation in my life". He was 25 at the time, and had yet to write a single verse. But, even though he followed his master, the differences are plain to see: "The philosophy of Ricardo Reis is that of Caeiro, but hardened and falsified by civilization". Reis has a "gigantic, pagan soul"; and that paganism of his (much like Caeiro's), driven by his devotion to nature, isn't far from that which António Mora preaches in *Regresso dos Deuses* (Return of the Gods); nor are their aesthetic differences substantial. Because, to Pessoa, according to Jairo Nogueira Luna, *Christianity was a religion begotten by the decadence of the Roman Empire, and, as such, carries a decadent spirit in its genesis, turning Man's life into a state of contempt towards the grace of God. Paganism, on the other hand, was more human, in that the gods weren't poles apart from humans, but rather a superior stage they too could attain, while still conserving their human aspects.*

"The philosophy of Ricardo Reis' entire oeuvre can be summed up as a sad Epicureanism", according to his brother Frederico. Mora elaborates: "The artist doesn't express his emotions. With them, he expresses those which are common among other men... Others' emotions. Humanity has nothing on his own emotions". Words which could just as easily have been said by Reis. "There are sudden, deep sentences, because they come from depth, that define a man, or, rather, with which a man defines himself. I'll never forget the one Ricardo Reis once defined me with. We were talking about lying, and he said: I abhor lying, for it is an inaccuracy". To sum it up, "his inspiration is straight and dense, his thoughts are compactly sober, his emotion is real". Other than poems, Pessoa also tasked Reis with translations for a *Greek anthology* he

8 Andresen began an "Homage to Ricardo Reis" by saying: *Trust not, Lydia, that any of the summers/ That we lost might ever return/ Handing us the flower/ We'd postponed picking.*

planned to publish, including Sappho's *Poems* and Aeschylus'[9] *Alcmene,* as well as Aristotles' *Politics.* Those books were part of the editorial projects of his publishing house, Olisipo, as we will see. Reis is the one *Pessoa would have liked to be,* according to Ángel Crespo. Whatever the case, Pessoa himself acknowledges that, with Reis, he reached "the apex of literary maturity".

His exile

In the beginning of 1914, an insurrectionist monarchical movement takes power in the north of Portugal. Less than a month later, it was quelled, and its proponents were pursued, among them Reis. On the 12th of April 1919, he voluntarily exiles himself in Rio de Janeiro, a choice owing to the fact that his friend Luís de Montalvor lived there; other illustrious Portuguese followed suit – Casais Monteiro, Paulino de Oliveira and Jorge de Sena (some after Pessoa's death). His conservative ideas became problematic in a now clearly republican country, and so he lived out the rest of his days in Brazil, though he did spend some time in Peru – in Cerro de Pasco, Arequipa, likely the "dirty and sterile remote republic". "I am under the impression that I live in this shapeless fatherland called the universe. It is then that, silently, slowly, the anticipated longing for an impossible exile dawns upon me". He stops writing on the 13th of December 1933, but, a few days before Pessoa's death, he would write one final poem:

> There are many living in us;
> I know not whether I think or feel
> Who, indeed, thinks and feels.
> I am merely the place
> Where one thinks and feels.
>
> I have more than one soul.
> There are more of me than myself…
>
> *Odes* (13/11/1935), Ricardo Reis

The death of Reis

Unlike in Caeiro's case, Pessoa doesn't kill him off. His end comes at the hands of José Saramago in his classic 1984 novel *The Year of the Death of*

9 Greek poet (525-456 BC), widely considered the first great author of Greek tragedy (created by Thespis). But perhaps Pessoa might have been mistaken, as the Alcmene he spoke of was probably the one which inspired Horace's odes, whereas Aeschylus authored a tragedy on Prometheus.

Ricardo Reis[10]. Therein, we are informed that one month after Pessoa's death, Reis abandoned his voluntary exile and returned to Lisbon. He lived through the political chaos of 1936, during which tyrants expanded their demesnes. Mussolini had already come to power in 1922; Hitler in 1934; and now Franco, with the advent of the Spanish civil war. Portugal was living through the harshest stage of Salazar's dictatorship, which had begun in 1933. Reis suffered during that time, leaving his hotel infrequently and falling in (platonic) love with a young woman, Marçenda, who had a lame arm. Lídia, a virgin "envied by death", a distant love for whom he "braided a crown of flowers", ends up as his lover and maid in the rented house he moves into at length. And she bears him a son. Also according to Saramago, Reis encounters the ghost of Pessoa. *He stands at the corner of Rua de Santa Justa, looking at him as if he were waiting, but not impatiently.* The two share *many and most strange conversations.* In their last one, at the end of said year, Pessoa comes to say goodbye. *Wherever you go, I'll go with you.* And the two then lose themselves *where the sea lands and land awaits.* The same sea that lay "far away, father than the gods", in which Reis once had conceived his own end. And so it had to be: "I entered, Lord, that door. I sailed, Lord, across that sea. I beheld, Lord, that inevitable abyss".

> I await with equanimity that which I do not know –
> My future and the future of all.
> In the end, all shall be silence, but
> For where the sea naught bathes.
>
> *Odes* (13/12/1933), Ricardo Reis

Selected texts

ODES

Come sit by my side Lydia, on the bank of the river
Calmly let us watch it flow, and learn
That life passes, and we are not holding hands.
(Let us hold hands)

Then let us reflect as grown-up children, that life
Passes and does not stay, leaves nothing, never returns
Goes to a sea far away, near to Fate itself,
Further than the gods.

---

10 Saramago would later jokingly refer to Ricardo Reis in the following terms: *An expatriated doctor whose whereabouts remained unknown, in spite of some recent, obviously apocryphal news.*

Let us hold hands no more: why should we tire ourselves?
For our pleasure, for our pain, we pass on like the river[11].
'Tis better to know how to pass on silently,
With no great disquiet.

With neither loves nor hates, nor passions raising their voice,
Nor envies making the eye rove too restlessly,
Nor cares, for if it knew care, the river would flow no less,
Would still join the sea in the end.

Let us love each other calmly, with the thought that we could,
If we chose, freely kiss and caress and embrace,
But that we do better to be seated side by side
Hearing the river flow, and seeing it.

Let us gather flowers, and do you take some and leave them
In your lap, and let their scent lend sweetness to the moment -
This moment when calmly we believe in nothing,
Innocent pagans of the decadence.

At least, should I first become a shade, you will remember me after,
Though remembered, I may not inflame nor hurt nor disturb you,
For we never hold hands, nor kiss,
Nor were we ever more than children.

And if, before me, you take the obol to the gloomy boatman[12],
I shall have not cause to suffer when I remember you.
You will be sweet to my memory if I remember you thus, on the river bank,
A sorrowful pagan maid, with flowers in her lap.

12/06/1914

The gods do not consent to more than life.
Let us then all refute which may lead to
Unbreathable summits,
Eternal and unbloomed.

Let us be aware through mere acceptance,
And, whilst our blood still pumps through our temples,
Nor does our love wither
From within, let us last,

---

11 Pessoa is evoking the metaphor of Heraclitus of Ephesus (540-480 BC): *In the same river we both step and do not step, we are and are not.*

12 Charon, the ferryman of the dead. He is also mentioned in *Disquiet:* "No surviving widow or son placed the obol in his mouth to pay Charon". In another ode (11-12/09/1916), Reis completes the thought: *Nor does the widow place in his mouth/ The obol due Charon/ And over his unburied corpse/ Not even the traveller will throw dirt.*

As clear panes of glass, transparent to light,
Allowing the sad drizzle to flow down,
Tepid beneath the sun,
Casting slight reflections.

There's a variant of this poem, which is as follows:

The gods do not consent to more than life.
And so, Lydia, let us lastingly
Do their bidding,
Among the sun and flowers.

Chameleons[13] placed in Nature,
Let us take its calm joy
Our lives' colour,
As a bodily shape.

As clear panes of glass, transparent to light,
Allowing the drizzle to flow down,
Tepid beneath the sun,
Casting slight reflections.

17/07/1914

Follow your fate,
Water your plants,
Love your roses.
All else is but
The shadow of trees.

Reality
Is ever more or less
Than what we wish.
Only we are always
True to ourselves.

Softly is to live on your own.
Grand and noble it is
To ever live simply.
Leave all pain on the altars
As an ex-vow to the gods.

See life from afar.
Never question it.
She cannot possibly
Give you an answer.

13 Pessoa's ever shifting nature in literature likely made him feel as one.

It is beyond the gods.
Do, however, serenely
Emulate Olympus
In your heart.
Gods are gods because
They do not think of themselves.

01/07/1916

Under the tutelage
Of careless gods
I wish to spend the awarded hours
Of this fated life.

There is naught I can do
About the being they made me into,
I can but wish that Fate
Has accorded me peace as my destiny.

In truth, I want nothing
More than life; as the gods
Grant life and not truth; and perhaps
They don't even know what truth is.

(Undated)

Ardua et præceps gloria vadit iter
(The path to glory is hard and dangerous) Ovid

ÁLVARO DE CAMPOS

Poor Álvaro de Campos, whom no one cares about.
Poor him, who feels so sorry for himself.
Untitled (undated), Álvaro de Campos

Who is Campos?

Álvaro de Campos was born on the 15th of October 1890, "at 1:30 in the afternoon, according to [Augusto] Ferreira Gomes" – as he wrote on the famous letter to Casais Monteiro (13/01/1935)[1]. The episode was later clarified by Gomes himself. According to him, one night, he arrived a little earlier at the apartment Pessoa lived in, at Rua Cidade da Horta, and they waited for the usual lot – Cunha Dias, Numa de Figueiredo[2] and Alberto Silva Tavares, who had been delayed by rain. The year was 1916 and it transpired during the holidays. The host tried to start a conversation and suggested: "With your intuition, try to ascertain the place, date and time of birth of Álvaro de Campos". Gomes laughed and took a wild guess based on what he knew: *He was born in Tavira*[3]*, on the 15th of October*[4]*, 1890*[5]*, at 1:30 in the afternoon...* Pessoa wrote it down and, the following day, gave exulting thanks to his friend: "You guessed it! Álvaro de Campos' horoscope matches perfectly!". Campos was tall for the standards at the time. According to his ID, he measured 1m75, two centimetres more than Pessoa. Thin and elegant, albeit "with a slight tendency to slouch", he wore "an overly belted coat" and used a monocle on his right eye. Vain,

1 In spite of that, he would later claim in a horoscope he had been born on the 13th of October 1890 "at 1:17pm".

2 *A Portuguese Black writing in French,* Sá-Carneiro wrote in a letter (31/08/1915), his words reminiscent of Pizarro, Ferrari and Cardielo.

3 The birthplace of Pessoa's paternal grandfather, general Joaquim António de Araújo Pessoa.

4 The day in which Virgil and Nietzsche, two of the literary men Pessoa most admired, had been born.

5 Given the years of birth of the heteronyms Jean-Seul de Méluret (1885), Charles James Search (1886), Ricardo Reis (1887), Alexander Search (1888, just like Pessoa) and Alberto Caeiro (1889), 1890 would naturally follow.

he confesses (in "The Passing of the Hours") that he spends three hours dressing up. His hair is straight and black, parted to the side. He is neither fair nor swarthy, "of a vaguely Portuguese Jew persuasion" – here Pessoa once again mentions his own descent, which included ancestors executed at *auto-de-fé*. His was a layman's education, but he began to study with an uncle who was "a priest from the *Beiras*"[6], who also taught him Latin. A "priestly great-uncle" from whom he'd inherit "an appreciation for classical things", their kinship appears to be ill-defined, as Campos describes himself as "a senseless teenager under the care of his priestly cousin, who he called uncle", and called him 'uncle' out of respect. In 1919, he visits Newcastle upon Tyne, much like Eça de Queiroz did in December 1874 to take on a role as a consul. Physically, heteronym Álvaro is perhaps inspired on the poet Ernesto Campos Melo e Castro (1896-1973) – also from the Beiras, a Jew from Covilhã, Libra and an engineer, just like Campos, with whom he also shared his surname[7]. When they were introduced in Lisbon, Pessoa brought the similarities between their noses to the attention of those present. He has a degree in nautical engineering from the University of Glasgow, a profession inspired by Raul Soares da Costa (married to Maria Madalena, daughter of aunt Anica), and Helena Freitas, his daughter, admits as much.

> Yes, I, the nautical engineer who is superstitious like a peasant godmother,
> And wears a monocle so as not to resemble the way I conceive of myself
> (...)
> I turn every corner of every street every single day,
> And whenever I think of something, I am thinking of something else.
>
> *The Passing of the Hours*, Álvaro de Campos

He doesn't finish his studies: "I left after I had concluded around a third of my engineering degree in Scotland". Still, he considered himself "an engineer by occupation, sick of all and everything else". He worked for Casa Forsyth, a name evocative of Edimburgh's medieval names, and was even hired as "director for Bragança's public works" – where he was tasked with "evaluating the road to Guimarães". But he is soon fired "for not working, as Bragança's workers will to this day concur" – which is why he wrote in "Opiary" that "doing nothing is my perdition". He lived in his old country house in Tavira, where he was "happy and content". But not for long, as he then moved to Lisbon, where he was free to indulge in his ill temper, as one can see in the

6 The provinces between the North and Centre of Portugal. Sancho Pessoa da Cunha, Pessoa's great-great-great-great-great-grandfather came from Beira-litoral.

7 Ana Rita Palmeirim told me that, in 1918, a company registered its offices close to the house Pessoa had been born in. The company was "Álvaro de Campos, Lda.", from one Álvaro Metrass Campos. A coincidence, surely.

following small poem, which begins thus: "Madam Gertrudes!... You haven't cleaned this room properly: Get these ideas off here". His mother and father dead, he lived off small rents "with an old great-aunt". Aunts, actually, as it stands in the verses in which he speaks of "the ample dining room of my old aunts", in which "the clock tick-tocked the passage of time in slower fashion" and where he indulged in "tea and toast in the province of yore, eternally a child, eternally abandoned". An image evoking the old great-aunts Maria Xavier Pinheiro and Rita Xavier Pinheiro da Cunha, with whom Pessoa lived in several stages of his life.

> My old aunt, who loved me because of the son she'd lost...
> My old aunt used to sing me to sleep
> (Even though I was already too old for this).
> The memory makes tears fall on my heart, cleansing it of life,
> And a light sea breeze wafts inside me.
>
> *Maritime Ode*, Álvaro de Campos

"An almost prototypical sinner in the matter of irregular verses", Campos is fundamentally a poet of sensations – rebellious, anguished, cosmopolitan. Someone who fully adopted the motto "feeling in every way, loving all in every form", always "infinitely yearning for the finite" and "the possible, impossibly". As he claims in "Salutation to Walt Whitman", he is also "pretentious and amoral". This "new individual" appears within him all of a sudden, when "in a burst and at the typewriter, with no interruptions or corrections, Álvaro de Campos' *Triumphal Ode* came to be". Sá-Carneiro, on the 20th of June 1914, proclaims: *You have just written futurism's masterpiece;* the same that he himself considered "a true wonder" in 1916 – the "Ode with that name and the man with the name he has". In "London, 1914, June". A false location, as he never went to the land in which his brothers lived; and a false date, as Campos had already been born in him much earlier. The man and his solitude.

> Poor Álvaro de Campos!
> So lonely in life! So depressed in his feelings!
> Poor him, sunken in the armchair of his melancholy!
> Poor him, with (real) tears in his eyes,
> Who today gave all he had, which wasn't that much,
> In a grand, liberal and Muscovite gesture,
> To a poor man who wasn't poor, but had sad eyes for a profession.
>
> *Untitled* (undated), Álvaro de Campos

Campos and Caeiro

"As I wrote certain passages of *Notes for the Memory of My Master Caeiro,* I cried real tears". Because "before meeting Caeiro, I was but a nervous machine of doing nothing". Heteronym Frederico Reis attests to that: "There is no doubt that Alberto Caeiro awoke, both in R[icardo] Reis and in Álv[aro] de Campos, the poetry both held within themselves". He was thus ready to live his own existence. "I saw paths and shadowy short-cuts everywhere, and I was the very shadow and the short-cuts. Ah, I am free… Master Caeiro. I have returned to your house on top of the hill. And I saw what you saw, but with mine own eyes". He then concludes: "Ah, if this whole bright world, and those flowers and light, this whole world with dirt and sea and houses and people, if this is all an illusion, then why is this here?". Caeiro was unmoved. To him, Campos was "a good man, but drunk". The response is swift: "O, master Caeiro, only you were ever right?"

Their heated discussions were probably owed to the fact that the differences between them were so marked. Once, while translating "with friendly perversity" a verse of William Wordsworth (1770-1850), Campos said "a flower by the river was a yellow flower and nothing else". To which Caeiro replies: "It depends if one considers said yellow flower as one of several yellow flowers or that single yellow flower". Once again, he asks: "Are you happy with yourself?", and Caeiro replies: "No, I am happy". Pessoa completed the sentence with a comment of his: "It was like the voice of the very earth, which is everyone and no one". In another conversation, Campos asks: "What is classical materialism?", to which Caeiro replies: "It is a thing of priests without religion, and therefore with no excuse". Campos challenges him, appalled, pointing out "similarities between materialism and his doctrine, save for the latter's poetic nature". Caeiro ended the conversation in professorial fashion: "But that which you call poetry is everything. It isn't even poetry, it is but the act of seeing". The following (abridged) dialogue became famous:

Campos – But can you not conceive of space as being infinite?

Caeiro – I conceive of nothing as being infinite. How could I conceive of anything as being infinite?

Campos – Imagine a space, then. Beyond that space, there is more space, and further beyond that one, and further still, and on, and on… It doesn't end.

Caeiro – Why?

Campos – Suppose it ends. What comes after?

Caeiro – If it ends, then nothing.

Campos – But can you conceive of that?

Caeiro – Can I conceive of what? That something has its limits? Naturally! That which has no limits does not exist. To exist is for there to be something else, and therefore all must be limited.

Campos – Look, Caeiro... Consider the numbers... Where do numbers end[8]? Let us take any number – 34, for example. After it, we have 35, 36, 37, 38, and so on, unceasingly. There is no large number that isn't followed by a larger one still.

Caeiro – But those are merely numbers. What is 34 in truth?

Notes for the Memory of My Master Caeiro, Álvaro de Campos

Campos and Reis

Theirs was a relationship rife with conflict. "Most peculiarly, Álvaro de Campos is an entirely opposite pole to Ricardo Reis. That being said, both are disciples of Caeiro and sensationists". According to Reis, "in all which is said – poetry or prose – there is idea and emotion; and the only difference between those two forms is rhythm"; said rhythm being "a gradation of sounds and lack of sound, much like the world in the gradation between being and not being". Emotion was thus reduced to the process which ideas make use of to convert themselves into words. With no great differences between poetry and prose. "What Campos truly does when he writes in verse is to write rhythmical prose". In turn, Campos questions Reis and his poetry, which he considered "overly orientated towards the cardinal point called Ricardo Reis"; only to see Reis lament "Campos' contempt for the precision of sentences". Among their many disputes, there was one about art which began with a text written by Campos, in which he criticized Reis' poem (published in *Athena* #1, October 1924), which begins thus:

I steel my haughty mind for the effort
From high above, and leave the verse
Up to luck and its laws;
Because, as high and regal thought may be,
The sudden sentence searches for it
And its slave, rhythm, serves it.

Odes (undated), Ricardo Reis

Campos makes an indignant criticism: "He may well steel his haughty mind from high above (whatever that means), although it appears to me as narrow, limited poetry... But the relationship between height and verses of a certain number of syllables eludes me". To him, "much like to say is to speak, and if one cannot speak while screaming, one must speak singing. As music is alien to speech, one feels music in speech when one arranges the words in a way

8 A reference to professor Serzedas, a character in the short story "O vencedor do tempo" (The winner of time) of heteronym Pero Botelho, in which that modern Socrates maintains that "the numerical infinite begins but does not end, the infinite zero is nothing".

in which they contain a musicality that isn't theirs, and is artificial in them". Because, for Reis, "poetry is music that is played with ideas, and thus with words". Campos counters that "with emotions, all you could do is music. With emotions walking towards ideas… you could make a chant. With nothing but ideas… you could make poetry". Therefore, "the colder the poetry, the truer it is". Reis is furious at that, and claims Campos "is a great writer of prose, a writer of prose with a scientific approach". In that veritable dance of opinions on the subject, Caeiro also chips in, mentioning "the prose of my verses"; as well as Bernardo Soares, who says that he prefers "poetry in verses to poetry that encompasses all of art", and concludes that "poetry would be for children before they got to the future prose". Whereas Pessoa himself could tell apart words and voice when writing: "Words express ideas, voice conveys emotion. Poetry, as an expression of ideas, is born of words. Verse, as an expression of emotions, is born of voice. Originally, poetry was oral, it was sung. The expression of an idea requires an explanation. The expression of emotion demands rhythm. To convey that emotion is to deprive it of thought, conserving that expression".

Campos and Pessoa

The two aren't always in agreement. Pessoa proclaims his "exalting of the institute of motherland"; whereas Campos replies in "The Passing of the Hours", declaring himself "internationalist and cosmopolitan". Pessoa calls him "my son" (letter to Côrtes-Rodrigues 04/03/1915); or "my abominable, yet fair friend Álvaro de Campos" (letter to José Régio 26/01/1928); or "my old but most dear friend" (letter to Casais Monteiro 26/12/1933). According to himself, he was "a Walt Whitman with a Greek poet inside" and even has fun with his creation – almost re-enacting his prank on Guisado, leading António Ferro to believe a poet named Alberto Caeiro actually existed. "In order to give an idea of Álvaro de Campos' individuality, even to those closest to us, I reminded Alfredo Guisado to claim having received one such collaboration from Galicia; and so we obtained blank paper from Cassino de Vigo, on which I wrote his compositions". They were the verses of "Steps of the Cross" – at the time, a poem which was still attributed to Álvaro de Campos, which was then published in *Centauro* (1916) as if Pessoa had written them. His friends fell for it, and he was overjoyed. Then, in time, he wrote "several compositions, generally of a scandalous, annoying bent, especially for Fernando Pessoa, who, in any event, has no other choice but to publish them, no matter how vehemently he disagrees". Teresa Rita Lopes emphasizes that *in creating Álvaro de Campos, Pessoa gave a person's shape to his fears and anxieties. Through him, he dared the gestures, the travels and the excesses that his apathetic temperament didn't allow him to experience.* But only at a first stage, it should be said.

In June 1930, in a meeting arranged by Carlos Queiroz, José Régio and João Gaspar Simões travel from Coimbra (where they resided) to Lisbon just to meet him. Pessoa greets them at Café Montanha in rather unfriendly fashion. According to Simões, *instead of attending the meeting in person, Pessoa sent through himself another, none other than Mr. Álvaro de Campos!* José Régio, from Vila do Conde, never made a secret of his open hostility towards the inhabitants of Lisbon, especially intellectuals from that city. And he does not enjoy the meeting. But he does acknowledge the genius of it and, in *Presença* #33 (1927), had already called him *master, the one with the greater embarrassment of riches of all our so-called modernists.* The two never met again, but they exchanged a good number of letters. The heteronym slowly gains a life of his own. Books are dedicated by Pessoa's friends, not to Pessoa, but to Campos himself: *Tanto,* by Samuel Dias; *Teoria da indiferença,* by António Ferro; *Fogueira eterna,* by Alves Martins; *Se Gil Vicente voltasse,* by Ponce de León – this one dedicated to *Álvaro Fernando de Campos Pessoa.* Letters are regularly sent to him by Sá-Carneiro, who once said: *I sent Campos two postcards and one for you;* and also by Alfredo Guisado, Ferreira Gomes, Côrtes-Rodrigues – with Rodrigues occasionally signing his letters as Violante de Cysneiros. A pseudonym writing to a heteronym. In 1910, Campos was a fully out of the closet homosexual, who screamed for "a revolt against duties and a revolt against morals". Throughout his oeuvre, there are even a number of poems which clearly spell out his sexual preference.

> Look, Daisy; when I die, you shall
> tell all of my friends in London,
> (…)
> tell that poor lad
> who gave me so many happy moments,
>
> Though you know not that I'm dead…
> even he, who I thought I loved so,
> will care not the least bit…
>
> *An old sonnet,* Álvaro de Campos

But, in 1920, Pessoa meets Ophelia, and from that moment on, he who had once dreamt of young boys and rough sailors would never be the same again. In a "communiqué of the nautical engineer Mr. Álvaro de Campos in a state of alcoholic unconsciousness", he even confesses to lusting after a woman: "Ah, Margarida/ Were I to give you my life/ What would you do with it?". Such is the change operated on him, that Campos ends up getting married. At least so it would appear when reading his final poems (such as "Holiday in the Country"), in which we find him in a domestic environment, quietly keeping company to the wife handling a pair of scissors, or with both talking sweetly to each other – evoking Pessoa's experience in Durban with his mother and stepfather.

> You mused, staring at me as if I were space.
> I reminisce to have something to think about without thinking.
> Suddenly, in a half sigh, you interrupted what you were being.
> You stared at me, unconsciously, and said:
> "Such a shame that not all days are like this" –
> Much like that day, which had been nothing.
>
> *Holiday in the Country*, Álvaro de Campos

On some occasions, Campos takes over his creator's role in his relationship with Ophelia. Like on the day in which he forbids her from "weighing less grams, eating little, sleeping less, having a fever and thinking of him" – Pessoa himself. Or when he says: "I have a task for you, my lady, namely plunging the abject physiognomy of that Fernando Pessoa into a bucket", after which he calls his own creator a "miscreant". Ophelia reacts: *I vehemently object to you referring to Mr. Fernando Pessoa, who I greatly esteem, as abject and wretched;* and also declares she cannot comprehend how *being his personal and esteemed friend, you can treat him in such degrading fashion.* Even the final letter Pessoa writes to her is only sent "with due permission from Mr. Álvaro de Campos". Ophelia comments: *He* [Pessoa] *was rather baffling, especially when he introduced himself as Álvaro de Campos. He would tell me, today it is not I, but my friend Álvaro de Campos. He would then behave in unrecognisable fashion, all keyed up and speaking nonsense.*

The many Campos

"Álvaro de Campos is the character of a play; all that's lacking is the play". Having been introduced to the world in two poems, "Opiary" and "Triumphal Ode", both published in *Orpheu* #1 (1915), he also wrote about other, varied topics. In *Malthusian Law of Sensibility*[9], for example, he preaches "the abolition of the dogma of personality (that we have a personality separate from those of others) and the abolition of the concept of individuality (that each soul is one and indivisible)". What that means: In politics, "abolishing any and all conviction that lasts longer than a state of mind"; in art, "abolishing the dogma of artistic individuality"; in philosophy, "abolishing truth as a philosophical concept". Campos defines himself in the following terms: "I am a technician, but I have technique only within technique. Beyond that, I am mad, and rightly

9 Pessoa's Malthusian reaction against modernist poets, which he hoped there were less of.

so". "I can imagine myself as anything, because I am nothing. If I were anything, I wouldn't be able to imagine". João Lobo Antunes, a doctor and the winner (in 1996) of the Pessoa Prize, put it thus: It was *the curse of intelligence.*

For Sá-Carneiro, *Álvaro de Campos is most certainly not greater than Fernando Pessoa, but he manages to be more interesting than him;* and goes even further: *To me, Campos is the one who exists, and Pessoa is his pseudonym* (letter from 30/08/1915). Almada Negreiros held a similar opinion. Pessoa himself recalls that, "after having read *Triumphal Ode* with enthusiasm", his friend shook him "forcefully by the arm at my lack of enthusiasm, and said in almost indignant fashion: *This may not be how you would have written it, but it is very much like life.* I felt that only our friendship spared me the implicit affirmation that Álvaro de Campos was worth much more than myself". Almada completes the description of that episode: *I came down and told Fernando Pessoa: Álvaro de Campos, I urge you to give Fernando Pessoa a good kick up the arse for me when you next meet him.* To António Quadros, *being the most complex of all heteronyms, he is simultaneously the most evident and the most hidden of all, the one closest to humanity and to divinity.* Pessoa considers a book consisting only of Campos' poems, and on the 3rd of February 1935 he writes the one which was meant for the end of it – adding in brackets *"end of the book".* Then, in one of his typical fits of fickleness, he would write six further poems. The one meant for said end of said books reads:

It's been quite a while since I've written a sonnet,
But that's OK, I'll just write one now.
Sonnets are childhood, and, for an hour,
My childhood is nothing but a big black spot;

It throws me off a train (well, really me…)
Onto a futile and unmoving track;
And the sonnet is like someone looking back
These last two days over everything I see.

Thank Heaven I still haven't forgotten the art
Of fitting fourteen lines together well
So folks will always know right where they are.

Where folks are, or where I am, I don't know…
I'd rather know no more about anything else
And it'll still be bullshit when I do.

I Come Back Home,[10] Álvaro de Campos

10 According to Pessoa, the poem which inspired him was "Soneto de repente", by (Félix) Lope da Vega (y Carpio, 1562-1635).

Opiary

During a trip to the East on a German ocean liner, *Opiarx*[11] was born. Initially, it was dedicated to Fernando Pessoa and, lastly, to "mister Mário de Sá-Carneiro". In real life, that voyage (the seaborne part of it) takes place in 1901, when, during his stepfather's sabbatical vacations, the entire family visits Portugal. Pessoa travelled across the entire western coast of Africa, passing by Zanzibar and Dar-es-Salaam (Tanzania's former capital), which Campos evokes in "The Passing of the Hours"; Port Sail (Egypt), the tip of the Suez Canal, which he mentions in that same poem; and Naples. In "Opiary", however, the travel was interrupted in Marseille, from which he then departed to Lisbon by land. An image reminiscent of Rimbaud who, in his youth, travelled all over Europe and, upon returning to Africa to die, he also disembarked in Marseille.

The title is explained by Campos' cocaine and opium habit, as did so many writers in his time, such as Huxley, Rimbaud, Thomas de Quincey and Manuel Bandeira. The poem consists of 43 stanzas in an ABBA rhyme scheme, it was written in a rush to be published in the first issue of *Orpheu,* in March 1915. "And so I wrote 'Opiary', in which I endeavoured to give all of Campos' latent tendencies, as they would later be revealed, but still without as much as a trace of contact with my master Caeiro". He would later conclude: "Out of all poems I've written, this was the most time-consuming… Oh, well, I believe it came out all right". A fair assessment, and his critics seemed to agree, especially considering the poem's topic matter. Joaquim-Francisco Coelho even suggested that, in a way, *we could and should read* Opiary *as a possible glorious afterword of* The Lusiads… *in which the anti-hero, sitting down and depressed, makes for a somewhat grotesque contrast with the erect and fierce hero of the national epopee.*

> With the soporific nudge of morphine
> I lose myself in throbbing transparencies,
> And on a diamond-studded night the moon
> Rises as if it were my Destiny.
> (…)
> What I really want is faith and peace
> And to get these sensations under control.
> Put an end to this, God! Open the floodgates!
> Enough of this comedy in my soul![12]
>
> *Opiary*, Álvaro de Campos

---

11 A neologism stemming from the Latin *opium.* But the title normally used is "Opiário" (Opiary), another neologism, but easier to understand.

12 There's a small inscription at the margins after that final verse, saying: "At the Suez Canal, aboard".

Tobacco Shop

On the 3rd of February 1927, a more mature Campos (and Pessoa, too) reveals the first inspirations for what would become his most renowned poem:

> In the squares – perhaps the same as ours –
> What elixirs will be touted and proclaimed?
> (…)
> In my own metaphysics, which I have because I think and feel
> There is no peace.
> (…)
> The weariness of thinking, going to the core of existing,
> Makes me old since before yesterday with a chill in my body.
> What of lost purposes and impossible dreams?
>
> *March of the Downfall*[13], Álvaro de Campos

After this first draft, 1927 would also see a "Draft for Tobacco Shop", which reads (abridged): "Man, wolf of his own inspiration[14], carries on in outraged disgrace as the Earth spins, unfazed, restless is he, with no other comfort other than his own illusions, he rules, wages war, leaves the memories of numberless battles, verses and sacrifices. The Earth shall go cold without any of it having been for aught. Other systems of planets and satellites might give birth to new mankinds. Other Christs shall in vain climb other crosses". Then, with the same inspiration, other small poems keep popping up until, on the 15th of January 1928, he finishes the largest of them all. The one which he will be remembered for. *An epopee of abject failure,* according to Rémy Hourcade. Published in June 1933 in *Presença* #39, it filled up its cover page and an interior one, its title typed in a peculiar *TaBaCaRia.*

The Tobacco Shop's tobacco shop

Which was "The Tobacco Shop"'s tobacco shop? That is the question. For some biographers, it was Tabacaria Costa, which still exists at Rua Áurea, 295 – as Pessoa always bought his cigarettes there. According to others, it was Casa Havaneza do Chiado, at Rua Garrett, 124-134, a *purveyor of cigarettes, assorted items for smokers, newspapers, lottery tickets,* right next to A Brasileira. Others still believe it was Leitaria Académica, *trader and seller of milk, dairy, pastries, wines, fruit, mineral water, etc.* This last hypothesis

13 The title had previously already shown up, written at the margins of one of "Lisbon Revisited"'s originals.

14 A reference to a quote of Plautus' (254-184 BC) *Aulularia: Homo homini lupus* (Man is Man's wolf), which Thomas Hobbes also used in his *Leviathan* (1651).

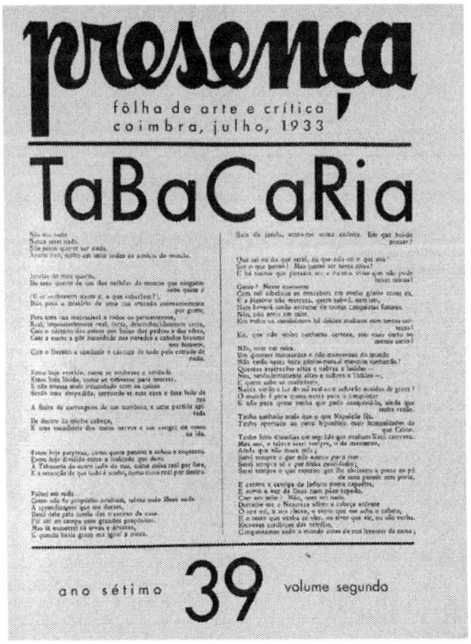
presença

fôlha de arte e crítica

coimbra, julho, 1933

TaBaCaRia

ano sétimo 39 volume segundo

Cover of *Presença.*

is an impossibility, as the place was only inaugurated on the 1st of January 1938, when Pessoa had already passed away. All opinions are equally bereft of any real historical source. Among authors, the most consensual place is A Morgadinha, at Rua Silva Carvalho, 13/15, on the corner of Coelho da Rocha – the street in which Pessoa lived when "Tobacco Shop" was written – as it was the only place nearby where he could purchase tobacco. The poem itself hints at it:

> Windows of my room,
> Of my room, one of the millions in the world
> no one knows who owns
> (And if they knew, what would they know?)

But even that guess doesn't hold much water. Firstly, because Pessoa's room at the time had no windows; his niece had the one room with a view to the street. Manuela Nogueira, who lived in said room, told me as much. And António Manuel Rodrigues de Seixas, the son of barber Manassés, who had (almost always) accompanied his father when he went to shave Pessoa every day, claims the same. The apartment was later destroyed from the inside for the construction of Casa Fernando Pessoa. But the floor plan that Manassés' son drew for me began with the dining room and the children's room, both of which had windows; then a hallway, the room for sister Teca and only then Pessoa's. Small. Dark. Hot. *Depressing,* according to him. And with no windows. Also, A Morgadinha was in a corner, beyond the sight of most of Coelho da Rocha's buildings, Pessoa's included. Even when stretching out from the window, craning one's neck to the left – as I did – the store couldn't be seen from that room's window. Which is why it couldn't possibly have been "the Tobacco Shop across the street, as a real thing outside".

Not only that: A Morgadinha didn't even exist at the time. According to Lisbon's city records, it was built (registry #32.082) only on the 3rd of June 1958, dedicated *to the trade of dairy, pastries, wine and fruits,* and would be dissolved not long thereafter, on the 17th of October 1971. According to the many statements I got from his neighbours of that time, its owners were Oliveira e Trindade, and the Ford automobile from one of the owners was kept inside the premises. But it probably wasn't quite so. Oliveira was certainly Manuel Santana de Oliveira, single, sales employee, residing at Avenida Padre Manuel de Nóbrega, 19-4th left – one of A Morgadinha's founding partners. The Ford brand was virtually unknown in Lisbon at Pessoa's time, and Oliveira probably stored his car there from 1958 onwards, which would likely have influenced the memories of the kindly old folk I talked with. What we know for sure is that, at the time of the poem's writing, in that address' corner, there was indeed another store which sold wine and chocolate, as well as *newspapers, tobacco, and stationery,* according to niece Manuela Nogueira. The owner was António Lopes, a name which Manassés' son remembered. Júlio Trindade, the employee who served Pessoa, lived at Rua Saraiva de Carvalho, 114, quite close to the address. He was the "chubby Trindade" Bernardo Soares spoke of.

As I searched for the true address, it is important to point out that, at the turn of the 19th century, Lisbon had 80 tobacco shops which sold cigarettes, cigarillos and cigars, as well as newspapers and lottery tickets (some even provided money exchange). It was there that began the age of the Havanezas, a symbol of Lisbon's *belle époque.* The most famous were the previously mentioned Casa Havaneza, at Chiado, which Eça spoke of in *The Crime of Father Amaro;* Nova Casa Havaneza, Rua dos Capelistas, 136-140; Tabacaria Bela Havaneza, Rua da Prata, 207; Havaneza do Socorro, at the corner of Rua da Palma with Rua de São Lázaro, which Pessoa mentions in a letter to Geraldo Coelho de Jesus (10/08/1919). Also, Havaneza de São Pedro de Alcântara, at Rua de São Pedro de Alcântara, 47, Oeiras, which sold tickets for the village of Sintra and Águas de Caneças, as well as stearin candles, which, unlike the regular ones, didn't produce smoke and smelled less of burnt lard. There was also Havaneza do São Carlos, Havaneza de Belém, Havaneza Central de Coimbra, Havaneza Áurea and Havaneza Bocage (in Setúbal).

Other than those, there was also Havaneza dos Retroseiros, founded in the latter end of the 19th century. It was right in front of the offices of Casa Moitinho de Almeida, at the corner of the then-called Rua dos Retroseiros, 63/65. "Across the street, as a real thing outside", as he recalls in the verses.

'Retrosaria' is the Portuguese word for 'haberdashery', and it was in that street that most such establishments gathered in downtown Lisbon; formerly, it had been Rua d'El-Rei and Rua da Madalena, and, after Rua dos Retroseiros, it finally settled on Rua da Conceição. Currently, the building hosts Peleira Pampas, a purveyor of furs, mainly Argentinian. Due to changes in the city's geography, said shop no longer has one of its sides turned towards Rua da Prata, and has only one door at number 63 at Rua da Conceição. According to 1900's Almanaque Palhares, Havaneza dos Retroseiros was defined as a purveyor of medicinal and imported tobaccoes, newspapers, lottery tickets, and assorted articles appropriate for smokers; its phone number was 21.004, according to the Lista dos Assinantes da Companhia of 1930. Its owner at the turn of the century was Manuel Alves Rodrigues – a slender gentleman with an upturned moustache, a goatee and hair parted at the middle, as was fashionable at the time. He wore a gummed collar with rounded tips and a Lavalliére bow-tie. In 1922 (according to the Anuário Comercial de Portugal), with Alves Rodrigues' death, the shop became owned by another Manuel, this one Gonçalves da Silva. That is the titular "Tobacco Shop".

At Casa Moitinho de Almeida, Pessoa typed his poems at night, after having finished his translation work. This information comes from poet Luís Pedro Moitinho de Almeida, who would comment on the verses in the morning with their author. On the first floor of the building, he had a room all to himself. A garret, in his own words: "I am, and may always be, the one in the garret; even if I don't live in one", as he lived at Rua Coelho da Rocha. And from his office's window, as I was able to ascertain, one can indeed see the building in which said Havaneza dos Retroseiros was found. The definitive piece of evidence comes from an untitled poem by Pessoa, which begins with the following verses:

> A cross at the tobacco shop's door!
> Who died? Alves himself? To the
> Devil with the well-being he outwardly showed.
> Since yesterday, the city has changed.
>
> Who was he? He was the one I saw
> Every day I say him.
> (…)
> He was the tobacco shop's owner
> A landmark of who I truly am.
>
> *Untitled* (14/10/1930), Álvaro de Campos

The poem's Alves is, naturally, Manuel Alves Rodrigues, the shop's former owner. We don't know if Pessoa already knew of his passing at the time of the writing of "Tobacco Shop", but it would hardly have been a surprise for him, as he always refers to him as "the pale tobacco shop owner". In the real world, the "cross at the tobacco shop's door" likely referred to an employee who always served Pessoa. Bernardo Soares tells us that it was the cashier, who "with crooked coat and all, was in a certain way the whole of humanity". He would later confess: "When I was told yesterday that the employee of the tobacco shop had committed suicide, it seemed like a lie. Poor man, he also existed! We had forgotten this, all of us, all who knew him in the same way as all those who never met him. Tomorrow we'll forget him even better. But he evidently had a soul, for he killed himself. Passion? Anxiety? No doubt... But for me, as for all humanity, there's only the memory of a dumb smile and a shabby sports coat that hung unevenly from the shoulders. That's all that remains to me of this man who felt so much that he killed himself for feeling, since what else does one kill oneself for? Once, as I was buying cigarettes from him, it occurred to me that he would go bald early. As it turns out, he didn't have enough time to go bald".

Tobacco Shop Characters

Five characters are mentioned in the poem. Other than Pessoa, whose traits are listed in almost every verse – his love of drinking, his fear of going mad, cigarette, dreams, anxieties. The first of those five characters can be found in the following verses:

> (Eat chocolates, little girl:
> Eat chocolates!
> See, there are no other metaphysics in the world beside chocolates.)

Said "little girl" is his niece Manuela Nogueira. As she told me herself, *the milk shop I bought chocolates at with the coins uncle Fernando gave me was about two buildings after number 16 of Rua Coelho da Rocha, perhaps number 10 or 12. The owner was Mr. Trindade, I remember it as if were yesterday.* The address was Rua Coelho da Rocha, 2/4, at the corner of Rua Silva Carvalho, 13/15, some 50 metres away from Pessoa's building. His niece could go buy chocolates without having to cross any street. And Júlio Trindade wasn't the owner, but only an employee. The second character is in the following verses:

> But the owner of the Tobacco Shop came to the door and stayed there.
> I look at him with the discomfort of a misturned neck
> And the discomfort of a misunderstanding soul.

As established, the owner was Manuel Ribeiro Alves. Two other characters follow:

(Maybe I'd be happy
If I married my washerwoman's daughter.)

Washerwomen can be found in some of Pessoa's poems. Such as in this one, from 15/09/1933: *The washerwoman at the washhouse/ Smacking clothes against solid stone/ Sings because she sings and is sad/ Because she sings, because she exists/ So she is happy as well.* His washerwoman at the time was Irene, and her daughter was Guiomar. Pessoa did ponder marrying her, during the two phases of his relationship with Ophelia Queiroz. That secret passion of his is explained by a fun story which begins when friend Thomás d'Almeida asks him to register his daughter with the name of *Múcia Leonor,* but Pessoa recorded it as *Múcia Guiomar d'Almeida*. The same name of the later Guiomar, who would almost change his life. Before that, in 1916, the spirits of heteronyms More and Wardour had also suggested that the woman he would fall in love with would be a governess – a description far more apt for Guiomar than Ophelia. And, in *The Education of the Stoic,* he confesses: "Once I had the chance to marry a simple girl who could perhaps have made me happy, but between me and her, in my soul's indecision, stood fourteen generations of barons", and "that soft and sad moment marks the beginning of my suicide".

The man came out of the Tobacco Shop (stuffing change into his pants' pocket?).
Hey, I know him: it's Esteves, who is without metaphysics.
(The Owner of the Tobacco Shop came to the door.)
As if by divine instinct, Esteves turned and saw me.
He waved goodbye, I shouted *So long, Esteves!*

Pessoa doesn't mention that Esteves in any other writing. The sole possible reference is in fragment 481 of *Disquiet,* in which he mentions "a rounded, ruddy old man, smoking a cigar at the tobacco shop's entrance". Perhaps it was him. It is not an unreasonable assumption, as in that very fragment, right after mentioning the "old man", he immediately recalls "the pale owner of the tobacco shop" – and, as Soares, finishes with "what has become of all those who, as I saw and saw them again, became a part of my life?". Two characters which are coincidentally together both in the poem and in the following two lines of *Disquiet:* "Esteves, who is without metaphysics" and "the owner of the tobacco shop". The problem is that there was no Esteves among his friends, nor any important artist of politician in Lisbon with that name. In search of a character he might be referring to, three names should be taken into account, as they were of (some) renown in Lisbon at the time: João Manuel Esteves Pereira (born in 1872), a public servant who, alongside Guilherme Rodrigues, wrote the *Dicionário de Portugal* and was a student at the Instituto Superior de

Letras, much like Pessoa. Francisco Romano Esteves (born in 1882) was a painter, an organizer of Casino Estoril's art salons and a director at Lisbon's Sociedade Nacional de Belas-Artes. And Raul Augusto Esteves (born in 1878), an army officer who fought in Flanders during World War I, held a measure of influence on the Movement of the 28th of May 1926 and was the target of an assassination attempt at the end of the First Republic.

But all three names can be safely discarded, as Pessoa had a very peculiar way of writing. Each and every reference he uses in poems and assorted writings stem from his personal life or the works he read; he would never use a random name, or that of someone unknown to him, in a poem which he felt was going to be immortal. I actually imagined it might be a wordplay of sorts, but, at length, decided to look for one who might have been part of his life. And I concluded it could only have been Joaquim Esteves, a neighbour of his at Rua Coelho da Rocha who lived almost next door, at Rua Saraiva de Carvalho, 200. One of those ciphers whose paths we cross in life without realizing it. Ergo, "without metaphysics". But close enough to the family that, at his request, he was the declarant of Pessoa's death certificate – number 1.609 at Lisbon's 7th Registry Office.

The death of Campos

After an initial profusion of texts, Campos goes silent. "Opiary" was written on the 1st of March 1914; "Triumphal Ode" on June 1914; "Two Ode Excerpts" on the 30th of June 1914; the monumental "Maritime Ode" in 1915; "Salutation to Walt Whitman" on the 11th of June 1915. All came from that first phase of his. Because *Álvaro de Campos is Álvaro de Campos only from March 1914 to the end of 1915,* according to Gaspar Simões. He then slowly matures. Caeiro is dead. Reis travels to Brazil. Campos is the only Pessoa consents he accompany him throughout his life. He resumes writing in 1922, but by then it is no longer Campos writing, but Pessoa himself. In the end, all we have is a tired, disheartened man. "To the devil with you, without me, or leave me alone with the devil!". The heteronym writes his own epitaph: "Here lies Álvaro de Campos; the rest can be found in the Greek Anthology". In *Mente-me: diz-me a verdade,* Adolfo Camilo Diaz mentions an alleged murder of Campos, in which he was *tremendously mutilated by a saw.* The murder suspect was Pessoa, covered up by Ophelia Queiroz, but then the victim turned out to be one Esteban Gracieli. In his novel *The Last Days of Fernando Pessoa,* Antonio Tabucchi imagines Campos visiting the poet at the hospital. *What time is it?, Pessoa asked. Almost midnight, Campos replied, the best hour to meet you, the hour of ghosts.* In that encounter, which would be their last, both share all their secrets. In the end, Campos told Pessoa: *I will not survive, I will go with you.* And so it was.

Selected texts

TOBACCO SHOP

I'm nothing.
I'll never be anything.
I can't wish I were anything[15].
Even so, I have all the dreams of the world in me.
Windows of my room,
Of my room, one of the millions in the world no one knows who owns
(And if they knew, what would they know?),
You open onto the mystery of a street crossed constantly by people,
Onto a street inaccessible to all thought,
Real, impossibly real, certain, unknowably certain,
With the mystery of things beneath stones and beings,
With death putting moisture on walls and grey hairs on men,
With Destiny driving the cart of everything down the road of nothing.
Today I'm vanquished, as if I knew the truth.
Today I'm lucid, as if I were about to die,
And had no more brotherhood with things
Than in a farewell turning that house and that side of the street
Into a row of coaches, a conductor's whistle
From inside my head[16],
A jolt of nerves and creaking bones in departure.

Today I'm perplexed, like someone who's thought and discovered and lost.
Today I'm divided between the loyalty I owe
The Tobacco Shop across the street, as a real thing outside,
And the feeling that everything's a dream, as a real thing inside.

I've failed in everything.
Since I've proposed nothing, maybe everything was nothing.
The learning they gave me,
I used it to sneak out the back window.
I went to the country with grand intentions,
But all I found there were grass and trees,
And when there were people, they were the same as the others.
I leave the window, sit in a chair. What should I think?
How do I know what I'll be, when I don't even know what I am?
Should I be what I think? But I think about being so many things!

---

15 A recurring theme in Pessoa's oeuvre. Álvaro de Campos: "No: I want nothing. I have already said: I want nothing" (Lisbon Revisited, 1923); Ricardo Reis: "Nothing comes of nothing. We are nothing" (Ode, 28/09/1923); Fernando Pessoa: "I am nothing, I can do nothing, I know nothing" (Untitled poem from 06/01/1923). As well as *Message,* which begins with "I was not anyone".

16 A reference to his mental state. He repeats that very image in a number of other texts and even in letters to his friends. A letter to Mário Beirão (01/02/1913) contains almost the same words: "You can hardly imagine what manner of Rua do Arsenal, pertaining to bustling activity, my poor head has been as of late".

And there are so many thinking they're the same thing–they can't all be!?
Genius? At this moment
A hundred thousand minds like mine dream themselves geniuses like me[17],
And history won't remember, who knows?, not even one,
Nor will there be anything but the midden of future conquests.
No, I don't believe in myself.
In every asylum there are so many nut-cases with so many certainties!
I, who have no certainties, am I more right or less right?
No, not even in myself.
In how many of the world's garrets and non-garrets
Are there dreaming at this hour how many geniuses-unto-themselves?
So many high and noble and lucid aspirations–
Yes, truly high and noble and lucid–
Who knows if they're plausible–
Will they ever find the light of day, the ears of people?
The world is for those who were born to conquer,
Not for those who dream they can conquer it, even if they're right.
I've dreamed more than Napoleon accomplished.
I've clasped to my hypothetical breast more humanity than Christ ever did.
I've made more philosophies in secret than Kant ever wrote.
But I am, and may always be, the one in the garret,
Even if I don't live in one;
I'll always be he wasn't born for this;
I'll always only be oh, but he had such qualities;
I'll always be the one who waited for someone to open the door at the foot of a doorless wall,
Who sang a ditty of the Infinite in an overgrown field,
Who heard the voice of God in a closed-up well.
Do I believe in myself? No, nor in anything else.
Let Nature pour over my ardent head
Its sun, its rain, the wind that finds my hair
And let the rest come if it comes, or is to come, or doesn't come.
Cardiac slaves of the stars,
We conquer everything before we get out of bed;
But we wake up and it's opaque,
We get up and it's alien,
We go out and it's the entire world,
And then the solar system and then the Milky Way and then the Indefinite.

(Eat chocolates, little girl:
Eat chocolates!
See, there are no other metaphysics in the world beside chocolates.
See, all religions teach no more than a candy store.
Eat, dirty girl, eat!

---

17 The same idea is reproduced in *Disquiet:* "Am I institutionalized in an asylum of vagrancy, happy for utter defeat, amidst the rabble of those who thought themselves geniuses but were nothing but beggars with dreams".

If only I could eat chocolates as truthfully as you do!
But I think and, tearing the silver paper, which is really only tin foil,
I drop everything on the ground, as I've dropped my life.)

But at least there remains from the sorrow of what I'll never be,
The rapid calligraphy of these verses,
Portico leading into the Impossible.
At least I consecrate to myself a tearless contempt,
At least I'm noble in the grand gesture with which I toss
The dirty clothing I am, without a laundry-list, into the course of things,
And stay home without a shirt[18].

(You, who console, who do not exist and so console,
Whether Greek goddess, conceived as a statue come to life,
Or Roman patrician, impossibly noble and malignant,
Princess of troubadours, most gentle and colourful,
Marquise of the eighteenth century, décolletée and distant,

Or celebrated coquette of our parent's time,
Or something else modern–I don't know quite what–
All of it, whatever it might be, be it, and let it inspire me if it can!
My heart is an overturned bucket.
As those who invoke spirits[19] I invoke
Me to myself and encounter nothing.
I go to the window and see the street with absolute clarity.
I see the shops, I see the sidewalks, I see the cars pass by,
I see the clothed living entities who cross.
I see the dogs which also exist,
And all of it weighs upon me like a curse of banishment,
And all of it is foreign, as is everything.)

I lived, I studied, I loved, I even believed,
And today there's no beggar I don't envy solely because he's not me.
I see his tatters and his sores and his lies,
And I think: maybe you've never lived, studied, loved, and believed
(Because it's possible to make reality of all this without making anything of all this);
Maybe you've hardly existed, like a lizard with its tail cut off,
The tail squirming just short of the lizard.
I've made of myself what I haven't known,
And what I could have made of myself I didn't.
The masquerade I wore was wrong.
They believed the mask; I didn't contradict them, and lost myself.
When I wanted to take off the mask,

18 Certainly a metaphor, as Pessoa was never at home without a shirt on.
19 Remembrance of the nights at aunt Anica's, when Pessoa lived there, when they would summon spirits with a board. More on that later.

It was stuck to my face.
When I finally got it off and looked in the mirror,
I'd already aged[20].
I was drunk, I didn't know how to put on a mask I hadn't even taken off.
I threw away the mask and slept in the cloakroom
Like a dog tolerated by the management
For not making trouble
And I'm going to write it all down to prove I am sublime.
Musical essence of my useless verses,
If only I could encounter you as something I'd made,
And not remain always in front of the Tobacco Shop in front of me,
Crushing underfoot the awareness of existing and existing,
Like a rug a drunkard stumbles on,
Or a doormat the gypsies stole, even though it was worthless.
But the owner of the Tobacco Shop came to the door and stayed there.
I look at him with the discomfort of a misturned neck
And the discomfort of a misunderstanding soul.
He will die and I will die.
He'll leave his sign behind, I'll leave my verses.
At a certain point his sign will die, and my verses will die.
After that, the street where his sign was will die[21],
And the language in which I had written my verses.
Then the turning planet, where all of this took place, will die.
On other satellites in other systems something like people
Will continue making things like verses and living under things like signs,
Always one thing across from the other,
Always one thing just as useless as the other,
Always the impossible just as stupid as the real,
Always the mystery of the depths just as certain as the dream of the mystery of the surface,
Always this thing or that thing or neither one thing nor another.
But a man went into the Tobacco Shop (to buy tobacco?),
And plausible reality suddenly falls on top of me.
I start up energetic, convinced, human,
And plan to write these lines wherein I say the contrary.

I light a cigarette while thinking about writing them
And the cigarette tastes like liberation from all thought.
I follow the smoke like a path all its own,
And enjoy, in a moment both sensitive and competent,
The freeing of all my speculations
And the awareness that metaphysics is a consequence of being cranky.

---

20 Perhaps an allusion to Dorian Gray. Here, due to the mask reference above it, it is likely an allusion to Portuguese masquerades, in which people asked passers-by in the streets *who am I?,* and would then take off their masks.

21 A very similar structure can be found in *Disquiet:* "Tomorrow, so too will I – the soul that thinks and feels, the universe I am to myself – yes, tomorrow so too will I be that which no longer crosses these streets, who others will vaguely evoke with a *whatever became of him?"*

Then I sit back in the chair
And continue smoking.
While Destiny grants it me, I'll continue to smoke.

(Maybe I'd be happy
If I married my washerwoman's daughter.)
That sinks in. I get out of the chair. I go to the window.

The man came out of the Tobacco Shop (stuffing change into his pants pocket?).
Hey, I know him: it's Esteves, who is without metaphysics.
(The Owner of the Tobacco Shop came to the door.)
As if by divine instinct, Esteves turned and saw me.
He waved goodbye, I shouted So long, Esteves!, and the universe
Reconstructed itself to me with neither ideal nor hope, and the Owner of the Tobacco Shop smiled.

POEM IN A STRAIGHT LINE

I never knew a soul who ever took a licking.
My friends have all been champions at everything.

And I, so often vulgar, so often obscene, so often vile,
I, so deliberately parasitical,
Unforgivably filthy,
I, so often without patience to take a bath,
I, who've been so ridiculous, so absurd,
Tripping up in public on the carpet of etiquette,
I, so grotesque and mean, submissive and insolent,
Who've been insulted and not said a word,
And when putting a word in growing still more ridiculous,
I who strike chambermaids as laughable,
I who feel porters wink sarcastically,
I who've been scandalous about money, borrowing and not paying it back,
I, who when the time came to fight, ducked
As far as I could out of punching range,
I who go into a sweat over the slightest thing –
I'm convinced no one's better than I at this sort of game.

No one I know, none of my speaking acquaintances,
Ever acted ridiculous, ever took insults,
Was ever anything but noble – yes, all of them princes, living their lives,
How I'd love to hear a human voice, from any one of them.
Confessing not to sins but to infamies,
Speaking not of violent but of cowardly acts!
But no, each one's a Paragon, to hear them tell it.
Is there no one in this world who'd confess to me he's been vile just once?
All you princes, my brothers,

Enough – I'm fed up with demigods!
Where are the real people in this world?

Am I the only scoundrel and bungler alive?

Maybe women don't always fall for them.
Maybe they've been betrayed. But ridiculous? Never!
And I, who've been ridiculous but never betrayed,
How do I speak before their Highnesses without stammering?
I, who've been vile, literally vile,
Vile in the meanest and rottenest possible sense of the word.

Ne Jupiter quidem omnibus placet
(Not even Jupiter can please all) Theognis

ALEXANDER SEARCH

The eagle said
'Can I fly?'
Moments, Alexander Search

Who is Search?

William Alexander Search was born during Pessoa's time in South Africa and wrote regularly, almost always in English, at least for two years after his return to Lisbon. The character was inspired by the crime novels of Arthur Morrison, Austin Freeman, Baroness Orczy, Conan Doyle "and others", chief among which American novelist Edgar Allan Poe. Pessoa was a member of Collins Crime and of The Albatross Crime Club, two English book clubs which provided genre novels to their members as soon as they were published. In a business card he printed, under the name *Alexander Search,* we have *Lisbon* at the left and *Rua da Bela Vista (Lapa), 17, 1°* – where Pessoa lived at the time. Search was "born on the 13th of June 1888, in Lisbon", same as Pessoa, and died on the 4th of February 1908. His *signature,* repeatedly trained, can be seen in 18 of the books that were found on Pessoa's bookshelf, at Rua Coelho da Rocha. Search wrote prose texts characterized by "a mystical, delirious ardour"; such as one in which he hailed the Regicide[1], claiming that power took "three shapes – strength, authority and opinion". Many are dialogues – with Pessoa, with friends (real or imaginary, with God. He wrote a diary, heralding Bernardo Soares, and short stories, the sole finished one was "A Very Original Dinner", which Pessoa defines as "the tale of a madman". Hardly surprising, coming from him. Dated June 1907, it begins with "someone's quote": *Tell me what you eat: I will tell you what you are*[2]. It would be his first detective story. Others followed, all of them left unfinished. He also wrote poems, and some

1 The murder of king Carlos I, on the 1st of February 1908. The episode is known thus because no other king had ever been murdered in Portugal.
2 Jean-Anthelme Brillat-Savarin (1755-1826), judge and gourmand, exiled in Switzerland who then made a living teaching French, playing the violin and cooking. The quote is from his *The*

were originally conceived for other heteronyms (such as Charles Robert Anon) but were attributed to him, such as this fun little sonnet:

ON AN ANKLE

A sonnet bearing the imprimatur of the inquisitor-general and other people of distinction and decency

Offered, but not dedicated to A.T.R.[3]

I had a revelation not from high.
But from below, when thy skirt awhile lifted
Betrayed such promise that I am not gifted
With words that may that view well signify.

And even if my verse that thing would try,
Hard were it, if that work came to be sifted,
To find a word that rude would not have shifted
There from the cold hand of Morality.

To gaze is nought; mere sight no mind hath wrecked.
But oh! sweet lady, beyond what is seen
What things may guess or hint at Disrespect?!

Sacred is not the beauty of a queen…
I from thine ankle did as much suspect
As you from this may suspect what I mean.

A pact with the Devil

His most renowned text is the peculiar *Pact With the Devil.* Perhaps inspired by Teixeira de Pascoaes – which begins his *Regresso ao Paraíso* with the following: *Satan consumes the fire of his days.* Perhaps inspired by a short story by Eça de Queiroz, who mentions a deal with the devil made by Saint Friar Gil. Or perhaps he was just being topical and following the lead of writers who were popular at the time, such as Goethe, Vigny or Beaudelaire, who wrote *The Flowers of Evil.* In that pact, Pessoa, who had previously considered Satan "a spirit of evil", now describes him as one who does good. In a note, he considers "the Devil as God's spirit" who rises against he who created an imperfect world, the "proud and anything but sober Jehovah"; he also hailed the "Satanic Trinity", which was "the World, the Flesh and the Devil". He acknowledges that "concerning

Physiology of Taste, published on the 8th of December 1825. Pessoa likely omitted his name just out of his passion for a good mystery.

3 His friend Alexandre Teixeira Rebelo.

the Devil, never did a Portuguese truly believe in him, emotion wouldn't allow for it"; and so he now conceives of another, delicate and generous, who says: "I am truly the Devil, and thus I do no harm". It is a character which has ever tormented Pessoa. In a short story by Search, "The Hour of the Devil"[4], a pregnant lady called Maria (like Pessoa's mother) dances in a carnival ball with a man dressed as Mephistopheles. Later, she returns home and has a "most interesting conversation" with the Devil – who leaves a message for her unborn son, which he foretells as "a poet gifted with genius" (Pessoa himself, probably): "Lady, do not be frightened. I truly am the Devil, and thus I do no harm. Do not fear me, and to not be startled. Certain pretenders of mine, on Earth and above it, are dangerous, much like all plagiarisms… Shakespeare, who I have at times inspired, forced me to take oaths" and "said I was a gentleman". After that, he further elaborates: "Yes, I do corrupt, because I stimulate the imagination. But God is worse". And he finishes with the following, uttered by a shadow: "Do you truly know what I feel? I feel tremendously sorry for you". According to Gnosticism, Satan is also the *serpent;* or, in hermetic traditions, *Saturn* – a spirit of light. But, in *Pact With the Devil,* he is Jacob – and let us not forget Pessoa considers himself half-jewish.

> Pact made between Alexander Search, from Hell, from Parts Unknown, with Jacob Satan, Master although not king, of the very same place.
>
> 1. Never to give up or to abstain from the purpose of doing good for Mankind.
>
> 2. Never to write anything, sensual or otherwise detrimental, which is evil and does harm to those who read it.
>
> 3. Never to forget, when attacking religion in the name of truth, that religion cannot be replaced, and that poor Man weeps in the dark.
>
> 4. Never to forget the suffering and ailments of men.
>
> † Satan
His brand
>
> 2nd of October 1907
Alexander Search

The Role of Search

Despite his writings, he remains a mysterious figure among the other heteronyms. Pessoa held him in special esteem; proof of which is the fact that all of his manuscripts in the Chest were carefully and neatly written down. And it certainly wasn't by chance that Pessoa wrote the first lines of his *Faust* in the

4 His drafts showed an alternative title: *Devil's night,* at times written in Portuguese *(Noite do Diabo).*

very same year he began to say goodbye to Search, 1908; or that he pondered compiling his writings in a book which would be titled *Documents of Mental Decadence* – which hardly comes as a surprise from one who considers himself mentally ill, "with a confused imagination", "a victim of the ineffable schism between thinking and feeling", "solitary", "miserable and mean". Someone for whom "thinking and writing has ever been a scourge and a misfortune". The heteronym himself confesses: "Here lies a poet who was mad and young". In "Agony", it reads: "Oh God, let me not fall insane!" – which makes sense, as both the heteronym and Pessoa lived in a constant fear of madness. Search, in 1906-1908, wrote a series of poems on the matter, such as this one:

Weep for the ruin of my mind
Weep rather, child, that things so deep should move me
To lose the clear thoughts that could prove me
One worthy of mankind.

Flashes of Madness IV, Alexander Search

The death of Search

Pessoa claimed Search had one "task: Everything which isn't under the purview of the other three" (Caeiro, Reis, Campos). In spite of that, he ended up abandoned. Deep down, Search disappeared because he was no longer necessary to one who already returned to his country, his people and his language. But he doesn't fully abandon him. Around 1911, he scribbles a poem in Portuguese, and still writes the odd one in English, with his last one published in *Contemporânea* magazine (1923). He also co-signed "Poèmes Intersectionistes" with Sá-Carneiro for *Europa* #1. In French! To himself, he wrote two epitaphs. One of them generic, in which he considers himself "a poet of the world who had no joy nor peace in life", and another, which was rather more specific:

Here lieth A[lexander] S[earch]
Whom God and man left in the lurch
And nature mocked with pain and woe
He believed not in state or church
Nor in God, woman, man or love
Nor earth below nor heaven above.
His knowledge did to this about:
(…) and love is not
Nothing is everywhere sincere
Save sorrow, hatred, lust and fear

Epitaph, Alexander Search

Selected texts

SOUVENIR

How sweetly sad it is sometimes to hear
Some old loved sound to memory recalled,
To see, an if in dreams, some old dear face,
Some landscape's stretch, some field, some dale,
some stream
A memory so sudden, sad and pleasant,
Aught that recalls the days of happy youth.
Then spring in happy pain the tears that wait,
Those subtle tears that wait on thought, and all -
Field stream and voice – all that we hear or see -
Goes from the sense, adorned with mem'ry's hand
And merges slowly into dreamy light.
I wake; alas! by dreams I was betrayed.
'Tis but a semblance that I feel and hear
Because the past, alas! cannot return.
These fields are not the fields I knew, these sounds
Are not the sounds I knew: all those are gone,
And all the past – alas! cannot return.

BLIND EAGLE

What is thy name? and is it true that thou
A land unknown of men inhabitest?
What pain obscure is figured on thy brow?
What cares upon thy heart contrive their nest?
Of human things the purest and the best
No constant beauty doth thy soul allow;
And through the world thou bear'st thy deep unrest
Lock'd in a smile thine eyes do disavow.

Being of wild and weird imaginings,
Whose thoughts are greater than mere things can bind,
What is the thing thou seekest within things?

What is that thought thy thinking cannot find?
For what high air has thy strong spirit wings?
To what high vision aches it to be blind?

BUILD ME A COTTAGE

Build me a cottage deep
In a forest, a simple, silent home,
Like a breath in a sleep,

Where all wish maybe never to roam
And a pleasure all smallness may keep.

A palace high then build,
With confusion of lights and of rooms,
A strange sense to yield,
Whither my desire from the cottage's glooms
May go, to return, unfulfilled.

Then dig me a grave,
That what cottage nor palace can give
I at length may have,
That the weariness of all ways to live
May cease like the last of a wave.

SONG OF DIRT

Come, let us speak of dirt!
God's curse is on our head.
Let our lips irreverence blurt!
We are sufferers all; let us, instead
Of prayer, offer God the sacrifice
Of our minds that he curst with crime and vice,
Of our frames that diseases make dread!

Let us offer the tyrant of all,
To hang in the hall of his palace of pain,
A funeral pall,
And a bride's white dress with a stain,
And a widow's weeds, and the crumpled sheets
From the bed of the wife.
Let them be symbols of human strife!
Give we God the dirt of the streets
Of our spirit, made mud with our tears,
The dust of our joys, the mire of our fears,
And the rot of our life!

Omnia fui, nihil expedit
(I was all. It availed me naught[1]) Severus

BERNARDO SOARES

My soul is impatient with itself, as with a bothersome child; its restlessness keeps growing and is forever the same.
Book of Disquiet, fragment 10, Bernardo Soares

Who is Soares?

Bernardo Soares is a "semi-heteronym" who "appears whenever I feel tired or sleepy" (letter to Casais Monteiro, 13/01/1935). In his last year of life, he claims "although he doesn't have my personality, it is, not differently than mine, a simple mutilation thereof". "A literary personality", as he admits in a letter to Gaspar Simões (28/07/1932). *Ber-nár-do,* Nelly Novaes Coelho suggests, *has the same rhythmical and sonorous flux of Fer-nán-do;* and *Soares* was, according to her, much like an anagram of *Pessoa* – with the R exchanged for the P. Bernardo is also the name of a sentry in Shakespeare's *Hamlet,* a work Pessoa had always been fascinated by. The heteronym gains a semblance of life, with no dates of birth or death; neither is his story original. His cultural influences are French, reflecting the upbringing *dona* Maria had given Pessoa, and he loses his mother at the age of 1. "All that is dispersed and useless in my sensibility stems from the absence of that warmth and the useless longing for the kisses I cannot recall". At the age of 3, his father kills himself, "I never knew him". In both cases, Pessoa draws parallels between them: the loss of his father when he was 5, and of his mother, who chose another man, her second husband, over him. "You who hear me and barely listen, you know not what such tragedy is like! To lose one's father and mother".

Much like Pessoa, he smokes "cheap cigarettes", suffers from insomnia and almost has the same profession, taking care of mercantile bookkeeping in trading houses. And he even makes a comment about (José Joaquim) Cesário Verde (1855-1886) which could just as easily have been said about Pessoa and Soares: "When Cesário Verde told the doctor that he wasn't Mr. Verde who

1 Pessoa quoted the same sentence in *Book of Disquiet,* without naming the author.

worked in commerce, but rather the poet Cesário Verde, he made use of one of those verbalities of useless pride which drip with the scent of vanity. What the poor bastard had ever been was Mr. Verde, who worked in commerce". All things considered, "I do not believe I will ever cease to be an assistant bookkeeper. I truly wish, with a fierce sincerity, to never be anything more than an assistant bookkeeper". A profession for those bereft of ambition. Or hope. "What use to dream of princesses, rather than the office's front door?".

The office he works in

Soares worked in a fabric warehouse, where he fills up the products' prices, "hunched over the book I write on, the useless story of an obscure firm". Said firm was Casa Vasques & Cia., the "cheapest heights for an assistant bookkeeper", actually Casa Moitinho de Almeida (where Pessoa worked at). From there, looking out of one of the four windows, he beholds "the blonde sheen of the golden moonlight". *It was what he saw from the balcony of his father's office, which oversaw Rua da Prata,* according to the son of the company's owner, Luís Pedro Moitinho de Almeida. "I am alone at the office", says Soares. *That was because his father gave him a key,* explains Luís Pedro; sometimes, he spends the entire night on his boss' typewriter, at the time of Rua Coelho da Rocha, when he didn't have his own. In one large office room, aligned across two rows, employees pack shipments. In it, "people who habitually surround me, the souls who know me through conversation and daily contact without knowing me at all – they're the ones who cause a salivary knot of physical disgust to form in my throat. It's the sordid monotony of their lives, outwardly parallel to my own, and their keen awareness that I'm their fellow man – that is what dresses me in a convict's clothes, places me in a jail cell, and makes me apocryphal and beggarly"; and "I then wonder how it is I survive myself, how I dare have the cowardice of being here, among these people".

> Invoices are made by people
> Who have loves, hates, passions, politics, crimes at times
> And are so well written, so much to the point, so independent of all this!
> There are some who look at an invoice and do not feel this.
>
> *Maritime Ode*, Álvaro de Campos

The characters he socializes with are gradually introduced in *Disquiet.* "Vasques my boss is Life – monotonous and necessary, imperious and inscrutable Life. This banal man represents the banality of Life. For me he is everything,externally speaking, because for me Life is whatever is external". "Medium height, stocky, a bit coarse but affectionate, frank and savvy, brusque and affable", "pleasant, hard face, firm stare", "stiff moustache", "his jokes always inappropriate and his soul outside the universe as a whole". "We all have a Vasques who's the boss – visible for some of us, invisible for others". In real life, said boss was Carlos Eugénio Moitinho de Almeida. *Vasques the boss is my father,* Luís Pedro confirms. Little by little, details of his daily life emerge. Such as when he remembers that his boss "closed a deal that brought a sick man and his family to ruin. *I feel sorry for the fellow,* he told me. *He's going to wind up destitute.* But his boss "isn't a crook; he's a man of action". "Mr. Vasques is like all men of action, be they business leaders, industrialists, politicians, military commanders, social and religious idealists, great poets, great artists". Despite that description, he holds his boss in high esteem. "I already remember him in the future with the nostalgia I know I'm bound to feel"[2].

Bookkeeper Moreira, the one who hands him his direct orders, is "the essence of monotonous constancy". "When I see the face of Moreira it's as if I had finally docked at a port". But, "when all is said and done, I prefer Moreira to the astral world; I prefer reality to truth". Another employee, Sérgio, takes care of shipments and marks down "the numbers of the rail-road vouchers". Cashier Borges always asks for his blotter. "They all have boxes before them", "even if it's the woman they married". Vieira, the travelling salesman, is "a happy lad who holds rosary beads to his heart". The other travelling salesman, Sousa, is much younger, "ordinary in his singularity"; and António, the office boy, is "the errand boy". "If I were to write down the literary influences my spirit is owed to, I would be remiss in not mentioning Mr. Vasques, bookkeeper Moreira, travelling salesman Vieira and errand boy António". Two of them worked at Casa Moitinho: António and Vieira. With those very same roles. The others came from other places he worked for, especially, I believe, *Palhares, Almeida e Silva Ltd.,* at Rua dos Fanqueiros, 44, 1st floor, but couldn't check, as Lisbon's Registry Office no longer has the record books of those companies. Luís Pedro recalls how Pessoa would read him out loud some excerpts of what he'd written the night before. One day, as he heard their names, António looked at Vieira (the real ones from Casa Moitinho) and said that Pessoa *was writing a book with us as the characters.* Other than his work colleagues at Casa Vasques, there was also a "gentle cat", "which stares at me with eyes full of life". Not "a cat toying with pleasure", nor like those that "rub themselves against my legs and feel as unto tigers during sex". In an anthology organized by Carl von Vechten, *The tiger in the house,* there is an epigraph by Fernand Méry evoking a similar image: *God created cats to give Man the pleasure of petting tigers.* But the one from Casa Vasques was likely just a common cat[3].

---

2 It was not to be in real life. Soares/Pessoa died well before boss Vasques/Moitinho de Almeida.

3 The inspiration for those verses might have come from Apollinaire's "Le Chat", which goes: *In my house I want:/ A reasonable woman,/ A cat passing among the books,/ And friends in every*

O cat playing in the street
As if it were in bed,
How I envy your luck
As it cannot even be called that.
(…)

You are happy because that's what you are
The whole nothing you are is yours.
I see myself and I am without myself,
I know myself, and I am not myself.

Untitled (January 1931), Fernando Pessoa

Rua dos Douradores

"How many Caesars have I been at Rua dos Douradores". The office of Casa Vasques is in that street, which "contains the meaning of everything", "the whole of humanity", "the answer to all riddles, except for the riddle of why riddles exist". It is there that, without any remorse, he consumes his existence. "If I had the world in my hand, I would surely exchange it for a ticket to the Rua dos Douradores". The choice of that street for the offices of Casa Vasques is (likely) owed to Casa Pessoa – a canteen where he regularly had lunch, and where he met Soares. Or because he had worked there, at F.A. Gouveia (number 126, 1st floor), the predecessor of Gouveia e Carvalho Lda. Or because Eça de Queiroz had placed there the offices of *Alves e Cia.* Or maybe simply because the buildings' layout there reminded him of his first home. Nearby, at the crossing of Rua da Conceição and Rua dos Fanqueiros, there is also a church (Madalena), the tolling of which likely reminded him of that of the Church of the Martyrs, which little Fernando heard as a child. It's as if he were searching for his past. Caeiro dreamt of nature, Campos imagined new lands, Reis lived out his last days in Brazil, while Soares lived in a village of sorts, much like Pessoa, who all but confined himself to little more than a single street, stretching out from Rua da Alfândega all the way to Praça da Figueira, present in so many of his verses:

Praça da Figueira in the morning,
Whenever it is a sunny day (as it always is
in Lisbon), is something I never quite forget,
Vain memory as it may be.
There is so much more interesting

---

season,/ Whom I cannot live without. Or, more likely, from Bocage's "Os dois gatos", in which Bocage mentions a *mean, poor cat,* and ends with the following verses: *Strike down that pride/ Cantankerous creature/ You are not more noble than I;/ Just more fortunate.*

Than that logical, plebeian place,
But I do love it, even here… Do I
Know why I love it? It doesn't matter.

Untitled (October 1913)[4], Álvaro de Campos

The room he lives in

His apartment is also at Rua dos Douradores, "right after a market, the owner of which I know as people know other people". That market, the most important one in Lisbon until 1940, is that of Figueira, situated behind Rossio Square, where Rua dos Douradores meets Praça da Figueira, which is why Soares' building is farther away from the Tagus. The apartment is at a "4th floor [2nd in some texts], above infinity", much like the one Pessoa was born in. "The four walls of my poor room are simultaneously cell and distance, bed and coffin". In that "narrow", cheap room, "rented monthly, and where nothing happens", the furniture is crude and "the sun can be seen through dusty panes", all of it in accordance with "the poverty of the intermediate streets of ordinary down-town". And if "the office represents life for me", the apartment "represents Art for me. Yes, Art, residing on the very same street as Life". The room's description is different from that of Vicente Guedes, the previous author of *Disquiet.* Guedes' room, at Rua dos Retroseiros, 17, 4th floor (once again), was larger – "with two rooms", and better – "with a luxury of a kind", decorated with noble "deep armchairs" that "conserved the dignity of tedium". Almost as if Pessoa were playing out the apartment change he lived through during his childhood, exchanging the luxury of his place of birth for the simplicity of Rua de São Marcal, where he later moved to.

If I raise my eyes, I'll be confronted by the dingy row of buildings opposite, bythe grimy windows of all the down-town offices, by the incongruous windows of the upper floors where people still live, and by the eternal laundry hanging in the sun between the gables at the top, among flowerpots and plants.

The Book of Disquiet, fragment 437, Bernardo Soares

Deep down, Bernardo truly is Fernando. "I looked at the mirror in my room and saw the poor, pathetic face of an unpoor beggar; and then the mirror turned away, and the spectre of the Rua dos Douradores opened up before me". Early in the morning, he gets up and goes to work. "One of my favourite

4 Published in *Tempo Presente* magazine, in December 1959, under the title of "A somewhat old sonnet" – the title of another poem, written in 1922, which begins thus: "Look, Daisy: When I die…"

strolls, on mornings when I dread the banality of the approaching day as if I were dreading jail, is to walk slowly past the still unopened shops and stores". He arrives at the office, "sordid down to the marrow of its employees", and there he spends his normal working days, every one much like the other. His table is next to "unwashed windows", from which he can see "a joyless street", where the throws his used matches to. To him, it is "the window of my life" in "the silence of my disquiet". His paycheck is small, but enables him to "carry on". At six o'clock, "boss Vasques says you can go", he bids the other employees goodbye at "the late afternoon disquiet" and goes back home. At night, "in my quiet room, alone as I have always been, alone as I will always be", all he feels "is weariness, and the disquiet that is its twin". It is then he writes "words as if they were the soul's salvation" and gilds himself "with the impossible sunset of high and vast hills in the distance". The gilding part is an obvious reference to Rua dos Douradores, and probably to the Tagus, which had a golden sheen when he saw it from the balconies of the offices of Casa Moitinho de Almeida or the windows of his room at Largo de São Carlos at sunrise and sunset. And only those who have seen it like that can truly understand what he meant.

> Today I was struck by an absurd but valid sensation. I realized, in an inner flash, that I'm no one. Absolutely no one.
>
> *The Book of Disquiet,* fragment 262, Bernardo Soares

On the days in which there is no work to be done at work, he remains at home meditating; or walks along "the sad streets extending eastward from where the Rua da Alfândega ends (…) the Rua da Prata, the Rua dos Douradores, the Rua dos Fanqueiros". All those streets are at Lisbon's Pombaline Lower Town area. Prata and dos Fanqueiros run parallel to Rua dos Douradores, and both lead to Rua da Alfândega. "Sometimes I spend hours at the Terreiro do Paço, next to the river, meditating in vain"; or, as it reads in other writings of his, "on the riverfront", "on the waterfront", "on the wayside", "on the edge of pain". Soares too walks around Rossio, formerly known as *Ressio* or *Recio* (Commons) – "Praça do Recio", as it stands in several of his texts. It is the most important square in Lisbon. A place where all sorts of weekly fairs, bullfighting, riots, executions and *autos-de-fé* took place.

> He passed me by, came across me in a street at the Baixa
> That poorly dressed man, beggar by trade, as can be seen
> on his face,
> He sympathizes with me, as do I with him;
> And, in reciprocity, in overflowing largesse, I gave him
> all I had

(Except, of course, what was in my purse, where I carry
most money: I am not a fool, nor a Russian novelist,
Romanticism, certainly, but in measured fashion ...)

Untitled (undated), Álvaro de Campos

The beginning of The Book of Disquiet

The first reference to *Disquiet* is a note titled *Rumor ou Desassossego,* dated 1910. Two years later, in his correspondence with Sá-Carneiro, he already has a project in mind. Paper 380 of the Chest reads: "Book of Disquiet: 1) Peristyle (13 excerpts), 2) Dance, 3) Last Swan, 4) Weaver, 5) Charm, 6) Apotheosis (or Epiphany) of the absurdity (of lying), 7) Morn, End". In 1913, signed by Pessoa himself, a fragment titled "Na floresta do alheamento" (In the forest of obliviousness) in *A Águia* magazine, identified as *from The Book of Disquiet, in preparation.* In 1914, he still harbours the notion of crediting "that sick production" with his own name, but it would quickly become *The Book of Disquiet, written by one calling himself Vicente Guedes, published by Fernando Pessoa.* Vicente Guedes is the one he always meets with in Casa Pessoa, "the usual cheap restaurant". But he "died young" and Pessoa doesn't even mention him in his final years. He told Côrtes-Rodrigues (04/10/1914) that "for a couple of days now, I've been up to *The Book of Disquiet",* but confesses that "it's all fragments, fragments, fragments"[5].

That *Book of Disquiet* was written by hand with a quill (70% of the fragments) and with a typewriter (the remaining 30%), "composed by Bernardo Soares, assistant bookkeeper in the city of Lisbon, by Fernando Pessoa", and is defined throughout his life as a "diary", an "intimate diary", a "random diary", "this diary of mine made for me", "confessions", "inane impressions", "non-rushed ramblings", "book of Fate", "a book with a progressively unstitched spine", "my lifeless story", "an autobiography of one who never existed", "the biography of one who never had a life"; or, as in the title he had planned for the first part of the book, "a factless autobiography". In a letter to João Lebre e Lima (03/05/1914), he confesses it stemmed from "a sterile fury of dreaming". It has as appendixes the "Great excerpts" – a compilation of writings scarcely bigger than the fragments, which are consensually attributed to Soares: "Divine envy", "Cenotaph", "Sentimental education", "Funeral march", "The art of effective dreaming", "Our lady of silence", "The visual lover", "Peristyle", "Symphony of the restless night" or "Advice to unhappily married women" – in which he suggests that "unhappily married women include all who are married and

5 Likely just a coincidence, but the cadence hearkens to *Hamlet's* famous monologue – *Words, words, words.*

some who are single", before giving said ladies a bit of advice: "Cheat on your husbands in your imagination". In his reveries, he plans to publish those "Great excerpts" as an independent book, but he would never get around to it, like with so many other projects in his life.

Only 12 "fragments" were published in literary magazines. The rest remained in envelopes in the Chest. Petrus (Pedro Veiga) edited in 1961 almost all of the fragments Pessoa published in life. Jorge de Sena, first in 1961 and then in 1969, tried to edit *Disquiet* and gave up; it would finally be released by Ática (1982) in two volumes, organized by Jacinto de Prado Coelho, Maria Aliete Galhoz and Teresa Sobral Cunha. During the process, it became clear that there was a first phase of the book, from 1912 to 1921, which is attributed to Vicente Guedes; and a second, from 1928 to 1934, which was Bernardo Soares'. With so many differences between those two phases, both in inspiration and in style, it wouldn't be amiss to speak of two different Books of Disquiet, written by two distinct authors. Still, *Disquiet* is here treated as one book by a single author, as that's the consensus between its readers – and Pessoa himself, it bears remembering.

The book's style

Soares tries his hand at poetry, but Pessoa thinks there's no future in it for him, as "Soares isn't a poet. His poetry is imperfect, and without the continuity of his prose, the verses are the trash of his prose; the pen nibs of what he writes well". The relationship between Soares and the other heteronyms is also clear. "The assistant bookkeeper Bernardo Soares and the Baron of Teive are two oblivious figures. I compare them both because the two are cases of the very same phenomenon – the maladaptation to the reality of life". This because "Soares writes in a style that, good or bad, is mine". "On the other hand, there are remarkable similarities between Bernardo Soares and Álvaro de Campos", especially as the end draws near. "But, in Campos, we soon see the Portuguese's sloppiness, the unconnected images, more intimate and less purposeful than Soares". It would have been the finest example of a new genre, which he claims to have created: The "novel without a plot" – an idea which, to be fair, had already occurred to Flaubert. The character is conceived under many influences: Mallarmé's *Poésies,* in which he says: *A book neither begins nor ends, at most it pretends to;* Henri-Frédéric Amiel's *Fragments d'un journal intime;* or Rilke, with *Die Aufzeichnungen des Malte Laurids Brigge,* his intimate diary attributed to another, the story of a lonely man, an aspiring author with an age and occupation similar to Soares', who notes down reflections and the facts of his daily life. That is the path Pessoa chooses. He even tells Sá-Carneiro that he means to insert in *Disquiet* some sentences of the letter he is writing him. According to Georg Rudolf Lind, *Disquiet* is synthesis *of decadentism.* According to Eduardo Lourenço, it is *a suicidal text, which disarticulates all the fictions which vainly separated him from the one true love he ever harbored... death itself.* Soares himself is almost simple-minded in his definition: It is but "a whimper", the "saddest book"[6] in Portugal.

What might have been

A passage from *Disquiet* reads: "The feelings that hurt most, the emotions that sting most, are those that are absurd: the longing for impossible things, precisely because they are impossible; nostalgia for what never was; the desire for what could have been; regret over not being someone else; dissatisfaction with the world's existence". It is a recurring theme for poets. "Ah, it's my longing for whom I might have been that distracts and torments me". In 1913, Sá-Carneiro (in "Estátua Falsa") speaks of *the sadness of the things that weren't;* and, in 1925, Manuel Bandeira (in "Pneumotórax") speaks of *the life that might have been and wasn't* (and would reproduce this verse verbatim in his *Antologia* of 1965). The poem takes place in a doctor's office: *Say thirty three... thirty three... thirty three... thirty three... Breathe.* And ends with a vision of his own life: *So, doctor, can we try a pneumothorax? – No. The only thing we can do is play an Argentinian tango.* Despite their similarities in form, the inspiration for these verses was quite different. Sá-Carneiro was preparing his suicide, and Bandeira's body was racked by tuberculosis, so he had no hope for a normal life. Whereas for Soares, especially with World War I, *the horror of death got progressively more attention in* Disquiet*... anonymous, random heroes disembarked without having chosen the time of their departure,* acknowledges Teresa Sobral Cunha. In him, as in Álvaro de Campos and Pessoa himself, there is but resignation with defeat. The idea is made plain in a number of texts, such as the following poem:

> And all that's left for me is the undefined anxiety
> Of what might have been and was not.
>
> *Untitled* (08/08/1910), Fernando Pessoa

And in many others, such as the following:

> Ah, who will write the history
> Of whatever might have been?

---

6 Again, likely just a coincidence, but it is nevertheless intriguing that, when Gustave Flaubert wrote *Salammbô* (1862), he said that *a man needs to be sad in order to resurrect an entire city in a book.*

If someone wrote it, that would be
The true history of humanity.

Original Sin, Álvaro de Campos

But what I wasn't, what I didn't do, what I didn't even dream of;
What I only now see I should have done.
What I only now see I should have been –
That is what it means to be dead beyond all the Gods.

Untitled (11/05/1928), Álvaro de Campos

Of what might have been, all that remains is what is.

The man from Porlock, Fernando Pessoa

The purpose of the ideal is for us to be others, but the price is high – such as not even being what we might have been.

Untitled ("Os Outros Eus"), Fernando Pessoa

Sadder than what happens
Is what has never happened.

Untitled (09/06/1930), Fernando Pessoa

There are so many things which, without even existing,
Exist protractedly in existence,
And, protractedly, it is ours and us…
(…)
Over the soul, the pointless beating of wings
Of what wasn't, nor could be, is everything[7].

Untitled (19/11/1935), Fernando Pessoa

Finally, Soares sums it up thus:

That which I was and will never again be! That which I had and will never again have!

The Book of Disquiet, Bernardo Soares

7 Pessoa would die 11 days after writing these verses.

Soares' fate

In one of the published fragments, Soares says: "It is not death I want, nor is it life". But he soon ceases to publish, and nothing else comes out from him during Pessoa's final years, except for a last, isolated fragment, on the 23rd of June 1934. According to Bréchon, *Discovering* Disquiet *was an even more astonishing find than Caeiro, twenty years before.* One cannot remain indifferent to it. For a few, it was a minor work, as it had no literary genre to speak of. It was but *a false diary,* as per Gaspar Simões. Conversely, in a literary survey conducted by *The Independent* (in 1999), British writer Paul Bailey held it up as *the book of the century.* As one reads its pages, it is as if an entire life were stripping down, exposing the misery and greatness that compose the duality of the human soul. For many, *Disquiet* was Pessoa's ascent to literary greatness, bordering on the sublime. Many consider Soares the best of Fernando Pessoa; and the most demanding readers consider it a work of genius at its highest level. I share the sentiment, and I suppose Pessoa did likewise: *"The Book of Disquiet* and the character Bernardo Soares are the uppermost level". Perhaps because, more so than any other heteronym, it was himself. Both sharing the same dread of death. "So too, it sometimes happens in life that a soul weighed down by living suddenly feels relief, for no apparent reason. The empty immensity of things, the tremendous oblivion in the sky and on earth". And both carry on together through life. Until the end.

Selected texts

THE BOOK OF DISQUIET, fragment 6

I asked for very little from life, and even this little was denied me. A nearby field, a ray of sunlight, a little bit of calm along with a bit of bread, not to feel oppressed by the knowledge that I exist, not to demand anything from others, and not to have others demand anything from me – this was denied me, like the spare change we might deny a beggar not because we're mean-hearted but because we don't feel like unbuttoning our coat. Sadly I write in my quiet room, alone as I have always been, alone as I will always be. And I wonder if my apparently negligible voice might not embody the essence of thousands of voices, the longing for self-expression of thousands of lives, the patience of millions of souls resigned like my own to their daily lot, their useless dreams, and their hopeless hopes. In these moments my heart beats faster because I'm conscious of it. I live more because I live on high. I feel a religious force within me, a species of prayer, a kind of public outcry. But my mind quickly puts me in my place… I remember that I'm on the fourth floor of the Rua dos Douradores, and I take a drowsy look at myself. I glance up from this half-written page at life, futile and without beauty, and at the cheap cigarette I'm about to extinguish in the ashtray beyond the fraying blotter. Me in this fourth-floor room, interrogating life!, saying what souls feel!, writing prose like a genius or a famous author! Me, here, a genius!...

THE BOOK OF DISQUIET, fragment 40

Sometimes I feel, I'm not sure why, a touch of foretold death... Perhaps it's an indefinite sickness which, because it doesn't materialize in pain, tends to become spiritualized in nothingness, the end. Or perhaps it's a weariness that needs a slumber far deeper than sleeping affords. All I know is that I feel like a sick man who has been getting steadily worse, until at last he calmly and without regret extends his feeble hands over the bedspread he had been clutching. And then I wonder what this thing is that we call death. I don't mean the mystery of death, which I can't begin to fathom, but the physical sensation of ceasing to live. Humanity is afraid of death, but indecisively. The normal man makes a good soldier in combat; the normal man, when sick or old, rarely looks with horror at the abyss of nothing, though he admits its nothingness. This is because he lacks imagination. And nothing is less worthy of a thinking man than to see death as a slumber. Why a slumber, if death doesn't resemble sleep? Basic to sleep is the fact we wake up from it, as we presumably do not from death. If death resembles sleep, we should suppose that we wake up from it, but this is not what the normal man imagines; he imagines death as a slumber no one wakes up from, which means nothing. Death doesn't resemble slumber, I said, since in slumber one is alive and sleeping, and I don't know how death can resemble anything at all for us, since we have no experience of it, nor anything to compare it to. Whenever I see a dead body, death seems to me a departure. The corpse looks to me like a suit that was left behind. Someone went away and didn't need to take the one and only outfit he'd worn.

Silence emerges from the sound of the rain and spreads in a crescendo of grey monotony over the narrow street I contemplate. I'm sleeping while awake, standing by the window, leaning against it as against everything. I search in myself for the sensations I feel before these falling threads of darkly luminous water that stand out from the grimy building façades and especially from the open windows. And I don't know what I feel or what I want to feel. I don't know what to think or what I am. All the pent-up bitterness of my life removes, before my sensationless eyes, the suit of natural happiness it wears in the random events that fill up each day. I realize that,while often happy and often cheerful, I'm always sad. And the part of me that realizes this is behind me, as if bent over my leaning self at the window, as if looking over my shoulder or even over my head to contemplate, with eyes more intimate than my own,the slow and now wavy rain which filigrees the grey and inclement air. To shrug off all duties, even those not assigned to us, to repudiate all homes, even those that weren't ours, to live off vestiges and the ill-defined, in grand purple robes of madness and in counterfeit laces of dreamed majesties… To be something, anything,that doesn't feel the weight of the rain outside, nor the anguish of inner emptiness… To wander without thought or soul – sensation without sensation – along mountain roads and through valleys hidden between steep slopes, into the far distance, irrevocably immersed… To be lost in landscapes like paintings… A coloured non-existence in the background…A light gust of wind, which I can't feel on this side of the window, breaks the even fall of rain into aerial discrepancies. A part of the sky hidden from view is clearing. I notice this because I can now make out the calendar on the wall through the less than clean window that faces my own. I forget. I don't see. I don't think. The rain stops, and for a moment a fine dust of miniature diamonds hangs in the air,like tiny crumbs from an enormous tablecloth bluely shaken on high. I can feel that part of the sky has cleared. I can see more distinctly the calendar through the window opposite. It has a woman's face, and the rest is easy because I remember it, and the toothpaste is the brand everyone knows. But what was I thinking about before I got lost in seeing? I don't know. Effort? Will? Life? A huge onslaught of light reveals a now almost entirely blue sky. But there is no peace – ah, there will never be! – at the bottom of my heart, an old well in a corner of the farm that was sold, a dust-coated memory of childhood shut up in the attic of someone else's house. I have no peace, nor even – alas! – the desire to have it…

THE BOOK OF DISQUIET, fragment 225

So many times, so many, like now, it has oppressed me to feel myself feel – to feel anguish just because it's a feeling, restlessness because I'm here, nostalgia for something I've never known, the sunset of all emotions, myself yellowing, subdued to grey sadness in my external self-awareness.

Ah, who will save me from existing? It's neither death nor life that I want: it's that other thing shining in the depths of longing, like a possible diamond in a pit one can't descend. It's all the weight and sorrow of this real and impossible universe, of this sky like the flag of an unknown army, of these colours that are paling in the fictitious air,where the imaginary crescent of the moon, cut out of distance and insensibility, now emerges in a still, electric whiteness.

It all amounts to the absence of a true God, an absence that is the empty cadaver of the lofty heavens and the closed soul. Infinite prison – since you're infinite, there's no escaping you!

GREAT EXCERPTS (OUR LADY OF SILENCE)

Sometimes, when I feel discouraged and depressed, even my ability to dream loses its leaves and shrivels, and the only kind of dreaming I can have is to muse on my dreams,and so I leaf through them, like a book one leafs through over and over, finding nothing but inevitable words. And then I ask myself who you are, you this figure who traverses all my languid visions of unknown landscapes and ancient interiors and splendid pageants of silence. In all of my dreams you appear, in dream form, or you accompany me as a false reality. With you I visit regions that are perhaps dreams of yours, lands that are perhaps your bodies of absence and inhumanity, your essential body dissolved into the shape of a tranquil plain and a stark hill on the grounds of some secret place.

Perhaps I have no dream but you. Perhaps it is in your eyes, when my face leans into yours, that I read these impossible landscapes, these unreal tediums, these feelings that inhabit the shadows of my weariness and the caves of my disquiet. Perhaps the landscapes of my dreams are my way of not dreaming about you. I don't know who you are, but do I know for certain who I am? Do I really know what it means to dream, such that I can know what it means to call you my dream? How do I know that you're not apart of me, perhaps the real and essential part? And how do I know it's not I who am the dream and you the reality, I who am your dream instead of you being mine? What sort of life do you have? By what manner of seeing do I see you? Your profile?It's never the same, yet it never changes. And I say this because I know it, without knowing that I know it. Your body? It's the same whether naked or dressed, and in the same position whether seated or standing or lying down. What is the meaning of this that means nothing?

My life is so sad, and I don't even think of weeping over it; my days are so false, and I don't even dream of trying to change them. How can I possibly not dream of you? Lady of the Passing Hours, Madonna of stagnant waters and rotting seaweed, Tutelary Goddess of the sprawling deserts and the black landscapes of barren cliffs – deliver me from my youth. Consoler of the disconsolate, Tears of those who never weep, Hour that never strikes –deliver me from joy and happiness. Opium of all silences, unplucked Lyre, Stained-Glass Window of distance and exile –make me hated by men and scorned by women. Cymbal of Extreme Unction, Caress that doesn't touch, Dove lying dead in the shade,Oil of hours spent dreaming – deliver me from religion, for it is sweet, and from unbelief, for it is strong. Lily drooping in the afternoon, Keepsake Box of wilted roses. Silence between prayers– fill me with loathing for being alive, with resentment for being healthy, and with contempt for my youth.

Make me useless and sterile, O Shelter of all hazy dreams; make me pure for no reason,and indifferently false, O Running Water of Sad Experience; let my mouth be a frozen landscape, my eyes two dead ponds, and my gestures the slow withering of decrepit trees, O Litany of Disquiet, O Royal Mass of Weariness, O Corolla, O Holy Fluid, O Ascension!

Ecce homo
(Behold the man) Pilate to the Jews

FERNANDO PESSOA

Fernando Pessoa feels things
but he doesn't move, not even inside.
Notes in Remembrance of my Master Caeiro,
Álvaro de Campos

Who is Pessoa?

Fernando Pessoa often signs his texts with his own name. He is an *orthonym.* But, in writing, he was but another heteronym of that other Pessoa – the real, "impure and simple", who lives and suffers in Lisbon. Jorge de Sena was the first to realize that. The same Sena who wrote him a letter, six years after his death, saying: *When you wrote under your own name, you were no less of a heteronym than the others,* later suggesting that Pessoa *had created himself as a heteronym of himself.* So too believed Casais Monteiro, accepting some of the differences between the heteronym and the man. For Bréchon, *neither Caeiro, nor Reis, nor Campos, nor any of the other heteronyms is, on his own, Pessoa;* but *neither is Pessoa "himself".* Because that *seductive hypothesis,* now according to Antonio Tabucchi, *is absurdly also the most logical.* Many others share similar opinions. Pessoa himself mentions "Fernando Pessoa's works", as, for him, "Fernando Pessoa doesn't exactly exist, as it were". Recalling, in that plurality, "Alberto Caeiro, Ricardo Reis, Álvaro de Campos, Fernando Pessoa, and however many there are, have been, or will be".

How many lost victories
Out of not having wanted them!
How many lost lives!
And the dream that wasn't…
(…)
Lament of futile dreams,
Which memory has awakened,
useless, so useless –
Who will tell me who I am?

Untitled (27/05/1926), Fernando Pessoa

Symbolism

Between 1910 and 1912, when he begins to write more in earnest, he is still strongly influenced by the French symbolism of Beaudelaire, Mallarmé, Rimbaud, Verlaine. The movement would begin in Portugal with Eugénio de Castro and his book of poems *Oaristo* (1890), and was followed by Camilo Pessanha and his followers. In his early days as an author, Pessoa would be one of them. But he soon changes and abandons that style of his "third adolescence", in which he lived "in the atmosphere of Greek and German philosophers, as well as the decadent French [symbolists], whose action was suddenly swept from my spirit by Swedish gymnastics and by reading [Max] Nordau's *[Critique de la] Dégénérescence* – a reference explained by the fact that he read the book by that Hungarian Jew in the office of Luís Furtado Coelho, his Swedish gymnastics teacher. After that, he reads *Regeneration, a reply to Max Nordeau,* by an anonymous author, and concludes the following: "Some works, like Nordeau's and Lombroso's, belong to scientific charlatanism". During that period, he writes "Beyond God – which, for Sá-Carneiro (letter from 03/02/1913), *wields mystery, interrogates the beyond. And what a thing of wonder, that second stanza... "What is it, river-being flowing?"*. That stanza is in one of "Beyond God's first poems, which begins thus:

I watch the Tagus in such a way
That my watching forgets I'm watching
And suddenly this strikes me
Against my daydreaming
What is it, river-being flowing?
What is it, my-being-here and watching?

Beyond God (I/Abyss), Fernando Pessoa

Paulism

Symbolism, which marked the old guard of Portuguese literature at the time, soon gives way to the "new literature" which consisted of "one one sole discipline: To feel everything in every possible way". Because "all literary movements are born of a reaction against previous movements". Teixeira de Pascoaes' and Guerra Junqueiro's "archaic nationalism" and "nostalgia" are left in the past, as are their talks of *a new chant,* of a new *Lusiad* era which the *nostalgic motherland* ought to create. His opinion on Junqueiro – author of the monumental *A velhice do Padre Eterno, Finis Patriae* and *Oração à luz* – slowly changes. In the beginning, he was "a great poet"; later, nothing but a "notorious con artist"; and lastly "I am largely indifferent to his oeuvre";

until, in the end, "Junqueiro is dead". That Paulism of his, to Gaspar Simões a *duskism* of sorts, was characterized by three elements: A "vague ideation", which "holds whatever is undefined as a constant", inspired by Mallarmé; the "subtle ideation", which "translates a simple sensation with an expression that makes it vivid", an evolution of that same sentiment; and "complex ideation", which "translates a simple sensation with an expression" which "gives it new meaning", in a final and superior stage. He is joined by Alfredo Guisado, Côrtes-Rodrigues and Sá-Carneiro. Deep inside, he becomes quite agitated. "Let us create Portuguese literature". On the 29th of March 1913, giving shape to that idea, he writes "Swamps of yearning". The inspiration came from André Gide's French masterwork *Paludes* (1895). A book written in Africa, once again Africa, in which the author reflects upon his life. Pessoa's manuscript is passed out among his friends before being published (along with "O church bell") in February 1914, in the one and only issue of *Renascença* magazine.

> Swamps of yearnings brushing against my gilded soul…
> Distant tolling of Other Bells… The blond wheat paling
> In the ashen sunset… My soul is seized by a bodily chill…
> (…)
> Horizons shutting our eyes to space, where they are false
> links…
>
> Fanfares of future silences… Faraway trains…
> Gates in the distance… seen through the trees… so utterly iron!
>
> *Swamps of yearning*, Fernando Pessoa

Intersectionism

But "Paulismo is, as J[oão] C[orreia] de O[liveira] told us at Brasileira, *an intoxication of artificiality";* and that attempt at "emotionalizing ideas" soon became a search for a space amidst the European vanguard. The path opened up when Sá-Carneiro brought attention to new tendencies which, according to him, were going to change art. Then, bit by bit, he sloughed off all that was "vague" and found "plasticity". And so the intersectionist aesthetic was born, "an exact expression of the exterior as the interior", an adaptation of sorts of poetry to the cubist vision, anticipating the great surrealist movement that would soon emerge. "It might perhaps be useful, I think, to launch intersectionism as a movement, not with merely artistic ends, but thinking it through as a series of ideas that must be publicized so they may effect the national psychism, which must needs be worked on and shot through with several new ideas and emotions which might jolt us out of our stagnation". Almada Negreiros, José Pacheco, Rui Coelho, Santa-Rita Pintor and D. Tomás de Almeida all joined the movement. Pessoa was thinking of publishing one large volume, *Antologia do Interseccionismo,* which would include Sá-Carneiro's "Manicure"; Almada Negreiros' "Manifesto Anti-Dantas", and Pessoa's "Oblique Rain", "Triumphal Ode", "Ode to Walt Whitman" and the monumental "Maritime Ode".

> And my happy childhood awakes, like a tear, in me.
> My past rises up, as if it that sailor's hail
> Was an aroma, a voice, the echo of a song
> Which was calling to my past
> By that happiness it would never have again.
>
> *Maritime Ode*, Álvaro de Campos

Atlantism

In the beginning of 1915, a variant of Intersectionism was born, dubbed Atlantism by specialists, which was mainly present in his prose texts. A movement with a prophetic bent, inspired by Sebastianism, which understood art as "a lie which suggests a truth". On the social field, he wishes for "the replacement of religion by patriotic mysticism, not by creating a national God… but a national Christ – which already exists in the transcendentally representative figure of Sebastião I". He plans a *Manifesto* with the multiple senses of that Atlantism. "Any Empire that isn't founded on the Spiritual Empire is dead on its feet, a Corpse in charge". It would be a reaction against traditionalism and the monarchy, "because it is connected to Rome". Deep down, he wishes to create a spiritual civilization able to subjugate "all peoples; for there is no resisting the arts and the forces of the spirit". But those intentions, brief as a sigh, soon simmer down.

Sensationism

On the 21st of November 1915, already after "the most important day", he decides to "scorn the notion of the plebeian socialization of myself, of Intersectionism". He is then influenced by Futurism and other similar movements. "Call the intersectionists, intersectionists. Or paulists, if you must. Myself, I am neither intersectionist [or paulist] nor a futurist. I am myself, and only myself, concerned with none but myself and my sensations". A natural reaction from one who had confessed that "literature, like all art, is a confession that life isn't enough". Because Pessoa, as Jerónimo Pizarro observed, *wanted to be unto a whole literature, to live all movements within himself.* Which was why he immediately assumes that it would be "the first manifestation of Portugal-Europe, the one grand literary art which has revealed itself in Portugal", defined as "a decomposition of reality in its psychic, geometrical elements" in order to "raise human self-conscience". According to said movement, "sensation is the only truth", which *points to an art that, in turn, intends to raise the self-awareness of those who aestheticize it,* according to Fernando Alvarenga.

Sensationism was fundamentally "born of the friendship between Pessoa and Sá-Carneiro; as, for both of them, "to feel is to create. To act is but to destroy. To comprehend is to delude ourselves"; and "the only reality is the fact that the word reality makes no sense at all". "The one true reality, therefore, is sensation". With it, one of Campos' mottoes would be implemented: "Feel everything in every possible way". Its core tenets were "a) sensation, purely as such; b) the awareness of sensation which gives it worth, and thus an aesthetic slant; c) the awareness of sensation, from which an intellectualization can stem, which is to say, the power of expression". "Sensationism defends the aesthetic attitude in all of its pagan splendour". "Alberto Caeiro, the glorious young master, was the one who founded it. Dr. Ricardo Reis made it logically neoclassical. The intense poet Álvaro de Campos modernized it. Those three names are an entire literary epoch's worth".

Two works belonging to Sensationism are "16", by Sá-Carneiro, published in *Orpheu* #2; and Pessoa's "Triunfo", which was dedicated to Sá-Carneiro. In a text he wrote on the movement, he ends by saying that "the rest is Portuguese literature", signing off as "Fernando Pessoa, sensationist".

> I am nothing, I follow nothing.
> Deluded, I bring myself with me.
> Comprehending not how to comprehend, I don't even know
> If, being nothing, I can even be.
> (…)
> Dreaming is nothing, and not knowing is futile.
> Sleep in the shadows, uncertain heart.
>
> *Untitled* (06/01/1923), Fernando Pessoa

Neopaganism

In 1916, he begins writing texts which, although contradictory among themselves, no longer have that style so typical of sensationism. Essentially, these "reaffirm the superiority of Portuguese neopaganism over neoarabism", in a movement centred around five works: "1. Alberto Caeiro's "The Keeper of Sheep", 2. Ricardo Reis' *Odes,* 3. António Mora's *The return of the gods,* 4. Ricardo Reis' *New odes,* and 5. António Mora's *The basis of paganism – Theory on objectivist duality".* Also, in December 1917, he writes "Fundamental theses of Portuguese neopaganism":

I. There is no deep national movement, no deeply renovating national movement, that isn't a cultural movement.

II. There is no deep cultural movement that isn't a religious movement.

III. There is no deep Portuguese cultural movement that isn't an Arab movement, as the Arab soul is the bottom of the Portuguese soul.

IV. There is no deep Arab cultural movement that isn't a deep movement.

But there would be no future for all those -isms, and those movements were soon forgotten. As if Pessoa no longer had any need for literary trends or heteronyms, now that he was treading different paths with his master Caeiro. Little by little, his poetry becomes more refined, and, from 1918 onwards, he begins to use his own name more and more when writing.

His mamma's boy

Of the poems which ensue, one of the most renowned ones is "Mother's little boy", published in *Contemporânea* magazine #1, series III, in 1926, and subsequently in *Notícias Ilustrado* #22, series II, in 1928. It all began in 1926 when, while having dinner in a boarding house, he sees hanging from the wall the lithography of a dead young soldier. The image stuck with him, and so "Mother's little boy" was born, according to José G. Herculano de Carvalho, inspired by Rimbaud's "The sleeper in the valley". Upon comparing both, I had to concur.

The sleeper in the valley	Mother's little boy
A little valley bubbling over with light	On the abandoned plain
A young soldier	So young! How young he was!
There are two red holes in his right side	Run through by bullets – Two, from side to side

The idea likely began to take shape in 1925, when his mother died. From then on, he understood he was well and truly alone; deep down, he was mother's little boy. Eduardo Freitas da Costa, a cousin of Pessoa, disputes that notion, as does Augusto Ferreira Gomes, declaring Pessoa hadn't *the faintest relations with his family,* certainly out of a sense of duty to protect an old friend, as the poem makes no secret of such intimacy. Such as the verses *An only child, his mother had given him/ A name that she kept always;* as Pessoa, an only child after the death of brother Jorge, kept his own name and used it when referring to his mother, who had abandoned her former surname in favour of her new husband's Rosa.

On the abandoned plain
Warmed by the tepid breeze,
Run through by bullets[1]
– Two, from side to side -,
Lies dead, and goes cold.

Blood stripes his uniform.
Arms outstretched,
Niveous, blond,[2] blood-drained,
Gazes with a languid look
Blindly at the lost skies.

So young! How young he was!
(Now how old is He?)
An only child, his mother had given him
A name that she kept always
"His mother's little boy".

Fallen from his pocket
A small cigarette box.
Given to him by Mother. It is whole
And good, the cigarette box,
It is he who is no longer wholesome.

From another pocket, winged
Tip grazing the earth,
The sheathed whiteness
Of a handkerchief… Given to him by the old maid
Who carried him on her lap.

Far away, at home, there is a prayer:
"May he return soon, and well!"
– Meshes that the Empire weaves!
Lies dead and rots,
Mother's little boy.

Mother's little boy, Fernando Pessoa

Shortly thereafter, he is taken by a similar bout of inspiration and publishes also in *Notícias Ilustrado,* series II, 1929, a poem which is strikingly similar:

The child with the golden hair
Lies on the crown of the road
Has his guts outside

1 On the 27th of February of that same year of 1926 in which the poem was published, he had written almost the same words in "To the memory of president-king Sidónio Pais".

2 Based on the lithography's figure.

And, by its bit of cord,
A train, and is unaware.

His face is now a mish
mash of blood and nothing
There glitters a small fish
– the kind for a bath-tub –
Over by the kerb.

Dark swathes of the street featureless.
One gleam still, far-off, gilds
The upbringing of the future…

And the golden child's?

We took the town after an intense bombardment, Fernando Pessoa

The theme reappears in a poem in which Pessoa evokes France. There are two possible explanations for that reference – and, this being Pessoa, both are probably equally as valid. The first and most obvious suggests the only battle Portugal took part in during World War I – at La Lys, between the 9th and the 29th of April 1918, with a humiliating defeat for the Portuguese troops. 7.500 (or 12.000) were made prisoner, wounded or killed, among them 327 officers, out of a total of 20 thousand (or 50 thousand) men of the Expeditionary Corps. The quote makes sense, even though the valley of La Lys is in Flanders, Belgium, as it's quite close to France. Thousands of Portuguese were buried in the French cemetery of Richebourg, close to *La Couture.* He mentions the battle in "Songs of Defeat": *Best to fall in Ksar el-Kebir/ Than to win at La Lys.* However, the poem likely simply evokes the memory of his friend Sá-Carneiro, who had taken his life in Paris: *He who was so much to you, everything, everything, everything...* A phrase Pessoa certainly would use in memory of his friend.

For those, mother, who died and fell in battle…
Gong-ong-ong-ong…
For those, mother, who were maimed in combat
Gong-ong-ong-ong…
For those whose bride shall ever wait in vain…
Gong-ong-ong-ong…
Seven times seven shall the flowers wilt in the garden
Gong-ong-ong-ong…
And their corpses shall be of the anonymous, universal dust
Gong-ong-ong-ong…
And they, who knows, mother, ever alive, hopeful…
Mad they are, mother, mad because their bodies died but pain doesn't…
Gong-gong-gong-gong

What of he whom you held to your chest?
Gong…
Who knows which of those unknowns strewn about is your son
Gong…
You still have the bibs he used as a child, stored in a drawer…
His old toys remain in boxes in the pantry…
Now he belongs to rot, somewhere in France
He who was so much to you, everything, everything, everything…
Look, he is nothing in the general holocaust of History
Gong-gong…
Gong-gong-gong-gong…
Gong-gong-gong-gong…
Gong-gong-gong-gong-gong-gong

Untitled (undated), Fernando Pessoa

The idea of writing poems based on everyday life would often be repeated by Pessoa – and, to be fair, by most poets as well. And so it was when he saw in a newspaper the photo of a laughing family as they got a check to compensate them for the hit-and-run death of their son. The dead son and the family members smiling at the sight of money so outraged him, that he wrote:

I know full well it is normal
But I still have a heart…
Good night, and shit!
(Crack, o heart of mine!)
(Shit for the whole of humanity!)

In the house of a mother whose son was killed,
Everyone laughs, everyone jests.
And there's a loud sound of countless blaring horns reminding us
That they got their due compensation:
Baby equals X,
Enjoy X right now,
Eating and drinking the dead baby,
Bravo! You are people!
Bravo! You are humanity!
Bravo: You are all fathers and all mothers
Who have children who can be killed by a car!
All is forgotten when there is money involved.
Baby equals X.

So much of it, they could have used it as wallpaper.
With it, they paid the final instalment of their furniture.
Poor little baby.
But, if he hadn't been killed by a car, how would their finances be?

Yes, he was beloved.
Yes, he was dear to them
But he died.
Too bad, he died!
But at least now they can pay the bills
And that is something.
(Of course it was a tragedy)
But now they can pay the bills.
(Of course that poor little body
was mangled)
But at least now they don't owe any money at the grocer's
(Too bad, yes, but there's a silver lining).

Baby is dead, but now there's ten contos[3].
Yes, ten contos.
You can do a lot (poor baby) with ten contos.
Pay plenty of debts (poor, dear baby)
With ten contos.
Sort out plenty of things
(Beautiful and dead) with ten contos.

Sure, it is sad
(Ten contos)
Our child, killed by a car
(Ten contos)
But seeing our house refurbished
(Ten contos)
A home rebuilt
(Ten contos)
One can forget plenty for that (how we mourn him!)
Ten contos!
It seems they received it from God's own hands
(Those ten contos).
Poor mangled baby!
Ten contos.

Untitled (undated), Fernando Pessoa

All is worthwhile if the soul is not small

Pessoa's three most oft-quoted verses are *Sailing is necessary, living is not necessary, The poet is a faker* and *all is worthwhile if the soul is not small.* Except Pessoa never wrote the first, as we've already established. The second, as we've previously clarified, doesn't suggest what the

3 A *conto* was the equivalent of a thousand *escudos.*

readers think it does. And the third, almost always wrongly quoted – with "when" frequently used instead of "if" – is from *Message* ("Portuguese sea"), transcribed below. It is an image which often appears throughout his oeuvre. For example:

> Other times when I hear the wind blow
> I feel that just hearing the wind blow makes it worth being born.
>
> *Discontinuous poems* (07/11/1915), Alberto Caeiro

> Great are the deserts, and all is desert.
> Great is life, and life isn't worth having.
>
> *Untitled* (04/10/1930), Álvaro de Campos

> Better to write than to dare live, even if living means merely to buy bananas in the sunlight, as long as the sun lasts and there are bananas for sale.
>
> *The Book of Disquiet,* Bernardo Soares

> Living isn't worth our while. Only seeing is.
>
> *The Book of Disquiet,* Bernardo Soares

> Let's talk of the past – that should be beautiful because it is useless and makes us feel sorry… It is never worth doing anything… I well know it wasn't worth it… That is why I thought it beautiful. No, my sister, nothing is worthwhile… Nothing is worthwhile, o distant love of mine, other than knowing how soft it is that nothing is worthwhile.
>
> *The Sailor*, Fernando Pessoa

> Life seems to be worthwhile after all. And therein lay the tragedy, but there was no one to write it.
>
> Letter to Ronald de Carvalho (29/02/1915), Fernando Pessoa

> Better to see something for the first time than to get to know it.
>
> *Untitled* (12/04/1919), Fernando Pessoa

> I was all, nothing is worthwhile[4].
>
> *Elegia na sombra*, Fernando Pessoa

4 These verses were written on the 2nd of June of his final year.

Maturity

Time passes. Search has long since been left behind. Caeiro is dead. Reis, in exile, is silent for many years. Campos had already abandoned his initial sensationist phase; he writes little now, and when he does, it is Pessoa who writes. Bernardo Soares, as already established, was him; tearing any semblance of intimacy, as texts of his were occasionally attributed to Soares. "I live in the present. I know not the future. I no longer have the past". In 1932, Pierre Hourcade defined Pessoa as *the worthiest of the universality of all Portuguese poets of our time, who still gravitates around the edges of any literary circle, lonely planet and ironical witness of the clan's customs.* Mother's little boy finally begins to be Fernando Pessoa.

Selected texts

PRAYER

Lord, you are heaven and earth, that thou art life and death! The sun and the moon thou thou art thou and the wind! Thou art our bodies and our souls and our love are you well. Where nothing is you dwell and where everything is – (your temple) – this is your body.

Give me soul to soul to serve you and love you. Give me sight to see you forever in heaven and on earth, ears to hear you in the wind and the sea, and hands to work on your behalf.

Make me pure as water and high as the sky. That there is no mud on the roads of my thoughts or dead leaves on the ponds of my intentions. Grant that I know how to love each other as brothers and serve you as a father.

(…)

My life is worthy of your presence. My body is worthy of the earth thy bed. My soul may appear before you as a son back home.

Make me as big as the sun, so that I may worship me, and makes me pure as the moon, so that I can pray for me, and makes me clear as day that I can always see pray for me and you and love you.

Lord, protect me and sustains me. Give me that I feel yours. Lord, deliver me from me.

STEPS OF THE CROSS (XIII)

Emissary of an unknown king,
I carry out the formless instructions from beyond,
And the brusque sentences that come to my lips
Sound to me as something entirely different and anomalous…

Unconsciously, I divide myself
Between myself and the mission my being was entrusted with,
And the glory of my King gives me disdain
For this human folk I must deal with…
I know not if the King who sent me exists.
My mission is to forget it,
My pride, the desert I find myself in within me…

But they exist! I feel grand traditions
From before time and space and life and being…
My sensations have beheld God…

MESSAGE (PORTUGUESE SEA)

Oh salty sea, so much of your salt
Is tears of Portugal!
Because we crossed you, so many mothers wept,
So many sons prayed in vain!
So many brides remained unmarried
That you might be ours, oh sea!

Was it worthwhile? All is worthwhile
When the spirit is not small.
He who wants to go beyond the Cape
Has to go beyond pain.
God to the sea peril and abyss has given
But it was in it that He mirrored heaven.

SCAFFOLDING

How many years have I
frittered away, dreaming!
How much of my life was
But the living lie of
Some imagined future!

Here, standing at the river's edge,
Strangely, I feel at peace
Watching its ceaseless pointless flow,
Cold and nameless, it represents
A life lived in vain.

How little do hopes achieve!
Much better to seize the moment!
Even a small child's ball bounces
Higher than all my hopes.
It rolls further than any of my wishes.

The ripples of the river, so slight
They are hardly ripples at all,
Hours, days, years, quickly pass by,
The green shoots and the snows; all is
Consumed by the burning Sun.

I spent all that I never had.
I am older than my years.
The fantasy that sustained me -
The queen upon my stage;
Standing naked, her reign is over.

The gentle murmur of slow waters,
Reaching out for the bank passed by,
Carrying dreamlike memories
Of hazy hopes!
Life and dreams, only a dream!

Whatever became of me? I found myself
When I was already lost.
Instantly I recoiled from myself
Like a madman who is afraid to see
The reality of his own insanity.

Dead sound of gentle waters
Flowing because flowing is their destiny,
Take with you not only my memories,
But my dead hopes too!
Dead because they must die!

I am the future dead,
Only a dream connects me to myself -
A dark and dragging dream
Of what I might have been -
A wall in my deserted garden.

Rippling waters of the past take me away
To the sea's soft oblivion!
Join me forever to what I never will be,
I who surrounded with scaffolding
The house that I never built.

Trahit sua quemque voluptas
(Each one is drawn by his own delight) Virgil

EVERY HETERONYM

I, the contradictory,
The scar of the sourpuss sergeant,
That bastard, José, who promised he'd come but didn't.
The Passing of the Hours, Álvaro de Campos

A biography of the 127 heteronyms

What follows is a numbered list of the heteronyms – as well as some other names which, despite having been written by Pessoa, are not considered as such – in alphabetical order, for ease of consultation.

1. A.A. Crosse – He wrote in English about Portuguese myths which were dear to Pessoa, although that activity was summed up by a single, unpublished text. He also took part in riddle contests – such as one at the London *Times*[1] (13/07/1920), in which he'd hoped to win the prize of a thousand pounds so that Fernando might think of marrying Ophelia. The potential bride-to-be supported the idea, praying a novena to St. Helen and making a promise to Jesus, as per Pessoa's suggestion. According to her, *mister Crosse is very smart and isn't nearly as unlucky as he thinks... I will hope he beats my dear Fernandinho, dearest love of my life.* In letters, Ophelia says: *I won't forger Mr. Crosse* (22/03); laments that *after all that, mr. Crosse won't win anything* (25/04); and mentions *it's 11 pm, I shall pray for mr. Crosse and go to bed.* (27/04/1920). But neither saint nor Christ, amorous sighs, contrite prayer or miraculous novenas would help, as losing was indeed written in the stars as Crosse's fate. And Pessoa's.

– A.A. Rey da Silva – How António Augusto Rey da Silva also signed his name[2].

1 According to some biographers, crossword competitions as well. Which is impossible, considering that, even though they had existed in England since 1762 (at *London Magazine),* they were only published in *Times* in 1935, the year of Pessoa's death.
2 Names used by Pessoa which weren't heteronyms will be listed in this format.

– A. Couto – How Armando Couto also signed his name.

– A. Rey da Costa – He was to illustrate Marvell Kisch's novel, *A riqueza de um doido*.

2. A. Francisco de Paula Angard (Fr. Angard) – Author of scientific texts in *O Palrador*, a newspaper that was allegedly printed at Tipografia Angard, which he owned, at the imaginary Rua Divem, 8. Among Angard's texts, written in a naïve style, one "Monstros da antiguidade" (Monsters of ancient times) of his *Leituras científicas* stood out. It begins thus:

> Everything that Man's fantasy can conceive of cannot ever approach the prodigious shapes created by nature in the beginning of the age of earth.

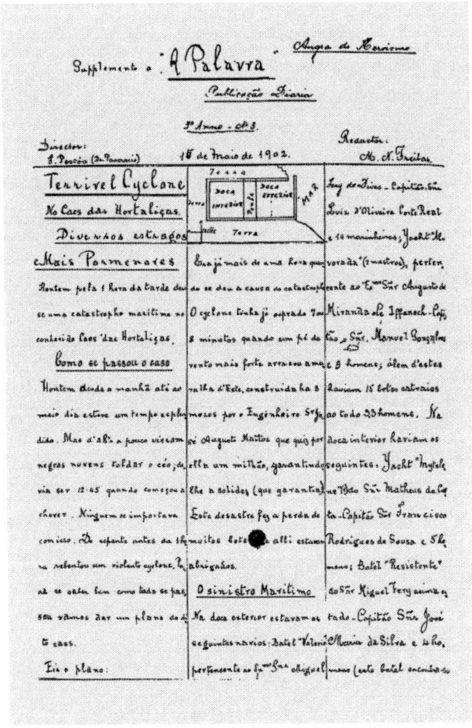

Supplemento a "A Palavra" — Angra do Heroismo

Publicação Diaria

1º Anno - Nº 3.

Director: F. Pessôa (Dr. Pancracio) — 15 de Maio de 1902. — Redactor: M. N. Freitas

Terrivel Cyclone

No Caes das Hortaliças

Diversos estragos

e Mais Pormenores

Hontem pela 1 hora da tarde deu-se uma catastrophe maritima no conhecido Caes das Hortaliças.

Como se passou o caso

Hontem desde a manhã até ao meio dia esteve um tempo esplendido. Mas d'ahi a pouco vieram negras nuvens toldar o céo; devia ser 12.45 quando começou a chover. Ninguem se importava com isso. De repente antes da 1h [illegible] rebentou um violento cyclone. [illegible] se sabe bem como tudo se passou vamos dar um plano do [illegible] caes.

Eis o plano:

Terra — Doca interior — Doca exterior — Mar — Terra

Era já mais de uma hora quando se deu a causa da catastrophe. O cyclone tinha já soprado 7 ou 8 minutos quando um pé de vento mais forte arrasou a muralha d'Este, construida ha 3 mezes por o Engenheiro Sr José Augusto Mattos que quiz por ella um milhão, garantindo-lhe a solidez (que garantia!). Este desastre fez a perda de muitos botes [illegible] alli estavam abrigados.

O sinistro Maritimo

Na doca exterior estavam os seguintes navios: Batel "Victoria" pertencente ao Ex.mo Snr Miguel [illegible] de Dives - Capitão Snr Luiz d'Oliveira Corte Real e 14 marinheiros; Yacht "[illegible]" (3 mastros), pertencente ao Ex.mo Snr Augusto de Miranda [illegible] - Capitão o Snr. Manuel Gonzalves e 9 homens; além d'estes haviam 15 botes catraios ao todo 23 homens. Na doca interior haviam os seguintes: Yacht "[illegible]" do Snr Matheus da Costa - Capitão Snr Francisco Rodrigues de Sousa e 5 homens; Batel "Resistente" do Snr Miguel [illegible] - Capitão Snr José Maria da Silva e 4 homens (este batel encontra-se

Newspaper made by Pessoa

It bears remembering that, in his younger years, Pessoa had fun making newspapers, much like Sá-Carneiro, who had published *O Chinó* during his school years. The first of those was *A Palavra* (The Word) – when he visited his mother's family in Tavira. He was 13 at the time. Then, *O Palrador* (The Prattler), which he began editing in Lisbon, during his vacation from Africa in 1901. After #7 (05/06/1902), for no obvious reason, a new series followed with a new #1 (17/09/1905). Those newspapers were written by hand, with pencil or Indian ink on foolscap folio, so thin (and with such wear and tear nowadays) that I feared they would crumble in my hands while perusing them in Lisbon's National Library. All of them in Portuguese, even though he still lived in Durban at the time. Later, other newspapers still would be born: In 1907, there was *O Phósforo;* and, in 1907/1908, *O Iconoclasta;* followed by *O Progresso* and its rival, *A Civilização* – a "miniature newspaper, as its boss [Humberto Ferreira] is one himself – both printed in a mimeograph and already resembling neighbourhood newspapers.

3. A. Moreira – Co-author of *Essay on intuition,* with reference to heteronym Faustino Antunes. In that text, Moreira made claims such as:

> Upon profound examination of existence, we can but surrender to the evidence that there is little else we can hope to know than to acknowledge men through their own experience.

4. (Dr.) Abílio Fernandes Quaresma (Quaresma Decifrador, Tio Porco) – His first name, Ambrósio, was promptly discarded, and he became Abílio Ponciano Nogueira, like Pessoa's great-grandfather; or Abílio Nunes dos Santos Júnior, a trailblazer for radio in Portugal (at the P1AA station – Rádio Lisboa). "Born in Tancos in 1865, passed away in Lisbon in this our year of 1930" (or "died in New York"), "man of average height, bordering on tall, thin and frail without being sickly, with no elegance or distinctiveness, he was, in the worst sense of the word, harmless". "He wore a grey suit which was either badly tailored, badly kept, or both, with a soft collar, low, unkempt, and a simple black tie with a sloppy knot" and "light brown beard and moustache with grey hairs". "His face, sucked-in and with bad skin, lay between pale and swarthy; his nose, slightly hooked; his mouth, medium-sized, gave a modicum of strength to his weak, depressed physiognomy". He had "the look of habitual depression and obliviousness". Single, doctor without a clinic, he lived on the third floor of Rua dos Fanqueiros, in a small, untidy room with a window looking out to Lisbon's roofs.

He always had "a cigarette in his mouth". Not the dark Peraltas of yore, which were too rich for his blood, but rather the type one must roll oneself, as well as the occasional cigar. "Quaresma smiled at him [boss Guedes] and puffed his cigar". His fingers, much like Pessoa's, were yellowed by smoke. He "looked old for his age", hunched, had a cadaverous cough and "a furrowed brow underneath his ill-fitting hat". His age was at odds with his apparent advancing years, as Quaresma couldn't have been over 40. In the beginning, he was conceived as the character of another heteronym, Pêro Botelho – reproducing a period of transformation which took place in other stages of his heteronymy. He translates letters written by Edgar Allan Poe and writes crime novels he calls *Contos de raciocínio* (Tales of reasoning). He intended to publish his works "in books of separate booklets, of different sizes and correspondingly diverse pricing", adding that they would come out "one per month". Those unfinished novels would have been:

1) *O caso Vargas* (The Vargas Affair)
2) *O pergaminho roubado* (The Stolen Scroll)
3) *O caso do quarto fechado* (The Case of the Closed Room)
4) *O desaparecimento do Dr. Reis Dores* (The Disappearing of Dr. Reis Dores)
5) *O roubo na Quinta das Vinhas* (The Robbery at Quinta das Vinhas)
6) *O caso da janela estreita* (The Case of the Narrow Window)
7) *Três episódios: A carta mágica, etc.* (Three episodes: The Magic Letter, etc.)
8) *O caso do triplo fecho* (The Case of the Triple Lock).

He was also to have written the following:

9) *Tale*[3] *X/A morte de D. João* (Tale X/The Death of D. João)
10) *Cúmplices* (Accomplices)
11) *Crime*
12) *O roubo da Rua dos Capelistas* (The Robbery at Rua dos Capelistas)
13) *O caso do barão de Viseu* (The Case of the Baron of Viseu)
14) *O crime da Ereira* (The Crime at Ereira)

Pessoa actually pondered editing one of his *police novels* with a "preface by Quaresma", according to a letter to Casais Monteiro (13/01/1935); which is rather strange, since he found him "a dull, lifeless individuality", "a frail attachment to humanity". In his words, "and now to the flaws of philosophical intelligence in general and Abílio Quaresma's in particular". Still, he writes: "I think fondly of Quaresma; remembering him is truly distressing to me", as everything in him "was an idea that dovetailed into decadence". "He lived alone, smoking and meditating", "closed in his alcoholism, impertinent and with an almost automatized reasoning". "His seclusion was now absolute. His naturally dour nature, radically so, his slovenliness had gotten worse, and the sloppiness in his gestures and attitude were now absolute". Still, "he was miraculously energized whenever he solved a problem… he stepped on an imaginary pedestal, drank deeply of unseen forces, and was no longer the weakness of a man, but the strength of a conclusion[4]". Quaresma created a

3 In English in the original title.
4 Andrea Camilleri, Italy's greatest editorial hit nowadays, is a professed admirer of Fernando Pessoa. In his novel *La vampa d'agosto,* the character of Commissioner Montalbano, a gourmand and refined reader, makes several references to Quaresma.

character which would end up becoming his master, Tio Porco, inspired by Poe's Monsieur Dupin, who could all but read minds and uncover the most intricate mysteries by putting himself in the minds of criminals. "Riddles, chess problems, geometrical and mathematical brain teasers – he fed off such things and lived with them as one would with a woman. Applied reasoning was his abstract harem". Conan Doyle put an end to his Sherlock Holmes in an abyss in a fight against Moriarty (which he would later regret); whereas Poe died before he could kill off Monsieur Dupin. The same would happen to Quaresma, who died little by little of *delirium tremens*, far away from his homeland. While walking across Lisbon's Baixa, the heteronym invariably met Bernardo Soares and Pessoa himself – who, when informed of his death, said: "My soul was made more bitter by knowing a man like Quaresma had never attained a single day of renown."

5. Accursio Urbano – Pessoa wrote riddles, puzzles, metagrams and logogryphs for the newspapers he made during his teenage years, without ever providing the answers. Not even in subsequent editions of said newspapers. The reader was to guess – that is, if there even was a solution. He would occasionally mention facts such as: "Someone has yet to guess riddle #1"; or Riddle #5 was guessed by few". In *O Palrador,* Urbano was the author of riddles dedicated to heteronyms Morris & Theodor, Pad Zé and Scicio, such as the following one:

> To kiss her unequalled mouth
> And jubilantly return with her
> To the motherland of Brazil.

6. Adolph Moscow – A collaborator at *O Palrador* and author of *Os rapazes de Barrowby* (The Barrowby Lads), a text in Portuguese by an author with an English name. Only two chapters from that book were ever written. In Chapter I, A vida e a escola de Barrowby (Life and School at Barrowby), he even makes a drawing for the first page, describing the work as a "humoristic chronicle". In it, he narrates the life of a Jewish stranger at the school of the village of Barrowby (there is a map of it in the text) and his struggles with a stupid schoolmate called Gyp. "Explain yourself! – Gyp yelled at the Jew", before punching him in the nose at the lack of an explanation. The novel doesn't continue after that. Perhaps because Pessoa, then 14, was no longer studying at Durban High School.

7. Alberto Caeiro – Already described in his own chapter.

8. Alexander Search – Already described in his own chapter.

9. Alfred Wyatt – Lived in Paris – *14, Rue Richet*[5] – where he socialized with Sá-Carneiro. In the letters Pessoa wrote him, his name is always preceded by *monsieur*. His role remains unclear.

10. Álvaro de Campos – Already described in his own chapter.

– Álvaro Eanes – But a name quoted by Michaël Stoker.

– António[6] Augusto Rey da Silva (A.A. Rey da Silva) – Administrator of *O Palrador*.

– António Caeiro da Silva – He and his brother, Júlio Manuel Caeiro, were tasked with caring for the works of their dead sibling Alberto Caeiro. Interestingly, among Pessoa's papers, there were also to be found the initials of those two brothers, which don't quite match their names: A.L.C. (instead of A.C.S.) and J.C. (instead of J.M.C.).

– António Cebola – Literary director of *O Palrador*. Pessoa and his sister Teca made up stories in Durban, which both acted out. Some of the characters in those stories had vegetables as surnames and only answered when called such. Brother João Maria remembers two, *Mr. Nabo* (turnip) *and Mrs. Cenoura* (carrot). The same that then featured in the stories he told niece Manuela Nogueira when playing with her, according to herself. Due to the age difference with brother and niece, these characters and plays lingered on – and perhaps that's why that peculiar nomenclature endured with some of his heteronyms (Gaudêncio Nabos, Pimenta) and others (António Cebola, Rabanete).

11. António de Seabra – A critic of "ideas and mores", he wrote booklets which he called *Pamphleto lixa – periódico de crítica de ideias e de costumes* (Pamphlet file – journal of critique of ideas and mores). His convoluted explanation for such a title was: "The wise critic cannot have any scruple other than slightly striking down ideas with a careful hand wielding the file of opinionated levity. For this reason, and none other, the title of these brief pamphlets could be no other than *Lixa* (file)". Perhaps he was being groomed as a future author, but his role ended up being secondary. The heteronym is António, Pessoa's second name, and Seabra, one of his father's surnames. In this case, it should be pointed out how curious it is how some heteronyms end up reproducing real people. There was indeed an António de Seabra

5 Perhaps a reference to Charles Robert Richet, physiologist and specialist in allergies, Nobel Prize winner in Medicine in 1913.

6 There are altogether four Fernandos and nine Antónios (first or second name), in Portuguese and English, among the heteronyms (and the like) of Fernando António Nogueira Pessoa.

(1798-1895), knight of the Order of Christ, viscount, minister of Justice and of the Supreme Court; a Henry More, English philosopher; a Jean-Seul, victim of Salazar's government, on account of Pessoa's heteronym's verbal incontinence; a José Rodrigues do Vale, from Lisbon, and 12 years Pessoa's senior; the professor or Marnoco e Souza, as we will see further up ahead. One of António Seabra's texts reads: *What name more apt than File for a pamphlet which aims to critique, especially as File is the female form of Trash*[7]*, and this society is indeed nothing but trash?* His writing style is exotic. In a reference to sensationists, he had the following to say:

> During the times of transition in societies, there is wont to be at the surface of elaborations a measure of contradiction and incoherence which one might metaphorically call roughness and rugosity.

12. António Gomes – His original fate was to become the heteronym of heteronym Pantaleão, but he gained a measure of autonomy around 1913. Pessoa intended to transfer to him the entirety of that other heteronym's oeuvre: "With a degree in Philosophy from the University of the Useless", he is the author of *História cómica do sapateiro Afonso* (The Comical Story of Shoemaker Afonso) – an imaginary book with a critique of Afonso Costa, the minister of justice in Teófilo Braga's government. In 1915, he also wrote *A Universidade de Lisboa,* a pamphlet in which he ridiculed Pessoa's former teachers and illustrious members of that institution such as the doctor Queiroz Veloso and (Joaquim Fernandes) Teófilo Braga, Portugal's first president. Although aprocryphal, the project of a correspondence school should be attributed to that *António Gomes, of the Portuguese Animal Protection Society:*

> We teach the idle, people of society and merely decorative personalities – all those who, in truth, have no true purpose in the world. We teach them to keep the dignity of idleness.[8]

13. António Mora (Dr. Garcia Nobre) – Given birth in the end of 1914, he was to "continue the work of Caeiro" and to be the mouthpiece for Ricardo Reis. His name is likely a mix of one of his own names with the surname of Madame la Comtesse de Mora (the empress Eugénie, wife of Napoleon III) – to whom Félix Goidefroid dedicated his music "Un soir à Lima", which his mother played on the piano in Durban; or a reference to the municipality of Mora, in Évora. "An imposing figure, tall, all-white beard and a lively, haughty stare", he wore a white tunic and sandals much like a Roman, although he is a voracious reader of the Greek Aristotle. A cultured man, he could recite in "a beautiful voice" the

7 *Translator's note:* 'Trash' is 'lixo' in Portuguese.

8 A reference to Cicero's (106-43 BC) *Cum dignitate otium* (Leisure with honour), the ideal of those who retired from Roman public life.

lamentations of Aeschylus' *Prometheus* (and held that "the race of gods and Man is one"); and another Greek poet, Pindar (518-438 BC), of which a single work survived, his *Victory Odes* – almost the title Álvaro de Campos ended up using for his "Triumphal Ode". He wrote more pages than Caeiro and Reis together. Mora is "a clandestine editor" of *Athena* magazine, administrated by Ruy Vaz and Pessoa himself. As per the Chest's papers, these were the plans for Mora:

Athena	– *Cadernos de reconstrução pagã* (Notebooks of pagan reconstruction) 64 to 128 pages per issue Price: 300 réis (?) Editor: António Mora. Irregular publication.
First Notebook	– Preface: António Mora (…) *O regresso dos deuses* (Return of the Gods) – António Mora
Second Notebook	– *Introdução ao estudo da metafísica* (Introduction to the study of metaphysics) – António Mora
Third Notebook	– *Milton superior a Shakespeare* (Milton greater than Shakespeare) – António Mora
Fourth Notebook	– *Ensaio sobre a disciplina* (Essay on discipline) – António Mora

His output consists of *Prolegómenos a uma reforma do paganismo* (Prolegomena for a reform of paganism); *Tratado da negação* (Treaty of Denial) – in which he claims "Lucifer, the lightbearer, is the nominal symbol of the spirit which denies"; and, above all, *O regresso dos deuses* (Return of the Gods), originally meant for Ricardo Reis. Texts which Álvaro de Campos holds up as "wonders of originality". He was a rationalist, philosophical, a sociologist and theoretician of neopaganism. "With the fall of Arabism[9], its lesser facet remains – that of religious fanaticism". He offers his work to Apollo, as, according to Mora, it was "against Christ", even though Pessoa held the former as "the great bastard"[10]. "My mission was to explain. I explained. I did not initiate, I followed!". In Mora, "the demonstration of paganism is complete", as evidenced in texts such as the following:

9 The Iberian Peninsula had been under Muslim occupation for over 500 years.

10 Apollo was Zeus' illegitimate son with the Eastern goddess Latona. A bloodthirsty god, he decimated armies with the plague, murdered Cassandra and killed Laertius' two grandsons.

> The so-called pagan religion is the most natural of all. The first distinctive trait of a religion is that it is natural. That which is most acceptable for the pagan in Christianity is the popular faith in miracles and saints, the rites, the pilgrimages. Thus, the pagan is the conscious creator of his own gods, whereas the Christian does so unconsciously.

In search of an art of all arts, Pessoa realized that the only feasible plan for his ideas was to conceive it, not as a space, but as a time, which was why he leaned on the discovery of relativity by Lithuanian Hermann Minkowski (1854-1909) and Albert Einstein (1879-1955). In that fourth temporal dimension, which Sensationism adopted, "a living medium and a writing medium" would be able to project themselves into another world. "For António Mora, the soul is immortal because it is atemporal, and the soul is less real than the body, *so much so, that it cannot see"*. Mora would then move on to defend the two main tenets of Sensationism: "To feel everything in every possible way" and "to be all and everyone". He had the following outlined in chapter 3 of *Prolegómenos:*

1. Dimension – point – reality – soul
2. " – line – movement (time) – feeling
3. " – plane – space – representation
4. " – figure – space – time
5. " – …

Mora also wrote numerous texts on politics. In one of them he stood "for Germany", expressing his admiration of that country's cultural movers and shakers, such as Goethe, Hegel and Kant. Pessoa reacted with *Resposta to A*[ntónio] *Mora* (A Response to António Mora), in which he said: "It is a most cruel irony that such a race, which considers Latins degenerate and stupid, would find in a Latin spirit its greatest justifier. I do believe Dr. António Mora hasn't quite grasped the psychic phenomenon which is conventionally called German culture". Committed to a hospice in Cascais, he suffered from "interpretative mania" – a condition which causes the patient to "formulate a theory, or what he supposes to be a theory, and interpret every fact according to it, even those that have little bearing to the matter the theory is concerned with". Mora was "clinically, not very far from what one might consider paranoid" and was "also hysterical. But paranoia is sometimes accompanied by intercurrent psychoneurosis". Occasionally, he uses a different name, Dr. Garcia Nobre. When Pessoa met him, shortly before his death, his head "was already all white". As Campos summed it up: "António Mora was a shade with speculative whims, but he found Caeiro and found the truth. My master Caeiro gave him the soul he did not possess". As if that weren't enough, Mora also wrote poems like "Aforismos" (Aphorisms, 10/10/1919), in which the following two verses stand out:

We want one thing
We do another.
We are the ones who want
We are not the ones who do.
(…)
We are others. We die
The life we live.
The us we are is nothing.
Those who are pass by the road
Of our consciousness.
There is no science for this.

– António Passos – Another name quoted by Stoker.

14. Anthony Harris – This name appears three times in the margins of unpublished texts. Among them, according to Stoker, a poem in which Alexander Search is criticized. Of a naive temperament, his style is tormented and dynamic.

15. Arcla – Chronicler of *Civilização* newspaper. One of his texts, "Secção alegre" (Joyful section) reads:

Down Rua da Imprensa went
A hurried congressman
(…)
He shoved the door open, went up the stairs
And then, oh, lordy! This is what I heard
Amidst great shouting and yelling
(…)
And, hugging the other, he wept
(…)
Oh, the ministers! Oh, the presidency!
Come to the arms of these disgraced wretches
We promise we shall be honourable
And govern with great intelligence
(Huddling, crying and swinging to and fro).

– Armando Couto (A. Couto) – One of the owners and main editors of *A Civilização* newspaper – the newsroom of which was at Rua da Escola Politécnica, 19, Lisbon. That newspaper, first published on the 16th of April 1909, amused itself with news such as: "Mr. Mário Freitas [Pessoa's cousin] suffers from mental alienation"; "congressman Pessoa published some verses in English", or "the current Treasury minister attempted suicide, throwing himself off the bottom of his bed". Against it soon rose *O Progresso,* which Armando accused of having had "a bout of acute laziness".

– Augusto Magenta – Author of the (imaginary) book *O amor* (Love), announced in *O Palrador.*

– Augustus Search – One of the Search brothers. He appears in a letter by Charles. It is unknown which projects Pessoa had in mind for him.

– Augustus (Augustus Bernard, Augustine) West – It is unclear who he might have been. The heteronym signed a poem with a pen; on the margin of the verse "cry when you remember me", his name is scratched out – this according to Stoker. He appears in several documents in the Chest, with different handwriting. His surname was inspired by Martin West, the first governor of the Cape, the name of the street in his Durban address: West Street.

– Author of the Letter from Argentina – This text (1912-1913) only recently came to light. The author's name is unknown, as the letter is unsigned, in which he wrote touching words for a friend called Guilherme, consul at Buenos Aires. In that letter, he says "it might be interesting to write to someone and tell them my life". The author, "a commercial clerk" much like Pessoa, had made acquaintance of the addressee in "a night café". He also confesses: "I left my wife six months ago. Did you know I was married? Of course you didn't". In the end, he declares: "I leave life bereft of hope, longing and remorse". The text is titled "[Uma] Carta da Argentina" ([A] Letter from Argentina). It might just have been a project for a short story, but it remains unknown what sort of role this letter played in Pessoa's oeuvre. Nor could its author be considered a true heteronym.

– August Wyatt – Just the name identifying him as a (supposed) writer.

– Aurélio Biana – Just a name quoted by Stoker.

17 – Baron of Teive – His final heteronym, who only came to light well after Pessoa's death. His first name was Carlos, followed by the three letters of a middle name: "Fer" or "Fon". Perhaps Ferreira (as Jerónimo Pizarro believes), or Fonseca (as per Richard Zenith). Even when holding the original in hand, and bearing in mind the quirks of Pessoa's handwriting, it is hard to say which. His surname is illegible, scratched out beyond all recognition, other than the "M" it begins with. Perhaps Morais, which is quite a common surname in Portugal, or a reference to Mora (like António Mora), or probably Macieira, where the heteronym is to have been born. Pessoa mentioned him in a letter to Gaspar Simões (28/06/1932) in a list of heteronyms "still to come". His first writings survived in a black notebook, and are dated the 6th of August 1928. Álvaro Coelho de Athayde, son of a distinguished family, was the twentieth (or

fourteenth) Baron of Teive. That name, Teive, was supposed to be temporary, but Pessoa ended up never changing it. The inspiration (likely) stemmed from one Diogo Teive, a humanist who wrote verses in Latin, a shieldbearer of Prince Henry, who discovered the isles of Terceira and Corvo, and magistrate at Terceira, where *dona* Maria was born.

The character reproduces Pessoa's life in many ways. "I could never contain the influx or heredity and the upbringing of my childhood". "As a child, I feared neither man nor beast; but I was afraid of dark rooms... I remember how that apparent distinctiveness disoriented the simple psychology of those around me". His mother died, which led to disillusionment. "My mother's death broke the last of the external bonds which still connected me to life's sensibilities". An aristocrat, much like Pessoa liked to consider himself, and wealthy, as Pessoa could only wish he were. He spent some periods in a psychiatric clinic in Lisbon, where Pessoa often tried to visit him. They met there once, which is why he said: "To Teive I bequeath the speculation concerning the certainty that madmen have more than we do". He is obsessed with his oeuvre, "this incoherent pile of as of yet unwritten things". And keeps his distance from others. "I have never been mistreated by anyone, in any way, shape or form. All have ever treated me well, but with distance. I soon realized the distance was of my own doing, emanating from me". "Thus, I can freely say I have always been respected. But not loved or cherished, never that". Teive is Pessoa himself. Even in his sex life, vowing never to marry out of fear of loving. Shy with women, sexually frustrated, he can't even relate intimately to the maids who served in his farmstead, in the outskirts of Lisbon. In his own words: "There was no maid in my house I couldn't have seduced. But some were large, others were small, others were ugly. And so the peculiarity of love passed me by, as did most of life". The notion of such hypothetical conquests would become more distant still when the Baron's leg was amputated, much like Rimbaud. Bravely, he refused anaesthetics during surgery. "I never feared suffering; rather, I held it in contempt".

Close to the end, he burned all of his manuscripts in an oven – a gesture inspired by Pessoa's friend, Santa-Rita Pintor, who had died in 1918. "For the past two days, I spent my time burning them, one by one – and it took me two days, because I would read a manuscript here and there". "I do not regret having burned the drafts of my oeuvre. This is all I have to bequeath to the world". *This* was his sole work to survive the fire, *A educação do estóico* (The Education of the Stoic), the subtitle of which was *A impossibilidade de fazer arte superior* (The Impossibility of Creating Superior Art). To him, it was almost "a will". Underneath the title, he scribbled with a pen: "The lone manuscript of the Baron of Teive". Richard Zenith contends he meant to have written "last", but changed his mind mid-writing. An impression I also shared as I analyzed the word. That reference to a "manuscript", which is present in every publication, might not have been Pessoa's definitive choice, as he also wrote "script" above it. A habit of his, of writing two (or more) words in the text, so he could later pick the one which seemed most appropriate. In this case, he forgot to cross off one of them, and the choice became the later editors'.

When compared to Bernardo Soares, who wrote *Educação sentimental* (Sentimental Education) in 1910, Pessoa believed "their style differs, in that the nobleman's is intellectual, bare of images, whereas the farmer's is fluid. The nobleman thinks with clarity, the bookkeeper can barely hold his emotions and thoughts in check". Their sole points of contact were the themes, their "incompetence in living" and their "feeling of exclusion". And they wrote with the same substance of style, the same grammar. They wrote in a style which, "good or bad, is mine". In the end, Teive wasn't Soares' counterpoint, but rather Álvaro de Campos', who had reached his zenith by then. The two share a number of bits of imagery, especially when one compares *Estóico* to "Tobacco Shop", as in the following examples:

Stoic	Tobacco Shop
Whenever I feel certain of something, I remember that all madmen felt even moreso.	*In every asylum there are so many nut-cases with so many certainties!*
Rather to dream than to be.	*I'm nothing Even so, I have all the dreams of the world in me.*
From my window… which isn't even one.	*Windows of my room, Of my room, one of the millions in the world no one knows who owns*

At the end of *Stoic*'s ante-penultimate chapter, it reads: "I believe I have attained the peak of the employment of reason. That is why I must kill myself" – a gesture inspired by Pessoa's friend Sá-Carneiro. "I put an end to a life which I believed able to contain all manner of greatness, and which I saw contain but the inability of wanting them". "That which will drive me to suicide is an impulse akin to that which drives us to go to bed early. I have an intimate slumber of all intentions. Nothing can transform my life now". But he soon realizes there is "something sordid, and even more ridiculous than sordid, about this habit of the weak of making universal tragedies out of the sad comedies of personal tragedies". In the end: "If the loser is the one who dies and the winner the one who kills, with this, confessing myself beaten, I declare myself a winner". Richard Zenith suggests that *Pessoa was frightened and created the baron to save him from himself. And so, the Baron of Teive was born to die.* At Quinta da Macieira, where he lived. On the 11th of July 1920, according to Pessoa. Which is probably why the initial date of 1928 for *Estóico* was changed to 1920. News of his death appeared "in the obituary of a common newspaper" – *Diário de Notícias.*

– Benjamim Vizetelly-Cymbra – Administrator of *O Palrador.*

18. Bernardo Soares– Already described in his own chapter.

– Bi – A nickname he used for heteronym Íbis. And also a pet name for his nephew Luís Miguel.

19. C. Pacheco – He was but "a half-ruined aristocrat, an idle nobleman of sorts, somewhat maniacal". Despite having so few qualities, in 1917, Pessoa entrusted him with the mission of expressing his "mental automatism". He wrote obscure, visionary poems for *Orpheu* and *Europa,* which he titled "Notas" (Notes). Among them, the only one of which a copy remains, "Para além d'outro oceano" (Beyond another ocean) – dedicated *to the memory of Alberto Caeiro,* destined for *Orpheu 3,* which begins thus:

> In a feverish feeling of being beyond another ocean
> There were positions of a clearer, limpid living
> And appearances of a city of beings
> Nut unreal, but livid of impossibility, enshrined in naked purity.

The "C" probably stands for Coelho, thus, Coelho Pacheco, which was part of a long list of Portuguese authors typewritten by Pessoa. In this case, there did indeed exist one José Coelho de Jesus Pacheco (1894-1951), from Lisbon, son of a drugstore's assistant and a housemaid. Self-taught in languages, he dreamed to be an aviator or playwright, and attended the first years of an engineering degree (at Instituto Superior Técnico). He was the nephew of a good friend (and business partner) of Pessoa's, Geraldo Coelho de Jesus, as well as the editor of *A Renascença* magazine – which only had one issue published, in February 1914. The same Pacheco that Fernando Carvalho Mourão dedicated a poem to ("Sonhos") from his book *Pétalas de rosas* (1913). But his interest in literary endeavours was to be short-lived, as he soon showed a preference for the art of getting rich. He began working in the automobile business right after his wedding in 1919. In the 20s, he was already connected to the firm J. Coelho & Germano, at Rua Borges Carneiro 25, Campo de Ourique, dedicated to the *manufacturing of chassis and carriages;* and, on the 21st of March 1947, he would become senior partner of J. Coelho Pacheco Lda. – with an *office, stand, garage, and section of Ni-Fe accumulators,* as per an ad, at *Rua Braamcamp 92/94, near Largo do Rato.* According to its constituent acts, it was dedicated to *the industry of repairing automobiles and the like* and, due to its actual business, was better known as Stand Graham Paige. António Luís de Seabra Palmeirim – *de Seabra,* like Pessoa's paternal family – was a minority partner. Coelho Pacheco would pass away in 1951.

The assumption that C. Pacheco was a heteronym stems from a series of respectable hints. The fact that the real José Coelho Pacheco had been unknown as a writer, and only now has evidence thereof emerged, thanks to granddaughter Ana Rita Palmeirim. As well as his letter to Pessoa, on the 20th of February 1915, in which he declares to have known him *since the times of* Orpheu *and* A Renascença *(you might not even remember that one, even though you were a collaborator);* and another one, on the 20th of March 1935, in which he thanked Pessoa for having sent him *Message* and claimed to know it by heart and that he had *recited it to several people,* after which he bids his goodbye with *a big hug from your old friend J. Coelho Pacheco.* It is known that he wrote "Para além d'outro oceano" for a magazine run by Pessoa, it would stand to reason that he would mention it in at least one of the letters. Another hint is the fact that JCP never signed his name as C. Pacheco; the two texts in his magazine were signed as J. Coelho Pacheco, and the other as Line (a heteronym). To add another layer of mystery to this character, a to-do list by Pessoa of 1913 included the following note: "Check (C. Pacheco) if the trenchcoat is lost". Also, the fact that "Para além d'outro oceano", written in 1916, had been dedicated "to the memory of Alberto Caeiro", when Caeiro's first text would only be published in 1922. Thus, only someone close to Pessoa (as we now know to be the case) could have known at the time that Alberto Caeiro would some day be published. Or the fact that he had already *died* (in 1915). Or that, in his poem, JCP spoke of sheep's flocks much like those from Caeiro's "The Keeper of Sheep". To say nothing of the fact that, in "Falou com Deus" (01/02/1913), Pessoa had already used the words of that very title:

> What boat do I sail in
> Beyond the ocean
> God spoke to Human…
> I am even that which I am not.

As it happened, after this book's first edition, on the 3rd of May 2011, *Jornal de Letras* published an article from Teresa Rita Lopes, in which some clues on the character's identity were handed out. The source was the abovementioned granddaughter of JPC, Ana Rita Palmeirim. When I came in contact with her, she showed me the original. Or more than an original, as I realized it was a draft of the poem, which could only mean it truly was his. Thus, and with the data we have available today, there seems to be a reasonable amount of certainty that the poem isn't Pessoa's, but the real Coelho Pacheco's. This being the case, we can definitely cross this one from Pessoa's extensive list of heteronyms.

20. Cæsar Serk – Initially, it was to be a character for *Ultimus joculatorum* (The Last of the Mockers), ergo the Latin name. Pessoa thought of giving said name to another heteronym and wrote "Cæsar Serk (= Alexander Search)". But Cæsar would gain a life of his own, "oblivious to laughter, always between deep meditation and tortured bitterness".

21. Dr. Caloiro – He wrote texts for *O Palrador* (1902), which appropriate for his 14 years of age, such as "A pesca das pérolas" (Fishing for Pearls), which ends thus:

> A being classified on the lower rung of the scale of creation is able to produce a marvel of beauty – an incomparable jewel to shine on a monarch's diadem, to be the symbol of all that is most precious and pure to the poet!

Next to the signature, a comment by Pessoa: "Should be more serious".

22. Capitaine Thibeaut – "I couldn't have been older than five [in other texts, six], and, being an isolated child who didn't wish to be so, I was accompanied by some figures from my dreams". Perhaps that is why he considers that "imaginary figures are more important and truthful than real ones"; and recalls "somewhat less vividly, a rival of Chevalier de Pas". It is Captain Thibeaut. While playing, he said sister Teca was a *lieutenant.* One rung below, as she was younger than *captain* Pessoa.

– Carlos de Teive – This name was simply crossed under *Carta da Argentina.* Likely Barão de Teive.

23. Carlos Otto – A satirical poet and a collaborator at *O Phosphoro,* he had also been entrusted with the translations of Arthur Morrinson. He penned *Tratado da luta livre – método Yvelot* (A Treaty on Wrestling – The Yvelot Method), which, as per instructions, was to be published with a photo of the author on the cover (with no indication as to which photo, exactly. The book is a detailed repertoire of moves – with special emphasis on "the leg sweep", which could be "sideways, frontal" or even "posterior, applied to the back of the leg". Upon perusing the text, one gets the feeling that it was Angolan capoeira. In one of his poems, "Sonho de Górgias" (Gorgias' Dream), Otto said:

> I dreamt a colossal, eternal[11] city
> Beyond the feeling and idea of existing
> Which not even love could smile at.
> So peculiar to that which we nicknamed real.

11 The variant was *shapeless.*

In 1909, he wrote "Epigram":

> One day, feeling itchy
> To play the biggest prank
> Blunder made religions.
>
> The sceptre of Horror had fallen off one boat
> And, nearby, they were making the hollow and broken
> Statues of Having, Time, and Space[12].

On the 8th of March 1910, he scribbled the beginning of a poem, in which he says: "I love that which the notion of gods daren't". In that same year, Otto writes to Mário Nogueira de Freitas (Pessoa's cousin) on the back of an envelope about "the tutelary goddess[13] of decadent things", and that was the last that was ever heard from him.

– Catherine Search – Another Search, this one the sole sister among four siblings. Much like Augustus, she shows up in an annotation made by Charles. No further references exist of what plans Pessoa had for her.

– Caturra Júnior – An author mentioned in *O Palrador.*

24. Cecília – She wrote riddles for *O Palrador* (1902). Such as this one, dedicated to the heteronym Velhote:

> I am as much beast as I am man.
> In the garden I can be found
> In the living room, on a divan
> My locations positively abound.

25. Cego que faz quadras à maneira de Bandarra (Blind Man who writes quatrains in Bandarra's style) – In the 20s, Pessoa wrote dozens of quatrains on the typewriter, most half-improvised, sometimes paying no attention to metric, perhaps because "he who writes popular quatrains communes with the soul of the people". Casais Monteiro called them *a collection of little bland quatrains, as the people write them (hmm), which should have remained where they were found.* To the commentators of his oeuvre, those *Quatrains of the Bandarrist blind man* have a style unlike any other heteronym's. They are much like *trovas,* their style messianic, such as this one:

---

12 Another reference to *The Divine Comedy.* In the annotations preceding Chant XIV, an image with clay feet is called *Statue of Time* by Dante.

13 Some ancient gods had them, such as the sons of the Egyptian god Horus: Isis was Imseti's, Nephtys was Hapi's, Neit was Duamutef's, and Serket was Kebehsenuef's. Pessoa likely created his own, as there is no record to this one's identity.

I feel closely that which lies distant
When I do not believe I see
My body sits on today
My soul wanders infinity.

The presence of simple quatrains amidst the elaborate poems Pessoa wrote shouldn't in any way feel peculiar. In January 1927, he complimented "perfect poems with four verses", claiming that "a well-wrought sentence in a quatrain adds something to the system of the universe". He would also mention the blind man in quatrains of his own, on the 26th of February 1931:

I went to the window
Because I heard singing.
A blind man and his guitar
Both of them weeping.

Both worthy of pity
They are as one
Wandering the world
Eliciting pity.

I, too, am a blind man
Singing on the road,
The road is larger
And I ask for nothing.

He seemed not to have decided what to name the character, and didn't even give him a specific name.

26. Charles James Search – Born on the 18th of April 1886, supposedly[14] a year before Ricardo Reis. Thus, he was "two years older than his brother Alexander Search". Pessoa pondered attributing to him the book *The Portuguese regicide and the political situation in Portugal.* But he would end up with menial tasks, such as "writing prefaces" for his brother's works. He was also "only to translate" into English and anthology of Portuguese authors: Almeida Garrett, Antero de Quental, Eça de Queiroz, Guerra Junqueiro; as well as the odd work such as the poem *El estudiante de Salamanca,* by Spanish writer Espronceda y Delgado (1804-1842), a translation which ended up signed by the heteronym Herr Prosit. Showing just how little regard he held for him, Pessoa admitted he might "write the prefaces for his translations", but only "if they offer no analysis".

14 An English word amidst the Portuguese text. He would use it for Jean-Seul de Méuret as well, as we will see further up ahead.

27. Charles Robert Anon – He showed up around 1903, unworthy of a place or date of birth. In a diary written in English, which Pessoa penned in 1906, his stamp appears on every page. "At the age of eighteen", and "single (with the odd exception)", he is Anglo-Portuguese – "an English-styled Portuguese", with "traces of dipsomania, *dégénéré supérieur,* poet". Anon evoked his own family drama. "I remembered my mother, who I had lost in my first childhood". A letter of his contained the address of Rua de São Bento, 98, 2nd left – aunt Anica's house, where Pessoa was living at the time. He tried several letter closings, settling for "yours very true, Anon". His surname is an evident shortening of *anonymous,* and it was how he signed his texts for Durban's *Natal Mercury,* wondering whether C.H. Hagger (director at the Commercial School) should use the title of doctor; commenting the translation of one of Horatio's odes; or writing riddles by way of short poems. A writer of short stories, he claimed to be "a citizen of the world and a philosopher". Upon his return from Africa, he wrote sonnets in English and philosophical meditations such as *Death,* in which he says:

> Beauteous Earth, it seems impossible that one day we shall have to leave you. Before the dead, especially when they led happy lives, we realize how fragile life is. The long process of dying is more painful than death itself.

The first heteronym to deserve an extensive oeuvre, he meant to write *The world as power and as not-being, Metaphysics of power, Philosophical essays,* and to produce a *Book on physiognomy.* He wrote drafts for a comedy *(Marin),* as well as an essay (06/04/1905) on that literary genre. His is the phrase that Pessoa liked so much: "The possible is the real". He hated "priests and kings, a hate which grew in my like an overflowing flood" and soon turned against "an eminently stupid and eminently mean god". In 1906, trying to articulate what he truly felt, he wrote two *epitaphs:*

From the Catholic Church:	Here lies the devil The world hath now but little evil.
And from God:	He's dead now And the world hath no more evil.

He would also confess to having rid himself "of the immoral, false influence of Christ. I could take pity on kings and priests, as they were but men". It was also at that time that he wrote *Excommunication,* of which only a fragment remains (abridged):

> I, Charles Robert Anon,
> Being, animal, mammal, tetrapod, primate

Placental, ape (...)
In the name of TRUTH, SCIENCE and PHILOSOPHIA,
Not with bell, book and candle, but with pen, ink and paper,
Pass sentence of excommunication on all priests and all sectarians
of all religions in the world.
Excommunicabo vos.
Be damned to you all.
Ainsi-soit-il.
Reason, Truth, Virtue
By C.R.A.

C.R.A. would, however, be short-lived, and would become Alexander Search in 1908. In *Elegy* (1905), under that convoluted original signature of his, it reads "C.R. Anon, *id est* Alexander Search", and it was Search who wrote some of the poems previously attributed to him, such as "The death of the titan", "Sonnet" and "Rondeau". Angolan writer José Eduardo Agualusa says in "Catálogo de sonhos", an amusing short story, that Search went to live in Bahia, where he was often visited by Aleister Crowley, who we will read up on further ahead. *Dona* Inácia, a maid who served him for 35 years, says he died of heart failure in 1970. He remained a bachelor, as doctor *Carlos Roberto* [Charles Robert] *is a serious person, very respectful, and doesn't indulge in sin, not even in thought.*

28. Chevalier de Pas – His first heteronym, first conceived when Pessoa was still living at Rua de São Marçal. Born in France, he evoked the upbringing Pessoa received at home. Niece Manuela Nogueira showed us a *Floral Birthday Book* from her mother, which today remains locked in a closet in her living room. According to Manuela, Pessoa penned in it his first ever writing, *Cavaleiro de Pá* (1st of July) and *Chelavier de Pá* (11/07/1894). In both cases it is only the sound of the name *Pas,* without the "s" it would later acquire – not the French noun for *step* (as per Irene Ramalho Santos, who calls it *Cavaleiro do Passo),* but the adverb of denial. In several texts, Pessoa recalls "one Chevalier de Pas[15] from when I was six, by way of whom I wrote letters to myself", "retelling daily events" and "whose figure, while not entirely vague, still earns that part of my affection which most resembles longing". Likely a double of his father, whose absence was so keenly felt in his life.

15 Likely just a coincidence, but in his travels, Eça de Queiroz used a calling card saying *Le Chevalier de Queiroz.*

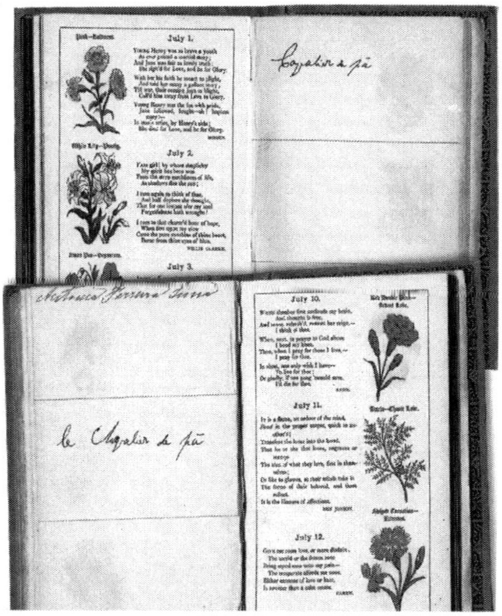

Pessoa's mother's book

29. Claude Pasteur – French, translator of *Cadernos de reação pagã* (directed by António Mora). The name is perhaps allusive to Louis Pasteur (1822-1895), the inventor of microbiology and the rabies shot, who also studied the fermentation process of beer – a drink which Pessoa never particularly favoured.

30. Dare (Erasmus) – In *Ultimus joculatorum,* he defines him as "a philanthropist, a good friend of [Cesar] Serk's", sometimes also signing as Erasmus. But Pessoa could never really decide which was his name.

– Darm Mouth – Another name quoted by Stoker.

31. David Merrick – A literary critic during Pessoa's time at Durban, he is to have written *Epitaph of the Catholic Church, Satan's Soliloquy, The Devil's Voice, Tales of a Madman* and *Pieces in sub umbra* – among which is the short story "The Atheist", which fancied itself as "a study of religion". All of them unfinished. Pessoa had also reserved *The schoolmaster tale* for him, but Charles Robert Anon ended up co-opting it. In an 89 page notebook which ended up known as *The David Merrick Notebook,* he wrote "sonnets, legends, etc." in English, as well as projects for odes. In a Mark Twain book, he noted down "David Merrick, 1903". Everything points to Merrick having metamorphosed into Charles Robert Anon, and Anon, in turn, into Alexander Search, as we've previously established. To Robert Bréchon, *Merrick embodies the obscure phase*

of Pessoa, the tragic feeling of a life which, already at the time, was tearing his heart. In one of his poems, "Inês de Castro", we have the following lament:

These hands I've kissed, how cold they are
These lips (…) where mine lived
In my absent-minded thoughts
How pale and livid!
Oh, the horror of looking upon you![16]

32. Detective Ingês (English Detective) – The sobriquet of the one who was to write "the crime novel *A Boca do Inferno*" – based on the faked death of Aleister Crowley at Boca do Inferno, in Cascais. The novel had a completed first draft, and had the following index:

Preface
Chapter I – The path of the Devil
Chapter II – Preparing the deed
Chapter III/IV – The case begins/Aleister Crowley in Portugal
Chapter V – In which mystification occurs
Chapter VI/VII – The unexpected alibi/Mr. Cole
Chapter VIII – The duality Crowley-Cole
Chapter IX – Case closed
Chapter X – Murder and an epitaph

The end of that novel reads: "The doubtlessly humble grave is certainly bereft of any and all inscription. If any were to be carved, and if one in English should do, then it ought to be searched for in Shakespeare".

33. Diabo Azul (Blue Devil) – Around 1908, when he wrote for Lisbon's weekly newspaper *O Pimpão,* Pessoa used that name. His writings were quite diverse, however, which leads one to suspect some might have been written by his uncle Henrique Rosa. He also wrote odd riddles for *O Palrador,* such as this one:

In the first, you shall see
An animal
In the second, you shall revisit
Said animal
On the whole, you shall find
That animal.

16 Inês de Castro was a Galician noblewoman who became the bride of Peter I (1320-1367), future eight king of Portugal, and who was killed by order of Peter's father due to adultery. After becoming king, Peter ordered his court to kiss the bones of his beloved, and had her killers executed, which is why Merrick ends the poem with the verse "I had them killed, Inês".

334 Diniz da Silva – A modernist poet who, much like Sá-Carneiro, lived in Paris. In *Europa* magazine, under the collective title of *Loucura* (Madness), he published a set of three poems, among which "Eu" (I), which begins thus:

I am mad and recall
A distant, unfaithful memory
Of one transitory thing
Which I dreamed of having as a child.

And ends as follows:

Like the starry canopy of a beggar
In the useless bend of the road I linger in
Of the uncertain road I do not follow.

35. Eduardo Lança – Born on the 15th of September 1875, in Salvador (Brazil). The place was inspired by Father António Vieira, who lived, suffered and died there. An orphan (like Pessoa), he went to live in Lisbon (like Pessoa). The studied administration in Brazil (much like Pessoa did, in Africa), and was employed at a trading house in Lisbon (just like Pessoa). He was to have written the 1894 book *Impressões de um viajante em Portugal* (Impressions of a traveller in Portugal), almost akin to Pessoa's *What the Tourist Should See*, which was "wonderfully written, in a beautiful and truly Portuguese style". The following year, he was to have published "a book of beautiful verses", *Folhas outonais* (Autumn leaves). In 1897, another one, *Coração enamorado* (Enamoured heart). In 1902, *Ao luar* (Under the light of the moon). But his best book of poetry, written in 1900, was to have been *Os meus mitos* (My myths). Initially, Pessoa had also destined him *Sonetos de amor* (Sonnets of love), which was later signed by F. Nogueira Pessoa instead. He was a collaborator for some Brazilian newspapers, "which we can hardly specify, so many were they". During Pessoa's trip to Terceira, between May and July 1902, he signed two poems under this heteronym's name. One is "Estátuas" (Statues), which ends thus:

'tis why I look back and see myself as Dust
The green illusions of my past
And, much like the wife of faithful Lot[17]
I linger, petrified, weeping.

The other was "Enigma"; a simple quatrain published in *O Palrador:*

I, who have declared open war to human respite
Know thousands of lovers who envy me!
I feed off blood, and drink of life
In the arms of whoever wishes to give me death!

17 The nephew of Abraham. Upon fleeing Sodom, his wife (the Bible does not specify a name) looked back, in spite of the angels' prohibition, and was turned into a salt statue.

36. Efbeedee Pasha – The name is a play on the sound of the letters F, B and D in English. Pessoa did not write what it might have meant. As a guess, I assume it might have been Familial British Disorder, a malady akin to Alzheimer's, which was unknown at the time, and that it might have alluded to Pessoa's time in Durban: F for Fernando, B for Blackmore House, the name of his school's dormitory, and D for Durban. Should that be the case, the name would mean something like Fernando, the Pasha of of Blackmore-Durban. The heteronym meant to write "a book no respectable lady should be seen reading, but which many of us would like having a peek at", *Stories of Efdeebee Pasha* – "copyright in Great Britain, San Marino and Andorra". He wrote an index and frontispiece for it, as well as newspaper reviews of it, which "while pre-emptive, were nonetheless carefully edited". Such as this one, for the *Sunday School Magazine:* "A copy of this book was acquired for the purposes of its review. Attracted by an unusual ruckus, accompanied by laughter, we had a hard time tearing it off the hands of our deliverymen". Or this one, for *The Sporting Times:* "Such a shame that the author carefully omitted his real name and address, as we count among our staff a number of competent assassins".

– Erasmus – Another name for the heteronym Dare.

– Ex-sergeant William Byng – A heteronym created by heteronym Horace James Faber, in *The case of the science master,* who "was incompetent on common matters". According to Faber, that former sergeant was "an alcoholic, a reasoner, incompetent at daily life", "obscure and reserved" and displayed "an inability to reason with common matters". The character stood out among the others from that book – Inspector Williams, John Lewis, Robert Johnson, Dr. Travers, Francis Jeane, John Blaver, which is why many consider him to be an autonomous heteronym. Much like Pessoa, Byng had bouts of *delirium tremens,* and, much like Pessoa feared would happen to him, died of excessive alcohol consumption, just like fellow heteronym Abílio Quaresma.

37. F. Nogueira Pessoa – He appears on the cover page of notebook 144, which contains the editorial projects of Empresa Íbis. In a list of authors, by order of appearance, we have F. Nogueira Pessoa, Alexander Search and Jean-Seul (de Méluret). It contains the fair copy of the sonnet "Antígona" – the character of Sophocles' tragedy, who stood up to Creon and was sentenced to death for it. Judging by the papers of the Chest, we know that Pessoa destined *Sonetos de amor* (Sonnets of love) to him in June 1902, but he never finished the book, which had originally been meant for Eduardo Lança. Using parts of his full name to form another entity wasn't an isolated case, as we also have António de Seabra, Fernando António and António Nogueira de Seabra.

38. F.Q.A. – He wrote logogryphs for *O Palrador,* such as this one:

> I contain precious stones and gold
> Shining things like silver and ivory
> Large… huge treasure that I hold
> In my exchequer of endless finery.

39. Faustino Antunes – A psychologist who wrote "letters of information concerning my character" to professors in Durban, of which some drafts in English remained, but not the copies of those which were sent. He lived at "Rua da Bela Vista, in Lapa, Lisbon", the address of his great-aunts and grandmother Dionísia (number 17, 1st floor). He left a notebook with attempts at a signature on the back page; as well as an *Essay on intuition,* co-written with fellow heteronym A. Moreira. According to Antunes, "the poet is egocentric, builds others from himself. Falstaff is Shakespeare, as are Pudita[18], Iago, Othello and Desdemona". He further elaborates: "Distance and intuition are identical. It is commonly believed that the poet who creates, the merchant and the diplomat[19] all make use of the same faculty. One might excuse the error, but it is still an error. A more thorough analysis will reveal the difference". He wrote the following comment:

> Great minds know humanity by knowing themselves, whereas small minds are forced to know Man through their own existence.

– Fausto – The main character of an incomplete dramatic poem, which pondered knowledge, the world, pleasure, love and death. He was Pessoa's version of that hero of numerous literary works, of which the best known is Goethe's (1749-1832) – who, in Pessoa's estimation, was "Shakespeare disguised as a sphinx and with his movements impeded by the disguise". The character wins Gretchen's affections, and, as fate would have it, ends up killing her brother, Valentin, in a duel. Maddened by grief and remorse, Gretchen later kills her own son and dies in prison, while Mephistopheles claims the soul promised to him by Faust. By way of reference, Goethe projected and wrote two *Fausts;* whereas Pessoa projected three and finished none. The text is written throughout his life; Goethe began writing his definitive *Faust* in 1773 and only finished it in 1832, the year of his death. In Portugal, some believe the story of Faust was inspired by Friar Gil, the Portuguese Dominican Gil

18 This character does not exist in Shakespeare's oeuvre. Likely a mistake from the person who transcribed Pessoa's text, who misspelled Perdita from *The Winter's Tale.*

19 An ambiguous sentence, like so many others written by Pessoa. He could just as well have meant Shakespeare, a *poet,* who created a *merchant* (in *The Merchant of Venice)* and a *diplomat* (in *Anthony and Cleopatra,* or *Henry IV),* or himself, a *poet* who created, a *tradesman,* is his several attempts at being a businessman, and a student who gave up on the notion of being a *diplomat.*

Rodrigues (1190-1265), who allegedly made a pact with the Devil in exchange for magical powers, and was only freed by the Holy Mary. Eça de Queiroz wrote a short story about it, "São Frei Gil, o Fausto Português", in which he said: *His name was Gil Rodrigues e Valadares, and he is said to have been "Faust" – because he made a pact with the Devil – and "Saint", first by the voice of the people, and then by the Church's (he was canonized in 1749).* Pessoa's Fausto expressed anguish and pain more akin to the author than the character. For Teresa Rita Lopes, Fausto was to be *the starting point of all other characters, the raw matter from which Pessoa retrieved his heteronyms.*

40. Ferdinand Sumwan – A heteronym that Pessoa projected himself into. Another name for him, perhaps, as he wrote in the aforementioned *Ultimus joculatorum* "Ferdinand Sumwan (= Fernando Pessoa, since Sumwan = some one = Person = Pessoa)". Symptomatically, he is described in English as a "normal, useless, careless, lazy, negligent and weak" individual.

41. Fernando António – He took part in some newspaper competitions and even won a small prize, along with ten other contestants, in *Pearson's Weekly*'s[20] *Picture words.* Nothing else is said about the award.

42. Fernando António Nogueira de Seabra – He wrote an untitled book in English about the occult sciences, which would be part of a *Theosophical and esoterical collection* (1926) meant for Livraria Clássica Editora, defined as "an essay and other select fragments of the book of golden precepts translated (into English) and with annotations by H.P.B." – the initials of Helena Petrovna Blavatsky. The translator (of this and the remaining volumes of the collection) was Fernando Pessoa, as stated on the frontispiece. The heteronym also answers for *Cartas do outro mundo* (Letters from the Other World). Those two books, along with a third by one M.C.R., are listed under the numbers V, VIII and X in Pessoa's estate. They name no author, unlike all other books from the collection, and so it seemed legitimate to attribute their authorship to Pessoa himself. The heteronym reproduces his name, putting only his registered surname (Pessoa) in place of the paternal surname he didn't get (de Seabra). He never expounded upon the book and the reasons he attributed its authorship to this name.

43. Fernando Castro (Fr. Castro) – Translator of C.W. Leadbeater's *Servants of the Human Race.* The name was inspired by *dona* Fernanda Castro, wife of his friend António Ferro, a very special presence in Pessoa's life. After this book's first edition, I was made aware of an article written by Maria de Fátima de Sá e Melo Ferreira, in which it is revealed that one Fernando de Azevedo

20 An English newspaper with a circulation of 250 thousand copies at the beginning of the 20th century, created by newspaper magnate Sir Cyril Arthur Pearson.

e Castro had existed (1898-1922), and had translated Leadbeater's book. That being the case, we can count one name less for Pessoa's collection.

44. Fernando Pessoa – Has a chapter all of his own.

45. (Dr.) Florêncio Gomes – Psychiatrist, (likely) brother of António Gomes. His was a long text of 55 handwritten and 8 typewritten pages, *Tratado de doenças mentais* (Treatise on mental illness), in which he "clearly showed the evolution of the persecution complex". He was the one who studied the life of the miserable heteronym Marcos Alves, who ended up committing suicide, as we'll see further on.

– Fr. Angard – Another name for A. Francisco de Paula Angard.

– Fr. de Castro – The name is quoted by Stoker, but is likely just a variation of Fernando Castro.

– Francis Neasden – Editor of the humour section of *O Palrador.*

– Frederick Barbarossa – Another name quoted by Stoker. Here, though, it's a mere reference to the eponymous Holy Roman Emperor, who greatly impressed Pessoa.

46. Frederick Wyatt – Another Wyatt brother, who came about around 1913 and earned an extensively practised signature. He lived in Paris and wrote poems and prose in English. Pessoa's friends asked him about his *poor friend,* as Frederick was "the greatest dreamer of all. He was ever incompetent at handling the truth", "always swinging from one extreme to another point of view or action". "Of morbidly childish shyness, or an impetuous, clumsy boldness", "in some occasions, he would shrink; in others, he would shed off his shyness in odd, wild fashion". To sum it up, Wyatt went "from excessive anarchism" to "the arrogance of a perfect aristocrat". But "there was something inexplicable about him which inspired pity". Pessoa believes, perhaps thinking of himself, that "would that he were mad instead; it would have been better for him", and concluded that he was a "poor thing". In a notebook from 1914-1915, he attributed 20 poems to him, which had been written from 1907 to 1908 by Alexander Search, after which Wyatt was consigned to oblivion.

47. Frederico Reis – Essayist, brother of Ricardo Reis, Sá-Carneiro called him *brother Reis* (letter from 18/07/1914). Pessoa drafted a *Crítica de F.*[ernando] *P.*[essoa] *a F.*[rederico] *Reis* (Fernando Pessoa's Critique of Frederico Reis), in which he describes him as "brilliant, combative and lucid", albeit "of intermittent

lucidity, an excessive enthusiasm", as Frederico lived "out there". He left us a text on Ricardo Reis' poetry, which he deems to be of "a sad epicureanism". Deep down, "it is the affirmation of a critic". He wrote a long pamphlet "about the Lisbon school, the heir of the avant-garde spirit of the Coimbra school". His philosophical thoughts were summed up in a brief notation:

> Each of us should live his own life, isolating himself from others and seeking whatever pleases him within the bounds of individual sobriety. He should not seek violent pleasures, nor flee from any painful sensation that isn't extreme.

48. Friar Maurice – An English friar who desperately wishes to be and do good, but who lives in a crisis of faith. In an annotation dated November 1907, he confesses himself "a godless mystic, a Christian bereft of a creed". Pessoa says: "Poor Friar Maurice, you were present, and all was cold, cold, cold, poor Friar Maurice. Friar Maurice is mad. Don't laugh at Friar Maurice". Patiently, he wrote his *The book of Friar Maurice,* of which there are a number of texts, such as the following:

> Half of me is noble and grand, half of me is petty and vile. I am both. Whenever the grand part of me triumphs, I suffer because the other half – which is also truly me, which I didn't manage to alienate from myself – hurts due to it. When the petty part of me triumphs, the noble part suffers and weeps. Ignoble tears or noble tears – all are tears.

49. Gabriel Keene – Author of a novel announced in *O Palrador,* the title of which was to be *Em dias de perigo* (Days of Peril). But apparently, not a single chapter was written.

50. Gallião – He wrote odd riddles for *O Palrador,* dedicated to Gallião Pequeno (a son of his, perhaps), such as this one:

> The Lusitanian plant is thump – 2.

51. Gallião Pequeno – He wrote riddles for *O Palrador,* such as this one:

> 3 – This bashful man is where the wheat is kept – 2

52. (Dr.) Garcia Nobre – Another name for António Mora – "Dr. Garcia Mora, as the patient said".

– Gaud – Another name for Dr. Gaudêncio Nabos.

52. (Dr.) Gaudêncio Nabos (Gaud) – An Anglo-Portuguese comedian, journalist and literary editor of *O Palrador,* "whose character oscillated from

anarchy to open laughter". Since the heteronym expressed himself in English, Pessoa sometimes indicated how his name should be pronounced –"NAY-boes, in fact". He came about when Pessoa made his definitive return to Lisbon (1905), and, unlike his creator, he very much enjoyed using words at odds with the rigid mores of his time, as did Joaquim Moura Costa. In "Salutation to Walt Whitman", for example, Álvaro de Campos says: "Let no son of a… cross my path" – whereas Nabos or Costa would freely have employed the cuss word. For example, one of his writings reads: "Some people seem not to be aware that a courtesan is a whore", to then conclude that: "An individual of scant imagination will take a while until he can understand the meaning of this sentence".

Despite his lack of interest for politics, Nabos had plans for "a project to reorganize slavery", but stopped writing in 1913 and never got around to beginning the text. He was also an "original and brusque" doctor, who "had few patients, as, in his own words, a man would have to be very patient to have him as a doctor". Pessoa says: "I remember the unpleasant feeling he once caused me to feel (I still didn't know him that well), when he stared at me intently for a few seconds and said in a sure voice: *You're either phthisical* (I was chilled to the bone and greatly afraid) *or… or… you're not".* In another passage: "Nabos standing at someone's deathbed, everyone in tears, etc., witnessed: *Where there is life, there is the hope to live.* Appalled, I raised my eyes, his face was livid. I felt a hysterical urge to start laughing". In an (undated) note, he wrote:

> 'tis a nice and glorious thing, to have been in a shipwreck or in a battle; the worst part is that one needs to be there to have been there.

Reflecting upon death, he wrote what he considered his *Metaphysics* (excerpt):

> – To die is for us to die.
> – The horror of dying is that of us dying.
> – Who knows if two parallels don't meet when we lose sight of them?

53. Gee – This one's name is the sound of the letter 'G' in English, was tasked with replying to decipherings at *O Palrador* and wrote metagrams such as the following:

> The Grand element
> Should be in the house
> And his place
> Is greater among the family.

54. George Henry Morse – A spirit who came to him whenever he was in a trance. Less assiduous than others, he always wrote in English.

55. Gervásio Guedes – (Likely) brother of Vicente Guedes, he was the author of *A coroação de Jorge V* (The Coronation of George V), initially attributed to L. Guerreiro; and, before him (or her), to Jim Crown. As said coronation took place on the 22nd of January 1911, the text was most certainly written after that. The heteronym was borne of his attempts at creating the literary magazine *Lusitânia,* later converted into *Orpheu.* But he would be short-lived, as, given his traits, Pessoa would occupy himself with more serious matters. The coronation text reads (excerpt):

> King George has the physiognomy of a fish. It is, however, useless to explain via maritime life that which is much easily and democratically explained by the equivalent of that which gives the fish its peculiar expression.

– Gomes Pipa – Another name for José Gomes.

56. H.H. Fletcher – A companion of Charles Robert Anon's in Durban. Among the books on Pessoa's bookshelf signed by him are *The revised Latin primer,* by Benjamin Hall Kennedy. Reproducing that which also happened with Alexander Search, Charles Robert Anon, Martin Kéravas or Sidney Parkinson Stool. His name was inspired by J(oseph) S(mith) Fletcher, of whom Pessoa had 27 different books. On the margins of a drawing, Pessoa wrote the name differently: Letcher.

57. Henry Lovell – Another not particularly assiduous spirit who wrote in English. At times, it's Henry Lovell = Henry More, with kaballistic signs underneath. His surname was perhaps inspired by James Russell Lowell (1819-1891), a romantic poet and an abolitionist, of whom Pessoa had two books on his bookshelf: *Essays and belles lettres* and *The English poets.*

58. Henry More – Pessoa believed he rubbed shoulders with Henry More (1614-1687), one of the Cambridge Platonists and opponent of Thomas Hobbes' (1588-1679) mechanical philosophy, and called him "Henry More, the Platonist". Together with his signature, there are often two intersected triangles. Astrologer, poet, philosopher and professor, the prose texts of his séances were something akin to "novels of the subconscious". There are some comments by More in some of Pessoa's manuscripts. In *Crepúsculo em Deus* (Twilight in God), which is attributed to Wardour, it reads "no good", followed by a kaballistic sign. In his séances, he says things like: "You are my disciple"; or "You'll soon know that which you have courage for, namely to copulate with a girl"; or "You've been thinking of the girl, leave her alone, she will appear in due time". In a text psychographed the 9th of July 1916, he warns: "You are the centre of an astral conspiracy – the meeting place of elementals of an evil kind. A woman can imagine what your soul is". In another: "My son,

this world we live in is a tangle of incongruence and voracity. Your fate is too grand for me to reveal it to you. You must discover it for yourself. But man is feeble and so too are the Gods. Fate – the nameless God – lords over them from his unreachable throne. My name is mistaken and so is yours. It is not what it seems. Understand this, if you can, and I know you can". After which he signs "More, Henry More, RC Frat" – a reference to the *Rosicrucian Fraternity.* At times, he adds after his signature: "Farewell, my boy".

59. Homem das Nuvens (Man in the Clouds) – Pessoa addressed postcards to his family with this name – including one from Las Palmas to his great-aunt Adelaide Pinheiro d'Andrade Neves. In others, besides the signature of Homem das Nuvens, what appears to be a large, stylized H. Or even only said H, as he did in a postcard given to him by his stepfather, from the *Ran Pa Er* (the ship in which commander Rosa travelled to Durban, still a single man).

60. Horace James Faber (Ex-Sergeant William Byng) – A teller of tales and an essayist, he left us 49 handwritten sheets, unnumbered, almost all archived as *Fragments of tales,* all but six sheets spread out among other envelopes of his estate; plus *Prosa de C.R. Anon* (C.R. Anon's Prose), *Eusem, Considerações e apreciações literárias* (Literary considerations and appraisals), as well as a fragment titled *Almanac of the illustrated diary*[21]. Faber is a crime novelist in the vein of Edgar Allan Poe and Arthur Conan Doyle. He and Anon were "two inseparable friends". But, whereas Anon wrote stories *of the imagination,* his were *detective stories* whose main character was a deductive genius by the name of ex-sergeant Byng. In an annotation on the margin of *The case of the science master,* he wrote: "Ex-Sergeant Byng, title", which is a sign that he pondered giving that romance another title. As it so happened, several texts initially attributed to him ended up as Abílio Quaresma's.

– Humberto Ferreira – Editor and co-owner (along with Armando Couto) of *A Civilização.* In another newspaper he created (this time for the opposition), *O Progresso,* the victim was invariably Ferreira, even though he had "the support of the president and of the Public Opinion".

61. I.I. Crosse – Another Crosse brother. He wrote *Caeiro and the pagan reaction,* revealing the unearthing of "the mysticism of objectivity". In it, he claims "mystics attribute meaning to everything", whereas "Caeiro sees an absence of meaning in everything". He also wrote *The very great rhythmist,* in which he claims Álvaro de Campos is "the most violent of all writers". "His volcanic emotion, his swinging from violence to tenderness, is yet to be

21 Inspired by the illustrated almanac that newspaper *O Século* published annually from 1897 onwards.

equalled in the histrionics of our era". Pessoa considered entrusting him and his brother Thomas with defending the Fifth Empire and the Freemasons, though he ended up putting his name on those articles at the end of his life, as we shall see further up ahead.

62. Íbis (Bi) – "I am an Ibis". *He used to say that at home,* according to brother João Maria. Ever since he was a child, Pessoa pretended to be that Egyptian bird. And did so at any time and any place, even in busy streets, provided there were children around. In such moments he said "now I'm going to be an Ibis" and would then emulate the bird with gestures, surprising passers-by and embarrassing adults who accompanied him. On the margins of some letters, he would occasionally draw a stylized human figure with one leg up. At least two poems of his remain, one of which for sister Teca, which begins thus:

> Go away, sun from the skies,
> The eyes of my sister
> Were made by God
> To cover for mornings.

63. Isaías Costa – According to Stoker, he comes up once, signing typewritten articles. He was meant to be the author of three books of riddles. It bears remembering that, in Pessoa's authors list, there is one Isaías Coelho. Interestingly enough, among the sentences left behind by this Costa, there is one "We are the devil", very similar to Sartre's (1905-1980) *Hell is other people.*

– J.G.H.C. – Another name for J.G. Henderson Carr.

64. J.G. Henderson Carr – Came from his time at the Commercial School and shows up twice in a tachygraphy manual, *Pitman's shorthand instructor,* according to Richard Zenith. His name and that of another heteronym, Tagus, show up in a set of texts which were supposed to be compiled under the title of "Rags". In *Natal Mercury,* he took part in a riddle contest. According to Zenith, the abovementioned J.G.H.C. would send the newspaper riddles which would then be solved by another heteronym, Tagus.

65. J.M. Hyslop – A poet who came to him in séances. His sole text with a handwriting all his own is a short poem (untitled and undated) which ends thus:

> It moves at sea
> It can be tamed at sea
> The hurt that was present
> In the shadow and the aroma.

Here too, heteronym Henry More wrote at the margin "no good". Pessoa agreed with the comment, crosses it with a pen and bids his creature goodbye. But, oddly, instead of going into the trash, the poem ended up in his creator's Chest.

– Jacinto Freire – Only a name quoted by Stoker. In this case, it might have been Jacinto Freire de Andrade (1597-1657), Portuguese historian and the author of *A Vida de Dom João de Castro, vice-rei da Índia.*

– Jacob Dermot – Another Jacob for the collection. In his diary (16/03/1900), it reads: "Difficulty in the mental execution of Jacob Dermot."

66. Jacob Satã (Satan) – In a rather contradictory text in English, Pessoa says he was a "spirit of M[22] and a master of tenderness". His first name could perhaps be inspired by Jacob Fusul, a Sephardic Jew and prophet of Sebastianism, who claimed to be *the incarnation of divine power.* We have already previously seen Satan in Search's pact and in *Ultimus joculatorum.* In the beginning, Pessoa had a noble role in mind for him: "The Satanist is but the materialization of the divine"; only to utterly contradict himself by describing Satan as "a spirit of evil, the owner of the house and the one actually in charge"; Pessoa would add at the side "bad part".

67. James Joseph – Another spirit who would appear to answer his questions. Sometimes only to say "No. No. No. No.", after which he signed the text and left.

68. Jean-Seul de Méluret – This Jean-Seul (Lonely John) was created by Pessoa around 1907, "supposedly born in 1885, on the 1st of August". He was thus "a year older than Charles Search and three years older than Alexander [Search]". An annotation spelled out his address: "Place Octave Mirbeau, between Rue Felicier Champsau and Rue Lacenaire". All imaginary names, a rather unusual thing for him, probably owed to the fact that it was a Parisian address. "At the age of 17, Jean-Seul is an antianarchist. His task is to write poetry and satire of scientific writings in French, for a moral and satirical purpose", and to publish "the French edition of a non-existent magazine". An aristocrat and a man of the *Ancien Régime* – the old French monarchy which was toppled during the Revolution of 1789 – he railed against egalitarianism, feminism and free love, which he considers a manifestation of decadent spirits. He has three uncompleted books to his name.

The first, from September 1908, is *Cas d'exibitionnisme,* in 17 fragments, in which he classifies exhibitionism as a female malady. The preface begins with "Là, à Lisbonne", which he used to accentuate the differences between

22 Out of decency, he preferred not to spell out *merda* (shit).

the still provincial Lisbon and "Paris of the naked women", "of pederasty and flashing of genitalia". In that preface, he says: "If we were a grand and strong spirit, we would approach the matter of Western civilization's degeneration, and especially that of France, in all of its amplitude, all its shapes and tendencies. We would study the aetiology, the interests, the therapeutics, we would make a diagnosis to the extent possible". And concludes: "There is no excuse for the most modest spirit in its sincerity, whether it's to dream, to wait or to wish to ignore".

Then came two satires. *La France à l'an 1950,* narrated by a Japanese, had some of its eight fragments published in *Europa* #1. They were about "corruption, lust, pornography, prostitution in the streets, but I know that the worst is that which resides in the souls". He also described how France had a Hymen-less Institute, a School of Masturbation and a School of Sadism. As if that weren't enough, "mothers bed their sons, fathers their daughters". In *La France,* we have: "Our civilization is dying, especially the French", and "the death of a society is more dreadful than that of an individual organism. Society decomposes in life". The text begins with the phrase: "There are no normal people here", but only "people two times aberrant, sexual, two times inverted" and ends up recommending "shame to those who consider this satire funny. Woe upon he who laughs with it", concluding with "end".

Finally, *Messieurs des souteneurs* – the original title of which was *Litt*[érature] *des souteneurs.* That condemnation of the literature of decadence featured the famous French author Anatole France, the Nobel Prize winner in Literature in 1921, as a member of the Management Board (he first wrote and then crossed "Director") of the Company of Pornography, Foolishness and Shittery, which was a Public Limited Company of Very Limited Liability. It should come as little surprise, considering that in *Ultimatum* he had already said: "Get out, Anatole France, you Epicurus of homoeopathic remedies, Jaurès[23]-coloured tapeworm of the *Ancien Régime,* wilted Renan[24] tossed with Flaubert and served in a phony seventeenth-century salad bowl!". He then affirmed, in a typical platitude of the time, that "art has nothing to do with morality".

His texts were signed JS (Jean-Seul) and mentioned where they were written, *Lisbonne.* What is fascinating is that, at the time, there was indeed one Jean-Seul living in Lisbon, who ended up a victim of the bad blood between Pessoa and Salazar, because Pessoa signed a letter as that heteronym, in which he stated the "exact date" and the circumstances of the dictator's death "in 1968", according to what the stars had told him. "I see a chair, then

23 Jean Jaurès (1859-1914) was the murdered founder of the French Socialist Party.

24 Ernest Renan (1823-1892) was a famous author who lost his faith and abandoned his ecclesiastical vocation.

a bed, and then... a circus[25]". And so, the real Jean-Seul ended up arrested. The heteronym wrote a single poem (August 1910) in French, which was meant for *La France en 1950:*

Nothing is, everything passes,
All is in its due course
The day tires
Of being day.
The tears that fall
Will soon be ruined.
The eyes which...
The time-vulture
Coos and swells
Rises and coos
Always, always.

69. Jerome Gaveston – He appears in seven of Pessoa's manuscripts, according to Stoker, close to the names of Anon and Search. His signature also appears in a notebook of 1907. Still according to Stoker, the surname could have been inspired by Piers Gaveston, lover of Edward II (1284-1327) of England, who then became baron of Cornwall. Edward married princess Isabella of France, daughter of Phillip IV, and had four sons. But Gaveston was a regular in his bed, up until his assassination in 1312.

70. Jim Crow – *A reply to Jim Crow* was to be the subtitle of *A coroação de Jorge V* (The Coronation of George V). But at list V of his works (1911), Pessoa had already attributed the latter to L. Guerreiro (and then to Gervásio Guedes). Perhaps because he considered "Mr. J[im] C[row] is one of the abilities with notions of humanism circumscribed to the usage of short sentences and saying unpleasant things". With the generic name of *Jim Crow,* he wrote several notes in English on racial prejudice, which Pessoa had witnessed in South Africa, and it was doubtlessly an allusion to the Jim Crow laws in the USA, which enforced racial segregation.

71. João Craveiro – He wrote texts defending then president-king Sidónio Pais for *Acção* newspaper, after Pais' murder in 1918. Pessoa also destined "Comentários" to him, which were to be published in *Athena.*

72. Joaquim Moura Costa – A republican activist who considered the monarchy "a chamber pot without a lid" in a "sea of piss". It makes sense,

25 Salazar died on the 27th of June 1970, but the beginning of his end was indeed in 1968, on the 3rd of August, when he fell off a *chair,* which caused a subdural hematoma, was brought to a *bed* at the Cruz Vermelha Hospital, and the Carnation Revolution on the 25th of April 1974 that followed might be described as a *circus.*

considering Pessoa was an ardent republican upon his return to Portugal in 1905, and could well have created this heteronym in a spasm of patriotism. A collaborator at *O Phosphoro,* he was also a satirical poet, having dedicated the following verses to the poet Augusto (César Ferreira) Gil (1873-1929)[26]:

I see he rhymes effortlessly
That his verses come out flowingly
All of such easy interpretation,
To be a poet, Augusto, verily
All you lack is a poet's foundation.

Moura Costa is also a "rabid" protester of the Church, which he holds to be "a trap from God", which is why he begins his *Ladainha negra* (Dark litany) saying: "Damned be the Catholic Church everywhere". He also has the habit of handing out Diplomas of Blunder, one of which was given to the count of Samodães (Afonso Costa). With Moura Costa and Nabos, Pessoa learned how to use swear words. He dedicated another poem to his fellow heteronym Padre Mattos, which ends thus:

Well, then, that leading figure
One day (sad day) gave out a fart.
...and the sad effect of divine flatulence
Falling into dirt on which cats pissed
From which father Mattos spontaneously sprouted.

– (Professor) Jones – Another name for Professor Trochee.

73. José Gomes (Gomes Pipa) – Collaborator at *O Phosphoro,* he also wrote about politics. In a somewhat obscure text, "Na farmácia do Evaristo" (At Evaristo's Pharmacy) – published in *História* magazine in 1979 – Pessoa recalls a conversation between the owner Mendes, republicans Justino dos Doces and Coimbra de Barbas, colonel Bastos and José Gomes, the topic of which were facts which might legitimize a republican insurrection. The text might have been born during the revolt of the 14th of May 1914 (or, perhaps, on that of the 18th of April 1928). In that short story, Pessoa gives "two reasons" for José Gomes' nickname of "Gomes Pipa" (Barrel Gomes): "One was patent on the bulge of his formidable corpulence. The other, if anyone cared to know, was easily understandable just by hearing him speak, as Gomes wiped his mouth and said: 'I've drank better'. Barrel of wine, clearly.

26 Pessoa criticized Gil for having written *Alba plena,* a 123 page-long book of religious verses, in which the word "Christ" doesn't appear even once.

74. José Rasteiro – He wrote proverbs and riddles for *O Palrador.*

75. José Rodrigues do Valle (Scicio) – Partner and literary editor of *O Palrador,* he wrote riddles such as this one:

> Changing the last vowel,
> Perhaps you can dress it.
> And, with the appropriate instrument,
> You might be able to whip it.
> In rather old-fashioned manner
> You will write kinsman;
> Without the concept,
> You shall never guess.
>
> This is how the thought
> Bounds leagues in a moment.

It bears pointing out that there was a Portuguese poet and essayist called José Rodrigues do Vale (only one 'L'), born in Monção 12 years before Pessoa, and who had 14 pseudonyms, among them Fuão, João Seco, Marcos de Portela, Rip and Roque.

– Joseph Balsamo – This English adaptation of the count of Cagliostro's name (Giuseppe Balsamo) was also used by the heteronym Voodooist.

– Júlio Manuel Caeiro – He and his brother, António Caeiro da Silva, were supposed to look after the posthumous work of their brother, Alberto Caeiro.

– Kapp de Montale – But a lost note amidst Pessoa's estate, awaiting his fate as a heteronym. Montale is the surname of Eugenio, a renowned Genoese poet born in 1896, who eventually won the Nobel Prize in Literature in 1975.

76. Karl P. Effield – Supposedly born in Boston, USA, and the author of *From Hong Kong to Kudat,* a book which was never even written, according to Richard Zenith. That American adventurer travelled all over the Far East and Australia. In a notebook from Pessoa, in a section titled "Trifles", is the primitive version of the beginning of a poem titled "The miner's song". According to Zenith, that episode mentions *a European lad* [Pessoa] *who makes up a man* [W.W. Austin] *who travels to Australia, where he discovers a poem attributed to an American pre-heteronym (Effield), who had also been in Asia – it is vertiginous, literally speaking.* Zenith published the poem, translated by Luísa Freire, and its first stanza is as follows:

We leave the grassy paths we tread,
We leave the shadowy lake we sailed,
We leave our beloved mother in the distant fatherland
And live with hope, though we might fail.

– L. Guerreiro – *The coronation of George V* is attributed to him (or her) in list IV of works to be published, and also in list V *(post 1911),* part of Pessoa's *Contemporary studies,* instead of Jim Crow, whom it had been meant for initially. In another list (annex 484-8r), that very title is now attributed to Gervásio Guedes. There are no further references to Guerreiro.

– Letcher – Another name for H.H. Fletcher.

77. Lili – The name of this heteronym is inspired by a china doll belonging to sister Teca. Lili wrote incomprehensible riddles for *A Palavra,* such as this one:

How radio this animal is – 2.

78. Lucas Merrick – (Likely) brother of David Merrick. Pessoa had five short stories in store for this heteronym, the last one, "A escapada do malandro" (The scoundrel's escapade) about Lisbon's police. 20 others, which were originally meant for him, ended up with Charles Robert Anon. Including *The schoolmaster's tale,* in which he says: "My inability wasn't owed to a lack of scholastic preparation, but from my lacking the most useful virtue that is patience".

– Lucian Arr – Was meant to illustrate Marvell Kitsch's *Os milhões de um doido* (The Madman's Millions), along with A. Rey da Costa.

79. Luís António Congo – Chronicler and copywriter at *O Palrador* (1912). In one of his texts, he presents the "exquisite poetry" of luso-brazilian poet (and fellow heteronym) Eduardo Lança. In another, evoking the African origins made apparent by his surname, he wrote about "an imaginary disease, the evil eye", a fake malady which was quite common in the 17th and 18th centuries, which was assumed to be caused by envy. Pessoa used the Spanish version of the malady, *quebranto,* instead of the more typically Portuguese *mau-olhado.*

– M.N. Freitas – Editor of *A Palavra,* but really just his cousin, Mário Nogueira de Freitas.

80. M.V. du Saussay – Secretary of one Company for the Embellishment of the World, a name which was later changed to Company of Pornography,

Foolishness and Shittery, the advisor of which was Anatole France. Perhaps he intended to use the character to reply to Jean-Seul's critiques of France, but Saussay wrote nothing but satires before being abandoned by his creator.

– Major Bastos – Another name indicated by Stoker, who considered it *a person reserved for signing texts.* It should be pointed out that there is another serviceman with the surname of Bastos in Pessoa's *Na farmácia do Evaristo,* albeit with a higher rank (colonel). There was also one Mr. Bastos in a propaganda text he wrote for Tintas Berryloid.

– Manuel Maria – In the texts he wrote for his newspapers, Pessoa spoke of "Manuel Maria's visions", but never elaborated upon who he was or the significance of said visions.

81. Marcos Alves – According to a note in his diary (16/02/1913), it was on that date that "the whole character of Marcos Alves" was fixed. He claims to be from Lisbon, despite having been born in the Algarve, much like Pessoa's paternal family, which is why he recalls "the native landscape of the Algarve, the long-lasting longing for a lost life". An uncle of his died of tuberculosis (much like his uncle José). His paternal grandmother suffered from mental alienation (much like grandmother Dionísia). On the mother's side, nothing seems to have been amiss. His sex life is non-existent (much like Pessoa's). "His was a mission which had been imposed upon him by life. Like Buddha's and Christ's, it was one of peace, decency and love". Alves revealed generous impulses of tenderness in every small gesture. "His old dreams were predictions, not dreams or wishes". In his room, alone, he cried when thinking of hungry children and the world's injustices. He then felt the ambition to be a new Christ, or to preach sublime, eternal love to sad and suffering humanity. He fancies himself wishing well to those who hate him, giving bread to his enemies, raising the small daughter of one of the men who assaulted him, giving alms to those who will betray him. And then he sleeps, "to cry some more, happy and sad with the dolorous love burning in his heart" and feels sorry for himself. In *A carta mágica* (The magic letter) of heteronym Abílio Quaresma, he appears in one of the dialogues, which ends thus:

> Quaresma – It was my pleasure to make your acquaintance, professor Marcos Alves.
> Marcos Alves – Likewise, Dr. Quaresma.

In letters signed by Alves, it is as if Pessoa were speaking about his own life: "Seeing what I wanted to be, a tremendous anguish rises up to my head. Everything I loved ended up hurting me sooner or later. I can only feel whole by claiming I am at least two[27]". In one of those letters, Marcos Alves says: "I have no soul. I sold it to myself in exchange for false coins, bought kisses, useless friendships, despicable admirers, enemies who've forgotten me". In time, he comes to understand the futility of it all. "The sick man felt the depression of defeat, the agonizing sadness of being aware that he did nothing, that his intentions were useless". He twice tries to commit suicide, and Pessoa describes the third attempt: "He put the revolver into his mouth and trembled as he felt the iron against the roof of his mouth. But he then recalled, not without a measure of relief, that this was how Antero de Quental had committed suicide" – in 1891, three years after Pessoa's birth, due to a severe neurasthenia. "The apathy was absolute. He had become another. He already was death. All that was missing was the final gesture. He closed the eyes and pulled the trigger". He was 24, one year older than Pessoa at the time.

– Maria Aurélia Antunes – Another name quoted by Stoker.

82. Maria José – Maria José is a miserable 19 year-old girl, hunchbacked and suffering from tuberculosis. Evoking her name, she claims "I am neither woman nor man". Maria, like Pessoa's mother, and José, like his father's great-grandfather – José António Pereira de Araújo e Souza, artillery captain who was granted nobility in 1799. The use of those family names is constant throughout his oeuvre. In *The hour of the Devil,* for example, two women are talking: One is Maria, and the other, Antónia, the female form of António, Pessoa himself. Maria and Antónia, mother and son. Maria José spends her days by the window, crying over her unhappy lot and watches those who walk by in the street, especially a locksmith she only ever refers to as *senhor António.* Lost in the Chest, the text is titled "Carta da corcunda para o serralheiro" (The hunchback's letter to the locksmith). Manuela Parreira da Silva maintains that it is either *a short story or a draft for one, while keeping its epistolary form.* And perhaps it really is. The letter is rather unserious, and Pessoa seems to amuse himself with the thought of all the world's woes on the back of a miserable young woman. The text ends with a handwritten signature, in a handwriting which was meant to be the author's. It reads (abridged):

Mr. António,

You don't know who I am, or rather, you do, but not really. You must have always thought little of the hunchbacked girl living on the first floor of the yellow house, but I think of nothing but you. I know you have a lover, that tall, beautiful blonde; I envy her, but I don't feel jealous of you, as I am entitled to nothing, not even jealousy. I feel sorry for not being another woman, with another body and another temper. You are all

27 As a variant, *at least two and many.*

that has sustained me in my illness. I am entitled to liking others, even if they don't like me back, and I also have the right to cry. They say all hunchbacks are mean, but I never wished ill upon anyone. I am nineteen, and could never understand why I've lived this long, only to be ill and have others pity me for my deformed back. I would like to know how your shared life is with your girlfriend, as it is a life I can never have. I still remember that day when you passed by on a Sunday with your light blue suit. You looked beautiful as the day itself, and never have I envied your girlfriend more. Margarida, the seamstress, says she spoke to you once, and that time I also felt great envy. I am neither woman nor man, as no one thinks I am anything more than a person who is occupying space at the window, good grief. Goodbye, mister António, I have but days to live and write this letter only to hold it against me as if it had been written by you to me, and not by me to you. There you have it, and I am crying.

Maria José

To Victor J. Mendes, *the hunchback shares some similarities with Ophelia Queiroz* – evoking that frequent scene in which he walked by her house and she saw him from her window. She is also 19, as was Ophelia when she first met him. *The syntax and the vocabulary of Ophelia's letters are comparable to the syntax of Maria José's letters.* To say nothing of the locksmith, who, according to Mendes, *is similar to Fernando António Pessoa* – even in name, *António.* Álvaro de Campos says in "Reality": "From that window on the second floor, still identical to herself/ Bending over, a girl older than myself". Perhaps it was her, with the ages switched. According to Pessoa specialists, the inspiration came from a *cripple* who always stood at a window at Rua Coelho da Rocha. Teresa Rita Lopes suggests it might have been a hunchback who lived in an apartment in front of him, and whose name is unknown. But none of the papers in the Chest as much as mention her. In search of confirmation, I spoke to his neighbours at the time, who still lived in the same apartments at Rua Coelho da Rocha, and none of them recalled such a woman. Which, to be fair, proves nothing, really, as all neighbours were already over the age of 80 and had only witnessed the last years of Pessoa. It's perfectly possible that one such hunchbacked girl might have lived there at the start of the 1920s. They did say she was spoken of by *dona* Eunice, widow of the owner of Paris Cinema, who lived further down, at Rua Domingues Figueira. But no other records of her existence could be found.

Inês Pedrosa later continued that sad story. According to her, the letter was never sent to mister António. Delirious and in poor health, Maria José wouldn't let go of that piece of paper. They gave her a shot and she fell asleep. The seamstress Margarida then decided to deliver the letter, and the moved locksmith replied in a style with which Pedrosa sought to emulate the letter of Pessoa's last breakup with Ophelia (abridged):

> Miss Maria José
>
> I would like to be able to lie to you, but it'd be disrespectful to the sincerity you displayed in the letter you wrote while thinking of me. If I truly were the whole man you imagine I am just from seeing me pass by your window, I would find the courage for that lie your pretty little heart deserves and give it to you like a bouquet of roses. That window I saw you at days ago was your loneliness and your company. I feel bad for not seeing you on it now. We are all worthy of pity, due to flaws of the body or the soul. I feel so sorry that I cannot say I love you like you would like me to tell you, but I can say I do care enough about you not to lie, and that is a kind of love unto itself. Whenever I told a woman I loved her, it was to get something from her in exchange, it was never authentic or from the heart. You can gloat about the fact that you are the one woman I ever wrote a letter to, even if I see you more as a child or an angel than as a woman. That which people dream of is better than what happens to us, and now I have learned to dream of another life because of this love of yours. Do make an effort not to die, you are still far too young, and many would surely miss those lovely sentiments of yours. I would like to see you again at your window, happy to see me. My wishes for a quick recovery, yours
>
> António

No further was said about this fake fairytale.

– Marino – According to scholars, he was an official heteronym. But he doesn't appear to have had much autonomy. The character appears in fragment VII of a draft by David Merrick, which ends up in Search's hands (1903), with the title of *Who am I?* In it, in a dialogue with his master Vicenzo, he says:

> Marino – Who am I? Good question, but I know not how to answer. A month ago, or even a week, I might have been able to promptly and cheerfully reply "I am Marino…". But now I cannot speak. I have asked that same question so many times, and reason couldn't give answer to what I was saying.

Marino bids life goodbye by jumping off a cliff into the sea. Like he himself says: "The mystery of all – it is around us, underneath, above, all over the earth, the entire sky and more". It was the draft for the profile of Faust, a character which would hound Pessoa his entire life.

83. Marnoco e Souza – Another spirit which communicated with him, this one with childish calligraphy, very different from Pessoa's at the time. The name was inspired by professor José Ferreira Marnoco e Souza (1869-1916), mayor of Coimbra from 1904 to 1910. In the texts, we also find answers by Pessoa to questions posed by Marnoco.

– Martin Hewitt – Just a name quoted by Stoker. Only here it's just a reference to Arthur Morrinson's *The adventures of Martin Hewitt* (1896).

84. Martin Kéravas – Another one who Pessoa simply mingled with, like he did during his childhood with Chevalier de Pas, Quebranto D'Oessus and Capitaine Thibeau. At first, he was just the character of a short story by David Merrick (the title of which was the character's name), but he eventually gained a life of his own and signed with a stamp a book at Pessoa's bookshelf: *Pitmanis shorthand*. The stamp says: *F.A.N. Pessoa, Durban, Martin Kéravas.*

85. Marvell Kisch – The name is (perhaps) inspired by classical figures. A friend of Milton's, the Englishman Andrew Marvell (1621-1678), was the one who, according to heteronym Adolph Moscow, "elevated physiology to a science"; and (even less likely), the Prague-born Czech Egon Erwin Kisch (1885-1948), journalist and later objector to Hitler in Germany, who also took part in the Spanish Civil War. Marvell Kisch is the author of the (imaginary) novel announced in *O Palrador, A riqueza de um doido* (The wealth of a madman), of which one sole chapter was written – with a title that, according to its author, should be changed to *Os milhões de um doido* (A madman's millions). The novel begins, recalling "the first ladies of the evening" who walked "imperceptibly across the city of London", and was supposed to be illustrated by A. Rey da Costa and Lucian Arr.

– Mariano Zeca – Editor of the remaining sections of *O Palrador*.

86. Master of Voodooism – This voodoo master is a minor spirit that appeared during his séances and was born quite close to another one, Voodooist.

87. MCR – The author of a book about the occult sciences, written for the Philosophical and Esoterical Collection, translated by Pessoa himself. In that collection, that book and two others attributed to heteronym Fernando António Nogueira de Seabra are listed as volumes V, VIII and X.

88. Miguel Otto – He was meant to translate the previously mentioned *Tratado da luta livre – método Yvelot* written by his brother Carlos Otto.

89. Morris & Theodor – He (or they) wrote riddles for *O Palrador*, such as this one:

> Such a stunning set!
> Life, light, song, love
> Who could, at the appropriate time,
> Treat the subject on the canvas?

From divine art to painting
An eminent cultivator.

– Nat Grande – Editor of the short story section of *O Palrador.*

90. Navas – Translator of the short stories of Horace James Faber. In the list of his translations, the page has them numbered 1 to 12 by hand. But only three were worthy of titles inspired by Poe's work: "The case of Mr. Ariote", "The case of the science professor" and "The case of the quantum equation".

91. Néant – Néant (French for *nothing)* was meant to write the preface for *Peints par eux-mêmes* (Painted by themselves), a book which was never written and never had a heteronym attributed to it.

92. Nynfa Negra – She wrote riddles for *O Palrador,* such as this one, dedicated to Gallião Pequeno:

> Luísa walked in a firm step across the terrace, waiting for her mother. Where is this thing that can be found in music?

– Olegário Andrade – Just a name quoted by Stoker. But here, and strange as it may seem, it is but a reference to Brazilian-born Argentinean writer Olegario Victor Andrade (1839-1882), author of *El arpa perdida.*

– Oswald Kent – Editor of *O Palrador's* sports' section.

93. Padre Mattos – The name is (likely) inspired by forensic psychiatrist Júlio Xavier de Matos (1857-1923), author of *Os alienados nos tribunais* and of the reform of psychiatric assistance in Portugal, as well as the founder of the Campo Grande Asylum in Lisbon, which would then be renamed after him in 1942. Heteronym Joaquim Moura Costa railed against him, dedicating to him the poem "A origem metafísica do Padre Mattos" (The metaphysical origin of Father Mattos) (see nr. 72). By way of this heteronym, Pessoa replied to a survey by *A Águia* magazine, calling "individualists" to all Portuguese poets who still showed appreciation for Spain and Germany. To Pessoa, this republican is "a disaster", and he was swiftly abandoned.

That particular diatribe's author claimed that Father Mattos, whom I had labelled as a heteronym, had been a real person. According to the sage, he had gone by the name of father José Lourenço Matos (only one "t") – born on the 7th of December 1893, in the village of Folques (Arganil, Portugal), where he died on the 11th of December 1916. The same man who, according to the blog, had written for the newspaper *A Palavra.* The blogger, however, seemed unaware that that particular newspaper had been made of foolscap folio, like the one children write in. Written with a pencil. By Pessoa himself. Crossing the father's date of birth with those of Pessoa's writings attributed to that particular heteronym (1902), in order for the good blogger to be correct, that meant a 9 years-old priest had somehow managed to have been ordained, written seven books, fought the monarchy, been arrested and sent into exile. But mainly because Pessoa's sole references to said father consisted of an article he himself wrote for *A Palavra* in 1902. When our priest would have been 9 and should still be learning how to read with his mother. Besides, Moura Costa's poem dates from 1909, when the future priest would have been 13 and the republic was yet to replace the monarchy. In short, even if someone with that name were to have existed, it would have been a mere coincidence.

– Pad Zé – Another name for Pedro da Silva Salles.

94. (Dr.) Pancrácio (Pancratium) – He appears in 1902, in the Azores. This English writer resides in Durban and is editor at *A Palavra,* a collaborator and later literary editor for *O Palrador,* and also published texts for *O Pimpão.* One of his tales for the book *Brancos e pretos* (Whites and Blacks) says how he "was waiting for a letter from Rachel" and claimed "nothing is greater than love. As the beautiful April afternoon ends, the April night comes, then another April day, and still nothing from Rachel". At length, as fate would have it, "the lottery ticket seller came in her stead". After that, as if abruptly changing his mind, he switches course and ends the short story with: "I was wrong earlier, friends. There is one thing greater than love: Dough". Pancrácio reacted fervently against the orthographic reform that was being bandied about in Portugal: "Falar [to speak] has but one L/ Now the donkey won't run off"; or "The accent, I say, is ever changing (like the wind's scent)". He left a number of poems, at least seven of which were published, chief among them "Quando ela passa" (When she passes by), the margin of which had the following scribbled on it: "For music". Written on the 5th of May 1902, still at Angra do Heroísmo, it is usually published as if it were Pessoa's, and begins thus:

When I sit by the window
Athwart the snow-fogged panes
I see her sweet sweet image
As she passes by… by… by…

– Pancratium – The name Dr. Pancrácio signed his erudite writings with from 1903 on. Among them a long *Essay on poetry,* which was "written to edify and instruct pretentious poets", in which he says:

> After some studies, I found out that poetry can generally be considered as such when each line begins with a capital letter. Should the reader manage to ascertain another difference, I would be most grateful if he would share it with me.

In spite of his apparent affection for him, the text was eventually attributed to Prof. Trochee.

95. Pantaleão – A "sybaritic idealist of integrity" in spirit, "a comedian, a dreamer, a pedagogue, an essayist with a talent for agitation and a visionary", as well as a journalist, a militant republican, a pamphleteer (against the monarchy and the Catholic Church) and a poet who came up around 1907. Pessoa attributed to him some writings about "our colonial administration", and considered criticizing the government in a book which was to be "rough and brutal". By writing in Portuguese, Pantaleão was almost as unto Pessoa himself, at a time in which most of his heteronyms were either English or French. In *Consciência do mistério do mundo* (Awareness of the world's mystery), he says "life is the eternal rumour, and death, all death, the eternal rebuttal". He had planned *Fábulas para adultos* (Fables for adults), in which he'd seek to attack the powers-that-be with irony. At the side of the signature he practised, Pantaleão wrote his motto: "Life is an evil worthy of being mocked". The name might have changed. In a draft of his oeuvre he titled *The Transformation Book,* under his name, Pantaleão wrote in parentheses "if necessary, give true name". Perhaps that of fellow heteronym António Gomes.

96. Parry – Wrote riddles for *O Palrador,* such as this one:

> What is the sound the animal calls the reader?

97. Pedro da Silva Salles (Pad Zé) – Collaborator and editor of the humour pages of *O Palrador,* he wrote texts such as the following:

> In an alehouse, a poet told a painter who was showcasing a painting: Allow me to congratulate you on the success of your painting. You are an exquisite artist, a true talent. By the way, can I borrow ten tostões28?

98. Pêro Botelho – His *signature* appears in a notebook from 1915. The name is reminiscent of a renowned Spanish character from the 14th and 15th centuries, mentioned by Francisco Gómez de Quevedo y Santibáñez Villegas (1580-1654) in his *El entremedido, la dueña y el soplón.* In it, he describes Pero Gotero and his

28 Pessoa likely evoked a famous character of Lisbon's café scene, one Burnay do Pataco, whose name was inspired by one of the wealthiest Portuguese at the time, Henri Burnay (1838-1909), a banker and art collector. This beggar plied his trade at cafés, approaching his victims and presenting them with a card which said: *Would the kind sir lend me five mil-réis?* At the expected refusal, he would then turn his card, which read: *And what about five tostões?*

boiler – the Devil himself and the boiler from hell. Even in Portugal, the character is often referred to by his Spanish (or archaic Portuguese) name – *careful, boy, or you might end up in Pero Gotero's boiler.* Arnaldo Gama, a friend of Camilo Castelo Branco's, gave the quote a more Portuguese touch in his *A caldeira de Pedro Botelho.* The expression *Pedro Botelho's boiler* is still used to this day in Portugal's inner regions, mainly to frighten children. Thus, a better version of the name would be Pedro Botelho. But Pessoa preferred to *portuguesefy* just the surname, Botelho, and refrained from giving him the demonic nature of the original character. Botelho wrote minstrel acts such as the following:

> Such damage she causes
> With her tender stares…
> Yet I'm the one who tempts souls,
> I am the one who's Satan!
> What changes you manage to wreak
> With those libertine eyes of yours!
> You make young men of the elderly
> And manage to age the young…

The heteronym was to sign *Cartas de Pêro Botelho* (Letters of Pêro Botelho). In one of them, ("for nobody"), he says: "Today, I am old, save for the intensity with which I feel. So that, today, my spirit is indifferent to sexual desire. It exists in my soul, but it doesn't care for him. This state of mind is more painful than mourning of the most…", and then the sentence is cut, with only a loose sentence to the side letting us know how the train of thought would end: "It is the death of us to ourselves". He also wrote short stories, philosophical ones, which he hoped to compile under the title of *Contos de Pêro Botelho* (Tales of Pêro Botelho). Only fragments of those remain, chief among which is, without a shadow of a doubt, "O vencedor do tempo" (The winner of time), initially meant for Vicente Guedes. Narrated by professor Serzedas, it begins thus:

> Whence comes the Truth-plus-error of all philosophical theory? Each of us is God being him, God thinking of himself. Thus, as each of us is God, each of us sees truth, has truth in himself. But, as each of us is, according to God's thought, not-God, to not-be is a mistake. We think of ourselves as God. We are free because we are God.

99. Pimenta – He wrote riddles for *O Palrador,* such as this one:

> In the beginning, the warmest feeling burns 1.2.1.

100. Pip – Author of jokes and riddles in *O Palrador.* This heteronym paved the way for the birth of another, (Dr.) Pancrácio. But he still managed to sign ten poems, among them one written when Pessoa was 13 (31st of March 1902), the humorous "Os ratos" (Mice), which begins thus:

They lived ever content,
Stuck inside their holes,
Four brave little mice,
Four fearless mice.

It's one of the earliest ecological poems on record. In it, Pip elaborates upon the fate of the four mice, who "one day woke up feeling peckish" and died from what they ate. The first, because of "the aniline someone coloured the sausage with", the second due to "the alum in the flour", and the third because of "lime in the milk". Finally, the fourth, "inconsolable, was sought by grim death" when he took poison, except "the merry rat got fat", as

Except in this tract of land
As it was at the time
The very poison itself
Was also counterfeit!

101. Portugal – He wrote a number of notes on racial prejudice in English. But this heteronym was also given to writing poems. And the opportunity to do just that came on the 14th of December 1918, when president Sidónio Pais was shot to death. On the upper floor of the Rossio train station, when he was about to board the Expresso do Norte. In his homage, he published a compilation of texts, *Em memória do Grande Morto e grande Português que foi o Dr. Sidónio Pais* (In memory of the Great Dead and great Portuguese that was Dr. Sidónio Pais), claiming to be *a humble homage... of friends and admirers of the unforgettable President.* Pessoa, as we will later find out, also respected him. And perhaps even more than that. And he coordinated that small book, *O Bem-Amado* with the help of friends António Botto, Silva Tavares, Branca Gonta Colaço, and others. However, oddly enough, it doesn't contain a single poem of Pessoa's, even though page 39 has a sonnet by *Portugal,* the same title Pessoa considered for *Message* at the time. *And reading this sonnet promptly hearkens to "Mother's little boy" and "To the Memory of the President-King Sidónio Pais", such are the similarities,* according to Dr. Celestino Portela, who firmly believes it to be a new heteronym. It should also be noted how coincidental the title *O Bem-Amado* (The Beloved) is, considering the words of Pessoa in the poem he wrote in homage to the late president.

In our soul the faith endures
That, beyond the world and fate,
He still thinks of us and is
The beloved.

To the Memory of the President-King Sidónio Pais, Fernando Pessoa

And now for the collection's poem, as originally published:

Between the four walls of a room,
The Hero's body disappears,
Amidst the alluvion of roses, he proffers
Lusitania, which he dreamt of saving!

Sleep, let him sleep, as God rocks him,
And the Race lives and dreams in a prayer.
That which yet shines through on his face,
And his cold mouth stifles!

Gentle shape of he whom death mocks,
Victorious the steel chest in which beat
A most high and beautiful dove's heart…

Oh, no! from his dream there yet shines,
As if from a felled colossal cedar,
A flash of Epopee in the Elegy!

Untitled, undated (1918), Portugal

102. (Herr) Prosit[29] – A German name for Pessoa's gallery, originally a character of Alexander Search's in the previously mentioned *A Very Original Dinner.* He might have been meant to be a heteronym of Search, but was entrusted with a most noble task: To sign the translation of Espronceda's *The Student of Salamanca.*

– Quaresma Decifrador – Such a name (Decipherer) was appropriate for Abílio Quaresma, given his notorious knack for solving riddles. Pessoa considered converting him into the main character of *O profeta da Rua da Glória* (the Jew Borjara Salomão), which was later entrusted to Pêro Botelho.

103. Quebranto D'Oessus – A character of his tender childhood and an almost intimate friend of his. Sister Teca tells her children of a game Pessoa played when their parents were out. Pessoa clad his siblings in sheets and painted their faces black with white around the eyes, as if they were ghosts. He then turned off the lights and rang all the bells in the house. The black servants fled in terror and only returned the next day because his stepfather went into their township, carrying the sheets and the bells in his hand. According to Teca, *these sorts of pranks, in which he embodied the horror character Quebranto D'Oessus, were repeated in several occasions, in the most varied situations.*

29 A toast in German.

– Rabanete – He answers riddles of *O Palrador* and was thanked by the editors for three (unspecified) letters of his.

104. Raphael Baldaya – Pagan, astrologer and antispiritualist, he aimed to publish *Trovas de Bandarra em comentário interpretativo* through Olisipo – Pessoa's publishing house. His surname (perhaps) stems from his mother's great-great-great-great-great-grandfather, Afonso Gonçalves Baldaya, who sailed the seas with Gil Eanes. Baldaya is confusing, and his texts are difficult to read. All on purpose, naturally. Sá-Carneiro (in a letter from 24/12/1915) comments on that heteronym: *Most curious, him being an astrologer. Hopefully, you'll go ahead with it. What an extraordinary and picturesque biographical note.* And concludes: *His incarnation in Rafael Baldaya, long-bearded astronomer, is simply hilarious.* Baldaya leaves a number of astrological writings, among which a *Treaty of Denial and some principles of esoteric metaphysics,* in which he claims to believe "the great occult destiny Portugal has in store, carrying on with what it has already accomplished". In this treaty, he refers 11 theses which would lead to conclusions such as "God exists for himself, but God is wrong", or that "being itself is the Not Being of Not Being, the mortal affirmation of life". Signed by Baldaya were also a number of ads published in Lisbon newspapers, written in English, offering mail-sent horoscopes, "absolute satisfaction" guaranteed, and in three models: "Experienced horoscope, 500 réis (a brief outline and general considerations on a person's life); Full horoscope, with a detailed reading of life and fate, 2,500 réis; Detailed horoscope, 5,000 réis". There are no records of any clients.

105. Ricardo Reis – Already described in his own chapter.

– Roberto Kola – Editor of riddles at *O Palrador.*

106. Sableton-Kay – Author of a novel announced in *O Palrador, A luta aérea*, of which not a single chapter was written, unlike fellow heteronym Gabriel Keene's *Em dias de perigo.*

107. Sanches – "Literary chronicler of Diário da Manhã" who narrates the sad life of a few heteronyms, such as Marcos Alves.

– Scicio – Another name for José Rodrigues do Valle.

– Saveston – A mere signature that Pessoa repeated ceaselessly, with no concrete fate to speak of.

– Serradura – Just a name quoted by Stoker. But, here, it must be a reference to the eponymous poem of Sá-Carneiro's.

– (Professor Serzedas) – A character of Pêro Botelho's in the tale "O vencedor do tempo" (The Winner of Time), who waxes philosophical about space, will and the existence of God. The tale's narrator is someone who speaks to him. In style, Serzedas uses a contradiction as a springboard to prove a concept; thus, every thesis brings some measure of denial with it. For example, for him, God is all that is and is not. In the permanent opposition between truth and error of his writings, one sees that "reality nullifies itself"; or that "Kant saw but half the facts". According to scholars, he was important enough to merit autonomy. For instance, Bréchon believes *he is more of a species of heteronym* – although he isn't listed as such here. Serzedas also held that "the notion of infinity came from the notion of the number"; but, as numbers begin at number 1, "infinity itself starts, but does not end, it has a point of departure, but not of arrival".

108. Sidney Parkinson Stool – In Pessoa's library, he signed Harry Fielding's (1707-1754) *The history of the adventures of Joseph Andrews, and his friend Mr. Abraham Adams,* both the preface and the last page, his names scratched out and with the year 1903 at their side.

– Sileno Ladino – Editor of the caricatures section of *O Palrador.*

109. Sher Henay – Englishman, compiler and author of the preface of an (imaginary) *Sensationist anthology.* It is unknown what 'Sher' stands for, which he also wrote before the name of Arthur Morrisson. Perhaps some equivalent to a maharajah, something like the *Lion* [Sher] *of Punjab.* Pessoa mentions a letter addressed to him on the 24th of December 1917 by "a lady from Famalicão", Matilde Alice de Faria, asking for news of him; the letter had been sent to a company Pessoa worked at, A. Xavier Pinto & Cia., at Rua S. Julião, 101, 1º, Lisbon. Therefore, the doubt remains whether he was a heteronym or a real person whose name wasn't remembered.

110. Souza – Another spirit of his séances. Different than the others, he also wrote texts in Portuguese – *Annotations,* in his own words. Among them, one which has a small drawing and a peculiar caution: "Try to walk like this".

111. Tagus – It was with this pseudonym from his times at Durban that Pessoa was "awarded a Molière" on the 12th of December 1903 by *Natal Mercury* for riddles he sent. That award consisted of *Les oeuvres de Molière* – which remained in Pessoa's personal library. Zenith still recalls a peculiar incident, when the newspaper referred to the winner as *Mr.,* when, due to Pessoa's age,

he should have been addressed as *Master.* Tagus succeeded J.G. Henderson Carr and preceded A.A. Crosse.

112. Thomas Crosse – The third Crosse brother, he lived in Lisbon and wrote in English about topics that were near and dear to Pessoa's heart, such as Judaism, occultism and the Freemasons. He'd also write about Salomão Malcho, who tried to convert Charles V and the Pope himself to Judaism. Cross came from his time in Africa and accompanied him throughout his life, even translating a couple of sensationist poems into English, which were "of little renown and unjustly forgotten", as well as a couple of Caeiro's, to be published by Olisipo in an *Anthology of Portuguese Sensationist Poetry.* He wrote part of a "Preface" for the translation of those poems and critiques, also in English. Much like Pessoa, at first, he supported the military coup of 1926. In the Chest there is a long list of themes Crosse was to write about – *The Origin of Discoveries, The Myth of King Sebastião, Kings That Will Return.* Envelope 143 of Lisbon's National Library attributes 14 originals to him.

– Tio Porco – For some specialists, he was indeed a heteronym, but it was but a character of Abílio Quaresma's, which quoted German philosopher Immanuel Kant all the time. In *Janela indiscreta* (Indiscreet Window), he confirms his profession with the following exchange:

> – Does the gentleman write?
> – No. I am an artist, said Tio Porco.

113. Torquato Mendes Fonseca da Cunha Rey – Author of an untitled writing, which he entrusted Pantaleão with, asking him to publish it. For specialists such as Madalena Dine, *it appears to be a character of the character Pantaleão.* When Rey died, Pantaleão announced he intended to fulfil "the last wish of by dearly mourned friend" – declaring even not to "know the value of what he wrote, let the learned ones pass their judgement". A monarchist, he left a number of texts in which he expresses his ideas, such as this "Prefácio às visões" (Preface to Visions):

> I do not fight the monarchy, I fight Portuguese monarchy. In most countries, Monarchy has become compatible with the greater civilization. Portuguese monarchy has not. One need but look at it. There is no better argument.

114. (Professor) Trochee (Professor Jones, Troqueu) – He signed a comedy text which was originally meant for Dr. Pancrácio *(Pancratium),* one *Essay on poetry,* "written to edify and instruct pretentious poets", in which he says:

> When I think about the abundant number of lads and the suberabundant number of young girls in the current century… whenever I consider the large number of poetic compositions which emanate thereof… I am convinced that, were I to write an essay on poetic art, I shall be contributing greatly to the common good.

– Troqueu – Another name for Professor Trochee. A "trochee" is a Greek (or Latin) verse consisting of a long syllable and a short one.

– Trapalhão – An author referred to in *O Palrador.*

115. Um Irregular do Transepto (An Irregular of the Transept) – It was under this name that Pessoa sent a letter (28th of January 1934) to Fernando de Sousa (1855-1942), editor of Catholic newspaper *A Voz,* and better known as Nemo, author of *A doutrina maçónica.* In it, he railed against an article published on the 24th of January 1934, titled "Freemasonry in Germany". In it, he corrects the newspaper at having used the term "lodges" with what were supposed to be "grand lodges", and cannot comprehend how a "manifestly Christian newspaper can rejoice at the praise for yet another offence by the spirit inimical to Christ". Subsequently, in a text about the *Orders of the atrium, the cloister and the temple,* the heteronym explains the origins of the name he signed the letter with;

> Having passed the Transept – whether in regular fashion, by plenary initiation in either of the two quoted orders; or in irregular fashion, via direct contact with the High Initiators, and thus with no need to resort to either of those orders – what follows are the so-called Orders of the Cloister, or High Orders.

116. Um Sonhador Nostálgico do Abatimento e da Decadência (A Nostalgic Dreamer of Dejection and Decadence) – In his later years, Pessoa's dislike for Salazar had become absolute. He begins writing harsh texts against that "little tyrant who didn't drink wine", as well as poems, one of which the censored "Liberdade", and none of them published in Pessoa's life. But his friends typed them and handed them around Lisbon's cafés, among them three signed by one *Sonhador Nostálgico do Abatimento e da Decadência,* such as this one (29th of March 1935):

> This Salazar fellow
> Is made of salt and ill fortune
> Should it ever rain
> Water shall dissolve
>
> The salt
> And under the sky
> There shall remain but ill fortune.

The inspiration for this heteronym's name came from a speech by Salazar in the awards ceremony where *Message* was awarded: *That which edifies and that which destroys, that which educates and demoralizes the creators of civic or moral energies and the nostalgic dreamers of dejection and decadence, cannot possibly be of equal value for society.* Coincidentally (further reason for him to have chosen this name), the words are almost the same as those in a text by Pessoa (04/05/1915), which speaks of "ultradecadent movements, interpretative of dejection".

117. Vadooisf – Yet another poet revealed in séances, with a name which perhaps wasn't meant to be definitive, as, after naming him, Pessoa added a question mark in parentheses. One of his poems ends thus:

> By sheer chance
> In the undecided
> Setting sun
> In the wisdom
> Of knotty delay.

118. Velhote – He wrote riddles for *O Palrador,* such as this one:

> In man they say I am
> And in verse I should be
> In the wind someone tried
> To say they would find me.

119. Vicente Guedes – Born around 1907 to be a shadow of Pessoa. In the back of the paper which contains the plan for Caeiro's oeuvre, Pessoa defined him thus: "A dandy in spirit, he strolled across the art of dreaming through the chance of existing". "Of V[icente] G[uedes], none know who he was or what he did". "For Vicente Guedes, being self-aware was an art, and knowing was a religion. He definitely lived the inner anaesthesia, that attitude of the soul which more closely resembles the very attitude of a bona fide aristocrat's body". He signed a poem in 1910 and, besides the writings of several heteronyms, he also translated the works of Morrisson, Byron, Aeschylus, Shelley, Stevenson, to be published by Íbis. He intended to write *Contos de um doido* (Tales of a madman), narrating the life of heteronym Marcos Alves, and, given his penchant for "glasses of aguardiente", he wrote "R, nunc est bibendum" (now one must drink), in which he says:

> What else is the spirit to do
> Aside from drinking until it forgets life.

On the 22nd of August 1914, he edits what he called *A decorative Chronicle,* subsequently rebaptised as *Diary of Vicente Guedes,* and finally *The Book of Disquiet.* In it, aside from noting down everyday facts, are considerations on life, such as this obituary: "The figure of Almeida's son is comprised of three elements: He was a man of the people, a pederast and a boor. Other than his love for landscapes and men, nothing else attracted him". Then, the author of the book became Bernardo Soares – the one which Pessoa began to "see", as he claims in his famous letter to Casais Monteiro about the genesis of his heteronyms. He also changes the author's address: From Rua dos Retroseiros, 17, 4th floor (Guedes), he moved to Rua dos Douradores, unnumbered, 4th floor (Soares), after which Guedes began to be declared as dead. "It is that which remains and will remain of this soul of most subtle reasoning, more debauched in pure dreaming, the likes of which has seldom been seen in this world". And so was "the great and conscientious Vicente Guedes reaped by death". Tuberculosis, much like Caeiro and so many others around Pessoa.

120. Voodooist (Joseph Balsamo) – An evil spirit, in life, the herald of Egyptian Freemasonry, Count Alessandro di Cagliostro (1743-1795) himself. A charlatan which began to manifest around 1916. But this Voodooist, which was to have been famous in the French court, was eventually exposed and abandoned Pessoa shortly thereafter.

121. W. Fasnacht – A German graphologist who offered to "decipher people's character via their handwriting" for 200 réis, plus 25 réis for the answer via postal note. Letters were supposed to be addressed to *W. Fasnacht, Posta-Restante, Lisbon.* Underneath the ad's draft, which can be found at Lisbon's national library, there is a *true* signature of the graphologist.

122. W.W. Austin – Two signatures of Austin are in the Chest (without the W.W. initials). He lived in Australia for a while, and there he met a group of miners, according to Richard Zenith. He was tasked with presenting another heteronym, which he did in a letter to the editor of *The Natal Mercury,* in which he says (abridged): "I heard plenty of his stories and songs, almost all of them interesting. I'm sending you the best of them all… crafted with care and all due attention to the metric. Here is the song which the author, a young man called [Karl P.] Effield, titled 'The Miner's Song'". After the letter, nothing else was ever said about Austin.

123. (Rev. or Sir) Walter Wyatt – Another Wyatt brother. A priest, his name was occasionally preceded by Rev(erend), and other times by Sir. He wrote two volumes of poetry in English, and his signature was clearly practised. In that long list of heteronyms, Pessoa has the habit of writing in families. Father and

son, like Gallião and Gallião Pequeno. Or brothers: In pairs – such as Ricardo and Frederico Reis, David and Lucas Merrick, António and Florêncio Gomes, Carlos and Miguel Otto, Gervásio and Vicente Guedes; in threes – such as A.A., I.I. and Thomas Crosse; or Alberto, António and Júlio Manuel Caeiro; or even fours – like Alexander, Augustus, Catherine and Charles James Search; or Alfred, Augusto, Frederick and Walter Wyatt.

124. Wardour – Another poet which came to him in séances; except, unlike the episodic nature of the others, this one was persistent. In poems, his signature simply says Wardour or Wardour + Pessoa. Some dated, mainly those from 1916. Perhaps aware of the mediocre quality of texts such as "Crepúsculo em Deus" (Twilight in God), the spirit at times notes down at the margins "this poem is yours; I give you my part in it, my boy"; and signs with a kaballistic sign, *8,* amidst scribblings of *yes* or *no.* One of them begins thus:

> O mere whiteness
> Of spreading moonlight
> O river of fairness
> Of the moonlight flailing.

Besides horoscopes, Wardour was involved in Pessoa's life, to the point he insisted he lose his virginity: "Monastic life is for monasteries", he said on the 1st of July 1916. His was the mission of announcing the woman who was to "introduce him to virility". Later, he informed him that said woman, "strong and immensely masculine in her willpower", would make Pessoa "her slave"; he knew it well, for she was to be Margaret Mansel – in the past, Wardour's own wife in "an unhappy marriage". At times, Pessoa seeks to know more of Wardour, but in those moments, the heteronym always says "don't ask me any questions":

125. Woman in White – Another minor spirit from his séances. For Pessoa, she was one of the "obscure spirits".

126. Willyam Links Esk – A character which signed a letter on the 13th of April 1905, meant for an imaginary newspaper in Durban. His English reproduces the sound of the words rather than their orthography, as is the case of his surname, in which Esk corresponds to Esq. of *Esquire.* In that letter, the author protests against a report that he had been arrested for seven days, when, according to him, he was only detained for six days and 23 hours.

127. Zé Fininha – Author of texts for *O Palrador,* such as "Carta de um provinciano" (Letter from a hick). One of this character's traits is the fact that he writes as if he were barely literate.

Other names

Some scholars mention other names as heteronyms. Among them poet António Botto – who, in his homosexuality, according to Jorge de Sena, *was also a heteronym of Fernando Pessoa, in poetry and in its corresponding life.* Or D. Sebastião, who professor Luís Felipe Teixeira held as *doubtlessly his most complex heteronym, especially considering he represents the transcendental vanishing point of his "geometry of the abyss".* Joel Serrão suggests likewise, that the heteronym was *covertly returning to the homeland.* Robert Bréchon quotes Sá-Carneiro *as a type of supplemental heteronym.* Richard Zenith goes so far as to suggest that Ophelia Queiroz herself could, in certain moments, be *some sort of anti-heteronym, a real character converted into a historical figure.* Eliezer Kamenetzky should also be included in that category, as we shall see further up ahead. Jorge Luis Borges claims to have met him when he was young (Pessoa would have been 21 years old, and Borges 20) in September 1919[30], at Martinho da Arcada, and that they made a pact that he'd become one of his heteronyms, after which Pessoa would dictate him his poems. According to him, *it all began as a joke between us, but as time went on, it became a habit and, after that, all but second nature;* which is why he confesses that, *from time to time, I still feed Pessoa's famed Chest with new works.* For the record, Borges was the grandson of a Jew from Torre de Moncorvo, Bragança.

As we've established, 127 names are heteronyms. Were we to add a further 75, which – according to the adopted criteria of classification – aren't considered true heteronyms, there would be even more: 202 in all. Not to mention the abovementioned five real characters, which would bring the total up to 207. The one thing all the heteronyms have in common is the fact that they were all defeated. *Beaten in life,* as the literary movement founded by Eça de Queiroz, Guerra Junqueiro and Ramalho Ortigão was designated as. In that list, there isn't a single big name, no eminent hero, no successful man or a member of nobility; no one who is acknowledged or praised by his fellow countrymen. Quite the opposite, what we have is a small crowd of ciphers, minor figures who mirrored their creator's life. In his *Poetics,* Aristotle says *the difference between the historian and the poet lies not in the fact that the former writes in prose and the latter in verse (for, if Herodotus'*[31] *work had been composed in verse, it would still be a work of history). Rather, it lies in the fact that one writes about what happened, and the other about what might have happened.* Pessoa, as if taking that description to heart, asks himself in "Original Sin": "Who shall write

30 An imaginary encounter, as Borges only came to Lisbon in May 1924, and gave the year of 1919 to characterize his farce. It also bears mentioning that Pessoa only truly came to Borges' attention much later, when, around 1960, the Argentine co-wrote an article on Portuguese literature in the 20th century with his friend, Alicia Jurado.

31 Greek historian (484-420 BC) who, in his books, narrated the differences between barbaric peoples (Egyptians, Medes, Persians) and the Greeks.

the history of what might have been?". He did: African, German, Brazilian, French, English and Portuguese; monarchist and militant republican; decipherer, philosopher, geographer, graphologist, journalist and madman; physician, psychologist and psychiatrist; man, woman and spirit; aristocrat, Roman emperor, mandarin, maharajah and pasha; soothsayer, alchemist, astrologer, warlock, Christian convert, reverend, sir, man of the people and mama's boy. In all those faces and many others, he told the story of this unhappy man who dreamt of being so many – and couldn't even manage to be himself.

> All I think
> All I am
> Is an immense desert
> I am not even at.
>
> *Untitled* (18/03/1935), Fernando Pessoa

ACT III

IN WHICH HIS MANY TASTES AND TRADES ARE DESCRIBED

Vivit sub pectore vulnus
(The wound rests deep within the chest) Virgil

PESSOA AND BRAZIL

Sociologically speaking, there is no Brazil.
Letter to Eurico de Seabra (31/04/1916), Pessoa, Fernando

Longing for Brazil

The presence of Brazil in the life and oeuvre of Fernando Pessoa is fragmentary. To him, Brazilians were but a part of a shapeless whole, "an undifferentiated amalgam of several races subordinated to the original sin of speaking Portuguese"; and "even those who know Brazil exists can conclude that, in literary terms, it doesn't exist"[1]. He certainly acknowledges the country's importance, though: "As far as we can today ascertain, there are but two nations of European origin outside of Europe which have the soul to be an empire – the United States and Brazil", as "Brazil has a life of its own, much like the United States do with regards to England"[2]; and believed that "the need to strengthen the natural spiritual bonds between us and Brazil necessitates propaganda for that republic". Thus, "Portugal, determined to support its cultural imperialism, must first seek out Brazil"; so much so, that he pondered creating a company, Cosmópolis, which should concern itself with "everything that is Portuguese and Brazilian, and seek to aid the news of both countries in any way it can". He also planned an *Album of Portugal* about the Portuguese colony in Brazil – even knowing that "the Portuguese and Brazilian public", "of average culture"

---

1 Aldous Huxley (1894-1963) said something similar of Brazil: *It is one of the unlikeliest countries I am aware of.*

2 American poet (Irving) Allen Ginsberg (1926-1997) does not reply in kind and, in "Salutations to Fernando Pessoa" (an obvious allusion to "Salutation to Walt Whitman"), badmouths him: *Every time I read Pessoa I think/ I'm better than he is.../...he's only from Portugal/ I'm American greatest country in the world/...his mostly Portuguese, but that's not his fault.* It could be that such ill will stemmed from Ginsberg having read some of Pessoa's texts, such as "Americans deal with everything as if it were a joke"; or even worse, his definition of the US in *Ultimatum* as a *bastard synthesis of Europe's scum, garlic of the transatlantic stew, nasalized pronunciation of tasteless modernism.*

has “traditionally few readers”. In the survey *Portugal, vast empire,* he claims “the Portuguese have created the modern world” and that “in the darkest hours of our decadence, our imperial action carried on, especially in Brazil”. Despite that apparent regard, he had some less than flattering words for Brazilians in one of his manifestos:

> And you, Brazil, “sister republic”, jest of Pedro Álvares Cabral, who didn’t even want to discover you![3]
>
> *Ultimatum*, Fernando Pessoa

In 1928, he publishes *Interregnum – defence and justification of the military dictatorship in Portugal;* taking care to explain in a letter to brother Luís Miguel (07/01/1929) that, although it was “representative of what one might consider *the current political thought of Latin countries...,* more rigidly conservative than that which my opuscle contains”, the position is valid “only in Portugal – it [the book] has no reference to other similar systems”. On the 6th of May of that same 1929, he wrote for *Notícias Ilustrado* the article “Brazil, sister nation and friend”, in which he compares the two people, who are headed for “the common fate, hit by the same light, attracted and guided by the same mysterious call”; and sees that so too do the stars bring us together, as the “six marriages of the twelve energies” of the Zodiac, are carried out in “six axes” in horoscopes. Astrologer Paulo Cardoso explained the quote to me: *These unions are made between opposed and complimentary signs, such as Pisces and Virgo, namely those of Portugal and Brazil; and, as that relationship evolves, so too does the voyage towards the New Time, to the Era of Aquarius of the Fifth Empire.* He also mentioned Brazil in a favourite quote of his: “All else is to inherit from your Brazilian uncle, or not to be where the grenade fell”. The latter was an expression of luck after World War I, when to evade a grenade was indeed lucky, whereas the former alludes to when João VI stayed in Brazil in 1808 with his retinue of noblemen, merchants, wastrels, exiles and robbers, some of which preferred to remain instead of travelling back to Lisbon, and never married on account of their acquired taste for the perfume and supple flesh of black female slaves. As they had no sons, whatever wealth they accumulated went to the children of their siblings in Portugal, who *inherited* it. Thus, Brazil was but a place to make your fortune in. To say nothing of the fact that, even though there is no overt reference to Brazil, the country is present in his most important book:

3 Pessoa would later downplay it, saying: “Fortunately, our ridiculous mocking of the Brazilians no longer takes place”.

With two hands – Act and Fate –
We unearth. In the same gesture, one
Raises the flickering, divine torch
And the other parts the veil.

Whether it was the hour to be or that was
The hand which tore off the West's veil,
Science was the soul, and Boldness, the body
Of the hand that unveiled it.

Whether it was Chance, or Will, or Storm
The hand that raised the torch which shone,
God was the soul and Portugal, the body
Of the hand that drove it.

Message ("The Occident"), Fernando Pessoa

Native language

Portugal and Brazil are united in Pessoa's soul in two main matrices. The first would be the empire of the language, as Portuguese is "far too complex to be easily assimilated and learned by peoples of other nations". It would be "the Fifth Empire in spirit"; as the nation could be "more than one, and spiritually [both] are the same, as they share the same language". And "Portugal, in this case, means Brazil as well". Finally, he proudly proclaims: "I have no feelings, political or social; I do, however, hold a highly patriotic sentiment, to a certain extent", as "my homeland is the Portuguese language". *Last flower of the Latium, uncouth and fair* – as Olavo Bilac put it, as if complementing the thought, and for whom *you are both splendour and grave.* Had he been more generous, and, like Eça, he might have said that the language spoken in Brazil was *Portuguese with sugar.* Consistent with his beliefs, Pessoa then presents five reasons why Portuguese should be considered the "literary language" of the entire world:

1. It is the richest and most complex of all Romance languages.
2. It is one of the five imperial languages.
3. It is spoken, although not by that many people, from the East to the West, contrary to all other languages but English and, to a certain extent, French.
4. It is easy to learn for whomever knows Spanish and, to a degree, Italian – ergo, it's not an isolated language.
5. It is the language spoken in a great growing country: Brazil (it could be spoken from the East to the West and not be spoken by a great Nation).

Sebastianism in Brazil

A second common point with the "New Portugal", represented by Brazil, would have been Sebastianism. He knew Brazilian historical figures which reminded him of Sebastião I, mainly messianic figures from the northeast. The first such man, in 1819, was former soldier of the 12th militia battalion of Alagoas, Silvestre José dos Santos, self-proclaimed Master Quiou, The Envoy, who founded the city of Paraíso Terrestre (Earthen Paradise), at today's Bonito, in Pernambuco, 136km away from Recife. Before his people, he proclaimed the imminent resurrection of Sebastião I, who would share his treasure with the faithful. The religious ceremonies took place in a shed covered with dry leaves of a local palm tree called *catolé*. Inside, a mysterious woman clad in white, Our Lady herself, gave orders to the prophet Quiou. The community, a small state set apart from the official country, was a dangerous example of independence for the crown, which was why the militia of governor Luís do Rego (25/10/1820), commanded by *bold marshall* Salazar Moscoso, soon destroyed it. Silvestre ran off and was never heard from again. On the ground, scattered about the burning houses, lay the bodies of 79 men and a couple of women. The Prata river ran red from all the blood. Worried about the unfolding developments of the 1817 Republican Revolution, which had installed an interim government in Pernambuco, emperor Pedro I proclaimed in a manifesto on the 1st of August 1822: *Remember, people of Pernambuco, the fires of Bonito.* Words to the wind, as not even a month later, the fires of Bonito would light up the placid shores of the Ipiranga creek.

Then, in 1836, came the Enchanted Kingdom of the mamluk João António dos Santos, at Pedra Bonita, today known as Pedra do Reino, at the border between Pernambuco and Paraíba, then district of Vila Bela. To his faithful, João António promised that *the ugly shall be rendered fair; the poor, wealthy; the ill, healthy; and the black, fair;* but his story fizzled out and his fate remains unknown. His successor, brother-in-law João Ferreira, implemented the right of *pernada,* wherein brides were forced to give themselves to their governors, thus reviving the Roman *primae noctis.* In his deranged preaching, he assured all that *Sebastião would come from the Veiled Isle with two thousand galleons laden with guns and gold, accompanied by King Arthur of England and the nine hidden tribes of Israel.* So that the bowels of the Earth might open themselves at the passage of such majestic retinue, victims' throats were slit or their skulls were dashed on rocks. Between May 14 and 17 1838, 30 children, 12 men and 11 women were sacrificed, including João António's father, his wife (queen Josefa) and sister-in-law (Isabel). Besides 14 dogs which were to one day return as dragons for the royal entourage. In the end, João II, as he called himself, ended up immolated by his own companions, who tied his body between two trees so it would stop thrashing. The following day, what was left of that slum was destroyed by major Manoel Pereira.

The most notorious of all came from Bahia: António Vicente Mendes Maciel – known as Bom Jesus Conselheiro (Advisor), Santo António Conselheiro, or just António Conselheiro. He was described by Câmara Cascudo as *frugal, austere, demanding, disciplined and chaste.* There, from 1893 to 1897, in a hamlet by the bank of the river Vaza-Barris, he gathered between 20 and 30 thousand followers. In his visions at Arraial de Canudos, he proclaimed that *the hinterlands shall turn to sea and the sea to hinterlands.* Some of his predictions would become famous: *Verily, I tell you that, when nation battles nation, Brazil against Brazil, England against England, Prussia against Prussia, then shall Sebastião from the waves of the sea emerge with his army.* Euclides da Cunha, in his *Os sertões,* transcribed some annotations he found at Arraial, such as:

> The Antichrist was born
> To rule over Brazil
> But lo, there is the Advisor
> To rid us from him.
>
> Then shall come to visit us
> Our King Sebastião
> Woe betide he
> Under the rule of the Dog.

His followers, among which there were some monarchists to be found, were promptly fought by the recently established republican government. Arraial was levelled by harsh and successive expeditions, but these weren't without their cost: In the second one, for example, colonel Moreira César, chief of the official troops, was killed. In the end, it was inevitable, and the official country imposed his might on those ragamuffins. Conselheiro, killed on the 22nd of September 1897, was first buried at the altar of the Holy Trinity, next to the New Church; exhumed on the 6th of October by general João da Silva Barbosa, so that his body might be identified by a commission presided over by medical major José de Miranda Cúrio. His head was lopped off, treated with virgin lime and brought to Salvador, where it was examined by the most famous Brazilian psychiatrist at the time, one Raimundo Nina Rodrigues, professor at Bahia's Medical Faculty. Pessoa knew Canudos well from reading Euclides da Silva and revered "the memory of António Conselheiro, bandit, madman and saint, who died in Brazil's hinterland in exemplary fashion, with his companions, without surrendering, as those ultimate Portuguese fought for the hope of the Fifth Empire and Sebastião, who shall come when God wills it, our lord, the emperor of the world".

The heteronyms and Brazil

Brazil was also where some novels of heteronym Abílio Quaresma took place, such as *The Vargas Affair* – in which agent Guedes says: "Whether or not I go to Brazil, I wish you the best of luck"; or in *The case of the narrow window* – which had a projected chapter (which remains to be found among his papers) titled "Departure to Brazil". It also bears remembering three other heteronyms: Accursio Urbano, in his riddles for *O Palrador,* claims Brazil as his "homeland". Writer Eduardo Lança was born in Bahia. And Ricardo Reis lived out his voluntary exile in Rio de Janeiro. The choice of such a place was owed to Luís de Montalvor having lived there, working as an aide for Bernardino (Luís) Machado (Guimarães), who, at the time (1912-1915), was plenipotentiary minister at Rio, where he was born, and subsequently president in 1915/1917 and 1925/1926. A citizen of Rio, the president of Portugal. How that must have amused Pessoa[4].

Catulo da Paixão Cearense

Pessoa made plenty of references to Brazil. In a letter to William Bentley (undated, but certainly from 1915), editor of *Portugal* magazine, he says that "the Brazilian spirit isn't particularly bright and, in literary matters, has the counterproductive habit of keeping up to date with the present of twenty years ago". Brazilian diplomat (Manuel de) Oliveira Lima (1865-1928), frowned upon in Portugal by the *Orpheu* group ever since his compliments of Júlio Dantas, was criticized for his dissertation at the Royal Society of Literature: "The statements he made are so incorrect, the lack of precision he conveys so remarkably false, that it is impossible, within the bounds of decency, to correct the mass of criticism". Among his Brazilian friends could be counted Ronald de Carvalho, "one of the most interesting Brazilian poets", and Eduardo Guimarães, who Gaspar Simões said to be of a *mallarmean*[5] *aristocracy.* But the one Brazilian Pessoa ever mentioned in his poems is another still:

> My life has been, in brief,
> Lowly and obscure,
> Neither fortunate nor unfortunate,
> Shadows of tatters in the murk.

---

4 Although he wasn't the first Portuguese governor born in Brazil. Before him, Maria II, daughter of Pedro I (IV in Portugal), had been queen in Portugal without having renounced her Brazilian citizenship.

5 Reference to the *prince of poets,* Stéphane Mallarmé (1842-1898), who gathered the cream of the crop of Paris' intellectual elite in his house.

Much like a lowly clerk
I've remained at a null counter
Neither Catullo is enamoured
Nor the political position a council of state.

Catullo of Passion, Fernando Pessoa

This "Catullo" was theatrologist, poet, musician, singer and composer Catulo da Paixão Cearense, the famous author of *Luar do sertão,* who, in spite of his surname, was actually born in São Luís do Maranhão (1863) and died in Rio de Janeiro (1946). Pessoa wrote the name with two l's, according to the occasional Brazilian norm, or perhaps to better rhyme with *nullo* [null] at the time also written with two l's – even though the orthographic reform agreed to by Portugal and Brazil at the time had already established that only one 'l' was to be used. Such is his admiration, that he intends to translate some of Catulo's texts into English. In *Herostratus and the search for immortality*[6], he even predicts that history would preserve Walt Whitman, as he embodies "all of the northern dementias, much like all of Latin America is to be found in Catullo"; and celebrates that "great poet, who dramatizes his poems in the lingo of the Brazilian hinterlands", and also mentions him when he remembers São João "with lamb in hand, as Catullo saw you".

Cecília Meireles

At the end of 1934, Cecília Meireles went to Portugal for the first time for a number of conferences in Lisbon and Coimbra. With her came her first husband and an old friend of Pessoa's, Portuguese painter Fernando Correia Dias, who would commit suicide in the same month in which his poet friend died[7]. In her estimation, Pessoa was *the most extraordinary case of Portuguese letters,* and her most famous poem "A arte de ser feliz" (The Art of Happiness), has a style rather similar to his[8]:

There was a time in which my window
Opened to a city which appeared to be
Made of chalk. Close to the window, there was a small, almost dry garden.
(...)

6 Herostratus of Ephesus achieved the immortality he sought by burning down the temple of Artemis, goddess of wild animals and hunting in 356 BC – one of the seven wonders of the ancient world. He was tortured by Artaxerxes, and the Ephesians forbid the mere utterance of his name, which ironically ended up increasing his infamy.

7 Cecília (1901-1964) wrote, thinking of him: *But whomever saw eyes, arms and dreams so torn, and died for his sins, shall speak to God.* She would remarry in 1940 with Dr. Heitor Grillo.

8 In a letter to Ruy Affonso (17/09/1946), Cecília acknowledges *similarities between us* [her and Pessoa]*, of rather deep nature, both in spirit and in our upbringing,* but disagrees he influenced her in that specific poem.

When I speak of these small
Bits of happiness standing before
Each window, some say such things
Don't exist, others that they exist
Solely before my windows, and others
Still, that one needs to learn how to look,
To see them as such.

Cecília called one of the offices Pessoa worked at and they set up a date, around midday, at Brasileira do Chiado. After waiting for two hours in vain, she returned to the hotel she was staying at, probably Borges (at Rua Garrett, quite close to the café) and found there a copy of *Message,* dedicated "to Cecília Meireles, high poet, and Correia Dias, artist, old friend and accomplice (see *Águia*[9], etc.), in the invocation of *Apolo* and *Athena* [both magazines], Fernando Pessoa, 10-XII, 1934". With it, a note explaining his absence: He had felt psychic vibrations and had decided to do his horoscope that day, where he saw that "the two were not to meet"[10]. Cecília would never meet Pessoa, "sadder than what happens is that which never happened". Back in Brazil, she wrote the first critiques on his poetry for the anthology *Poetas novos de Portugal* (1944) and later, at *Jornal do Brasil* (21/09/1968), she signed the first chronicle "Fernando Pessoa helping me" – in which she reflects upon notions of honesty and pretence, based on Pessoa's sentence "To speak is the easiest way of becoming unknown". Fate just wouldn't have them meet.

If, at one point
I had turned to the left rather than the right,
If, at a certain moment
I had said yes instead of no, or no instead of yes;
If, in a certain conversation
I had uttered the sentences which only now come to me –
If everything had been that way,
I would be different today, and so too would the universe
Perhaps have become quite another.

Untitled (11/05/1928), Álvaro de Campos

9 Dias was copyist and illustrator of *Águia* magazine, in which Pessoa published a number of articles, and had been invited to collaborate with him in *Orpheu.*

10 Far from an unusual occurrence with Pessoa. In a letter to Aleister Crowley (06/01/1930), for example, he says that "January and February are straight out" and that "March is a propitious month for meeting you, as the base solar direction (Sun, sextil, Neptune) is in remarkable harmony with the circumstances". The Chest has astrological calculations which suggested September for Crowley's visit, and so it was in 1930.

Pessoa's fame in Brazil

His life was ever marked by two facts. One of them political, when, at the beginning of the Portuguese Estado Novo, he showed his support for a right-wing government in numerous texts, which earned him the antipathy of those intellectuals committed to democracy. Then, he turned on Salazar, which merited a reaction from conservatives of all stripes. Another is related to mores, as in more than one occasion, he took the side of overtly homosexual poets. To say nothing of his defence of slavery, critiques of communism and Christianity. Those unconventional attitudes likely led him to be more esteemed outside of Portugal than in his own country. Or, perhaps, as Teresa Rita Lopes told me in a conversation, it was so because *Portugal is a small country, where intellectuals rub shoulders and all envy each other.* I mention these facts dispassionately, in the interest of detailed analysis, but must mention that perhaps it wasn't by chance that the first of his biographers, João Gaspar Simões, was born in Portugal – all others are, in chronological order, a Spaniard (Crespo), a Frenchman (Bréchon), and an American (Zenith). What is certain is that, in time, a better understanding of historical context opened the doors to the limitless admiration he deserves, even among his own. And especially in Brazil, where he is esteemed like no other Portuguese poet.

> If he who created
> The world had wished
> For me to be different
> He would have made me differently.
> (…)
> If to see is to fool myself,
> To think, to misguide,
> I know not. God granted me them
> In truth and on my path.
>
> *Untitled* (02/01/1932), Fernando Pessoa

Esse oporte ut vivas, non vivere ut edas
(One should eat to live, not live to eat) Cicero

THE FLAVOURS OF PESSOA

Oh great men of the Moment!
(...)
Pad your fame and bellies–
Tomorrow's for the madmen of today!
Neighbourhood Gazette, Álvaro de Campos

Culinary in Pessoa's texts

Arte de cozinha, Portugal's first cookbook came out in 1680, written by Domingos Rodrigues, Pedro II's cook. One hundred years later, *O cozinheiro moderno* came out, written by Lucas Rigaud, a Frenchman who came to Portugal to cook for queen Maria I. Neither of which indicated the ingredients' amounts, unlike modern cookbooks, a style which endured in Europe until 1870 at least, when Alexandre Dumas released his monumental *Grand dictionaire de cuisine,* which was one of his most important books, along with *The Count of Monte Cristo* (which wasn't a count) and *The Three Musketeers* (which were four). At that time, Almeida Garrett wrote *Travels in my Homeland, Dona Branca* and *A conquista do Algarve,* all with an emphasis on gastronomy; Eça Queiroz published *The Crime of Father Amaro, Cousin Bazilio, The Mandarin, The Illustrious House of Ramires* and *The Maias,* going so far as claiming in *Contemporary Notes* that *Man puts as much of his character and individuality in his kitchen inventions as he does in art.* Also Camões in his *Lusiads,* in which Marques da Cruz remarks upon the *many victuals which embarked in the armada's ships.* But none of that moves Pessoa; in his works, the table always has a secondary role. Circumstantial. Nor was he much of a gourmand, always preferring simpler recipes, perhaps because "this ritual of mine of the palate is far less solemn". "Let us eat, drink and love (without getting overly attached to food, drink and love, as that would later bring elements of discomfort)".

First flavours

Pessoa was born amidst the smoke of the Saint Anthony festivities. Sardines roast at the coals (they are fatter and tastier around that time), consumed by the public over slices of bread; trays of Lapa cookies, chorizo, grilled pork meat, quesadillas, fried cod dough and spoonfuls of rice pudding. "Oh, the plates of rice pudding/ With their cinnamon strips!/ Oh, the white hand that brought them!/ Oh, that it was her hand!". The same scene plays out in every street in Lisbon: "Who sells the truth, and in which corner? Who is the peppermint to season it with?". To drink, colourful jars of red wine, elixirs and sangria, with ice cubes and slices of lime floating in that mix of wine and sugared water. But, in that time, he wouldn't have attended many such celebrations, as he soon was to travel far away, and so not many flavours became imprinted in his memory. Perhaps mainly sweets, such as chocolate, which is present in so many texts of his: "A mere piece of chocolate can shake up my nerves with the surfeit of memories it provokes. Childhood! And as my teeth sink into the dark, soft mass… Tears well up in my eyes, and… I can taste my bygone happiness, my long lost childhood".

> Buy chocolate for the child I succeeded by mistake,
> And take off the sign, for tomorrow is infinite.
> (…)
> Large are the deserts, and all is a desert.
> Unless I am mistaken, of course.
> Poor human soul with an oasis only on the desert next to it!
>
> Might as well pack it up.
> Fin.
>
> *Untitled* (04/10/1930), Álvaro de Campos

Nor did he retain any of Africa's flavours, even having spent there the rest of his childhood. In that new continent, we only know he enjoyed curry. And so did many Portuguese, to the point that in the abovementioned Domingos Rodrigues cookbook already had recipes for meat and fish curry. Every family has its own way of doing it, usually with saffron, cinnamon, cardamom, clove, tumeric, rice paper, bay leaf, masala, nutmeg and seeds – coriander, cumin, sweetgrass, sesame, mustard. And also allspice, powdered red pepper and black pepper. But he soon drops that habit, according to Alfred Margarido, as, upon, his return to Portugal, *he was disappointed with the curry served in Portuguese restaurants, due to the absence of coconut and the mild spices.* Except for the curry served at a tavern called Casa Pessoa, at Rua Santa Justa, where he *met* Bernardo Soares. In his own words: "We met often at the same cheap, secluded restaurant. We knew each other by sight; nodded naturally in silent greeting. Once, we almost met at the same table, and as fate would have it, we exchanged a couple of sentences, and conversation followed. After that, we met there every day for lunch and dinner". Among the dishes with curry he enjoyed, one stood out:

CURRIED ROOSTER WITH RICE

Ingredients: 1 medium rooster, 1 small coconut, 2 small chilli peppers, 2 teaspoons curry, 1 teaspoon ginger, 2 teaspoons cumin, 20g coriander (seeds), 150g tomato juice, 1 large onion, 4 cloves garlic, 60g butter, 500g rice, salt and pepper to taste.

Directions: Braise the rooster, chopping it with the onion, garlic and butter. Set aside. Grate the coconut and boil it for 15 minutes. Squeeze the coconut. Temper the coconut's milk with salt, tomato juice, chilli pepper and curry. Add cumin, coriander seeds and ginger (ground). Add the rooster to the sauce. Cook it properly. Serve with rice cooked in water, salt and curry.[1]

Flavours at home

His family's bill of fare wasn't particularly refined, but quite varied nonetheless: Dried *açorda* with bread, cod dough, lamb with potatoes, Portuguese boiled dinner, custard, stuffed meat slices, white beans, fish fillets, pork loin – "where is the casual girl bringing the pork chops and the wine to? To which heaven she doesn't believe in?". Also slices of chorizo garnished with carrots, green beans and other vegetables. Cabbage, too, "sink number nine, for those who look like a cabbage". He invariably remembers his home meals fondly: "The table set with more sitting places, with better sets of china, with more glasses, the sideboard with many more things – sweets, fruit, the rest in the shadow – the old aunts, the cousins". And, in those moments, he feels "nostalgia of eating the past like hunger bread". Also "fruits whose name was a sinking of teeth into their flesh's soul", among them Almeirim melon with prosciutto, much more in line with what he considers "a simple, studied diet", or even by itself: "I ate chopped melon/ And drank wine after/ The more I look at you/ The more I know we are not meant to be". Cakes, too, even knowing that "one cannot eat a cake without losing it". "Sink number six, for those who comb their hair with fruitcake". The typical crown-shaped fruitcake contains a fava bean and a small prize, which earned a wish to whomever got it. Born in France during the reign of Louis XIV, the recipe came to Portugal with Baltazar Rodrigues Castanheiro for the inauguration of the Confeitaria Nacional at Rua do Bestega, in 1869. Called *bolo-rei* (king cake), it is usually eaten at Epiphany, called 'Kings' Day' in Portugal.

1 This recipe and the following ones stand to this day.

BOLO-REI

Ingredients: For the risen dough: 14g baker's yeast, 3 spoons lukewarm milk, 100g wheat flour.

For the cake: 250g wheat flour, 100g risen dough, 1 spoon salt, 4 eggs, lemon zest, 150g sugar, 100g butter, 150g dried crystallized fruit (plum, cherry, fig, walnuts), 1 chalice Port wine, flour, 1 yolk to baste.

Directions: Prepare the risen dough and let it ferment for 4 hours. Set aside. Chop the dried crystallized fruit and soak them in Port wine. Set aside. Place the flour on the table. Make a hole in the middle. Place the risen dough and knead well. Add the eggs (one by one) at room temperature, the lemon zest, the sugar, the butter (previously churned until creamy). Mix. The dough should have a soft consistency. Cover it and let it rest until the following day. Add the crystallized fruits. Split the dough in two. Give both the shape of a crown (first making a ball, and then a hole in the middle), with around 30cm diameter. Add the fava bean and the prize. Let it rest in an enclosed space for an hour. Baste it with the yolk (diluted in water). Bake it at medium temperature (180º C). As it bakes, decorate it with more crystallized fruits and sugar. Leave it in the oven until it acquires a golden tone.

Breakfast

"Waking up in the city of Lisbon later than the others, waking up at Rua do Ouro, waking up at Rocio, by the doors of the cafés". During his time at Rua Coelho da Rocha, he had his breakfast at home, but only when sister Teca was around. Whenever alone, he always ate out in the street, Azeitão and Alverca cheese and a large glass of wine. Or in cafés. Most of his life, he patronized Casa do Carmo, at Largo do Carmo, while he read "the newspaper on the table". It was there he supposedly met Sá-Carneiro, who lived close by at Travessa do Carmo. Sá-Carneiro once recited him the following verses in 1915:

Cafés of my laziness
Today you are – such encomium!
The entirety of my field of action
And all of my covetousness.

Lunch

Pessoa has his "dinner (and breakfast) sent" from nearby taverns; or goes there – whenever he can afford to, at least. In his diary, there are a number of entries of that constant lack of funds: "I had lunch at Pessoa, thanks to a loan from João Correia de Oliveira" (27/03/1913); or "At home without dinner, as I had no money" (14/11/1915). As a follow-up to that annotation, "I wasn't bothered much, as I drank some wine at Pedro de Lima's exhibit" – after attending the inauguration of the artist's art studio at Avenida da Liberdade. For lunch, he invariably favours steak. "To this day I recall the steaks in the palate of longing; steaks, I know or suppose, the way no one does them today or I don't get to eat". At the time, there were many famous ones. Such as Nicola Steak, prepared at the eponymous café, or the grilled steak served with a thick sauce, known as Brasileira Steak – the Brasileira do Chiado, naturally, and not the "vile den or grave of artistic utilities and purposes known as Brasileira do Rossio"[2]. To him, the latter was "the inferior Brasileira", a *double entendre,* as Rossio lies lower than the hill atop which Chiado is found. But the one steak he favoured above all others was served at Cervejaria Jansen, at Rua do Alecrim, the meeting point for modernist poets, where he discussed the birth of *Orpheu* magazine from 1914 onwards.

JANSEN STEAK

Ingredients: 400g sirloin steak (sliced in two steaks), 4 cloves of garlic (crushed), 2 bay leaves, 2 spoons pork lard, salt and pepper to taste.

Directions: Season the steaks with salt, pepper, bay and garlic. Place lard and garlic on a frying pan, and then the steaks. Flip the steaks. Ratify salt and pepper, if necessary.

In his frequent comparisons with England, he mentions that it's a place where people "eat marmalade at breakfast" and that "the moon (or so the English say) is made of green cheese". The same moon, according to Pessoa, "is blue every once in a while", in a clear allusion to the idiom. Still on that note, he confesses that "the English eat their eggs, which we classify as *warm,* not in cups and cracked open, but in small egg cups in the shape of half an egg, in which said half fits, and then crack the egg's exposed end, eating it with a teaspoon after adding salt and pepper". Luís Oliveira Guimarães witnesses: *He liked fried egg, which he would offer to share, saying 'care for some of my fried sun'?*

FRIED EGGS WITH CHEESE

Ingredients: 6 eggs, 6 thick slices of cured cheese, 50g of butter, salt and pepper to taste.

Directions: Cut the cheese in thick slices. Melt it in a frying pan with butter. As soon as it melts, add the eggs. When the whites begin to thicken, season with salt and pepper. Bring to the oven for 5 minutes. To be served immediately.

The Leão d'Ouro was invariably frequented by plastic artists which became known as Grupo do Leão, as well as employees of the National Theatre and its

2 Today, at the same address, is the shoe shop Seasize, which, at the time of my visit (2007) had an autumn/winter collection at very reasonable prices.

regulars. "That night, I went to Leão to sup". The house specials were *seafood, lamprey, cod and fishes in general.* Today, Leão d'Ouro has moved from its original address at Rua 1° de Dezembro (formerly Rua do Príncipe), numbers 95-97-99, to the almost adjoining 103-105-107 of the old Café Restauração, wherein gathered a group formed around Edmundo (Alberto) de Bettencour (1899-1973), a poet from Funchal, 11 years Pessoa's junior and friend of Miguel Torga, who signed his works as António Serafim. The current rooms of Leão still boast the same tiles of the original location, portraying hunting scenes. The owner, Manuel de Abreu Sousa, took us through the labyrinthine kitchen to the abandoned salon Pessoa used to frequent, still with the same stone arches on the walls and the same wooden beams on the ceiling, after which he offered us a round of brandy. The place was untouched. All that was missing was the poet. Or perhaps not. One of Leão d'Ouro's specialities is shrimp, much to Pessoa's taste. "I peeled the shrimp/ took off its whole head/ When love isn't right/ Is when love annoys". Seeing as we were there, we had the shrimp casserole, served since the poet's time, which is definitely worth it.

SHRIMP CASSEROLE

Ingredients: 500g of small shrimp, 300g of wheat bread, 4 spoons milk, 750g tomatoes, 2 large onions, 3 spoons dry white wine, 2 spoons lemon juice, 5 spoons olive oil, 1 slice of cheese, salt and pepper to taste.

Directions: Sauté the onions (rings) in olive oil and tomatoes (diced). Add the peeled shrimp. Boil for 10 minutes. Cut the bread in thin slices. Add milk, salt, pepper and drops of lemon. In a large casserole with olive oil, place alternating layers of bread and sautéed shrimp. Put wine, what's left of the milk the bread marinated in, and cheese over the last layer of bread. Cover the pan and bring it to boiling point. Serve hot.

Dinner

"It's all a jumble – childhood lived at a distance, tasty food at night, moonlit scenery". In those occasions, the ritual is always the same: First, dinner, and then a cigarette. But only when he's short on cash, as provided the funds, he invariably smokes a cigar, a necessary complement to good food. Said dinner always begins at 7 with a soup. According to Alfredo Margarido, *they gave him cabbage soup at home, but they didn't have that in Durban, as cabbages wanted nothing to do with that harsh coast.* Niece Manuela Nogueira concurs: *Uncle Fernando greatly enjoyed the soup we had at home, mainly cabbage soup.* It's not a typical Lisbon dish, but rather from Douro and Minho. The soup, initially yellow due to the potatoes, becomes green with the admixture of thinly sliced cabbage.

CABBAGE SOUP

Ingredients: 500g potatoes, 1 bologna, 2 cloves of garlic, 4 spoons olive oil, 200g cabbage, salt.

Directions: Boil the potatoes in 2l of water with sliced bologna and salt. When the potatoes are cooked, squash them and put them in the broth. Add cabbage and half of the olive oil and let it boil until the cabbage is cooked. Add the rest of the olive oil before serving.

Sometimes, he goes to Café Martinho at Largo Camões, then known as Martinho do Camões, where Eça de Queiroz and friends met. It was there that the creation of Solução Editora was discussed, and where Almada Negreiros recited for the first time his *Manifesto anti-Dantas.* For Marina Tavares Dias, it was *the most elegant and luxurious place in Lisbon, an à la carte restaurant.* Founded in 1845, it closed in 1959 and BPI bank was built in its former premises. But, taking his tastes into account, one cannot think of soup without mentioning *açorda.* The word appears quite often in "Ultimatum" and in many other texts. "To me, Chiado tastes of *açorda".* The dish is usually made with fish, lobster or shrimp; like this one, served at Irmãos Unidos, the meeting spot for futuristic poets, at Praça do Rossio, 112.

SHRIMP *AÇORDA*

Ingredients: 400g shrimp, 1l water, 1 bunch of parsley, 3 spoons dry white wine, 500g hard bread, 4 spoons olive oil, 3 cloves of garlic, 1 small chilli pepper, 1 bunch of coriander, 3 egg yolks, salt and pepper to taste.

Directions: Cook the shrimps in water tempered with salt, parsley and white wine. Sift and peel them. Add bread to the liquid in which the shrimps were cooked. In a large, deep pan, put olive oil and the already crushed garlic. Add shrimp, chopped chilli pepper and squeezed bread. Bring it to boil and mix it with a wooden spoon, until achieving a uniform mush. Season with salt, pepper and diced coriander. Add the yolks, mix it some more and it's ready to serve.

His favourite dish

Once per week, he shares a meal with cousin Mário Nogueira de Freitas. Thursday night, at the home of Lobo d'Ávila, teacher at the universities of Lisbon and Coimbra[3]. Saturday, at "the home of that friend of mine I usually have dinner at" (letter to Ophelia, 02/10/1929). Sometimes with an *uncle,* his second cousin António Maria Pinheiro Silvano; or his cousin José de Almeida Neves and his wife, Titita. Funnily enough, to honour his nationality, his

3 Perhaps by way of repayment, Pessoa translated a text of his into English for it to be published in the *Financial Times.*

favourite dish should be cod – but there is absolutely no reference to it in any of his writings. He only quotes a "Salazar cod" waxing ironically about the prime-minister, and one "Guedes cod", which was to be a chapter in his novel *The Vargas Affair,* of which but a sentence exists: "He hasn't the constitution to drink aguardiente, it's bad for him, the intrigued seller said". But his dish of choice is Porto style tripe.

PORTO-STYLE TRIPE

Ingredients: 1kg cow stomach lining (all parts), 1 veal hand, 150g chorizo, 150g pork belly or prosciutto, 150g pepperoni, 150g pork head meat, 1 chicken, 1kg butterbeans, 2 carrots, 2 large onions, cooking oil (or olive oil), parsley, 1 bay leaf, salt and pepper.

Directions: Wash the stomach lining well, rubbing salt and lemon. Cook in water and salt. Set aside. In another pan, cook the other meats and the chicken. Set aside. Cook the beans with onions and sliced carrots. Put cooking oil (or olive oil) in a large pot. Add all the meats cut in large bits, then the beans. Season with salt, pepper, bay leaf and parsley. Leave in the stove for half an hour. Serve in a clay or porcelain terrine with white rice.

He enjoys the dish so much, he even dedicates a poem to it, written in one of the few restaurants around the area, Ferro de Engomar, which is still open to this day at Estrada de Benfica. There remain some controversies concerning the meaning of the poem. *Metaphors,* according to Tereza Rita Lopes. *A possibility to love,* as per Eduardo Lourenço. Because, for those who comment his oeuvre, that "love like a cold tripe" is homosexual love.

One day, in a restaurant beyond time and space,
They served me love as cold tripe.
With utmost delicacy, I told the delegate from the kitchen:
I'd rather have it hot.
I told him tripe (and it was Porto style) is never eaten cold.

They got impatient with me.
You're never right, not even in a restaurant.
I didn't eat, I didn't ask for anything else, I paid the bill,
Went outside, and walked up and down the street.

… if I asked for love, why did they bring me
Cold Porto style tripe?

Porto Style Tripe, Álvaro de Campos

The dish is one of the reasons the inhabitants of Porto are called *tripeiros,* a term on the origins of which there is no consensus. The most popular version claims that Prince Henry the Navigator needed to supply his ships in a journey to take Ceuta (1415) and asked the inhabitants to provide him with all the food they had, and so the city had to subsist on tripe for a good while. The people of Lisbon, on the other hand, are known as *alfacinhas* (little lettuces). In the Greek city of Athens, women sowed lettuce on the roofs to ensure a bountiful harvest, but there is no record of any such legend in Portugal. Journalist José Carlos Vasconcelos of Lisbon's *Jornal das Letras* recalls the version according to which the name was a reference to the neighbourhood of Alfama, Lisbon's very first – which, according to him, *flourished with the trade of unsavoury wares.* Others believe it's an endemic plant of the Azores, the *Lactuca watsoniana trelease,* vulgarly called *alfacinha,* which actually looks quite different than the lettuce. Probably incorrect, as there is no actual record of such a plant in Lisbon. Thus, as the name suggests, *alfacinha* must have come from the lettuce, bequeathed by the Moors to the Portuguese culture. According to the Bureau of Lisbon Studies, the origin of the designation was lost in time. Some claim it was because lettuce once flourished on Lisbon's hills. Others that, during one of the city's sieges, the inhabitants could only eat the lettuces planted on their gardens. Another unlikely story. Perhaps it's because the city has for the longest time been supplied by the produce planted by the poor, among which lettuce. Especially Sintra, *altar of clouds over the mountain range,* for Mário Beirão; a city "ever enveloped by a thin foggy veil, bathed at times by a grand splendour of light". The same Sintra which led Lord Byron (1788-1824) to say that, due to its food and its boys, *Lisbon is at Paradise's doors.*

> At the wheel of a Chevrolet[4] on the road to Sintra,
> Through moonlight and dreams, on the deserted road,
> I drive alone, drive almost slowly, and it almost
> Seems to me, or I almost force myself to think it seems,
> That I'm going down another road, another dream, another world,
> That I'm going on without having left Lisbon, with no Sintra to go to,
> That I'm going on, and what is there to going on but not stopping, but going on?
> (...)
> On the road to Sintra in moonlight, in sadness, before the fields and night,
> Forlornly driving the borrowed Chevrolet,
> I lose myself on the future road, I disappear in the distance I reach.
> And in a terrible, sudden, violent, inconceivable desire
> I speed up...
> (...)
> On the road to Sintra, near midnight, in moonlight, at the wheel,
> On the road to Sintra, oh my weary imagination,

4 This is (likely) the first case of advertising in a poem. At the time in which he wrote this verse (11/05/1928), Pessoa was working at Empresa Nacional da Publicidade, an ad agency controlled by General Motors, home of the Chevrolet. It also bears remembering that one of Pessoa's few refined tastes was to drive a car. "Shall I leave dreams behind me, or will the car do it?".

On the road to Sintra, ever nearer to Sintra,
On the road to Sintra, ever farther from me...

Untitled (11/05/1928), Álvaro de Campos

Restaurants and cafés in Lisbon

Pessoa enjoys places "in which there is a mezzanine with the outward appearance of a decent tavern", where one is served "a hearty, homemade meal akin to that of a restaurant at a village without a train", out of "a desire for peace and convenience of price". These were, according to his friend Gaspar Simões, *the most intimate place he knew, as he had forever lost his true home at a tender age.* According to Maria Aliete Galhoz, *through its cafés, in friendship and its emptiness, Lisbon relives all that youth in a burst.* There, one finds "curious fellows, faces with no interest, a series of side notes of life"; which was why he compares "those figures at the cafés" to "some dream gnomes, the memories of which leave the aftertaste of a past mourning", quite different from "the authentic men who pass by the streets". But those he met with weren't always anonymous. From 1905 on, as we've previously seen, he spends many nights with uncle Henrique Rosa in Lisbon's cafés, where they meet important names of the Portuguese letters, among them Raimundo António de Bulhão Pato (1824-1912) – as legend has it, at least, albeit retold by waiters who weren't even alive at the time.

Superstitious to a fault (he never sat at a table with 13 people), he was *the fatal man of his generation, a virile type, the ideal incarnation of romantic appetites who lorded over women,* as José Quitério defined him. *A mediocre poet and a second-rate writer, with no real oeuvre to speak of,* according to Vitorino Nemésio. The selfsame Pato who was caricatured by Eça: First in *The Maias,* via the character of the poet Tomás de Alancar – a hunter who bragged of his true aim, *with long, romantic whiskers* and lover of women; and then in the short story *José Matias,* where he disdainfully reproduces Pato's poems (from his books *Versos).* In spite of their age difference (Pato died in 1912, at the age of 84), they were united by their literary tastes. Not so much by his books, of which the most renowned (and not always acclaimed) was *Paquita* (1866), mainly for his Shakespeare translations – *Hamlet* (1879) and *The Merchant of Venice* (1881). A compulsive gourmand and a respected cook, he left famous recipes such as Andaluzia style *açorda,* opulent rice, Bulhão Pato hare and Castillian quail. Ironically, he became known for a dish that wasn't even his, but belonged to his friend João Mata, a restaurateur in Lisbon. Forjaz Sampaio sums up his fate: *It's more than likely that bookworms ate all copies of* Paquita *and that the worm is the final reader of his books, but there is always someone ready to eat the clams.* Whether or not he knew the writer, this was one of his favourite recipes:

BULHÃO PATO CLAMS

Ingredients: 2kg clams, 2dl olive oil, 4 cloves of garlic, 1 bunch of coriander, 1 large lemon, salt and pepper.

Directions: Leave the clams in salted water for 2 to 3 hours. Before cooking them, drain them off and run them through water abundantly. Cut the garlic in slices and dice the coriander. Put a pan with olive oil and the garlic on the stove. When it's hot, add the coriander and leave it there until it begins to pop. Add the clams and cover it with a lid, turning the clams at intervals. As soon as they're all open, take them off the fire and season with pepper and lemon juice to taste.

Pessoa also patronized simpler restaurants, which specialized in codfish cakes; dive bars which served appetizers and barrel wine; and eateries for meals in general. Almost always, according to Albino Forjaz de Sampaio (1884-1949) owned by *honoured workers from Galicia. None can prepare pig's feet with herbs, cow's foot, or "hake canoes" quite like them. It was the Galician who provided the* alfacinha *with cooked cod and cod with chickpeas, the tasty tripe, the rich pork and beans and chickpeas with spinach, all for a low price.* Said Galicians replaced the Black labour force which had disappeared with the abolishment of slavery. They performed domestic services, sold water in casks and lit the streets' gas lamps. Little by little, they began opening modestly-priced, popular restaurants. "After eating [and drinking], people sit on rocking chairs, cuddle up to the pillows, close their eyes and let themselves live".

Sundays, he's always at Montanha, first opened in 1864 and closed in 1952. It was there he met José Régio and João Gaspar Simões in the 1930 encounter which gathered those three writers – the one in which Pessoa pretended to be Álvaro de Campos. Sometimes, he also goes to Tavares Rico, at Rua da Misericórdia, 35-37-39, in Chiado. Eça de Queiroz's favourite restaurant. Created in 1784 under the name of O Talão, it has three doors (one of which gives access to the upper floors), protected by a stylized balcony, the second floor boasting green iron-grated verandas, arches and a tiled façade – a bit of luxury to polish its modesty. The mezzanine has a tea room, Tavares Pobre. At Pessoa's time, it no longer belonged to the Tavares brothers, Manuel and Joaquim, who always addressed their customers in verse. Thinking of Tavares, friend Georges Courteline told him one *would sooner change one's religion than the café he goes to.*

There were others. Café Gibraltar, where Almada Negreiros could always be found at night; Chave d'Ouro, where politicians of all stripes gathered – "From the terrace of that café, I shakily stare at life"; and A Tendinha do Rio, next to Cerco da Bandeira, famous for being patronized by painter José Malhoa (1855-1933) and writer Júlio Dantas (1876-1962). In the latter, an honorary plaque was later placed in homage of the *Orpheu* group, which also gathered there: Fernando Pessoa, José Pacheco, Armando Côrtes-Rodrigues and José de Almada Negreiros, with the odd absence of Luís de Montalvor, Eduardo Guimarães and Ronald de Carvalho – the latter two perhaps on account of being Brazilian. Also, Nicola do Rossio, where politicians and men of letters such as Bocage met. In their places, we can nowadays find Nicola (new and refurbished as a snack bar) and Pic-Nic. Close by is Café Gelo, patronized by young revolutionaries during the monarchy, which then moved on to Café Áurea Peninsular, at Rua do Arco da Bandeira. He also frequented Café Royal, at Cais do Sodré; Café-Restaurant Gibraltar – *breakfast, dinner and supper, billiards;* Adega Vale do Rio; Café La Gare; Café Suíço, where he was introduced to Camilo (de Almeida) Pessanha (1867-1926); Hotel Alliance; and only didn't go to Café Fernando Pessoa, at Praça Cid Luso, because it didn't exist at the time. The only ones missing are the two cafés which had the most impact in his life.

Brasileira do Chiado

First, Brasileira do Chiado, at Rua Garrett (formerly do Chiado), 120-122. At the time, its name was written with a *z* – *A Brazileira, Casa Especial do Café do Brasil* (Special House of Brazilian Coffee) *Lisboa, Porto, Sevilha, Câmbios e Tabacos* (Exchange and Tobacco). According to an ad published at *Diário de Notícias,* on the day of its inauguration (19/11/1905), it sold *tea, flour,* goiabada, *tapioca, pepper, wine and olive oil.* According to Marina Tavares Dias, *the name was a clarion call for those who wished to drink Brazilian coffee,* as every patron was entitled to a free cup of freshly ground coffee. All others were paid, however. And *O Jornal* reacted to a price increase: *Crime most foul! A* pataco *of coffee at Brasileira costs now half a* tostão. *Indignation, notable declarations, silence, protests.* Whenever he mentions A Brasileira, he means the one at Chiado. "At night, at Brasileira, speaking with Corado, and at night, at Brasileira do Rossio, with Côrtes-Rodrigues and Lacerda". The entrance looks like a horseshoe – but a single door (today, there's three) with an iron frame and glass playing the part of a welcome rug. In a way, and on a minor scale, it resembled the Rossio train station, at Largo D. João da Câmara. Right in front of the café, is a bronze statue to scale – a bar table with two chairs, Pessoa sitting on one and the other empty. Its author, Portuguese sculptor (António Augusto) Lagoa Henriques (1923-2009), explains: *I thought it necessary to take the sculpture off the pedestal and put it closer to people. So much so, that I even added another chair, so others could keep him company (Diário de Notícias,* 18/03/2006). And so it was, with tourists happily taking their seat on that empty chair for the inevitable photo or selfie. Many of them unaware of who that sombre man even was, or his predictable habits, such as never sitting with strangers.

A Brasileira do Chiado

Martinho da Arcada

The other was Martinho, at Terreiro do Paço 3, at the corner of Rua da Alfândega, the oldest café in Lisbon. From there, one can see the Tagus, between the building's archways. Inaugurated on the 7th of January 1782 as Casa da Neve[5], it belonged at the time to Martinho Bartolomeu Rodrigues, *official contractor of ice sold in Lisbon.* Back then, it was lit by olive oil lamps and had its chairs and tables on the pavement outside, which isn't exactly a sidewalk, but a 5m space between the entrance and the building's outer columns – said columns are separated at the curb by a proper sidewalk. Two years later, it changed its name to Casa de Café Italiana, in homage to the father of its owner; in 1795, to Café do Comércio; in 1824, Café Arcada do Terreiro do Paço; in 1830, Café Martinho; and only in 1945, when another Martinho opened (at Camões), it stuck with the current name of Café Martinho da Arcada. According to Luís Machado, it was *a place of conspiracies, a meeting place for jacobins, liberals, freemasons, anarchists and republicans. On its tables, regimes were discussed, politics were contested, revolutions were reneged.* The café *was reminiscent of the 18th century, at the time in which the French invaders*

5 'Neve' means 'snow' in Portuguese and, at the time, was the term used for ice as well.

of [Jean-Andoche] *Junot* [in 1807] *dragged their sabres over here and came to dissipate their tedium,* recalls Pierre Hourcade, who describes Pessoa *sitting at a high marble table, where the eternal Portuguese coffee steamed. I try to ignore the scene and keep my eyes focused on the magician's entrance. I thought him puny, melancholic and swarthy, chained to the fateful charms of longing which intoxicate the whole of his race – and, suddenly, I am met with the liveliest stare, a firm, malicious smile, a face brimming with a secret life... My heart beat faster, my attention was excessively focused but also confused, as if*

At Martinho da Arcada, Pessoa (right), Augusto Ferreira Gomes (standing), António Botto and Raul Leal.

the air breathed around Fernando Pessoa were richer in oxygen, in the murk of Martinho da Arcada. There, he sups with the owners, the Sá Mourão family. In time, his dinner becomes only soup. The old Mourão, worried about his friend, whips up some fried eggs with cheese to put on it and make it a bit heartier. At Martinho da Arcada, the most famous soup is the Juliana.

JULIANA SOUP

Ingredients: 2l water, 3 spoons olive oil, 2 leeks, 2 large carrots, 2 cloves garlic, 1 large turnip, 2 medium onions, 1 stalk celery, 5 leaves cabbage, 2 leaves lettuce, 100g peas, 50g butter, 1 spoon sugar, salt and pepper to taste.

Directions: Place the water, olive oil, salt, pepper and sugar in a pot. In another pot, sauté the onions and garlic with olive oil. Add peas, leeks, peeled carrots and turnip, celery, cabbage leaves and lettuce. Add the sauté to the broth. Season with salt, pepper, olive oil and butter. Leave in the stove for 10 minutes and serve.

Pessoa also used Martinho as an office. He invariably arrives at 7pm, always sits at the same marble table and spreads all over it the papers from the inseparable briefcase he always carries under his arm. The current owner, António Barbosa de Souza, makes a point of showing the table to tourists and admirers (as well as another, which Saramago used to sit at). Heavy furniture, parquet floor, a small ventilator on the ceiling, even at the time, the scenery was as obsolete as Pessoa himself. In the months preceding his death, he abandons every other café "where I have seldom gone to lately" and only patronizes Martinho. It was to be the last café of his life.

It is as if I waited eternally
For your arranged and certain arrival
Down there, at Café Arcada –
Almost at the edge of that continent.

Sá-Carneiro, Fernando Pessoa

Donec eres felix, multos numerabis amicos
(As long as you are happy, you shall have many friends) Ovid

THE PLACES HE LIVED AT

But where the heart-dim sailor knows
Homes are happy because not his.
Desolation, Fernando Pessoa

His homes

"Our life had no inside. We were outwards and otherwise". He also consumed that *outwards* life in the places he lived at. Always in rented homes, as he never had the funds (or the will) to buy one. For most of his life, his clothes were washed by *dona* Irene, mother of Guiomar – the simple lass he thought of marrying in "Tobacco Shop". When he lived with his family, he invariably made a financial contribution for room and board. A list of debts (1913) reads *10 months and a half of rent* owed his aunt Anica. At the house of his great-aunts, there's a receipt for *fourteen months of food.* Not with his sister Teca, however, as her daughter Manuela Nogueira assured me. And he moved so often that, for many years, he had to resort to a post office box – *PO box 147.* As he told Carlos Lobo de Oliveira (17/05/1928), it was his "perpetual address". Gaspar Simões (26/05/1931) was given an address for his letters: "Those addresses are, of course, *postally* invalid, there is but PO Box 147, as ever". Also, a rather odd missive sent to Côrtes-Rodrigues (04/08/1923) in that regard: "Should this letter go astray, and you forget 147, remember it suffices to write *Fernando Pessoa – PO Box – Lisbon.* Even without the number, it shall reach my hands". With no explanation of how Côrtes-Rodrigues could possibly know it if the letter went astray. No one is perfect.

In September 1905, when he was making ready for his permanent return to Lisbon, his stepfather *wrote to his brother* [general Henrique Rosa], *asking him for support,* according to sister Teca. But he never lived under his roof. His first shelter back home was with his great-aunts Maria and Rita and grandmother Dionísia; first in their summer house at Rua Pedrouços, 45 (Pedrouços), ground floor; then in their main residence – Rua da Bela Vista, 17, 1st floor (Lapa). Then, he lived with aunt Anica, already a widow, at Rua de São Bento, 98. Today, a plaque reminds passersby that, *on the 2nd floor left of this house, the poet Fernando Pessoa lived between 1905 and 1906.* At the beginning of October 1906, during yet another sabbatical of his stepfather's, he went with his family to Calçada da Estrela, 100, 1st floor, where his sister Maria Clara died at the age of 2, on the 11th of December 1906. The family returns to Durban in May 1907, and Pessoa went back to his great-aunts and mad grandmother, who would die shortly thereafter, on the 6th of September, at the Rilhafoles hospice. The next day, the *O Século* newspaper read: *Fernando António Nogueira Pessoa fulfils the painful duty of informing his relatives and close friends of the passing of his beloved grandmother* dona *Dionísia de Seabra Pessoa.*

In time, things back home became strained. Especially because his great-aunts didn't take kindly to his decision not to finish his studies and asked him to become more responsible. And they also wanted him to exercise more, as he was the son of a consumptive. A diary entry of his (July 1907) reads: "I've just had some sort of a scene with aunt Rita" – he hadn't followed the instructions of his Swedish gymnastics teacher, Luís da Costa Leal Furtado Coelho. And so many were such incidents, that in November 1909, as he already had the means to do so (from his grandmother's inheritance), he finally decides to live on his own. He then moves to an apartment at Rua da Glória, 4, ground floor, close to where he'd open his publishing house Íbis, at Rua Conceição da Glória, 38-40, ground floor. Afterwards, with his publishing house no longer in operation, he moved to Largo do Carmo, 18/20 – the same address of the International Mining Agency (where he worked at), owned by cousin Mário de Freitas. He would remain there until February 1911, when aunt Anica returned from the Azores with her sons Mário and Maria Madalena. Pessoa was their godfather. His two great-aunts also went to live with Anica, but not for long, as one of them, Maria, would pass away on the 21st of September 1914, in the rented apartment they lived in at Rua de Passos Manuel, 24, 3rd floor left. The "third floor of my aunts [now only Anica and Rita], the peace and quiet of yesteryear". In February 1914, they moved to Rua Pascoal de Melo, 119, 3rd floor right. But, in November of the following year, aunt Anica departs to Switzerland with her daughter and son-in-law, Raul Soares da Costa, who got into a naval specialization course – Álvaro de Campos' occupation. With no explanation whatsoever as to how one could possibly specialize in anything of naval nature in a landlocked country like Switzerland. "Now that the family I had here moved to Switzerland, all sorts of possible challenges have crumbled on me. And so I find myself in absolute, or almost absolute aboulia". The other great-aunt, Rita, would die alone in 1916 at her home in Pedrouços. Pessoa had gone back to rented apartment hopping since the previous year. According to Miguel Real, *he doesn't commit physical suicide, like his old friend Sá-Carneiro, but rather social suicide, loafing across fifteen rented rooms* [more, actually] *in twenty years* [also more] *of a solitary existence, inebriating himself with aguardiente and poetry.*

Here, in this deep apartment
In which I am, not in body, but in mind,
The cloister of being me, in this moment
In which I find myself, feel myself defined,

Here, now, I remember
When I stopped being me
And, uselessly, I weep tears so tender
At what I am and could not be.

Untitled (1924), Fernando Pessoa

Rua Coelho da Rocha

Finally, on the 29th of March 1920, he moves in with his mother (once again a widow) and his three half-brothers to a house belonging to colonel Carlos Augusto Chicorro da Costa, at Rua Coelho da Rocha, 16, 1st floor right, at Campo de Ourique. It was there, in the first parish of Lisbon (Santa Isabel), that took place the riots presaging the liberal regime of 1834. The tenancy agreement was signed on the 1st of April, but was already valid since the 1st of January – signed by Pessoa as his mother's proxy, as she was qualified as a resident of *Pretoria, Transvaal, South-African Union.* His next door neighbour, Virgínia de Sena Pereira, is the great-aunt of the poet Jorge de Sena. With her also lives the daughter of her first marriage, who had the same name. Nephew Jorge called them *the Sena-Pereiras.* Sena authored a curious poem, "Portugal, Brazil", one of the shortest ever written, with but a single verse – *Like father, like son.* But it wasn't due to that poem that he made history, as Oswald de Andrade would write an even shorter one, titled "Amor" (Love) and with but a single word – *Humour.* It's likely just a coincidence, but Frederico Valsassina announced *Amor e bom humor* (Love and good humour), his book of verses, on numbers 3, 4 and 5 of *Athena* magazine (edited by Pessoa). Afterwards, Agostinho da Silva (1906-1994) wrote "Soneto de Álvaro de Campos a seu heterónimo Pessoa" (Sonnet of Álvaro de Campos to his heteronym Pessoa) with the same inspiration: *I wished to be your father, and became your son/ The creature took to its creator/ A feeble love made a beloved out of a lover/ I kneaded the bread and made corn of myself – here, now, Pessoa, remake it all/ And cast me again into the storm/ Instead of the well inside of which I overhear you.* Sena's words ended up in Pessoa's hands in the following poem:

That Robertson[1] fellow, says Jesus Christ
To his divine father
Is so bold as to claim I do not exist.

Leave him, Father God said. Here is the truth:
Like father, like son; so it ever is
And not to exist[2] is a quality
You've inherited from me.

Tal pai, tal filho, Joaquim Moura Costa

Pessoa often visits the apartment of Virgínia; so often, that his neighbour António (son of barber Manassés) confided in me that rumour in the streets had it that Pessoa and her had an affair, when those visits were solely meant for the exchange of books and to converse in English, as she had lived in Boston for years, as the wife of the Portuguese consul. And to use her phone. One of his cards had the number 41.350, with the instruction of "please call mister Fernando Pessoa next door". When he began to live with Teca in 1925 and his niece Manuela was born, the front room was meant for the baby, the other one for his sister and brother-in-law, without any windows, and the third for Pessoa, also windowless. Small like that of a servant and *a little sad,* as described by António Manassés, who so often went inside with his father to help shave him. *As bad as could be.* But, as it was more secluded than the others – especially in a city with cold winters – it was the most appropriate for his fragile constitution. So much so that, when the family went to Évora or Estoril, *he didn't move to the front room* (with a window), as Manuela Nogueira recalls. "My room is a dark thing with vaguely white walls". To the left, a short space that only allowed for walking next to the bed's side, with the shoulders almost rubbing against "the crummy walls of my ordinary room". To the right, next to the door's wall, a high dresser on which he wrote from a standing position. Between it and the bed, a chair like the one he abundantly mentions in "Opiary": "Let me stay here, in this chair/ Until they pack me into a casket". The chair was replaced by an armchair in "The White House is a Black Ship" (1916): "I'm leaning on the chair, it's night, Summer has faded away". Or a throne, as in "Abdication" (1920): "I'm a king/ Who relinquished, willingly,/ My throne of dreams and tedium"

For more than half an hour
I've been sitting at my desk
With the sole intent

1 John MacKinnon Robertson (1856-1933), philosopher, literary critic and liberal politician. Pessoa had 23 books of his in his bookshelf, second only to J.S. Fletcher (27). Teixeira de Pascoais had 17, and H.G. Wells, 13.

2 In a first draft, "you not existing".

Of looking at it.
(These verses are outside my rhythm.
I'm outside my rhythm, too.)
Inkwell, large, in front of me.
Pens and nibs a little in front of it.
Closer to me, very clean paper.
To my left, a volume of the Encyclopedia Britannica,
To my right–
Ah, to my right!–
My paper knife–yesterday
I didn't have the patience to use it to finish cutting
An interesting book I'll never read.

Untitled (03/01/1935), Álvaro de Campos

It was there that Casa-Museu Fernando Pessoa was built, created in 1993 by Lisbon's city hall, to exhibit some personal objects (such as his last glasses) and pieces of furniture (like the writing table on which he penned "The Keeper of Sheep"). From the apartment's inside itself, nothing further remains due to renovations, much like what happened to his birth home, as both buildings only retained their outer walls. At the end of 1927, his sister accompanies her husband to his new military position in Évora, "four hours by train". Pessoa spends some weekends with them, a ritual they maintain until their return in the last months of 1930. Luís Miguel, his second and last nephew, is born on the 1st of January 1931. The following year, sister and brother-in-law build a house at Rua de Santa Rita, 5 (later 331) in São João do Estoril, right in front of today's Rua Fernando Pessoa. A plaque at the gate today reads: *Here lived Fernando Nogueira Pessoa.* He'd always have a room available there. Still, he felt nothing was truly his in either place. "Throughout my life... everyone has always seen me as an intruder. Or at least as a stranger. Whether among relatives or acquaintances, I've always been regarded as an outsider. I'm not suggesting that this treatment was ever deliberate. It was due, rather, to a natural reaction in the people around me. Everyone everywhere has always treated me kindly. Rare is the man like me, I suspect, who has caused so few to raise their voice, wrinkle their brow, or speak angrily or askance. But the kindness I've been shown has always been devoid of afection. For those who are closest to me I've always been a guest, and as such treated well, but always with the kind of attention accorded to a stranger and with the lack of affection that's normal for an intruder".

Of the time he spent at Estoril, his family registered but one occurrence. It was late, almost dark, and Pessoa still hadn't arrived for dinner, and was later found sitting motionless at the edge of a cliff, looking at the sea below. His intentions remained forever a mystery. He could just have been staring at the sea, naturally. But it is rather suggestive that Marino, his heteronym, threw himself into the sea. "Woe is me – I slip – away, o terrible sea!". As if reproducing what he had formerly written to Ophelia in a letter (09/10/1929): "I have a growing urge to go to Cascais – Boca do Inferno and its teeth, head down, and there, no more Íbis". Even with the house at Estoril, they all keep living at Rua Coelho da Rocha. But not for long, as on the 29th of November 1935, Pessoa goes to São Luís dos Franceses hospital. In 1939, now deprived of his company, the family moves to Rua das Praças, 43, at Lapa, and, in 1953, to Avenida da República, 48, 4th floor, where Teca, already a widow, would die in 1992.

Leitaria Alentejana – a legend

On the topic of places he lived at, it would be remiss not to mention the legend that, between 1916 and 1916, he lived at *the murky attic of Leitaria Alentejana.* The one responsible for this romanticized version is first biographer João Gaspar Simões. That room over said dairy was a single windowless division over the kitchen, accessed by a narrow set of stairs – no more than 2m wide and 2,5m long, where *a cot would barely fit.* At night, so he could read (according to Simões) he would make use of the lamp that was lit inside, and, during the day, whatever sunlight seeped through the lobby's door. So he wrote almost always on a marble table at the corner. Simões suggests Pessoa lived there *out of special deference* of the owner, *an illiterate admirer of his social gatherings at cafés.* The spirit Wardour once actually recommended: *Move to Sengo's house.* To make matters even more confusing, Eduardo Freitas da Costa assures *Pessoa never even met this Mr. Sengo.*

But said Mr. Sengo, as Simões calls him, never did Pessoa any favours, wasn't that illiterate, and never took part in any of his gatherings. After transforming the dairy into a barber shop, Manuel António Sengo was the landlord of two rooms he had at Rua Cidade da Horta, 58, 1st floor right – where also lived *dona* Emília (Sengo's lover and Pessoa's governess), her daughter (and Sengo's), Claudina and one *dona* Júlia, a former lover of Sengo's who, after abandoning him, took every belongings she could. Pessoa knew him well, having been introduced to him by his cousin Mário de Freitas, who was readying *a firewood deal* with him, for which he needed *Pessoa's technical collaboration.* The two were close enough for Pessoa to defend his interests before the abovementioned Júlia. Simões' conclusion was based on the fact that Pessoa used stationery of the *Leitaria Alentejana / Manuel António Sengo / butter, pastries, confectionery, fine wines and taverns / Rua Almirante Barroso, 12* for some of his letters – among which one for Silva Tavares, on the 16th of December 1916. After selling the building, Sengo kept an office for commissions and brokering right next to one of Pessoa's companies, F.A. Pessoa, and both used said stationery with the old address for letters or drafts – as recalled by Augusto Ferreira Gomes, friend and business partner of Pessoa's. The dairy was then turned into a glass and mirrors shop. When I last saw the place in 2006, it was abandoned, with no indication whatsoever that a poet had dreamt between its walls in the past. Old ladies by the sidewalk informed me that it was condemned. When it is, another bit of his past will have died.

A list of the houses he lived at

In all literature written about Pessoa, there are the occasional discrepancies in some finer points, such as the places he lived at. For that reason, almost every address mentioned in this book stems from those he indicated in his own correspondence; in declarations to public bodies like registry offices; or, whenever more than a number is mentioned by authors, and whenever possible, after *in situ* verification. What follows is a list of places of address in chronological order.

Lisbon (childhood)
– Largo de São Carlos, 4, 4th left; from 1888, the date of his birth, to 1893.
After his father's death, the family moves to a cheaper location.
– Rua de São Marçal, 104, 3rd floor, 1893 to 1895, when his mother marries and goes to Durban (beginning of 1896).

Durban
– Hotel Bay View, at Musgrave Road, 1896.
– Tersilian House (head office of the Portuguese Chancellery), Ridge Road, West Street, 157, 1896 to 1901.

Lisbon (on holiday from Africa)
– Rua Pedrouços, 45, ground floor, 1901, with his family.

Tavira (on holiday from Africa)
– Travessa da Rua Direita (unknown number), ground floor, from 1901 until the middle of 1902.

Azores – Angra do Heroísmo, Terceira Island (on holiday from Africa)
– Rua da Palha (currently Rua Padre António Cordeiro), unknown number, 1902.

Lisbon (still on holiday from Africa)

– Rua (today Avenida) Dom Carlos I, number 109, 3rd floor right, at Santos, from 1902 until his return to Durban that same year. A majestic home, much like the one at Calçada da Estrada – both rented by his stepfather.

Durban

– Tenth Avenue (unknown number), Perea, 1902 to 1905.

Lisbon

– Rua Pedrouços, 45, ground floor (his great-aunts' and grandmother Dionísia's summer house),1905.

– Rua da Bela Vista, 17, 1st floor (main house of his great-aunts and grandmother Dionísia), address as given in the letters written by C.R. Anon, 1905.

– Rua de São Bento, 98, 2nd floor left (house of aunt Anica), the address was printed on Alexander Search's calling cards, 1905 and 1906.

Lisbon (his family's new African holidays)

– Calçada da Estrela, 100, 1st floor (with his mother, stepfather and brothers), 1906 and 1907.

Lisbon (now for good)

– Rua da Bela Vista, 17, 1st floor (once again the house of his great-aunts and grandmother Dionísia, who passes away in the first year of his second stay), 1907 to 1909.

– Rua da Glória, 4, ground floor, 1909 and 1910.

– Largo do Carmo, 18/20, 1st floor left, 1910 and 1911.

– Rua Passos Manuel, 24, 3rd floor left (once again the house of aunt Anica, where great-aunt Maria would pass away on the 21st of September), 1911 to 1914.

– Rua Pascoal de Melo, 119, 3rd floor right (new house of aunt Anica's, until her departure to Switzerland), 1914 and 1915.

– Rua D. Estefânia, 127, ground floor right (room rented from a housemaid), 1915 and 1916.

– Rua Antero de Quental (unknown number), 1916.

– Rua Almirante Barroso, 12, 1916.

– Rua Cidade da Horta, 58, 1st floor (two rooms), 1916 and 1917.

– Rua Bernardim Ribeiro, 17, 1st floor, 1917 and 1918 (*dona* Emília, Sengo's lover, was his governess in this address and the next).

– Rua de Santo António dos Capuchos (a house with furniture, unknown number), 1918 and 1919.

– Alto da Boa Vista (Benfica), at the time the outskirts of Lisbon, beginning of 1919.

– Rua Capitão Renato Baptista, 3, ground floor left (as it reads on the proxy given him by his uncle Henrique Rosa), from May to August 1919.

– Avenida Gomes Pereira (again in Benfica, unknown number), from 1919 to 1920.

– Avenida Casal Ribeiro, 35 (house of his cousin António Maria Silvano), 1920.

– Rua de Santa Rita, 5 (today 331), Estoril, his sister's house, where he stays at during the weekends from 1932 onwards.

– Rua Oriental do Passeio, door two, Cascais, where he resides "temporarily" – as he says when applying to the call for curator for the museum-library Conde de Castro Guimarães, in 1932.

– Rua Coelho da Rocha, 16, 1st floor right, from March 1920 until his death in November 1935.

Audentes fortuna juvat.
(Fortune favours the bold) Virgil

HIS OFFICES

Making good use of time!...
Honest and superior work...
But it's so difficult to be honest and superior!
Marginalia, Álvaro de Campos

Offices in Lisbon

At the beginning of the 20th century, three out of four of Lisbon's inhabitants couldn't read. And very few speak a foreign language. Unlike that multitude of borderline illiterates, Pessoa is fluent in French, having been taught by his mother. His diary (20/04/1906) reads: "I started learning German"; he actually began to translate an anthology of German poetry, and also often made use of German expressions in his writings. And he got his education in an English school, at a time in which 70% of Portuguese exports went to England. Also, in Africa (at the Commercial School), he studied commercial arithmetic, accounting, tachygraphy and bookkeeping techniques. He was, indisputably, a cultured man. Qualified as he was, he could well have aspired to a well-paying job. But he refuses a number of invitations, such as Dr. Coelho de Carvalho's, the dean of the University of Coimbra, who offered him a professorship of English Language and Literature at the Faculty of Letters. Or that of general António Maria Silvano, who offered him a job to the tune of 80 mil-réis per month. Or, as recalled by cousin Eduardo Freitas da Costa, a position *with what was, at the time, an astounding salary: 200 mil-réis*[1]. He would subsequently also refuse a job offer at the Portuguese section of Vacuum Oil Cº. All because he wanted time to write. As he said in a letter to Olavo Pinto (29/07/1913), he'd rather work independently and be paid for his work "in the various offices where I translatingly spread my English knowledge".

At the time, the city's commercial offices were little better than a gathering of employees in the same workroom. Lit by lamplight, the smudged ledgers

1 For reference, Pessoa's rent at the time was 11 mil-réis per month, according to Costa.

recorded gas bills and the cost of Fénix handcuffs. The first electric lamps only made their appearance at such companies in 1909; and, when one ordered a pair of chandeliers, they usually came with two light bulbs *on a trial basis.* At the time, the invention was still a big mystery. *O Século*'s illustrated almanac announced the marvels of the future, claiming that *The electric lamp has a powerful purifying effect, both due to the light and ozone, as well as an as yet undefined emission of vapours. It is said that a lamp placed in an ill-smelling site is enough to dissipate the odours.* When progress puts out the final lamp, for good and ill, Lisbon loses part of its romanticism.

> Around the desolate lamp
> Whose oil illuminates my life
> A butterfly flits, as is the wont
> Of its undefined inconsistency.
>
> And, o vague wind
> Of solitudes,
> My soul is a lake
> Of indecisions.
>
> *Untitled* (01/09/1928), Fernando Pessoa

Commercial practises

At *Revista de Comércio e Contabilidade,* in 1926, he theorizes about knowledge he acquired while working in those offices: "The trader is a public servant; he must study the public, and the differences from public to public; he cannot have an opinion as a trader; he has no personality, he has trade". He also holds that "in practical life, there are three kinds of men – those born to order, those born to obey" and, as if speaking of himself, "those who were born neither for one nor for the other". Also, "most traders quote a price, for that price will ensure them a measure of profit, and will look no further beyond that. And why? Because the trader lives solely for the present, and his trading house has no tomorrow". Only the present and no tomorrow – once again, as if speaking of himself. "In order to succeed, one needs three definable things: Knowing how to work, making use of opportunities, and forming relationships. Everything else is under the purview of that undefinable but nonetheless very real element that we, for lack of a better name, call luck". He acknowledges that "the world belongs to those born to conquer it, not for those who dream of being able to conquer it, however right they may be". He reminds us that "the precept, be it moral or practical, lies somewhere between the Sermon on the Mount and the Manual of the Perfect Crook". He concludes by saying that the entrepreneur's most important quality is that which he never had: A sense of opportunity.

> Nothing holds me.
> I want fifty things at the same time.
> I long with meat-craving anxiety
> For I don't know what–
> (…)
> All abstract and necessary doors were closed in my face.
> Curtains were drawn across every hypothesis I could have seen from the street.
> I found the alley but not the number of the address I was given.
>
> *Lisbon Revisited (1926)*, Álvaro de Campos

It is amusing to read in those writings his admission of not understanding just how England works: "After eight o'clock in the evening, it is a crime to purchase apples, bananas, grapes, pineapples and dates, although it is allowed to buy apricots, figs, peaches and raisins". "Canned soup, which is provided by a number of dealers, cannot be purchased after eight o'clock", nor could "a cigar or pack of cigarettes at a railway kiosk, save if one also buys food for consumption during the train ride"; and "chocolate, sweets, sorbets cannot be purchased after nine thirty". "One also cannot buy aspirin or any other type of analgesic after eight o'clock, unless, as per the law, the pharmacist deems it reasonable to suppose one is suffering from a headache". Said law was World War I's Defence of the Realm Act. Still, he laments the fact that some of his English poems were never published in England, although, deep down, he accepted the reasons given to him by editor John Lane (23/10/1915), according to whom his writings couldn't possibly have been "printed in a country where there is an active public morality".

Having had an English upbringing, he considers some of the habits of Lisbon's inhabitants "fit for vulgar people", and concludes: "I am not vulgar". Nor was it vulgar for him to consider himself more English than Portuguese – deep down, he felt like an "English-styled Portuguese". For him, "there are four bases which European civilization is founded on, four principles on which its individuality and essence are based. They are Greek Culture, Roman Order, Christian Morality and English Politics". He goes further still: "20th century England was one of the countries in which it truly was worth living in". This from one who had written (in 1905) to *Mercury Natal* newspaper to say: "We, English, [are] the most selfish of all men". To say nothing of the fact that, shortly thereafter, he had harsh words for that country's colonialism:

The fallen lion every ass can kick,
That in his life, shamed to unmotioned fright,
His every move with eyes askance did trace.
I'll scorn beseems us, men for war and trick,
Whose groaning nation poured her fullest might
To take the freedom of a peasant race.

To England, II, Alexander Search

Henry Ford

Among all businessmen, he had the most regard for Henry Ford – "the world's supreme millionaire". Much like he held himself to be "Super-Camões", Ford was "Super-Rockerfeller", and he compares the American with "that clerk I am somewhat acquainted with, who has lunch every day just like he now is having, at the table at the end of the room. Everything that millionaire had, so too did this man; to a lesser degree, of course, but proportionally speaking. The two men accomplished the same, there isn't even a differential of celebrity, as so too do environmental differences establish one's identity. Everyone in the world knows the American millionaire's name; but everyone in Lisbon's square also knows the name of the man having lunch over there. These two men got all that the hand could obtain by stretching their arm. Their arm length might be different; in all else, they were just alike". He reproduces that same idea later, exchanging the actors:

> Some govern the world, others are the world. Between an American millionaire, a Caesar or Napoleon, or Lenin, and the Socialist leader of a small town, there's a difference in quantity but not of quality. Below them there's us, the unnoticed.
>
> *The Book of Disquiet,* Bernardo Soares

Despite his initial passion towards Ford, owed mainly to the fact that he was the one who instituted the five work days per week system in two of his automobile factories, he soon concludes that his theories stemmed from idle capacity. Which is why he says that "the practical precepts come not from the most practical intelligent men, but, and the difference bears pointing out, the most intelligent of practical men"; and "proclaims to the world" that "Ford's economical and moral motto was inspired by Machiavelli's"[2] – according to whom "what we do out of need should be made to appear as if made of our

2 Despite his somewhat unsavoury life, Pessoa had no problems quoting Machiavelli, going so far as to say that "his precepts mainly highlight that which is vile and mean in all men".

own accord"[3]. Thinking of his own vicissitudes, he recalled Ford's words in an article for *Revista de Comércio e Contabilidade* (1926), in which he said "one can breathe easier when one is wealthy"; and some of the American's thoughts were compiled by Lord Riddell[4] in "nine industrial commandments, which would be "the result of but half of his experience, which he deemed fit to share with us". They are:

> I. Seek out simplicity. Examine everything constantly, to see if you can find a way to simplify it. Don't respect the past. The fact that something was always done in a certain way isn't proof that there is no better way of doing it.
>
> II. Do not theorize; experiment. The fact that past experiences didn't work doesn't mean that future experience won't. Experts are slaves to tradition. It is therefore preferable to entrust the investigation of new projects to energetic people of lucid mind. Let them make use of the experts.
>
> III. Work and the perfection of work take precedence to money and profit.
>
> IV. Carry out your work in the most direct fashion, with no regard to rules and laws, nor the vulgar divisions of discipline.
>
> V. Install and maintain every machine in its best condition, and demand absolute cleanness everywhere, so that a man learns to respect his tool, his environment, and himself.
>
> VI. If you can manufacture something which you must use in large quantities, and do so at a cheaper price than you can buy it with, manufacture it.
>
> VII. Whenever possible, replace man with machine.
>
> VIII. The business doesn't belong to the owner or the employees, but to the public.
>
> IX. The fair salary is the highest salary the boss can pay regularly.

Translations

For the American-born London editor Warren F. Kellogg (Pessoa called him "Mr. Killoge"), who had just established himself in Lisbon as the representative of the International Library of Famous Oeuvres (at Rua do Comércio, 31, 2nd floor), he translated an *Anthology of universal authors* (in 1911), at the rate of 700 réis per printed page[5]. Even though Kellogg always complained that the ordered translations were never on time, he acknowledged Pessoa's *angelic temper,* and even invited the young poet to accompany him on a business trip to England – Pessoa refused, and, in his stead, went his friend Armando Teixeira Rabelo. Cecil Palmer made him an offer on the 30th of April 1914 to translate

---

3 I couldn't find any such sentence in Machiavelli's oeuvre. *The Prince* contains some phrasal constructions that convey a similar sentiment, such as *a prudent Prince neither can nor ought to keep his word when to keep it is hurtful to him.*

4 George Allardice Riddell, the first baron of Riddell (1865-1934), was the owner of some of London's newspapers, chief among which *News of the World.*

5 By way of comparison, in 1920, fathers gave their sons allowances to the tune of 5 mil-réis per month.

Provérbios portugueses into English, a project which was derailed by World War I. He offered to translate Shakespeare's oeuvre for João de Castro Osório on the 20th of June 1923, for 20% of the cover price, but nothing came of it.

In 1932, Pessoa (might have) translated reports of Banco Espírito Santo – the bank itself has no records of any such activity; but, the following year, he became the official translator for the Ministry of Finance, according to the minutes of the Lisbon House of Mercy (09/02/1933) – a brotherhood created in 1488 by *dona* Leonor, the wife of João II, the Perfect Prince, with the mission to *rescue the infirm, visit the incarcerated, bury the dead and accompany to the gallows those meant to die for their crimes.* He also translated *The treasure of São Roque,* by W. Telfer, for which he was paid 2,500 escudos. António Valdemar suggests that he might even have translated some of Salazar's speeches for the ministry. The Chest also contains seven typed pages of bill 22.789 translated into English, as well as several literary works, among which six books of theosophy – two of which published in 1915, and four others in 1916. According to the latest survey, he translated 11 books from English to Portuguese; and a poetry book and a correspondence book from Portuguese to English.

Commercial correspondent

The first record of this activity of his – his main one – is the draft of a letter in French (09/06/1906) to Entreprise Génerale de Luvisy (France) "concerning the job you are offering" – in response to the note of an Ads Agency published at *Diário de Notícias.* There are no records which confirm the letter was received or even sent. On the 13th of November 1913, he replies to an ad at *Diário de Notícias* (the same day the letter was written) which requested an English translator; as the newspaper read, letters were to be sent to an *Ads Agency at Rua do Ouro, 30*[6]. At that time, he was already working at at least three offices, as one can glean from his diary – "the two *Lavados* [Lavado, Pinto & Cia. Lda. and Martins Lavado Lda.] and to *Mayer* [Lima, Mayer & Perfeito de Magalhães Lda.]". Work is intense, but well paid. An annotation of his services at A. Xavier Pinto Lda., belonging to Alfredo Augusto Xavier Pinto and cousin Mário (1915 or 1916) enumerates 14 letters in January, 44 in February, 137 in March, 65 in April, 105 in May, 67 in June, 64 in July, plus 84 assorted texts: 580 tasks in all. In November 1915, he receives 39,50 (American) dollars per month, not counting what he earned from his translations for other clients. Three years on, and in only two offices, he makes 31 dollars per month. In clothes, it could be measured in about 11 suits. More than enough for him to live comfortably, since the rent for a room in Lisbon was 8 dollars at most. Except, for him, such a life would be akin to prison. "Unfortunately, I cannot

6 Pessoa didn't mention it, but it was Agência Havas.

abandon the offices I work at"; deep inside, he felt the bitterness of *having to resort to services coming from abroad to survive,* according to his friend Francisco Bourbon, who saw in him *a sacred revolt.*

Casa Moitinho de Almeida

Out of all the offices, the most important by far was undoubtedly Casa Moitinho de Almeida – founded in 1790 by Lucas Xavier Ferreira as a jewellery store, at Rua da Prata 62-69-71. In Pessoa's time, it was already Moitinho de Almeida & Cia., purveyor of commissions, based at Rua da Prata, 71, telephone 1056. Its four windows opened to Rua dos Retroseiros. On the first floor, he had a room all to himself, where he remained after office hours, typing poems and his personal correspondence. "I am alone in the office", he says, as his boss, Carlos Eugénio, had entrusted him with a key. Once, he got mad at him for having dropped cigar tips into the typewriter's keyboard, rendering it unusable the following morning. The word "Tabacaria" (Tobacco Shop) was written on on said typewriter.

Luís Pedro, the boss' son, declares: *He always had a friendly word, and everybody in the office wanted, respected and liked him as a good colleague and a magnificent correspondent in English and French. Even my father, who didn't take him seriously as a poet, had great esteem and appreciation for him.* A similar description to that of colleague Maria da Graça Ferreira do Amaral, according to whom *he arrived whenever he pleased, and when he did show up, he'd always ask me in a slow, amused tone: Many people looking for me? I'd tell him: This and that called, mister so and so, and thought to myself: He's going to take care of all this now, but no such thing; he'd just sit with me to chat, as if there was nothing for him to do, he had always something to talk about, and that's how he always made it relaxed and happy at the end of the day... Some days, he'd bury himself on the couch and would then show up to say: I was resting from not doing anything. He'd often come up in the middle of the afternoon with the jovial look of one who had just started his day. He probably went to bed late... I never heard a harsh word from him, he treated everyone with kindness, even those who were of more humble station.* "The office becomes a page with words of people". He worked there from 1923 until his death.

A list of the offices he worked at

Pessoa wrote many of his texts using company papers – mostly because they were at hand, at work. Some bear no proof that he truly worked there, such as F. Caetano (his brother-in-law's), Leitaria Alentejana (from his landlord António Sengo), M. Ávila Lima X. or A. Lima, at Rua dos Pragais, 150 (Porto). The following list of the offices he worked at is based largely on the studies of António Mega Ferreira and João Rui de Souza.

– *A. Soares Franco & Cia.*
Rua da Prata, 267, 1st floor. No proof of how long he worked there.
– *A. Souza*
No proof of the address or how long he worked there.

– *A. Xavier Pinto & Cia.*
Campo das Cebolas, 43, 1st floor; and later Rua de S. Julião 101, 1st floor. 1915 to 1917.

– *Agência de Publicidade de Manuel Martins da Hora*
Rua da Prata, unknown number; and Av. da Liberdade 18, 4th floor.
From 1925 on.

– *Agência Internacional de Minas*
Rua 1° de Dezembro, 45, 2nd floor right. No proof of how long he worked there.

– *Agência Mineira Anglo-Portuguesa*
Largo do Carmo, 18-20. No proof of how long he worked there.

– *Anjos & Cia.*
Rua dos Fanqueiros, 71, 1st floor. 1918.

– *Banco Burnay*
Rua dos Fanqueiros, unknown number. The bank has no record of him actually working there.

– *Banco Espírito Santo*
Rua do Comércio, 95-111. He wasn't an employee, according to the bank's records. But he likely did perform some sort of service, as he was acquainted with António Júdice Bustoff Silva, one of its controllers.

– *Casa Moitinho de Almeida*
Rua da Prata, 71. Previously described.

– *Casa Serras (E. Dias Serras, Lda. Importação, Representações)*
Rua da Madalena, 109, and later Rua Agusta, 228, 1st floor – today it operates at Rua da Palmeira, 1, ground floor, in the securities branch. From 1934 until his death.

– *Companhia Industrial de Portugal e Colônias*
Rua do Jardim do Tabaco, 74. No proof of the year he began working there, and until 1919.

– *Félix, Valladas & Freitas, Lda.*
Rua da Assunção, 42, 2nd floor, the office in which he met Ophelia Queiroz. 1919.

– *Francisco Camello*
Largo do Corpo Santo, 28, 1st floor – still exists and is owned by Francisco Castello Bueno Camello, a grandson of the former owner. From 1934 until his death.

– *Frederico Ferreira & Ávila, Lda. (R. Ferreira & Cia., Sebastião Lino Ferreira & Cia., M. Ávila Lima)*
Rua da Victoria, 53, 2nd floor left. In 1919 and during the decade of 1920.

– *Garantia Social e Agência Mineira Anglo-Portuguesa*
Rua do Carmo, 25, 2nd floor – created in 1901 and headed by cousin Mário Freitas. His first job as a commercial correspondent. From 1909 to 1913.

– *Gouveia e Carvalho, Lda.* (perhaps a branch of *F.A. Gouveia, da Rua dos Douradores)*
Rua da Prata, 93. From 1933 until his death.

– *Lavado, Pinto & Cia.*
Rua da Prata, 267, 1st floor right; later Campo das Cebolas, 43, 1st floor (where A. Xavier Pinto e Cia. was also based at). From 1913 to 1915, and from 1924 until his death.

– *Lima Mayer & Perfeito de Magalhães*
Rua da Betesga, 75, 3rd floor – currently Fritz Mayer, headquartered at the previous address Toscano e Cruz Lda. From 1913 on.

– *Mário N. de Freitas*
Rua Bela da Rainha (currently da Prata), 81, 3rd floor. Between 1909 and 1913.

– *Martins Lavado*
Rua Augusta, 75, 2nd floor, dedicated the the sale of typewriters. From 1913 on.

– *Palhares, Almeida & Silva, Lda.*

Rua dos Fanqueiros, 44, 1st floor – part of *The Book of Disquiet* was written here in the decade of 1920.

– *Pancada, Moraes & Cia.*

Rua Augusta, 85. In the decade of 1930.

– *R.G. DUN & Cia.*

Rua d'El Rei (currently do Comércio), 99, 3rd floor left – an American agency of commercial informations (with 21 branches across the world), later Dun & Bradstreet, nowadays Informa D & B. It was likely his first job, which Aniceto Mascaró, the husband of his cousin Laurinda Neves, got him, as he was the company's Portuguese manager. He stayed there a year at most. It is the last of the four offices which are still currently in operation. But he wasn't exactly an employee there, as his work was that of an intern, coordinating the informations of Portuguese companies and paid a pittance which only allowed him to buy cigarettes and books and have small expenses. In 1907.

– *Sebastião Lino Ferreira & Ávila Lima*

Rua da Vitória, 53, 2nd floor left. No proof of how long he worked there.

– *Sociedade Comercial Rebelo da Silva Lda.*

Rua dos Franqueiros, 44, 1st floor. Between 1909 and 1913.

– *Sociedade Portuguesa de Explosivos*

No proof of the address or how long he worked there.

– *Toscano & Cia. Lda. (Duarte Almeida Toscano)*

Rua de S. Paulo, 117-121. From 1920 on.

– *Xavier, Pinto e Cia.*

Campo das Cebolas, 43, 1st floor (until the building was sold to Lavado, Pinto e Cia.), later Rua de São Julião, 267, 1st floor right. It was in that office that Pessoa got news of Sá-Carneiro's death. From 1915 to 1917.

Fortuna, valete
(Hope and luck, goodbye) Latin version of a Greek epigram

THE MANY PROFESSIONS OF "MR. PESSOA"

I want I shall have
If not here,
Somewhere I know not where yet.
I have lost nothing.
I shall be all.
Untitled (09/01/1933), Fernando Pessoa

Little income

"Fuck my life! Having a profession weighs one one's shoulders like a paid-for burden", as "an ideal, a creed, a wife or a profession – the cell and the handcuffs, all of it". His ID card lists *commercial clerk* as his profession. The job description he also gives upon requesting a patent for his Indicative Yearbook, as we shall see further up ahead. In a letter (20/01/1935) to Casais Monteiro, he suggests: "What I am, essentially – behind the poet's involuntary masks and those of the thinking man and whatever else's might be the case – is a dramatist"; and he asks the following of Ophelia: "Never tell anyone I'm a poet. At most, I write verses". In a biographical note from 1935, closer to the end, he acknowledges: "Occupation: The most apt designation would be translator, the most precise, though, would be foreign correspondent in trading houses. Being a poet and a writer is no proper occupation, but rather a calling". Because, deep down, "being a poet is no ambition of mine, it is my way of being alone". Lastly, when he applies for the job at the museum in Cascais, he only describes himself as a writer. The same profession listed on his death certificate.

When I was a child
I lived, unknowing,
Only so that, today,
I might have that memory.

Because it is only today
That I feel what I was.

My life flows
Made of my lies.

But in that prison
Singular book, I read
The oblivious smile
Of what I then was.

Untitled (02/10/1933), Fernando Pessoa

Commercial ventures

With his grandmother Dionísia very ill (she would pass away on the 6th of September 1907), Pessoa knew the inheritance would be his, as her only grandson. Thus, as soon as he came of age, he would have the funds for small dreams. *Dona* Dionísia's tutor in hospital was Dr. Jaime Neves, but the inventory's tutor became António Maria Pinheiro Silvano, the same distant cousin who had evaluated the goods of the Pessoa family's first house, which were then auctioned off. According to the inventory's tutor, out of a total of 600,005 réis, minus 416,540 – the advances given to her grandson for food and the purchase of a suit (15,000) – there remained exactly 183,565. *A year's worth of food,* as per Mega Ferreira's calculations. The inheritance also included 24 stocks of Banco Portugal – with an exchange value of 167 mil-réis each – and young Pessoa earned around 4 million réis from them. Enough to purchase a house in Lisbon, depending on the location, and more than enough for him to risk a commercial venture.

It all began in 1909, and not 1907, as posited by his first biographer, João Gaspar Simões. The mistake, as confirmed by Mega Ferreira and Richard Zenith, stemmed from a letter in English sent to his friend Armando Teixeira Rabelo, on "August 24th, 1909"; in which the handwriting can easily lead one to assume the last number is a seven, especially since the last nine isn't as rounded as the first. On August 5th of that same month, in a barber shop, he reads an ad in *O Século* titled *Typography – For sale: Large printing machine with cylindrical dyeing and its belongings,* all of which were described in the ad. It was equipment belonging to the old Minerva Central typography, appropriated by businessman José Maria Martins. Brother João Maria confirms: *Apparently, he ran off, his face only half shaved and his hair only partly cut.* He promptly buys the machine by phone (as well as some other office automations from Spain, then at the hands of Aniceto Mascaró e Domènec) and picks it up at Portalegre. He spends the night at Hotel Brito, owned by João Maria da Silva e Brito[1]. The 200km trip was the only one he ever made after having returned to

1 On the 30th of December 1934, Álvaro de Campos mentions that he found on a hotel nightstand "a Portuguese Bible (most curious thing) made for Protestants", in which he reread "the First

Lisbon for good. On the train, he writes a letter to his friend Armando Teixeira Rabelo, as well as a small poem in English:

> Nothing with nothing around it
> And a few trees in between
> None of which very clearly green,
> Where no river or flower pays a visit.
> If there be a hell, I've found it,
> For if ain't here, where the Devil is it?
>
> *Alentejo seen from the train*, Fernando Pessoa

Íbis Printing House

Now the proud owner of the appropriate machinery, he founds in October 1909, with his cousin Mário Nogueira de Freitas, Empresa Íbis, Tipografia e Editora, Oficinas a Vapor, headquartered at Rua Conceição da Glória, 38-40, perpendicular to Rua da Glória, where he lived at the time. The decision is made in feverish delusions of grandeur, in order to fight "priests and kings", "to provoke a revolution here, write Portuguese pamphlets, edit old national literary works". Almost like an obsession. "Yes, let it be written here that I painfully love my motherland". The only problem was that, in the arts of printing, he had but a mimeograph with which to print his little newspapers; while there were around 95 printing houses in Portugal at the time, according to 1909's commercial yearbook. Competition which didn't suffer upstarts like him.

Time passes, "hour by hour, the will falters", and the printing house never actually begins operations, except to print his own papers and a couple for his cousin's Agência Mineira Anglo-Portuguesa. The Commercial Yearbook of 1910 shows us that, by that time, a new printing house had already taken its place, one Rodrigues e Piloto. On the 21st of November 1914, he writes: "My last vanity of being a man of action has vanished – the end would be the useless disaster inaugurated by the printing house". The rest remains a mystery, as there are no records of him having even registered his constituent acts. At Lisbon's Commercial Register, the reply I got was that, if Pessoa did register anything, the records would be found *in books considered closed, as they only contain extinct companies,* and those books, I was told, are archived in such a way that they are (all but) impossible to find. Pessoa died, without knowing that the brand ÍBIS would later become the banner of one of the largest hotel chains in the

Epistle to the Corinthians" in "the excessive quiet of the countryside's night". Having frequented no other hotel in his adult age, and with this one being "in the countryside", the mystery is promptly solved. As is the fact that he'd find it *curious* to find a Bible, as he had no way of knowing how common it was to find one in hotels.

world. With the company shut down, what happened to the machinery? And the employees? Did he owe the building's owner? What is known is that in 1913, with his family, he paid off debts to the tune of 40 and 100 mil-réis. "Practical life has ever appeared to me as the least comfortable of suicides".

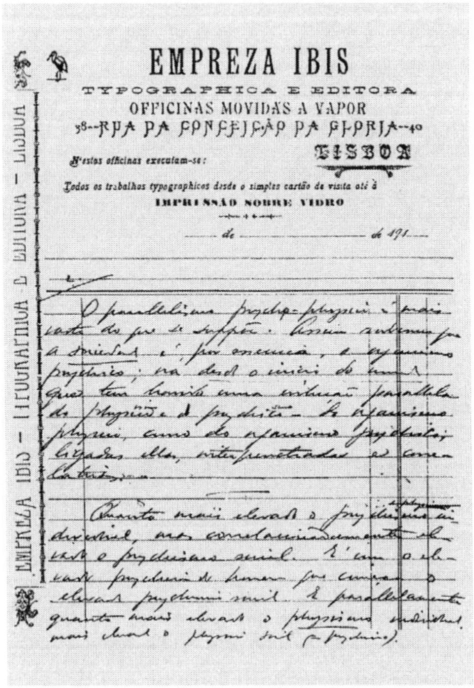
EMPREZA IBIS
TYPOGRAPHICA E EDITORA
OFFICINAS MOVIDAS A VAPOR
38--RUA DA CONCEIÇÃO DA GLORIA--40
LISBOA
N'estas officinas executam-se:
Todos os trabalhos typographicos desde o simples cartão de visita até á
IMPRESSÃO SOBRE VIDRO
de de 191
EMPREZA IBIS - TYPOGRAPHICA E EDITORA - LISBOA

Form of Íbis printing house

Cosmópolis

Pessoa considered Cosmópolis for the denomination of his Olisipo (which would come later) – according to his own words in a letter to Côrtes-Rodrigues (19/01/1915). But Cosmópolis would be an autonomous project with a much broader scope, intending to provide daily information about the arrivals and departures of ships and trains, translations "to and from all languages", heraldic and genealogical research, letter writing and ads. The project included a club with a restaurant meant solely for traders, a "leading library" (for book rental) and jobs agency "except for waiting staff". In all, 88 activities. A part of Cosmópolis went to Olisipo. The other, to Revista de Comércio e Contabilidade – which he released with his brother-in-law in 1926. Everything else remains but a dream.

F.A. Pessoa

On the 1st of September 1917, he registers as a self-employed trader dedicated to commissions, headquartered at Rua do Ouro, 87, 2nd floor. Later, in an interview to *Diário da Manhã,* Augusto Ferreira Gomes would say that he and Geraldo Coelho de Freitas had been his partners at the company. Which wouldn't go very far, as, on the 2nd of May 1918, he sends a letter to Fábrica Metalúrgica do Lumiar, noting that he'd already transferred all assets and liabilities to Numa de Souza Reys Ribeiro de Figueiredo. Part of the liabilities, as least, as he retained the rest; so much so, that on the 25th of January 1919 he took a loan of 62 mil-réis.

Olisipo Publishing House

In 1919, inspired by his cousin Mário, he decides to dedicate himself to a new undertaking. The Chest contains the three lines of action he outlines: "Editing", "propaganda of Portuguese products", and "all other matters handled individually, from the sale of patents in individual name to special imports and odd services, whenever expedient". And also provide tourists and traders with information about translations, legal assistance, advertising and copywriting, as well as serving as a middleman between English mining companies and owners of Portuguese uranium, chalcocite and wolfram mines. He then leaves his job at Companhia Industrial de Portugal e Colónias and installs Olisipo Agentes Organizadores e Editores Lda. – headquartered at Rua da Assunção, 58, 2nd floor, its logo designed by Almada Negreiros. According to commentators of Pessoa's oeuvre, his partners were Geraldo Coelho de Jesus and Augusto Ferreira Gomes, with no documents to prove it or otherwise. The partnership made sense, as Pessoa had solid theoretical knowledge of trading, which he learned in Durban, while the two supposed partners brought to the table actual experience, which Íbis' bankruptcy had proven he lacked. Jesus, for example, wrote *Basis for an industrial plan* in 1919. The company's registry dates from the 11th of October 1921 – book 9, sheet 24, at 15h50, at the Industrial Property Division of the Ministry of Commerce and Communications.

In spite of those many projects, Olisipo functions mainly as a publishing house. In 1921, it published Pessoa's *English poems I-II* and *English poems III,* as well as Almada Negreiros' *A invenção do dia claro.* In 1922, there was also a reprint of António Botto's *Canções,* with texts by Teixeira de Pascoais and Jayme de Balsemão; he also pondered publishing an "album of Portugal", as the centennial of Brazil's independence was being celebrated in Rio de Janeiro at the time with an exhibit. Also a weekly newspaper "with cosmopolitan news", fairly obviously titled *A Semana* (The Week); an "edition of illustrated postcards", and a "guidebook for tourists" – likely his unedited *What the tourist should see.* The following year, in February 1923, he would still print an opuscle by Raul Leal, *Sodoma divinizada,* which all but lauded *lust and pederasty* – according to its own author, *a divine work.* Botto's and Leal's books would be responsible for the end of Olisipo, as Portugal wasn't ready for such boldness, and both the authors and Pessoa himself started receiving hostile treatment in the streets. In March 1923, as was inevitable, Lisbon's civil government took both books – which kept on being sold, as forbidden items, by the city's booksellers. As for Leal's work, there were generalized restrictions. On the 6th of March 1923, the Lisbon Students' League of Action, headed by Pedro Theotónio Pereira (1902-1972), who would later become Salazar's minister of Foresight and ambassador at Rio de Janeiro, handed out in the streets a *Manifesto of the students of Lisbon's universities* against the book. Pessoa defended his friend and replied with *Concerning a manifesto of students,* signed by Fernando Pessoa and also distributed in the streets (excerpt):

Sobre um manifesto de estudantes

FERNANDO PESSOA.

Pessoa's manifesto

There are three things a noble spirit, whether young or old, never toys with, as to toy with them is the hallmark of a lowly soul; the gods, death, and madness. If, however, the manifesto's author wrote it in earnest, he either believes Dr. Raul Leal to be mad, or, not believing it, pretends to believe it so as to slander him. Only the lowliest of street churls would insult a madman in public. And it takes a even lower level of churlishness to spread such an insult, knowing it to be a lie… It is in part because of this, as these students are – especially in their actions, which I greatly appreciate – the living symbol of this society, that, in a way, publishing this protest is worth it, even if its intent is beyond them. This is social duty... Mad are the heroes, the saints, the geniuses, without which mankind is but a mere animal species, postponed corpses procreating[2].

Pessoa would later use a similar sentence in other texts, such as *Message,* on the 20th of February 1931:

My madness, let others take it up
Along with all that went with it.
Without madness what is man
But a healthy beast,
Postponed corpse that begets?

Or in one of Ricardo Reis' "Odes", on the 28th of September 1932:

Nothing of nothing remains. And we are nothing.
In the sun and air we put off briefly
The unbreathable darkness of damp earth
Whose weight we'll have to bear
Postponed corpses that procreate.

As for Botto, *Contemporânea* magazine published an article written by Álvaro de Maia – "Mr. Fernando Pessoa is Portugal's aesthetic ideal" – criticizing the *dreadful demonstration of Thracian love* and denouncing *the filth published by Mr. Pessoa,* which was a mere manifestation of *romantic rot. A literature of Sodom.* Álvaro de Campos replies with a letter to José Pacheco, the magazine's editor (17/10/1922), in which he said: "In every work of human literature, we seek but two things: Strength and balance. It isn't even an immoral book. It is a book broaching an immoral subject, which is quite different". Maia replies in *O Dia* (16/11/1922), defining Botto's book as *the throbbing lustful anxiety, made of pleasure and pain in Spirit-Flesh, vibrating incessantly.* Followed by another manifesto by the League of Students, this time *Against the inversion of intelligence, morals and sensibility.* Olisipo closed doors shortly thereafter, still in 1923; and Pessoa began offering Shakespeare translations which he had meant to publish on his own. But before that, he replied with another manifesto, *A warning on morals,* signed by Álvaro de Campos, in which he says (excerpt):

When the public knew that Lisbon's students were committed to moralizing others during their breaks of yelling obscenities at passing ladies, it let out an exclamation of impatience. Yes – the very exclamation the reader has just let out... To be young is to not be old. To be old is to have opinions. To be young is to not care about opinions. To be young is to let others go to Hell in peace with whatever opinions they might hold

2 In 1982, *Antígona,* an anarchist newspaper in Lisbon, wrote about the writings which continued to emerge from his Chest, and published a pamphlet titled *Fernando Pessoa, the postponed corpse that begets.*

– good or bad, as one never knows which he carries with him to hell. The schoolboys are butting into the affairs of writers who aren't even passing by, much like they butt into ladies who do pass them by. If they know not the reason before blurting it out, then neither would they know it afterwards. If they could know, they would interfere with neither writers nor ladies... Here, now, boys, study, have fun, and shut up. Have fun with women, if you like women; have fun in some other way, if it strikes your fancy... But, as for the rest, shut up. Shut up as quietly as you possibly can. For there are but two ways of being right. One is to shut up, which best suits the young ones. The other is to contradict oneself, which only elders are qualified for. Everything else is a great bore to whomever might be assisting. Europe, 1923.

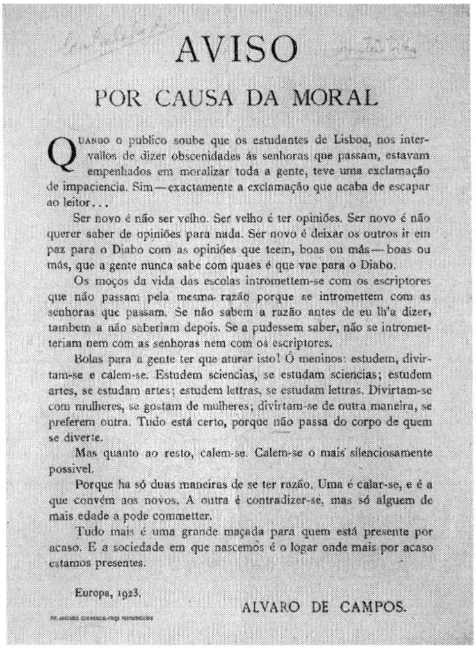

AVISO

POR CAUSA DA MORAL

Quando o publico soube que os estudantes de Lisboa, nos intervallos de dizer obscenidades ás senhoras que passam, estavam empenhados em moralizar toda a gente, teve uma exclamação de impaciencia. Sim—exactamente a exclamação que acaba de escapar ao leitor...

Ser novo é não ser velho. Ser velho é ter opiniões. Ser novo é não querer saber de opiniões para nada. Ser novo é deixar os outros ir em paz para o Diabo com as opiniões que teem, boas ou más—boas ou más, que a gente nunca sabe com quaes é que vae para o Diabo.

Os moços da vida das escolas intromettem-se com os escriptores que não passam pela mesma razão porque se intromettem com as senhoras que passam. Se não sabem a razão antes de eu lh'a dizer, tambem a não saberiam depois. Se a pudessem saber, não se intrometteriam nem com as senhoras nem com os escriptores.

Bolas para a gente ter que aturar isto! Ó meninos: estudem, divirtam-se e calem-se. Estudem sciencias, se estudam sciencias; estudem artes, se estudam artes; estudem lettras, se estudam lettras. Divirtam-se com mulheres, se gostam de mulheres; divirtam-se de outra maneira, se preferem outra. Tudo está certo, porque não passa do corpo de quem se diverte.

Mas quanto ao resto, calem-se. Calem-se o mais silenciosamente possivel.

Porque ha só duas maneiras de se ter razão. Uma é calar-se, e é a que convém aos novos. A outra é contradizer-se, mas só alguem de mais edade a pode commetter.

Tudo mais é uma grande maçada para quem está presente por acaso. E a sociedade em que nascemos é o logar onde mais por acaso estamos presentes.

Europa, 1923.

ALVARO DE CAMPOS.

Aviso por causa da moral

F.N. Pessoa

In November 1922, he pondered founding F.N. Pessoa – at Rua São Julião 52, 1st floor, sharing the space with Olisipo, with partners Augusto Franco, Albano da Silva and Júlio Moura. It was never anything more than a flight of fancy, as there are no records of any such company – rather, one Companhia União do Príncipe was headquartered there at the time. He also tried contacting many trade representatives at the time – Gaupin de Souza, Júlio Moura, Nicolas de Hehn, Zia Reshid, but it is unknown what his intentions were with them, or if they were even successful. On the 23rd of May and the 1st of July 1925, he wrote letters to a German company named Cellon-Werke, for the attention of Dr. Arthur Eichengrün, concerning the representation of chemical products. If it ever existed, F.N. Pessoa was only in operation until 1925.

Mining

In 1910, Mário Nogueira de Freitas founds Agência Mineira Anglo-Portuguesa (the invoices of which, as previously seen, were the only work carried out by Íbis). And he brings his cousin along. In the beginning of 1921 with Olisipo already operating, Pessoa published an ad at *Primeiro de Janeiro,* "concerning an incumbency set upon us by an English company" – the National Mining Corporation. He proposes the "usual commission of 10% "of the mine's final sale price", and actually gets a letter from engineer Mendes da Costa (02/05/1921), who was interested in showing him "pewter mines". But, despite replying (letters dated the 5th of May and the 6th of October), the English company's representative thanks him and declines the offer, as it wasn't "sizeable enough". Pessoa's activities in this branch were between 1918 and 1923; but he carried on until the 12th of August 1935, the year of his death. In total, it consisted of 112 letters (sent and received), all of them stored in the Chest. With no record of a single successful operation.

Advertising

At the end of 1924, Pessoa met Manuel Martins de Hora at a trading house in Rua de São Paulo, where he sold motors, machines and automobiles. Martins de Hora would found the following year the first Portuguese advertising agency, with capital from General Motors and João Pereira Rosa (controlling shareholder at *O Século* newspaper): Empresa Nacional de Publicidade – which represented J. Walter Thompson, then the largest company of its kind in the USA. They would later meet at Toscano, to define the commercial bases of their agreement. Pessoa worked for him between 1925 and 1929, mainly as a publicist and correspondent, and the two maintained their relationship until the poet's death. According to Martins, *he was quick to find the best sense of things, and would improvise about anything, whether cars, fridges, or fashion items.* José Blanco recalls that *one of the products they launched were "cornflakes"; and Fernando Pessoa translated a book of oat recipes for the company.* He also prepared texts for the thematic developmental project called Costa do Sol, which included Cascais and Estoril – a small fishing village where the wealthy bathe in, the royal family among them, and the place where golf, casinos and football were born in Portugal. Luís Pedro Moitinho de Almeida assured me that Pessoa was very apt at the business, which seems a less than respectable evaluation, taking his results into account.

Coca-Cola

In 1928, Casa Moitinho de Almeida was named an agent of Coca-Cola in Portugal. Which ended in disaster. Luís Pedro Moitinho de Almeida's statement helps us understand why (summed up): *My father made several orders, which came from the US in bottles and little bottles. The market was stocked with them.* As it so happened, the company preferred a different slogan in every country, and didn't want to use its North-American *The pause that refreshes,* which led to Almeida to ask Pessoa to come up with a new one for the product. Pessoa might have remembered what he wrote in "Maritime Ode", "when our insides tighten into a ball"; or, and the coincidence is rather thought-provoking, Unamuno's *Life and Death of Don Quixote and Sancho* (1905), which read: *Most great and terrible thing it is for the hero to be the only one capable of seeing his heroism from the inside, in his own insides, and that none other can see it on the outside in his strangeness.* Whatever the case, the following was born

First it's strange, then it gets into you.

It wasn't his only slogan, either. Another one which also reached notoriety was "a Pompadour corset fits well and helps the rest fit as well". Except Coca-Cola wasn't a corset. *The product sold well at first, but Pessoa's slogan helped to kill my father's representation of Coca-Cola through his company,* according to Luís Pedro. All because a scientist, Ricardo Jorge (1858-1939), who was the Head of Health in Lisbon at the time, voiced his protest, and the Ministry of Health ended up considering the beverage a hallucinogen, on account of the slogan expressing *the product's toxicity, as a feeling of strangeness followed by the ingested substance getting 'into' someone is exactly what happens with narcotics. If the product contains coca, out of which cocaine is extracted, then it must not be sold, so as not to intoxicate anyone; but, if the product doesn't contain coca, then advertising it with such a name would be fraud.* According to niece Manuela Nogueira, *Salazar didn't want a beverage which reminded people of 'coca'.* Pessoa's explanation is roughly the same. The product's bottles which were stocked in Portugal were confiscated and then thrown into the Tagus. Coca-Cola would only return to Portugal in 1977, after the Carnation Revolution, in Mário Soares' socialist government.

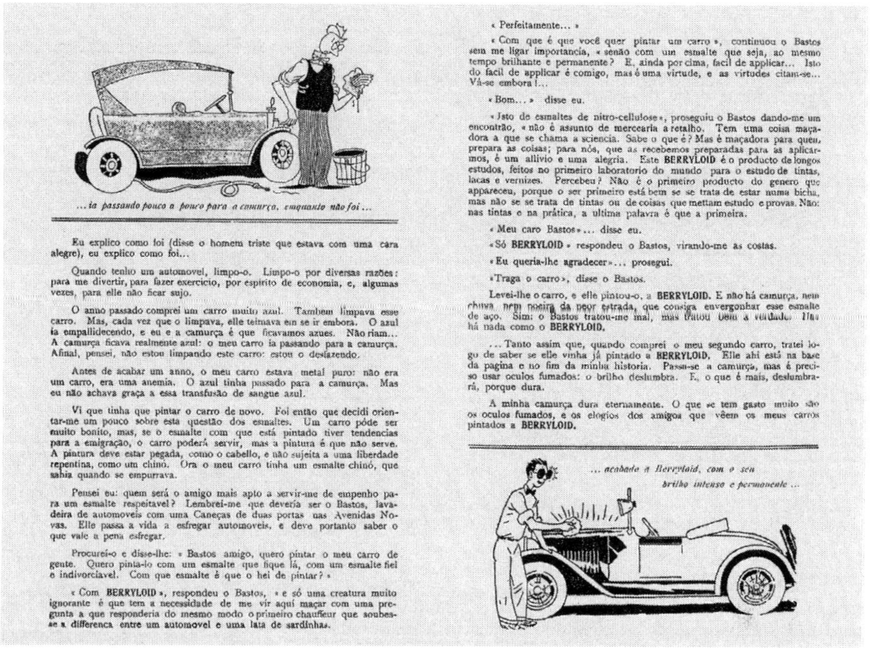

Ad for Berryloid inks

Berryloid inks

Pessoa also did a bit of suggestive advertising for Berryloid inks. The text, which was later published in *Folhas de poesia* (1959), is presented as a large and strange short story (abridged):

> I shall tell you how it was (said the strange man with a happy face)... This past year, I bought a very blue car. But, whenever I washed it, the colour faded. The blue was fading, and myself and the suede became rather blue. Don't laugh... The suede did indeed get blue: My car was slowly seeping into the suede. Deep down, I thought, I'm not washing this car; I'm dissolving it. Before the year ended, my car was pure metal: It wasn't a car, it was an anaemia. The blue had seeped into the suede. But I found that transfusion of blue blood anything but amusing. I realized I had to paint the car all over again. It was then that I finally considered the matter of enamel. A car can be very beautiful, but if the varnish it was painted with has a tendency to emigrate, the car may very well do, but the painting most certainly won't.

At this point, one Mr. Bastos comes into the story, the owner of a repair shop which suddenly shows up in the plot to reprimand the sad man with a happy face.

> Only a most ignorant creature would feel the need to come and bother me with a question which would get the same reply from a chauffeur who knew the difference between a car and a can of sardines.

After that putdown, Mr. Bastos recommended Beryloid inks to the sad man, provided he afterwards didn't forget to "wear tinted glasses, as the shine can dazzle". The text was accompanied by naive drawings of shining cars. Another commercial disaster.

Inventions

A somewhat unknown trait of Pessoa is his taste for inventions. There were many of them, almost all of which were devised in his mind, duly catalogued, and then promptly abandoned, without him ever deriving any profit from them:

– Five-letter code. With this code, information could be classified, which would allow for some economy in telegraphic communications. The idea was to "condense each unit (word of sentence) into half a word, based on a five-letter code". On the 20th of October 1915, he wrote a letter to London's Eden Fisher & Co. and actually got a reply on the 14th of November, in which his offer was refused, on account of the serious depression in the code market due to World War I.

– Crosswords (or advertwords). Some sort of "advertising crosswords" for English stores. The public would have access to them via the acquisition of stamps, priced at a shilling each, which would then be glued to an entry form. If 300 thousand people took part, it would be possible to offer prizes up to 4 thousand pounds, a veritable fortune at the time.

– Aristography. A new system of tachygraphy, which consisted of a "task list" of 1913, based on a code which could be used in Portuguese, Spanish, French and English – the typewriters. He tried to sell his idea "preferably on the basis of immediate payment + a stipulated monthly payment", but, also due to the war, he found no buyers.

– Paper paste. A common paste, with three strips of cloth glued to each of the three covers, with specific signs (A, B and C). He justifies the idea by saying that "the paste remains entirely sealed by a simple process". But he then gives it no further thought.

– New typewriter spool. Said spool would be a small iron roll, the cogs of which fit into some cleat systems, "such as the Blickensderfer's" – "however, the wheel has but a single line of digits". He first thought to apply the model to a cash register, drawing numbers and a drawer; then, it evolved into a typewriter. In it, spool B slides under the impulses of spool A, which contains the letters and signs. "The spool on which printing occurs doesn't slide, but rather the system that writes". Although his plans were lost, it is reasonable to assume they were a forerunner to the spheres which would later replace the typebars of old electric typewriters, and so the glory of an invention which would be successful the world over eluded him.

– Death of the envelope. Pessoa defined this paper ingeniously folded into six as a "letter-superscript", or "paper-letter-envelope". Part 1 was for the addressee, part 2 for the sender, and parts 3 to 6 were meant for the text. The paper's purpose was to "forgo the use of an envelope", and could be closed "via a simple process". A precursor to the aerogram, which was widely used during World War II. A drawing of said envelope can be seen in a letter sent to Frederico Ferreira & Ávila Lda. (03/11/1919), where he would later work at, and it is largely similar to the letter-envelope today used in Brazil.

– Table football game. This innovative initiative had already figured in two "task lists" of 1913, but football ended up being patented later (January 1937) in Barcelona by Alejandro Finisterre. Had he lived longer, Pessoa would certainly have lamented the fact he hadn't invested in the commercialization of a product that time ended up converting into an absolute success.

– Other games. The Chest contains a list of four other games – among them one of cricket and another of astrology, both of which he meant to acquire a patent for, and later commercialize; as well as a number of annotations on football results of the English league, as well as their respective stadium audiences – on which he hoped to base potential buyers for some of those games.

Indicative yearbook

But his best hopes of becoming rich lay in a *Yearbook of synthetic indicator, by name and any other classification* – an alternative to the two huge volumes of Portugal's Commercial Yearbook, with less than half the page count. In that invention of his, "all linguistic indications are replaced by conventional signs, which makes the book accessible in any language, by means of a font table in any given language". In his words, "the Yearbook would thus be redacted in no language at all". Anticipating what would later come with Windows. From those beginnings, he also considered editing a dictionary which would be called the *"Orthographic, prosodic and etymological dictionary of the Portuguese language,* and would serve as the basis for a full dictionary"[3]. The yearbook was registered at Portugal's Department of Property, under the number 14,345, on the 27th of October 1925, and he actually made a commercial proposal with it on the 27th of November to Banco Angola e Metrópole. A natural choice, as he had already dealt with that institution to acquire the rights to negotiate a loan for motorways and another one for construction work in Lisbon via F.N. Pessoa.

The bank would soon go bankrupt, however. Its director, Arthur Virgílio Alves dos Reis, had already forged his Oxford diploma. As an adult, he set up an ingenious scheme which defrauded authorizations from Banco de Portugal to London's Waterlow & Sons, so as to emit duplicate banknotes worth 500 escudos, which were then delivered to Alves Reis' bank. Two months after having registered his Yearbook, in December 1925, the fraud investigations began. The trial started on the 6th of May 1930, and Pessoa attended three of the five hearings, writing about that "rumorous process" of "seventy-eight volumes and twenty-six annexes". Alves dos Reis ends up convicted, acknowledging full responsibility and thus freeing his co-defendants. In 1945, he leaves prison, stops smoking, suffers from haemorrhoids, becomes an evangelical pastor and sees his wife die in an asylum. Shortly thereafter, on the 10th of July 1955, bald and paralytic, he is buried in a common pine coffin – with his family having to make quite an effort to pay for the funeral (800 escudos). Upon feeling that negotiations wouldn't move forward, Pessoa prepared a French version of the text (30/01/1926), which was originally written in English, describing how his Yearbook functions – with the title of *A brief explanation of the patent of Portuguese invention #14,345.* On the 6th of March 1926, he writes to Guérin Frères, at 10, Rue Laborde in Paris, suggesting its commercialization. No reply was forthcoming and, from then on, his dreams of becoming rich off his inventions became definitely archived.

> Yes, I well know
> I'll never be anyone.
> I well know
> That I shall never have an oeuvre.
> I know that, in the end,
> I shall never hear of myself.
> Yes, but now,
> While this hour lasts,
> This moonlight, these branches,
> This peace we're in,
> Let me believe[4]
> That which I can never be.
>
> *Untitled* (08/07/1931), Ricardo Reis

3 In the original, over the word *full,* stands the variant *comprehensive.*

4 In a first draft, "Let me believe *until I see"*. Reis had already anticipated that idea in one of the "Odes" of 1914: "This moment in which we quietly believe in nothing, innocent pagans of decadence".

Habent sua fata libelli
(Books have their own fate) Terence

THE BOOKS

God wills, man dreams, the work is born.
Message, Fernando Pessoa

His yearning

Pessoa has the (not so discreet) ambition to win the Nobel prize in Literature. "I think nothing of Caeiro, of Ricardo Reis or Álvaro de Campos. I won't get to do any of that, in a publishing sense, until I get the Nobel prize. Or even think, my dear Casais Monteiro, that all of them would be passed over by Fernando Pessoa" (letter from 13/01/1935). Deep down, he dreams of being renowned, which is why he writes so often in English, going so far as suggesting that "we should make of English the Latin of the entire world". But, in his case, and even with absolute technical mastery of the foreign language, he never attained the natural flow he had in Portuguese. He even acknowledges it, in 1932, when he writes the preface for Eliezer Kamenezky's *Alma errante:* "Eliezer isn't Portuguese, and so one cannot expect him to deftly wield one of the world's most complex, subtle and opulent languages". Nor was that choice of his owed to the notorious influence writers like Poe, Shakespeare or Walt Whitman had over him, but mainly so that his verses had "European odds (and let not this sentence be taken in the sense of an imminent Nobel prize)". All because, so he believed, it was the one language capable of guaranteeing him that award. José Saramago would prove him wrong in 1998, writing in Portuguese; Pessoa, on the other hand, wouldn't even have the privilege of so much as being nominated, like other Portuguese authors: João Câmara (1901), João Bonança (1907), Sebastião Magalhães Lima (1909), António Correia de Oliveira (15 times, from 1933 on), Maria Madalena de Martel Patrício (14 times, between 1934 and 1947), Teixeira de Pascoaes (5 times, between 1942 and 1948), Júlio Dantas (1950) and Miguel Torga (1960). "The sole moral compensation I owe literature is the future glory of having written my present works".

If I die young,
Without having been able to publish a book,
Without having seen how my verses look in print,
I ask those who would protest on my account
That they not protest.
If so it will have happened, then so it should be.
Even if my verses are never published,
They will have their beauty, if they're beautiful.
But they cannot be beautiful and remain unpublished,
Because roots may be hidden in the ground
But their flowers flower in the open air for all to see.
It must be so. Nothing can prevent it.

Uncollected poems, Alberto Caeiro

Organization of his writings

In 1929, he senses the end is near and begins to carefully organize his papers, to complete poems and type texts from his Chest. Perhaps because, as Yvette Centeno told me, *Pessoa didn't want to separate his life from his oeuvre, making of his oeuvre his true life.* "First, I thought to publish those works anonymously". But "no one should leave behind himself 20 different books, save if he is capable of writing 20 different books"; and "none of us, from the cat to myself, truly leads the life imposed upon them". He knows he is "the one who got too far up ahead from his travelling companions"; and realizes "all I got from the time I wasted with what I did was the now broken illusion that it was worth doing". *Presença* magazine wishes to publish a book with his poems. He promises *The Keeper of Sheep,* but asks that, in exchange, they publish one entrusted to him by Sá-Carneiro before his death, *Indícios de ouro.* A handwritten note contains the initial plans:

(1) Caeiro, complete;
(2) Ricardo Reis, several book from Odes;
(3) Notes for the memory[1] (as he speaks of Campos himself);
(4) A book by Álvaro de Campos;
(5) The family discussion.[2]

In the year of his death, as can be read in the letter to Casais Monteiro (13/01/1935), he opts for "a large book of verses – some 350 pages long – which encapsulates the several personalities of Fernando Pessoa". "The heteronyms (according to the latest intention I formulated concerning them)

1 *Notes for the Memory of My Master Caeiro.*
2 Dialogues of his heteronyms with himself.

must be published by myself and under my own name (it is already far too late, and therefore absurd, to keep such absolute secrecy). They shall form a series titled *Fictions of the interlude,* or some other, more fitting thing. On the first book of the heteronyms, it will in all likelihood contain not only Caeiro and Álvaro de Campos' *Notes,* but also three or five books of Ricardo Reis' *Odes"*. With all of them thus gathered, "I return to myself. I travelled for a few years, gathering ways of feeling. Now, having seen and felt all, I have the duty to shut myself at home and in spirit, and work as much as I can in all things I am capable of, for the progress of civilization and the broadening of humanity's consciousness". A simple explanation for such attitude: "The mask, if it could be kept, the mental effort required to maintain it would be useless". In a preface he wrote, he says: "I can enjoy the vision of the future upon reading this page, for I am indeed writing it; I can take pride in the fame I shall have, much like I would in a son"; and fully expects to see the book "printed by October". In another letter to Casais Monteiro (20/01/1935), he says that "until then, I should manage to publish *The anarchist banker,* a crime novel and one or the other writing most appropriate to the circumstances". But it was not to be; his complete works (only part of his writings) would be published only seven years after his death, thanks to the effort of Luís de Montalvor and João Gaspar Simões at Ática publishing house.

A list of the books he wrote

"Some works die because they are worth nothing. Others have the brief life of a fleeting spirit. Others coexist with an entire epoch. Others, still, last as long as a civilization does. But others endure beyond that. Those are the ones that reach the maturity of life that is as deadly as the Gods". And perhaps that is why he had so few books published. For not accepting anything less than the best. Even knowing that, as Mallarmé said it, *everything exists in the world to end up in a book.* Except it isn't easy to even define what a book is. The most commonly accepted definition is Unesco's, namely that of *a printed publication, not periodical, with a minimum of 49 pages, not counting the covers.* Which leads to paradoxical situations. "Maritime Ode" (930 verses), for example, wasn't published as a book, even though it is almost twice as large as *35 Sonnets* (490) or *Message* (581). Whatever the definition, it's perhaps fairer and most reliable to consider here only those works he himself named. In *Presença* (#17, December 1928), he recalls the works he had written up until that point: *"Antinous* and *35 Sonnets,* together, in 1918, and *English Poems I-II,* and *English Poems III,* also together, in 1922. He also published in 1923 *On a Student Manifesto...* and, in 1928, *Interregnum – In Defence and Justification of the Military Dictatorship in Portugal."* He deems fit to make the disclaimer, that "none of these texts is definitive. The author prefers to consider them as merely approximately existent". A biographical note written later, on the 30th of March 1935, reads: "Works he published: His oeuvre is essentially scattered, for now, among several magazines and occasional publications. Those which he holds as valid from among books or pamphlets are: *35 Sonnets* (in English), 1918; *English Poems I-II* and *English Poems III* (also in English), 1922; and the book *Message*, 1934, which earned the Poem award from the Bureau of National Propaganda". And then it reads: "Fernando Pessoa doesn't intend to publish any book or pamphlet. As there is no audience to read them, he feels he should be relieved of uselessly spending money he doesn't have in publishing same". Still, all things considered, the following list probably isn't far off:

Ultimatum. The text was originally meant for *Portugal Futurista,* the magazine born at the São Luís Theatre's futurist sessions. Along with many other manifestos which were also published in it: *Futurism* (interpreted by B.R.), *Manifeste de Peintres Futuristes* (Boccioni *et al.), Futurist Ultimatum* (Almada), *Futurist Manifesto of Lust* (Saint-Point), *The Music-Hall* (Marinetti). But few of the magazine's 10 thousand copies were commercialized, as the police was quick to impound the publication. *Ultimatum* was then published as an autonomous edition by Tipografia P. Monteiro. Perhaps on account of being a *separata,* he didn't actually consider it a book. Style-wise, that manifesto reproduces Marinetti's *Le futurisme* (1911), *Tripoli italiano* (1911), *Manifesto tecnico de la letteratura futurista* (1912); but, in its substance, it is mainly an act of protest against the humiliation of the British *Ultimatum* of the 11th of January 1890 (as we shall see up ahead). Against the small-mindedness he could feel taking hold of Portugal. In *Athena* #2, he says that "my aesthetic and social theory in *Ultimatum* can be summed up as follows: The irrationalization of activities which aren't (yet) rationizable. Much like metaphysics is a virtual science, as is sociology, I propose the irrationalization of both – which is to say, to make an art out of metaphysics, and politics out of sociology. That is, in a nutshell, what I defended in my *Ultimatum".* With not a semblance of modesty, he holds it up as "the most intelligent literary piece produced by the Great War" (excerpts):

> Eviction notice to the mandarins of Europe! Get out!
> (...)
> Ultimatum to all of them, and to all the rest who are just like them!
> And if they don't want to leave, then make them take a shower!
> Parade of nations, I spit on you!
> (...)

Give me some air!
Open all the windows!
(…)
Strong men of Lilliputian Europe, pass by as I shower you with my Contempt!
(…)
Pass by, epileptic dung-heap without grandeur…
Pass by, mildew of the New…
(…)
Come before my utter Loathing…
Proclaim loud and clear that nobody's fighting for Freedom or Justice! They're fighting in fear of everyone else!
Men, nations, objectives: all a huge zero!
SHIT!
Europe is thirsty for Creativity! She's hungry for the Future!
What we have now cannot endure, because it's nothing!
I, from the Race of the Navigators, declare that it cannot endure!
I shout this out at the top of my lungs, on the European coast where the Tagus meets the sea, with arms raised high as I gaze upon the Atlantic, abstractly saluting Infinity.

Ultimatum, Álvaro de Campos

35 Sonnets, by Fernando Pessoa. Lisbon, Monteiro & Co., 190 Rua do Ouro, 192, 1918, 20 pages long. The poems are believed to have been (mostly) written between 1908 and 1912, and were continuously corrected until their publication in 1918. Written in the style of the Shakespearean sonnet – 12 sequential verses with the rhyming scheme ABAB CDCD EFEF, plus two others further to the right in GG rhyme – they were borne of the fact that Pessoa saw in the English writer's 154 sonnets "a complexity that I wished to reproduce in a modern adaptation". Still, he occasionally made use of approximate rhymes, such as *are* and *for, abroad* and *ignored* ("Poem I"); *hole* and *soul, world* and *hurded* ("Poem III"), and so forth. He subsequently made a number of corrections (dated 06/11/1920), which were incorporated into later editions. He also planned on adding 15 poems to compose what would be his *50 sonnets,* and then pondered increasing that number, first to 71, then to 80 *English sonnets.* On the back cover of a copy, he wrote *Other sonnets* and a list of the eight *first verses.* It is unknown where those new sonnets might fit in the book. Not in sequence to those which had already been published, in any case, as poem XXXV feels very much like the book's end. The poem reproduced here expresses a sense of isolation that the poet desperately seeks to overcome.

Whether we write or speak or do but look
We are ever unapparent. What we are
Cannot be transfused into word or book.
Our soul from us is infinitely far.

However much we give our thoughts the will
To be our soul and gesture it abroad,
Our hearts are incommunicable still.
In what we show ourselves we are ignored.

The abyss from soul to soul cannot be bridged
By any skill of thought or trick of seeming.
Unto our very selves we are abridged

When we would utter to our thought our being.
– We are our dreams of ourselves, souls by gleams,
– And each to each other dreams of others' dreams[3].

Sonnet I, Fernando Pessoa

Antinous, A Poem by Fernando Pessoa. *Lisbon, 1918,* also edited by Monteiro & Co., 16 pages. Subsequent editions also contain the note that the first one (one thousand copies) had been revised by Pessoa himself. "An older and rather imperfect version was published in 1918. The current version aims to nullify and replace same, from which it differs on an essential level". As previously described.

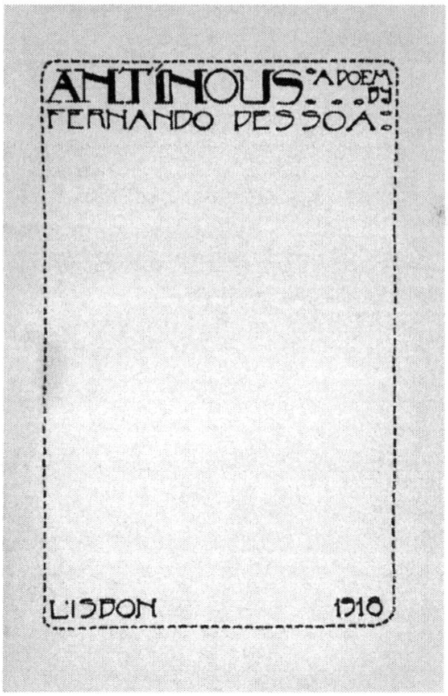

3 Pessoa makes frequent use of this image. "Each of my dreams, as soon as I start dreaming it, is immediately incarnated in another person, who is then the one dreaming it, and not I". In "The Sailor", for example, the *Watchers* dream that they're dreaming of a sailor, while he sees those who dream of him.

English Poems I-III, by Fernando Pessoa, Lisbon. Olisipo, 1921. A reprint (one thousand copies) of two writings published in 1918. According to Pessoa, "it takes knowing it well [the English language] to fully grasp the complete and compact text of those poems". The chosen poem mirrors the eternal play between life and death.

I love this world and all these men because
I shall not love them long. That we do die
I believe not, bound fast to higher laws,
But that we lose this world do not deny.

This light that in the sea makes many a light,
This breeze so soft when least we feel it most,
May be replaced by a diviner sight
Or by a truer breeze; but these are lost.

Like some strange trick of childhood that was ill
Yet had the childhood, in it I regret
Perchance in some far world sublime and still,
The childhood that I never shall forget –

No, nor these toys of sense –this world, these men –,
Dear now when had, dear when finally lost.

Poem 82, Fernando Pessoa

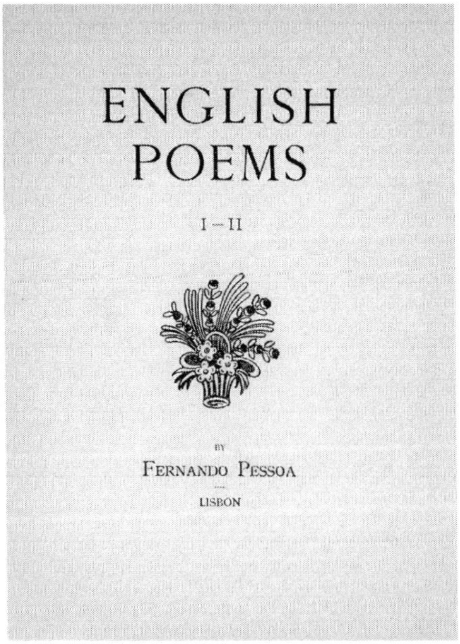

English Poems III, by Fernando Pessoa. Olisipo, 1921. Once again, 1,000 copies. It contained *Epithalamium* (already elaborated upon) and *Inscriptions,* including the following two:

I

We pass and dream. Earth smiles. Virtue is rare.
Age, duty, gods weigh on our conscious bliss.
Hope for the best and for the worst prepare.
The sum of purposed wisdom speaks in this.

VII

I put by pleasure like an alien bowl.
Stern, separate, mine, I looked towards where gods seem.
From behind me the common shadow stole.
Dreaming that I slept not, I slept my dream.

Inscriptions, Fernando Pessoa

Interregnum – In Defence and Justification of the Military Dictatorship in Portugal. Lisbon, Sociedade Nacional de Tipografia, 59, Rua do Século, 1928. A political pamphlet written at the behest of the Nucleus of National Action and sold in the streets at 50 centavos[4]. "In its original form, *Interregnum* should have been but an anonymous manifesto. The Interior Ministry forbid the manifesto's edition, unless it came out signed and converted into a book – or, rather, a pamphlet – which was the only way to prevent it from being censored, as there were a number of objections raised against it". Also, "it bears reviewing this all, and perhaps disavow plenty of it". In a note written in 1935, he claims it "should be considered as non-existent". Up to the reader to decide whether or not it should be in this list, then.

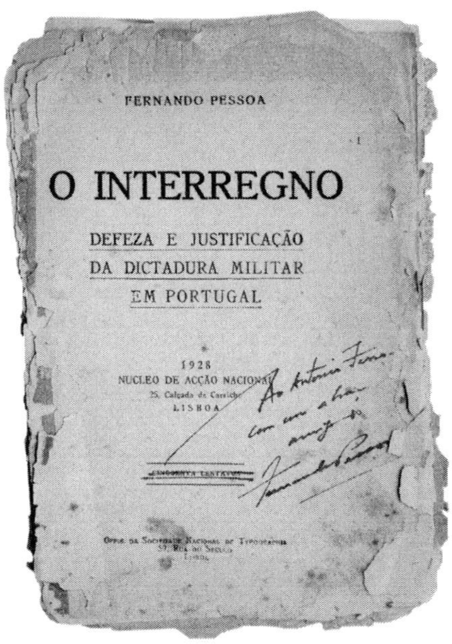

Message. The cover is bare, orange in the centre and with a small light yellow frame. Above, only the author's name, *Fernando Pessoa;* beneath it, in a larger font, the title *Message,* on the upper third of the page, and *Lisbon, 1934, Parceria António Maria Pereira, 44 Rua Augusta, 54* below. More on it in a later chapter.

4 A copy that Pessoa signed for António Ferro has the price scratched out with a pen. As if he were embarrassed of charging anything at all for a text of such nature. Said copy also had several pencil notes, whether by Ferro or by Pessoa (who often did so with books he offered), it is impossible to say.

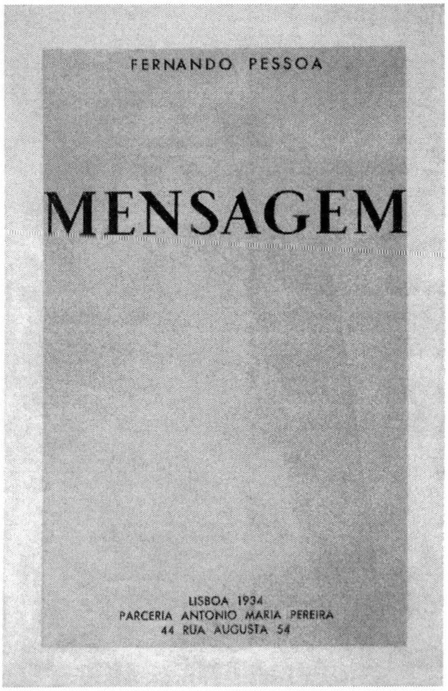
FERNANDO PESSOA
MENSAGEM
LISBOA 1934
PARCERIA ANTONIO MARIA PEREIRA
44 RUA AUGUSTA 54

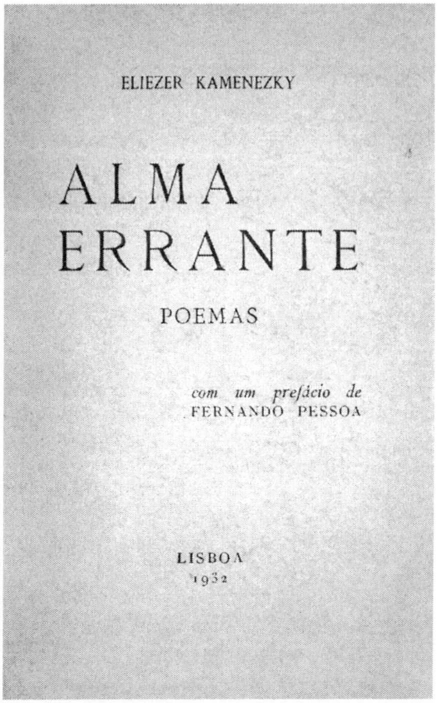
ELIEZER KAMENEZKY
ALMA
ERRANTE
POEMAS
com um prefácio de
FERNANDO PESSOA
LISBOA
1932

The mystery of Alma Errante

In 1932, *Alma Errante* [Wandering Soul], the book by the emigrated Russian Eliezer Kamenezky, is published in Lisbon. *Preface by FERNANDO PESSOA,* as it reads on the cover. "Eliezer is a Russian Jew, a temporarily settled wanderer, idealist and romantic as are all Jews, when they aren't the opposite" Pessoa says right off the bat. Born on the 7th of April 1888 (the same year Pessoa came into the world), in the Russian city of Bachmut (today's Artemivsk, Ukraine), he departed at the age of 15 from the port of Odessa as a stowaway, knowing not where the vessel was headed. And so began his journey across the world, with a stop at Brazil, and it was only in 1917 that he visited Portugal, deciding to take up residence in Lisbon in the 20s, at Travessa da Mãe-d'Água, 26, third floor – according to Ernesto Martins, who worked with Kamenezky and visited the apartment almost every night. Bearded like Rasputin, with a wild head of hair, a corpulent body, vegetarian and always wearing sandals, he was decidedly a peculiar figure. So much so, that he even played secondary roles in three Portuguese films: *Revolução de Maio, O pai tirano* and *Aldeia da roupa branca* – directed by António Lopes Ribeiro, who would be the godfather at Ophelia Queiroz's wedding. Later (in 1939), he would cry at the stillbirth of what would have been his only son, and lived out the rest of his days with close-cropped hair, with no beard and no laughter, until his death in 1957.

In order to survive during his early days in Lisbon, he first gave conferences on the virtues of natural food habits and nudism, but soon dedicates himself to selling antiques at São Pedro de Alcântara, 71, at Bairro Alto (above Elevador da Glória) – where it is said that Pessoa often napped on a chaise longue in the shop's basement. That well described *basement* was a tight affair, about 1m30 of height, in which there was an iron frame and a mattress which Pessoa made use of, not after lunch, but at late afternoon, to recover from his *glasses of aguardiente* and prepare himself for the alcohol-fueled nights with his friends. When Ernesto Martins took over that space (as part of a transaction with Kamenezky) to install his own bookstore/antique shop, he found there scribbling by Pessoa on the walls; the writings now covered by unwary painters, and the efforts to recover those texts have been fruitless.

Alma errante was Kamenezky's only book, marked by illusions of love and a longing for the past. Nothing wrong with the lyricism of such sentiments, but for a small detail: At the time of the book's writing, and even though he already spoke Portuguese with some fluency, he simply could not write in the language. Nor did he ever know anything of English, French or Spanish, as Ernesto Martins claims. Whenever he signed copies for customers, underneath his signature, he's simply scribble what others took to be indecipherable words[5]. Proof of that endures in a copy of *Alma errante* he signed on the 22nd of August 1952 to one *Mister José Pereira dos Santos,* in which he still reveals little intimacy with Portuguese grammar almost 20 years after having published the book, with a number of spelling mistakes and handwriting more akin to that of a schoolboy. According to Martins, and as told to him by Kamenezky himself, the Russian would write some memos and notes in his own language, folding them and storing the papers in empty shoe boxes (he had over 15 of them) – Martins can still point out where they were, on shelves nowadays occupied by rare books. Whenever Pessoa came to the store, he would read him (in Portuguese) those papers (written in Russian). His friend took notes and, days later, would hand him poems for 20 escudos each.

This wasn't the only such episode in Pessoa's life, as in March 1931 Carlos Eugénio Moitinho de Almeida's *O tabaco, vício brando e útil* was published by Lisbon's Rotary Club, having been written by Pessoa at the behest of his friend, according to sister Teca. Except this case was more serious, as he had written out of friendship for Moitinho, but, for Kamenezky, it was for money. In order to verify the origin of those verses, I searched for their trail, despite the low quality of the book's verses. Pessoa might have written them, imagining how Kamenezky would have, in an intentionally mediocre style. Perhaps even to cover up the small transactions between them. And the book's words provide us with valuable information, such as references to *Beethoven's sonatas, Chopin's preludes, Mendelssohn's idylls* or *Schubert's music,* all four very much to Pessoa's tastes, whereas it would have been far more understandable for Kamenezky to have mentioned Russian composers, for instance. Or verses declaring that violets are his *favourite flower,* when the national flower of Russia is the chamomile. Or even the rather pessoan habit (to be fair, a common one at his time) of capitalizing some words mid-sentence, such as Love, Justice, Mystery, Death (three times), Nature (four), Ocean and Thought. To say nothing of the quatrains which, in both inspiration and style – *watered down by the asymmetries of the heptasyllabic verse and the transgression of the rhyme style,* words by Teresa Sobral Cunha – are reminiscent of "Quadras ao gosto popular".

> Like you, I am alone in life:
> Like you, I have no one:
> Like you, I cry singing,
> Wondering if anyone exists.
>
> My life is a sad fate,
> Born of bitter pain.

5 According to Martins, he asked Kamenezky to write something legible when signing copies, to which the Russian replied: *That is precisely the point, Martins. Otherwise, people will realize I cannot write in Portuguese.*

My soul prays, singing,
Remembering lost love

In some cases, we also have borderline references to poems by Pessoa himself: A hail Mary of sorts; a memory of the lark's dialogue (Shakespeare), which Pessoa had long pondered writing himself; the idea that those who die aren't the ones dying, but rather those we no longer remember; or a hug to *little sister moon,* reminiscent of his distaste of Saint Francis (who used to call water *my sister).* There are also a couple of verses which, with some good will, could pass off as his – a distraction, in that case, as it's borderline impossible to write so much with nary a good sentence to show for it. Like, for example, *I love the silence and the mystical darkness of the night/ Which envelops me in its dark cloak*[6]*;* or *In that dark, dark night/ Sad as night, sad as the sea*[7]. In others, it's as if Pessoa were writing about parts of his own life. Like the one poem, one of two dedicated to Judite F. (Kamenezky's wife was a woman from Alentejo called Arnilde), which is more like a description of the beginning of his relationship with Ophelia:

> Do you remember the day of our first date. When, gazing upon me, you laughed uncontrollably – do you? If you don't, well, I do…
>
> I thought you were a dream of my dream[8]. And I lived dreaming of you.
> I sent you a couple of verses.
>
> Pieces of my dreaming soul.
> Verses filled with tenderness and spiritual love
> I wrote you some letters
> Sincerely narrating the state of my soul,
> The utmost fondness I felt for you…

Carrying on with my research, I then examined the book's title, inspired on the poem which comes right after the opening one: *Wandering soul, light as the wind! I wander around the world.* Hearkening back to Kamenezky's own life, naturally, before he set roots in Lisbon. Or perhaps evoking Ukrainian writer (Nicolai Vassilievitch) Gógol (1809-1852), and his *Dead souls.* Or maybe even Guerra Junqueiro, who wrote in *Pátria*[9]*: Gone, gone it goes! Wandering, chimeric soul!* However, Pessoa himself had used the expression in a number of verses – the oldest of which (around 1915) in Álvaro de Campos' monumental "Maritime Ode":

---

6 In "Two Excerpts of Odes", the cloak had a different colour: *Come, silent, static night/ Come envelop death with a white cloak/ My heart…*

7 In a 1911 "Ode", Ricardo Reis recalls the *Dead Sea,* a *Sea without a harbour, as unto a non-place.*

8 Very much a Pessoa tell, as previously established.

9 A book which Pessoa, in some moments, deemed more important than *The Lusiads.*

> O wandering, restless soul of people who live in ships,
> Of symbolic people who come and go, and for whom nothing lasts,
> For when the ship returns to port
> There's always some change on board!
>
> O never-ending flights, departures, drunkenness from Diversity!
> Eternal soul of navigators and navigations!
>
> *Maritime Ode*, Álvaro de Campos

I then attentively reread Pessoa's preface. Not a single word on the book's poems, only a mention to how intimate the *author* was with the language of the country he had chosen to live in. "Eliezer isn't Portuguese, and so one cannot expect him to deftly wield one of the world's most complex, subtle and opulent languages". Almost as if saying that the author could never have hoped to express, in that other language, "the idea and the emotion" which "reflect on the vocabulary and syntactical game" of poems. The text ends with suggestive words: "No Jew, no matter how great a poet, could ever write… the profound logical movement of the Greek ode"; or "to write like Aeschylus"; to say nothing of the fact that "clearly, no Jew could possibly have written this preface". Or the book, as he appears to suggest (because he didn't know how to write in Portuguese, naturally). As if Pessoa were leaving fingerprints on the paper, hoping someone might later notice them.

Following through with my research, I still pondered the likelihood that this wasn't the only book he had written for the Russian Jew. Which brings us to the novel *Eliezer,* ostensibly written by Kamenezky – published in Italy (Lucarini publishing house) by Amina Di Munno, who ascribed its writing to Pessoa. Just like Antonio Tabucchi would. The hypothetical dating of the text is based on the narration of a meeting between the Russian with the one who would later become president of the United States of Brazil, Washington Luiz (Pereira de Souza, 1870-1957) – elected in 1926 and deposed in 1930. As it so happened, in 1918's *Almanaque Vegetariano* (Vegetarian Almanac) in Brazil, a brief biography of Kamenezky was published, which doesn't mention said meeting. Therefore, the novel must have been written between 1918 and 1926. The thesis that it was of the Russian's writing seems untenable. For starters, the originals were typed in four typewriters, all of which were familiar to many other of Pessoa's writings. And in an English similar to that which Pessoa used in his prose, according to Luciana Stegagno Picchio. A copy of the book remained in the Chest, made of carbon paper, clocking in at 322 pages (13 to 86 are numbered with Pessoa's handwriting). According to "Team Pessoa", it is similar to Pessoa's *in the disposition of the text on the page, as well as the general traits of the dactylography.* To say nothing of the stylistic details, all of which point to *the one who typed the novel in English was Pessoa.*

An original text of his, or a mere translation? There can be no doubt about that, either. As we've already established, Kamenezky could never have written it in Portuguese, or in any other of the three main European languages (as he couldn't even speak them). Only Russian and Hebrew are left, two languages that neither Pessoa nor virtually anyone else in Lisbon spoke at the time. Which would have entailed a number of different translations before Pessoa could begin translating it into English. Besides, given that he was already living in Lisbon, it was unlikely that there was an English translation of the book before it was even published in Portugal. And, if Pessoa had only taken care of the translation, why would he have spent so much time correcting the original manuscript and adding to it? It's also somewhat less than credible that the (supposed) original and the (supposed) first translation were lost, as Kamenezky's devoted widow would never have parted with such manuscripts, which were so valuable to her. So much did this woman love him, that she wouldn't consent to figure alone in the street that was named after her, and insisted that her husband's name was also included – Rua Arnilde e Eliezer Kamenezky, at Redondo, district of Évora. Taking all this into account, the most likely probability is that Kamenezky told Pessoa about his life, and the poet was compensated for the service – and he most certainly needed it, given his ever precarious financial situation.

As if that weren't enough, I also researched the poems of *Alma errante* which Pessoa had stored – as he kept a copy of everything he wrote. A search made easy by the fact that Yvette Centeno had already rummaged through Envelope 91 of the Chest and had found 37 of *Alma errante's* 57 poems there, and a list of their first verses had been published at *Colóquio/Letras* magazine #56 (July 1986). A good part of those poems stored in the Chest had a number of corrections and variants; the rest (or some of them, perhaps) are likely in other envelopes yet to be identified – such as the poem "À memória de [In memory of] Florbela Espanca", which wasn't in Envelope 91 and ended up in the book (raising the initial count to 37). Or they might even not be Pessoa's, especially those with drab verses such as *I envelop you in my arms;* or *The best way to pray/ Is to do good every day;* or *The graveyard of dead souls/ Is the bodies of the living,* far too distant from any semblance of a pessoan touch. Thus, it is likely that some other hand was at work in the editorial process. All things considered, the mystery of the *Eliezer* novel and *Alma errante* poem remains, though both were very likely written by Pessoa.

Second mystery, What the tourist should see

At the end of 1925 or shortly thereafter, Pessoa wrote an English guide to Lisbon: *What the tourist should see.* Undated, the age of the text can nonetheless be inferred from a number of references to the "monument to the journalist França Borges (inaugurated in 04/11/1925); or the journal "*A Ilustração,* which recently began publication", also from 1925. The guide was neither published nor proposed to any publisher, and remained in silence in the Chest, only coming to light 71 years after his death, thanks to Teresa Rita Lopes. With a small change in the title's translation – *What the tourist must see*[10]. It's a fairly conventional and banal text, lost in *adverbial forms of intensity...,* which overdoes the superlatives which would be a better fit for an ad: "One of the biggest theatres", "total splendour", "the most remarkable of its kind in Europe", "an admirable handrail" – as Gilda Santos highlighted. With nary a truly pessoan sentence in the entire text. Bréchon defined it best: *A poor text, bereft of emotion, poetry, humour or trace of his genius.* The book ends abruptly, as if the text were supposed to continue, after speaking about "the tram at Gomes Freire", where the author let pass the chance of writing at least one noteworthy final sentence. Or, perhaps, as per Teresa Sobral Cunha, *the book was unfinished for representing so little to him.*

The details that point to it being of his writing include the fact that it was doubtlessly typed by Pessoa, stored in the Chest, and the probability that it was one of the patriotic projects he had conceived of, like the idealized (and never finished) *All about Portugal.* Other than that, nobody, not even his friends, even knew of its existence. Also, in 1924, there had already been released the first volume of a guide to Portugal, prestigiously published by Lisbon's National Library. Organized by Raul (Sangreman) Proença (1884-1941), a collaborator at *A Águia* magazine and co-founder of *Seara Nova* magazine. Thus, there wasn't really an audience for another guide, nor any good reason to write one. António Valdemar, professor of journalism, previously awarded with a medal by the Portuguese Authors' Society, suggests the book wasn't Pessoa's, but rather an English version of someone else's text – perhaps Raul Proença, or Gustavo Matos Siqueira, or Nogueira de Brito. Except the originals of said guide never materialized to support Valdemar's hypothesis. And no other author claimed it as his. With no further data available, we are reduced to mere speculation which holds no real aesthetic interest and wouldn't even be worthy of including in a biography, given its low quality: An unpublished book which would surprise no one to know it had originally been written by some author specializing in guides.

Uncompleted or unedited books

Pessoa wanted to write many other books, some of which he partly wrote, such as *The transformation book (or Book of tasks), Book of war* or *From Portugal,* all three in English, or [translated from Portuguese]*; The German War; The Aristocratic Republic; The Seven Rooms of the Abandoned Palace; Breviary; Chants of Defeat; Songs of Lisbon; Raining Gold; Pre-revolutionary*

10 As opposed to the more correct *should.*

Considerations; From Dictatorship to the Republic; Legends; Monarchy; Symphonies; Arab Suite; A Dictionary of Orthography, Prosody and Etymology of the Portuguese Language or *The Black Diamond* – after which he wrote (in English) *Some Title Like This.* Other books he actually did conclude, but never got to publish, such as the English *The Mad Fiddler* (1917), which was inspired by the legend of the Pied Piper. It is an allegory in five parts (corresponding to 37 poems), written in a rather modern English (distant from the archaic tone of his first English poems), and tells the story of a fiddler who passes by a village and plays for its complacent inhabitants, awakening "a luminous restlessness" in them stemming from the awareness of their failure, that "every soul is a lamentation", awakening the desire for a different future "like the unfurled flag which appeared". He appraises his own creation in a note: "The Mad Fiddler gathers the infantile, inferior oeuvre of my undisciplined imagination". As he says in "Four Sorrows", "no matter what we dream, what we dream is true". He sent the originals to London's Constable & Co. publishing house, which replied on the 6th of June 1917: *Having examined the poems, we cannot commit to their publication.* Instead of sending the manuscripts to another publisher, he put them in the Chest. Here, a poem expressing a beautiful vision of death:

The angels came and sought her.
They found her by my side,
There where her wings had brought her.
The angels took her away.
She had left their home, their God-bright day
And come by me to abide.

She loved me because love
Loves but imperfect things.
The angels came from above
And bore her away from me.
They bore her away for ever
Between their luminous wings.

'Tis true she was their sister
And near to God as they.
But she loved me because
My heart had not a sister.
They have taken her away,
And this is all there was.

Nothing, Fernando Pessoa

Fama volat
(Fame flies) Virgil

THE MAGAZINES

What good is freedom of
thought to those who, on account of their
social condition, cannot think?
Freedom of the Plebs, Fernando Pessoa

Writing in magazines

Brazil had its first brush with modernism in the beginning of the 20th century. Graça Aranha spoke of the communion between the *three races* – Portuguese *melancholy,* the native *metaphysics of terror* and *African childishness in all its cosmic terror.* Almost the same sentiment expressed by Ronald de Carvalho, for whom the very Brazilian soul was formed of *Portuguese longing, sweetened by Iberian sensibility, the indigenous disquiet and the taste of African sentiment of resignation.* Gilberto Freyre unveiled the mysteries of the Brazilian soul, understanding the process of integration effected on it by Portuguese colonists. Câmara Cascudo gave hints of his primitive bias. Oswald de Andrade released an *Anthropophagic Manifesto.* Menotti del Picchia inflamed audiences with his *warrior aesthetic.* Mário de Andrade, plus a group of vanguardists, organized the *Week of Modern Art* between the 11th and the 18th of February 1922. Villa-Lobos presented his *African Dances* at São Paulo's Municipal Theatre, wearing a jacket and flip-flops – on account of an injured foot, but the audience took it as being somehow *futurist.*

In Portugal, the futurist wave that was sweeping the world would also contaminate literature. A *new generation* began meeting at cafés, especially Brasileira. *Funny fellas,* as they were called at first. Literary magazines were the chosen path to express that vision of *structure, strength and death,* as Maria Aliete Galhoz defined it. "Fernando Pessoa has been a constant collaborator, always prompted by friendly requests, in magazines and publications of all sorts", as she claimed in *Presença* #3 (1927). "I have thoughts which, were I to realize and make them alive, would add a new light to the stars, a new beauty to the world, and a greater love to the hearts of men", he wrote in 1907.

At the time, Pessoa was already preparing to be Pessoa. But that yearning for novelty made itself more clearly felt from 1910 on, after the proclamation of the Republic. The same year in which Porto saw the birth of a magazine of the *Saudosismo* movement – an arm of *Renascença Portuguesa.*

A Águia magazine

Said magazine was *A Águia,* whose literary editor was Teixeira de Pascoaes – according to Júlio Brandão, *a pig's bladder bursting with vanity;* whereas, for Pessoa, he was "one of the finest living poets, and the greatest lyrical poet in Europe today". In #4 (April 1922), Pessoa published his first article meant for a larger audience: "The new Portuguese poetry, sociologically considered". The text was the opening for the magazine – which is remarkable, considering his age at the time (23) and that of the other collaborators in that issue, enshrined names one and all, such as Alexandre Herculano, Camilo Castelo Branco and Coelho Neto. In that article, after establishing comparisons with Victor Hugo's France and Shakespeare's England, Pessoa forecasts the coming of an Over-Camões, to whom "even the eminent figure of Camões shall play second fiddle to". Pessoa himself, he likely imagined. For Eduardo Lourenço, in that article, he presented himself as *an exterminating angel hailing from Anglo-Saxon culture, showing up with great fanfare in placid Portugal.* Shortly after, in issues 11 and 12 (November and December 1912), he published *New Portuguese Poetry in its Psychological Aspect,* in which he claims that poetry should be based "on vagueness, subtlety and complexity". This was a more sizeable text (50 pages long), more elaborate and creative. But his relationship with the magazine was on borrowed time, as the following year (03/03/1913), in *Teatro – Revista de Crítica,* edited by Boavida Portugal, Pessoa wrote a scathing review of Afonso Lopes Vieira's book, *Bartolomeu Marinheiro* (excerpt):

> Mr. Lopes Vieira means to write like a child, writing for children. Writing like a child is tolerable, provided one is a child, as being a child makes one vulnerable. Seeing as these childrens' books are his sleep, one might as well say he sleeps like an animal. Mr. Lopes Vieira is a criminal, for the following three reasons: He tries to sell a pig in a poke of simplicity, he is ridiculing matters which should be addressed with a simplicity stupidity can never manage, and because whoever writes "what was the sea before? A dark room where boys feared to tread" deserves an inquisition of teachers. Raised in stupidity by reading Mr. Lopes Vieira's infantile works, tomorrow's men of Portugal will hold Mr. Júlio Dantas as Shakespeare and Mr. Lopes Vieira as Shelley... and shall be Spaniards.

As it just so happened, Vieira was one of *A Águia's* most assiduous contributors, and such a rude review would come with a price. The magazine would still publish in August 1913 a text Pessoa had sent earlier – "At the Forest of Obliviousness", presented as a fragment of *The Book of Disquiet, in preparation.* But they refuse to publish a *static drama* titled "The Mariner" – in which a maiden is mourned in her coffin, on a table, as three women on a vigil talk about life and death. Pessoa would later comment on it in a letter to Côrtes-Rodrigues (04/03/1915): *"The Mariner* has been changed and perfected... The ending, in particular, is much better now... It isn't something I'd be embarrassed by, nor – I believe – that'd ever embarrass me". Indignant at such refusal, Pessoa wrote a pamphlet (which, thankfully for him, wasn't published), in which he opposed "the orientation of [the magazine's] lusitanist or *saudosista* spirit", recommending that its members "learn Portuguese, read the classics" and "make use of women on a regular basis and without shyness". Nothing surprising from one who, at the time, was still testing his limits. But he didn't finish the pamphlet, realizing that the magazine would never be the vehicle of such boldness. And he would never publish it.

A Renascença magazine

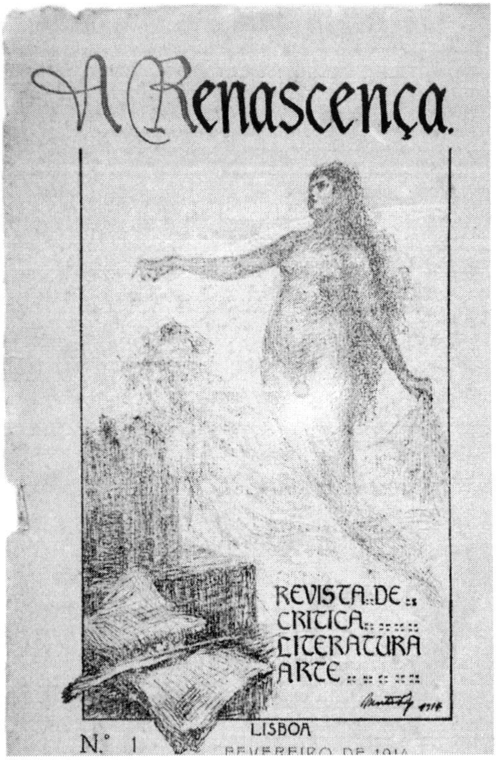

Searching for different paths, it was at *A Renascença* – directed by Carvalho Mourão and edited by (José) Coelho Pacheco – that he would publish “Impressions of Twilight”, which consisted of an untitled poem beginning with the verse “O bell from my village”; and “Impressions”, which begins with the verse “Marshes brushing anxiety against my gilded soul”. Interestingly, the magazine requested its readers to send books for commenting, warning beforehand that *only on exceptional circumstances will we review books we haven't gotten.* To say nothing of the fact that its very editorial claims: *“My* [the magazine’s] *yearning is you! My life shall be my yearning!* A yearning which wouldn’t go very far, as the magazine which considered its subscriber a *cruel reader,* ceased publication right after its first issue. *“Renascença* [Rebirth] died at birth”, Pessoa mused. And he wouldn’t miss it, as, deep down, he felt ready to stand on his own feet. His “other Is” began to pop up, and that *heteronym eruption prepared the explosion of* Orpheu, according to Octavio Paz.

Orpheu #1

Cover designed by José Pacheco

At the latter end of 1914, one could feel that a new dawn in Portuguese literature was fast approaching. Some projects were dropped along the way, like *Diogène* magazine – which was alternately written in English and French, to “make Europe aware of our irreverence towards it”. It was then that discussions took place to create an intersectionist magazine. In February 1915, Luís de Montalvor had just returned from Brazil and, during a night out at Montanha, he suggested to Pessoa and Sá-Carneiro they make a quarterly magazine. The idea gains hold. In their group, the eldest is Raul Leal (28); the youngest, António Ferro (19), with Pessoa (26) as the culturally most relevant member – *the basis of the pyramid,* as per Almada. The others were Alfredo Guisado, Almada Negreiros, Amadeu de Sousa Cardoso, Augusto de Lima, Côrtes-Rodrigues, Eduardo Guimarães, Eduardo Viana, José Pacheco, Luís de Montalvor, Ronald de Carvalho, Sá-Carneiro and Santa-Rita Pintor. While pondering the title, they first consider *Contemporânea,* due to their commitment to modernity; or *Lusitânia,* in that it was meant to represent Portuguese and Brazilian literature – a title which would later be used by José

Pacheco; or *Europa,* to go beyond the parochial Lisbon. On the 28th of July 1914, Sá-Carneiro wrote: *Europe! Europe! How necessary it would be.* The group had been discussing the title since 1912, but Montalvor's suggestion of *Orpheu* would gather the most consensus. For Maria Aliete Galhoz, it was *a symbol of how foreignly intimate literature, chance and life were.*

The magazine was headquartered at Rua do Ouro, 190, Lisbon, in Portugal, and Rua Humaitá, 104, Rio de Janeiro, in Brazil. It was registered under the name of Sá-Carneiro, its first editors were a Brazilian living in Portugal, Ronald de Carvalho, and a Portuguese who would later live in Brazil, Luís de Montalvor. The same who, in the introduction, describes the sentiment of those responsible for the magazine as *an exile of temperament, of art that is conceived of as a secret or a torment.* The one legally in charge of the publication was António Ferro. Pessoa confessed to being "most pleased with our illegality", as "little Ferro" was still a minor. In a note recalling the conversation with Sá-Carneiro, he clears up the matter: "Ferro doesn't mind?, I asked. Ferro? Do you think I consulted Ferro? I then burst out laughing. But, in fact, Ferro had been informed thereof, and he didn't mind his involuntary role as editor, nor its illegality". This because, according to Alfredo Pedro Guisado, *if any complication were to occur, his responsibility would have no real consequence,* as, being a minor, Portuguese law couldn't charge him with anything. The magazine was sold for 30 centavos. In Brazil, 1,500 réis fracos. The first quarterly issue, with 83 pages, is ready by the end of March. The print run was 450 copies, when similar magazines (such as Boavida Portugal's *Teatro)* numbered 1,000.

YEAR I – 1915 / #1 JANUARY-FEBRUARY-MARCH

SUMMARY

Luís de Montalvor	*Introduction*
Mário de Sá-Carneiro	*To the "Inklings of gold" (poems)*
Ronald de Carvalho	*Poems*
Fernando Pessoa	*The Mariner*[1] (static drama)
Alfredo Pedro Guisado	*Thirteen sonnets*
José de Almada Negreiros[2]	*Friezes (poems)*
Côrtes-Rodrigues[3]	*Poems*
Álvaro de Campos	*Opiary* and *Triumphal Ode*

1 The text refused by *A Águia.*

2 Negreiros described himself as the magazine's *illustrator.* Pessoa wrote him the following dedication (13/01/1935) in a signed copy of *Message:* "Hail, *Orpheu*'s baby".

3 Shortly before, in a letter to *A Águia* (for the attention of Álvaro Pinto, 24/02/1913), he says in a P.S.: "The boy's name is Côrtes-Rodrigues. Make sure to write it correctly in the Summary, so people don't think him Cortês (Courteous).

The cover of a woman between two sails standing in for a pair of pillars, evokes the tarot's Priestess – which Pessoa would later evoke himself in "Songbook" in the figure of the *Great Goddess.* After the summary, the magazine mentions the upcoming *(on sale at the end of April)* Sá-Carneiro's *Céu em fogo,* and a list of *works of our collaborators,* among which one by Álvaro de Campos, announced as *Arc de Triomphe, in preparation.* It is unknown what text it corresponds to. Perhaps it was a collection of poems, as the end of "Triumphal Ode" mentions it belonged to a book called *Arc de Triomphe, to be published.* Other than "The Mariner" (written on the 11/12th of September 1913), Pessoa published two other unplanned poems – Álvaro de Campos' "Opiary" and "Triumphal Ode", both of which read *published by Fernando Pessoa.* In a letter to Casais Monteiro (13/01/1935), he explains: "It was a last-minute need to find something to fill the pages. Sá-Carneiro suggested I write an *old* poem of Álvaro de Campos – a taste of what Álvaro de Campos would have been like before having met Caeiro and fallen under his influence". In a letter to Frank Palmer (undated, 1915), addressing a "supplement in English" he was planning to edit, he confesses "our magazine contains certain poems and works of prose which are *reprehensible* from a strictly moral standpoint". The first copy is sold on the 26th of March 1915.

The press' reaction is harsh and corrosive. Right off the bat, *A Capital* had two first page columns on the 30th of March, titled *"Orpheu's* poets have already been scientifically studied by Júlio Dantas 15 years ago, when he busied himself with the Artists of Rilhafoles" [an asylum]. The following day, André Brun dedicates the magazine a tidbit of his own, also in *A Capital: When I saw* Orpheu *in the hands of Praxedes, I assumed reading it had altered his mental faculties.* In *A Vanguarda* (06/04), José Barcelar asks: *Let us leave the new, infatuated loons of the native letters in peace.* After that: *The Bards of* Orpheu *are madmen with sense, Exotic art, The poets of* Orpheu *and the alienists (A Luta,* 08/04); *Orpheu in Hell, From fiancé to future father-in-law (A Capital,* 14/04); *Rilhafolesically... humanity advances... in 200 years, the entire world will be a madhouse (O Povo,* 12/04); "Paranoid poets", by Júlio Dantas *(A Ilustração Portuguesa,* 19/04); "A Worm's dream" *(A República,* 10/05). Not even its authors are spared. They were, at best, *harmless futurists.* Psychiatrist Júlio de Matos (1857-1923), dean of the universities of Lisbon at the time, and later director of Rilhafoles, declares Pessoa and friends *are boys, are they not? But those things they write are rather crude,* and concludes that their writings are *asylum literature.* In Jorge de Sena's estimation, *eminent psychiatrists* were consulted *to ascertain whether or not they are mad.* A small newspaper asks that, in the magazine's second issue, the first one's texts are translated into Portuguese.

There is tremendous scandal. Even acknowledging that "some of the sales were solely due to a desire to laugh", as he admitted to José Pacheco,

Orpheu was nonetheless "an absolute triumph". He exultantly wrote to Côrtes-Rodrigues (04/04/1915): "We are the talk of the town in Lisbon". *Orpheu*'s success was the scandal itself. Previously, only 100 copies had been sold in bookshops, but the remaining 450 were soon sold out. He had the following to say about *Diário de Notícias'* critiques (June 1915): "It is not the critique I am addressing, for none can hope to be understood if others don't even know the language they speak. To rebuke them for that would be absurd. So it has ever been with innovative geniuses: They were either considered mad – like [Paul] Verlaine and [Stéphane] Mallarmé[4] – or fools – like [William] Wordsworth, [John] Keats and [Dante Gabriel] Rossetti[5] – or fools, enemies of the state, religion and morality, as was the case with Antero de Quental[6]".

Orpheu #2

4 Verlaine shot his lover Rimbaud, and Mallarmé wanted to write an *Absolute book.*

5 Romantic authors all.

6 Antero Targino de Quental (1842-1891) took part in socialist revolutionary conspiracies throughout his life.

Between the first two issues of *Orpheu,* the political situation in Portugal took a considerable turn for the worse. Portugal entered World War I and lived through a number of contradictory insurrectional, conservative and revolutionary movements. On the 14th of May 1915, part of the army joined the Democratic Party and took over. General Bento de Castro, the head of government, ends up arrested and deported. Manuel de Arriaga, the president, is replaced by Teófilo Braga. The magazine suffers amidst all the uncertainty and fear in the streets. Issue 2 (April-May-June) is already presided over by Pessoa and Sá-Carneiro, who replaced their companions, their relationship having soured – to the point that, later on, already in Paris, Sá-Carneiro would refer to *little Montalvor's thievery.* Or, more likely, the change was owed to tremendous differences in temperament. Ronald de Carvalho was the magazine's representative in Brazil, which proved to be rather unimportant a role, while Montalvor was chiefly an organizer. None of them shared Pessoa and Sá-Carneiro's taste for scandals, and the latter two had decided they'd make a magazine which would endure as long as they could break rules and routines. The second issue had a larger print run at 600 copies, and was released on the 28th of June 1915. The black cover had nothing but the name on top and a large silver '2'.

YEAR I – 1915 / #2 APRIL-MAY-JUNE

SUMMARY

Ângelo de Lima[7]	*First poems*
Mário de Sá-Carneiro	*Unsupported poems*
Eduardo Guimarães	*Poems*
Raul Leal	*Atelier* (a vertiginous novel)
Violante de Cysneiros (?)[8]	*Poems*
Luís de Montalvor	Narcissus *(poem)*
Fernando Pessoa	*Oblique rain* (intersectionist poems)

With a special collaboration by the futurist
Santa-Rita Pintor
(4 double *hors-textes)*[9]

7 Lima (1872-1921) was a patient at the Rilhafoles asylum, after having been arrested at D. Amélia Theatre for having *uttered obscenities* in 1901. He tried to prove he understood his deviance in an autobiography, but was unsuccessful and would end up dying in the asylum.

8 Actually, it was Armando Côrtes-Rodrigues, who was studying at the time and opted for the pseudonym on account of *the professors' hostility towards the magazine.* At the end of his life, Côrtes-Rodrigues would clarify that the name had been Pessoa's idea, alluding to one of Camões' loves. Côrtes-Rodrigues later made another use of the name as a heteronym in the weekly *O Autonómico.*

9 Alfredo Pedro Guisado's collaboration isn't featured in this list, as the original manuscript of a cycle of poems of his – titled *Queda* – was lost.

The critiques continued unabated: *The Artists of Rilhafoles (A Capital,* 28/06, the release date), describing Sá-Carneiro as *a mastodontic boy with the soul of a child; The misunderstood (O Século,* 01/07); *It takes all kinds (A Capital,* 05/07); *The boys from Orpheu (O Século Cómico,* 08/07); *The proof of madness (O Sport de Lisboa,* 17/07). As if that weren't enough, Pessoa also amused himself by writing some more of his own: "The second of a woman's magazine called *Orpheu* has just been released. The goons clad as artists pretend to be men, determined to achieve social literature, the first of its kind since the world came to be. It remains to be seen what this lot of degenerates aims to attain with this literature of theirs. One must needs know who is reading".

Mutual ill will with Dr. Afonso Costa

On the night of the 3rd of June 1915, Afonso Augusto da Costa – leader of the Democratic Party *(the hard left),* minister of Justice and Cults of the Teófilo Braga government, suffers a serious accident. Fearing an attempt on his life, as soon as he heard the sound of an explosion, he jumped off a moving tram and fractured his skull in the ensuing spectacular fall. Pessoa had already written a number of poems with harsh critiques of the man, describing him as a "painfully ridiculous" reactionary of the spirit. Thinking of him, he even imagined an opuscule which was to be titled *The oligarchy of beasts* – as the governors of the First Republic came to be known in Portugal. Costa reacted with an article that was published at *A Capital,* quoting a modernist recitation *represented by... legs* meant to ensure resources for *Orpheu.* For him, it was but a *dynamic drama titled "The bender"* – a reference to Pessoa himself, naturally. The day after his fall, *A Capital* got a letter for the attention of Miguel Guimarães, signed by "his respectful servant Alavaro de Campos[10], engineer and sensationist poet". In it, alluding to Costa's mockery, he says "the drama we intend to present is titled *The journalists",* in which "all that can be seen are the twelve feet of three journalists"; and ends up applauding "the deliciously dynamic hour in which Divine Providence makes use of trams for its high teachings". He would finish with the following: "Riddlc me this/ What comes in through the door/ And leaves through the window?". Almada reveals that, *at the moment he wrote the article,* Pessoa *was extremely drunk.* Then, and in many other occasions in his life.

A Capital reacts on the 6th of July, saying that *Orpheu's poets are but creatures of ill intent;* referring to *Orpheu*'s futurists as *poor maniacs, creatures of vile and base sentiment... ridiculous and mean.* Underneath the scathing review, ironically in a futurist illustration, the ad for a restaurant – *Do you wish to snack well and dine better? Go to Argentina, Rua 1º de Dezembro, 75.* Except the snack, here, was the magazine's future. Some of *Orpheu*'s collaborators

10 Interestingly, the misspelled name is typed in blue, while the rest of the letter is in red.

protested against the violence of the text and went to *A Capital* to express their solidarity, among them Alfredo Pedro Guisado and António Ferro – who would pen a letter for *O Mundo,* in which they disavowed the writing and cut off ties with the magazine. Sá-Carneiro wrote a letter to *O Jornal* from Paris in defence of Pessoa. The letter was published on the 7th of July, but all he asked his friend was *is Afonso Costa dead or not?* Pessoa would write an even more violent text in reply to *A Capital*'s text (abridged): "The leader of the Democratic Party doesn't deserve the consideration due a regular member of mankind. A frog which mysteriously became a beast… His actions have been those of a cyclone, devastating, spoiling, disturbing all; with the difference that the cyclone, at least, doesn't muddy and sully". But that reply, which was only found among his papers much later, would never be sent. While preparing a later essay, he compares Costa to João Franco, head of the previous monarchic government: Franco was "a shitty tyrant", whereas Costa was "a tyrant of shit", defined as "Lenin in a cloak and kerchief", "Judas", "traitor", "vile as a vile actor", "a man of no spiritual standing or character", "sinister head of regiments of assassins and thieves". The year after the episode, on the 27th of June 1916, he still had the following to say about Costa (excerpt):

> Well, poo!
> Neither the king came, nor did Afonso Costa die when he fell off the tram!
> Everything remained the same, with only a couple of Germans less…
> And this is what Portugal was founded for!
> God, how little for so much!
> God, how little people for so many beasts!
> God, is this all Portugal is?
> Let us see the Portugal you won't let us see!
> Let us see that's what Portugal truly is!
> Period.
>
> Now begins the Manifesto:
> God!
> God!
> Listen to me:
> GOD!
>
> Well, shoot!
> Is the Portuguese press truly
> the Portuguese press?
> Is it this the shit we have to
> drink with our eyes?
> Sons of bitches! No, there isn't even
> a whore who'd bear them!
>
> *Manifesto*, Álvaro de Campos

A note in English was later found in the Chest, in which a supposed journalist reports on the incident: "A sensationist was almost lynched for having written an insolent letter to a Lisbon newspaper, in which he congratulated himself on the fact that Afonso Costa – the most popular Portuguese politician – had fallen off a tram and found himself at death's door". In the 30s, however, his opinion of Costa changed. Mainly because, as much as he disliked the man, he liked Salazar far less: "I deny you my support, but I cannot deny you my respect"[11]. Also: "If all political power had remained in the hands of Afonso Costa, the country would have been well governed and administered". "Credit where credit is due, no matter how much it discomfits me, as I'd rather speak ill of him".

The end of Orpheu

For Eduardo Lourenço, *Orpheu was the most radical experience in the history of our poetry... In fact, it was as if* [those responsible for the magazine], *in disbelief, they had seen God in poetry.* Pessoa wants to continue. But the political climate, some editing troubles and the lack of resources would prove to be fatal. The first issue earned 95 mil-réis. The second fell short of that. The bills at the typography remain unpaid. Sá-Carneiro resorts to his father, but the man is broke and living in Africa, and can do nothing. *Orpheu*'s death was thus an inevitability. Sá-Carneiro tells Pessoa in a letter (13/09/1915) that, *unfortunately,* he *must give up.* Worried about his friend, he suggests: *Place the blame for* Orpheu'*s death squarely on my shoulders. Say that, living in Paris, I do not wish to busy myself with the publication, that I am the one to blame;* and asks him to continue on his own, should he find the means to do so. Apparently, the debts were paid off by Sá-Carneiro's father, after his son had assured him he would take on no further financial responsibilities with the magazine. Pessoa supposedly wrote in September (there is no copy of the letter) that he still held hopes for the magazine. Sá-Carneiro replied: *You have thousands of reasons:* Orpheu *isn't dead.* And he believes that, *eventually, it shall resume publication.* The future would prove them both wrong.

Orpheu #3

From August 1915 on, according to Nuno Júdice, *no further was said about the magazine.* Pessoa registered the title, to keep it from being appropriated by Santa-Rita Pintor, who might intend to continue with it, and he registered as his own the title "3". Sá-Carneiro expresses what would have positively

---

11 Costa defended poet Guerra Junqueiro in court (1907) and then, during Sidónio Pais' dictatorship (1918), he went to exile in France and never again returned to Portugal.

horrified him: *Santa-Rita, maître of* Orpheu, *is a thought far worse than death;* and, from Paris, he suggests a *summary of* Orpheu *#3* (30/08/1915). Despite it having ceased publication, the third issue was indeed prepared and drafted:

SUMMARY
Introduction

Mário de Sá-Carneiro	*Poems from Paris*
Albino de Menezes	*After the kidnapping*
Fernando Pessoa	*Gladius and Beyond God*
Augusto Ferreira Gomes	*Across the twilight, Death of a faun...*
José de Almada Negreiros, sensationist poet and Narcissus of Egypt	*The scene of hate*
D. Tomáz de Almeida	*Eyes*
C. Pacheco[12]	*Beyond another ocean*
Castelo de Moraes	*Fog*

The edition would also contain four *hors-textes* by Pessoa, and paintings by Amadeu da Silva Cardoso, and was partially printed at Monteiro typography. Pessoa typed a text in purple ink which begins thus: "Ho there! The third issue of *Orpheu* has just been published. This magazine is, today, the sole bridge between Portugal and Europe, and, verily, the one true reason Portugal has to exist" as an independent nation. But the third issue is sold by weight, much like old paper, and would only be published 69 years later, based on the originals. Shortly after that typed text, he penned another, also in purple (abridged): "Several circumstances, mainly of financial nature, have led to the temporary suspension of *Orpheu* magazine". Not long after that, he replaced that draft with a typewritten text, this time in blue: "Financial motives, which are chiefly (or exclusively) motivated by the climbing costs of printing paper, have led *Orpheu* to temporarily suspend publication".

The story of *Orpheu* reached its end after a short run, as was the fate of most literary magazines at the time. Still, the volcano of a futurist generation wouldn't disappear. He announced to Côrtes-Rodrigues (04/11/1916) that "a new edition" would be "coming soon", "made with roses and stars in a new world". Sá-Carneiro laments: *What a beautiful* Orpheu *#3 we would have made! What a disgrace!* In a letter to Côrtes-Rodrigues (04/03/1915), one can see that the aim was "to keep at it with the magazine until #4, so that at least a volume can be compiled". In the Chest, there remain two small school notebooks prepared by Sá-Carneiro (plus seven others of clippings, glued by Pessoa himself) with articles about the magazine, 79 in the first and 24 in the second. In September 1917, Pessoa still pondered carrying on with it, as can

12 Pessoa's heteronym. The text is "dedicated to the memory of Alberto Caeiro".

be read in a note in the final page of *Ultimatum* – *"Orpheu* is finished. *Orpheu* lives on"[13]. But it would do so only in the hearts of those who had dreamt it up.

Acção newspaper and Contemporânea magazine

Later, some more literary magazines are released: *Exílio,* by the Santa-Rita brothers; *Centauro,* by Montalvor; *Portugal, a monthly review of the country, its colonies, commerce, history; Portugal futurista,* by Almada, which was promptly apprehended by the police. All of them had but one issue. In 1919, the newspaper *Acção* was also born, in honour of the "great dead" president-king Sidónio Pais. Geraldo Coelho de Jesus was the managing editor and Pessoa the editor. Copies are burnt in the streets. "The democrats I know are indignant at me". And the newspaper would only ever release three issues. In 1922, by the hands of José Pacheco (managing editor) and Agostinho Fernandes (editor), the magazine *Contemporânea* was born – the same name that had been considered for *Orpheu.* In it, Pessoa publishes "António Botto and the aesthetic ideal in Portugal", "The Anarchist Banker" and the 12 poems of "Portuguese Sea" (one of which ended up being replaced in *Message,* as we shall see farther up ahead). The following year, "Trois chansons mortes", "Letter to the author of *'Sáchá'*"[14], "Lisbon revisited (1923)" and "Spell". For Pessoa, it would be "in a way, the same as *Orpheu.* But what a difference! What a difference!".

What he truly doesn't like to see is an homage by the Ministry of Public Instruction on the magazine's very cover. So very different from the previous rebelliousness. All that was left was the longing, "such longing, ever more longing for the old times of *Orpheu"*. After that, he would still be content editor for another important magazine, along with painter Rui Vaz (who took care of the visual programming and ensured the necessary resources for the edition. It was *Athena.*

13 The sentence would be repeated in *Sudoeste* #3, published the year he died.

14 *Sáchá, comentários à vida moderna,* was written in 1923 by Francisco Manuel de Mello.

CONTEM PORANEA

MINISTÉRIO DA INSTRUÇÃO PÚBLICA

SECRETARIA GERAL

Considerando que a revista literária CONTEMPORANEA tem prestado relevantes serviços á propaganda e difusão da literatura portugueza ;

Attendendo que é necessário estimular iniciativas desta ordem, pelo que nelem e representam ;

Manda o Governo da Republica Portugueza, pelo Ministro da Instrução Pública, que seja dado público testemunho de louvor ao director e editor da referida publicação, respectivamente os cidadãos José Pacheco e Agostinho Fernandes.

Paços do Governo da Republica, 6 de Abril de 1923. — *O Ministro da Instrução Pública, João José de Conceição Camoesas.*

Portaria de Louvor publicada no número 85 — 6 Serie do Diario do Governo de quarta-feira, 11 de Abril de 1923.

numero
OITO
1 9 2 3

PORTUGAL
FUTURISTA

Santa Rita Pintor —José de Almada-Negreiros — Amadeo de Souza-Cardoso

Appollinaire

Mario de Sá-Carneiro —Fernando Pessoa — Raul Leal — Alvaro de Campos

Blaise Cendrars.

Athena magazine

Created to give civilization "a creating end", inspired by "the goddess of harmony and science in art", its first issue (October 1924) had the *Art magazine* subtitle. In the editorial, Pessoa says "one cannot learn how to be an artist. Each of us has within him the Apollo he seeks, and must seek his Athena". The magazine would have five issues released, from October 1924 to February 1925 (the latter only released in June). Some friends were invited to take part in the project, such as Almada, Botto, Ferreira Gomes, Leal, Mário Saa, Montalvor. It also had new writings by Sá-Carneiro and Henrique Rosa; as well as Poe's "The Raven", which Pessoa deems to have translated "rhythmically, to the beat of the original". Deep down, he wished to give his heteronyms a voice through the magazine: Ricardo Reis ("Odes") in #1, the only issue without ads; Álvaro de Campos ("What is Metaphysics?") and the poem "Mário de Sá-Carneiro" in #2; Pessoa himself (some poems) and Campos ("Notes for a Non-Aristotelian Aesthetic") in #3; Caeiro (poems from "Detached Poems") in #5. After that final issue, the magazine ceased publication for lack of funds. Or because it was no longer deemed necessary, as his other Is were now out there for the world to read. He still ponders releasing *Revista de Lisboa,* for which he prepares a summary which would contain Sá-Carneiro's last poems and more works by Raul Leal, Almada Negreiros and himself, besides a translation of Shakespeare's *The Tempest.* But, by then, he was already busying himself with another magazine, this one with businessmen as its target audience.

Revista de comércio e contabilidade

In January 1926, *Revista de Comércio e Contabilidade* was born – headquartered at Rua Coelho da Rocha 16, 1st floor, where Pessoa and his brother-in-law lived. Francisco Caetano Dias (1897-1969) was *administrative director and editor,* as well as *lieutenant of the military administration,* as per Portugal's Commercial Yearbook of 1922. The following year (1923), when he marries Teca, he becomes captain and, later, lieutenant-colonel. He has an (unfinished) degree in economics and accounting and, after retiring, dedicates himself to forensic accounting – for companies and stores such as Corticeira Robinson, Fábrica de Tapeçarias de Portugal and Ouriversaria do Carmo, where he buys jewellery for his wife with a *friend's discount,* as Manuela Nogueira put it. He published books on techniques and reading of balance sheets, was head of accounting at Lisbon's City Hall and even became (in 1962) head of finances of Cia. Portugal e Colónias. His daughter Manuela Nogueira explained that all those activities were a necessity, because *his pay wasn't enough for his family's needs.* The magazine took up the project of Cosmópolis, which Pessoa had conceived for a company and had never taken off. A cursory glance is enough to discern who the text's authors were. Those on commercial techniques, in normal typeface, are his brother-in-law's, while a couple (different in style and theme), as well as every note in italic, are clearly Pessoa's. And it had plenty of ads: Typewriters (Fortuna, Remington, Royal, Smith Premier, Torpedo, Underwood), Tudor accumulators Italiano, J. Anão, Ellans chemical papers, Soennecken writing quills, Cúria soap, Enil inks, and Kardex filing cabinets – fire, theft and error-proof.

The first issue's editorial penned by Pessoa reads "all theory must be conceived so as to be put into practice, and all practice must hold to a theory". Among the texts he wrote there, some strayed a bit from the conventional: "Example of a moral precept: *Do unto others as you would have them do unto you.* Example of a rational precept: *Know thyself.* Example of a practical and less than moral precept: *If you wish to fool someone by way of an envoy, you must first fool the envoy, as he shall then lie with conviction.* Example of a less than wise precept: *He who leaves nothing to chance will do little wrong, but will do precious little.* The first precept is common to several faiths in one way or another. The second is an inscription on a Greek temple[15] and is attributed to a Greek wise man who probably never existed[16]. As for the latter two, the first is from Florentine [Francesco] Guicciardini [1483-1540] and the second from Englishman [George Saville, 1633-1695, marquis of] Halifax". But, after six issues, and despite all the ads, the magazine ceases publication. Pessoa depends on said *commerce* and *accounting* to survive, even though those two topics are foreign to his soul, and he would soon after return to literary editions.

Presença magazine

On the 10th of March 1927, the first issue of *an art and critique pamphlet* is published in Coimbra, headed by João Gaspar Simões, José Régio and Branquinho da Fonseca, plus Adolfo Casais Monteiro (until #26). It was to be *the second modernism* – with Pessoa been responsible for the first, it bears remembering. Thus, there was a continuity link between the generation of 1915, *the most literally aware of all Portuguese literary generations.* Instead of *Orpheu's aesthetic revolution,* this one was a *moral revolution* – as the magazine defined itself. José Régio, head of the movement, signed the first issue's editorial. In the third (April 1917), in an article also signed by Régio, the magazine pays homage to the one held as the greatest figure of Portuguese contemporary literature: *Fernando Pessoa has the makings of a master and is the richest in directions of our so-called modernists.* Régio and Simões travel to Lisbon to meet the master – that one meeting at Montanha, where Pessoa pretends to be Álvaro de Campos. Régio isn't pleased, but from then on exchanges a number of letters with Pessoa (12). Simões has a better understanding of his fickle character, and the two remain close friends until the end, with Pessoa writing him 51 letters (two of which were lost). *Presença* was the magazine which lasted the longest, despite having few ads, with 54 issues between 1927 and 1938; plus two others in a second phase, between 1939 and 1940; and a special issue in 1977, to celebrate its 50th anniversary. Issue #47

15 The Oracle of Delphi.
16 Pessoa erred here, as it was Socrates.

(December 1935) had a plea by José Régio to Salazar's censors: *Allow us to humbly and provisionally exist.* In it, Pessoa publishes a significant part of his oeuvre: The eight poem of Caeiro's "The Keeper of Sheep"; Ricardo Reis' "Odes"; Pessoa's "Scaffolding", "After the fair" (from "Songbook"), "Eros and Psyche"; and Álvaro de Campos' "Maritime Ode", "Any Song", "Written in an Abandoned Travel Book", "Neighbourhood Gazette", "Anniversary" and "Tobacco Shop".

presença
fôlha de arte e crítica
coimbra, julho, 1936

Éste número consagrado a Fernando Pessoa, em quem «presença» se orgulha de ter reconhecido sempre uma das mais ricas e originais individualidades da literatura portuguesa. Não podendo ser o que sonharíamos fôsse, (é bom sempre sonhar mais!) nem sendo a personalidade de Fernando Pessoa para caber quer num número de revista quer num volume ou cento de volumes, «presença» promete nunca deixar de se ocupar do grande poeta. Será mais um modo de se afirmar fiel à missão, de que não desiste, de proclamar e defender quaisquer valores espirituais em geral, estéticos em particular, contra tôdas as antipatias violentas mas impotentes que se lhes opõem.

ano décimo 48 volume segundo

A Revista

In 1929's *A Revista,* by Solução Editora, he publishes Álvaro de Campos' *Delay* in issue #1, and excerpts of *Disquiet* in issues #2 and #4, besides a critique by Campos of Pessoa's "The Mariner". The editor was his friend José Pacheco, who soon gave up to relaunch *Contemporânea.* According to some specialists, Pessoa had a stake in the magazine – due to the fact that it was printed in the same typography as *Athena.* But, taking his personal finances into account, it's rather unlikely.

Norma magazine

In 1935, close to death, he makes plans for a final magazine which would be titled *Norma,* a fortnightly magazine of literature and sociology, which was to be released at *Orpheu's* 20th anniversary. He even drafted the first issue's contents, which would begin with the article "Fátima". In an editorial he scribbled, he explains: "The word *Norma* [norm] which I chose as the magazine's title, means *rule,* as we know; not just any rule, but a mental rule, imposed by the individual upon himself. If anyone infers that *norm* doesn't mean that, then it certainly won't be someone as tolerant ["liberal" as a variant] as myself who shall deny him the right of believing that". But he wouldn't have the time to carry it out.

Newspapers

Pessoa also wrote for newspapers. He wrote a lot, in fact. An often unstable relationship. In an incomplete text, "The hour of the Devil", this is how the Devil replies to a provocation by one D. Marco: "But let us leave that, which is purely journalistic. Let us remember I am the Devil. Thus, let us be diabolical". Hardly surprising from one who believes "journalism has the direct influence of the inferior arts in men". On account of some butting of heads with newspapers throughout his life, he says "there is a near complete split, if not utterly complete, between journalism and intellectual superiority"; or "the public doesn't wish for the truth, only for the the lie that pleases it the most".

> When one says journalism is akin to priesthood, it is well said, but the meaning is not the one which is usually attributed to the phrase. Journalism is a priesthood, because it has the religious influence of a priest; it is no priesthood in a moral sense, for there is none in journalism, nor could there ever be.
>
> "The Journalist's Argument", Fernando Pessoa

A memorable episode in his life began when, on the 4th of April 1915, *O Jornal* began publication in Lisbon. He wrote ten texts for it, four literary reviews and six chronicles – alternating with writer Albino Espiridião de Menezes and journalist Nuno de Oliveira. According to cousin Eduardo Freitas da Costa, he too (the cousin), Tomás de Almeida and Fernando de Carvalho wrote there. The first of those chronicles (5th of April) says that "politics, religion and social life are but inferior, plebeian degrees of aesthetics". The second (11th of August), concerned "the Portuguese's excess of imagination". The fourth (5th of April) was about "the Great War" taking place in Europe. The fifth (18th of April) concerned "popular protests". So far, so good, although they were controversial opinions. But the sixth[17] (21st of April) made reference to "my friend João do Amaral [a monarchical journalist and editor of *Aqui Del-Rei!* magazine]... a terrific lad, intelligent, even" and other figures from the right such as Crispim (Eugénio Severino de Azevedo), who had ganged up against *Orpheu.* In it, he rails against a recently inaugurated Monarchical Centre of

17 Pessoa would write a seventh about *the sadness of celebrities.* It remained unpublished and said: "It takes great coarseness to be at ease with celebrity".

Lisbon and compares its members to Lisbon's drivers, who were "bad drivers due to a lack of training".

> When the automobile industry appeared, it necessitated the creation of the driver class. No one but the odd clipped plebeian spoke against the initial lack of driving skill of the drivers. They were still learning the ropes – which is natural – and making a living – which is respectable. They then became aware of their art and, though most still drive badly, the fact is that they are most certainly drivers now. Now, as for the criterion of human tolerance which is applicable to drivers… it would be a sad day if it weren't also applicable to monarchic artists.

It wasn't his best idea. The next day, drivers who didn't understand that the object of his irony was the monarchists and not themselves, organized a loud protest in front of the newspaper's premises. As for the monarchists, who still felt the sting of hostility in Portugal, they reacted no less ferociously. Members of the Carbonari, one of the largest Portuguese secret societies, wanted revenge. The Irmãos Unidos restaurant was besieged by people looking for *Orpheu loons.* But Pessoa had already sneaked away through the back door, taking refuge in a chicken coop at Praça da Figueira. This was how he justified his retreat to painter and ceramicist Jorge Nicholson Moore Barradas (1894-1971): "You see… I don't have the constitution to endure the beating that was to be administered". The following day, instead of Pessoa's chronicle, Boavida Portugal and Baramoura Trajoso, the editors of *O Jornal,* published *A necessary explanation,* which read: *Due to the lack of forbearance evinced by the rude writings of Mr. Fernando Pessoa, which were printed in error in these pages yesterday, the gentleman is no longer a collaborator for this newspaper.*

A list of newspapers and magazines he wrote for

Throughout his life, Pessoa wrote for 50 different newspapers and magazines, publishing 134 prose texts and 300 poems. The National Library holds part of those writings in envelopes 135-135D.

- *A Águia*
- *A Capital*
- *Ação*
- *A Galera*
- *A Ideia Nacional*
- *A Informação*
- *A Renascença*
- *A Revista* (of Revista Editorial)
- *A Revista* (of Solução Editora)
- *Athena*
- *A Vida Portuguesa*
- *Centauro*

– *Contemporânea*
– *Descobrimento*
– *Diário de Lisboa*
– *É Real!*
– *Exílio*
– *Fama*
– *Folhas de Arte*
– *Fradique*
– *Girassol*
– *Ilustração Portuguesa*
– *Jornal do Comércio e das Colônias*
– *Litoral*
– *Mensagem*[18]
– *Momento*
– *Mundo Português*
– *Notícias Ilustrado*
– *O Heraldo*
– *O Imparcial*
– *O Jornal*
– *O Raio*
– *Orpheu*
– *Portugal*
– *Portugal Futurista*
– *Presença*
– *República*
– *Ressurreição*
– *Revista de Comércio e Contabilidade*
– *Revista Portuguesa*
– *Revolução*
– *Sol – Diário Independente*
– *Solução Editora*
– *SW (Sudoeste)*
– *Teatro: Jornal d'Arte*
– *Teatro: Revista de crítica*
– *Terra Nossa*
– *The Athenaeum*
– *The Durban School Magazine*
– *The Natal Mercury*

18 According to the editors, the title represented *an homage of our generation to the one Portuguese poet who can be compared to Camões, even though* Mensagem *magazine isn't a magazine in homage to Fernando Pessoa.* The magazine ran for six issues, having changed the title in the second to *Manifesto de uma geração* (Manifesto of a generation).

Davos sum, non Oedipus
(I am Davos and not Oedipus) Terence

ALEISTER CROWLEY

The man and the hour are one
When God makes and history is made.
The rest is flesh, whose dust
The earth awaits.
Message ("King João, The First"), Fernando Pessoa

The worst man in England

In 1930, Pessoa met "the English poet, mage, astrologer and *mystery* vulgarly known as Aleister Crowley. Edward Alexander Crowley, born in Leamington Spa (12/10/1875), was the son of a brewer of the Brotherhood of Plymouth (a Christian sect dissident of the Church of England) and *a dull pious woman* who was constantly upset with the son she considered the Beast itself. The Bible was the only book he ever read during his childhood. He was known by many names: Allick, Antichrist, Warlock of Thelema, Count Vladimir, Devil, Lord Bolekine, Master Therion (in his books), Perdurabo, Svareff, or just 666. "He who is endowed with intelligence calculates the number of a man, and the number is 666". In occultism, *666 is the light of the sun.* And it probably hadn't gone unnoticed by Pessoa that, in 1666, father António Vieira had been inspired by Bandarra and the prophet Daniel to declare 666 to be a sign of the Apocalypse itself, which would be followed by Redemption. As a child, Crowley would spit into holy water and martyred flies in defiance of God. He is alleged to have killed a native in the Far East to drink his blood and feel the pleasure of something he hadn't yet tasted. He was given to sexual excesses and alcohol, and, from 1919 onwards, to drugs too (cocaine, heroine, mescaline), having also initiated friends like Aldous Huxley – who wrote *Heaven and Hell* and *Doors of Perception* under the influence of those drugs. He was a contradictory figure, and his fellow countryman (William) Somerset Maugham (1874-1965) described him in acerbic terms in *The Magician.* With all those predicates, Crowley was considered by British newspapers as *the worst man in England.*

Crowley had three passions: Rock climbing – he climbed mount Kanchenjunga of the Himalayan mountain range, with no equipment or oxygen tanks; chess, in which he actually won some minor competitions; and above all black magic. At the age of 20, he already knows Greek and Latin. He doesn't finish his studies in Cambridge, studies Buddhism in China and changes his name to Aleister. In 1898, he began his initiation into the Hermetic Order of the Golden Dawn, founded two years prior by MacGregor Mathers, in which he assumed St. Rabelais' motto – *do what thou wilt shall be whole of the Law.* But he soon comes to despise it. He then fancies himself the reincarnation of Edward Kelly, John Dee's psychic and Queen Elizabeth I's astrologer. To his eyes, the sister of one of his friends would be the Scarlet Woman – the one sitting on the seven-headed and ten-horned beast, holding a gold chalice with the impurities of her prostitution in Apocalypse (XVII, 3:8). He would marry her in 1902 and make her his assistant. But life was cruel to the woman, Rose Edith Kelly, who became an alcoholic after the loss of the daughter she had with Crowley and died in an asylum. The Scarlet Woman then became Maria Tereza Ferreira de Miramar (his second wife), followed by Hanni Jäger. Crowley claims to be the latest incarnation of count Alessandro di Cagliostro, creator of the Egyptian Order of Freemasons in Vienna, who ended his days in a Roman jail, where he kept repeating the same sentence – *I wish to end among the roses, as I loved them during my childhood.* In Cairo, he comes into contact with Aiwass, minister of Hoor-Paar-Kraat – a superior being who dictated him the book *Liber Al vel Legis* ('Book of Law' in pseudo-Latin). Commentators of Aiwass' oeuvre claimed he was Horus, the Egyptian god of Heaven – represented in form of a hawk, with the sun and the moon for eyes. During World War I, he is admitted to the famous Lodge 33, which had an influential presence among the German high command. In 1929, he is expelled from Italy by Mussolini and took refuge in Fontainebleau. The following year, he'd also be kicked out of France, where newspapers described him as *an English Rasputin.* In the USA, he wrote an opera, *Sexualis;* and, in 67 uninterrupted hours, the dramatic poem *Tannhäuser* – about the life of that wandering German minstrel (1205-1268) who ended up converted into a legend by his people. After the end of World War II, he was considered a German spy, but prudently claimed to be an agent of the English Intelligence Service. As if all that wasn't enough, Crowley also claimed to confer with forces from beyond. To Pessoa, above all, he was a Freemason in the 33rd degree of the Ancient and Accepted Scottish Rite. All documented by Luís Miguel Rosa, in his important monograph on the matter.

Their meeting

On the 6th of March 1917, Pessoa ordered Crowley's *Book 777* from editor Frank Hollings. But their relationship would take another 12 years to actually come about, beginning on the 4th of December 1929, when he sent a check to Mandrake Press (London) to pay for two books he had ordered – among them the autobiography *The Confessions of Aleister Crowley.* In the exchange, he adds: "If you have any means of reaching Mr. Aleister Crowley, as I'm sure you do [he was the publishing house's owner], perhaps you'd be so kind as to inform him that his horoscope is incorrect; if, according to his calculations, he was born at 11 p.m., 16m, 39s, on the 12th of October 1875, with Aries 11 in his half-sky, with its associated ascendant and cusps". The Englishman replies a week later, confessing to knowing little of astrology and thanking him for the information. In it, and in the subsequent letters, he addresses him as *care frater* (dear brother), begins with the motto of the Abbey of Thelema and ends with his own, *love is the law, love under will.* In a reply (15/12/1924) to *carissime frater,* Pessoa sends him his *English poems* and, in a *post scriptum,* asks him to "kindly request your typist to detach Portugal from Spain".

As Pessoa tells him he cannot travel (letter dated 29/05/1930), Crowley says he shall visit him, but to tell no one about it. In his diary, Crowley notes: *I was forced to depart to Lisbon post-haste, so as to establish a delegation of the Order under the responsibility of* Dom *Fernando Pessoa.* On the 28th of August, a telegram says: Crowley arriving by Alcantara please meet. The ship arrived late from Vigo and had to stop close to the harbour, due to dense fog. "Let D. Sebastião come with the mist", and arrives in Lisbon, not on the expected 1st of September, but a day later. Crowley notes in his diary the impression the city makes on him: *God once tried to wake up Lisbon with an earthquake; he had to give up, as it wasn't worth it.* Finally with feet on dry land, that large, odd man wearing a black cloak advances upon a trembling Pessoa and tells him: *What was the idea of sending that fog upon me?* But, at that point in his life, Pessoa could scarcely have a hold on his life, let alone the weather.

Crowley first stayed at Hotel L'Europe, and then at Hotel Paris do Estoril, sharing a room with a suspicious lady, the (supposedly) German Hanni Larissa Jäger, 19 years of age, whom he had met as she served as a model in the studio of fellow German painter Steiner. The girl who was responsible for the end of Crowley's second marriage. Of *fully loaded heredity,* as Crowley is to have confided in Pessoa, although probably not in those terms, as the expression had already been used in old texts by Pessoa. They had lunch on Sunday, the 7th of September, and Pessoa marvelled at Hanni, to the point he wrote an erotic poem three days later, comparing her "pert bosom" to "two dawning mounds"; and wondering in the last verse "o, hunger, when shall I eat?". Nothing but a metaphor, of course. She also enjoys getting to know him, and, under the notes Crowley sends Pessoa, she writes sentences like *you are wonderful,* signing as *Anu,* not short for Hanni, but, as she insists on saying in letters, the part of the anatomy favoured by her lover: The anus. In a note to Pessoa (14/10/1930), she says she cannot accept the fact that one were to ever doubt her virginity, claiming she also wishes she had been born a boy. On the 30th of October, she declares that Crowley was, *in fact, two people: Himself, and a brother. They are twins playing each other's roles. Now that the evil one is dead, as was his due, the secret has been unveiled. But, then, which of them have I loved?* With characters such as these two, one really should expect everything.

Crowley's mysterious disappearance

On the 25th of September 1930, Crowley disappears. Without paying the hotel bills, as usual. According to the 27/11 edition of *Diário de Notícias,* he was to have committed suicide at the cliff of Mata-cães, in Cascais. London psychic A.V. Peters declares having psychographed a communication during a trance, according to which Crowley claimed to have been pushed down the cliff by an agent of the Roman Catholic Church. Scotland Yard sends an agent to Lisbon to investigate. In the place of the alleged murder, journalist and poet Augusto Ferreira Gomes found a cigarette case which allegedly belonged to Crowley, as well as a letterhead from the first of the hotels he had stayed at (L'Europe):

> L G P Year 14 Sun in Libra
> I cannot live without you. "The other Mouth from Hell"[1]...
> It shall catch me
> – and shall not be as warm as yours.
> Hijos.
> Tu Li Yu

A note dated the 21st of September says that Crowley wishes *to do a suicide stunt to annoy Hanni,* and ends with the sentence *arrange details with Pessoa.* But that wasn't all. He also aimed to escape the creditors which were chasing him for having bankrupted his publishing house. According to family members (brother-in-law and niece) and (almost all) commentators of his oeuvre, Pessoa himself is to have taken part in that stunt, choosing the place and all – perhaps because, on the 4th of January of that same year, poet Guilherme de Faria (1907-1929) had killed himself there. The plot also included Brazilian Pedro Carvalho Monteiro, a friend of Crowley who lived in Sintra and was the owner of the famous Quinta da Regaleira. Perhaps from when he travelled to Sintra to meet with chess player Eduardo Pelleu, who had a house there. Also his assiduous companion Ferreira Goes, coincidentally connected to the newspaper which published the disappearance; the same one

1 Boca do Inferno is a maritime cave in a nearby cliff, so called because it never returns the bodies of its victims.

who found the cigarette case – exotic, eastern, which could only belong to a man such as Crowley. When asked to identify the object, Pessoa declared it as Crowley's – when he knew full full well it had been lent by his brother-in-law Caetano Dias, who had purchased it in Zanzibar. The version is corroborated by the object's true owner to a number of friends. Pessoa deciphers the mysterious note (abridged):

> The year 14 is clearly the present year (1930). I don't know what LGP might be. But likely Mrs. Jäger's artistic name. Hijos I also don't know what it might mean,[2] and can only suppose it to be a magic word. Tu Li Yu is the name of a Chinese wise man, who lived three thousand years before Christ,[3] and whom Crowley claimed to be a reincarnation of. Important: Sun in Libra.

The conclusion was that it was all a fraud, as Pessoa explained: "The sun enters the sign of Libra at 18 hours and 36 minutes of the 23rd of September", concluding: "An astrologer might put up false dates; what is unacceptable is to forge a date written in astrological signs". He later declares to *Notícias Ilustrado* (05/10) to having seen "Crowley or his ghost turning the corner at Café La Gare" on the 24th of September; and, the following day, that "Crowley or his ghost went into Tabacaria Inglesa". Interpol soon found out that Crowley placidly crossed the border at Vilar Formoso on the 23rd of September, headed for Germany, where his lover had departed to, understandably incensed. Three days before Crowley's departure, following the advice of a friend of Pessoa's (Lawrence Shepard Armstrong, the American consul in Lisbon), he departed from Terreiro do Paço in *S.S. Werra* to Bremen, after the consul provided him with tickets. But only after bidding the poet goodbye. At the end of the year, Pessoa was still amusing himself with the episode, saying in a letter to Gaspar Simões (06/12/1930) that "Master Therion is gone, and none knows if he committed suicide (as at first I believed), if he simply went into hiding, or if he was murdered (an odd proposition, to be sure, but, as it appears, it is – or at least was – the one put forth by the English policeman who investigated the case)". Later, he would still translate some of his poems from which, according to Helena Barbas, he left out some epigraphs and *overtly erotic images,* or even changing *the meaning of certain passages.* Among them, "Hymn to Pan", the preface of Master Therion's *Magic in Theory and Practice,* published in *Presença* magazine (#33, July-October 1931), which ends thus:

> Flesh to thy bone, flower to thy rod.
> With hoofs of steel I race on the rocks
> Through solstice stubborn to equinox.
> And I rave; and I rape and I rip and I rend

2 Pessoa knew full well it was an imperfect variant of *Hanni Jäger Save Our Souls.*

3 Actually, it was just a phonetic play on *toodle-oo.*

Everlasting, world without end,
Mannikin, maiden, Maenad, man,
In the might of Pan.
Io Pan! Io Pan Pan! Pan! Io Pan!

The true end of Crowley

Pessoa wrote part of the ten chapters of the crime novel he had envisioned, "The Mouth of Hell", in direct reference to the place of Crowley's alleged suicide. In it, an English detective tries to describe the suicide. But he soon abandons the project and, by the end of the following year (1931), holds no further correspondence with Crowley. Shortly thereafter, he gets a letter demanding a promised translation, which also reads: *After committing suicide, I changed residence to Germany.* Pessoa reports it in a letter to Gaspar Simões (01/11/1931): "After committing suicide, Crowley changed residence to Germany". He would then eventually return to England, squalid, his head shaved and with a white goatee, and makes ends meet with tremendous sacrifices: He writes horoscopes, sells pills of an elixir of life made of his own semen, and elaborates a *thoth tarot,* painted by (Marguerite) Frieda Harris (1877-1962), which remains in use in Europe to this day. He spends the rest of his days in his hometown of Hastings, poor and all but friendless. On the 1st of December 1947, he utters his final words, *I am perplexed,* after which he dies. Later, a photo of his would appear on the cover of The Beatles' *Sgt. Pepper's Lonely Hearts Club Band,* in the illustrious company of names such as Bob Dylan, Carl Jung, Einstein, Fred Astaire, Laurel & Hardy, Karl Marx, Lawrence of Arabia, Marilyn Monroe, Marlon Brando and Shirley Temple; besides Hitler, who is supposedly hidden behind Ringo Starr's drawing.

Ad astra per aspera
(Through hardship to the stars) Latin proverb

THE ESOTERIC WORLD

I am the Black Christ
He who neither believes nor loves.
First Faust (The Mystery of the World, XX), Fernando Pessoa

Psychic gifts

Pessoa loved the occult sciences. According to sister Teca, he tried to know peoples' character by the shape of their head, read their palms, and tried to hypnotize himself, looking intently at a source of light. That passion of his would endure well past his childhood. From 1912 to 1914, as we've seen, Pessoa lived with his aunt Anica. The "revolutionary"; as he called her, was an aristocrat, a cultured woman "of nervous temper", with a shock of white hair (already by the age of 50), and wrote deplorable love sonnets. She was also very much into the beyond, and was the one who gave Pessoa a taste for the mysterious. At night, she conducted psychic sessions to communicate (or try to) with the dead, using a board brought by her nephew. Very popular at the end of the 20th century, said board had a pencil resting on it, which was used by spirits (or the hands of those sitting at the table) to transmit messages from beyond. Reminiscing about those times, and considering himself but an initiate, he laments the fact that he was "a delaying element in the semi-psychic sessions". In a letter to his aunt (24/06/1916), who was living in Switzerland at the time, he confesses: "By the end of March (if I am not mistaken), I became a psychic. Imagine that. I was sitting at home at night, having come from A Brasileira, when I felt the need to literally grasp a quill and place it upon a piece of paper. There was more curiosity than fear, even though some things are definitely intimidating. What bothers me a little is the fact that I know what it all means, more or less. Do not think it madness. It isn't: In fact, just so you know, in matters *of mental balance,* I am as well as I've ever been. Besides, the very dawning of such faculties in me came with a mysterious feeling of isolation and abandonment which fills me with bitterness to the bottom of my soul", which is why he considered himself "a prophet of the Devil, or a black bird". Aunt Anica would only see him again at the end of 1923, but, by then, all traces of psychic ability in him had vanished. Yvette Centeno brought a small document to my attention, having found it in his estate, in which he claims that *psychic abilities diminish intellectual faculties, and should therefore not be exercised.*

According to astrologer Paulo Cardoso, 2,700 *papers in his Chest concern astrology, and nothing in his oeuvre was due to chance*. "From the study of metaphysics to sciences, I began to concern myself with more violent spirits" and "spent terrified nights hunched over mystical tomes". In an attempt at systematizing that evolution, Antóno Quadros suggested a first phase, *the philosophocal stage* (1905/6-1915/6), followed by a *neo-pagan stage* which lasts until 1920, after which came a *gnostic stage,* which would last until the end of his life. José Manuel Anes simplifies, considering there to have been a *First Esoteric Phase,* which lasted until 1920, with an emphasis on astrology and theosophy, and a *Second Esoteric Phase,* with emphasis on gnosis, alchemy, magic, the Kabbalah, Templar, Rosicrucian and Freemason order. Pessoa himself confessed to feeling attracted to the mystical world, claiming his fate "belongs to another law, the existence of which little Ophelia can scarcely fathom, and is ever subordinate to the obedience of masters who neither suffer nor forgive".

> Question – What do you believe in?
> Answer – I am blind.
> Q – Who are you?
> A – I am naked.
> Q – What do you have?
> A – Only myself.
> Q – Do you wish to be taken in by this order to see the light in it?
> A – I do, if you will show it to me.
> Q – Do you wish to be clad in it?
> A – I do, if you dress me with it.
> Q – Do you wish to have safe harbour in it?
> A – I do, if it is granted me.
>
> *Initiation rite*, Fernando Pessoa

Automatic writing

During that initial phase, he begins to practice "automatic writing", going so far as psychographing a text from his uncle Manuel Gualdino da Cunha (who had passed away on the 25th of January 1898), a "signature I well knew" – communicating with his esteemed uncle but once before letting him return to his eternal rest. "Who is this?", he asks in distress, "who is drawing me

Kabbalistic or Masonic drawings, or writing me numbers as replies?". Other times, the spirits answer in an infantile writing to questions about businesses, literature, whether or not he should move to another place, or his (lack of a) sexual life. "This and that, nothing of any real interest or importance" were the "anonymous, so to speak" communications which he could not comprehend, "things which perturb me somewhat" – according to the spirits themselves, as no communication has permission to be correct in all details. He asks questions out loud, and the spirits reply via his hand:

> – Yes. No: I say it because it's true.
> – You don't know any of them.
> – No. Totally wrong.
> – I am telling the truth. No mouth speaks lies.
> – Never question me.
> – There are two facts to consider: What you think and what I know. Blend them both, and make the truth appear.
> – Your fate is far too elevated for me to utter it.
> – Fate, the nameless God.
> – You shall be arrested in 1917.
> – Maggot. Enough! Brilliant maggot.
> – Now go and work, post-haste.
> – Leave.
> – No more.

Some of those psychographed texts are scratched; so many, and so often, do not appear to be true communications with the beyond. He consults with a friend who was "an occultist and a magnetizer" in search of an explanation for the phenomenon, one Fernando de Lacerda, a renowned figure of the occult at the time, according to Gaspar Simões and Ángel Crespo; or Mariano Santana, according to cousin Eduardo Freitas da Costa. Whoever the friend was, from the information that one of his given numbers has four figures, he concludes that there must be five people in the room. Four of them were but listeners. "Who is the fifth person in this room, who stretches out his arm and interrupts us?". He is satisfied with the answer: It was himself, which confirmed it wasn't "a form of autosuggestion, but genuine psychic ability". The spirits thus assured him, claiming there was both a substance and a shape. *The shape comes from you and the substance from me. No communication is entirely mine. None is entirely your creation.* Then, little by little, Pessoa begins to discard automatic writing, which becomes increasingly less frequent from 1916-1918 onwards, featuring only next to poems and prose texts.

> Whose is the glance
> That peeks through my eyes?
> When I think I see,

Who keeps seeing
While I am thinking?
Along what roads follow,
Not my sad steps,
But the reality
Of my having steps with myself?

Sometimes, in the dimness
Of my room, when I
Scarcely exist for my
Very own self in soul,
The Universe changes
Directions in me.

Episodes/The mummy (III), Fernando Pessoa

Astral sight

His "writing psychic ability" is replaced by a "clairvoyant psychic ability", and he soon begins to experiment with "that which occultists call *astral sight* and *etheric sight"* – in which his eyes turn all substances to ether. He closes his eyes "and there is a succession of small paintings, very fast, very clear (as clear as anything from the outside world"). He even senses the impending death of his friend Sá-Carneiro in the distant Paris, and writes him a letter about it: "The fact is that your great crisis was a crisis of my own, and I felt it, as I've explained, not just through your letters, but also telepathically via the astral projection (as they say) of your suffering". That letter would never be sent, as Sá-Carneiro found the repose he so wished in "the *Mater dolorosa* of the anguishes of the shy and the sadnesses of the scorned". He can also see "some people's magnetic aura"; his own, "radiating from the hands"; and others' – like at Brasileira, "the ribs of a fellow through his coat and skin". Then, his own body begins to rebel against him. His right arm moves with a will of its own. His entire body "drops to one side, as if magnetized" or drunk – which, given the rivers of alcohol he was prone to imbibing, would hardly be surprising.

The very birth of his heteronyms was, according to him, a manifestation of those psychic abilities. "I know enough of the occult sciences to understand the so-called superior senses awakening in me, for an end known only to the unknown Master, who in this way initiates me, imposing that superior existence upon me, and causing me a suffering greater than any I've ever experienced, as well as the deep sorrow that comes with acquiring these high faculties". He also knows that "mystics of ill hour and sacrifice can at least feel the magical presence of mystery with their bodies and in their everyday lives". He writes "Um caso de mediunidade" (A case of psychic powers), in which he theorizes about "communicating spirits", "dancing epidemics of the Middle Ages" and how "spiritism should be forbidden". He analyses his own situation and concludes it is a "morbid state", declaring that "psychic abilities result from a mental imbalance, not unlike that which is produced by alcoholism, often the prodromal state of declared madness", noting down episodes of "hysteroneurasthenia"and "auto-suggestion". Those visions manifest in him in manifold ways. Once, as he gazed upon a mirror, he realized "my face disappears and the shape of a bearded man appears – four in all show up". One might imagine the first three were Alberto Caeiro, Ricardo Reis and Álvaro de Campos. The fourth, Raphael Baldaya (who had "a long beard"); or likely António Mora (who "had a white beard"). His heteronyms. People who existed solely in his imagination. As he finished that letter to aunt Anica (24/06/1916), in which he retells those episodes, he says: "Oh well, whatever will be, will be".

> Once more I see you,
> But, oh, I cannot see myself!
> The magic mirror where I always looked the same has shattered,
> And in each fateful fragment I see only a piece of me –
> A piece of you and of me!
>
> *Lisbon Revisited (1926)*, Fernando Pessoa

Astrology

Astrology is a doctrine which allows one to better understand Man and nature; forming alongside magic and alchemy the foundations of esoterism – thus his natural interest in it. In a note from 1906, he already confessed his "great love for all things spiritual, for the mysterious and the obscure", but his first astrological texts would only be written in 1908. In one of them, he says "the number representative of evil is number 1, because it is what divides; the number representative of good is number 3, because it is what unites". Three, just like his main heteronyns – Caeiro, Reis and Campos. Through the stars, he seeks to better understand his past and his future. "We shall have great financial losses, with an absence of amusement and outer glow, a lack of help, and perhaps even betrayal from friends. Venus is opposed to *Pars fortuna* in the 2nd, which intensifies the evil action against money"[1]. But "astrology is but the name we give to a facet of imagination; novels and the treatise on astrology are novels about different subjects, but not as different as the swashbuckling novel

1 The text was written on Friday, the 16th of August, with no indication of the year. Judging by the calendar, it was likely 1918, by excluding years in which Friday was on the 16th – namely 1912 (a long time before he began writing such texts) and 1929 (much later).

is from the urban novel, or the crime novel than the romance". In February 1915, after aunt Anica had already travelled to Switzerland, he decides to try his hand at writing horoscopes, penning 318 of them and publishing three: One for a woman (1916), one for friend Raul Leal (also 1916) and one for an unknown person (1934). The Chest also contains a list of finished and unfinished horoscopes – 98 documents, in all. From 1916 on, he also draws astral maps for characters like Cesário Verde, Chopin, John III, Sebastião, Goethe, Isaac Newton, Marinetti, Napoleon, Shakespeare, Victor Hugo, Yeats; friends like Alberto da Cunha Dias, Almada Negreiros, Amadeu de Souza Cardoso, Armando Côrtes-Rodrigues, João Camoesas, Raul da Costa, cousin Vitoriano Braga; heteronyms – Caeiro, Reis and Campos; events, such as the French Revolution, and even entities like Portugal (several, in search of the right one) or *Orpheu* – its date of birth was "the 26th of March 1916, at 7pm, 1st issue

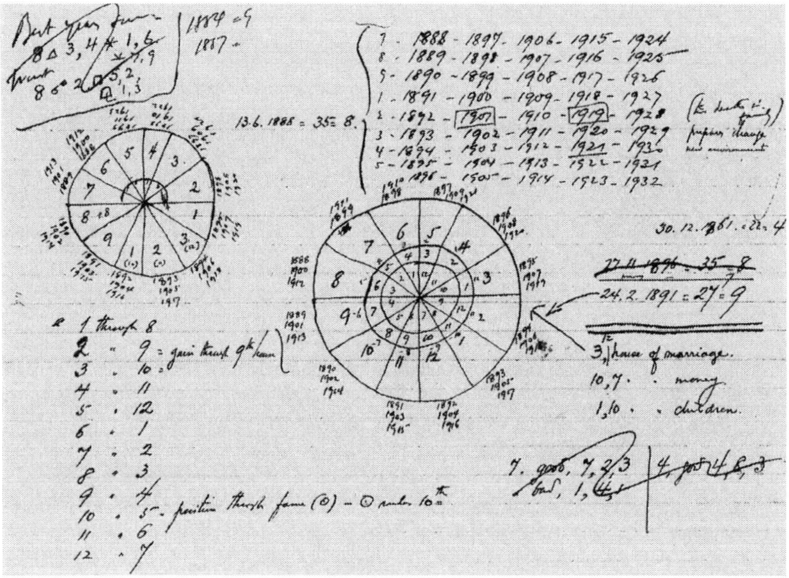

Pessoa's astrological calculations

sold". In the Chest, there is also a *Treatise on astrology,* signed by Raphael Baldaya; a *System of astrology* and *Introduction to the study of occultism;* as well as a text in English in which he attempts to discover the celestial body which shall be responsible for his death (abridged):

> What can be considered the fatal aspect in my horoscope? As a matter of opinion, the giver of life belongs to the sun, with moon and ascendant, which are those freest of malefic aspects; and, when a definitely malefic aspect affects that freer point, death occurs. According to this criterion, the giver of life is the sun; as both the moon and

the ascendant are affected by Saturn, respectively by the conjunction and the square. Which of the sun's aspects can be considered obscure? If we consider the ascendant as a definer of life in general, we should then seek the malefic aspects of the ascendant.

Essays on Astrology, Fernando Pessoa

Theosophy

Pessoa was also fascinated by that set of mystical or initiatory religious doctrines. In a letter to Sá-Carneiro (06/12/1915), he says: "Theosophy terrifies me with its mystery and occult grandeur". "I know the system's essence. It shook me to a point I wouldn't believe possible with any other religious system. The extraordinarily vast character of this religion-philosophy; the notion of strength, of dominion, of superior and extra-human knowledge present in the works of theosophy greatly disturbed me". "The possibility that there, in theosophy, might reside the truth, has taken hold over me". "The real meaning of initiation is that this visible world we live in is a symbol and a shadow, that this life we know through the senses is a death and a slumber, or, in other words, what we see is an illusion". He realises that "Man must discover on his own what the symbols show, as, in so doing, he shall live their lives, instead of limiting himself to comprehending the words they are shown in"; and warns that those topics "are not meant to be administered to any individual but he who has been prepared to received them. That preparation was and is called initiation".

The movement is created by Helena Petrovna Hahn – prematurely born in Ekaterinoslav (Russia) on the 30th of July (12th of August, according to the Russian calendar) 1831. Granddaughter of princess Helena Dolgotouki of the Romanoff bloodline, after she married the old general Nikifor Blavatsky (in 1848), governor of the province of Lirivan, she starts to sign her name just as Helena Blavatsky. But she would leave her husband after only three months of marriage, to live a stormy life. She supports Garibaldi in Italy (1866), works with spirits in Cairo (from 1870 to 1872), founds the Theosophical Society in New York (September 1875), takes the five vows of Buddhism in Ceylon, and returns to London to die in 1891. A woman of peculiar psychic constitution, she appeared to write what was dictated to her by superior entities. As the story goes, she could do so in Greek, Latin, Hebrew, Sanskrit and other exotic languages, which she wasn't even able to read in her normal state. She had the gift to communicate with invisible worlds, including that of the dead. She "undeniably got a message and a mission from unknown superior beings". Pessoa translates *The voice of silence and other select fragments of the book of golden precepts* in 1915 for Livraria Clássica Editora, and also *Light over the path* and *Karma* from one of her disciples, MC (the initials of Mabel Collins, 1851-1927).

From 1915 on, he oversees and translates *Theosophical and esoteric collection* for Clássica Editora, and during the course of that year also manages to translate *Ideals of theosophy,* by Annie Wood Besant – born in London (1847), married to the vicar of Sibsey, Frank Besant, who she soon split from; she was sentenced for obscenity, having published a book in favour of birth control (1877), joined the freethinker Charles Bradlaugh (1833-1891) and adhered to socialism as she associated with Bernard Shaw. After embracing Blavatsky's theosophy, she founded the Central Hindu College (1897) and joined the fight for India's self-determination, preaching that freedom is always acquired through love, and was arrested for it. She presided over the English session of the Theosophical Society and died in Aydar, India (1933). Besant adopted as her son the child who would one day become one of the greatest Indian philosophers, Krishnamurti Jiddu.

In 1915, he also managed to translate Charles Webster Leadbeater's *Compendium of Theosophy;* and, in 1916, from the same author, *Invisible helpers* and *Clairvoyance.* Leadbeater was an extraordinarily prolific writer, with more than a dozen important works to his name. Born in England (1847), he came to Brazil as a child, where his father got a job in a railroad company. Back in his home country, he received the sacrament of the Anglican Church (1878), adopted theosophy (1883), became a vegetarian and became the disciple of Jinarajadasa, in Ceylon. In Aydar, he teaches theosophy and English to Besant's adoptive son (1903). He investigates his previous lives and concludes he is meant to be a vessel for lord Maitreya (or Christ), the World's Instructor, a long-awaited event for theosophists. In the end, Leadbeater was anointed bishop in Australia and passed away in Sydney (1937). From 1913 on, Pessoa writes his first esoteric poems about these themes, mainly in English. In a letter to Sá-Carneiro (06/02/1915), he considers that theosophy contains "the high Christian principles"; and confesses in a letter to Gaspar Simões (26/10/1930) that "the same cloud hangs over the five poems which comprise what I call BEYOND-GOD"[2].

From my notion of the world
I fell...
Beyond-God! Beyond-God! Dark calmness...
Flare of the unknown...
All has a different meaning, o soul,
Even meaning-having itself...

Beyond-God IV, The Fall, Fernando Pessoa

2 In all caps, in the original.

But, little by little, the appeal of the movement's creator is lost, and the scant esteem for Blavatsky is reflected on her disciples. On one of them, Irish writer William Butler Yeats (1865-1939), Nobel prize in Literature in 1923, Pessoa had the following to say in *Ultimatum:* "Out with you, Yeats of the Celtic Mists, spinning 'round a sign with no directions, sack of dirty secrets beached after the shipwreck of English symbolism". Defined at times as a misunderstood martyr of the 19th century (according to Mário Roso de Luna), Pessoa had no doubt whatsoever: "Madame Blavatsky was a confusing, fraudulent spirit".

Initiation rites

From 1920 on, now a more mature man, he began to develop other occult interests. In notes for an *Essay on initiation,* he says magic seeks to "transcend intellect via power", and that "gnosis transcends the intellect via a superior intellect". That gnosis results in a religious and initiatory movement which preached salvation through spiritual knowledge, freeing Man from the earthly realm and leading him to superior planes. He also takes up alchemy – the union of opposites, a science of holy art which seeks the transmutation of bodies on account of their spiritualization; except, and *despite what has been said* (specifically, comments by Kuzawsk and Centeno), *the poet of* Message *was never an alchemist,* according to Manuel J. Gambe. Centeno would later confirm to having been but *an attentive* reader concerning that topic. He was equally fascinated by the Kaballah. Pessoa defined himself as "faithful to the secret tradition of Israel (the Holy Kaballah)", "source of all enlightenment". In a letter to Gaspar Simões (16/10/1930), he sends a poem which he describes as a dramatic interpretation of "transgressive magic" and reminds him that "if, for any reason, you deem best not to publish it [in *Presença],* then do not do so". The following letter (22/10/1930), he gives his reasons: "It might very well be that those topics were repulsive or unpleasant to you"; and, in the following one (26/10/1930), "truly, I can give you no explanation on the particular genesis of that poem". With no clear reason for such secrecy, as the poem is mainly an homage to Virgil, having been written on his birthday, on the 15th of October, two thousand years later. The same day on which Álvaro de Campos was born. Written in three slightly different versions, it was titled "The Last Sortilege":

"The gift others loved me with is dying.
I no longer become the shape and end of life
To those who, seeking them, sought me out.
Now a beach, the sea of arms no longer floods me.
Nor can I see myself rising to the saluted sun,
Or, lost in magical ecstasy,
Under the moonlight, at the mouth of the deep cave.
(...)

"Convert me in my last spell
In a statue of me in a living body!
Let who I am die, but let who I made and was,
The anonymous presence one can kiss,
Flesh of my abstract, captive love,
Be the death of me in which I revive;
And, much like I was, being nothing, let me be!"

The Last Sortilege, Fernando Pessoa

The Order of Christ

In all paths he tread, Pessoa chose "to defeat the love of life as life and the fear of death as death", and managed it by "beating the world, the flesh, the Devil". Always with no great commitment. In 1932, he claims in a letter to be unaffiliated with regards to institutions, and confirms as much in the famous letter to Casais Monteiro (13/01/1935): "I belong to no order whatsoever"; although, in a biographical note (March 1935), he contradicts himself by claiming to be "an initiate, via direct communication between Master and Disciple in the three minor degrees of Portugal's Templar Order" – a congregation which had been made extinct by king Diniz in the beginning of the 14th century. As if confirming previous declarations, in which he claimed to belong to the Order of Christ – the successor of Portugal's Templar Order, also extinct in the very year the poet was born (1888). The accepted explanation among pessoan scholars stems from his own words: "A Divine Initiate is, for example, a Shakespeare. This type of initiation is vulgarly known as genius", as "genius contains an obscure element – that obscure, real but hard to define obscure element called psychic ability when it takes on certain aspects". Deep down, poetry was a rite for his initiation, then. This phase of his saw the writing of delirious texts such as "The duke of Parma", in which the three elements of the Holy Trinity argue among themselves, seeking to know which of them truly exists.

For some scholars, this taste of his for Hermeticism was a central element of Pessoa's oeuvre. One of them is Paulo Costa, for whom *esoterism isn't a simple case of appropriating "esoteric themes" to illustrate his poetry; it was his way of being a poet.* While others, with considerably more weight behind their opinion, consider it but one of his many tastes. Octavio Paz, for example, says that *for every poet of the modern tradition, poetry is a system of symbols and analogies, much like the hermetic sciences. Parallel, not identical: The poem is a constellation of signs of light of their own.* Pessoa himself confirms it: "Do not seek nor believe, all is occult". In *Faust,* he says that "the one mystery, in all and everything, is that there is a mystery in the universe"; capping it off with Campos' irony: "Yes, of course, the universe is dark, especially at night".

Certum es quia impossibile est
(Although correct, it is impossible) Tertullian

THE FREEMASONS

When, awakened from this sleep called life,
We find out what we are...
Will we finally know
The hidden truth?

The Tomb of Christian Rosenkreuz (I), Fernando Pessoa

The Rosicrucian Order

In order to understand the importance of the Freemasons to Fernando Pessoa, one needs to turn back in time. It all begins with a sect founded by a pilgrim born in 1378 by the Rhine, German Christian Rosenkreuz. Son of a noble but poor family, he was educated by a monk who taught him Greek, Latin and Hebrew. After his tutor died in Cyprus during a pilgrimage they were making to the Holy Land, he studies with mystic masters in Damascus, Egypt, Morocco and Arabia. In 1407, he returns to Germany, founds House Sancti Spiritus (a hospital for those in need) and establishes the foundations of what would become the Rosicrucian Order, "a fraternity of those who await the day in which roses shall bud on mankind's cross". As legend has it, the order had already been created before Rosenkreuz, in the German city of Kassel around the year 46, when wise Ormus and six disciples were converted by Marcus, the Evangelist. But it was likely only structured in 1614 with the manifesto *Fama fraternitatis R.C.* Other important manifestos for the order, all of which preached the need for change in human society, were *Confessio fraternitatis* (1615) and *Chemische Hochzeit Christiani Rosenkreuz* (ostensibly from 1616, even though it was written in 1459, when Rosenkreuz was 81 years old). He passed away in 1484, and his crypt's location remained a secret for 120 years.

But though it feels its form is wrong, the Soul sees
At last in itself–mere Shadow–the glowing
Word of this World, human and anointed,
The Perfect Rose, crucified in God.

(...)
Lying before us, calm in his false death
And with the shut Book pressed against his chest,
Our Rosy Cross Father knows, and says nothing.

The Tomb of Christian Rosenkreuz (II and III)[1], Fernando Pessoa

"In the formula of the synod, sanctity is genius. Thus, man can be god. But only being entirely what he humanly is... Each man is but himself. He cannot belong to any Order. The RC's formula is as follows: Freedom, equality, fraternity. Freedom means not to subordinate oneself to anything. Equality means that, having this freedom, every man is equal to any other. Fraternity means not to oppose anyone, as long as he is what he is". The order's symbol is a red rose in the middle of a golden cross, with five "petals" which "contain the elements of martyrdom or suffering, which are the thorns". It is "God's double essence, masculine and feminine – the Cross". Thus, "he who was the crucified rose and crucified the Rose in himself imposed a crown of thorns upon his martyrdom; thus, it follows that this element in five parts is the Rosicrucian symbol". According to the order's belief, seven brothers come to the world as men whenever they are needed; while five others never leave the temple, dedicating themselves to internal works. Seven roses and five star tips represent those Twelve Grand Creating Hierarchies. Plus another one, the Head of the Order, which is only felt by the faithful. Inspired by it all, Pessoa wrote: "Christ forbids us from judging, for we see actions but not hearts. The Christian religion pays no heed to the world of actions, of the done deals, it sees but what man is what his actions reveal. *Render unto Caesar the things that are Caesar's,* as Christ said it, unto the real world what belongs to it. Human experience has taught us that the best of us is, much like Christ, crucified and tied to the cross of the real world, with its pains and its evils. He, the Rose of Emotion".

What fertile symbol
Comes with the restless dawn?
On the Dead Cross of the World,
Life, which is the Rose.

What divine symbol
Brings the day already seen?
On the Cross, which is Destiny,
The Rose which is Christ.

What final symbol

1 The three sonnets which comprise *The Tomb* were sent for publication in 1935 in *Sudoeste* magazine, but were vetted by Salazar's censorship.

Shows the sun already awakened?
On the dead and fatal Cross
The Rose of the Hidden One.

Message ("The Hidden One"), Fernando Pessoa

This understanding of the world is revealed in him in a grandiose dimension: "We must live intimately that which we repudiate. It costs nothing to those who are incapable of feeling Christianity to repudiate Christianity; what is difficult is to repudiate it after having truly felt it, lived it, been it. What is difficult is to repudiate it, or to know how to repudiate it, not as a lie, but as a truth. To acknowledge the truth as truth, and as an error at the same time: To experience opposites without accepting them; To feel everything in every way and, in the end, be nothing but the understanding of everything – when man has reached this summit, then he is truly free, as in all summits, he is lonely, as in all summits, he is one with the sky, with which he never truly is one, as in all summits". Famous Rosicrucians were Bacon, Camões, king Dinis (Portugal's poet king), Giordano Bruno, Goethe, Hermann Hesse, Isaac Newton, Johann Sebastian Bach, Leonardo da Vinci, Martin Luther, Nostradamus, queen Elizabeth, René Descartes, Richard Wagner, Shakespeare, Spinoza, Victor Hugo. Even so, this magical dimension slowly loses importance for Pessoa. "Mysticism is but the most complex way of being effeminate and decadent. The one useful side of uselessness". He then begins to consider religion and politics inferior manifestations, when compared to philosophy and sociology. "Religious leaders and politicians appeal to that which is least elaborate in men – his feelings. With it, they manage to manipulate and create fanatics", also proclaiming that "there are no saviours" and "there is no Messiah". But "the so-called Rosi-crucian Fraternity" manifests itself in him in another more important level. As confirmed by Yvette Centeno, *it would have been absurd to mention this Christian undercurrent, if its importance to the story weren't considerable, hidden as it might be.* To Pessoa, it had transcendental importance, as the Freemasonry stemmed from it, "entered through the Order of the Temple, passed through by the Rosicrucians, raised by the Order of Christ".

The power of the Freemasons

It all began with the old medieval guilds of master builders of churches and cathedrals. The term 'freemason' was first recorded in London (1375), and referred to stonemasons who were free to travel around England. With its origins in the legends of Isis and Osiris (in Egypt), carried over by the Templars, that ancient secret order, "which was an outgrowth of Rosicrucianism", renews in him a broader vision of faith. "All religions are real, as opposite as they may seem to one another. They are different symbols of the same reality. They are the same sentence uttered in different languages". "Thus, there must be tolerance for all religions. A Mason can be anything but an atheist"; while he himself is one who "knows the mystery made flesh. I am Hell". "I am the black Christ nailed to the fiery cross of myself". But perhaps Pessoa never truly joined them. "I am not a Freemason... nor am I, however, an anti-Freemason". There is no record for or against the possibility in any of his papers. Nor in any Freemason document that has been made public. The one reference is him saying that he was "an initiate, via direct communication between Master and Disciple in the three minor degrees of Portugal's Templar Order". An order which no longer even existed in Portugal, no less. Still, he proclaimed the following commandments for it (abridged):

1 – Have no firm opinion, and do not put too much stock in the value of your opinions.
2 – Be tolerant, as you can be sure of nothing.
3 – Judge no one, as you cannot see motivations, only the acts.
4 – Await the best and prepare for the worst.
5 – Do not kill or despoil, as, since you know nothing of life, other than it is a mystery, you know not what you do when you kill or despoil
6 – Seek not to reform anything, as, since you know not which laws things abide by, you cannot know if natural laws are in agreement, or if justice is, or our idea of justice.
7 – Strive to act like others, but to think differently than them.

"Commandments for a new law of God", Fernando Pessoa

Freemasonry and Salazar

The most expressive evidence of such an alliance occurs on the 15th of January 1935, when salazarist councilman José Cabral presents a bill to the National Assembly which would forbid all secret societies, including the Freemasons. Attending to Salazar's wishes, as he no longer intended to suffer the (according to him) evil influence of the Masons in Portugal. The Grandmaster of the Portuguese Freemasons, Norton de Matos, went to the National Assembly on the 31st of January, asking its president to reconsider the bill, but he was unsuccessful. Not quite as polite, Pessoa reacts vehemently and rather publicly in *Diário de Lisboa,* for which he wrote an arraignment against the initiative on the 4th of February – *Secret societies, a serene and thorough analysis of a bill presented to Parliament,* in which he says: "Right off the bat, there is a secret society I can denounce to Mr. José Cabral: The Council of Ministers". It is unknown how the Censorship Committee let that article slip. "The one who presented the bill was Mr. José Cabral, who, if not a Dominican, should most certainly be one[2], as his work is as comparable in nature and content to the finest traditions of the Inquisition... There are no more than two secret societies, the Company of Jesus and the Freemasons". For Pessoa, Freemasonry was more than a "secret society", it was above all an "initiatory order", and the government didn't have the means to eradicate "an international organization more powerful than it". He then said that Freemasons of every country should just boycott Portugal. The text was subsequently independently published – with a quizzical deletion of entire parts of it and changes to several other passages – *Freemasonry as seen by Fernando Pessoa.*

On the 8th of February 1935, the Censorship let it be known that *any reference... to that matter* concerning Pessoa was forbidden. The reaction was swift and unequivocal. José Cabral responded *to Fernando Pessoa and like-minded churls* with the article "Rain in the Temple", which was published in *Diário de Lisboa* (06/03/1935), in which he calls him *a delicate amphibian.* The following day, in the same newspaper, journalist Alfredo Pimenta wrote "The truth about Freemasonry", denouncing the harm they allegedly caused. Pessoa already held him in low regard before, ever since (in a letter-preface) he had praised Vasco Reis' book – the one which beat *Message,* as we shall see further up ahead. And he wrote a response on a sheet which remained in the Chest (as its publication was prevented due to censorship), criticizing Pimenta and Cabral: "I was addressing neither the foolish councilman [Cabral] nor the charlatan of a journalist [Pimenta], but rather the one behind both of them– the Missus [Salazar]... I hope both servants can forgive me". Both the government and the Freemasons then attacked him. Only Francisco Rolão Preto, leader of the blueshirts, shows a measure of sympathy for his cause when he wrote the article "No" – not so much due to solidarity, but because Salazar had prevented the unionist movement he had founded in 1932 from functioning. The bill was unanimously approved on the 21st of May, and became Law nr. 1.901 – Outlawing of Secret Societies. And even managed to get Freemason votes. The Chest holds the following note in the form of a poem:

> Solemnly
> Sheepily
> Seemingly approved by everyone
> Who are, one and all, animals
> At the National Assembly
> A bill by José Cabral.
> It is clear
> That everything
> Was this austere heel's doing
> He who studied so very hard
> And did many other ugly things

2 A reference to Salazar, who, at the time, was said to be a Jesuit, was actually a Dominican.

To become council president.
Chief of internormal animals
And star of a rather old new state
(…)
Go to Salazar, all of you
Whore who birthed you all.

Untitled (undated), Fernando Pessoa

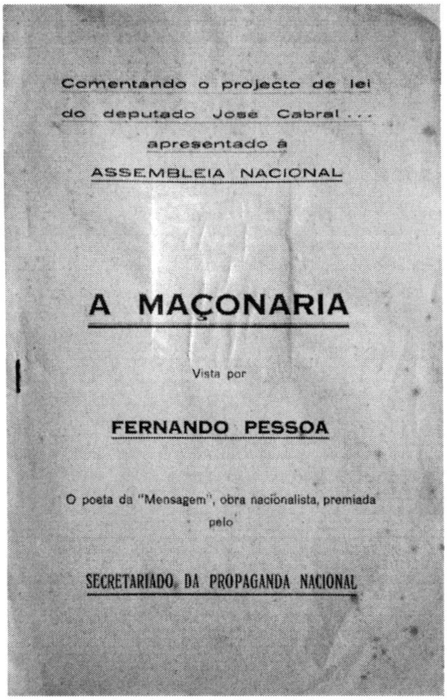
Comentando o projecto de lei
do deputado Jose Cabral …
apresentado a
ASSEMBLEIA NACIONAL

A MAÇONARIA

Vista por

FERNANDO PESSOA

O poeta da "Mensagem", obra nacionalista, premiada
pelo

SECRETARIADO DA PROPAGANDA NACIONAL

Biographical note

Deep down, Pessoa didn't fully believe in any of the abovementioned doctrines. Richard Zenith ponders: *When someone says with conviction that he believed in astrology, in Rosicrucianism, in the Kaballah, in mysticism, in spiritism or in any other -ism, it just means they haven't read his entire oeuvre.* Such was the case with the poet, who believed in all those doctrines and doubted them all. But, even if Rosicrucianism or the Freemasonry were important in his civil life, they had no real repercussions in his writings. On the 30th of March of the year of his death, he reaffirmed his beliefs in this biographical note (abridged):

Political ideology: English-style conservative, which is to say, liberal within the bounds of conservatism, and absolutely anti-reactionary.

Religious stance: Faithful to the Secret Tradition of Christianity, which is intimately connected with Israel's Secret Tradition (the Holy Kaballah) and with the occult essence of Freemasonry.

Initiatory stance: Patriotic stance: Supporter of a mystical nationalism, a new sebastianism which might spiritually replace all Roman Catholic infiltration, if there ever was any measure of spirituality in Portuguese Catholicism. All for Humanity; naught against the Nation[3].

Social stance: Anti-communist and anti-socialist.

Summary of these last considerations: To always bear in mind the martyr Jacques de Molay, Templar grandmaster, and fight on all fronts his three murderers: Ignorance, Fanaticism, and Tyranny[4].

---

3 As opposed to Salazar's motto: *Naught against the Nation, everything for the Nation.*

4 In a later text, he replaced them with Stupidity, Routine and Lack of Culture.

Ante victoriam ne canas triumphum
(Do not celebrate your triumph before the victory) Latin proverb

THE OVER-CAMÕES

I've never aspired to be more than a dreamer.
I've always belonged to what isn't where I am
and to what I could never be.
The Book of Disquiet, Bernardo Soares

Establishing a style

As years went by, Pessoa felt his writing mature. "I am now fully confident in my grasp of the fundamental laws of the literary art. Shakespeare can no longer teach me to be subtle, nor Milton how to be thorough. I am no longer interested in people who are merely intelligent – Wells, Chesterton, Shaw". The same (George Bernard) Shaw, a contemporary of his, who (in *Maxims for revolutionists)* says, as if addressing him: *It is bold to be sincere, unless one is equally as stupid.* In *Ultimatum,* as if by way of response, he declares that Shaw is a "charlatan of sincerity and a minor artist", and considered him "the lining of an inside out tailcoat". And he carries on with his life. "Today, after finally making the decision of being Me, to live up to my calling, I have reentered the divine conscience of my Mission. Today I wish to be exactly as my innate character wishes me to; and my innate genius demands it to be so". As if he knew, and well, of the "terrible and religious mission every man of genius is entrusted to by God". Plain in appearance, almost anonymous in the streets he walked in, he is "increasingly aware" of his superior gift; and finally decides: "If I must dream, why not dream my own dreams?

Even the armies I dreamed of were defeated.
Even my dreams felt false while I dreamed them.
Even the life I merely long for jades me – even that life…

Lisbon Revisited (1926), Álvaro de Campos

Pessoa and Portuguese poetry

In May 1912, in *A Águia* magazine, he publishes his second important article, "Reincidindo" (Relapsing). In it, he names the poets which would lead Portugal's literary rebirth – Antero, Junqueiro, Nobre, Pascoaes – and categorizes four phases of literature, which are related to "the soul of the people producing them": "The creating period, that of the forerunners, that of the initiators and that of decadence, which may be brilliant". According to him, "great literature is elitist" and "doesn't express the people's soul, it represents and interprets it"; after which he again foretells an "awe-inspiring resurgence for Portugal". After that, Boavida Portugal's interviews in *República* newspaper. The initiative is converted into a book, *Literary inquiry,* which Boavida dedicates to Pessoa, *intelligent and loyal comrade.* Gomes Leal, Lopes de Mendonça, Malheiro Dias, Teixeira de Pascoaes and other figures of the time are all interviewed as well; his was titled "From Agostinho on Pessoa". Among the four questions asked of the interviewees, the third one is of special interest for Pessoa: *Will there be a literary renaissance in Portugal?* The answers start being published in September, to some educated reviews, some not so much. Teixeira de Pascoaes, converted into Molière's hypocritical character, is considered a *vain and ignorant Tartuffe,* who writes *nonsense in sophomoric prose.* Pessoa gets contradictory reviews – some bludgeoning, others rather generous. For him, at the time, the vision (he'd later have) of the Fifth Empire wasn't clear yet, but he knew that the promised future wouldn't be brought about by guns. To complement his thoughts, in closing another article published in *A Águia* in December 1912 ("New Portuguese poetry in its psychological aspect"), he says: "And our great Race shall depart in search of a new India, which doesn't exist in space, in ships which are built from what dreams are made of. And its true and ultimate fate, of which the navigators' accomplishment was but a mockery, shall be divinely brought about".

From then on, the change is radical. The "Over-Camões" foretold in *A Águia,* acquires structure. At times, he changes the term, "Super-Camões, as we call him and shall call him". For him, "Portugal begins to shake off the heavy letter of the anti-nationalist tradition, as represented by the italianized Camões, by the followers of Spanish literature and the gallicized nonsense of which Bocage is a disgraceful representative; which was why he predicted "the imminent appearance of the Supreme poet of our race, Europe's Supreme poet of all times". The image gains broader and less obvious tones. In *Message,* for example, the Portuguese crown is represented by a man without a lineage, Nuno Álvares Pereira (1360-1431) – a deeply religious shieldbearer of queen Leonor, and a warrior who later entered the Carmo monastery as a layman brother, taking on the name of Nuno de Santa Maria. For the people, he became the saint constable, beatified in 1918 and canonized in 2009. According to Pessoa, true nobility lies in the spirit, rather than blood. In annotations which remained in the Chest, one can read that one Dr. Alonso Cavalheira predicted "that a new king shall come, who shall be the son of neither king nor queen, and whose name had been no king's until now". Pessoa himself, naturally, king of a realm of language. Although there had already been kings with the name of Fernando; nobody is perfect.

Around 1917, he begins to realize that Portugal is living through "a period of poor and depressed social life" and "petty politicking". By then, Sá-Carneiro had already died and, deep down, so too had his master Caeiro. He is in search of new paths. He writes Campos' violent *Ultimatum;* and, considering the influence Camões still held over his countrymen, he criticizes "the petrarchism[1] of the sad poets of our Renaissance", voicing his contempt for "those people's italianism". They had been "original writers but once, inevitably. After that, they did not evolve, nor did they grow". "The paucity and monotony in our men who show talent for literature grips the heart and oppresses intelligence". He goes further still. "All classical Portuguese literature can hardly be considered classical". "It is seldom Portuguese. It is Provençal, Italian, Spanish and French, occasionally English". For him, an author should be first and foremost committed to his land. For example, he can recite by heart Camilo (d'Almeida) Pessanha (1867-1926), author of *Clepsidra* and one of the greatest figures of Portuguese symbolism – the one who general Henrique Rosa had introduced him to at Pastelaria Suíça. He even wrote a poem about him, "À la manière de Camilo Pessanha" (26/07/1914), which ends in a lament: "Your flute cries"[2]. In 1915 (the letter is undated), he writes to Pessanha: "You, sir, did me the honour and gave me the great pleasure of reciting a few of your poems. I remember that spiritualized hour as a religious memento". After which he takes on serious topics related to journalism. At the time, Pessanha was already living in Macau, where he marries (in truth, buys a wife) and raises a family. There is no record of any reply, but several poems of his were among those to be published in *Orpheu* #3 (1916). He also admires (with caveats) and translates into English the one who was considered the greatest Portuguese poet of all, Luís Vaz de Camões. In a letter to William Bentley (undated, 1915), he sums up his feelings: "Camões is a great epic poet and a reasonably good lyrical poet. But he is markedly bereft of all purely intellectual qualities out of which the most elevated poetry is build from. He has no depth; no profound metaphysical intuition. He has no fantasies. And no true imagination to speak of. One needs but look at Adamastor[3], which was the best he could do. Note the extraordinary inability to conceive the greater details, how he falls back on the superficial and the petty, even in the very centre of his inspiration. Camões

1 Here in the sense of *antiquity.* Ironically, (almost) all of Pessoa's oeuvre which he wrote under his own name (save for mystical or nationalist texts) was later compiled under the title of Petrarch's best known book: *Songbook* (1470)

2 A reference to the first verse of one of Pessanha's poems, "Os barcos de flores", which reads: *Alone, unceasing, the sound of a flute cries.*

3 A giant representing the Cape of Good Hope in *The Lusiad's* Canto V.

is as unintelligent as he is unimaginative". To wit, "he is far from a Dante or a Shakespeare". Even more dryly, he was but "an italianized one-eye". Which is why, deep down, he considered himself greater than him. "I have tremendous admiration for Camões (the epic, not the lyrical), but I know not of any camonian element which has influenced me in any way, as impressionable as I am. Because that which Camões could have taught me had already been taught to me by others. The exaltation and sublimation of the homeland instinct are unteachable phenomena in their substance". To say nothing of the fact that "the construction and amplitude of the epic poem was already present in Milton (which I read before *The Lusiads),* and to a greater degree than Camões'". He then says that "as great as he is, Camões is not the literary equivalent of Prince Henry the Navigator or the Viceroy of India, Afonso de Albuquerque[4]". Or, with even more dryness, "Camões is *The Lusiads",* and that work, according to him, didn't even "occupy a place among the greatest sagas of the world; only the *Iliad, The Divine Comedy* and *Paradise Lost* have earned that distinction". His influence couldn't even affirm itself in Portugal, where he considers (Abílio Manuel) Guerra Junqueiro's *A pátria* "the greatest work our literature has produced". *The Lusiads* were in an "honourable second place".

Communism and Christianity

For Pessoa, "communism is a dogmatism bereft of a system. If the moral and mental filth could be wiped and gathered off all brains, and then be moulded into a gigantic figure, it would be the figure of communism, supreme enemy of freedom and humanity, as is all that which lies sleeping in the basest instincts hiding within us all". Still, his oeuvre shows an instigating relationship between communism and religion, and he believed "Bolshevik mysticism" was an offshoot of Christianity. "Communism is avowedly – both in theory and in practice – anti-national and anti-liberal. Catholicism, due to the strictness of its dogma and the intolerance of its action, is contrary to freedom of thought and freedom of expression". He goes further still: "The Roman Catholic Apostolic Church is an institution of ostensibly religious ends, but its real action is to prevent any and all integration it might have in mankind's progress and well-being. The Roman Church is the Anti-Man and the Anti-Nation. Both share fanaticism and dogmatism". And he even establishes a connection between the miracles of Lourdes and communism.

> How so, the miracles of Lourdes, friend?
> Miracles of Russia.
> Curing paralysis!

---

4 One of the greatest conquerors for the Portuguese crown in the 16th century (1453-1515), having taken Goa, Malacca and Ormuz.

Curing selfishness, now that is a miracle,
Ah, Lourdes, Lourdes, how many of you out there!

Untitled (undated), Fernando Pessoa

From 1917 onwards, with the creation of the Sanctuary of Fátima, he realizes a "Portuguese Lourdes" was being born. "What is miraculous is that the people want, and that the people understand. Whether it is Our Lady doing it in Lourdes or Fátima, or whether it is of Lenin's doing – therein lies the sole difference". In 1935, he wrote: "Fátima is the name of a tavern in Lisbon where I used to drink *aguardiente*. One moment… No, it was nothing of the sort – Fátima is the name of a place which was called Cova of this or another saint. In that place, a bunch of kids one day saw Our Lady appear, which, as everyone knows, is one of the privileges of childhood one cannot deny".

Bandarra

Little by little, he begins to have grandiose visions. "My dreams were of all kinds, but they represented manifestations of a single state of mind. I could dream I was Christ sacrificing myself to redeem humanity, or Martin Luther, breaking conventions, or Nero, bathing in blood and enjoying the lusts of the flesh. I either saw myself in a hallucination, beloved of the crowds, applauded, or beloved by women, seducing them into leaving their homes and hearths". In his estimation, those dreams foretold his grand fate. "I belong to a generation which is yet to come". He then proclaims in 1928, "let us abandon Fátima in favour of Trancoso" – the birthplace of someone who would be tremendously important in his life: An odd reader of the Bible called Gonçalo Annes (1500-1545, or 1556, or 1560), known as Bandarra, which history would remember only as a poor shoemaker. Pessoa had already previously expressed admiration for him, having translated some of the poems he had written in Latin in the 14th century. He was the one "in whose soul lived, none knew how, the Atlantic mystery of the Portuguese soul". Pessoa had two books of his, *Trovas de Bandarra* (1866) and *Profecias* (1911), which contained texts such as the following:

After the passing
Of ninety plus thou shall see
I saw the yearned-for
Who shall found new laws.

Shall see the fatal lion
Coming at him from Portugal
Which shall do him harm
To him, the hidden king.

Bandarra evoked a number of characters in Pessoa's imagination. Ling's King Gesar. Saint Isidore's Hidden One. England and Wales' legends of King Arthur. As well as those sung in Valencian coplas: Jean de Riquefaillarie, friar Pedro de Frias or the Calabrese Cistercian monk Joaquim de Fiore – who reinterpreted the Fifth Empire as the Eternal Gospel, describing the myth of the three ages in his Book of Figures. To him, the history of humanity would go through three stages, as per the three elements of the Trinity: Mosaic law, the age of the Father; Evangelical Law, the age of the Son; and the future law of the gospel, of the Holy Spirit. Each would be comprised of 42 generations of 30 years each, the first beginning with Adam, the second with Jesus and the third with the birth of the Antichrist, in 1260. Essayist and professor Joel Serrão adheres to the prophecy and proclaims: *The true patron of our country is that shoemaker, Bandarra.* Pessoa believed with all his heart in the prophecies written by Bandarra and his followers (though all were attributed to him) between 1530 and 1531.

He was neither saint nor hero,
But God made sacred with His sign
This man, whose heart was
Not Portuguese, but Portugal!

Message, "Bandarra", Fernando Pessoa

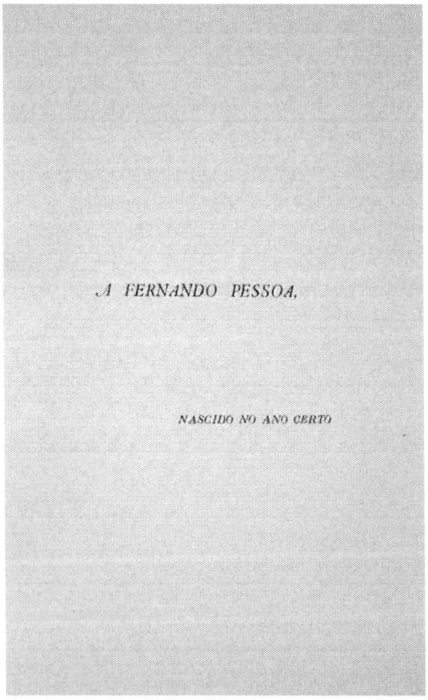

"Bandarra is a collective noun by which not just the seer of Trancoso is known, but all those who saw the same Light by his example". In 1934, in the preface for Augusto Ferreira Gomes' *Quinto Império* (Fifth Empire), he proclaims: "There are two sorts of prophecies. Those that have a great light in them, and those that have great darkness. The former are the string for the labyrinth, whereas the latter are the labyrinth itself. Both complement each other, however, for light casts away the darkness, but without darkness one could not perceive light. The best light we have in this world is nothing but visible darkness". More than anything else, Pessoa is impressed by ballad XI of Book Two:

> Presage, ye coming people
> Or the king who is to come
> Shall come again before you
> At the passage of thirty scissors.

He explains the expression *scissors* through Raphael Baldaya, for whom prophetic rules always refer to numbers. "In Roman numerals, there are three: The two (II), which is like the scissors yet to be fused as such; the five (V), which is part of the fused scissors; and the ten (X), which is the open scissors". Those thirty scissors of prophecy, then, would be 1640, 1733 and 1888. The first date was the year of the Portuguese Restoration. The second, "the apex of our period of rich sterility, of our repose of power". The third, the extinction of the Templar order, as well as his own birth. Also of relevance was the freeing of the slaves in Brazil, although Pessoa didn't put much stock in it. Finally, based on those dates, he summed up the scissors as "Independence, Greatness and Empire". Keeping the first and the third (now converted into second) original dates, and consigning the remainder to the future. In any event, the key to understanding the meaning behind the prophecies lay in the first quatrain of Book Three:

> On you, who shall be the Fifth
> After the Second's death
> I base my prophecies
> In these letters I paint for YOU.

Therein lie the three ages of the prophecies, according to the letters. "The word VOS [YOU], in the fourth verse", represented the time of strength (Vis), idleness (Otium) and science (Scientia). Depending on the transcriptions, "that word [VOS] has the variant AQUI [HERE] in some texts", written in capitals in both cases and representing variants for the same concepts as before: The time of arms (Arma), quietude (Quies) and intelligence (Intellectus). The texts contain dreams which Pessoa felt as his own: A ship "bringing king Sebastião aboard, raising aloft the pennant of the Empire as if it were a name". The essence of the prophecy lies in the first two ages, which represent the history of Portugal; with the third, science (or intelligence), foreshadowing the Fifth Empire which was to succeed Rome.

According to the rule of the third book of Bandarra's prophecies, Pessoa believed that, in the year 1888, "the supreme poet of all times" would be born. João da Silva Tavares dedicated his *Vida amorosa de D. Pedro IV* to *Fernando Pessoa, the yearned-for who finally appeared.* And occultist Augusto Ferreira Gomes dedicates his book of verses *Quinto Império* (1934) – the one with a preface by Pessoa himself – *To Fernando Pessoa, born in the right year.*

António Mora wrote about the man Portugal was longing for: "Through this man and through this oeuvre, we find ourselves on the cusp of a new era, even if none can feel it". Because "the future of Portugal is already written, for those who can read it, in Bandarra's ballads, and also in Nostradamus' quatrains". It is a grandiose dream. "That future of Portugal is that we become all. We've already conquered the Sea: We have but to conquer the Sky, leaving the Earth for the Others, the eternally Others, Others by birth, the Europeans who aren't Europeans because they aren't Portuguese". Later, spurred on by his discoveries, he foresees the following at the end of an article published in *A Águia* ("New Portuguese poetry in its psychological aspect):

> And our great race shall go in search of a new India, which doesn't exist in space, in ships built from "what dreams are made of". And its true and ultimate fate, of which the navigators' accomplishment was but a mockery, shall be divinely brought about.
>
> *Prophecy*, Fernando Pessoa

In his premonitions, he believes that "upon studying historical eras, one notices that geniuses appear more often in times of social disintegration. At first sight, one might say that disorder is what creates them". He speaks of his own country, his time and himself. "Between life and that which lives, which side does the river flow to?". Pessoa's river flows towards the future. "I belong to the nation of navigators and creators of empires". But, impatient, he wonders: "What will I be in five years' time? My friends tell me I will be one of the greatest contemporary poets". In 1928, he predicts that "within 10 years, Bandarra's prediction shall come true". He was wrong on both accounts, if only by the number of years, as before that he would experience "slumber, peace, being nothing, the long-awaited death". The prophecy wouldn't come true, at least not in his life. Bandarra himself didn't have much of a future, either. Arrested by the Inquisition in Lisbon (23/10/1541) and accused of being a Christian convert, he was interrogated during an *auto-de-fé* and was sent home on condition of delving no more into the mysteries of the Scriptures. He was a nobody. And he was never heard from again. Until father António Vieira came along.

Father António Vieira and Nebuchadnezzar's dream

This "Emperor of the Portuguese language", a messianic figure and theologist of the Fifth Empire, was for Pessoa "the greatest artist in our land". "António Vieira is in fact the greatest prose writer – dare I say it, the greatest artist – of the Portuguese language. And I don't just say this because his name was António" – like himself, Fernando António, it bears remembering. "Having to choose between Chateaubriand and Vieira, I would choose Vieira without need for much pondering". In *Apologia das coisas profetizadas* (Apology of prophesied things), Vieira deals with two main issues. *The first concerning the past, in which he affirms Bandarra was a true prophet, and having spoken with true prophetic spirit in his writings. The second concerning the future, in which he claims as a certainty that what Bandarra predicted will come to pass, such as the resurrection and second coming of the true king.* Next, he declares that Bandarra, *in life or after his death, had restored the sight of the blind and feet to the limp, and had resurrected the dead in confirmation of his prophecies.* In the vision of a new time, Vieira focuses on his *Five consequences* (of which the third has been lost), the most important being the fifth (abridged): *With the destruction of the Ottoman empire, a new empire and monarchy shall rise in the world, so says and supposes Bandarra.* From that belief, Vieira proclaims, in 1642, that Portugal would be the Empire of the World. Pessoa is particularly fond of the dream of the Babylonian king Nebuchadnezzar, as interpreted by the prophet Daniel. *The first and most important prophecy we have concerning this kingdom is Daniel's.* The text is part of the *Sermon of thanksgiving* for the birth of prince João. In the preface, Vieira explains the meaning he gives his own book: *Other stories tell of things which have occurred; this one promises to tell of those which will come to pass,* and describes his dream thus (abridged):

> Nebuchadnezzar, the great monarch, one night pondered whether or not his empire would be eternal; and, falling asleep with such thoughts, he saw the famous statue which is so often nailed to pulpits, its head made of gold, its chest of silver, its belly of bronze, its feet of iron. A great rock knocked it down and ground it to dust, and the same rock grew in a mound of such greatness, that it covered the entire earth. Daniel declared its meaning. The head is the first empire, that of the Assyrians; the second, the Persians'; the third, the Greeks'; the fourth, the Romans'; the fifth shall rule the world and be owed obedience by all. All which is hugged by the sea, all which is lit by the sun, all which covers and surrounds the earth will be the subject of that Fifth Empire.

Vieira's text covering the bases of the Fifth Empire is *História do futuro* (History of the future), which was likely written between 1642 and 1662. Pessoa confesses he "read it until the end, shaking, confused; then I erupted in tears of joy". As it so happened, "my master Vieira", placing his faith in Bandarra's prophecies, believed that said Fifth Empire would simultaneously be Christ's and the King of Portugal's – João IV, the Restorer, who had named Vieira *court preacher.* After the king's death on the 6th of November 1656, he wrote a letter to King Afonso VI, the Victorious, referring to João as one who had inaugurated a time of greatness *like his majesty in the sky* (Sebastião).

> Heaven spangles the blue and has splendour.
> This man, who once had fame and now glory has,
> Emperor of the Portuguese language,
> Was to us a heaven too.
> (…)
> But no, 'tis not moonlight: 'tis light ethereal.
> 'T is a day, and, in the sky ample with desire,
> The unreal dawning of the Fifth Empire
> Gilds the banks of the Tagus.
>
> *Message* ("António Vieira"), Fernando Pessoa

The utopia of the Fifth Empire as described by Vieira hearkens back to Judeo-Christian mythology. According to that biblical tradition, after Babylon came the empires of the Medes, the Persians and the Greeks. The fifth would have been the Kingdom of God. Moving forward in time to the Middle Ages, the belief was also that first came the Medes, the Persians and the Greeks, and the coming Fifth Empire was to be God's, that of the Eternal Gospel, with a new incarnation and a new Pentecost. For Vieira, the four previous empires had been the Assyrian, the Persian, the Greek and the Roman, after which would come the one true empire under Christ's cross. For Pessoa, they were "early", Greece", "Rome", "Britannic" and an undefined "?". "As for what Rome means… I won't say whether or not I know it… Whomever is able to understand, let him understand". Then, in 1934, the list is shortened to Greek, Roman, Christian and European Renaissance; which would be followed by the Empire of Culture, the Portuguese Fifth Empire.

> And so, past the four
> Ages of the being that dreamed,
> The world will be the stage
> Of the bright day, that in the dark
> Of the empty night began.
>
> Greece, Rome, Christianity,
> Europe – the four go
> To where all age goes.
> Who wants to live the truth
> For which Sebastião died?
>
> *Message* ("The Fifth Empire"), Fernando Pessoa

In a copy of *Message,* with the same ink he had used to write a dedication "to cousin Victoriano" (Braga), Pessoa underlined the words "four Ages", "Greece", "Rome", "Christianity" and "Europe".

That empire would unite very different forces: "The left side of wisdom, which is to say science and reason; and its right side, or occult knowledge, intuition, mystical speculation, the Kaballah". It would be thus because "only in a small nation can a spiritual Empire truly come to be, as it does not develop any attempts at territorial absorption". Vieira's innovation consists of giving a real sense to that incorporeal myth, claiming that the first emperor of the world would be Portuguese, though he mentioned no names. But Pessoa had no doubt: The king was certainly Sebastião; and he says as much in a letter (20/04/1930) to Keyserling[5].

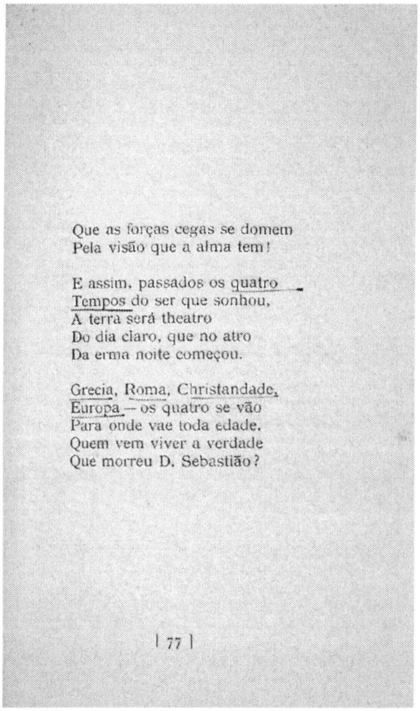

Que as forças cegas se domem
Pela visão que a alma tem!

E assim, passados os quatro
Tempos do ser que sonhou,
A terra será theatro
Do dia claro, que no atro
Da erma noite começou.

Grecia, Roma, Christandade,
Europa — os quatro se vão
Para onde vae toda edade.
Quem vem viver a verdade
Que morreu D. Sebastião?

[77]

Notes on *Message's* copy

After the battle of El-ksar el Kebir, where our King and lord Sebastião was ostensibly killed – but, being a symbol, he could not die – the Portuguese soul, inheritor of the

5 Hermann Alexander Keyserling (1880-1946) was a German count and philosopher, who founded a School of Wisdom in Darmstadt (1920), in which he proclaimed the superiority of intuition over intelligence, and had a series of conferences in 1930 in Lisbon, in which he spoke of Portugal's soul.

> Hellenic soul for reasons and lack of reasons that it wouldn't be legitimate to discuss now, fortified itself in the shadows and the abyss… for the first divine movement… of the second stage of the Secret Order which is the hieratic basis of our life.

"My brothers are the creators of the world's conscience – messy playwright W. Shakespeare, schoolmaster J. Milton, the layabout Dante Alighieri, and, if I may be so bold as to write it, that Jesus Christ who was no one of consequence in the world. What I write today is much better than even the best could have aspired to write". Pessoa truly believed his fate was to give continuation to Sebastião's grand dream. Not by chance, *Message* has three Warnings: The first being "Bandarra", the second "António Vieira" and an untitled third would be himself, Pessoa, who even suggests as much:

> I write my book at the brink of despair.
> My heart has nothing to hold.
> I have my eyes warm with water.
> Only you, Lord, give me a reason to live for.
> (…)
> When, my Dream and my Lord?
>
> *Message* ("The warnings, Third"), Fernando Pessoa

Arma virumque cano
(I sing of arms and the man) Virgil

THE LEGEND OF KING SEBASTIÃO

Mad, yes, mad, because I wanted greatness
Such as Fate does not grant.
Message ("Sebastião, King of Portugal"), Fernando Pessoa

And Portugal came true

In order to understand the oeuvre, one needs to first know the set of influences surrounding it – in this case, "Portugal rising from the deaf depths of fate" with "the very earth's soul, emotive without passion, clear without logic, energetic without synergy, which can be found in every Portuguese, and which is truly a reflection of this blue-green sky, the infinity of which is truly greater close to the Atlantic". Pessoa witnesses the tremendous transformations the country undergoes: The tragic end of the monarchy after the murder of king Carlos (1908), the chaotic beginnings of the Republic (1910), the pain of World War I (1914-1918), the social atmosphere which leads to the rise of Salazar (1928) and the institutionalization of the Estado Novo (1933). But, deep down, the dimension of "Infinite Portugal" began much earlier – at the very formation of the country.

He who hallowed you, made you Portuguese.
Of the sea and us, in you he gave us a sign.
The Sea was accomplished, and the Empire was undone.
Lord, Portugal is yet to be accomplished!

Message ("Prince Henry"), Fernando Pessoa

The Iberian Peninsula had been successively occupied by a number of peoples. According to legend, a full century and a half after the Great Deluge, Túbal founded at the mouth of the Sado the city which was to have the name of that grandson of Noah's: Setúbal. And Ulysses founded on the shores of the Tagus a settlement which would eventually become Lisbon. The legions of Rome also settled it, as did the Suebi, the Visigoths and several other barbarians. From the sea came the Phoenicians, and the Celts came by land, after a devastating drought had ruined their crops. But the greatest invaders of that area would be the Moors, who after 711 occupied the peninsula for over 500 years before being definitively cast out of Portugal (1257) and Spain (1492). There were also the apostles of Christianity, who were initially led there by James the Greater, in whose honour Santiago de Compostela would later be named. For Teixeira de Pascoaes, *saudade,* that oh-so-very Portuguese form of longing, *was born from the fusion between the Lusitanian people, the Romans and the Semites,* and is therefore both pagan and Christian. The Lusitanian tribes who lived there – "Lusitania" stems from "luz" (light) – eventually gave shape to the kingdom of Spain, which remained strong and united until Afonso VII ascended to the throne. With him, the empire devolved into a civil war, and Portugal's birth became imminent. Pessoa even claimed that the birth occurred in 1096, when Henrique took over the County of Portugal, but eventually conceded that Afonso Henriques (1110-1185), the Conqueror, was "the first king of Portugal", "the only emperor who truly had the entire world in his hands" – although, for the Roman Curia, he was mostly a very good exterminator of the enemies of Christendom. Christ himself appeared on the cross in a ray of light to Afonso (in 1289), at the dawn of the battle of Ourique, and rallied him into defeating five Moorish kings, associated to the five blue shields on the country's flag, which represent the five wounds of Christ. It is in that magical moment that the story of an entire people begins.

> Neither king nor law, neither peace nor war,
> Define with outline and substance
> This dull brilliance of the land
> That is Portugal sinking in sadness.
>
> *Message* ("Mist"), Fernando Pessoa

A few centuries pass until the reign of João III, the Pious. He had already mourned eight children, and was about to do the same with his last – João, married to Joana, daughter of Karl V of Austria. The wan skin of that frail prince, the hallmark of those who have no future to speak of, was cause for everyone to expect him not to have any children, and the Portuguese feared that "absent a male heir to the throne", the crown would be handed to a Spaniard. But, as luck would have it, a boy was born on the 20th of January 1553, the day of Saint Sebastian – although poor João, who died 20 days prior, would never know that he indeed had it in him. "After the death of the prince's father, he is anxiously awaited by the people, and became known as the Yearned-For". In 1557, his grandfather also passes away, and the heir to the throne is a fragile 3 year-old child baptised as Sebastião in honour of the saint's day. He would become a definitive presence in Pessoa's life and oeuvre.

The Yearned-For

Before the future king came of age, Portugal had Catherine of Austria, the widow of João III, as regent. But not for long, as she would soon return to her home country. Unaccostumed to the complex game of palatial intrigue, she handed over the reigns to her brother-in-law, Sebastião's great-uncle, cardinal Henrique. A man who had a brilliant career in the Church; he spoke Greek, Hebrew and Latin, and had been the prior of Santa Cruz de Coimbra before the age of 15; at the age of 22, he was already archbishop of Braga and; at 27, the grand inquisitor of Portugal and overseas territories; and, at 34, a cardinal. But time was cruel to him. In 1562, at the age of 50, he was a rag of a man awaiting "she who embraces all vague dreams". Pressured by the court, on the 16th of June 1557, Sebastião took the throne earlier than expected, on the very day he became 14 years old, as well as the sixteenth king of Portugal, the seventh and last of the dynasty of Avis. A Jesuit priest, Luís Gonçalves da Câmara, is chosen as his tutor and makes him into all but a monk in the mould of Ignatius of Loyola's Jesuits. One of the rules of his education was that *our lord and sovereign shall, from the age of nine onwards, be removed from the presence of women and left to the care of men.* He also undergoes strict military training under a manservant, Aleixo de Menezes, son of a veteran of the wars in Africa and India. That training, along with the rigours of his education, had all the makings of an epic. The child was fascinated by the romanticism of the crusades and dreamt of knightly heroes. In a blank sheet, he wrote: *Upon coming of age, he shall conquer Africa.* Miguel de Menezes, count of Vila Real, commented: *A noble enough sentiment. But only if Your Highness leaves us six or seven sons.* It was a premonition of sorts.

The new king also proved to be a strange man. In Alcobaça, he has Afonso II, Afonso III and his two wives exhumed, only to have the pleasure of gazing upon their faces. At the church of Batalha, he has the skeleton of João II, the Cruel, removed from his tomb, takes his sword off his skeletal hands and slashes at the air in a macabre ritual of glorification. According to historian Costa Lobo, *his eagerness for spasmodic sensations was only appeased with violent exercises of bullfighting, tourneys, or the creaking of the boat battered by stormy waves.* The young king enjoyed heading out into the Tagus during storms, only for the pleasure of showing his lack of fear. The heir of Joana, the Mad, he is thus described by Álvaro de Las Casas: *Fair-skinned as the field of snow, hair blonder than gold, skin finer than silk and eyes bluer than love. An ample front, a thin nose, lordly hands, mouth small and red like a beautiful strawberry.* Every morning, he experiences a discharge which is zealously verified by his chamberlain, and which leaves the court most worried. According to popular belief, it was due to gonorrhoea. To Gregorio Marañón, it was rather nocturnal emissions. According to Costa Lobo, *he was repulsed by female caresses.* Pedro Calmon sums it up: *He never wished to marry.*

Preparing for his adventure

According to Oliveira Martins, Portugal was *a nation of lost madmen,* and the young king embodies his people's madness. *Both nation and king were cheerfully dancing at the edge of the cliff.* For António Sérgio, another historian, *that which we regret the most about Sebastião isn't his recklessness, but his stupidity, his crazed antics, the morbid explosiveness, the useless ferocity, the constant swaggering of degenerate impulses.* A dispassionate run-through of his short reign, especially on the administrative front, gives us a different impression, however: That he was concerned with controlling public spending, with defining limits for the power of the state and for being even-handed in all his actions. But that wasn't nearly enough for the likes of him; the Yearned-For considered it his duty to conquer new lands for Portugal, honouring the "foundation of the first Empire, where the sun never set". In order for his homeland to retake its divinely set fate, he wishes to be *captain of Portugal in Africa* – in his words. *A captain of Christ.* Historian Antero de Figueiredo sums it up: *Sebastião was a medieval king, dressed in Renaissance garb. There was a century's worth of distance between himself and the people.* Despite all that evidence of thoughtlessness, he was still supported by many, including intellectuals such as Pedro António Coimbra, and poets like António Ferreira.

He was also praised by a limp nobleman born of a Galician family, who left his right eye in the beaches of Ceuta. A rabble-rouser and a spendthrift bohemian, who often slept in the jails of Tronco or Goa, he survived by managing the properties of deceased soldiers and writing verses for food. One who had been shipwrecked at the mouth of the Mecon river (Cambodia), losing all of his possessions and managing to save himself by swimming with only one arm – as the other was keeping his draft of *The Lusiads* safe, so it would be published in 1572. For that work, Luís Vaz de Camões was awarded three years' worth of an annual pension of 15 mil-réis by king Sebastião, also taking into account his services in India, provided he complied with courtly duties as well. A modest sum, roughly what a stonemason or carpenter would earn, and half the annual wages of a clerk. By way of comparison, the court's official chronicler (as historians were then called), João de Barros, who wrote *Décadas da Índia,* received 300 mil-réis per year for life. After Camões' death in 1580, his mother asked the court for the final instalment of the pension, with no record of her having ever received it. In *Canto I* of *The Lusiads,* Camões exalts the young king:

> Thou young, thou tender, ever-flourishing bough,
> true scion of tree by Christ beloved more,
> than aught that Occident did ever know,
> "Caesarian" or "Most Christian" styled before
> (...)

Thine acts so forceful are, told simply true,
All fabled, dreamy feats they far exceed;
Exceeding Rodomont, and Ruggiero vain,
And Roland happily born of Poet's brain.

And in *Canto* X, he exhorts him into action:

They crowd the mighty Mount whereof Meduse
robbed his body who the skies upbore
They flock in thousands from Cape Ampeluse
and from Tangier, Antaeus' seat of yore.
Abyla's dweller offereth scant excuse;
who with his weapon hasteth him the more,
when heard the Moorish clarions shrilly-toned,
and all the reign high Juba whilom owned.

The Moorish epic

The king also got advice from prudent men, such as the cardinal Henrique, a former regent of the kingdom, who warned him about the risk of losing *navigation and trade with Brazil, which is turning into a great state,* and thought it wiser to *defend the acquired rather than acquiring the new.* But Sebastião would heed no one. He asks the duke of Alba whether he knows the colour of fear[1], to which the good duke replied: *It is the colour of prudence, my Lord.* João Mascarenhas recommends that, if he is to go to Africa, then he should bring a shroud with which to bury his kingdom. In response, the king calls him *old, foolish and cowardly.* His intelligence assures him that the Moors are divided, as Abd el Melike, the legal heir of the Moroccan throne, had been banished the year prior by the usurper Muley Ahmed bin Abdullah. Melik had requested the king's help to retake the throne, and, to his eyes, that was the chance of starting off a new glorious age in the Moorish continent. The young king suddenly decides to undertake the quest and, on the 14th of June 1578, the royal standard is baptised, and the people are fascinated at the sight of so many colourful garbs. All of Portugal's most important families are represented in the expedition. On the 25th of June, "the last galleon sailed away, under a sun of ill-omen, forsaken, 'mid weeping of anxiety and ominous mystery". With not a single military plan. Such is the foolhardiness of the undertaking, that some of the court's members even ponder arresting him. As they should have. The idea of a divided Moorish land was a serious mistake, as the two kings would soon join forces against

1 Pessoa asked a similar question of Sá-Carneiro in a letter (13/04/1916): "What colour the act of feeling?"

the common enemy represented by the Portuguese invading army. The battle is a foregone conclusion, and only the maddened king seems not to realize it.

> Night covers the field which Fate
> Come death, left abandoned.
> Thus ceasing all the folly.
>
> By cover of moonlight, the tattered pennants
> Spangle the absurd, desolate field
> With a defeat of unknowns.
>
> *Folly*, Fernando Pessoa

Ksar El-Kebir

On the 4th of August 1578, on the eve of Our Lady of the Snows, both armies stare at each other on the opposite shores of the Mahazon river. The silence is terrifying. One can hear the buzzing of flies, which almost always seem to come with such stifling heat, as well as the crying of 200 Portuguese babies in the arms of their mothers – 800 youngsters had come with their parents in the expedition, to occupy the land after the certain victory. In all, the Portuguese numbered 17 to 18 thousand men – *a thousand or so noblemen,* as estimated by Joaquim Ferreira, plus 3 thousand German and Dutch mercenaries, 1,500 (or 3,000) warlike Spaniards, 500 noblemen from Castille and 600 (or 900) Italians sent by the Pope, as well as adventurers, whoremongers, beggars, daredevils and glory hounds, according to Oliveira Martins. What the young king hadn't counted on was a sea of 40 thousand (or even 120 thousand) Moors on the other side. He then decides to cross the river, even knowing that, in the chaos of battle, his troops would have no support. But, if he didn't attack, all those who accompanied him would starve to death. And so, the battle before the walls of Ksar El-Kebir *(great castle,* in Arabic), the heart of Morocco, was joined. Sebastião led a troop of ill-equipped and ill-trained knights. Surrounded by Moorish troops coming from everywhere, defeat is inevitable. Even so, with the rallying cry of *Saint George!,* he charges against that sea of men, *drunk with blood and heroism.* The battle's final scene is described thus by historian João Ameal:

> Many fall, more and more, in tragic clearings. After each charge by the unlikely cavalry, only half remain, and then half of that; by the end, all that remains is a bunch of fantastical centaurs, whose bloody swords swing unceasingly, shining red under the African sun. The horses die one after the other; weapons snap. Knights change mounts and return jubilantly, delirious, unfeeling, cutting down swathes of the Moorish cornfields. Defeat is all but certain. Cries ring out to keep the king safe, but Sebastião does not listen, does

> not think, does not consider any course of action other than battling to the death. Once again, he switches mounts, this one given to him by Jorge de Albuquerque Coelho, who was grievously injured. And he carries on with his hallucination, cleaving at empty air in barely conscious ecstasy. "My lord, what can avail us now?", his protégé Cristóvão de Távora asks, to which the young king replies, triumphant amidst defeat, trusting his eternal reward – "Heaven, provided our deeds have earned it".

It is a pointless battle, lasting from 30 minutes to 6 hours. For the standards of the time, it was a very quick affair. 7 (or 42) thousand bodies lie on the ground. After the slaughter, comes the work of tying up prisoners – so many, that there isn't enough rope for them all. "The concept of empire we had fell at Ksar el-Kebir". It was, as Ameal put it, *the grandiose outcome of Portuguese madness.* A genuinely medieval ending – an epic suicide of the cavalry. The records concerning that followed are rather imprecise. Nobleman Sebastião de Resende claims he clad the king in a fine white linen tunic, dropped him over his horse's saddle and rode off on the beast's hips. Another, Francisco de Souza, declares he returned to Portugal with a document signed by Belquior do Amaral, ensuring he himself buried the monarch's body. Many other versions would ensue, and the young king's fate would forever remain a mystery. The man was gone, and the legend was born.

> It never returned. To what undiscovered island
> Did it call? Will it ever return from the unknown fate
> It met?
> God hides the body and the shape of the future
> But His light projects it, a dream clouded
> And brief.
> (…)
> I know not the hour, but I know there is one,
> Even if God delays it, or the soul calls it
> Mystery.
>
> *Message* ("The Last Galleon"), Fernando Pessoa

And king Sebastião disappears

On the 29th of August 1578 (the battle took place on the 4th), Portugal would receive the news of its now vacant throne: "Our King and lord Sebastião was hit by the appearance of death", as Pessoa said in a letter to count Keyserling (20/04/1930). But did he truly die in that battle? Doubts persist, on account of there never having been any evidence, but, considering that kings were always surrounded by retinues in battle, it would have been almost impossible for him to as much as be injured without it being witnessed by a group of companions. And many are the testimonies which attest to him having escaped. Vincent Leblanc, one of the few survivors of the Marseille battalion, even claims to having seen his corpse in a coffin of quicklime, but then clarifies: *I heard it was the corpse of a Swiss, and that king Sebastião, upon being knocked off his horse, had run away.* So too claims friar Bernardo da Cruz, who had accompanied the expedition: *The king retreated and left the battlefield, without being chased by any Moor.* Other statements confirm that Portuguese fugitives had first arrived at the fortress of Arzila (Morocco), among them a masked man, who disguised themselves before boarding a ship of the armada which then set sail to Portugal. The fort's captain attests to that. The physician João Mendes Pacheco is to have treated him at D. Cristóvão de Távora's house, in Guimarães, having been summoned by the latter's widow. Dr. Mendes Pacheco would later be arrested and sent to the galleys by the king of Spain, with no precise accusation of the crime he committed.

According to other stories, Sebastião is to have lived in Sinai for 20 years, and that he wanted the Church to pressure the king of Spain (and now of Portugal too) into giving him his throne back. Robbed on his way to the Holy See and dressed like a beggar, he then ended up in a Venetian jail. But such is his insistence in getting an audience with the Pope, that the Roman Curia dispatches respected Dominican friar Estêvão de Sampaio, who had been successful in previous investigations and had the cardinals' trust. And friar Estêvão had no doubts that it truly was the missing king. The letter he wrote to Rome is impressive:

> I swear to thee on the Passion of Jesus Christ that he is king Sebastião as I am friar Estêvão. Should it not be so, then let me be condemned not only as a liar, but a renegade, a blasphemer and a heretic as well. I went and returned. I secretly ascertained that, of the sixteen marks he had on his body since childhood, he bears them all, to say nothing of the scars of battle.

Said marks were, among other, *a right hand larger than the left, thick lip on the right side, brown, hairy birthmark on the left shoulder blade, a large callous on his pinky finger, a missing tooth on the back of the jaw, his entire right side larger than the left, an extra finger on his foot.* These two rather different characters would have equally different fates. Friar Estêvão was executed at Barrameda's Sanlúcar Square, while Sebastião continued to claim his lost crown. Three different popes attested to his identity: Clement VIII (1598), Paul V (1617) and Urban VIII (1630). By the time of the third attestation, Sebastião would be 76 years old. And would be living in Morocco, according to Urban VIII, with children and a wife, a prostitute called Estrela, whom he addressed as 'princess'. According to others, he ended his days in the monastery of Limoges, in shame of his defeat at Ksar El-Kebir, and telling God in his prayers that he was a king without a kingdom. But those versions are unimportant for Portugal's history. The fact of the matter is that the young king does not return.

The nation made ready for the prisoners' ransom. At the end of July 1579, 80 noblemen arrive in Morocco, led by Francisco da Costa, who had been sent by the realm as ambassador. His mission was to free the most distinguished of the prisoners, many of which were children. A sum of 400 thousand cruzados is agreed upon; the ambassador lacks 150 thousand. He himself remains in Morocco as a hostage until the rest of the payment arrived, and would die there, along with all others who didn't return. Portugal lived under Spanish rule for years, but the people still hoped that Sebastião might be among the prisoners, that he was biding his time to reclaim the throne, perhaps waiting in one of those "Isles at the End of the World" – according to Pessoa, the "Fortunate Isles"[2].

What voice is this emanating from the waves
Which isn't the voice of the sea?
It is the voice of one who speaks to us,
But, if we listen, it falls silent
At having been heard.
(…)
'tis the fortunate isles
'tis a land without a place,
Where the King dies in wait.

Message ("The Fortunate Isles"), Fernando Pessoa

Three main facts contribute to the enduring legend of a still-living Sebastião. First, on the year of his disappearance (1598), blood dripped for 18 days from his father's tomb, indicating that he was suffering for his son, as the Portuguese believed. Second, the fact that only the missing king's portrait escaped unharmed from the fire at the All Saints Hospital in Lisbon. Third, his staged burial. The new Spanish king had the Moors send from Morocco a body which clearly wasn't that of the Yearned-For, which was then slowly dragged in a procession from the Algarve to Lisbon. The theatrics of the funeral procession's arrival at the Jerónimos Monastery only caused the Portuguese people's suspicions to increase, which is reflected on the Latin inscription on his mausoleum:

If rumours be true, here lies Sebastião
Whose life was prematurely taken on African shores
And say ye not that the king is wrong if he believes to be alive still [as] according to a revoked law, death [to him] was as unto life.

2 Said *Fortunate Isles* were to be found in the Atlantic and changed location depending on the legend – Azores, Cape Verde, Canary Islands, Madeira; or perhaps they were Saint Brandon's Isle, in a sea wherein dwelt monsters, demons, angels and birds which sang in Latin. The garden of Eden was to be found there, as was King Arthur.

The young king's succession

After Sebastião's disappearance, the Portuguese throne is occupied by cardinal Henrique, who, at the age of 66, was already making ready to meet his maker. He was known as the Chaste, but his celibacy proved to be a terrible mistake. The Senate of Lisbon asked him to marry, and the old man takes heart at the prospect of a love life he hadn't really counted on any more. Like a teenager, he sought the one to share his bed with, refusing the widow of France's Charles IX, as she was too old for him, as well as Isabel, second daughter of emperor Maximilian II, who was too ugly for him. He settled for the young flesh of Maria, eldest daughter of the duke of Bragança, who wasn't even 14 at the time, and requested pope Gregory III for permission to marry on the 7th of October 1578, as soon as he ascended to the throne. But his old body was no longer up to the task, weak to the point that he had to be breastfed, his wet nurse one *dona* Maria da Mota, of noble birth and married to Rui Fernandes Cota. Afterwards, embarrassed and plaintive, he gives up on his intent, realizing he is no longer physically able. The terrible year of 1580 then began. Plague and hunger weakened Portugal. In Lisbon alone, 25 thousand were buried on account of the outbreak. The cardinal disappears on the 31st of January. According to historian Manuel Amaral, none mourned his death. *Dom* António, Prior of Crato, took to the throne, but proved unable to unite the clergy or anyone of real influence, and was king for but a month, enough time to stamp coins with his face and employ a couple of family members.

Filipe II of Spain, Sebastião's cousin, then made his move. He takes the fortress of São Gião, the key to the Tagus, and gathers his army at the border in a show of force. His galleys enter the Tagus and he decisively defeats the Prior of Crato's troops on the 25th of August 1580 at the battle of Alcântara. Afterwards, he would still face a number of masqueraders claiming to be Sebastião: A potter from Alcobaça, who said he was the king of Penamacor (1584), and ended up sentenced to the galleys; stonemason Mateus Álvares, the king of Ericeira (1585), who handed out titles of nobility, gathered a small army to attack the Castillian sympathizers and ended up decapitated in Lisbon; and friar Miguel dos Santos tried to anoint king Gabriel, who was known as the Baker of Madrigal (1595), but the latter only managed to make Ana of Austria fall for him, and both the baker and his mentor ended up hanged. Lastly, in 1598, came the turn of one Marco Túlio Catizone, known as the Calabrese, who claimed to be an emissary of Sebastião. Catizone ended up decapitated (or hanged) in 1603. The Spanish dynasty endured for a while: After Filipe II, the Prudent (from 1580 to 1598), came Filipe III, the Pious (until 1621), followed by the last, Filipe IV, the Great, "three filipine dynasties" – until the 1st of December 1640, the Portuguese Restoration, when Portugal once again became a sovereign realm.

"While it freed us from the greatest of external shames, the Restoration did not free us from internal shame, nor did it bring anyone able to free us from it. We became independent as a country, and dependent as individuals". On the 9th of March 1808, still under occupation by Junot's French troops, the people saw yet another sign that Sebastião would return. José Carlos da Costa, from Lisbon, found an egg on which were stamped the initials V.D.S.R.D.P. – which everyone knew to be *Viva Dom Sebastião Rei de Portugal* (Long Live *Dom* Sebastião King of Portugal). An omen. Pessoa felt that "years pass, and its people dream of having a Portuguese king once more". Because, "in a symbolic sense, Sebastião is Portugal. Portugal lost its greatness with him, and would only regain it after his return – a symbolic return – much like his own life had been symbolic, an amazing and divine mystery". The Portuguese longed ever more intensely for the return of the Hidden One. And that longing came to be known as *sebastianism.*

Ad perpetuam, rei memoriam
(For a permanent record of the matter) Formula used on papal bulls

NEW TIMES

Ring, o clarion, whose voice says
That once you uttered the royal cry
For Dom *João, Master of Aviz,*
And Portugal!
Fifth Empire, Fernando Pessoa

The decadence of Portugal

At the end of he 19th century, the Industrial Revolution had changed the Old World, reaffirming the peripheral role of economies such as Portugal's. As if that weren't enough, the end of the slave trade would also interfere with the political logistics of the African continent, with tremendous repercussions for the countries who held lands there. Slavery would only end in the Portuguese territories in 1878 – its abolishing having been set in motion almost a century before with the marquis of Pombal – well after the English Slavery Abolition Act of 1833, and France's Decret de L'Abolition de L'Esclavage of 1848. And that was not all, as profound changes were also being operated on the field of international relations. The Treaty of Zaire acknowledged the Portuguese ownership over the river Icomati, but laws wouldn't be enough to preserve a dominion which had long since deteriorated. The English government of Lord Salisbury hands out the Ultimatum on the 11th of January 1890, proclaiming that all Portuguese military forces in Chire and the Country of the Macololos and Machonas[3] should withdraw or be decimated. War was imminent. An English dreadnought lay anchor on the shores of Portugal. The episode is nowadays known in Portuguese schools as *pink map*[4]. For historian Victor Eleutério, that *pink map was the colour of a ruinous dream of grandeur, much like the Fifth Empire.*

3 Peoples ostensibly under British protection who lived in a region between Angola and Mozambique.

4 Thus called because it was the colour of the map annexed to the accord of 1886 between France and Portugal, in an attempt at creating a Portuguese dominion which included the territories of Angola and Mozambique – which had previously agreed upon in the Berlin Conference (1884-1885).

On the night of that fateful 11th of January, king Carlos, the Diplomat, announced he would yield to the demands in order to save the interests of the state. In so doing, he all but ended the last hopes for a grand Portugal. In the streets, there is frustration and hate. *Gazeta de Portugal* agitates for *swift justice against those people.* A bulldog edition of *A Província* publishes Antero de Quental and Luís de Magalhães' "Manifesto for the Homeland". At Martinho da Arcada, mobs shout down the pirates. Republican revolts are suppressed. "Why is the nation divided thus against itself? The reason is easy to ascertain, as the case is of the sort that can have but one reason. We are divided because we don't have a Portuguese notion, a national ideal, no concept of a mission for ourselves". Before his own subjects, king Carlos becomes a *natural ally of England,* or an *accomplice for the outrage.* And *Ultimatum,* according to Nuno Severiano Teixeira, *attains the tragic dimension of a nationalist defeat.* Pessoa, in 1917, would use the name for a title of the manifesto in which he flips off "those who conform to a smallness of spirit".

The people's reaction

In Lisbon, street name signs are torn off and names are switched. Travessa dos Inglezinhos (Englishmen Lane) becomes Travessa dos Ladrões (Thieves Lane), and Travessa do Enviado de Inglaterra (England Envoy Lane) becomes Travessa do Diabo que o Carregue (Devil May Take Him Lane) – but only in common parlance, as the municipality never formalized those changes. The pound becomes known as the 'pilferer', an *inglesada* (something typically British) becomes known as a 'theft', and a beef is now a 'caitiff'. Even teaching English in public schools is questioned. José Alberto de Vasconcelos publishes in *O Século* "The Seven Deadly Sins – An Acrostic of *O Inglez* ('The Englishman', according to the spelling of the time):

sOberba (Pride)
luxúrIa (Lust)
iNveja (Envy)
preGuiça (Sloth)
guLa (Gluttony)
cólEra (Wrath)
avareZa (Avarice)

In 1890, renowned musician and painter Alfredo (Cristian) Keil (1850-1907) composed "A Portuguesa", with verses of sea captain Henrique Lopes de Mendonça (1856-1931), which was sung in the streets, especially the following refrain:

To arms! To arms!
On land and sea!
To arms! To arms!
To fight for our homeland!
Against the British
we march, we march!

"A portuguesa" becomes the national anthem on the 19th of June 1911, though the refrain was altered on the 16th of June 1957 by the Council of Ministers, replacing 'British' with 'cannons', as it'd hardly be appropriate for a national anthem to contain such strong words against a country with which it was on good terms once again. To the detriment of the refrain's meaning, of course, as one could hardly be expected to just march against cannons.

Pessoa felt deep in his soul the degradation of nationhood. "Every day, the newspapers bring me news of facts which are humiliating to us, Portuguese. None can conceive how I suffer with them. None can imagine the profound despair, the enormous pain that takes over me before such things". Ill-will against the monarchy intensifies. The military and political failings of the House of Bragança are plain for all to see, and one can feel the smell of blood in the streets.

The regicide

Saturday, February the 1st, 1908. Shortly after lunch, at Terreiro do Paço, two men made ready to change the course of Portugal's history. Primary school teacher Manuel (dos Reis da Silva) Buiça (1876-1908), with a dashing black beard, hides a Mannlicher rifle under his floor length coat; and Alfredo (Luís da) Costa, a frail trading clerk who carried a Browning FN 7.65 in his pocket. Minutes before, they were quietly having lunch and drinking beer at Café Gelo – which is still open at Praça Dom Pedro IV, at Rossio. With them, three other fellows of the Carbonari, which was opposed to the monarchy. The royal family is having a peaceful vacation at the palace of Vila Viçosa, in Évora, 150 kilometres from Lisbon. King Carlos rests in that ducal palace, having been proclaimed king on the 28th of December 1889, after Luís, the Popular's death. *Dom* Carlos was, according to republican Fialho de Almeida, *superior, intelligent, cultured, brave and even generous; the most intelligent politician of his time and the only one with a measure of character.* Carlos had been amusing himself since January, hunting deer on his property's grounds, completely unaware that he was about to become prey himself. Upon his return to Lisbon with his wife, Amélia – whom Pessoa called "D. Amélia d'Orleans" on account of the family she was born to – and his firstborn, prince Luís Filipe, who would be 21 in a couple of weeks. His other son, Manuel de Bragança, duke of Beja, was little over 19 and awaited his parents in Lisbon. The king's wife tries to convince him to remain a few days longer, but in vain. Had she managed to do so, both the family and Portugal's fate might have been very different. "At midday, a dire expectation hung in the pallid atmosphere. Towards the Castle, the sky was clear but with something ominous in its blue". The family arrives at Lisbon in the afternoon aboard the *D. Luís* steamboat. The king's life was in danger, everyone knew it; but, as if nothing could truly happen to him, he intends to go see Wagner's *Tristan and Isolde* at the São Carlos. The talk of the town is the uncovering of a republican revolutionary plot led by the so-called Group of 18. The court was of the opinion that no revolution would be forthcoming. But, in the words of historian João Ameal, *since revolution had failed, all that was left was crime.* Dr. António José de Almeida (1866-1929), who would later become president (1919-1923), was under arrest. On the eve of that terrible day, Teixeira de Abreu, the minister of Justice, went to Vila Viçosa with a decree-law of execution to authorize the deportation of those sentenced for the conspiracy, who would be exiled to the distant overseas colonies (Timor among them). The king picked up the quill and said: *I am signing my death sentence.* As if he predicted what was about to happen. João Franco (1855-1925), chief of government, retaliated against his opposition with an iron fist. Pessoa wasn't all too fond of him.

> A God tired of being God…
> In order to do something
> And not spend eternity idly
> Made João Franco.
>
> *João Franco*, Fernando Pessoa

Concerned with the possibility of the usual delays of parades such as the one he would be appearing in, the king asked his retinue to head immediately to the palace. Benedito Caparica, the coachman, held the reins of an open type carriage with the top down, called a landau. Prince Luís Filipe goes up first, the Colt 38 on his pocket undisguised by his livery. After him, *Dom* Manuel. Both go in front. The king stays in the back seat, to the left. The queen, after getting flowers from a child, stays on her husband's right. The smile on her face wouldn't be staying there for long. *Dom* Carlos puts his hand in his coat's pocket and fondles the grip of his Smith & Wesson 32, which he is never parted from. The parade begins. People respectfully take off their hats. But not all. Almost in front of the Treasury Department (today a post office), a shot is heard coming from the middle of the plaza. It was the sign for the attempt. Close by at the corner of Terreiro do Paço and Rua do Arsenal, right next to the statue of *Dom* José, Manuel Buiça leaves the green kiosk he was waiting at, walks a couple of steps and kneels down. He is in the middle of the street, 5 metres behind the carriage. He then takes the rifle from his coat and calmly takes aim at his king. The royal escort, unprepared and stunned, doesn't react. The dry crack of the first shot is heard, followed by others. The first hits *Dom* Carlos in the neck, severing his spine and leaving through his lower jaw. The king motions for his neck. The next hits him on the shoulder, and the third shatters one of the landau's lamps. "Two criminal bullets killed him". He then collapses over his wife, anticipating what TVs the world over would show on the 22nd of November 1963 with president Kennedy. Almost the same scene described by António Machado in "O crime foi em Granada":

> Dead, collapsed Federico [Garcia Lorca]
> – Blood on his brow and lead in his innards –
> …the crime took place in Granada
> Know ye – poor Granada – in his Granada…

Alfredo Costa climbs over the carriage's step, on the left side, and shoots the already lifeless body twice more on the back. The queen launches herself against the aggressor, still holding her flowers, trying to prevent him from taking more shots. Her screams can be clearly heard – *Villains! Villains!* Prince Luís Filipe stands up and aims at Costa with his Colt, but, before he can shoot, the man shoots him in the lung. Even so, he manages to take four shots. Costa falls down, to be killed by sword and pistol by the police. As he got up, though, the prince became an easy target, and Buiça kept shooting. One of his bullets hits the prince on the left side of his face, right underneath the cheekbone, and leaves through the back of his head. *Dom* Manuel tries to hold his brother and is hit on the arm. The coachman, even with a wounded hand, spurs the horses on towards the Navy Arsenal by the Tagus, between Terreiro do Paço and the Praça do Município. Infantry soldier Henrique da Silva Valente tries to get at Buiça, who shoots him in the thigh, but the killer was then felled by the sword of lieutenant Francisco Figueira Freire. The royal escort still shoots him a number of times. Pessoa sums up the scene in a text by heteronym Méluret: "Nothing more understandable than the murder of king Carlos of Portugal".

Nearby bystanders are herded by the police and savagely beaten. An innocent man, Sabino Costa, is killed by two shots to the head. The attack is immortalized in a drawing by Bestrame, which was published at *Ilustração Portuguesa* and then reproduced at *Petit Journal de Paris.* According to a report by José Brandão, who witnessed the scene, the carriage was covered in blood. The queen mother, Maria Pia de Saboia, recalling the decree her son had signed the day prior, addresses João Franco and says: *This is your doing, mister president.* The bodies of Buiça and Costa are left in a corner at city hall. According to Pessoa, they spoke "for the defeated" and had been "the soul of an entire people". Later, a public subscription is opened in favour of those two, who were heroes for the people, and their tombs were filled with flowers.

"The wonderful beauty of political corruption... and, every now and again, the comet of a regicide". The prince is left on an iron gurney and raw canvas. The king, right next to him, over a mattress and pillows. No sheets or pillowcase. His lips are already pale, and a rivulet of blood runs from the corner of his mouth. In his pockets, the revolver, a handkerchief, an Águilas cigar he would never get to smoke and a rusty watch hanging from his belt by a gold chain, marking the hour of his demise – five o'clock. The set is completed by two lamps and an old crucifix, plus a priest and sexton. Art imitates life. In 1935, the year of Pessoa's death, Federico García Lorca wrote a poem dedicated to a bullfighter, "Capture and death" (from *Lament for Ignacio Sánchez Mejías),* almost reproducing the scene (excerpt):

> At five in the afternoon
> It was five o'clock sharp.
> (...)
> A coffin with wheels is a bed
> At five o'clock in the afternoon.
> Bones and flutes sound in his ears
> At five o'clock in the afternoon.
> (...)
> The wounds burned like suns
> At five o'clock in the afternoon.
> (...)
> It was five o'clock on every watch.
> It was five o'clock in a shadowy afternoon.

The last king

The prince is crowned king. At the carriage, he is alleged to have fearfully whimpered: *Let us leave, let us leave,* but his austere mother had him pull himself together, reminding him he had a duty to fulfil until the end. His will to leave would only be delayed, however. At night, Manuel II had João Franco relieved from his duties and formed a new ministry. But the time of nobility was definitely at an end, and that young man was far too polite, kind and unprepared to govern a land that had descended into chaos. To say nothing of the fact that, according to Henrique Rosa (Pessoa's uncle), *he let his mother lord over him, as well as the priests and the cronies at the court.* During his short reign, there were six ministries. Word in the street goes that António Teixeira de Souza (1857-1917), the chief of government, had sold out to the republicans. According to Pessoa, "to say that Mr. T[eixeira] de S[ouza] had thrown the M[onarchy] under the bus is akin to saying that a patient's death is caused by the contagious state which precedes it". The example of Brazil, which had become a republic in 1889, excites the imagination of the Portuguese.

Two years after the attack, on the 3rd of October 1910, chief republican Miguel Bombarda (1851-1910) is murdered. By some madman, according to the government. The people don't buy it, however. The following day, on the 4th of October 1910, the king heads to the palace of Mafra and embarks with his mother and paternal grandmother (Maria Pia) to Plymouth, where he would exile himself to and where he would marry (in 1913) Augusta Victoria of Hohenzollern-Sigmaringen. He would later become known, not only as the Patriot, but also as the Unfortunate (for having lost his crown), the King-Longing (after the proclamation of the republic), or the Studious (out of his love for old books). On the 19th of January 1919, the monarchy would be newly proclaimed in Porto, but the kingdom of Traulitânia – as it became know – which actually spread across the entire north, lasted all of 25 days. *Dom* Manuel would end his days in Twickenham, where he wrote three volumes of *Ancient Portuguese Books 1489-1600* before his death, 22 years after that grey day in which he departed from Portugal. Without ever having returned to that nation which was no longer his.

The republic

On Tuesday, the 4th of October 1910, the first page of *O Século* announces: *At that time, on the castle of São Jorge, which had the blue and white flag, the republican flag was raised.* A day later and, on the central balcony of the city hall, much like in the regimes of France and Switzerland, the parliamentary republic was officially proclaimed. The members of the new regime came from the aristocratic bourgeoisie, which was made up of traditional families at the time. "Democracy is the upper floor neighbour (who throws trash into my yard)". Troubled times follow. Old grudges flare up. Positivist writer and philosopher Teófilo Braga (1843-1924), one of the founders of the republican party, becomes president of the republic of an interim government which lasts until the 3rd of September 1911. The government's strongman is Afonso (Augusto da) Costa (1871-1937), the young minister of Justice and Cults, whom Pessoa would later be terrified of. On the 28th of May 1911, 226 councilmen are elected. The National Constitutional Assembly abolishes monarchy on its inaugural session and declares *eminent patriots* all those who fought for the republican flag, and on the 18th of August 1911, they voted for a short, parliamentary and democratic constitution with only 87 articles. For historians such as António Reis, that constitution's sole original merit was replacing the king with the president.

The republic's new president was politician and lawyer Manuel de Arriaga (1840-1917). But that "constitutionalism did nothing but bring us a political regime entirely foreign to all material and cultural conditions of our true nature. It destroyed and despoiled uselessly and stupidly, aiming solely at our impossible adaptation to a regime no Portuguese sentiment wished for, and all truly Portuguese intelligence despised". Its first years are almost as complicated and unstable as the monarchy's last – barracked by the press, protested in the streets, mired in strikes and deceptions. "We are incapable of revolt and agitation. When we did have a revolution, it was only to establish something exactly like the thing we meant to replace". The government had "thieves of the worst kind (often good lads and good friends in the personal sphere)", "crooks with an inkling of true ideals, natural-born anarchists or great internal patriots, all of that was to be seen in the fake hodgepodge which followed the republic". "The country was prepared for monarchy, but certainly not for the republic". As he says in *Ultimatum,* the "Portugal-pittance" is but "the remains of the monarchy rotting as a republic".

Pessoa's enamourment with the republic wouldn't last long. Even so, "in a referendum on regimes, I would vote, albeit sorrowfully, for the republic". Those changes had tremendous repercussions on his understanding of the world. "Increasingly, I place on the psychic essence of my blood the impersonal purpose of aggrandizing the nation and contributing to the evolution of humanity. It is the shape which the mysticism of our race has taken in me". Deep down, he begins to feel revolted and disheartened. "I belong to a generation which has lost all respect for the past and all belief or hope in the future. Therefore, we live in and off the present, with the eagerness and hunger of one who has nothing else". The Portuguese sentiment becomes that of emptiness. "We are a great people of adjourned heroes. We bash in the faces of those who aren't present, conquer the hearts of all women we dream of, and wake up joyfully late in the morning, fondly remembering all the grand feats we have yet to accomplish. In the midst of it all, the republic doesn't end. It is hard to tell whether our past is out future, or if the future is our past".

World War I

In texts he psychographed as More, Pessoa has a favourable disposition towards Germany, as he could see "no other open path as disciplined individualism than to see Europe ruled by a strong people who were crushed". Writer João de Barros makes an appeal to Portuguese intellectuals in *O Mundo,* asking them to close ranks with the allies. Pessoa wrote a reply to Barros, which wasn't sent to the papers: "I do believe the time has come to say it loud and clear to the Portuguese that the Portuguese truth trumps war. Contrary to Mr. João de Barros' appeal, the Portuguese soul should align itself with her sister, the Germanic soul. For today's Portugal, oppressed and faded as it is, as for humiliated Germany of the beginning of the past century, what can lift both up is a tradition of Empire, and, in both cases, an entirely broken and wizened tradition". For him, there is "in both cases, a curious sentiment of national mysticism". "Among us, the mystical, national legend of *Dom* Sebastião; in Germany, the legend of Frederick Barbarossa, who is to return and restore the empire to its former greatness". But his country's story would play out rather differently. In the beginning of 1916, England asks Portugal to apprehend German merchant ships which were docked in Lisbon's harbour. The request is complied with on the 23rd of February. Following the subsequent failure of diplomacy, Germany declared war on Portugal on the 9th of March. The world would give notice the following day: *Germany declares war on Portugal, and Portugal haughtily accepts the German challenge.* The First World War begins for the Portuguese and, from the 28th of March on, all publications must undergo previous censorship.

How long shall the war last?, asks *Jornal da Mulher* on the 30th of June 1916. As a rule, European wars were short-lived. The ones between Bulgaria and Serbia (1885) and between Turkey and Greece (1887) were week-long affairs. The two Balkan wars (1912-1913) lasted roughly the same. The Franco-Prussian was settled in a month. But World War I would last for years. It had its importance for the cultural life, as a number of intellectuals who were residing abroad returned to Lisbon, names such as Almada Negreiros, Amadeu de Sousa Cardoso, José Pacheco, Luís de Montalvor, Raul Leal, Santa-Rita Pintor and, for a while, Sá-Carneiro as well. In Portugal, Afonso Costa's republican government falls. The energy with which he steers the fate of his nation is insufficient to grant him any sort of legitimacy. Even his party colleagues proved hostile. Brazilian Bernardino Machado (1851-1944) took his place for a short while (1915-1917), and soon new ministers were named under the stewardship of Victor Hugo Azevedo Coutinho. In the eyes of the people, they were as unto Victor Hugo's *Les Misérables,* and his was also a short-lived government, followed by Pimenta de Castro's (1846-1918) who, in 1915, went straight from the halls of government to prison. The writing was on the wall when "Time, eldest of the gods, granted them [the allies] victory", with the war ending on the 28th of June 1919 with the Treaty of Versailles.

In 1918, the next big thing in Lisbon is Carlos Gardel – with his different voice and slick hair combed back with pomade. In the cabarets of the Baixa and Praça da Alegria, especially Maxime, tango is all the rage. The city's social life resumes its course. The country is Europe's greatest producer of wolfram, an indispensable material for the production of armaments. With the war, fortunes had been made and spent by those newly rich known as *wolframists.* The same who light cigars with 100 mil-réis bills, purchase books by the metre and show off several ink pens in their coat pockets – even though (almost) none of them can write. Then came the time of the radio, and the first cement factories pop up. The country abandons its agrarian economy and begins its first great cycle of industrialization, importing steel, cars, coal, iron, oil, paper, equipment for trains and farm machinery. Change is in the air. And literature is no exception.

A new Portuguese literature

In 1914, Pessoa considers three open paths for Portuguese literature: "To deliver itself to the outside world and be absorbed by it…; to put itself aside, in an individual dream, reacting passively against modern life"; or "appropriating that noisy world, nature, all within the dream itself – and escaping reality in that dream. That is the Portuguese way (so very Portuguese"). The following year, he better details that vision (abridged): "Out of all three nationalisms, the first and lesser is the one stuck with traditions – the nationalism of Bocage and Castilho. The second is the one the soul of the nation is attached to – that of a Bernardim Ribeiro, in its lesser degree, or a Teixeira de Pascoaes at his most elevated. The third integrates all cosmopolitan elements – at its lesser degree, that of a Camões; we have yet to see it at its most elevated, but Shakespeare, Goethe and all other sublime representatives of the nations' literary peaks have attained it". He was speaking of himself, naturally: The Over-Camões.

Perhaps for the first time in his life, he knew where to go and how to get there. He picked the third path. From the death throes of the monarchy to Salazar's dictatorship, Portuguese literature reflects the yearning for a sebastianist redemption. "We have become Portuguese once again in nationality, but we shall never again become Portuguese in mind. Not Portuguese, not anything". To him, the Portuguese had inherited "a disbelief in Christian faith" and "created in themselves a disbelief in all other faiths". That mood explains the painful awareness of decadence and renews the yearning for greatness and hope, sentiments on which the search for a new identity would find purchase on, a "national idea". Pessoa believed the prophetic predictions of a glorious resurrection, an attempt at rebuilding history under the inspiration of the utopia of the Fifth Empire; the one which, in the end, would fulfil Portugal's grandiose fate. It begins as an act of faith, *Message.*

ACT IV

IN WHICH HIS DISQUIET AND FATE ARE RETOLD

Patriæ magnitudini
(For the homeland's greatness) Latin expression

MESSAGE

Arms crossed, he stares beyond the sea
(...)
The limit of the land dominating
The sea that may exist beyond the land.
Message ("King João the Second"), Fernando Pessoa

The consecration of Portugal

Pessoa had for a long time considered writing a great book dedicated to Homer's heroes: The *Odyssey's* Odysseus, son of Laërte and Anticlea, king of Ithaca and notorious for having devised the Trojan Horse; and the *Iliad's* Achilles, son of Thetis and Peleus, a cruel, bloodthirsty warrior who was only felled when Apollo guided an arrow shot by Paris' arrow, which hit him in his one vulnerable spot – the ankle, which his mother had held as he was bathed in the Styx. That book was initially titled *Homeridae,* but eventually became *Portugal – An Epic Draft.* Shortly before its edition, in a letter to Gaspar Simões (28/07/1932), Pessoa defined it as "a small book of poems, 41 in all". In the end, they would be 44 – and, perhaps not by mere chance, 4 + 4 = 8. Much like the eight letters of Portugal or *Mensagem.* The definitive title was inspired by Anchises, son of Capys and Themiste, who guarded flocks at Ida's Height (close to Troy), a character of Virgil's *Aeneid* who gave his son the very formula of the universe, which Pessoa scribbled in a number of variants:

MENS AG|ITAT MOL|EM[1]
MENSA GEMMARUM[2]
MENS AGEM[3]
ENS GEMMA[4]
MENS AGEM

1 The mind moves matter.
2 The table of gems.
3 The mind acts.
4 The gem being.

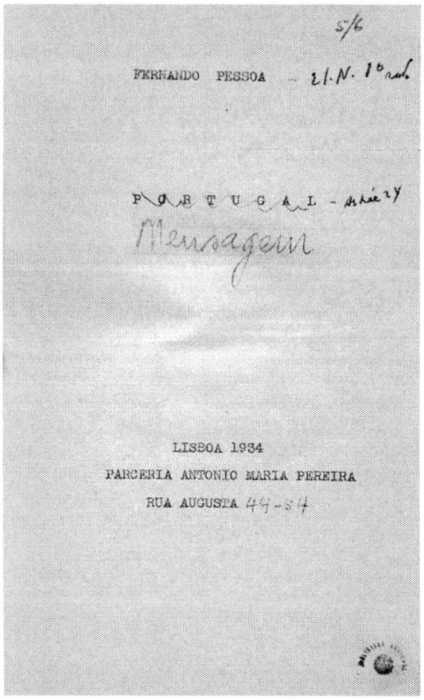

First page of *Message,* as sent to the publisher

The title is changed as the book is already being printed. The typewritten copy handed over to the publisher, dated 23rd of August 1934, has the original title scratched through with a pencil, and with *Mensagem* written underneath it by hand. This on account of "my old friend [Alberto da] Cunha Dias having brought to my attention – his observation patriotic and publicity-minded in equal measure – the fact that our country's name was nowadays prostituted to shoes[5], as its greatest dynasty was to hotels[6]. *Do you want your book to be titled after an analogy that portugalizes your feet?* I agreed and conceded, as I always agree and concede whenever presented with arguments. I take pleasure in being defeated when Reason is the victor, no matter the proxy". But that wasn't all. He was also afraid it might seem a little too pretentious to readers, as deep down he didn't consider his work was "up to the homeland's standards". All things considered, he acknowledged that "the title *Message* is an improvement over the first one". In its first draft, the book was meant to "represent how the wars between old and new gods dovetailed into the feats of Portugal – Hyperion and Apollo etc. (and what of Christianity? How does it fit here? As an *attrait* employed by the old gods to prevent men from having any faith in Jove's race?). Neptune with his storms, Jove with his bolts, Venus with corruption… Mars, seduced by Venus, with the conquests derived from the Discoveries". This reference to a *discovery* is curious,

5 A reference to *A Portugal, the country's oldest and most important shoe factory.*

6 The dynasty of Avis. Cleonice Berardinelli clarifies that the name was given to *a pretty villa in Lisbon, which was converted into a luxury hotel.* And Bragança was also the name of a Lisbon hotel.

as it doesn't necessarily refer to discovering new lands, but new languages. In the words of Lavoura Lopes, *whereas the humanists of the Renaissance discovered the ancient world in Latin, the 15th century Portuguese contributed to the Renaissance with the discovery of new worlds in the vernacular.*

Both *Message* and *The Lusiads* express the same idea of national exaltation; which is why, in his drafts, Pessoa jots down the very meaning of the book – "an epic fragment". For that purpose, and so as to give the text a tone from the past, he opts for an archaic orthography – *y* instead of i, silent letters, double consonants and exhortations in Latin. Camões revered king Sebastião in his challenging mission of building an empire, placing memory and hope on the same plane, whereas Pessoa, although he did respect the past, he foresees the grandiose future of his people – *a different conception of heroism,* in which *the object of one's hopes is transferred into dream and utopia.* Jacinto Prado Coelho was the first to feel it. Harold Bloom thinks it strange that Camões doesn't appear in *Message,* but that is easily explained by the fact that Pessoa fully intended to take his place as the epitome of Portuguese literature. The text is mirrored on classical works, such as the *Divine Comedy,* which takes place during the holy war of 1300. In it, Dante Alighieri (1265-1321), after having traversed the nine circles of Hell and standing atop the mountain of Purgatory, is led into Paradise by his (platonic) love Beatrice Portinari. The *Divine Comedy* is comprised of one hundred poems, divided in three *cantos – Inferno* (34)*, Purgatorio* (33) and *Paradiso* (33). *Message* shares the same structure – Coat-of-Arms (19), Portuguese Sea (12) and The Hidden One (13). As further proof of that inspiration, one need but look at the verses of *Inferno's canto* XXVI and compare them with *Message's* "The Bogey-Beast"

Comedy	"The Bogey-Beast"
52. To ask thee who is in yon fire, that comes	Whose are the sails over which I skim?
79. O ye, who dwell two spirits in one fire!	The bogey-beast that lives at the end of the sea[7]
132. Thrice it whirl'd her round	Three times from the helm he raised his hands

Message's structure

7 In a first draft, "the *bat* that lives at the end of the sea". The poem was originally meant to be published in *Contemporânea* magazine, vol. II, numbers 4, 5 and 6, under the title of *The bat* – as the Cape of Good Hope was known.

Underneath its title, a quote in Latin explains the work's historical sense: *Benedictus dominus deus noster qui dedit nobis signum* (Blessed be the Lord our God, who gave us the sign). It is the *signum* of the battle of Ourique, which pitted the Portuguese against the Muslims, and in which legend says that Christ appeared in front of Afonso Henriques, which was then converted into one of the five wounds of Portugal's arms. The first part, underneath the epigraph *Bellum sine bello* (War without war), is *Coat-of-Arms* – duly divided into Fields, Castles, Escutcheons, Crown and Crest – anticipating the glorious actions of Portugal's founders. With seven castles reproducing the *myth of the seven ages* – according to António Quadros – even though the seventh castle is split into two, King João the First and Queen Philippa of Lancaster, the couple who gave birth to the dynasty of Avis. It represents the ascension. The second part, under the epigraph *Possessio maris* (Possession of the Sea), is *Portuguese Sea* – with the characters who would honour their people in the discoveries of their great navigations, presaging new horizons. According to astrologer Paulo Cardoso, the 12 poems are *a rigorous transposition of the 12 signs of the zodiac.* It represents the apogee. The third part, under the epigraph *Pax in excelsis* (Peace in the heights), is *The Hidden One* – rife with symbols and warnings which prefigure new times, a third age of redemption which would begin with King Sebastião in the grandiose dream of the Fifth Empire and ends with the image of fog, where "all is uncertain and ultimate". It represents decline. At the end of the book, another quote, this one evoking Rosicrucian initiation rites – *Valete frates* (Farewell, brothers).

Message is also marked by the profound influence of celestial bodies the author believes to be under. As he writes in "Hour of the Devil", "We live in this world of symbols, simultaneously clear and obscure – visible darkness, so to speak; and each symbol is a truth which can replace truth until time and circumstances restore the true one". Which is why he writes a preliminary note, in which he clears up the matter:

> Understanding symbols and (symbolic) rituals demands the interpreter be in possession of five sorts of conditions, without which the symbols will be as dead for him, and him as dead to them. The first is *sympathy*. The interpreter must feel sympathy towards the symbol he means to interpret. The second is *intuition*, that understanding with which one feels what lies unseen beyond the symbol. The third is *intelligence*, which must needs go from discursive to analogical, so the symbol might be interpreted. The fourth is *comprehension*, as certain symbols cannot be properly understood if previous different symbols haven't been so. The fifth is least definable, and I'd tell some that it is *grace*, others that it is the hand of the *Unknown Superior*, speaking to others.

The beginning of Message

The idea of a book of this nature came about when Pessoa returned to Portugal. Jorge Nemésio recalls a draft of a similarly inspired poem, "Legends", from 1905. In 1910, he scribbles the draft of another poem, "Portugal", which, style-wise, *foreshadowed the coming* Message – in the words of Fernando Cabral Martins[8]. Gaspar Simões believed there to be an older reference still, the conception of the poem "Gládio", on the 21st of July 1913. In Paris (letter dated 07/01/1913), Sá-Carneiro approved the title Pessoa had suggested, and recommends he tell it no one else, lest *some imbecilic, anaemic platelet show up in the libraries with that name.* The "patriotic idea, always more or less present in my purposes, now swells up in me", he says in a letter to Côrtes-Rodrigues (19/01/1913). the first poem he writes is "Fernando, *Infante* of Portugal" (21/07/1913) – "God gave me his glaive for me to wage His holy war". Afterwards, "The Bogey-Beast" (09/09/1918), "*Padrão*" (13/09/1918), "Prayer" (31/12/1922) and "Ascension of Vasco da Gama" (10/1/1922). Around 1928, he aims for some unity between those poems, and writes 11 more, among them "Afonso de Albuquerque"; one in 1929, two in 1930, three in 1933, and 10 in 1934, the last one on the 2nd of April 1934, "The Columbus". Twelve of them are undated. Even after the first edition of *Message,* Pessoa keeps correcting his verses by hand – be it accents, punctuation or words. And not even in a single copy, as would be the sensible thing to do, making instead annotations whenever something occurred him. Proof of that criterion are at least three annotated copies: One can be found today at Casa Fernando Pessoa; another dedicated "to Eduardo Malta, a hug from your friend and admirer, FP 13/01/1935"; and a third dedicated "to [cousin] Victoriano [Braga]". The annotations do not, however, match the number of alterations in the second printing.

In *Message,* Pessoa asks his nation for compromise, as Portugal was living "one of the most critical (in the original meaning of the word) moments of refurbishment of its national subconscious". It was "purposely" on sale on the 1st of December (1934), the glorious date of Portugal's Restoration (in 1640), when the country got a Portuguese king after 60 years under Spanish yoke. Parceria António Maria Pereira, the publishing house, gave the book such importance, it occupied its entire shop window at Rua Augusta 44 with copies of *Message.* He would later bemoan that it had been the first book of his "mature stage", a sentiment marked mostly by disappointment. Augusto Ferreira Gomes

8 In spite of all the evidence to the contrary, for Ariano Suassuna, *Message* was inspired by Olavo Bilac's poem, "Sagres" (1898), which he took with him in a trip to Lisbon in 1912. According to him, the central idea of *Message* was already present in "Sagres", *including the symbolic value of capitalizing words such as Sea, and the deeper meaning of the Monster-World to beat, as a figure of Fate.* Let it be on record.

was in charge of proofreading. The graphic presentation, as the reader can see in the previous cover, is from Armando Figueiredo's *Editorial Império,* with Figueiredo later telling *Átomo* magazine that, when the author asked him to edit *Message,* he claimed "not to have the means to pay for the work upfront", but that he would do so "circumstances permitting". Perhaps it wasn't quite so, however, as José Blanco suggests António Ferro didn't have any qualms about appropriating some of the funds of the Bureau of National Propaganda to finance the book's printing. Blanco goes further still in a later text, in which he claims that it was painter Paulo Ferreira, at the time a collaborator of the BNP who told him as much. Despite all the credit owed his source, that is highly unlikely, however. Ferreira was almost certainly referring to the money Ferro had given Pessoa as an award (more on that below). In any event, the editor did indeed risk being a victim of what Pessoa called "process of the late Manuel Peres Vigário [Vicar]". Or, as the Portuguese expression goes, a true *vicar's tale,* the origin of which Pessoa sought to explain in an eponymous short story.

The Vicar's Tale

In Pessoa's version, *conto* (tale) referred to Portugal's currency (equivalent to mil escudos or a million réis), and Vigário (Vicar), a surname[9]. Purposefully chosen, of course, as the cunning tricksters of the time were known as *vigaristas*[10]. The explanation for the term is given in an amusing text, "To a Great Portuguese – Precise and Impassioned Narration Of What The Vicar's Tale Is", first published in the début issue of *O Sol* magazine (30/10/1926), and later in *Notícias Ilustrado* (a weekly supplement of Lisbon's *Diário de Notícias,* 18/07/1929), then titled "The Origin of the Vicar's Tale (summary):

> There once lived in Ribatejo a small-time farmer and cattle merchant named Manuel Peres Vigário. One day, a printer of counterfeit bills came up to him and said: "Mr. Vigário, I still have a couple of fake hundred mil-réis bills to hand out. Would you like some? I'll give them to you for twenty mil-réis each". As it so happened, in two day's time Vigário needed to pay off two brothers, cattle merchants like himself, whom he owed one conto de réis. On the first day of the fair, in which payment was due, the two brothers were dining in an obscure local tavern, when Manuel Peres Vigário stumbled through the door, clearly drunk. He pulled up a chair and asked the brothers if they minded getting everything in fifty mil-réis bills. The brothers were fine with that; but, as soon as the wallet was opened, the wariest of the two brought his brother's attention to the "bills", which were clearly hundred mil-réis. Manuel Peres shakily counted twenty bills, which he then proffered. One of the brothers immediately pocketed them, not even wasting time looking at the money. Then, as a natural effect of his drunkenness,

9 And not a very common one, at that. Lisbon's 2010 yellow pages lists but one Dr. Vigário.

10 *Translator's note:* Which can be roughly translated as *vicarists.*

Peres told them he wished a receipt. It wasn't something they usually did, but none of the brothers raised any objection. Then, Manuel Peres told of how, one day, at that time, at the tavern of who knows who, "we were having dinner (and so on, with all the stupid verbosity of a drunk), the two had gotten from Manuel Peres Vigário the due amount in fifty mil-réis bills.

The following day, as one brother tried to exchange the first hundred mil-réis bill, the man it was proffered to rejected it as fake, as he did the second and the third. And the two brothers, upon looking closely at the bills, realized not even a blind man would accept them. They filed a complaint, and Manuel Peres was summoned by the police, thanking the heavens for having been drunk to the point of actually asking for a stupid receipt, which, lo and behold, said: "One conto de réis in fifty mil-réis bills". If the two brothers had hundred mil-réis bills, then those most certainly weren't his. He well remembered, despite his drunkenness, to have paid twenty bills, and the brothers (according to Manuel Peres) weren't the type of men who'd take hundred mil-réis bills instead of fifty, as they were honoured men of renowned good character. And, as it was the only just thing to do, Manuel Peres Vigário was naturally let go.

The literary competition

On the 29th of November 1933, the Bureau of National Propaganda announced the creation of five literary awards, each with specific demands:

– Eça de Queiroz Award, Romance
Must be of amply constructive intent
Prize: 10 thousand escudos

– Alexandre Herculano Award, History
Firm patriotic criterion
Prize: 6 thousand escudos

– Antero de Quental Award, Poetry
A) For the best book of verses, no smaller than 100 pages, of undoubtedly Portuguese inspiration and, preferably, of a high sentiment of nationalist exaltation.
Prize: 5 thousand escudos
B) A poem, or loose poetry, in which the same qualities and intentions are present.
Prize: 1 thousand escudos

– Ramalho Ortigão Award, Essay
National innovative spirit
Prize: 4 thousand escudos

– António Eanes Award, Journalism
Matter of far-reaching national scope
Prize: 2 thousand escudos

The deadline for applications was the 1st of July 1934, but was extended until the 31st of October. According to José Blanco, *it was António Ferro's decision, so that Pessoa would have time to enter with his book.* Blanco goes farther still, admitting a conspiracy by friends Augusto Ferreira Gomes, Alberto da Cunha Dias, Almada Negreiros and Ferro himself, all of whom wished the poetry prize be awarded to him. The only name missing from Blanco's list is Luís de Oliveira Guimarães, *who worried about Pessoa's finances, and so* [Guimarães] *helped Ferro come up with some award to give him...* "As it [the book] was finished, I was spurred to publish it". Spurred by whom? Said friends? Or only Ferro? At night, Pessoa used to host them at home and read them his texts, and it bears remembering that previously, on the 17th of July 1923, he had signed a Portuguese intellectuals' protest against the prohibition of Ferro's book, *Mar alto* – the one he dedicated to *the beauteous talent and the beautiful soul of Pessoa, with friendship and admiration.* In another one, *Salazar,* the dedication was for Pessoa, Campos and Reis, *three great names of contemporary literature.* Pessoa, on the 11th of March 1933, thanked him "for the triply dedicated copy".

In the office he headed at the BNP, Ferro employed a number of Pessoa's friends: Almada Negreiros, Augusto Ferreira Gomes, Paulo Ferreira; and also (in 1936, Ophelia Queiroz, by request of her nephew Carlos Queiroz, who also worked there. In a letter from the 27th of April 1933, Pessoa wonders if there was "some proper position" for his friend Armando Teixeira Rabelo, appealing to their "old fellowship". The answer is precise: *There are few positions, and they are already filled.* The letter is then concluded with words which accurately portray the situation at the time: *You're not the only one who has to work double shifts... You're not the only one who is simultaneously Fernando Pessoa and Álvaro de Campos. I, for example, am António Ferro and director of the Bureau.* Followed by *the reply above was the director's. António Ferro took great interest in your request and shall do what he can at the earliest opportunity.*

The book "was ready by September, and I actually thought it would no longer be eligible for the contest, knowing not that the deadline – initially set for the end of July – had been extended until the end of October. However, since there already were copies of *Message* available at the end of October of the age of Nazareth's Christ, I delivered those demanded by the Bureau", he confesses in a letter to Casais Monteiro (20/01/1935). Pessoa's version doesn't hold up to scrutiny, as another one of the contest's requirements was that a book needed to have at least 100 pages, and *Message* had exactly 101[11] – systematically numbered only up to 100. Of those, only 52 contained poems, three had the final verses of said poems, many were blank or only had titles – which would normally be placed over the poems. Consequently, page 101 contained the index complement which was announced on page 97, and the name and address of Editorial Império was placed on 102. Such an amount of blank pages could only be explained by the huge increase in production costs, as it was necessary to comply with the 100 page requirement.

Many of *Message*'s poems had already been published. In 1922, the 12 poems of *Portuguese Sea* came out in *Contemporânea* magazine (volume 2, issues 4, 5, 6) – although one of them, "Irony"[12], was replaced by "The Columbus". "Prince Henry the Navigator", "King João the Second" and a first draft of "Afonso de Albuquerque" had also been published at *O Mundo Português* magazine (1933), and it bears remembering that, after having delivered the copies, he would still publish in *Diário de Lisboa*'s literary supplement "Prince Henry", "The Bogey-Beast" and "Prayer". But none of that presented a problem, as it wasn't a requirement for the poems to be unpublished – another hint that the contest was tailor-made for Pessoa. "The book was ripe for competition" – he said, referring to the requirement of *nationalist exaltation.* "I have entered the competition!". And complements it with: "I didn't do it, I must say, with my eyes on the possible prize, although there would be no intellectual sin in doing so" – as he explains on the 13th of January in the following year. On the 31st of December 1934, the first floor of Tavares restaurant would host a party, as described in *Diário de Lisboa: During lunch, between each dish, Dr. António de Menezes* [judge secretary] *read the minutes of the meetings concerning each award.*

Judging the other awards

The Eça de Queiroz Award (Romance) had no winner; even though the judges recognized *notable qualities in some of the submitted works.* Even João Gaspar's *Amorez infelizes* and Joaquim Paço d'Arcos' *Herói derradeiro* weren't up to the standard, and with it, the BPN saved 10 thousand escudos.

---

11 Pessoa erred as he estimated the space he'd have for the index after the book's edition, thinking it would end at page 100 – precisely the mandatory number of pages. The book's draft even has a handwritten notation of *edited and printed in Lisbon* in pages 101/102.

12 This esoteric poem did not make it to the final version of *Message,* and read: *One builds the house where the other lay the stone./ The Galician Colón, of Pontevedra,/ Followed us where we did not go./ We did not see our tree bear those fruits.// An empire he won for Castille,/ For himself, his due glory – the one/ Of having conquered great distance across the sea./ But having started it counted for little.*

The Alexandre Herculano Award (History) was given to Caetano Beirão da Veiga's *D. Maria I,* which was considered *a most worthy work.* The judges also gave an honourable mention to Quirino da Fonseca's *A caravela portuguesa,* and Vitorino Nemésio's *Alexandre Herculano.*

The Ramalho Ortigão Award (Essay) was given to João Ameal's *No limiar da idade nova,* a very interesting, critically acclaimed work. Though it bears remembering that Ameal was a Salazar supporter through and through.

The António Eanes Award (Journalism) was given to Augusto da Costa's *Portugal, vasto império,* a book of interviews that was *an exhaustive inquiry given weight by its testimonies... some of which about the meaning of Portuguese colonization and our future as Imperial Nation.* The judges also gave an extraordinary award to Fernando Pamplona's *Os voronoffs da democracia,* which was granted 2 thousand escudos – part of the abovementioned unpaid 10 thousand, which meant a total of 8 thousand pocketed for whatever other end.

According to *Diário de Lisboa, at the end of the feast, António Ferro declared that those literary awards were but an attempt at awakening spiritual struggle in Portugal;* and lauded the contest *for having revealed authors like Vasco Reis, or bringing them back from isolation, as with Fernando Pessoa.* Lastly, and with plenty of wine in the mix, *lieutenant-colonel Costa Veiga praised the work of António Ferro.* The winners *showed up at the end of the lunch, to great applause.* Only Pessoa wasn't among them.

The Antero de Quental Award (Poetry)

The jury for this award was composed of four members:

– *A nationally renowned poet.* Alberto Osório de Castro (1868-1946) of *Boémia Nova* magazine fame, lawyer, president of the Supreme Court of Justice and the Superior Council of Public Administration, was chosen.

– *A poet of the new literary generation.* Lawyer and poet Mário Beirão (1892-1965)

– *Two literary critics working for Lisbon's press.* The ones chosen were traditionalist Acácio de Paiva (1898-1989) and teacher and writer Teresa Leitão de Barros.

António Ferro took upon himself the role of jury supervisor and the right of a tie-breaking vote, if necessary. Yet another proof that the award was meant for Pessoa, as *Message* would need but two votes and Ferro would certainly benefit his old friend in case of a tie. But he wouldn't get the chance to do it, as the overwhelming majority of votes went for Franciscan friar Vasco Reis' *A romaria. A work of genuine Portuguese lyricism, which reveals a true artist's sensibility, and of markedly Christian and populist value,* in the words of the jury. *The most logical attribution of the award, as it was a poem which best embodied the most coherent attributes of a salazarist aesthetic,* according to Alfredo Margarido. *A collection of simplistic verses,* for Carlos Felipe Moisés. *A petty work for grocery clerks and seamstresses, of ridiculous literary value, a momentary abuse of holy water,* according to Gaspar Simões, who had harsher words still in a conference in 1977: *A grotesque poem.* Casais Monteiro wrote to Pessoa (10/01/1935): *I don't think it absurd – in fact, I think it absolutely normal – that a jury would find* "Romaria" *good and* "Message" *good. But that the same jury thinks Vasco Reis' book is good and thinks yours is good too, that's what leaves me gobsmacked. Message* would be officially disqualified, for not fulfilling the 100 pages requirement. But the real reason was certainly another, as the winner also had less than 100 pages of verses (93) and made use of the same blank sheets and solitary chapter names to fulfil the requisite number.

But how did the jury vote? As the contest's minutes are lost to us, we can only speculate. Osório de Castro certainly voted against. According to him, when reading "A romaria", he felt *a Cesário Verde or an António Nobre was about to manifest.* Another vote against would certainly come from old (former) friend Mário (Gomes Pires) Beirão, as Beirão no longer was the one who sent Pessoa books dedicated *with great friendship and the highest regard for your talent (Cintra),* or *in homage and the greatest admiration for your talent (O último lusíada).* Even though he had been close to Pessoa, and the latter had been his confidant between 1912 and 1914, when they exchanged letters regularly. In a letter, he speaks of his "spiritual kin John Keats" and says "you are as perfect and much more perfect" (06/12/1912). In another one, he considers him "a great poet and a great artist"; and, as a professor would a disciple, he comments on the poems he had sent, declaring that "none of them seems to set a new state within your oeuvre. I am most curious to see in which direction you will evolve" (19/07/1914). Had he known, he certainly wouldn't have liked that future. From 1914, Beirão begins to distance himself from the group of literary rebels led by Pessoa, remaining faithful to the nostalgia of *Renascença Portuguesa* – the same one which had edited his first four books. The two ceased writing to each other from that point on and, with time, the distance between them only grew. Pessoa was opposed to the Estado Novo, whereas Beirão, eternally candid, remained in love with Salazar's promises. So much so, that he even wrote the anthem of the Mocidade Portuguesa – a youth organization which taught young boys the ideology of the Estado Novo. That anthem, which exalted the "clamour of the tubas", was proof that Beirão's poetry had indeed stagnated, and begins thus:

> Off we go, chanting and laughing
> Carried, oh, yes carried by
> The tremendous, sonorous
> Unending clamour of the tubas.

> Off we go, the dream is beautiful!
> Towers and towers rising.
> Flashes, clearings opening wide!
> Dawn of immortal light,
> Shattered by purple mists,
> Gilding the sky of Portugal!

Beirão took revenge in his own, hidden way, discarding Oscar Wilde's *true friends stab you in the front.* Two votes for *A romaria,* thus. The book only needed one more, and I'd bet on Acácio de Paiva for it, on account of his old age, if nothing else. An excerpt of the lost minute, which was partially transcribed in *Diário de Lisboa,* gives us an insight into the jury's thought process: *The author is 23 years old and completely unknown to the public, and currently exercises his noble spiritual trade as a Franciscan missionary in Mozambique.*

An award for Message

The rest of the minute's transcript goes: *As for the second category, the award was given to Fernando Pessoa's* Message, *in the eyes of the jury a high poem of evocation and historic interpretation, which has been duly acclaimed by critics... Its author, voluntarily isolated from the public at large, is a renowned figure amidst Lisbon's intellectual circles, as well as one of the most original characters in Portuguese letters.* As Ferro, who coincidentally was also the coordinator of the government's expenses, would never have let his friend leave empty-handed, *Message* got the award meant for poems under 100 pages – *taking into account the high nationalistic sense of the work, and the fact that the book was passed to the second category only due to the matter of its number of pages;* and the director of the BNP decided to *raise the amount of the prize awarded to* Message *to 5,000 escudos.*

There seems to be no consensus on the matter. To this day, many believe that the consolation prize was offered by Ferro himself to Pessoa, to benefit a friend in need. But that notion doesn't hold up to scrutiny, as it is opposed by the declaration of Eduardo Freitas da Costa, who maintaned that such a *second-rate* award was indeed meant for *a poem or loose poetry in which the same qualities and intentions are present*, provided it had been published between the 1st of July 1933 and the 31st of October 1934. Besides him, António Quadros also claimed there was an award of a thousand escudos for books under 100 pages; all Ferro did was increase the amount to 5 thousand escudos. That, and awarding the prize to a book instead of loose poetry, as per the regulation, of course. What is certain is that those statements will ever be suspect, considering they came from Pessoa's cousin (Freitas) and a son of Ferro's (Quadros). Still, the fact is beyond dispute if one considers a text by A.N. (Albano Nogueira), titled "A cultural initiative" on page 15 of *Presença* #40 (December 1933), in which both categories are confirmed for the Antero de Quental Award. What legitimises that statement is the fact article's author, speaking on behalf of *Presença* magazine, harshly criticizes both the contest and Ferro himself. And he suggests the award should have been given to António Correia de Oliveira, which leaves right out the possibility that he might somehow be defending Pessoa or Ferro – since, at the time of the article's writing, the contest wasn't even accepting applications. Be that as it may, the prize was awarded. There is a receipt at the Torre do Tombo National Archive, which confirms the payment. Besides, there were funds available for such magnanimity, considering that, having withheld the 10 thousand escudos for the novel award, the BPN still managed to save many thousand escudos, even with the extraordinary award handed to *Message.*

Luís Oliveira Guimarães' statement is important to understand what really happened: *As the jury didn't choose* Message, *Ferro was rather pained. I also thought that the priest's book was nothing to write home about. We then tried to see if we could create an extra award, a sort of spare prize for Pessoa. And we did manage to whip up one to the tune of five contos, which was quite a sum... The mood at the time was rife for situations like that, on account of its sense of justice. Cafés, theatres, bookshops were spaces of solidarity and slanderous gossip. Chiado had become quite the den of hearsay.* It is true that Ferro made the decision to help a deeply indebted friend, but also because he was perhaps the only one in the jury capable of grasping the greatness of *Message.* An opinion shared by critics of his time. There was but one negative review, by Tomás Ribeiro Colaço, who thought the poems were excessively intellectual, *often mere telegrams of a remarkable poet... which few shall be able to decipher*[13]. All others were positive, even from salazarists like João Ameal and João de Castro Osório. *O Diabo,* a newspaper which stood in opposition to the dictatorship, for example, concluded its review of the book with the following: *Even if its author were to never write another verse, his name would forever be linked to the richest of Portuguese poetry.* And *Presença* #46 (October 1935) proclaims: *For its originality, the assuredness and the strength of the intentions, sentiments and ideas, or of its means of expression – it is one of those superior books which only come up every once in a long while.* The prize of 5,000 escudos was a sizeable sum, especially for one of uncertain sources of income like Pessoa. Not accounting for inflation, it would be something like 3,500 Euros nowadays. At the time, according to research conducted by António Mega Ferreira, *an eighteen carat "Longines" watch costed a thousand escudos;* with such a sum, he could purchase over a hundred tons of cod. Pessoa pays off all his debtors – among them Júlio Trindade, for the drinks supplied

13 Hardly surprising, coming from the editor of *Fradique,* a far-right weekly.

every night at the corner of his house. And actually manages to live in peace for a while without having to borrow from Casa Moitinho, according to the owner's son, Luís Pedro Moitinho de Almeida. But, when all is done, there is precious little left, and he soon gets into new debts. When he died a couple of months later, he already owed the same Trindade 600 escudos. Perhaps on account of all his debts, he considers the award "in special conditions, most honourable to me". In a brief "commentary" (untitled) published in *Diário de Lisboa* (04/01/1935), he goes further still and claims the award was "justly" handed to *A romaria,* an "adorable" poem from "an admirable artist". "I don't know of any other book, be it in prose or verse, that so paganly and christianly interprets Portugal's religious soul. That is no longer just Portugal. That is talent". José Blanco assured me he sees no irony in those words. As for me, I believe that such exaggerated compliments point to an opposite meaning; an impression given credence to when, in a later text, Pessoa claims to have "avenged" himself from his "rival with a white glove".

The award ceremony

The ball for the awards ceremony was initially scheduled for the 14th, but only took place on the 21st of February 1935. Only a few days after Pessoa wrote the explosive "Secret associations" article (04/02) in favour of the Freemasons, and having been forbidden by the censorship from as much as discussing the matter (08/02). According to *O Século,* all winners were present. Salazar gave an inflamed speech about the subordination of the arts to politics, reminding all of *the moral and patriotic principles which are the foundation of this reformative movement* [of the Estado Novo] *and which impose certain limitations to the mental activity and productions of intelligence and sensibility of the Portuguese, and should even establish some guidelines for them.* Manuela Nogueira recalls how, at the time of the awards, he sat shrunken in a train to Estoril. The invitation, which remains intact in the Chest, mentioned the need for an *appropriate vestment.* Pessoa told the barber Manassés that he didn't "have the accoutrements for the party". Like he'd said a year before in "And yet, and yet", "poor he who lost the offered place because he had no clean coat to show up with".

A romaria

Vasco Reis' *A romaria* is dedicated *to my mother.* A letter-preface by Dr. Alfredo Pimenta, monarchist and staunch opponent of the Freemasons, defines the book in the following terms: *Our country needs wholesome, beautiful books*

– a thing of rarity both among and outwards of us, for we pendularly consume ourselves between two poles: Either morbid beauty, or dull innocence. His book combines the two essential qualities: It is pure and beautiful. After having been criticized for his favourable position towards the Freemasons, he now had to endure this praise of Vasco Reis. Pessoa replied with a text which remained in the Chest, "Barrel of trash" (abridged): "Dr. Alfredo Pimenta is a man who reads by the kilo and studies by the metre. As a result: kilometric ignorance. Some psychiatrists hold that the foolish have a pronounced tendency to arithmetic. Dr. Alfredo Pimenta performs miracles. He reads books written in languages he doesn't know; he perfectly understands matters on subjects he knows nothing of. Without knowing any Latin, Dr. A[lfredo] P[imenta] is at least doctor *honoris causa* in misconduct". Ironically, *A romaria* reproduces Pessoa's proclivity for quotes in Latin, beginning with the cover, under the title, the inscription *Si quaeris miracula* (If you seek miracles); and, another irony, it begins by evoking the feast of the saint to whom Pessoa owed his name:

Golly gee!
Such joy about!
Saint Anthony had his day,
From up on high, such revelry!

What follows is a sequence of expressions of rather questionable taste: *Gilded, fair and divine are you, triumphant Chariot, soul of little bird;* as well as perplexing bits of dialogue such as the following:

BOLCHEVIK (whipping the donkey):
Ho, donkey! Ho, there, ho! You're sleeping, damn you!
You're fit for a friar, idle like a nabob!
Blasted be this life of mine!
CRIPPLE:
Oh, dear, be patient!
Pain is always a good in the hands of Providence!
BOLCHEVIK (brusquely):
Shut it, woman, or you're getting it!
If you can't see the donkey is dragging its hooves, you can walk!

The book ends with the following exhortation:

And he said to Friar Anthony:
"You are Portuguese;
You are a good human; you're a saint – come with me!
Be prodigal with us, attend to yours!"
– And Evil was a cloud which the sun dispersed…

To Gaspar Simões, Vasco Reis was *but a candid Franciscan, so poor in talent as the founder of his order was poor in worldly possessions.* His contemporaries didn't hold a much different opinion of him. Born Manuel Joaquim Reis Ventura (1910-1988), the author was, at the time of the contest, a missionary in Mozambique, but soon relinquished his habit. And his poetic name. He begins writing prose, signing as Reis Ventura, and articles on economy, with his full birth name. It was as if he felt embarrassed of having written *A romaria.* In 1973, he considers the contest *a mistake which deeply bothers me. There is absolutely no term of comparison between* "Message" *and the poem I wrote at the age of 19 called* "A romaria". *Even if it was awarded first place, there can be no terms of comparison between* "A romaria" *and the magnificent work of that genius;* and concludes in a letter to *O Jornal* (published in 19/11/1985), in which he says his *teenage verses don't even exist, and Pessoa was the one who truly won the award.*

Pessoa and the chaotic beginnings of the republic

In order to understand the reasons behind the jury's decision on *Message,* which included far more than mere literary merit, one needs to go back in time. Pessoa is living through the end of the monarchy, no longer believing in it; and just two years after the proclamation of the republic, he was already disaffected with the new court figures. "When we had a revolution, it was meant to implant something just like the thing it meant to replace... It was a childish, superficial, fake gesture". According to Joana Amaral Dias, Pessoa's obsession with *the notion of order* sent him in search of his father, an authority figure. Which is perhaps why he repudiated "those people's republicanism". He begins to elaborate on a *Theory of aristocratic republic,* after the Greek meaning of the work *aristos* (best), and yearns for "a Cromwell to come", as Portugal demanded such a man.

> With trash, other people's money and innocent blood,
> Surrounded by murderers, traitors, thieves (safe)
> In her French coffin, she passes beyond the world,
> In a cart pulled by a donkey (the State's)
> Most liberally, in a most disagreeing sight,
> The Portuguese Democratic Republic.
>
> "Funeral March", Fernando Pessoa

He believed three characters could be that Portuguese Cromwell. First, general (Joaquim) Pimenta de Castro (1846-1918), "one of the finest dictators in our history" – who governed Portugal in 1915 for little over three months. Second, general Sidónio (Bernardino Cardoso da Silva) Pais (1872-1918), "an indisciplinarian of souls" – a term Pessoa sometimes applied to himself. The "King Media", as Álvaro de Campos called him, was minister of Promotion and Finance in João Chagas' government (1911) and ambassador in Berlin (1912-1916). A member of Brito Camacho's Unionist Party, he led the military insurrection which opposed Portugal's participation in World War I. After the insurrection's victory and the formation of the New Republic on the 8th of December 1917, Sidónio dissolved the parliament, censored the press, promoted monarchists, had himself elected prime-minister of a Public Salvation Junta, and was finally elected president in Portugal's first democratic elections. According to José Blanco, Pessoa saw him as *the very reincarnation of King Sebastião.* "His regency was famous for its immorality, for the effrontery of its ulterior dealings, and its political crimes". He had the dangerous habit of mixing in with the crowd. An easy target, he survives a first attempt on his life on the 6th of December 1918, but not the three bullets of the second, "on the upper floor of the Rossio train station – on the night of the 14th of December 1918" when he was going to board a train bound for Porto. He was buried at Santa Engrácia Church, which was later elevated to the status of National Pantheon for containing the remains of other presidents, such as Teófilo Braga and Óscar Carmona; writers like Almeida Garrett, Guerra Junqueiro and João de Deus; and marshall Humberto Delgado. Sidónio Pais was the object of a song from Pessoa ("One day Sidónio shall return/ To be dead is to pretend"), and, on the 27th of February 1920, the following epic 240 verses poem:

Far from fame and blade,
Unaware of the mobs, he sleeps.
Around him, cloister or arcade?
Naught but tremendous night.

Because, to him, already turned
Towards the side wherein only God lays,
More than Shadow and Past, to him,
Both heaven and earth.

"To the memory of president-king[14] Sidónio Pais", Fernando Pessoa

Starting in 1925, the biggest crisis in the republic begins. A first attempt at a coup on the 18th of April fails, but others would follow. On the 11th of December, president Manuel Teixeira Gomes (1860-1941) resigns and goes into exile. Bernardino Machado, the president expelled by Sidónio Pais (1917), is elected for a second term of office, and the leadership of government went to António Maria da Silva (1872-1950). But only until the 28th of May 1926, when another coup brought a military junta to power, led by general António Óscar de Fragoso Carmona (1869-1915). Pessoa's reservations about parliamentarism explain his spiritual support of that coup. (Manuel) Gomes da Costa (1863-1929) is then named president. Also only for a short while, for he'd soon be exiled as well, on the 9th of July. Carmona was named president on the 16th of November 1926 – and subsequently elected as the sole candidate, in March 1928 – remains in office until his death, on the 18th of April 1928. And thus the historic conditions for the appearance of the third such character were put in place.

Salazar, the man and the hour

António de Oliveira Salazar was born on the 28th of April 1889 – north of Coimbra, in Vimeiro, Santa Comba Dão. Of humble origins and a former seminarian in Viseu, he was regent of Economy and Finance at Coimbra's Law Faculty. In 1921, upon being elected as a councilman by the Catholic Centre, he renounces on the very first day of his term, and, on the 27th of April 1928, he becomes the new government's Finance minister. At first, for Pessoa, he was "the right man at the right time". The accounting of every ministry is under his purview, and only he can authorize spending, directing the government without paying heed to anyone else. *I know very well what I want and where I'm headed,* as he was wont to say. The following year, and

14 When published at *Acção Magazine,* the poem had the word "king" censored, as, according to the government, it gave prestige to the monarchy.

against all Portuguese expectations, he actually achieves a surplus in public spending. And, on the 5th of July 1932, he all but became plenipotentiary dictator – even though he still was officially only president of the council of ministers. Salazar, much like Hitler and Mussolini, never became president. "I trust professor Salazar for a primary reason and two secondary. The former is the fact that he has two qualities which the Portuguese tends to lack, a firm clarity of intelligence and will. The latter two are that I have seen the accomplishment of things which previously just weren't done, and our growing prestige abroad. I said I trust him, because I do, and no more on that". In 1928, Pessoa writes *Interregnum – defence and justification of the military dictatorship in Portugal,* a *Political manifesto of the Nucleus of National Action.* Said "interregnum" is the period of time which separates the First Republic from the Estado Novo, and in it is plain to see the importance he placed on order. "If a nation were a village, the police would be enough; as it is a nation, it needs to be the entire armed forces", after which he declares "Yes, I am a situationist". But not for long.

Litte tyrant Salazar

Little by little, the government begins to display authoritarian traits, restricting the public freedoms of speaking, publishing and gathering. In 1932, reacting against censorship, Pessoa had already changed tune and spoke of "professor Oliveira Salazar's ironic hand". "We are at a singular time, in which all characteristic traits of decadence pop up". His first critical texts begin in 1930. Among them one, in response to a manifesto of the National Union, which begins thus: "I hereby wish to contest the principles expounded upon in a somewhat illiterate manifesto the government read on the 30th of July... The thesis of professor Salazar is a bunch of known political principles... My thesis, on the other hand, would have heretofore unknown results". The corporative Estado Novo was formed by the Constitution (of the 11th of April) and the Bylaw of National Work (of the 23rd of September, both in 1933). From then on, Pessoa begins to denounce "the right-leaning sovietism of the National Union", in which there was "a personal theocracy". To him, "the Portuguese dictatorship endures for two reasons: Fear of communism, and Salazar's irrepressible status. It is socialist alcoholism". According to Pessoa, he was "a seminarian of accounting" – having been both a seminarian and finance minister. Afterwards, when comparing Salazar to Mussolini and Hitler, he declares "we are witnessing the caesarization of an accountant", "the chief of government isn't a statesman, he's an usher", an "eccentric corpse, the perfect enforcer of order. Everything he does reeks of the shadow of unholy kings". At the time, one particular dish became famous in Portugal, Salazar style cod, thus named because it requires no olive oil – as, according to the people, *if it's lean, it doesn't deserve it, and if it's fat, it doesn't need it.*

Salazar Style Cod
Ingredients: ½kg cod, 1kg potatoes, 50ml vinegar, 2 cloves of garlic, pepper.

Directions: Wash and de-salt the cod. Place the cod, the peeled potatoes and enough water to cover it all. When it is cooked, strain the water and place the cod on a platter. Season it with vinegar and garlic, and serve.

His animosity towards Salazar would only increase at his reactions against the Freemasons. In a letter to Casais Monteiro (30/10/1935), he claims that the latter replaced the logical rule of censorship "you cannot say this or that" with the soviet rule of "you must say that or this". He then starts referring to him in public, albeit with restrictions: "'tis but a finger, a little finger. And by the finger one can recognize the Dwarf[15]. By way of an act of resistance, he wrote a poem on the 16th of Mach 1935, which would only be published posthumously, on the 2nd of September 1937, in *Seara Nova* #9. Underneath the title, a note in parentheses – "A Seneca quote is lacking". Impossible to know which one, but perhaps he was thinking of *The true goods are those which reason bestows, substantial and eternal* (Epistle 74).

Ah, how delightful
To leave a duty[16] undone,
To have a book to read
And not even crack it!
Reading is a pain in the neck[17],
And studying isn't anything.

The sun[18] shines golden
With or without literature.

The river flows, fast or slow,

15 The *Dwarf* was Salazar, ironically replacing the giant in the Latin proverb *Ex digito gigas* (through the finger, he giant).

16 Salazar demanded compromise from the country's intellectuals, and said as much in the abovementioned speech of the contest *Message* had been sent to. Even in the preface of his book, *Discursos,* Salazar declared that *Portuguese writers should, in every writing of theirs, follow the guidelines of the Estado Novo.* What is "delightful", then, is to not comply with a tyrant's demands.

17 In *Disquiet,* he says "to feel is a pain in the neck". Here, the sentence suggests that Pessoa thought that reading writings praising the Estado Novo were a pain in the neck.

18 Not the sun per se, the one Search loved "with personal glee" ("A Day of Sun", 1908), or the one he quotes in *Message,* personified by Odysseus ("The very sun that opens the sky"), but a metaphorical one which he refers to when quoting António Telmo – for whom *To say the sun or to say Portugal is one and the same.* The "sun" in this poem is his own country, which, instead of "creating" with democracy, "dries" under Salazar's censorship

Without a first edition.
And the breeze, belonging
So naturally to morning,
Has time, it's in no hurry.
Books are just paper painted with ink.
And to study is to distinguish, indistinctly,
Between nothing and not a thing.

How much better, when it's foggy,
To wait for King Sebastian,
Whether or not he ever shows!

Poetry, dancing and charity are great things,
But what's best in the world are children, flowers,
Music, moonlight and the sun, which only sins
When it withers instead of making things grow.
Greater than this
Is Jesus Christ,
Who knew nothing of finances
And had no library, as far as we know…

Freedom[19], Fernando Pessoa

The poem was duly sent to the Police for Vigilance and Defence of the State (later converted into Pide, in 1945), and the penultimate verse ("Who knew nothing of finances") was edited out[20], only seeing the light of day two years later, when different censors were in charge and Pessoa had already died. But café companions like Manuel Mendes got to see the original version. The year of his death, he would write three other poems, all titled "Salazar" – all dated the 29th of March, signed by the heteronym A Nostalgic Dreamer of Dejection and Decadence and published only after the Carnation Revolution. Many copies are made by Pessoa himself, and friends like Luiz Rei Santos (one of the participants of the 1st Salon of Independents of the National Society of Fine Arts), recite them by heart. Little by little, having been recited so often, some became variants of themselves, and thus the most trustworthy version is the one which remained in the Chest. The first is but a play on his name:

António de Oliveira Salazar.
Three names in regular sequence…
António is António

19 A title in the vein of Alexander Search's *Liberty,* which begins with *Oh, sacred Liberty, dear mother of Fame!* It was refused by *Natal Mercury,* due to the vehemence of his repudiation of England's policies in South Africa.

20 Pessoa replied with "Fado of censorship", which contains the following refrain: *In this field of politics/ Where we are kept in by the guard,/ Fado, replies censorship;/ I look, but cannot see.*

Oliveira [olive tree] is a tree.
Salazar is but a surname.
So far, so good.
What makes little sense
Is the sense of it all.

After which came the most famous of all:

This Salazar fellow
Is made of salt and ill fortune
Should it ever rain
Water shall dissolve

The salt
And under the sky
There shall remain but ill fortune.

Oh, confound it!
Looks like it already rained…

The third poem begins by pointing out the fact that Salazar doesn't much care for the bars Pessoa patronizes:

Poor him,
Poor little tyrant!
He doesn't drink wine.
Not even on his own…

He drinks the truth[21]
And freedom, too
And with such gusto
That both are now hard
To find in the market.

Poor him,
Poor little tyrant!
My neighbour
Is in Guinea

And my godfather
In Limoeiro[22]

---

21 In *Interregnum – defence and justification of the military dictatorship in Portugal,* Pessoa says: "The principle of truth lies in acknowledging the error"; and, in "The Mariner": "That is so strange, it must be true". Álvaro de Campos completes: "Today I'm vanquished, as if I knew the truth". But said "truth" was gone now, crushed under Salazar's heavy hands.

22 As previously mentioned, Limoeiro was a prison.

Here so very close[23].
And nobody knows why.

Oh, well,
What is true is that
This consoles us
And gives us faith.

As poor him
Poor little tyrant
He doesn't drink wine,
Or even
Coffee.

Which was followed by another (untitled) poem (29/07/1935), this one in a more serious tone and signed with his own name, criticizing not only Salazar, but the entire Estado Novo he represented. So the reader might have a notion of the text's vehemence, here are its first and last stanzas:

Yes, this is a New State[24]
For it is a state of affairs
The likes of which heretofore unseen.
(…)
May faith be everlasting
For hope is not vain!
Corporative hunger
Is defeatism! Joy!
Today, lunch is tomorrow.

He also released "Poem of love in a New State" (08-09/11/1935), also under his name, the first and last stanzas of which are:

You have the mysterious stare
With cloudy mien,
Indecisive, doubtful,
My Maria Francisca[25]
My love, my budget!
(…)
I well know: Because of how you are
You can never love me.
Do forgive me, please

23 The prison was close to Chiado.
24 *Translator's note:* Literally "Estado Novo".
25 Likely a reference to Queen Maria I, baptised as Maria Francisca Josefa Antónia Gertrudes Rita Joana – queen of Portugal between the 24th of March 1777 and the date of her death, on the 20th of March 1816. She was known as the Pious, for her religious devotion, and the Mad, on account of the mental illness that accompanied her in her final years. For Pessoa, Salazar's madness would be the equivalent of hers.

> I am but following the guidelines
> Of professor Salazar.

He had plenty of reasons for such critiques. A draft of a letter to president Carmona (1935) reads: "I didn't know that order in the streets, roads, bridges and police stations would have to be bought at such high a price – that of the retail sale of the Portuguese soul". This apparent relative freedom in cultural manifestations was owed to old friend António Ferro – the jury supervisor in the contest. But this coexistence between dictator and intellectual couldn't last. Ferro would soon be sent *(exiled,* according to Manuela Parreira da Silva) away from Portugal, to hold public office in Bern and Rome. Already during the contest, the jury was likely aware of how *Message* did not comply with the government's directives, and it certainly would have been a bad look to reward someone who so staunchly opposed it. His fiercest criticism hadn't yet reached the wider audience, true, but they were renowned in intellectual circles and among his group of friends, many of them with connections to the Estado Novo. A copy was sent to Salazar. The note of thanks came unsigned.

> One might as well publish a decree-law along the following lines:
> Art. 1. A[ntónio] d[e] O[liveira] S[alazar] is God
> Art. 2. Everything to the contrary is hereby revoked, namely the Bible
>
> *Untitled* (1935), Fernando Pessoa

The fate of Message

"I've been old on account of the Estado Novo" he wrote shortly before dying. "The main argument against a dictatorship is that it is a dictatorship". "Professor Salazar, having no prestige of his own, let himself be clad in its appearance. It is his tunic of Nessus[26]". Commenting Salazar's speech during the awards ceremony, he says "that peasant of letters cast off whatever Portuguese intelligence still looked upon him kindly, already with a measure of impatience, and an already vaguely disdainful tolerance, at that". "He sought to climb a pedestal he barely fit in, to ascend to a throne he knows not how to sit on". "António de Oliveira Salazar caused Portugal to stop being a country and turned it into a surname: Salazarist Portugal, and not the Portugal of the Portuguese". Pessoa already yearned for a truly democratic regime, more open to the changes the world was undergoing. He wants a free country. *Message* is also a reaction to that oppression. A cry for his homeland. As if predicting his fate, he ends the book with the following exhortation:

26 Much like the cursed tunic which killed Hercules, who could not take it off, so too did Salazar wear the garments of a prestige which was not his, like a second skin he could not remove.

Neither king nor law, neither peace nor war,
Define with outline and substance
This dull brilliance of the land
That is Portugal sinking in sadness -
Brightness without light or heat,
Like that which the will-o'-the-wisp confines.

Nobody knows what one wants.
Nobody is aware of one's own soul,
Nor of what is evil, nor of what is pure.
(What distant anxiety weeps nearby?)
All is uncertain and ultimate.
All is fragmented, nothing is whole.
Oh Portugal, today you are mist…

'Tis the hour!

Valete, Fratres.

Message, "Mist", Fernando Pessoa

"'tis the hour". Not the hour of *Message.* Nor that of Portugal. It's his time. *Vulnerant omnes, ultima necat* (All hours wound, the last one kills). *"Valete, fratres"* – goodbye, brothers, as he had precious little time left.

Fugit irreparabile tempus
(It escapes, irretrievable time) Virgil

THE MUSEUM OF CASCAIS

On a sad day, my heart sadder than the day...
On a sad day, every day...
On such a sad day...
Clouds, Álvaro de Campos

One last hope

As time goes by, and increasingly so, Pessoa wishes to live in some "quiet village in the countryside". In his dreams, he saw a "little country house", "whitewashed with lime and silence", "a ray of sunlight", "orchards and vegetable plots", "vineyards", "branches lulled by the wind", "trees by the road", "the farm's pine grove". There, he might "wake up amid the racket of roosters and hens and the early morning rustling in the country house", speak with "cheerful peasants and joyous girls", "hear the rivers flow", have his "outings in a countryside that never existed". The idea slowly gains shape in him, especially after 1919. In a "life plan" he writes, he notes down his intention to "rent a house outside of Lisbon – for example, in Cascais – put all my belongings there and leave it to the care of Emília[1], my life organized, with no fears or concerns". Cascais "means some point outside of Lisbon, although close by, and might just as easily mean Sintra". From 1931 onwards, with his sister now living in Cascais, he spends almost every weekend there. Close to his nephews. And "if one day I succeed in carrying the cross of my intention to the good Calvary, I'll find another Calvary on that good Calvary, and I'll miss the time when I was futile, mediocre and imperfect".

The matter is far from settled among those who study Pessoa. Richard Zenith, for one, told me with all conviction that he had never even considered living outside of Lisbon. An opinion shared by Yvette Centeno. But I believe that, in the end, he did wish to escape from that uncertain life he led, and Teresa Rita Lopes is in agreement with me there. His economic limitations are a growing

1 The maid (and former lover) of Manuel Sengo was working for Pessoa at the time.

martyrdom for him. "Unfortunately, I cannot abandon the offices and my work (I cannot, of course, because I'd have no income then". He feels doomed to be but "a poor, stagnated bibliophile, ever hunched over the book", serving "an archaic past". On the 29th of November 1929, in a letter to Ophelia, he announces his intentions of "leaving Lisbon" in order to attain "a measure of isolation" and reorganize his oeuvre. Ophelia reacts: *What are you on about, moving to Cascais? You're not going, are you? You only do it to scare me! You shall be a husband, won't you? Don't you want me as your little wife?* But none of those intents would materialize. He would neither have the means to write without financial concerns, nor would he make of her his *little wife.* Two years after his death, friend and poet António de Navarro (1902-1980) declared that Pessoa had confessed to him his desire to earn twice as much as he did, living in *a modest place he thought of but which he wasn't granted.* That place was the Museum of Cascais.

All this is nothing,
But in a road
Such as life is
There are plenty of things
Misunderstood...
(...)
And so the breeze
Whispers among the branches
Saying, without realizing it
An imprecise
Happy little thing.

Untitled (09/05/1934), Fernando Pessoa

Applying for the job

On the 1st of September 1932, he feels within his reach that peace he always sought, when he reads in *O Século* that there is a job opening as curator-librarian for the Conde de Castro Guimarães Museum, which had opened its doors two years prior, in 1930. The museum is in Cascais, in a majestic villa at Avenida Rei Humberto II de Itália. To its side, a small 17th century chapel (consecrated to Saint Sebastian). In front of it, a fountain and a nude statue of Joseph Bernard's *(Young woman dancing with her son).* Behind it, a large park which today belongs to the museum as well. It is almost like the perfect house he described in his dreams. On the 16th of September, he applies for the job, claiming to be a "writer" who lives "temporarily in Cascais, at Rua Oriental do Passeio, door 2"; pulls rank with his "Intermediate Exam at the University of the Cape of Good Hope"; claims to have been granted the

"English-style Queen Victoria Award"; and includes testimonies by Gaspar Simões and Pierre Hourcade – even though his friends were only 29 (Simões) and 24 (Hourcade) at the time.

To prove his linguistic knowledge, he attaches his poem *Trois chansons mortes,* and three English poems, as well as reviews of his works from London's *Times* and *Glasgow Herald.* He also refers the titles of the Portuguese literary magazines he writes for, adding that: "As to the literary merit of these writings, the gentlemen need but ask among the Portuguese literary and artistic mediums". Lastly, he declares to be "renowned in the country, mainly among the newest generations, to a borderline unjustifiable degree for one who has so far been loath to compile his works in books". As for the regulation's demand that all applicants have "accredited competence and good repute", he replies that such attributes "are not for documents to prove – much like elements such as physical appearance and education, which are undocumentable by nature". He also sends an English version, for no apparent reason.

Another trial

According to Pessoa's biographers, the museum's administrative committee is comprised of Cascais' mayor, secretary of finances and a delegate for the fine arts. No record of their names. But that probably wasn't the case, as, in 1932, Cascais didn't even have a mayor. After the 1926 coup, and until 1937, the city only had administrative committees – led by lieutenant António Rodrigues Cardoso. The delegate for the fine arts was Dr. José de Figueiredo. As for the secretary of finances, there are no records of him whatsoever, not even in the museum. Pessoa is the most qualified candidate and desperately wants the job. But "there's nothing I've wanted – and nothing in which I've placed, even for a moment, the dream of only that moment – that hasn't disintegrated below my windows like a clod of dirt that resembled stone until it fell from a flowerpot on a high balcony. It would even seem that Fate has always tried to make me love or want things just so that it could show me, on the very next day, that I didn't have and could never have them". And so it would be this time, as well.

On the 17th of October 1932, Carlos Bonvalot, a painter with paintings at the National Museum of Contemporary Art, is chosen (he died two years later, at the age of 40). Far from an inadequate choice, as the museum didn't only have a library, but also hosted art exhibits regularly, and Bonvalot's paintings had already been featured there. But the reasons for the choice remain a mystery. Perhaps Bonvalot had influential friends, or the library wasn't considered important enough to be under the care of someone from a literary medium. Or, who knows, perhaps the conservative museum didn't wish to have someone with the traits of the *Orpheu* lads on its payroll. Upon doing my research, I question Dr. Rui Trindade – the current holder of the job Pessoa sought – on the choice. He didn't know, but did say that the fact Pessoa didn't have a higher education degree might have been a factor. Luís Pedro Moitinho de Almeida said: *One day, he was in such a state of hopelessness, he actually collapsed on the table at café Montanha, and started to cry. It was when he knew he hadn't gotten the job at the Castro de Guimarães Museum.* His statement is corroborated by another friend of Pessoa's, Francisco Peixoto, who declares having seen him *awash in tears.* The museum would have guaranteed him a steady income, which would mean he no longer had to hop around offices, and would have spared him the embarrassment of having collectors at his doorstop. He would be able to pay off his debts, buy all the books he'd like and live in a spacious apartment to store his things in, without worrying about having to move again soon after; or, even better, he could pay for the room in his sister's house. Perhaps even marry Ophelia. And Cascais was close enough to Lisbon that, if he wished to meet his café friends, he could do so whenever he pleased. But defeat was his inseparable companion.

> I'm someone who failed to be.
> We're all what we suppose ourselves.
> Our reality is the one thing we'll never manage.
> (…)
> In soul, and with some truth,
> In imagination, and with some justice,
> In intelligence, and with some right–
> My God! my God! my God!–
> I've been so many Caesars!
> I've been so many Caesars!
> I've been so many Caesars!
>
> *Original Sin*, Álvaro de Campos

The beginning of the end

It was to be his final attempt at getting his life in order, according to António Mega Ferreira. After that, it was only a matter of waiting for fate to run its course. "I've witnessed, incognito, the gradual collapse of my life, the slow foundering of all that I wanted to be". "Perhaps one day they'll understand that I fulfilled, like no one else, my instinctive duty to interpret a portion of our century; and when they've understood that, they'll write that in my time I was misunderstood, that the people around me were unfortunately indifferent and insensitive to my work, and that it was a pity this happened to me". He no longer harboured any illusions of ever becoming wealthy. "My past is everything which I could not be". As he has no faith in luck, nor does he have any escudos left, he refuses Santa Rita's lottery tickets, as he hadn't "taken a ticket for life". It is said that, one day, at Martinho da Arcada, a lottery ticket seller asked him: *Would Mr. Pessoa like four hundred contos?* To which Pessoa replied: "No, thank you. Pay two coffees, and keep the change".

His business and inventions forays never amounted to anything. Now, he was afraid he wouldn't have enough to survive. He would always have a room at his sister's house, but what about "a little bit of calm along with a bit of bread, not to feel oppressed by the knowledge that I exist, not to demand anything from others, and not to have others demand anything from me"? The tendencies he had fostered hadn't gone beyond the few who had any interest in literary magazines in a small country such as Portugal. "All my writings were unfinished". Two years later, with *Message,* he would also fail to win the Antero de Quental Award for books. "I even shed my desire for glory, like a sleepy man who takes off his clothes to go to bed". In a letter to João de Lebre e Lima (03/05/1914), many years before, he had made "a dreamt confession of uselessness and dolorous sterile fury of dreaming". Now he's certain of it. Bandarra's prophecy wouldn't come to pass – not in his lifetime, at least. The Nobel prize never materialized. Nor would anything else. "Later, perhaps... Yes, later... Some other, perhaps... I don't know...".

> Whatever will be
> Will be, whether I want it to or not.
> (...)
> No more peace, nor less peace,
> For my waiting
> For what must not be
> Shall be, in time, if I thought of it. All else is dreaming.
>
> *Untitled* (28/12/1928), Fernando Pessoa

Stultum facit fortuna quem vult perdere
(Fate stupefies whom it wishes to destroy) Publilius Syrus

A CLINICAL CASE

I am at the depths of a bottomless depression.
The sheer absurdness of the sentence speaks for me.
Letter to Sá-Carneiro (14/05/1916), Fernando Pessoa

Forebodings of mental illness

"A voyage between souls and stars, through the Forest of Fright... and God, end of the infinite road, awaiting in the silence of His greatness" – is how he defines his state of mind in a letter to Côrtes-Rodrigues (19/05/1915). Not too dramatic. Sister Teca had the following to say on the matter: *He was always afraid of madness, Fernando spent his whole life terrified of going mad like grandma, or to die of consumption like father.* Pessoa knew he was different from others, and suffered with it. It was "hell itself that seems to be laughing inside me, it's the croaking madness of the dead universe, the spinning cadaver of physical space, the end of all worlds blowing blackly in the wind, formless and timeless, without a God who created it". The first signs manifest themselves early. Still in Durban, he complains of the lack of attention he got: "In my family, there is no understanding for my mental state – no, none. They laugh at me, they scorn me, they don't believe", "my family understands nothing". An unfair assessment, as there was little they could have done. In a note from the 25th of July 1905, at the age of 17, he recalls a "scene" between him and great-aunt Rita, at the end of which "I again felt one of those symptoms which become increasingly clearer and more horrible to me, a moral vertigo. In physical vertigo, there is a spinning of the inner world. For a few moments, it is as if I were losing the sense of the true relation of things". In notes from 1905, he realizes "these feelings are becoming routine" and "seem to open the path to a new mental life, which will end in madness". Two years later, on the 25th of July 1907, he almost reproduces the sentence in his diary, this time in English, showing concern for his "new mental life which shall of course be madness". The following year, his despair intensifies: "Let me not be insane, my God."

This old anguish,
This anguish I've held for centuries in me,
Overflowed its vessel
In tears, in grand imaginations,
In dreams the style of terrorless nightmares,
In great sudden senseless emotions.
Overflowed.
How will I ever get through life
With this unease putting creases in my soul?
If I'd at least gone truly mad!
But no: it's this being in between,
This almost,
This being able to be,,,
This.

Untitled (16/06/1934), Álvaro de Campos

Terrified at the scope of that he believes to be his madness, he writes letters to two former teachers of his at Durban High School, Belcher and Maggfor, and requests a diagnosis of himself, signing the letters as a doctor from Lisbon, Dr. Faustino Antunes. By way of marginalia, he notes at the margin: "Myself as a mental patient". Ernest A. Belcher was his master of languages, close enough to him that Pessoa even became sub-editor of a magazine he edited. Belcher replies (14/07/1907), recalling his former student's English compositions, which were remarkable as a rule, at times bordering on genius; he mentions Pessoa's passion for Carlyle and reproached him for it, as *Carlyle is the last man a still immature boy should seek to emulate*[1]. There is no record of Maggfor's reply. He wrote two drafts of letters for former schoolmate Geerdts (who was then teaching at Lincoln College). In one, he congratulated him on his scholarship. In the other, he notes on the margin "Myself presumed dead", and wrote "The ill-fated F.A.N. Pessoa, who we assume to have committed suicide, blew up the countryside home[2] in which he was living, killing himself and several others. A crime (?) which caused a tremendous stir in Portugal. I was tasked with inquiring about his mental health, insofar as possible. What was the general opinion on him?". The letter, a questionnaire of sorts in eight parts, concludes thus: "I must ask you keep the utmost discretion on his matter. Besides, it might have been (let us hope it indeed was) an accident. I am merely fulfilling my obligation to determine whether this catastrophe was a crime or a mere accident. I would be most thankful for your prompt reply".

1 Because Scotsman Thomas Carlyle interpreted history through the men he admired the most. In *Past and Present* (1843), for example, he maintained that every society should be led by a man of genius. Deep down, Belcher probably wished his student worried less about feats of greatness and were more dedicated to his studies.

2 The following year, Alexander Search wrote "Burn his house".

Geerdts sends his reply to Rua Bela Vista, where Pessoa was living with his aunt Maria, and defined him thus (04/10/1907): *I did not, in fact, have the opportunity to put his willpower to the test. He was shy and harmless and avoided socializing with his colleagues. I cannot recall any peculiarity which would as much as suggest mental imbalance. I can say he did own some rather indecent Portuguese and French comic strips. He dedicated all of his free time to reading. I ask you to please apprise me on Pessoa's illness: Is he fully mad, or is there still a chance he might recover?* Geerdts recognized him as the author of the letter, but replied in protocolar fashion, as if he believed the ruse. He recalls how *all of our colleagues got used to seeing him win every award* and has no diagnosis to give – though he well knew the tortuous paths his former colleague tread. At the age of 75, in an interview to colleague H.D. Jennings, he completes the description: *Yes, [I knew him] very well. Our tables were next to each other. A frail little boy with a big head. He had a keen intellect, but was rather mad. Far more intelligent than I was.*

The fear of madness

"I am mad, and that is what I find difficult to understand. I don't know whether to call it a privilege or a disease". All he was lacking was a correct diagnosis. In that search, he wrote (20/06/1919) to Hector and Henri Durville, two psychiatrists who were directors of the Institute of Magnetism and Experimental Psychism – 23 Rue Saint-Merri, Paris. He wished for information concerning a magnetism course by correspondence, and exposed his situation to them (abridged): "From a psychiatric point of view, I am hysteroneurasthenic. The neurasthenic element dominates the hysterical element, which contributes to my not displaying the outwards signs of hysteria. I change my mind ten times a day. Like most born neurasthenics, I can almost always control the outwards or dynamic results of those intimate manifestations. The fact is that, since this past year, I have been under the influx of nervous states of all shapes and sizes, which for a long period of time even deprived my will of the desire to do nothing". The specialists I consulted with assured me this description was technically correct. Previously, and in English, he wrote: "One of my mental complications – horrible beyond words – is the fear of madness, which is madness in and on itself". That note, signed by Search, is divided in three sections: *Agony, Delirium* and *Documents of Mental Decadence.* "The paradox is not mine: It is I". To wit, "I am neither evil nor cruel: I am mad". Studying the output of this heteronym, Luísa Freire says *one can almost feel the madness approaching.* Like in this 1908 poem:

Oh God, if Thou be'st anything
Hear this frail prayer that I fling
Like a flame leaping past control
From out the hell that is my soul:
Oh God, let me not fall insane!
(…)
Pour down on me all woes, all ills
All else that the strain'd spirit fills.
With horror and with terror mute;
But madness, madness absolute,
Keep from my trembling mind away.
(…)
Torture me in all ways that are,
Let me be scorned and crushed and trod,
Plunged in full conscious agony,
Let me become a fear, a care,
But madness, madness, oh my God,
Do not let madness come to me!

Prayer, Alexander Search

On the 15th of November, he experiences "a few small and curious frights of the spirit", and, shortly after, on the 26th, "thrice during the day and night, crises of a curious kind of vertigo – of physical nature – yet I have been lucid all day". In his delusions of grandeur, he dreams he is Nero, Martin Luther, Jesus Christ. Deep down, he compares himself to Shakespeare, in whom he saw "the deep understanding of the tragic states of life – intense passion, profound disturbance, madness". In *Faust,* he says: "I am the Black Christ, nailed to the fiery cross of myself". Yet "Christ was a madman, true. What is a madman?". "You, doctors, study all sorts of mental illnesses, symptoms, manifestations, etcetera and such, but you don't bother with determining what the subjects themselves might be thinking, what can't be seen in the symptoms. Psychiatry… psychiatry… I'm not quite sure how to say it". In French, he writes: "I am mad, I know it, but what does it mean to be mad? No one knows". The idea pursues him relentlessly. "I only regret not being a child, so I might believe in my dreams, or not be mad, so I could cast away all the [ghosts, perhaps] surrounding me". At that time, and mainly throughout the following years, a deeper anguish seems to take hold of him, without a stare or gesture that might have tipped others off. His niece Manuela Nogueira, for example, claims never to have seen him as much as appear unhinged.

"It takes a certain intellectual courage for a man to frankly recognize that he's nothing more than a human tatter, an abortion that survived, a madman not mad enough to be committed", "wishing to scream inside my head" and having "no one to trust in. I cannot bother my friends with these matters. I am shy, and it repulses me to make my anguishes known to others. Woe is me! Poor Alastor! Oh, Shelley[3], how I understand you! I feel abandoned like one shipwrecked in the middle of the sea. And what am I if not shipwrecked?". Later, it is as if he has made peace with his lot: "Madness, far from an anomaly, is the normal human condition. To not be aware of it and it not being considerable means to be a normal man. To not be aware of it and it being considerable means to be a madman. To be aware of it and it being inconsiderable means to be disappointed. To be aware of it and it being considerable means to be a genius". Like himself, naturally.

> What's become of your boy? He's gone mad.
> What's become of the one sleeping softly under your provincial ceiling?
> He's gone mad.
> Whose who was I? He's gone mad. Today he's who I am.
>
> If I at least had religion, any religion!
> If I believed, for example, in that fetish
> I had in that house, in that one brought from Africa.
> (…)
> Because what is everything, besides what we think of it?
> Crack, heart of painted glass[4]!
>
> *Untitled*, Álvaro de Campos

All that disquiet severely limited his relations. "Friends, none really. Only a few acquaintances who believe they empathize with me and might perhaps feel sorry if I were run over by a train and my burial took place in a rainy day". He limits his affections further: "I realized it was impossible for one to love me, unless that person lacked all manner of aesthetic notions – and then I would despise them for it". According to psychiatrists, a symptom of self-loathing. In a séance of 1917, heteronym Wardour advises him: "Start working on healing your mind". But that was too far beyond his strength. In 1920, he wishes to "go to a house of healing the next month, to see if I can find there some treatment which allows me to withstand the dark wave which is crashing over my spirit". In a latter to an unknown "Dear friend" (31/08/1920), he once again recalls: "The Decree of the 11th of May 1911 allows the patient himself

3 Alastor was an epithet of Zeus as the personification of a curse, and the title of a poem by Percy Bysshe Shelley (1792-1822) – "Alastor, or the spirit of solitude". Shelley, the greatest English lyrical poet, was first quoted by Pessoa in a letter to Boavida Portugal (undated, 1912); and, from that point on, rather frequently. He confided to José Osório de Siena (1932) that "the inspiration I consorted the most with it was perhaps Shelley's". In *Disquiet,* he says "like Shelley, I loved".

4 A typically Portuguese home decoration at the time: a glass painting of Christ's bleeding heart. Previously (01/10/1928), in an untitled poem, he had already said: *My heart has cracked/ Like a shard of glass/ It wished to live and had it wrong.*

to require internment… I wish to ask you to tell me how and to whom I shall present such a request, and which documents are needed". The letter is based on the fact that, due to that decree, his friend Dr. Carlos Dias was admitted to mental institution. Pessoa mentions that possibility on several occasions, even in conversation with Ophelia. On the 30th of May 1920, she writes: *Maybe you don't need the decree any more (13th of May, isn't it?).* Much later, already during the second stage of their relationship, she would once again address the matter (23rd of September 1929): *I remember when Fernandinho was trying to convince me he would be going to a nuthouse, and that he wanted Osório to buy the Decree of the 28th or 25th of May…*[5] *Would that you had at the time! Although it is true that this time might be better for me or for us.* In a séance in 1929, he goes as far as saying that "the soul is the face of the road", later wondering: "Is it foolishness, madness, crime or genius – this pain here?".

> This sort of madness
> To call it talent is to sell it short
> Which shines in me, in the dark
> Commotion of my thoughts,
> It brings me no joy;
> Because, in the end, there shall always be
> Sun or shadow in the city
> But, in me, I know not what there is.
>
> *Untitled* (undated), Fernando Pessoa

Anguish in his correspondence

Although reserved before those he doesn't know, he makes no secret of how he feels to those close to him. The theme, which is present in numerous passages of his oeuvre, is displayed in almost cruel splendour in his correspondence. According to specialists I consulted with, the language of those letters, technically precise and very much up to date (for the time) suggests Pessoa read extensively on the matter, as is plain to see in the following excerpts:

> "My faculties of analysis have become something I know I possess, yet know not where they lie. I am the involuntary Atlas of a world of tedium." (22/01/1913, letter to Jaime Cortesão)

> "I am currently going through one of those crises which, when they take place in agriculture, are wont to be called crises of abundance. You could scarcely fathom

5 The dates of the decree are wrong in the letter.

what manner of Rua do Arsenal[6] my poor head has been, with regards to movement." (01/02/1913, letter to Mário Beirão)

"I am beset by such deep tedium, I cannot express it other than to describe a hand strangling my soul." (03/05/1914, letter to João Lebre e Lima)

"It slowly approaches its end, this state of mind that has accompanied me for a while, in which I can't even collaborate with myself." (25/05/1914, letter to Álvaro Pinto)

"Everything around me is moving away and crumbling... Perhaps glory tastes of death and uselessness, and triumph smells like decay." (05/06/1914, letter to *dona* Maria, his mother)

"I am in a state of absolute aboulia. Doing anything requires from me an effort akin to lifting a heavy weight, or reading a book by Teófilo[7]." (19/11/1914) "This crisis of mine is akin to those great psychic crises." (04/01/1915) "I've been meaning to speak of you about my case of psychic nature for a while now" (19/01/1915, letters to Côrtes-Rodrigues)

"I am once again a prisoner of all sorts of imaginable crises, only now I am under a full-scale assault. I am psychically besieged." (06/12/1915, letter to Sá-Carneiro)

"I don't know if you will truly think me mad. I believe not. I'll ask you the favour not to mention this to anybody else. There is nothing to be gained from it, and much to be lost, some of which of unknown nature." (24/06/1916, letter to aunt Anica)

"Inwards-driven and cerebral, like most natural neurasthenics, I can almost always control the outwards or dynamic results of those intimate manifestations." (10/06/1919, the abovementioned letter to Henri and Hector Durville)

"I believe I am undergoing a bout of psychosthenic madness. Internment in an asylum is recommended." (31/08/1925, letter "to my dearest friend" – no record of who it was)

"The rope on the old automobile I carry in my head has snapped, and the sense I didn't have made the sound "trr-trr-r-r-r-r..." (09/01/1929, letter to Ophelia Queiroz)

"That light mental alienation, which is the most [Álvaro de] Campos of my privileges, has been constantly by my bedside." (06/12/1929). "I am hysteroneurasthenic with a predominant hysterical element in my emotions and the neurasthenic element in my intelligence and will (one thorough, the other callow)." (11/12/1931) "Intellectually, these past few months I have been on unpaid leave." (12/05/1932, letters to João Gaspar Simões)

6 One of the busiest in Lisbon, at the time.
7 (Joaquim Fernandes) Teófilo Braga (1843-1924) was twice president of Portugal and wrote dozens of books, all of them rather voluminous.

"I don't know if I am merely hysteroneurasthenic. I tend to this second hypothesis, as I display phenomena of aboulia which hysteria *per se* frames in the records of my senses." (13/01/1935, almost repeating an earlier report to José Osório de Oliveira; letter to Adolfo Casais Monteiro)

"The fact is that, since the year prior, I have been under the influx of nervous states of several shapes and sizes, which have even deprived me of the will to do nothing: I have felt like a psychic film of a psychiatry manual, chapter on psychoneuroses." (10/10/1935, one month before the end, letter to Tomás Ribeiro Colaço)

The neurosis and his characters

As a writer, it is only natural that his state of mind reflected itself on the characters he created. "It is in temperamental instability that we should assume the creations of heteronyms stemmed from, as they are but another face of depersonalization. It is under the light of the knowledge of mental care that one can explain the mythical transfigurations that haunt and deceive those who aren't prepared to penetrate an anomalous psyche", he wrote on June 1930. Search lived his life in fear of going mad and frequently used the expression "soul hell". From 1906 to 1908, he wrote "Flashes of madness", and intended to compile prose writings in *Documents of mental decadence.* Pessoa met Baron of Teive in a psychiatric clinic in Lisbon. António Mora had been admitted to Cascais' Casa de Saúde. David Merick wrote *Tales of a madman.* Marvell Kisch, *A madman's millions.* Diniz da Silva began a poem, confessing "I am mad". Florêncio Gomes wrote a *Treatise on mental illnesses.* On Frederick Wyatt, he said "would that he were mad". Friar Maurice is mad, although he never confessed as much. Former sergeant Byng, heteronym of the heteronym Horace James Faber, "displayed an inability to reason with normal things. And, in *The Vargas affair,* Abílio Quaresma compares "drunkenness with madness. The similarity, when one looks beyond external differences, is absolute: The same lack of self-control, the same emergence of repressed tendencies, due to that lack of control, the same lack of coordination of ideas, emotions and movements, or the false coordination of same". *Maktub,* it was written.

The first diagnoses

There is no consensus among the authors. For Dr. Mário Saraiva, doctor at Vilar and author of two books on Pessoa's mental health, he was *a happy psychopath, confused and contradictory, with symptoms of schizophrenia.* Dr. Luís Duarte Santos, professor at the University of Coimbra's Faculty of Medicine, suggests: *Personality? Schizoid (doubts concerning the existence of ciclothymic or cycloid traces). Psychosis? Paranoia and schizophrenia.* Dr. Taborda de Vasconcelos, likely the only doctor who treated him, had the following diagnosis: *Psychopath of schizoid nature;* defining 'schizoid' as *ultimately, an individual who defends himself by eliminating realities and distances himself thus, until he finds refuge in a final redoubt by way of an intimate exile, which Jung designates as an introvert.* To wit, Taborda believed he was *a suffering psychopath.* Graphology specialist Simone Evin, at the request of Armand Guibert (one of the first French scholars of Pessoa), analysed a page of his and, even though she declared she had no prior knowledge of his work (which is rather hard to believe), she considers his case *disaggregation and shattering of the personality, which often translated into the wind of madness,* and concluded that *the poet laughs about his contemporaries, but in a dangerous fashion. There is more than one title for him, there is cynicism, fortunately balanced with a great kindness, nobility, feeling of universal fraternity, qualities which allowed him to avoid a tragic fate (suicide or madness).* Dalila Pereira da Costa, commentator of Pessoa's work, is drier still: *A psychopath.* Whereas, for José Martinho, *he was lucid enough to know he was a madman who didn't need to be in an asylum.* But all those rushed opinions seek scandal rather than science.

The correct diagnosis

Searching for a correct diagnosis, I sought out specialists to discuss his case, and there was consensus among them in that Pessoa didn't fit the psychiatric definition of a madman. Had he been so, he wouldn't have made it to 47 without having been institutionalized. The proof is in his life. He has all genetic conditions to go mad, like grandmother Dionísia, but he defends himself with his neurosis – a gift of sorts for him, which allowed him to keep psychosis at bay. *A healthy neurosis saved him,* says eminent Brazilian psychiatrist Samuel Hulak. To him, Pessoa definitely wasn't schizophrenic. Bastos e Albuquerque shared the same opinion, and said that he had *egodisthonic disturbances of psychosexuality;* or Francisco Manuel da Fonseca Pereira, who feels that *admitting that Pessoa suffered from a more serious mental syndrome such as schizophrenia doesn't seem defensible*... It clearly sounds like a forced, unjustified exaggeration. In conclusion, he did not suffer from manic-depressive syndrome, nor any other psychosis which would alter his grasp on reality. His profile fits that of a schizoid personality – on with a behaviour dissonant from the average, which tends to display discontinuous traits of hysteria[8]. The specialists I consulted with consider that he was a schizoid with depressive, phobic and compulsive traits.

8 In his own words: "If I were a woman… But I am a man, and in men hysteria takes on mainly mental aspects; and so all ends in silence and poetry; or "Man is a hysterical animal, but not too hysterical in normality".

As it so happens, Pessoa is also a melancholic who seldom follows through on his tasks. He abandoned his university degree. Most poems are untitled and undated. He neither finishes nor structures *Disquiet* – the book as we today know it is a compilation of texts he left in envelopes, plus a few others which were later attributed to it by scholars, based on their style of thematic consistency. His life imitates a dream, with the decisive collaboration of alcohol. As an adult, it is as if he were another person. A character which invented its creator. He himself confesses: "Fernando Pessoa doesn't exactly exist". To say that the writer gave life to the man Fernando António Nogueira Pessoa is, therefore, far from an exaggeration. To paraphrase poet Jean-François Casimir Delavigne (1793-1843), *madmen are admirable in their moments of lucidity.* In many cases, like Pessoa's, revealing themselves to be true geniuses.

I requested a diagnosis of Dr. Samuel Hulak, which he elaborated in the style of Pessoa, writing a letter to *Dear Professor Sigmund S. Freud*[9]. In it, his supposed patient (abridged) *claims to suffer from anxiety attacks and drink copiously; he mentions phobias, including descending into madness (there are such cases in his family); he feels struck down by a deep sadness; and, besides the comorbidity which is par for the course in cases of melancholy and alcoholism, he has the classic complaints of asthenia, aboulia and anhedonia, mainly in the mornings, all three of which subside at night. Based on his report, I believe him to still be a virgin. Nothing about him would lead me to believe he is homosexual; rather, he appears to be asexual. The trap of his neurosis became the solution for his mental health, thus avoiding psychosis. I fear there is also a masochistic core which won't stop him in his search for chronic suicide by way of alcoholism or some consumptive disease.* Doctors use the image of existentialist philosopher Karl Jaspers (1883-1969) to define mental patients: *neurotic* would be the clock with an imperfect mechanism, whereas *mad* would be the broken clock. If that is so, then Pessoa's clock worked at all times, and perfectly so, although it didn't always give the right time.

9 The choice of Freud is ironic, as Pessoa had no regard for him whatsoever. In *Stoic,* Baron of Teive says: "This is one of those cases in which all of us should be like Freud. It is impossible for us not to individuate ourselves towards a sexual explanation". And a letter to Gaspar Simões (11/12/1931) reads: "Freud is, in truth, a man of genius, creator of a psychological criterion which is both original and attractive, provided it rests on a sexual interpretation. Now, in my estimation (always in *my* estimation), Freudism is a strict, imperfect system". And, in a loose text, he goes further still: "I proudly register that, as I spoke of Freud, I made use of both a phallic image and an ironic image, and so he would certainly understand it. What he might glean from it, I know not. In any event, damn his eyes!".

Neurosis and his oeuvre

Other than the search for diagnosis, there remains in the eyes of many a subtle relationship between the illness and his oeuvre, a mix of madness and awareness of madness. The expression "my science learn'd" *expressly signals the intimacy of the author with the "genius and insomnia" problem, and that intimacy exacerbates his state of crisis*, according to Georg Lind. And so, the phenomenon of heteronymy should be seen under that lens, as he himself says "the origin of my heteronyms is the deepest trait of hysteria within me". Some commentators have suggested one should contextualize his writings according to the illness. Mário Saraiva, for example, cannot see the oeuvre beyond the man who produced it. *To read Fernando Pessoa without the indispensable prevention leads to a false and delusional interpretation of what one reads and of the writer's personality.* His conclusion is that, once his condition is disclosed, *the literary and human figure of Fernando Pessoa doesn't come out looking good.* Duarte Santos accepts that, claiming that *a psychopathological study of Pessoa would be necessary to better understand his oeuvre.* Taborda de Vasconcelos goes further still: *Nothing kept him from conceiving and creating a sizeable oeuvre, the composition of which, odd as it may seem, was the fruit of the collaboration of all the anomalies in his life.* Celeste Malpique sums it up: *The schizoid tends to live in fantasy, in a transactional dream space... where... imaginary friends, characters... can be created. And when such a fantasy... is mobile, rich, and finds support in literary artistic expression, it can be a source of creativity, as was the case with Fernando Pessoa.*

Far from such positions, I believe the matter should be addressed with less emotion. *The figure of the narrator does not exist,* words of Saramago; *a book is, above all, the expression of its author.* Which is why, deep down, it is a senseless debate. "One writes verses, comes across as mad; and, later, as a genius, perhaps". There are mediocre mental patients, and those of a superior kind. The reasons which lead them to write are a sideshow. What counts is what is created, and the best of it. To know the man's weaknesses doesn't diminish the oeuvre; quite the opposite, it makes it special and speaks highly of the author. His fellow countryman Eça de Queiroz, for example, lived in constant conflict with family members – his mother was unknown to him, and he had a difficult temper. But his works are no less excellent because of that. Friend Ângelo de Lima once told Pessoa: *No poet in the world has ever supplanted or as much as equalled you.* Thus, it was "like a madman who dreams high, I perhaps contribute to the aggrandizement of the universe, as one who has left a beautiful verse behind has also enriched the skies and the earth, and made even more emotively mysterious the reason as to why there are stars and people".

Rubem Alves, when comparing Pessoa to others who also had *a rich mental life,* says none of them had mental health: *They were far too lucid for that.* According to him, the human body is like a computer, in which the hardware is the equipment and the software a set of symbols which were programmed from words, and a computer can go mad from either hardware of software flaws. The master's conclusion is that *the music coming from his software was so beautiful, his hardware couldn't stand it.* In a letter to Casais Monteiro (13/01/1935), speaking about his neurosis, Pessoa confesses: "These phenomena explode inwards, and I experience them alone with myself. Thus, everything ends in silence and poetry". Also, it bears noting that in his case too, the oeuvre is beyond the fragile condition of the poor man who wrote it.

> Someone committed to an asylum is at least someone.
> I'm committed to an asylum without an asylum.
> I'm clear and crazy,
> I'm coldly insane,
> I'm apart from everything and equal to all:
> I'm in a waking sleep dreaming dreams
> Insane because they're not dreams.
> That's how it is with me…
>
> *Untitled*, Álvaro de Campos

Bonum vinum lætificat cor hominis
(Good wine brings joy to Man's heart) Roman saying

THE AMAZING LUCIDITY OF DRINK

At times, a good bender
carries with it an astonishing lucidity.
Untitled (1931), Fernando Pessoa

An irresistible craving for alcohol

It is as if the two had been born for each other. At times, upon arriving home, Pessoa would pretend to be drunk. To amuse the children *or to annoy his sister, who was as conservative as he was radical, and was positively mortified by alcohol, and always said Fernando drank too much* – according to brother João Maria. Teca recalls how *often, at lunch time, I'd sit by the window and wait for him. As soon as he saw me, he pretended to be drunk, stumbling, tripping and throwing his hat on the chandelier. I'd tell him to just look at himself, how others would think him mad.* The problem is that Pessoa *drank too much* – according to niece Manuela Nogueira. And in increasingly larger quantities. "my most deliberate acts, my clearest ideas and my most logical intentions were after all no more than congenital drunkenness". He does it because his "mental activity" ceases "as soon as unassisted by the casual vapours of an alcoholic beverage". Baudelaire, in "Get Drunk", wrote: *Get drunk and stay that way. On what? On wine, poetry, virtue, whatever. But get drunk.* Throughout his life, Pessoa always acted upon those words. For Francisco Manuel Fonseca Ferreira, *those individuals who drink alcohol tend to become progressively adapted to increasingly high doses, and may even appear to be sober while presenting levels of blood alcohol content which would cause average to severe intoxication on those who don't have the habit.* So too was his case, having developed such a resistance to the secondary effects of alcohol, that he never publicly embarrassed himself without meaning to. His neighbours António Manuel Rodrigues de Seixas and Carlos *Bate-Chapa* Campos, who saw him pass by every day at Rua Coelho da Rocha, confirmed as much: *We never saw him drunk.* Some times, when the family hosted others for dinner, Pessoa stayed in his room, according to the words of Mário Soares, former president of Portugal; when he had already consumed part of his inseparable bottle, it is reasonable to assume. Or perhaps he only wished to keep his distance from strangers; so much so, that one day, according to Manuela Nogueira, *he asked me to tell a visit he was drunk, just because he didn't wish to see them.*

João Gaspar Simões corroborates the version that Pessoa was an inveterate drunk. His "necessary poisons" were *poisonous effluviants.* Because he drank much more than was reasonable. Not a very trustworthy testimony, as despite their lifelong correspondence, Gaspar Simões only resided in Lisbon from 1935 onwards, when Pessoa was already getting ready to die. Augusto Ferreira Gomes, for example, rails against such notion: *God forbid I tell you that Pessoa was a pure and wholesome teetotaller... He drank vigorously and copiously, perhaps a little more than he should in his final years. But to the level of what his biographer [Gaspar Simões] implies, almost seeming sorry that he didn't end up in a gutter like Poe... good Lord, that's quite a ways off!* But deep down, Pessoa might just have thought that his guilty pleasure was worth it. "Everyone has his alcohol. To exist is alcohol enough for me. Drunk from feeling, I wander as I walk straight ahead".

His favourite drinks

"With mortal hand, I raise to my mortal mouth in a fragile vessel the fleeting wine"; and "I don't consider wine – though I enjoy drinking it – to be a source of nourishment or a vital necessity". Of that particular beverage, he has particular appreciation for the so-called *Lisbon wines:* Some white – Bucelas and Gaeiras; or table red wines, especially Colares, from southern Estremadura, made from moscatel grape – *poisonous Colares,* as Eça said in *Cousin Basílio.* Ophelia, in a letter from the 6th of April 1920, mentions another preference of his: *It pleases me to know Mr. Crosse is in good health*[1]*, but he should be careful with his Madeira, and Mr. Álvaro de Campos should mind the bucket*[2]*, as he might drown if he doesn't know how to swim, the poor thing...* But his favourite wine is another, which is why he dreams with "bottles of that Port wine no one can buy". He also tries absinthe in the company of Sá-Carneiro, but finds it disagrees with his stomach. He enjoys brandy (Macieira) – "so I let my heart smart, and I drink brandy". But above all, he preferred the type of moonshine made out of the mash of grape skins

1 A reference to a previous letter by Pessoa, in which he mentioned that heteronym "A. [A,] Crosse in in good health – a pound of health thus far, enough not to having caught a cold.

2 Another reference to the same letter, in which Pessoa says: "Farewell, I'm putting my head into a bucket to rest my spirit. It is the way of great men – provided they have 1. spirit; 2. head; 3. a bucket to put their head in.

and stems known in Portugal as *bagaço. He'd have* bagaço *in the middle of the morning or the afternoon,* according to niece Manuela Nogueira. *Clear liquor,* for António Ferreira Gomes. *Glasses of aguardiente,* for Eugénio Lisboa. *Only aguardiente,* for António Quadros. *Preferably of the Águia Real brand.* "Ah, drink! Life is neither good nor bad". Poetry and alcohol always walked hand in hand with him.

> The drunkard was stumbling drunk
>
> And I, who was just passing by,
> Didn't help him, for he was stumbling drunk,
> And I was just passing by.
> The drunkard collapsed in a drunken stupor
> In the middle of the street
> And I didn't turn back, but I heard. Me, drunk
> And his fall in the street.
>
> The drunkard fell, drunk
> In the street of life.
> My God! I also collapsed, drunk
> God.
>
> *Untitled* (undated), Fernando Pessoa

The art of drinking

In a letter to Ophelia, he says: "Do not wonder at my peculiar handwriting. The reason for it is the fact that I unearthed at home a splendid Port wine, which I opened and already drank half from". In a letter he signed as Íbis, he claims to have written it in "Abel style" – Casa Abel Pereira da Fonseca, better known as Val do Rio cellar. Ophelia replies, asking him *not to go to Abel.* In another letter, Ophelia laments him having *preferred Abel rather than me. I well know my company is nothing special. But... at least I don't go to your head.* In another one: *You haven't been patronizing Abel, have you? It's not good for your health, it's poison you're imbibing, and then my poor little thing falls ill and it's no fun, ruining yourself by your own hand. It's bad for your liver, your stomach, your intestines, it's all bad for you.* In another one still: *Abel has sweet aguardiente, but Baby's mouth is sweet, and perhaps a little spicy, but it's as it should be.* All letters were written in September 1929, and it bears mentioning that, while Ophelia almost never mentioned drinking during their first stage, allusions to it became commonplace in the second stage, nine years later.

In a letter to Casais Monteiro (13/01/1935), in which he explains the origins of his heteronyms, he deems it fit to clarify: "I am interrupting [the letter]. I am neither mad nor drunk"; something that should come naturally to one who says "I find myself ever lacking a thing, a glass, a crisis, a phrase". He confesses to Gaspar Simões to having been encouraged by "a friend of mine, who is drunker than I am, does not feel like getting drunk on his own, and has insistently prompted me to stop typing and join him"; and, in another one, he claims to be "definitely tired and thirsty". Simões suggests he had *aguardiente colics, at any time of the day, on his feet, before the first tavern he came across";* and recalls how, when it happened, *he tended to write in English. Under the influence of alcohol, in the pleasant or unpleasant excitement that the friction with the landscape infused him with, he let the quill flow, much like it happened in Portalegre, when he wrote* Alentejo seen from the train. Still on that episode from Portalegre, in which he bought the printing equipment for Íbis printing house, José Blanco suggests *it shouldn't be taken too seriously, as for him it was but a joke.* "I have something of the spirit of a bohemian, of those who let life slip away, like something that slips through one's fingers", as well as a constant clearing of the throat, which can be heard from afar. "I ate and drank rather less than usual in the first-floor dining room of the restaurant responsible for perpetuating my existence. And as I was leaving, the waiter, having noted that the bottle of wine was still half full, turned to me and said: 'So long, Mr. Soares, and I hope you feel better". Mr. Soares is, of course, Bernardo Soares, Pessoa himself, and the waiter's words are rather telling – him leaving a bottle only half empty could only mean he wasn't feeling well. Soares appreciates "the waiter who just now demonstrated his camaraderie by wishing me well".

"If a man writes well only when he's drunk, then I'll tell him: Get drunk. And if he says that it's bad for his liver, I'll answer: What's your liver? A dead thing that lives while you live, whereas the poems you write live without while". He often "raises the head of his anonymous life" and finds out it is but "congenital drunkenness, inherent madness and huge ignorance" – an expression he repeatedly makes use of in his texts. He then experiences "a slight daze like the beginning of drunkenness" which "reveals to me the soul of things". In 1926, in *Revista de Comércio e Contabilidade* #2, in an article titled "The handcuffs", he protests against the United State's Prohibition, which he considers "an intolerable intrusion of the state in citizens' lives, a factor of disturbance in the free game of economics". Commenting on that law, he says "the anti-alcohol movement is one of the greatest enemies of the development of will". When it was revoked by president Roosevelt in December 1933, Pessoa must have been thankful, in his own way.

> Today is the day, today is the day
> In which Bacchus shall display
> All of his joy.

Come reap, come and reap
The flowers for your orgy.
Come reap to then lose
Come reap for your aches[3].

Act of the bacchantes, Fernando Pessoa

"Just by thinking of a word, I understood the concept of Trinity". Every morning, as he left home without breaking his fast, he stopped at the dairy his friend worked at, at the corner of Rua Coelho da Rocha and Rua Silva Carvalho. The establishment, as previously noted, belonged to António Lopes, but he is always served by an employee, his friend Júlio Trindade. He heads to the counter, placed his right index finger[4] over the corner and said: "headed me 7". Said "7" was a glass of red wine which cost 70 centavos. As soon as the sun set, he would repeat the gesture at the counter and simply say "2, 8 and 6", and soon Trindade came with a matchbox (20 centavos), a pack of Bons cigarettes (80) and a chalice of Madeira brandy (60). He pocketed the matches and the cigarettes and downed the chalice with a single swig. He would then produce a small black bottle he always kept in his briefcase and handed it to Trindade, who would soon return it with a new cork. Filled with aguardiente. His nightly dose. He put the bottle back into the briefcase and would leave without paying. Every morning, his room was a mess. On the table, papers scribbled with words gilded by "the impossible sunset of high and vast hills in the distance". According to Manuela Nogueira, those papers were read to her parents after lunch. The floor was dotted with cigarette tips and the little black bottle, empty and without a cork. When Mr. Manassés appeared for his daily shave, he always had the same request, which he made in almost reverential tone. *He was a very kind person, mister Pessoa was,* recalls Manassés. The request was always to head to Trindade to fill up his blessed little bottle.

Our boss is a father
He does good by us.
We drink to his health,
And ours, too!
Let there lack no grain for the seed
Medicine for the ill
And wine for us!

Medieval bacchanal, Fernando Pessoa

3 This poem's marginalia (written in English) reads: "No, no, no", which proves he was less than pleased with the verses.

4 The scene was described to me via gestures by António Seixas (son of barber Manassés) and Carlos *Bate-Chapa* – both witnessed the same scene every day from across the street (in front of the barber shop).

Friend Martins da Hora confesses that, *whenever he couldn't be found, there was only one thing to do: Leave a message at Abel Pereira da Fonseca, which was the only place he went to regularly, as he never had any set day or time for all other places. But never, during the many years we interacted, did I notice the slightest hint of dementia...* Another friend, Luís Pedro Moitinho de Almeida, says: *I often saw scenes such as this: Mr. Pessoa would be working, usually at the typewriter, would get up, pick up his hat, straighten up his glasses and say with a solemn voice: "I am going to Abel's". Nobody ever thought it strange. One day, he went "to Abel's" so many times, I couldn't hold it in any more, and just said: "Mister Pessoa," when he returned, "you can take it like a sponge!", to which he immediately replied, with his usual irony – "Like a sponge? Like a sponge store, with a warehouse attached". It was the only flaw – if a flaw it was – that I ever saw in him.*

A chronic alcoholic

In medical texts, drinkers are usually divided in three distinct groups: social drinkers – who do not display expressive psychic or organic manifestations; problem drinkers, who, despite their tolerance to alcohol, reveal secondary manifestations when drinking in excess; and chronic alcoholics, who end up suffering serious manifestations due to their dependence on the ingestion of alcohol. The World Health Organization defines a chronic alcoholic as *a heavy drinker who, displaying a physical or psychological dependence of alcohol, may develop symptoms of withdrawal such as tremors, agitation, anxiety and panic, which can evolve into* delirium tremens. Pessoa, having started drinking in large quantities from an early age, corresponds to that classical model of a chronic alcoholic. At the age of 18, as Charles Robert Anon, he confesses to already suffering from bouts of dipsomania, or an uncontrollable urge to drink. At the age of 19, in a letter written in English to Teixeira Rabelo (22/08/1907), he claims to find himself "amidst a few moments of concatenate mental activity, not without the assistance of the casual fumes of an alcoholic beverage".

Alcoholics are often only able to function with the aid of alcohol, and usually start drinking in the morning to make the alcohol-induced tremors stop. Hemingway would drink gin upon waking up, but he wasn't alone in that. Donald W. Goodwyn, chairman of the Kansas University Medical Centre, concluded a study on the matter, according to which *alcoholism is an epidemic among writers,* listing Charles Bukowski, Edgar Allan Poe, Emily Dickinson, Ernest Hemingway, Eugene O'Neill, Henry Thoreau, Lillian Hellman, Mark Twain, Mary McCarthy, [Gerard] Nerval, Paul Verlaine, [Francis] Scott Fitzgerald, Tom Wolfe, Truman Capote, William Faulkner. As it so happened, unlike most chronic drinkers, Pessoa did not display the expected physical or psychological signs of his addiction. The very quality of his writing attests to the fact that he had no pronounced neurological or psychological lesions, as the life he led was incompatible with neuropsychological disease brought about by alcohol.

President Mário Soares told me that, in 1985 – he was prime-minister at the time – during the 50th anniversary of the poet's death, he had his remains relocated to the Jerónimos Monastery. According to bureaucratic demands, his coffin would have needed to be opened so his bones could be collected, but his body was intact, as if embalmed. The conclusion of those who witnessed the scene is that, while he had none of the formaldehyde usually used in the process of mummification, his body contained alcohol. Copious amounts of alcohol. Alcohol which, in life, had soaked his flesh, preserving the body. Except that's not quite how it works. Chemically, formaldehyde isn't alcohol, but aldehyde. With distinct organic compounds. Alcohol contains a hydroxil functional group with an OH structure – an oxygen atom bound to hydrogen; whereas aldehydes contain a functional group with a CHO structure – a carbon atom bound to hydrogen and oxygen. A corpse's integrity always results from the body's physical constitution, the region's micro-climate, or the geological properties of the soil it was buried in. The Catholic Church, for example, no longer accepts bodily incorruptibility as evidence of one of the two miracles required for acknowledgement of sainthood.

This version was also defended by writer Emiliano Monge. For him, six years prior, a commission of notables had decided to move the remains. He even refers the reaction of one of its members, António de Sagadaes: *I will never forget how startling that unexpected vision was, it was as if I stood before the same man I had seen several times during my childhood, as if I were looking at a photo of his.* Except the scene isn't believable. Luiz Rosa, Pessoa's nephew, had been charged with monitoring the situation, and he confirmed the following to me: *All coffins placed in tombs have another coffin underneath, made of lead, with a sealed lid, where the body is buried. Therefore, no one could have just checked to see if the body was truly intact,* Which leads us to conclude that all was just another legend about Pessoa.

Delirium tremens

His dependency on alcohol worsens in time, and he actually begins to suffer from *delirium tremens* – reproducing the scene with heteronyms Abílio Quaresma and ex-Sergeant Byng. To better understand the severity of it, one should bear in mind that it is a progressive medical event. At the early, prodromal stages, it manifests through extreme anxiety – with sweating, tremors and sleep disturbance; followed by a period of mental confusion, disorientation, restlessness, hypo- (or, more frequently) hyperthermia and changes in sensory perception, with the presence of Lilliputian hallucinations (sight of diminutive elements) and zoopsia (seeing animals), with the patient also likely to experience convulsions. Pessoa felt all those signs. His first crisis was in Estoril, at his sister's house. There, he would later collapse several times on the floor. Another crisis took place at Rossio, at dawn, close to Café Gelo, where the telephone booths are. A third one might have been experienced at Rua Coelho da Rocha, when others had to break down the door to come to his aid because had lost consciousness in the bathroom. Against his own expectations, he resists those final crises and, a few days before his death, he writes an English poem titled "D.T."[5] – certainly *delirium tremens,* because, in *delirium,* the alcoholic feels disgusting animals close to his body and starts struggling to escape from them. All perfectly described in the following verses:

The other day indeed,
With my shoe, on the wall,
I killed a centipede
Which was not there at all.
How can that be?
It's very simple, you see -
Just the beginning of D. T.

When the pink alligator
And the tiger without a head
Begin to take stature
And demanded to be fed,
As I have no shoes
Fit to kill those,
I think I'll start thinking:
Should I stop drinking?

But it really doesn't matter…
Am I thinner or fatter
Because this is this?
Would I be wiser or better
If life were other than this is?

No, nothing is right.
Your love might
Make me better than I
Can be or can try.
But we never know
Darling, I don't know
If the sugar of your heart

---

5 Some publications omit the title.

Would not turn out candy…
So I let my heart smart
And I drink brandy.

Then the centipede come
Without trouble.
I can see them well.
Or even double.
I'll see them home
With my shoe,
And, when they all go to hell,
I'll go too.

Then, on a whole,
I shall be happy indeed,
Because, with a shoe
Real and true,
I shall kill the true centipede -
My lost soul!…

D.T., Fernando Pessoa

The poem is soon sent to his brother Luís Miguel, on the 15th of October 1935, and the Chest also contained a draft of a letter in English (summed up):

> Dear L…
> When I wrote to you the other day, my idea was to send you a copy of the alcoholic or post-alcoholic poem, of which I recited by heart the first verses for you and E…[6] Somehow, I forgot, but I am sending it now and wish to make it clear that it in no way approximates anything I'd even consider publishing in English, as it's clearly unfit for publication. It's just so you can see the damned poem's nature. For some ironical intervention of the typewriter or the carbon paper, the copy came out lopsided, which, however, is rather consistent with its disarray.

A slow suicide of sorts

Pessoa drank alcohol as soon as he woke up, and kept at it during the day, plus the inevitable night bottle. In time, he takes note of the increasing frailty of his body, but does nothing to change his routine. Which hardly comes as a surprise, taking his neurosis into account – and neurotics almost never commit suicide on a whim. It tends to be a slow and perfectly self-aware process. Much like alcoholism. "You ask me what I want. To drink to the point I no longer know

6 There are no records of who "L" was. But, according to Manuela Nogueira, "E" was likely Pessoa's sister-in-law, Eve.

if I'm drinking of if I already drank". He studies his condition in books and performs self-diagnosis, confirming the foreshadowing of his own horoscope. He believed his second crisis would be the end of him. "And do you see me, Ruy [Santos] foregoing aguardiente?". That friend in particular considered he was in a *sorry state.* He knew of MacGregor Mathers' story (of the Hermetic Order of the Golden Dawn fame) and his "terrible end, dulled by alcohol. It was a most pungent affair". And he fears something similar may happen to him. "I was drunk, I didn't know how to put on a mask I hadn't even taken off". Álvaro de Campos wrote a poem about that slow path towards suicide[7]:

> If you want to kill yourself, why don't you want to kill yourself?
> Now's your chance! I, who greatly love both death and life,
> Would kill myself too, if I dared kill myself...
> If you dare, then be daring!
> (...)
> You're needed? O futile shadow called man!
> No one is needed; you're not needed by anyone...
> (...)
> First there's anxiety, the surprise of mystery's arrival
> And of your spoken life's sudden absence...
> Then there's the horror of your visible and material coffin,
> And the men in black whose profession is to be there.
> Then the attending family, heartbroken and telling jokes,
> Mourning between the latest news from the evening papers,
> Mingling grief over your death with the latest crime...
> And you merely the incidental cause of that lamentation,
> You who will be truly dead, much deader than you
> imagine...
> Look at yourself in the face and honestly face what we are...
> If you want to kill yourself, then kill yourself...
> Forget your moral scruples or intellectual fears!
> What scruples or fears influence the workings of life?[8]
>
> *Untitled* (26/04/1926), Álvaro de Campos

Armando Ventura Teixeira, his barber at Chiado, said: *Fernando – nobody knew he was a great poet – drank bottles of aguardiente like one who wanted to kill himself.* Dr. Jaime Neves actually forbids him from drinking: *An extra chalice of aguardiente, and it'll be the end of you.* Pessoa pays him no heed. "Today I'm vanquished, as if I knew the truth". "And I, who timidly hate life, fear

---

7 Most specialists believe it was written for Pessoa himself. Conversely, and in what I believe to be a correct assertion, Cleonice Berardinelli brought to my attention the fact that that it was written on the 26th of April 1926 – the exact date of the suicide of dear Sá-Carneiro's suicide. In that case, the suicidal sentiment was related to his departed friend, and not himself.

8 A variant was "What scruples or fears can the workings of life have"?

death with fascination". There is no consensus among specialists on the matter. Teresa Rita Lopes maintains *he neither went mad, nor did he commit suicide, his Others went mad and killed themselves for him.* In a conversation we had, she reaffirmed her belief that he hadn't committed suicide. Teresa Sobral Cunha shared her opinion. Cleonice Berardinelli, in another conversation, told me *he slowly killed himself without meaning to, which isn't the same.* Conversely, Ireneu Cruz believes that, in a case such as his, *the most plausible form of suicide would indeed have been through alcohol.* Jorge de Sena thinks likewise. *It was an exemplary suicide, carried out in calculated fashion throughout twenty five years of poetry. A suicide through the gradual and copious ingestion of alcohol.* In Hiudéa Rodrigues Boberg's words, *it was a slow suicide.* According to psychiatrist Celeste Malpique, *the poet did not commit suicide; he faded away in bouts of delusion, a simmering depressive process which, in its unending cycles, ended up consuming him, soaked in alcohol by way of anaesthesia.* For Dr. Taborda de Vasconcelos, *Fernando Pessoa can and should be considered potentially suicidal. And he did carry out his impulse.*

> And today I am but a delayed suicide,
> A still living desire to sleep.
> But to really sleep, not in dignifying fashion.
> Like an abandoned ship
> Shipwrecked, alone amidst the darkness and the mist.
>
> *Untitled* (28/08/1927), Fernando Pessoa

Taking all the above into consideration, the notion that he did commit suicide can't easily be put aside; especially as, in so doing, he emulated his heteronyms Baron of Teive, Marcos Alves and Marino. Even though he did say in *Disquiet* that "suicide is cowardice". Because, and even if it weren't a conscious decision, deep down maybe he wished for a cleaner end. "Thus I lived, thus I died life, calm 'neath mute skies". He knew it was inevitable, the humiliation of dying in bed, prostrate and impotent. "Let us gleefully enter death! Damn it". And he prefers to shorten his old age by way of glasses of aguardiente. "I am left by what is feverish in simple life; an utter calmness takes hold over me". And it is increasingly common to see him drunk. "Consoler of the disconsolate, Tears of those who never weep, Hour that never strikes – deliver me from joy and happiness"

> Wise is the man who contents himself with the spectacle of the world
> And, as he drinks, he can barely recall
> He already drank once in life,
> He from whom everything is new
> Is imperishable.
>
> *Odes* (19/6/1914), Ricardo Reis

Acta est fabula
(The play is finished)[1]

HIS DESPONDENCY

Death hovers like a lost bird.
English notation (04/05/1922), Fernando Pessoa

A grim fate

Pessoa at the age of 40

The year is 1935, his last one, and all dreams of the past are far gone. "My poor life". Shortly before, in 1930, he had written: "At the age of 20, I laughed at my grim fate; today, I know my banal fate. At the age of 20, I aspired to the eastern principalities; today, I would be content, no questions asked or details required, with a peaceful end of life here in the suburbs, as the proprietor of

1 The words used to announce the end of plays in Roman theatre.

a slow tobacco shop". He feels abandoned as "one fated for defeat", doomed to while away precious hours working in offices that have little to do with his writing, reduced to "the interval between what I am and am not, between dream and what life has made of me". A harsh price to pay for survival. "I see life as a roadside inn where I have to stay until the coach from the abyss pulls up". In this final year of his, he says that "no one cares what an obscure poet does or thinks". Even the act of writing begins to be an ordeal for him. "Little by little, all bonds were broken. Soon, I shall be alone". It is only then that he truly understands that "my past is all I could not be" and "my fate is decadence".

> It's been a long time since I've been able
> To write a long poem!
> It's been years…
> I lost everything that made me conscious
> Of a certain something in my being…
> What's left for me today?
> The sun's without my calling it…
> The day costs me no effort…
>
> *Untitled* (1934, Álvaro de Campos

His friend Gaspar Simões travels to Lisbon for a conference at *O Século* (28/03/1933). Pessoa was invited, but didn't show up. "I regret that your coming to Lisbon during the conference coincided with a couple of days of greater invisibility on my part (letter from 02/04/1933). Simões knows the true motive for his absence and makes no big deal out of it. "As grand as tragedies are, none are greater than the tragedy of my own life", as "I am no longer myself. I am a fragment of me, preserved in a museum", "one of those rags used to wipe dirty things, which are left by the windowsill to dry, and there remain forgotten". He barely sees João Maria, who moved back to Lisbon from London with his wife Eve. His other brother, Luís Miguel, on a honeymoon with his wife Eileen, is impressed by the state he finds himself in. They take a few photos together in Spring 1935, and Pessoa says he will visit them in England, but knows well he won't. "I am sick of myself, objective and subjectively. I am sick of it all".

> I'm dizzy,
> Dizzy from too much sleep or too much thought,
> Maybe even both.
> (…)
> In the end
> What life have I made of my life?
> None.
>
> *Untitled* (12/09/1935), Álvaro de Campos

A future of uncertainties

The small world he inhabits has everything within his reach. To shave and get a haircut, he resorts mainly to Manassés, who visits him early in the morning. Several times, the barber found him with the previous night's clothes, unconscious, head resting on his working table. "As a child. I remember I saw dawn shining over the city. I saw morning, and felt joy. Now, I see morning and feel sad". So he becomes increasingly more of a shut-in. "The four walls of my squalid room are at once a cell and a wilderness, a bed and a coffin". His family is almost always in Cascais. Sister Teca asks friend Júlio Trindade to let her know in case something out of the ordinary happens, but he disliked such supervision, refusing to accept his growing health limitations. "When I get sick, what I hate most is if someone should feel obliged to take care of me, something I'd loathe doing for another. I've never visited a sick friend. And whenever I've been sick and had visitors, I've always felt their presence as a bother, an insult, an unwarranted violation of my wilful privacy".

> The sleep falling over me,
> (…)
> It's the sleep of the sum of all disillusion,
> It's the sleep of the synthesis of every despair;
> It's the sleep of holding the world in me
> Without having contributed to it.
> (…)
> My God, what weariness![2]
>
> *Untitled* (22/08/1935), Álvaro de Campos

"My pain is silent, like the part of the beach the sea can't reach". Cleonice Berardinelli says that, in that time, he experienced *a fever from beyond.* "In this borderless country known as the universe, I feel like I'm living under a political tyranny that doesn't oppress me directly but that still offends some secret principle of my soul. And then I'm slowly, softly seized by an absurd nostalgia for some future, impossible exile". In a first horoscope, he predicted he'd live until the age of "68 and 10 months, approximately". In another, he adds up the numbers of his birth, following a specific formula: "13.6.1988 = 35 = 8", the same eight which, in numerology, stands for success, prestige, arrogance; and, at the side, he notes the presumable date of his death: "30.12.1961 = 22 = 4", four, the sign of perseverance and rigidity. Perhaps he laughed at seeing how far those concepts of numerology truly were from his case. Putting no faith in such calculations, he redid his horoscope (in 1934) and realizes he is not

2 When it was published in *Presença* #52 (July 1938) as "A previously unpublished poem by Álvaro de Campos", it was dated 28/03/1935.

long for the world. In 1935, he sends his thanks for a book sent by journalist António Marques Matias (editor of literary magazine *Momento),* saying; "I know not your age, but I assume it has the virtue of being composed of a large number". Matias was only 24. In his case, one might well remember Shaw's words, that *youth is an ailment with a cure;* and, at the age of 47, Pessoa had long since been healed. He predicts his death for the following year's 30th of June, seven months after the actual date. An explanation was provided me by eminent astrologist, Professor Luís Filipe Teixeira, of Lusófona University in Lisbon: *The difference lies in the base hour of the genethliac map and the corresponding "progressions". And that difference was about twenty minutes, which caused the error upon projecting* (the sun circles around "progressions", a degree per year of life). In 1935, he reviews his horoscope. The new prediction pointed to 1937, this time off by two years. Believing he still had that time left, he resists having a doctor brought to his presence on the eve of his death. He asked his astrologist friends to confirm the numbers. One of them was Raul Leal, who didn't give him the answer he saw in the skies – according to him, *so I wouldn't sadden him any further.* Leal did tell Jorge de Sena that Pessoa's death would occur not in 1937, but closer to the poet's own prediction, in 1935.

> I believe I'm going to die.
> But the meaning of dying doesn't move me.
> I remember dying shouldn't have meaning.
> Living and dying are classifications like those of plants.
> What leaves or flowers have classification?
> What life has life or what death, death?
>
> *Detached poems*, Alberto Caeiro

In another letter (1957) sent to Sena, Leal claims his own death would be in 1967; he too got it wrong, as he would pass away on the 18th of August 1964.

The genius and his time

"The nobler the genius, the less noble his fate". Pessoa realizes that his life is coming to an end, and sees himself as a failure. Without the recognition he deep down feels he deserves, like so many other great men before (and after) him. Reflecting upon that matter, he seeks to articulate an explanation for it: "Each epoch reacts to the ways of the preceding epoch. And venerates the geniuses who lived in opposition to their own time. The one thing a genius can expect from his contemporaries is contempt", and "nothing is so deleterious for others' esteem for a man than the notion that the latter might be better than them. Dislike, colourless as it is, assumes shades of envy. The hesitation in acknowledging that a man might be better than us is as nerve-wracking as the possibility of something unpleasant happening to us". Therefore, "one can say that the genius isn't appreciated in his time, because he stands in opposition to it. The more universal the genius, the easier it is for the following epoch to accept him, as his critique of his own epoch will be deeper still". "They never become famous two or three epochs later. A small genius attains fame, a greater genius attains spite, a god attains crucifixion[3]. Pessoa feels much like said god, living in "a time prior to the one I am living in"; knowing he will live on through the notoriety of his writings. "How many times have I – I, who scoff at such seductions of distraction – found myself thinking how nice it would be to be famous, how pleasant to be cajoled, how colourful to be triumphant! But I cannot see myself in such lofty situations without having my other I laughing. Do I see myself being famous? The applause reaches where I live and collides with my cheap room's crude furniture, with the paltriness that surrounds me and belittles me from the kitchen to the dream. I shall die as I have lived, amongst the bric-a-brac". In a draft of an unsent letter to Gaspar Simões (1929), he confesses: "For me, only celebrity (true celebrity) would be the psychic synonym of freedom". A celebrity he would not attain in life.

> Don't try to persuade me otherwise: I'm lucid.
> It's like I said: I'm lucid.
> Don't talk to me about aesthetics with a heart: I'm lucid.
> Shit! I'm lucid.
>
> *Untitled* (undated), Álvaro de Campos

Memories of his mother

Shortly after losing *dona* Maria in 1925, he wrote "Mother's little boy" – "So young! So young he was! (how old is he now?)". As years go by, he misses his mother more and more. After all, "that man who was your boy grew old". "I'm so cold, so weary in my abandonment. Go and find my Mother, O Wind. Take me in the Night to the house I never knew". Now close to the end, he wrote her another poem, this one in French, so very different from the one he had written as a child:

> Mommy, mommy
> Your child
> Has grown
> And became sadder still
> (…)

3 Fittingly, one of the books in Pessoa's bookshelf was John Ferguson Nisbet's *The Insanity of Genius*.

Wherever you are listening from,
See, I shall always be your child
Your little boy
Who grew up
(…)
I shall return to your love
A child
In your arms
For ever
Mommy, mommy
Oh, mommy.

Mommy, Fernando Pessoa

The hour is nigh

He begins to prepare for death since the end of 1934, and started methodically organizing his papers in the Chest. The comparison with the previous chaotic state of affairs makes it all the more evident. "This was the tragedy, yet there was no dramaturge to write it". The following year, at Martinho da Arcada, friend Augusto Ferreira Gomes takes what would be his last photo. As background, perhaps due to a gut feeling, he chose a different table than the one he usually sat at – this one rounded, made of wood, and far more solemn.

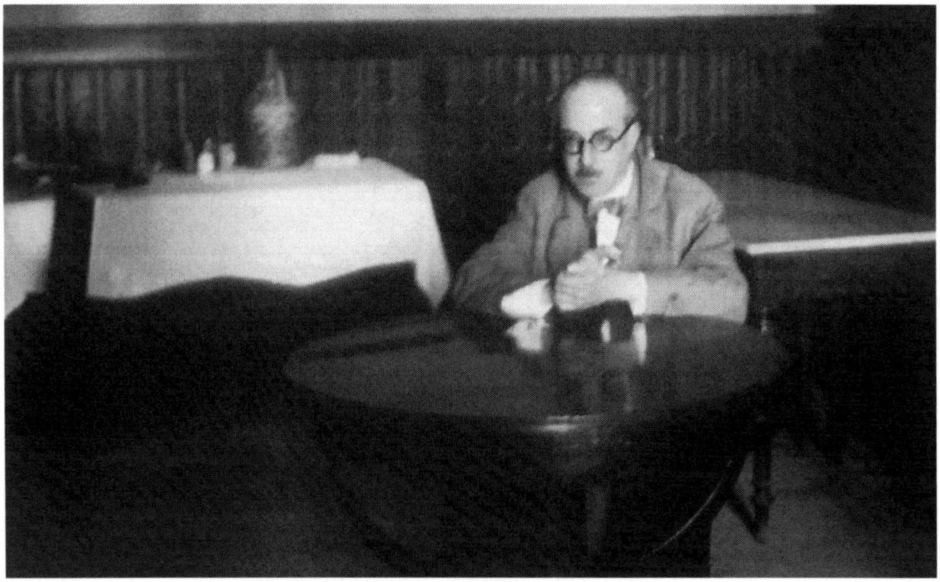

Last photo at Martinho

In this photo, taken in 1935, he looks fat, his shoulders hunched, his skin looking swollen, not much hair left, prominent forehead, flaccid lower lip, eyes no longer glinting. His Jewish nose acquires alcoholic shades of red and purple. Where he previously sat for the entire afternoon, writing poems, he now sits idly by himself. Sometimes, it's like he isn't really there, staring at an indeterminate spot on the wall. Only the typical smoker's clearing of the throat and the cough announce his presence. One night, he sees Carlos Queiroz and, misty-eyed, asks him "how is Ophelia?". He shakes his hands vigorously and tells him "a beautiful soul". Nothing else. As if he were talking to himself. And doesn't even wait for a reply, as Ophelia, if she had ever been a part of his life, had long since escaped from it.

Here, now, I remember
How much of myself I ceased to be
And, futilely… I cry
What I am and could not have.

Untitled (1924), Fernando Pessoa

Now, there, in his little world, he only awaits "the empty immensity of things, the great oblivion". Because "that thing, joy, lies in the Faraway Island[4], the one you know and none of us know of". Even his body feels different. "Once upon a time, I was a decadent poet; today, I believe I am but decadent". Summer is coming to a close. "I have nowhere to run to, unless I run from myself". Jorge de Sena thought he *looked old, even though he was only forty,* and elaborates: *Pessoa got old with vertiginous speed. Without losing his "British" mien, he seemed twenty years older than he really was.* His former sartorial elegance is gone. In a final meeting with Almada Negreiros, that friend of his recalls his *hat buried in his head, his white raincoat rather dirty.* Gaspar Simões' description is similar: *Wrinkled clothing, short trousers, his arms escaping his sleeves and a slightly rumpled hat on his head, which leaned ever slightly to the right, made a mockery of his former dignity and made him look like a vagrant, a beggar* – evoking a poem his friend had once written.

Yes, to be a vagrant and a beggar, as I am,
Is not to be a vagrant or a beggar, which is facile;
It is to be isolated in one's soul, and that is being a vagrant,
And having to beg days to pass and leave us, that
Is being a beggar.
All else is stupid like a Dostoyevsky or a Gorky.

Untitled (undated), Álvaro de Campos

4 Probably one of the Fortunate Isles in the Atlantic Ocean, where king Sebastião is to have lived out his years – for those who believe he didn't die in battle.

Pessoa's dead

"The dead! The dead who loved me in my childhood. Whenever I remember them, my whole soul shivers and I feel exiled from all hearts, alone in the night of myself, weeping like a beggar before the closed silence of all doors". Now it was only himself and "the ghosts of my dead Is". "For me, when I see a dead person, death seems like a prank. The corpse infuses in me the impression of a garb which has been discarded. Someone who left and didn't need to take that one suit he wore". And "all those I've loved have forgotten me in the shadow". When he feels that way, he "counted the dead I've had in my family". His father died of tuberculosis, at home, when his son was only 5 (1893). His brother Jorge (1894), in Lisbon. His maternal grandmother, Madalena Pinheiro Nogueira (1896), at Terceira Island. His uncle Manuel Gualdino da Cunha (1898), in Pedrouços. Two sisters: Madalena Henriqueta (1901), in Durban, and Maria Clara (1906), in Lisbon. His dear paternal grandmother Dionísia (1907), at the asylum of Rilhafoles. His stepfather's mother, *dona* Henriqueta Margarida Rodrigues (1909), at a nursing home in Belas. His great-aunt Maria and great-aunt Adelaide (1911), in Lisbon. His great-aunt Rita (1916), in Pedrouços. His stepfather (1919), in Pretoria. Veríssimo Caetano Dias (his brother-in-law's father) and niece Leonor, in Lisbon, plus uncle Henrique Rosa and his mother (1925), at Quinta dos Marechais. His "aunt" Lisbela (1929), in Lisbon. Cousin Mário, died of consumption in Lisbon (1932). "Where are the living?".

"Dead people are born, they do not die". He also misses his friends. Sampaio Bruno (1915), in Lisbon – the same one who, for Pessoa, "died as soon as he died". Sá-Carneiro (1916), in Paris. Santa-Rita Pintor, António Ponce de León and Amadeu de Souza Cardoso (1918), in Lisbon, in the same year that *president-king* Sidónio Pais died. Almada Negreiros wrote: *Our initial group is down to four: A writer, Fernando Pessoa; a musician, Ruy Coelho; a painter, Eduardo Viana; and myself.* After them, Gomes Leal and Ângelo de Lima (1921), in Lisbon, the latter also at Rilhafoles. Guerra Junqueiro (1923), in Lisbon. António Sardinha (friend of Unamuno's), in Lisbon (1925). Camilo Pessanha (1926), in Macao. Boavida Portugal (1931), in Lisbon. José Pacheco (1934), in Lisbon. Ronald de Carvalho, in Rio, victim of a car crash (1935). And many more. It is as if all around him were "dying amidst unfurled flags, in the final day of a flaming empire". And he cries because "when an old man sees his childhood companions dying all around him, he feels his time must be near".

> First watcher: Does every story have to have an end?
> Third watcher: Of course I know it wasn't worth the trouble... That's why I loved it...
> Second watcher: Only the dream is eternal and beautiful.
> First watcher: Why do we die?
> Second watcher: Perhaps from not dreaming enough...
> *The Mariner*, Fernando Pessoa

"And suddenly, here, I feel the cold from over there. It comes from my bones and makes my flesh shiver. I gasp and wake up. The man who passes me under the arcade by the Stock Exchange stares at me warily, without knowing why. And the black sky, closing in, pressed even lower over the southern shore ". He feels "all the unsuspected anguish of a human soul about to burst, all the incurable despair of a heart forsaken by God" and wonders "when will this all end, these streets I drag my misery across, and these steps on which I huddle, cold, and feel the hands of night slipping between my tatters?".

His last photo, at the age of 47

He still believes that, come October, he will publish his "great book". "But, one day, the sun, having given light, shall stop shining; having given light, it will bring an end to death; other sorts of faked eternities will feed souls of other species. Other useless Christs shall vainly climb on new crosses". In the end, "it shall be as luck wills it". And he would live out the rest of his days with no further hope, "unless some unforeseen complication comes up". And it did.

> Second watcher: Perhaps… It doesn't matter… What is this cold? Ah, come now–come now! Tell me this… Tell me one more thing…
>
> *The Mariner*, Fernando Pessoa

Ars longa, vita brevis
(Art is long, life is short) Hippocrates

THE END

I never supposed that which they call death
Would make any sort of sense...
Sá-Carneiro, Fernando Pessoa

His time comes

"And now, in clear day, face to face, let us tell our fortunes". The hour to decipher the "painful riddle of life" comes at last, and he is ready. "May I at least carry, to the boundless possibility contained in the abyss of everything, the glory of my disillusion like that of a great dream". Except "it is more painfully than that". It is "the malaise of living the weariness of having lived"; "the malaise of having to live, even if in another world, the weariness, not only of yesterday and today, but also tomorrow, eternity, if there is such a thing, and oblivion". The first warm winds announce the Spring of his last year, 1935. He feels he won't live to see another. "When Spring comes, if I am already dead, flowers shall bloom as they always do". Shortly before, he had written almost the same words: "Come Spring, I may no longer be here for this world". And so it would be. On the 2nd of June, he wrote another poem against Salazar's dictatorship, as if certain of the end; in which he laments the fate of Portugal as if he were speaking of himself:

> Slowly, the race wanes, and joy
> Is like another's memory.
> (...)
> The past and the future weigh upon us
> The present sleeps in us.
> (...)
> So much, so much! What of who has been?
> Doesn't anyone return?
> Nothing. Neither faith nor law, neither sea nor harbour.
> Only the lengthy stagnation of grief,
> Like the dull afternoons on the dead sea,
> The painful solitude of the waters.
>
> *Elegy in Shadow*, Fernando Pessoa

After Spring comes Summer, but soon "that Summer faded away" and Lisbon's windows no longer have lilies, carnations and basil on them. "The flowers of the my childhood's fields, I shan't have them eternally". "All that I've thought, all that I've dreamed, all that I have or haven't done – all will go in autumn, like used matches or papers crumpled into fake balls. All that constituted my soul, from my lofty ambitions to my humble rented room, all will go in Autumn, in the tender indifference of Autumn". An "Autumn which begins in us", "like a vague slumber surviving the final gestures of acting". Physically, all can see he isn't well. *He was bitter,* according to António Manassés. In a draft of a letter to Casais Monteiro, which was left unfinished, he warns he will write nothing else "for *Presença* or any other publication or book". And then began what would be his last November. Earlier, on the 22nd of April 1922, he finished a poem with: "Today, I expect neither the delight/ Of having expected, I want it to end". Finally, his wait was coming to an end. He published his last three articles: in *Diário de Lisboa* (11th), "Poetries of a prose writer", on the book of his friend Cunha Dias; in *Sudoeste* #3, Álvaro Campos' "Random note", discussing the matter of sincerity in art; and "We of *Orpheu",* exalting his former magazine companions, which ends "as for the rest, no more on that". His friends didn't realize he was speaking of himself. He also wrote his last poems in other languages. In English, there was "The happy sun is shining", a title rather incompatible with his state of mind; and, in French, "Le sourire de tes yeux bleus", addressed person unknown. In Portuguese, 11 days before his death, he wrote a final poem which he ends thus:

> There are illnesses worse than illnesses,
> Pains which do not hurt, not even in the soul
> But which are more painful than all others.
> There are dreamt anguishes more real
> Than those life causes us, feelings
> Which can only be felt by imagining them
> And are more ours than life itself.
> (...)
> Over the soul, the useless flapping of wings
> Of what wasn't, nor could be, and yet is all.
> Give me more wine, for life is nothing.
>
> *Untitled* (19/11/1935), Fernando Pessoa

His last days

26th of November 1935, Tuesday. He is sitting alone at home. His first bout comes in the form of stomach pains and fever. Nothing too serious yet, and he gets better the next day, and carries on with his exasperating routine, as if nothing were the matter. But, "as the hours pass, the expression fails me. As the hours pass, my will falters. As the hours pass, I feel time advancing over me. As the hours pass, I get to know myself, useless hands and butter stare, carrying with me into the cold ground a soul that could tell no stories, an already rotten, dead heart, and in the stagnation of undefined aspirations rendered moot". There remains no doubt that "today I'm vanquished, as if I knew the truth. Today I'm lucid, as if I were about to die".

> What became of it all?
> What have I done of myself?
> Let me sleep,
> Sleep with a smile
> And let this be the end.
>
> *Untitled* (04/11/1914), Fernando Pessoa

27th of November, Wednesday. After another regular day at work, as night approaches, he goes to Martinho da Arcada. In rather foreshadowing fashion, Sá-Carneiro once said of the place: *Martinho... I don't know why, but that café – and not the other cafés in Lisbon, only this one – has always impressed upon me the notion that it is a place where one goes to end his life: A strange refuge, perhaps, of those who no longer harbour any illusions whatsoever.* He sees Almada Negreiros go inside and, feel far too tired, doesn't get up to greet him as usual. Gaspar Simões soon joins them[1]. His friends think it strange to see him so dishevelled, with an untied black tie, everything so different from his usual self. He is agitated and clears his throat a lot. The pains of all anguishes weigh down on his body. And his fever does not abate. "The hour, like a fan, snaps shut". Teca has her birthday at Estoril, but actually going there for dinner, in his condition, was too much for him – even knowing that he'd be breaking a long-held tradition by not attending. He asks the newspaper salesman to send a congratulatory telegram in his name, but the man pocketed the money and didn't send it. At night, he heads over to his friend Armando Teixeira Rabelo. He feels stomach cramps, but doesn't make the others aware of it. According to António Quadros, *he had a serious hepatic crisis that night* (cousin Eduardo Freitas da Costa claims it was at dawn, between the 26th and the 27th). Upon departing, he stumbles and laughs in odd fashion, but Simões attributes it to the alcohol. He stares at the sky, as if looking for a star to wish for the impossible, and walks towards Rua dos Douradores, perhaps searching for the trail of Bernardo Soares. His condition is visibly serious.

1 According to Simões, who said as much at a conference in 1977, the meeting was actually on the following day – as, in his words, *Pessoa would die two days later in the hospital*

O daybreak, you're so late… Come…
Come, uselessly,
Bring me a day just like today, and a night just like tonight…
Come bring me the happiness of this sad hope,
(…)
Come on, daybreak, come!

Insomnia, Álvaro de Campos

28th of November, Thursday. "Dawn broke like a fall. Let us realize the truth. Let us, Velada, become aware of our own tedium, for it ages itself". Manassés goes to his apartment for his daily shave, and is horrified at his physical state. Both remain silent, as if Pessoa didn't even have the strength to talk. Or as if neither man had anything more to say to the other. Still, later on, he still manages to clean up and go to work. His brother-in-law comes looking for him, concerned about his not attending his sister's birthday; asked about the telegram, he says it never arrived and, seeing him up and about, assumes everything is fine. At the end of the day, Pessoa returns home at his usual leisurely pace. *Without stumbling,* according to António Seixas and *Bate-Chapa,* who remember having greeted him. At night, he is alone once more. He feels pain and is sorry that he has no one who can avail him. But, perhaps trusting his own horoscope, he imagines he should get better soon enough. "Soft, useless heart! Soft, there's nothing to hope for". The previous year, on the 9th of August, he'd written: "Today is Thursday in a week without a Sunday… No Sunday at all". It was to be his final week. And it was Thursday, like in the verse. The week had a Sunday, of course, "a topsy-turvy Sunday", which he wouldn't get to witness. "Always someone at Sunday", but not him, "not on my Sunday". His last day was to be a Saturday, in two days' time.

The day after tomorrow, yes, only the day after tomorrow…
Tomorrow I'll start thinking about the day after tomorrow,
Maybe I could do it then; but not today…
No, nothing today; today I can't.
(…)
The day after tomorrow I'll finally be what I could never be today.
Only the day after tomorrow…
I'm sleepy as a stray dog's chill.
I'm really sleepy.
Tomorrow I'll tell you everything, or the day after tomorrow…
Yes, maybe only the day after tomorrow…
By and by…
Yes, the old by and by…

Procrastination[2], Álvaro de Campos

2 In the original draft, the title was "Sigh from the air".

29th of November, Friday. The longed-for future is at hand. "My God, what did I do with my life?". Once again, he is alone in his apartment. "Life had no inner dimension". His sister was in Estoril, nursing a broken leg. His first stomach cramp comes quite early. His next door neighbour, Virgínia Sena Pereira, told the family that his condition inspired care. There is no consensus on the date; according to Taborda de Vasconcelos, the warning had been given two days before; or on the eve, according to the nephew of *dona* Virgínia (poet Jorge de Sena) and cousin Eduardo Freitas da Costa. Pessoa's cousin (and doctor) Dr. Jaime Pinheiro de Andrade Neves is summoned – *a good-for-nothing,* Robert Bréchon recalls one of his inner circle members having said, without identifying the comment's author. The cousin decided to take him to the hospital. At that time, he was in the company of close friend Armando Rabelo; Francisco Gouveia, an office work colleague; and Carlos Eugénio Moitinho de Almeida, owner of Casa Moitinho de Almeida[3]. Pessoa asks for a shave, and neighbour Manassés is called[4]. Upon remembering that his telegram never got to its destination, he asks one of his friends to send another. "I'll be packing up for forever". He puts on a pyjama and a jacket tied to the waist with a strap. He goes to his bookshelf and picks the smallest book he could find: Bocage's *Sonetos escolhidos* – given to him in 1921 *with the respect owed your talent* by intimate friend Alberto da Cunha Dias, who had written the book's preface[5]. He puts the book in his right pocket and is ready to go. He is taken on an automobile ambulance, away from the house he would never return to. "I have lost hope, like an empty wallet".

> Perhaps victory is death, and glory
> Is but the memory of it
> And perhaps to win is rather to die
> Than to survive… What is death? It is dusk…
> Life is to have it, live it, and lose it.
>
> *To a dead revolutionary*, Fernando Pessoa

São Luís dos Franceses Hospital

"Bring pages; bring virgins; bring, servants, the cups, the gun salutes and the garlands for the feast Death is attending! Bring them all and come clad in black,

3 Probably to protect his son Luís Pedro, who was 23 at the time and rather fond of Pessoa, Moitinho told him nothing of it, and Luís later said that, *on a cold December morning, I was surprised by the news of Fernando Pessoa's death.*

4 Despite the many records that Armando Ventura Teixeira, his Chiado barber, was called instead, Gaspar Simões' testimony that the *barber neighbour was called* is far more credible and logical.

5 Pessoa had dedicated "Gladius" to him, first in *Orpheu,* and then in *Athena.*

head crowned with myrtle. The King goes to dine with Death in his palace by the lake, between the mountains, away from life, oblivious to the world". But life doesn't always imitate art, as the "old palace" he dreamed with wasn't next to any lake. Nor is it close to any mountain. It is one of Lisbon's best and most expensive private hospitals at the time, São Luís dos Franceses. It was situated at Bairro Alto de São Roque, at Rua Luz Soriano, 182 – a calm, shaded place, surrounded by iron benches, less than a kilometre from the apartment he was born in. He had "just entered the hospital for an operation", is bought to room 30 (later renumbered 308) – the same in which, as we saw, friend Almada Negreiros would die (in 1970). A far cry from what he had sensed in "The Mariner", "a room in what is doubtlessly an old castle". Unlike in Summer, there is scant light in that small room – 3 metres by 4, iron bed like in all other hospitals, a tall closet, another, smaller, with a telephone on top, a couch for two, a chair and a modern headstand. Between the bed and the window is a mosquito net, dulling the surroundings from within, the perfect scenario for a verse he had previously written – "Between myself and the world, there is a mist keeping me from seeing things as they truly are"; or, almost the same first words of "First Faust", "there is a veil between myself and what is real". The walls are clean, covered with dark paint up until the ceiling; the ceiling is an immaculate white. Not a single painting in sight. Today, the room has in front of it the elevator which leads to the first floor. The wall is clear and rough, flecked with cement up until the height of 2 metres, and then smooths out. The ceiling is made of plaster. The couch sits between the bed and a barred window. Closet, austere headstand and three common wooden chairs complete the decoration. The room looks very much the same even today.

Question – Where do you come from?
Answer – I don't know.
Q – Where are you going to?
A – I wasn't told (I know).
Q – What do you know?
A – What I expected (nothing).
Q – What do you see?
A – I am blind.
Q – What are you wearing?
A – I am naked.
Q – What do you have?
A – Only myself.
Q – What do you want?
A – To see the light.
Q – What light?
A – Whichever is at hand.
Q – Which is at hand?
A – The one given to me.
Q – If it is given to you, how shall you see it?

A – With my eyes.
Q – If it is not given to you, how shall you see it?
A – Within me.
Q – What is hanging from your neck?
A – The past.
Q – What is it you feel on your chest?
A – The future.
Q – What is at your feet?
A – The present.
Q – What is it you feel?
A – Darkness, cold and danger.
Q – How shall you vanquish them?
A – The darkness, with day, the cold with sun, the danger with life.
Q – And how shall you obtain day, sun and light?
A – By not being blind, naked or myself, here, alone.
Q – Who created you?
A – I don't know.
Q – Why don't you know?
A – Because I was born.
Q – Do you wish to know it?
A – Yes, because I will die.
Master of the Atrium – You need but say yes.
The Neophyte[6] – Yes.
Master of the Atrium – Peace be with you.

Initiation rites, Fernando Pessoa

The feast is set. Instead of pages, virgins and serfs, he is only accompanied by austere nurses. No music or dancing, all one hears is that silence which foretells eternity. Luís Pedro Moitinho de Almeida confirms as much, quoting his friends: *He didn't complain once. He only said what he needed to.* "Who knows if will die tomorrow?". He feels his impending doom and asks for a pencil; lying down in bed, he couldn't possibly use his usual quill, as the tip has to be pointing down, and there was nowhere convenient for him to place the inkwell[7]. The family kept that pencil to this day. He then puts his inseparable black briefcase over his chest, places a sheet of paper on it, and writes down his final written sentence in English:

I know not what tomorrow will bring.

6 In "Initiation", published in *Presença* #35 (May 1935), the text ends with "Neophyte, there is no such thing as death".

7 In a letter from the 13th of June 1918, Pessoa's mother wrote: *As the chair is reclined, I am writing with a pencil, as I have nowhere to put the inkwell on.*

The intentionally archaic style accentuates the literary sense he wished to convey, although Pizarro, Ferrari and Cardiello believe it to be a clear echo of an epigram by Palladas of Alexandria *(To-day let me live well; none knows what may be to-morrow),* published in the first volume of *Greek Anthology* (1916) – a book that could be found in Pessoa's bookshelf. Jorge Monteiro, in turn, believes he wrote the sentence to evoke the Scriptures (Proverbs, 27:1): *Do not boast about tomorrow, for you do not know what a day may bring.* According to niece Manuela Nogueira, *it wasn't the first time he said those words.* And he did indeed write similar (incomplete) verses on the 28th of October 1920, which were later found in the Chest:

> I, that know not if I shall live tomorrow,
> How but my hope of that live I today.

In *Disquiet,* he feels "the torture of fate" and wonders: "Who knows if I will die tomorrow?". He knew that for a certainty, now. And so did everyone else.

The last day

> It may be the last day of my life.
> I saluted the sun by raising my right hand,
> But I didn't really salute it or even say good-bye to it.
> I showed it that I've liked seeing it before. Nothing else.
>
> *Detached poems*, Alberto Caeiro

30th of November, Saturday. "That after tomorrow" had finally arrived. His last sentence's "tomorrow" would indeed be tomorrow, the very next day. The non-metaphysical tomorrow. "Ah, what morning is this?". Hours pass. "I no longer fear the last afternoon". The afternoon gives way to evening, and "the setting sun, the colour of the pain of a distant god, can be heard weeping beyond the spheres". Darkness sets. "Night falls, the heat whelms down a little, and I'm as lucid as if I'd never thought". In *Disquiet,* he confesses: "All I asked of life is not to stand in the way of the sun". He would never again see it. And he trembles upon feeling what is to come. "Underlying everything, the hushed night was the tomb of God". So be it. "Lord, night has come", "with its dark mystery tattered with celestial bodies". It is a rainy night. And it was to be his last.

> Right before a trip, that bell,,,
> Knock off the racket, will you?
>
> I'd rather enjoy the repose of the *gare* of the soul I have,
> Than watch the advance, the iron arrival

Of the definitive train,
Than sense true departure in the gorges of my stomach,
Than stirrup this foot –
It never learned not to get all mushy every time it had to leave.

Là-bas, je ne sais où, Álvaro de Campos

"I gaze upon my end, which stares sadly at me, from the deck of the Boat of all boats" and "I close my slow, sleepy eyes". Around 7pm, thinking Pessoa is fine, and with his wife nursing a broken leg at home, his brother-in-law heads back to Estoril. Dr. Jaime Pinheiro de Andrade Neves and a doctor from the hospital, one Dr. Alberto António de Moraes Carvalho, remain in the room. Right after the brother-in-law's departure, his friends Francisco Gouveia, Vítor da Silva Carvalho and Augusto Ferreira Gomes arrive. And, according to the hospital, there was probably a chaplain and a nurse there, as well, as the hospital was under the administration of the Order of Saint Vincent de Paul[8]. According to António Quadros and Gaspar Simões, he still manages to ask in a loud and clear voice:

Tomorrow, at this time, where shall I be?

There was no answer forthcoming. "To depart! My God, to depart! I'm afraid to depart!", as he had written previously. Around 8pm, he begins to lose his sight. In an interval of lucidity, and thinking of reading the book he brought with him, he mumbles his last words.

Hand me my glasses.[9]

His request went unfulfilled. "Death shall come neither soon nor late". A far cry from the time in which he said "now that I am nearing death, I can see everything clearly". Or, like in "English poems XII", "life lived us, not we life". It then was "as if a window opened", and, half an hour later[10], "my heart stopped". Much like he had written in such premonitory fashion, "the river of my life ended". *A dream's Icarus,* as Montalvor defined him, finally departed towards the stars. "Long live me, for I am dead!". As per

8 I researched the hospital – which today belongs to the French government – for the chaplain's name and a list of nurses, but found no such records.

9 Leyla Perrone-Moisés compares the sentence to the one uttered by Goethe – an author Pessoa greatly appreciated – shortly before his death: *Mehr Licht!* (More light!). Pessoa all but describes the scene in "First Faust" (first theme, XXXIII): *But where am I? What house is this? Room/ Rugged, simple – I know not, I haven't the strength/ To observe – room filled with light/ Dark and protracted, which, in the afternoon/ I one... But what does it matter? Light is all./ I know it.*

10 Despite the many reports placing his death at 20h30, his death certificate reads only *20h.*

the verses of his past, now he too had "hands crossed over my chest, the halted gesture of wanting nothing". Due to a thunderstorm, all telephones in Estoril ceased to function for a while. His bedridden sister and his brother-in-law would only later be made aware of his death. The brother-in-law laments that he didn't get to see his family in his final moments, and asks for the burial to be scheduled for Monday morning, and that the obituary be written. He would later say he'd had *a wretched end.* "Remember, when death comes, that each day dies, and the sunset is beautiful, and so is the night that remains". Because "Death is the triumph of life". "Today, now, clearly, he's dead. Nothing else". He died as he lived, lost "in a nameless, mortuary horror".

His friends leave, and the body remains alone in the room. The hospital's nuns, aware of his relationship with Ophelia Queiroz, call her to ask if she wishes to say goodbye to her friend without being seen by others. After all, their relationship wasn't exactly a secret, and definitely not among Ophelia's family, or Pessoa's friends. Montalvor once caught them, and Almada Negreiros, on the night of Pessoa's burial, made the most famous drawing of Pessoa's face (this book's cover) and offered it as a present to Carlos Queiroz, Ophelia's nephew – according to Ophelia's grandniece, Maria das Graças Queiroz. He never would have handed him the drawing, if he wasn't aware of their relationship. It is thus not unreasonable to assume that one of the nuns was also aware of it. Ophelia arrives shortly thereafter and is brought to the room via a side door. The door is locked and both are alone with each other. "We'll keep vigil over the passing hours". She then places her hand over her beloved's brow and trembles, as if recalling verses she'd read in *The Mad Fiddler:* "Put my hair back from my brow's pain". It was as if Pessoa had foreseen the scene (excerpts):

Let thy hand set
My hair back. Look
Let thine eyes smile
Into the unrest
Of mine eyes now
Thine for a while.
I seem asleep
All things have failed.
All hopes are dead.
All joys are brief.
Ay, let thy hand,
Give me relief!
What life is now
Is worth so little
That pain seems brittle
Put my hair back

From my brow's pain.
What I regret
Hath never been.

Lest my rest fret,
True rest, come soon!

The Mad Fiddler ("L'inconnue"), Fernando Pessoa

After that, Ophelia places his right hand between hers, whispers to him all the things she ever wanted to tell him, and just stares at his face, knowing she'll never do it again. "A rooster crows. The light, all of a sudden, brightens. The three watchers remain silent, not looking at each other. Not too far away, along a road, a roving carriage groans and squeaks". Light begins to seep into the room as day breaks. The nuns return and warn her that his family might be arriving at any moment. She gets up and looks one last time at that face she once dreamt would be hers. One of the nuns puts her hand in Pessoa's pocket, takes Bocage's book and gives it to her. In order to persuade her to accept it, she says she believes Pessoa would like her to keep it. Ophelia puts the gift in her bag and silently leaves from whence she came. Then, so that nobody would know of what had transpired, she says she heard from Pessoa's death from her nephew, Carlos Queiroz. According to her: *I brought my hand to my face, let out a scream, and cried for a very long time.* She only didn't mention she cried next to him.

News of that last encounter almost became a novella. It all began in 1985, on the 50th anniversary of Pessoa's death. One of Rede Globo's most important directors, journalist Ronald de Carvalho (a homonym of Pessoa's friend, as capricious fate would have it), flew to Portugal on a mission to make a documentary on the event. He requested an interview with Ophelia, who refuses, in a letter the journalist kept to this day. But she consents to being filmed from her apartment's window, next to grandniece Maria das Graças Queiroz. The two wave at the camera, as seen on Brazilian TV. At night, now that he knew where she lived, he heads to the apartment. Ophelia opens the door, surprised (as he hadn't told her he'd be coming) and restates that she would give no interviews. Carvalho said he had only come to tell her she was a beautiful woman, handed her a red rose and asked permission to kiss her on the forehead. Ophelia, as if paralysed, doesn't even react. The journalist bid her a good night and leaves, his steps echoing across the silent hallway. It was then that Ophelia woke from her trance and suddenly said: *Please, come back. I will be dying soon, and no one will understand what happened between Fernando and myself otherwise. But only if you promise not to make these facts public until after my death.* Ronald did so, went into the apartment, and she told him about their encounter, feeling guilty at not having shared the story with Maria da Graça. The journalist confesses that, having anticipated that others might doubt him, he actually pondered typing the declaration down and having her sign it, but before he could do so, Ophelia said: *As no one will believe that anyway, I'll give you this as proof.* It was the little book inside a bakery's brown bag, where it had been kept since 1935. And where it still remains. In the inventory of *Fernando Pessoa's private library* (Pizzarro, Ferrari and Cordiello), it is considered a *Book of unknown whereabouts.* But, since then, it has been seen by over 500 thousand visitors on the exhibit "Fernando Pessoa, plural like the universe", which took place in São Paulo (2010) and Rio de Janeiro (2011). The dedication *(the prefacer of these pages offers Fernando Pessoa* [unreadable] *in his literary life with the respect owed his talent and his* [unreadable], *IV – 1921)* is signed by Cunha Dias, the organizer and prefacer of the book. I matched it with others, in other books, and consider both the handwriting and the signature to match perfectly. Ophelia then gave the journalist a photo of hers, when she was still young, and wrote a dedication on it. And the two said goodbye, never to see each other again. When asked why he didn't make her testimony public right after Ophelia's death, Carvalho said: *I was waiting for the right moment. As* (according to him) *the moment hasn't yet arrived, I have authorized it* in this book.

I, me myself…
Me, full of weariness,
As much as the world can give…
(…)
But me, me…
I'm me,
I stay me,
Me…

Untitled (04/01/1935), Álvaro de Campos

The burial

1st of December, Sunday. The coffin is carried to the chapel at Prazeres Graveyard for mourning. His friends tried to publish his obituary the previous day, but there were no newspapers being released on Sunday, nor Monday morning (02/12) due to the holiday of the 1st of December, date of the Portuguese Restoration, and only close friends and family know of it. "It's Sunday and I have nothing to do", as he wrote in *Disquiet* on Saturday, the 1st of February 1930. And he indeed had nothing to do on this Sunday. His only task was to remain lying down, mute, motionless, as "I mourn my own dead body in the night in me".

> What more do you want? I finished!
> Neither lacking the neighbour's canary, o morning of another time,
> Nor the full-basket sound of the baker in the stairwell,
> Nor the I don't know where I am anymore proclamations,
> Nor the funeral (I hear their voices) in the street,
> Nor the sudden thunder of wooden shutters in the summer air,
> Nor… so many things, so many souls, so few fixable!
> (…)
> My peaceful bread, the good butter by the window!
> Enough, now I'm blind to what I see!
> God damn it, I'm finished!
> Enough!
>
> *Cul-de-lampe*, Álvaro de Campos

2nd of December, Monday. At around 11, the funeral procession silently departs towards his final resting place at Prazeres Graveyard, where he is placed in a shelf of dear grandmother Dionísia's plot. "I went along with my grave". *Diário de Notícias* described: *The procession was composed of messrs.* Alfredo Guisado, Jaime Neves and Jaime Azanoal; António Ferro, José Marques de Oliveira, Manassés Ferreira [de] Seixas, Ângelo Martins Fernandes, Pedro Rodrigues de Oliveira, Joaquim A. da Silva Vale Lobo Fernandes, Moutinho da Silva Rodrigues, F.R. Dias, Raul Narciso da Costa, D. Sara Félix da Cunha, Armando Costa, F.N. Gouveia, A. Allem, Ângelo Duarte da Silva Ramos, Fernando Ramos, Vítor de Carvalho, Fernando da Silva, Moitinho de Almeida, Afonso Lucas, Francisco Costa, Albertino Soares, Nogueira de Brito, José Castelo de Morais, João Soares da Fonseca, Silva Tavares, António Pedro, Raul Leal, José Rato de Carvalho, Armando Teixeira Rebelo, António da Silva, Rozendo Jesus, Diogo Osório Ferreira Rebelo, José de Almeida Roque, José Bento dos Reis, Manuel Serras, Francisco Moreira da Silva Roque, José da Costa Freitas, Eduardo Freitas da Costa, António de Sousa, J. Araújo, Artur Narciso da Costa, Augusto Ferreira Gomes, Vitoriano Braga and Augusto Santa Rita.

> Goodbye, goodbye, goodbye, all the people who didn't come to see me off,
> My abstract, impossible family…
> Goodbye, today's day, goodbye, today's flagstop, goodbye life, goodbye life!
>
> *Là-bas, je ne sais où,* Álvaro de Campos

Missing from the list are *dona* Emília, Pessoa's housekeeper – according to Eduardo Freitas da Costa[11]; friends da Cunha Dias and Gaspar Simões, according to Luís Pedro Moitinho de Almeida; and Almada Negreiros, who made the most famous drawing of his face upon returning from the burial to Brasileira[12].

Almada's drawing given to Carlos Queiroz

Negreiros would later say that, *one day in 1935, the poet personally went to bury the body which had accompanied him his entire life.* And, of course, he was accompanied by his 127 heteronyms – his lifelong companions who weren't about to abandon him in his final hour. Gilles Germain goes so far as saying that *neither Álvaro de Campos nor the others attended the funeral rites.*

11 An exclusion likely owed to the fact that, at the time, it was uncommon for women to attend the funerals of men who weren't part of their family.

12 There are three nearly identical drawings. The one mentioned above was the first, which was soon given to Carlos Queiroz (according to painter Paulo Ferreira). Of the other two, one can be found today at the Calouste Gulbenkian Foundation, and the other was sold at an auction at Lisbon's Palácio do Correio Velho (20/05/2008).

The explanation most often offered is the fact that they never existed, which is patently absurd. Indeed, "it was all absurd, like mourning the dead". Montalvor gave the eulogy. 20 years prior, Pessoa had written for Montalvor a text which faithfully recreated what was now taking place: "Perhaps God listens to me, but he hears of himself, like all who listen. This was the tragedy, yet there was no dramaturge to write it". At his feet, his *dramaturge* friend, with his inseparable monocle and with an already very receded hairline, said (abridged):

> Those who were his peers and partook of his Beauty should not, and could not, see him being lowered into the earth or, rather, ascend and attain true Eternity – without expressing the calm but nevertheless human protest of anger at seeing him depart. His companions of *Orpheu,* his brothers, who shared the same ideal blood of his Beauty, could not, I repeat, let him be buried thus without having picked the petals off the white lily of his silence and his pain. We mourn the man taken from us by death, and with him the wonder that was partaking in his company, and the grace of his human presence. But only the man, as hard as it is to say it, as his spirit and his creative power, those were endowed by Fate with a strange, undying pulchritude. The rest is with the genius of Fernando Pessoa.

"Pray for me, Maria[13], and I shall feel a calmness of love over my being. Like moonlight over a stagnated lake". In that dialogue, Pessoa/Faust asks: "You cry? Did I make you cry?", to which Maria replies: "Yes… No… I cry at seeing you sad". Faust: "Do you love me, Maria?" And Maria: "I feel your fear when I think of you… Ah, how I love you". And Faust ends the dialogue thus: "Love! How that word embitters me to the core, empty as it is… No, don't cry".

> At first everyone feels relieved
> That the slightly irksome tragedy of your death is over…
> Then, with each passing day, the conversation lightens up
> And life falls back into its old routine…
> Then you are slowly forgotten.
> You're remembered only twice a year:
> On you birthday and your death day.
> That's it. That's all. That's absolutely all.
>
> Two times a year they think about you.
> Two times a year those who loved you heave a sigh,
> And they may sigh on the rare occasions someone mentions
> your name.
>
> *Untitled* (24/06/1926), Álvaro de Campos

---

13 Maria is the name of the Holy Mary, two Portuguese queens, his mother, Ophelia Maria Queiroz, and a heteronym (Maria José). But, in this case, it's just a character of *Faust.*

His death in the newspapers

"To die is simply to no longer be seen". The ceremony, as described by Gaspar Simões, *was discreet, with little to no tears. With no memory of tears,* as confirmed by Luís Pedro Moitinho de Almeida. The following day, most newspapers gave notice of his death as befit one of his importance in the world of letters, with 28 announcements in total: 12 in Lisbon, four in Porto, two in Coimbra, and one in Braga, Faro and Sintra, plus four more at the Azores and three in Madeira. Some with errors: That he died at Casa de Saúde das Amoreiras *(A Pátria);* that he had a degree in Letters from the University of England *(O Século);* that he had been an author at *Orfeu (O Comércio);* that he had left behind a novel *(Diário do Minho).* A few of those texts (excerpts):

> Fernando Pessoa was quoted in the *Times'* literary supplement as an English writer. As none can live off the letters in Portugal, he worked at a commercial office. He had taken ill three days ago and went to a hospital, where he died the night prior in silence, much like he'd always lived, fleeing the limelight and discreetly drowning in death, much like he had done in life.
> *Diário de Lisboa,* 02/12/1935

> From an early age, Fernando Pessoa dedicated himself to the letters, but never managed to live off them, as few do so in Portugal.
> *Diário do Minho (Braga),* 03/12/1935

> His passage through life was a trail of light and originality. At his literary gatherings at Martinho da Arcada, he was always the youngest of all young men sitting around him. Perplexing, deeply original and structurally true, his personality was as heterogeneous as the paths he took in life. Everything in him was unexpected. From his life, to his poems, to his death. Unexpectedly, as if it were a book announcement, one heard news of his death. Though he may have died, and matter might have abandoned his body, his spirit shall never leave the hearts and minds of those who loved and admired him.
> *Diário de Notícias* (Lisbon), 03/12/1935

> He wanted to be original, and in a certain way, managed to do so in *Orfeu.* He wished to be perfect, and attained that in *Message.*
> *Diário da Manhã* (Lisbon), 03/12/1935

> Fernando Pessoa, one of the gentlest spirits we've had the pleasure of knowing, passed away yesterday. He was a poet, not a mere writer of verses, like all those who swarm around and fill the displays at bookstores.
> *A República* (Lisbon), 03/12/1935

> Fernando Pessoa held within his extraordinary personality – without a doubt the most complex in all of Portuguese literature – all the elements of intellectual attraction. When the general public doesn't know of a great poet, it's never the poet's fault. There

are only occult geniuses among uncultured people. Therefore, the feeling of those who accompanied the man's remains was that the fairest of lights had been snuffed out.
Emissora Nacional (Lisbon), 05/12/1935

Photo of his funeral, with António Ferro behind the coffin

O Diabo wishes to convey the family its sympathies.
O Diabo (Lisbon), 08/12/1935

Fernando Pessoa has passed away. Night had already fallen. The eve of the 1st of December had been of glorious beauty, and the sun set to sing higher still its praises of Portugal on the following day.
Avante (the Portuguese Communist Party's newspaper), 16/12/1935

Fernando Pessoa is dead. This brief news wishes but to convey the cold in our hearts at your premature departure, Fernando Pessoa. But the poet never dies. The ones who die are those who spend their lives trying to deny eternity. Your soul remains.
Presença #47 (Coimbra), December 1935

Fernando Pessoa was perhaps this century's greatest Portuguese poet. Ennobled by his silence, made obscure by his partially published oeuvre, it is still to early to judge him.
Manifesto (Coimbra), 01/01/1936

"Life is the hesitation between an exclamation and a question. Doubt is resolved by a period". Nothing to mourn, then, as to him "to die is to carry on".

And his fate is thus fulfilled. “Be it the death of me in which I revive”. Sophia de Mello Breyner Andersen dedicated a poem to him (“Fernando Pessoa”), a collage of his verses – some complete, others used as inspiration, and ends it by adapting “Written on an abandoned book during a trip”, “I was like weed”, and the first two verses of “Abdication”. In it, the poet cries (excerpt):

> Your just chant which disdains shadow
> Your courage to dare not to be anyone
> Your navigation with a compass and no stars
> You’re just like a four-faced god
> You’re just like a many-named god
> You were like unplucked herbs.
> Take me, Eternal Night, in your arms
> And call me your son.

Pessoa died? Long live Pessoa!

Nunc dimittis servum tuum, Domine
(Lord, now lettest thou thy servant depart) Simon, after having seen the Messiah

WHAT DID PESSOA DIE OF?

The ghosts of my dead Is
Are now part of my flesh.
The Mad Fiddler, Alexander Search

A difficult diagnosis

What did Pessoa die of? That is the question. In order to answer it, firstly, one needs to consider the primitive state of medicine at the time. Imaging consisted strictly of x-rays (since 1895). Plasma was only beginning to be used in transfusions. Sulfa antibiotics started being used in 1936; blood banks in 1937; penicillin in 1944; sonograms, endoscopies, CAT scans, MRIs and other sophisticated exams would only appear in the second half of the 20th century, all well after his death. In Portugal, far from the developed centres of Europe, house calls are still common practice. Hospitals were meant only for serious – almost always terminal – cases, and looked more like asylums, where one went to alleviate the pain of chronic injuries, have limbs amputated, lancing abscesses and dying. With no detailed medical explanations available, one can but speculate on the diagnosis.

Cirrhosis

The most common cause of death among authors is cirrhosis, due to all the alcohol they consumed throughout their lives. Cirrhosis is the replacement of normal liver tissue by scar tissue, which hardens it and leads to its eventual failure[1]. It can also lead to a number of physical consequences – sexual dysfunction, testicular atrophy, breast enlargement, hair loss; as well as spider-shaped vascular lesions of the skin, known as talengiectasias, which aren't

1 According to Donald W. Goodwin, after barmen, *more writers die of liver cirrhosis than any other occupation.*

easily spotted due to their diminutive size. His case seemed to have no such symptoms. Still, Pessoa's history suggests a high likelihood of it having been cirrhosis, perhaps even more than highly likely. In fact, that was the diagnosis of Dr. Bastos Tigre after having examined him in the 20s. With today's knowledge, the direct epidemiological relationship between cirrhosis and alcoholism during a period of 25 years is well established. Practically zero up until a daily intake of 40 grams, it grows to 50 percent likelihood at 200 grams, with no further statistical increases. Pessoa drank more than those 200 grams. In an attempt at calculating his daily alcohol intake, Francisco Manuel Fonseca Ferreira came to a bottle of wine at every main meal, six chalices of aguardiente throughout the day, plus another bottle of wine during the night, sometimes a large one, even. The amount was probably even greater. Starting with the six chalices of aguardiente per day, which actually sounds conservative, especially during the period that preceded his death. Also, at night, instead of wine, he usually favoured the aguardiente kept in his bottle[2]. But cirrhosis or any other type of chronic hepatic disease wasn't the cause of his death. Had he actually suffered from it, he would hardly have exhibited the intellectual vigour and the high level of his output during his final year. We know he felt ill, that he had abdominal pain and went to the hospital. All very quick. But, for him to have died of cirrhosis, he would have to have previously displayed malnutrition and intense muscular weakness, as well as some of the classical symptoms which accompany the final stage of every cirrhosis, namely:

a) Jaundice – his skin would have acquired a yellowish tone.

b) Ascites – his belly would have swollen up. He would have needed to use his trousers unbuttoned, and they would have looked large in his legs, as ascites swells up the belly and causes the rest of the body to waste away.

c) Neuropsychological disturbances – alcohol would surely have caused an aggravation of neurological dysfunctions, such as shaky hands and obtundation.

d) High digestive haemorrhage – with loss of blood. If that loss followed regular bowel movements, his faeces would be darkened by blood; if not, he'd vomit blood – a symptom which would have immediately alarmed his friends, family and office colleagues, who knew his father had died of consumption.

d) Coma – due to liver failure of infection.

There are no references whatsoever of those symptoms in his friend's accounts during his last days. Nor in those of the doctors who tended to him. But that's not the reason his death surely wasn't caused by cirrhosis; rather, it is the fact that it doesn't cause acute abdominal pain.

---

2 These calculations were supported by sister Teca's declaration in an interview with *Jornal de Notícias,* in which she recalled that, at night, she'd *see big bottles of wine he bought and kept in his room.*

Other possible causes of death

The difficulty in making a diagnosis only increases from there. His death certificate (sheet 805, record 1,609 at the 7th registry office of Lisbon's Civil Registry) says *intestinal obstruction* – with no information whatsoever concerning what might have caused said obstruction. An unlikely event, due to the lack of any abdominal distension, of visible peristaltic movements or vomiting. Gastroenterologist Irene Cruz claims there's a possibility that he contracted *hepatitis B or C* in South Africa, and that it remained latent for over 30 years. But that's mere, hard to evaluate speculation, especially since that type of hepatitis doesn't cause the abdominal issue Pessoa experienced. It would also be reasonable to assume he died from tuberculosis, just like his father, or other lung ills, as he was an inveterate smoker. And it bears remembering how he constantly suffered from bouts of flu throughout his life – "sore throat", as he says in his diary. At first, he had three per year, and these occurred more often as time went on, to the point he preferred to live in a windowless room, far from the cold that would seep through the windows. But tuberculosis, even of the intestinal type, would never have resulted in his acute bout, so it can also be ruled out.

The record book of São Luís dos Franceses Hospital lists Dr. Jaime Neves' diagnosis as *kidney colic.* But kidney – or biliary – colics aren't caused by alcohol consumption, and it's not even related to the liver; rather, it's an obstruction of the gallbladder caused by a calculus, which results in intense abdominal pain which waxes and wanes in spasmodic contractions, irradiating up to the back or right shoulderblade. Also, *liver colic* entails continuous pain, not the one that comes and goes in spasms, like the one Pessoa experienced. Thus, Dr. Jaime Neves' diagnosis doesn't deserve much consideration. Had it been as he claimed, even with the primitive medical science of the time, the doctors would know that without surgery he would die in a matter of days – as septicaemia would inevitably occur, followed by organ failure. He would certainly have been operated in such a case, especially as gallbladder surgery was fairy common practice in Portugal at the time. It's thus most likely that, faced with an uncertain diagnosis, the first doctor just wrote down some random cause to justify his death.

Still in the realm of hypothesis, one should examine the variables which might have occurred, such as: *Aortic dissection,* with symptoms which weren't displayed by Pessoa – intense pallor, sweating, tachycardia, fainting, state of shock; *acute appendicitis,* which would have meant a moderate, continuous pain that would have accompanied him until the end, which, according to all witnesses, wasn't the case; *acute cholecysttis,* a longer evolution period which, had it been the case, would surely have compromised his awareness; *acute diverticulitis of the large intestine,* which would have caused lower abdomen pain, fever, intestinal bleeding and complaints of disturbances in his bowel rhythm, all of which suggestive of this event; *myocardial infarction,* no clinical elements to lend it any credence; *thrombosis of mesenteric vessels* – a hypothesis which could only be confirmed by an autopsy; *peptic ulcer,* which would cause rhythmical pain in the stomach during the ingestion of food, which never happened with Pessoa. Also, *peritonitis,* which would have entailed acute, constant abdominal pain, which also wasn't the case. Had it been so, he would have experienced a serious deterioration and would never have been able to write an archaic sentence with precise handwriting in a language not his own – "I know not what tomorrow will bring". Not would he have asked, with total lucidity, "Tomorrow, at this time, where shall I be?". Or have expressed a desire to read and ask for his glasses, as in such a state, he would have lacked the basic mental control to as much as ask for them.

The likely causa mortis: Pancreatitis

The most likely medical hypothesis is acute abdomen, resulting from pancreatitis, which generally isn't preceded by any type of clinical history. As was the case with Pessoa. Francisco Manuel Fonseca Ferreira also reached the same conclusion. A very common ailment in alcoholics, pancreatitis is characterized by a strong pain in the abdomen and usually is accompanied by serious shock and important metabolic disturbances. The fact that his pancreas wasn't exactly healthy only increases the odds of it having been the case. Also, pancreatitis frequently causes acute pain (similar to that of gallstones) in the upper abdomen, which could lead to fainting – due to pancreatic enzymes entering the blood flow in the abdominal cavity and/or omental retrocavity. When he was found unconscious in the bathroom, days before his death, it might have been an episode of hypoglycaemia – frequent in alcoholics who drink for days on end (almost) without eating – or *delirium tremens;* there's no way to know for sure, but it was most likely one of those characteristic fainting spells caused by pancreatitis. Which was probably also the cause for the waves of pain he experienced.

Supremum vale
(Farewell for the last time) Ovid[1]

POST-SCRIPTUM

Life is short, the soul is vast.
Message ("The Field of the Escutcheons"), Fernando Pessoa

His remains

Consummatum est. "I have finished. However, one oughtn't finish just now": With his death, Fernando Pessoa's life truly began. "Life is a god's sad infancy, the human desolation of envisioned immortality"; and "when the grass grows over my grave, let it be a sign for me to be utterly forgotten". Yet he did not truly die. He only took "the corpse of lost faith into the tomb of illusion"; and today he is consensually considered *unique, standing tall and above all other Portuguese poets of his age,* in the words of Casais Monteiro. Likely the greatest of them all. In a poll conducted by Portuguese channel RTP1 (2007), which listed the greatest Portuguese in history, he placed eight – with 2,4 per cent of the votes, and ended up inspiring a coin minted by the Bank of Portugal (2,50 euros). *It is entirely possible that, as an export product, Pessoa is worth more than Portugal Telefónica* – according to José António Pinto Ribeiro, minister of Culture. In the end, Bandarra's prophecy was fulfilled. "I have hope that some day, after my death, I shall find what few children I sired, and that I'll find them beautiful in their dewy immortality". And indeed he did. In 1954, Jorge de Sena wrote: *The country owes him a resting place alongside the great names of our homeland.* And so would it be. Fifty years after his death, in 1985, his remains were transferred to the National Pantheon at Jerónimos Monastery. In that monastery's beautiful cloister, at the edge of the Tagus, lies Pessoa's solitary tomb (by sculptor Lagoa Henriques, the same one who made his statue at the entrance of Brasileira)[2]. On the granite column next to it, the steel plaque is sober: "Neither statue nor tombstone may narrate he who was all of us". On

1 The final words of Orpheus as he lost Eurydice.

2 According to the original project, Pessoa's bones were supposed to be placed inside the column next to the tomb. But, during the course of the operation, it wasn't possible to open the lead coffin in which the body was, and so the coffin itself had to be buried in the cloister.

it stands *Fernando Pessoa, 1888-1935,* and, on the lower part, in bas-relief on the granite itself, the following verses:

> It's not enough to open the window
> To see the fields and the river.
> It's also not enough to not be blind
> To see the trees and the flowers.
>
> 20/04/1919 Alberto Caeiro[3]
>
> No, I don't want anything.
> I already said I don't want anything.
> Don't come to me with conclusions!
> Death is the only conclusion.
>
> 1923 Álvaro de Campos[4]
>
> To be great, be whole: nothing that's you
> Should you exaggerate or exclude.
> In each thing, be all. Give all you are
> In the least you ever do.
> The whole moon, because it rides so high,
> Is reflected in each pool.
>
> 14/2/1933 Ricardo Reis[5]

Final words

In "The Mariner", the First Watcher asks: "Does every story have to have an end?". Some do, such as those which tell of the paths of those chosen by the gods. And "whoever has read the pages of this book will by now surely have concluded that I'm a dreamer". So it was, indeed, but his fate was to dream of wonders. "The end: The Gods shan't speak to us, and neither will Fate. The Gods are dead, and Fate is mute". Be that as it may, the story has been written. After all these pages, perhaps the best way to end the account of his life is to recall an excerpt of the first of his "Excerpts from two odes", better known as "Ode by night". Delivered to Sá-Carneiro in 1914, the poem was posthumously published in Vitorino Nemésio's *Revista de Portugal* #4), in July 1938. Upon commenting on those odes, Sá-Carneiro said: *Come now, Pessoa… I maintain, my friend, that little Álvaro's productions are the best of… Pessoa.* They are "magnificent words" and, with them, the poet nearly touches the sky:

---

3 From "Detached Poems".
4 From "Lisbon revisited (1923)".
5 One of his last dated "Odes".

Come, ancient and unchanging Night,
Queen Night who was born dethroned,
Night inwardly equal to silence, Night
With sequin-stars that flicker
In your dress fringed by Infinity.
Come faintly,
Come softly,
Come alone, solemn, with hands hanging
At your sides, come
And bring the far-off hills as near as the nearby trees,
Merge every field I see into your one field,
Make the mountain one more block of your body,
Erase all its differences I see from afar,
All the roads that climb it,
All the varied trees that make it dark green in the distance,
All the white houses whose smoke rises through the trees,
And leave just one light, and another light, and one more
light
In the hazy and vaguely troubling distance,
In the distance that's suddenly impossible to cross.
(…)
When everything loses its edges and colours,
And high above, in the still bluish sky,
As a distinct crescent, a white circle, or just a sliver of
new light,

The moon begins to be real.

Excerpts from two odes, Álvaro de Campos

Pessoa's goodbyes

"I must write my book. I fear just to think which might be the truth. Even if it is bad, I must write it. God willing, the truth won't be bad", even as he knew that "this book is my cowardice". Here it is, "pages torn, on the typewriter of an unhappy present, in the immense longing for a better future". But, by way of final words, I prefer a vision of redemption; and so I gather for a brief instant, in a false but nonetheless coherent unity of effect, the words he wrote in numerous texts throughout his life, fully cognizant of the fact that his "path is now another, where there be no more stars and sunlight is neither law nor day". Over to him, then, for his goodbye:

The work is done. The hammer has been cast. I salute all those who read me, and leave the image of my dead intent written in this book. Farewell, farewell forever, queen of leaves. I lay down my quill, end my solitary pilgrimage. Life is the interval between what has happened and what will happen, the dead interval between Death and Death. And I have lived a full life. We are all mortal, with a fair duration, never longer nor shorter. Some die as soon as they die, others live on for a while in the memory of those who saw and loved them; others remain in the memory of the nation they were born in. But all are surrounded by the abyss of time, which causes them all to disappear in the end.

Why do I write this book? I write it to lie to myself. Let us ever seek the impossible, for such is our lot. You, you hear me but barely listen to me, you know not what manner of tragedy this is! Would that a sentence remained of me, one uttered thing of which one could say *Well done!* But none can. You shall have consolation, for you shan't have hope; you shall have oblivion, for you shan't have desire; you shall have repose, for you shan't have life. Then, and after then, shall come the day, but it will be too late, as always. Out of dealing in shadows, I have become one myself. And I miss me. What is fame after death? A life that's not a life, my dearest boy. Memories come, with their longing and their hope, and a smile of magic. All I am, or all I've been, or what I believe I am or have been, all is lost all of a sudden – the secret, the truth, perhaps fortune. Death – What is death? Death is the triumph of life. All dead, my nanny, all dead. Pray for me. I feel this same sun gilds the fields where I am not present. Such loneliness. Pray for me, my nanny.

I have fulfilled. *L'Heure est a Nous! Combattons!* Tomorrow, so too will I be that which no longer crosses these streets, who others will vaguely evoke with a *whatever became of him?"*. It is not death I want, neither is it life: It is that other thing which shines at the depths of yearning like a possible diamond. Vast sky, blue sky, sky close to the mystery of the angels. Let me sleep, let me forget, lady of Uncertain Design. The rest is up to Fate. The future… Yes, the future… Behind defeat lies pure, dark, ruthless solitude of the deserted sky. And, beyond, in the distance, the first star shines ever so small. The end[6].

Selected excerpts, Fernando Pessoa

And thus, in his own words, the glorious life of my friend Fernando Pessoa has been told.

6 Pessoa liked to end his texts in English with phrases such as "last chapter" or "end of the book". He also had a special proclivity to end poems in English or French, or even to use "end" amidst Portuguese, sometimes in imitation of American movies of his time, with an allegorical "the end". In most texts written in Portuguese, he wrote "fim" (end), sometimes incorporating it into the poem itself, like an untitled poem (28/08/1927): "I wrote on a blank page. End". As this book is his, it wasn't about to deviate from the norm, and thus his goodbyes are concluded with this end.

Non refert quam multos libros, sed quam bonus habeas
(It does not matter how many books you have, but how good the books you have are) Seneca

BIBLIOGRAPHY (SPECIFIC ON FERNANDO PESSOA)

Books are papers printed with ink.
Freedom, Fernando Pessoa

A Águia, complete series, Porto, Renascença Portuguesa, from 1912 on.
A Renascença #1, no publisher, 1914.
A Revista (Solução Editora), complete series, Lisbon, Imprensa Líbano da Silva, (from 1929 on).
Abreu, Maria Fernanda de. "Elementos para o estudo da recepção de Fernando Pessoa nos países americanos de língua castelhana: Argentina e México". In: Minutes, 4th International Congress of Pessoan Studies, Porto, Eng. António de Almeida Foundation, 1988.
Aguiar, Flávio. "A viagem e o exílio em Mensagem de Fernando Pessoa". In: Minutes, 4th International Congress of Pessoan Studies, Porto, Eng. António de Almeida Foundation, 1988.
Alcântara, Marco Aurélio. "A musa com Salazar". Recife, *Diário de Pernambuco*, 27th of Nov. 2010.
– "Fernando Pessoa contra Salazar". Recife, *Jornal da ANE*, Jan. 2009.
Almada Negreiros, José de. *O quadrado azul.* Lisbon: Assírio e Alvim edition, 2000.
– *Orpheu* 1915-1965. Lisbon: Ática, 1993.
– *Ultimatum futurista.* Lisbon: Ática, 2000.
Almeida, Beth. *Fernando e suas várias pessoas.* Jornal de Letras, Oct. 2010.
Almeida, Lindinalvo A. de. "Jogo do amor em Fernando Pessoa". *Estudos Portugueses* #5, Recife, Associação de Estudos Portugueses Jordão Emerenciano, 1995.
Almeida, Luís Pedro Moitinho de. *Acrónios.* Preface by Fernando Pessoa. Lisbon: Oficinas Gráficas, 1932.
– "Fernando Pessoa e a Coca-Cola". *Jornal de Letras, Artes e Ideias,* #28 (16-29 March), Lisbon, 1982.
– "Fernando Pessoa e a magia". In: Academia Portuguesa de Ex-Libris, Separata of *Boletim* #12, Lisbon, 1959.
– *Fernando Pessoa no cinquentenário da sua morte.* Coimbra: Coimbra Editora, 1985.
Almeida, Onésimo Teotónio. "Pessoa, a Mensagem e o mito em Georges Sorel". In: Minutes, 4th International Congress of Pessoan Studies, Porto, Eng. António de Almeida Foundation, 1988.
Alvarenga, Fernando. *A arte visual futurista em Fernando Pessoa.* Lisbon: Editorial Notícias, undated.
– "Do paulismo ao intersecionismo: O encontro com a arte da Europa". In: Minutes, 4th International Congress of Pessoan Studies, Porto, Eng. António de Almeida Foundation, 1988
Alves, Clara Ferreira. "Ode ao mar do norte". *Tabacaria*, v. 13, Lisbon, Casa Fernando Pessoa, 2004.
– "Os dias de Durban". *Tabacaria*, v. 11, Lisbon, Casa Fernando Pessoa, 2003.
Alves, Hélio J. S. *Fernando Pessoa, literary critique.* Casal de Cambra: Caleidoscópio, 2007.

Anes, José Manuel. *Fernando Pessoa e os mundos esotéricos.* 3rd ed. Lisbon: Esquilo, 2008.
Antunes, Alfredo. *Saudade e profetismo em Fernando Pessoa.* Braga: Faculty of Philosophy, 1983.
– "Três meditações sobre Fernando Pessoa". *Estudos Portugueses* #5, Recife,
Associação de Estudos Portugueses Jordão Emerenciano, 1995.
Antunes, João Lobo. "E no princípio era o mostrengo". *Tabacaria*, v. 12, Lisbon, Casa Fernando Pessoa, 2003.
Arbaizar, Philippe et alii. *Fernando Pessoa, Poete Pluriel.* Paris: Les Cahiers, 1985.
Areal, Leonor. "Hipertexto, literatura e Fernando Pessoa". *Tabacaria* #5, Casa Fernando Pessoa, 1997.
Arribat-Paychère, Elisabeth. "As quedas e os caminhos para o cais absoluto na obra poética de Álvaro de Campos". In: Minutes, 4th International Congress of Pessoan Studies, Porto, Eng. António de Almeida Foundation, 1988.
Athena, complete series, Lisbon, Imprensa Libanio da Silva, from 1924 on.
Auretta, Christopher Damien et alii. *Goethe e Pessoa, contemporaneidade de Fausto.* Lisbon: Colibri, 2006.
Avillez, Martim. *Os ensaios.* China: Lusitânia Press, undated.
Azeredo, Maria da Conceição Fidalgo Guimarães Costa. *Fernando Pessoa educador.* Braga: Appacdm, 1996.
Azevedo, Fernando de. "O poeta, a visão e o rosto". In: Fernando Pessoa e a Europa do século XX, Porto, Serralves Foundation, DL, 1991.
Azevedo Filho, Leodegário A. de. *Fernando Pessoa, seus heterônimos e a emergência do novo.* 2nd ed. Rio de Janeiro: Author's Edition, 2009.
– "Sobre as odes de Ricado Reis". In: Minutes, 4th International Congress of Pessoan Studies, Porto, Eng. António de Almeida Foundation, 1988.
Azoubel, Suzana. "Estudo patográfico de Fernando Pessoa", master's thesis in Neuropsychotia for the Federal University of Pernambuco, Recife, 2009.
Baptista, Jacinto Sérgio. *Pessoa, encontros e desencontros.* Coimbra: Quimera, 1992.
Barroso, Ivo. "Pessoa perdido". *Folha de S. Paulo,* 14th of Nov. 1999.
Bastos, Othon; Albuquerque, Suzana Azoubel. *Estudo ortográfico de Fernando Pessoa,* v. II. 2nd ed. Recife: EDUPE, 2010.
Belchior, Maria de Lourdes. "Deus e deuses na poesia de Fernando Pessoa e heterônimos". In: Minutes, 4th International Congress of Pessoan Studies, Porto, Eng. António de Almeida Foundation, 1988.
Belkior, Silva. *Fernando Pessoa-Ricardo Reis: Os originais, as edições, o cânone das odes.* Lisbon, Imprensa Nacional-Casa da Moeda, 1983.
Bene, Orietta Del. "Algumas notas sobre Alberto Caeiro". Separata of *Ocidente* (v. 74), Lisbon, 1968.
Berardinelli, Cleonice. *Estudos de literatura portuguesa.* Lisbon: Imprensa Nacional-Casa da Moeda, 1985.
– (org., introduction and notes). *Fernando Pessoa, alguma prosa.* Rio de Janeiro: Nova Aguilar, 1976.
– (org., introduction and notes). *Fernando Pessoa, obras em prosa.* Rio de Janeiro: Nova Aguilar, 1995.
– *Fernando Pessoa: Outra vez te revejo.* Rio de Janeiro: Nova Aguilar, 2004.
– (org.). *Poemas de Álvaro de Campos.* Lisbon: Imprensa Nacional-Casa da Moeda, 1990.
– (introduction and notes). *Poemas de Álvaro Campos.* Rio de Janeiro: Nova Fronteira, 1999.
– "Remexendo no espólio pessoano". In: Minutes, 4th International Congress of Pessoan Studies, Porto, Eng. António de Almeida Foundation, 1988.
– "Um Álvaro de Campos desconhecido". *Revista da Biblioteca Nacional, Lisboa,* #3, Sep.-Dec. 1988.
– Mattos, Maurício (orgs.). *Mensagem.* Rio de Janeiro: 7Letras, 2008.
Berrini, Beatriz. "As viagens do viajante poeta Fernando Pessoa". In: Minutes, 4th International

Congress of Pessoan Studies, Porto, Eng. António de Almeida Foundation, 1988.
Besant, Annie. *Ideias da teosofia* (translation by Fernando Pessoa). Lisbon: Livraria Clássica Editora, 1915.
Bidaine, Philippe; Reverdot, Jean-Philippe. *Fernando Pessoa.* Paris: Marval, 1990.
Blanco, José. "A verdade sobre 'Mensagem'", undated text.
– "Chronologie sélective". *Europe*, #s 710/711, Paris, 1988.
– Fernando Pessoa: *Esboço de uma bibliografia.* Lisbon: Imprensa Nacional-Casa da Moeda, 1983.
– "Fernando Pessoa ou os caminhos do futuro". In: Minutes, 4th International Congress of Pessoan Studies, Porto, Eng. António de Almeida Foundation, 1988.
– "O meu amigo Fernando Pessoa". *Tabacaria*, v. 11, Lisbon, Casa Fernando Pessoa, 2003.
– *Pessoana (bibliografia passiva, seletiva e temática).* Lisbon: Assírio e Alvim, 2008.
– "Variações pessoanas". *Foro das Letras* 9/10, Coimbra, Associação Portuguesa de Escritores Juristas, 2004.
Blavatsky, H.P. *A voz do silêncio* (translation by Fernando Pessoa). Lisbon: Livraria Clássica Editora, 1916.
Boberg, Hiudéa Rodrigues. "Estudo preliminar sobre as afinidades poéticas entre Fernando Pessoa e Cecília Meireles". In: Minutes, 4th International Congress of Pessoan Studies, Porto, Eng. António de Almeida Foundation, 1988.
Borges, Alexandre. "Caeiro e a filosofia da negação da filosofia". Atlântica, Angra do Heroísmo, 2007.
Borges, Paulo. *O jogo do mundo, ensaios sobre Teixeira de Pascoaes e Fernando Pessoa.* Lisbon: Portugália, 2008.
Botto, António. *Canções.* 2nd ed. Lisbon: Olisipo, 1922.
Brandão, Roberto de Oliveira. "Consciência e modernidade em Fernando Pessoa". In: Minutes, 4th International Congress of Pessoan Studies, Porto, Eng. António de Almeida Foundation, 1988.
Bréchon, Robert. *Estranho estrangeiro: Uma biografia de Fernando Pessoa.* Lisbon: Círculo de Leitores, 1997.
– "Pessoa e Lisboa". *Tabacaria* #7, Lisbon, Casa Fernando Pessoa, 1999.
– "Pessoa en France". *Europe* #s 710/711, Paris, 1988.
Brunetti, Almir de Campos. "Um Agostinho da Silva, uns Fernando Pessoa". In: Minutes, 4th International Congress of Pessoan Studies, Porto, Eng. António de Almeida Foundation, 1988.
Butler, David. "Joyce e Pessoa: Autores da polifonia". *Tabacaria*, v. 13, Lisbon, Casa Fernando Pessoa, 2004.
Cabral, Leonor S. "O método contextual-dinâmico aplicado a uma ode de Ricardo Reis". In: Minutes, 4th International Congress of Pessoan Studies, Porto, Eng. António de Almeida Foundation, 1988.
Câmara, Leônidas. "Vitória e derrota em Fernando Pessoa". *Estudos Portugueses* #5, Recife, Associação de Estudos Portugueses Jordão Emerenciano, 1995.
Candelária Maria. *80 poemas sobre motivos de Fernando Pessoa.* Lisbon: TIP. Henrique Torres, 1968.
Cardoso, Lúcio. "Fernando Pessoa", conference at the Law Faculty of Belo Horizonte, s.d.
Cardoso, Paulo. *Mar portuguez: A mensagem astrológica da mensagem.* Lisbon: Editorial Estampa, 1990; 2nd ed., 1991.
– *Mar portuguez e a simbólica da Torre de Belém.* Lisbon: Editorial Estampa, 1991.
Carvalhal, Tânia Franco. "Fios pessoanos na poesia brasileira". In: Minutes, 4th International Congress of Pessoan Studies, Porto, Eng. António de Almeida Foundation, 1988.
Carvalho, António Carlos. *Pessoa (figuras míticas).* Lisbon: Pergaminho, 1999.
– *Prefácio de Mensagem.* Lisbon: Caixotim, 2007.
Carvalho, João de. *Fernando Pessoa.* São Paulo: Casa de Portugal, 1993.
Carvalho, José G. Herculano de. "Pessoa leitor de Rimbaud". In: Minutes, 4th International Congress of Pessoan Studies, Porto, Eng. António de Almeida Foundation, 1988.

Castelo, José. "Um pastor para o século 21". Draft, Curitiba, 2006.
Castro, E. M. Melo e. "O intertexto em Pessoa, ou melhor, o interpessoa, ou melhor: nós". In: Minutes, 4th International Congress of Pessoan Studies, Porto, Eng. António de Almeida Foundation, 1988.
Castro, Ivo. "A casa a meio do outeiro". In: Minutes, 4th International Congress of Pessoan Studies, Porto, Eng. António de Almeida Foundation, 1988.
– *Editar Pessoa.* Lisbon: Imprensa Nacional-Casa da Moeda, 1990.
Cavalcanti (Filho), José Paulo. "Ainda que amar seja um receio". Massangana, Ed. Massangana, Recife, 2007.
Cavalcanti, Maria Lectícia Monteiro. "Os sabores de Fernando Pessoa". *Continente Multicultural* #59, Recife, CEPE, 2005.
Centeno, Yvette K. *A filosofia hermética.* Lisbon: Editorial Presença, 1985.
– "A filosofia hermética na obra de Pessoa". Separata of *Fernando Pessoa no seu Tempo*, Lisbon, National Library, 1988.
– *De Fernando Pessoa. Cadernos de Literatura,* Coimbra, INIC, 1979.
– *Fernando Pessoa: O amor, a morte, a iniciação.* Lisbon: A Regra do Jogo Edições, 1985.
– "Fernando Pessoa, Ophelia, bebezinho ou o horror do sexo". *Colóquio Letras,* Lisbon, Mar.-May 1979.
– *Fernando Pessoa: Os santos populares.* Lisbon: Edições Salamandra, D.L., 1994.
– "O envelope 91 do espólio de Fernando Pessoa". *Colóquio Letras*, *Lisboa* #56, Jul. 1980.
– "O Espólio / Escolha do Fernando Pessoa", *Colóquio Letras, Lisboa* #54, Mar. 1980.
– "Os trezentos". *Revista da Biblioteca Nacional. Lisboa* # 3, Sep.-Dec. 1988.
– ; Recikert, Sthephen. *Fernando Pessoa, tempo – solidão – hermetismo.* Lisbon: Moraes Ed., 1978.
Cirurgião, António. *Fernando Pessoa e a filosofi a humanística.* Lisbon: Presença, 1985.
– *Fernando Pessoa: Os trezentos e outros ensaios.* Lisbon: Presença, 1998.
– *O olhar esfíngico da Mensagem de Pessoa.* Lisbon: Ministry of Education, 1990.
– "Os castelos da Mensagem de Fernando Pessoa". In: Minutes, 4th International Congress of Pessoan Studies, Porto, Eng. António de Almeida Foundation, 1988.
– ; Reckert, Stephen. *Tempo – solidão – hermetismo.* Lisbon: Presença, 1991.
Citati, Pietro. "L'infini de Pessoa". *Europe*, #s 710/711, Paris, 1988.
Coelho, Eduardo Prado. "O Sena é o mais belo rio que passa na aldeia". *Tabacaria*, v. 11, Lisbon, Casa Fernando Pessoa, 2003.
– "Pessoa et la critique". *Europe* #s 710/711, Paris, 1988.
Coelho, Jacinto do Prado (preface and organization). *Fernando Pessoa: Livro do desassossego, por Bernardo Soares*, v. I and II. Lisbon: Ática, 1982.
– "O Fernando Pessoa de Leyla Perrone. Moisés". *Colóquio Letras, Lisboa* #71, 1983.
Coelho, Joaquim Francisco. "Da cadeira de Álvaro Campos". *Colóquio Letras, Lisboa* #71, 1983.
Coelho, Nelly Novaes. "O livro do desassossego: grau zero da heteronímia fernandina?". *Estudos Portugueses* #5, Recife, Associação de Estudos Portugueses Jordão Emerenciano, 1995.
Coelho, Odette Penha. "Leitura de Álvaro de Campos (Um percurso da modernidade: Da euforia para a disforia)". Minutes, 4th International Congress of Pessoan Studies, Porto, Eng. António de Almeida Foundation, 1988.
Colombini, Dúlio. "Pessoa e metafísica". In: Minutes, 4th International Congress of Pessoan Studies, Porto, Eng. António de Almeida Foundation, 1988.
Contemporânea, #s 8 and 9, Lisbon, Imprensa Libanio da Silva, 1924.
Corrêa, Sérgio. "Interseccionismo e sintaxe em Fernando Pessoa". In: Minutes, 4th International Congress of Pessoan Studies, Porto, Eng. António de Almeida Foundation, 1988.
Costa, Dalila Pereira da. *O esoterismo de Fernando Pessoa.* Porto: Lello Editores, 1996.
Costa, Horácio. "Sobre a pós-modernidade em Portugal: José Saramago revisita Pessoa". In: Minutes, 4th International Congress of Pessoan Studies, Porto, Eng. António de Almeida Foundation, 1988.

Costa, João Bernard da. "Reencontros". *Espaço Público*, 30th of Oct. 2005.
Costa, José Fonseca e. *Os mistérios de Lisboa (A Lisbon Guide by Fernando Pessoa).* DVD, JFC film, 2009.
Courteau, Joanna. "Fernando Pessoa: Às margens do século XX". In: Minutes, 4th International Congress of Pessoan Studies, Porto, Eng. António de Almeida Foundation, 1988.
Coyne, André. *Portugal é um ente, de l'être du Portugal, fribourg.* Lisbon: Lusiada Foundation, 1999.
Craveirinha, João. *E a Pessoa de Fernando ignorou África?* Lisbon: Editora Universitária, 2005.
Crespo, Ángel. *A vida plural de Fernando Pessoa.* Lisbon: Bertrand Editora, 1988.
– *Estudos sobre Fernando Pessoa.* Lisbon: Editorial Teorema, 1984.
– "Le sébastianisme de Fernando Pessoa". *Europe* #s 710/711, Paris, 1988.
Cruz, Ireneu. *A propósito da morte de Fernando Pessoa, diagnóstico diferencial de cólica hepática.* Lisbon: Acta Médica Portuguesa, 1997.
– "Fernando Pessoa, a propósito da sua patobiografia". *Boletim do Núcleo de Gastrenterologia dos Hospitais Distritais,* Lisbon 2004.
Cunha, Teresa Sobral. "António Mora: O heterônimo-filosófico". In: Minutes, 4th International Congress of Pessoan Studies, Porto, Eng. António de Almeida Foundation, 1988.
– *Cânticos do realismo e outros poemas.* Lisbon: Relógio D'Água, 2006.
– (org.). *Correspondência com Fernando Pessoa (Mário de Sá-Carneiro).* São Paulo: Companhia das Letras, 2004.
– *Fausto, tragédia subjectiva, Fernando Pessoa.* Lisbon: Editorial Presença, 1988.
– (org.). *Fernando Pessoa: Fausto, tragédia subjetiva (fragmentos).* Rio de Janeiro: Nova Fronteira, 1991.
– (org.). *Fernando Pessoa, quadras e outros cantares.* Lisbon: Letras Pessoanas, 1947.
– (org.). *Livro do desassossego.* Lisbon: Relógio D'Água, 2008.
– "Pessoa responde a Campos: Segunda carta a José Pacheco". *Revista da Biblioteca Nacional, Lisboa,* #3, Sep.-Dec. 1988.
– "Planos e projetos editoriais de Fernando Pessoa: Uma velha questão". *Revista da Biblioteca Nacional, Lisboa*, series 2, 2(1), 1987.
Cusastiz, Brunello de. *Esoterismo, mitogenia e realismo político em Fernando Pessoa.* Porto: Caixotin Edições, 2005.
D'Alge, Carlos. "Ressonância da Ode triunfal, de Álvaro de Campos, no poema Taxi, de Adriano Espínola". In: Minutes, 4th International Congress of Pessoan Studies, Porto, Eng. António de Almeida Foundation, 1988.
DaCosta, Fernando. *Máscaras de Salazar.* Lisbon: Casa das Letras, 2007.
Décio, João. "Para uma poética de Álvaro de Campos". In: Minutes, 4th International Congress of Pessoan Studies, Porto, Eng. António de Almeida Foundation, 1988.
Decker, Jacques de. "Pessoa como Pessoa". In: Homenagem a Fernando Pessoa. Eng. António de Almeida Foundation, 1991.
Deguy, Michael. "Complication à souhait". *Europe* #s 710/711, Paris, 1988.
Dias, Joana Amaral. *Maníacos de qualidade.* Lisbon: A esfera dos livros, 2010.
Deluy, Henri. "Traduction, avec F.P., d'un poème apocryphe de F.P.". *Europe* #s 710/711, Paris, 1988.
– *Quatrain complets (au goût populaire).* Perigeaux: Editions Unes, 1988.
Dias, Marina Tavares. *A Lisboa de Fernando Pessoa.* Lisbon: Íbis Editores, 1991 (reprint, 1999).
– "Fernando Pessoa e o milagre da fotografia". *Tabacaria* #10, Lisbon, Casa Fernando Pessoa, 2001.
– *Lisboa nos passos de Pessoa.* Lisbon: Quimera Editores, 2002.
Diaz, Adolfo Camilo. *Mentem-me: Diz a verdade; quem matou Álvaro de Campos.* Porto: Campo das Letras, 1998.
Dobzynski, Charles. "Les 4 vents de la poésie: tout Pessoa sauf rien... sauf Sá-Carneiro". *Eu-*

rope #s 710/711, Paris, 1988.
– "Sonnets des hétéronymes". *Europe* #s 710/711, Paris, 1988.
Dori, Salomé. *A vida sexual de Fernando Pessoa.* Lisbon: Palimpsesto, 2009.
Duarte, Luiz Fagundes. "Texto acabado e texto virtual ou a cauda do cometa". *Revista da Biblioteca Nacional, Lisboa,* # 3, Sep.-Dec. 1988.
Duarte, Zuleide. "Fernando Pessoa e as diversas expressões da modernidade literária portuguesa". *Massangana,* Ed. Massangana, Recife, 2007.
Durand, Gilbert. "Fernando Pessoa: a persistência europeia do mito e o reencantamento da modernidade". In: Fernando Pessoa e a Europa do século XX. Porto: Fundação de Serralves, DL. 1991.
Elia, Silvio. "O horaciano Ricardo Reis". In: Minutes, 4th International Congress of Pessoan Studies, Porto, Eng. António de Almeida Foundation, 1988.
Estibeira, Maria do Céu Lucas. "Uma introdução à marginália de Fernando Pessoa", masters thesis in Compared Literature, Lisbon, Faculty of Letters of the University of Lisbon 2002.
Fazzolari, Davi. "Olhares sobre Lisboa, Livro do desassossego" and "O que o turista deve ver", dissertation at the University of São Paulo, São Paulo, 2006.
Fernandes, Filipe. *Organizem-se, a gestão segundo Fernando Pessoa.* Cruz Quebrada – Dafundo: Oficina do Livro, 2007.
Fernandes, Jaime. "A tradição greco-latina nas odes de Ricardo Reis (uma análise quantitativa)". In: Minutes, 4th International Congress of Pessoan Studies, Porto, Eng. António de Almeida Foundation, 1988.
Fernandes, Maria João. "Do possível retrato". In: Fernando Pessoa e a Europa do século XX. Porto: Fundação de Serralves, DL. 1991.
Ferreira, António Mega. *Fazer pela vida, um retrato de Fernando Pessoa o empreendedor.* Lisbon: Assírio e Alvim, 2005.
– *O Comércio e a Publicidade.* Lisbon: Ed. Cinevoz/Lusomédia, 1986.
Ferreira, Antonio Mega. "Pessoa: propaganda, publicidade". *Egoísta* #24, Lisbon, 2005.
Ferreira, Ermelinda. *A mensagem e a imagem.* Recife: Editora Universitária, 2007.
– *Dois estudos pessoanos.* Recife: Editora Universitária, 2002.
– *Leituras, autores portugueses revisitados.* Recife: Editora Universitária, 2004.
– (org.). *Na véspera de não partir nunca.* Recife: Coleção Letras, 2005.
– ; Paiva, José Rodrigues de. *Em Pessoa.* Recife: Editora Universitária, 2007.
Ferreira, Francisco Manuel Fonseca. "Análise médica do alcoolismo de Fernando Pessoa". *Tabacaria* #11, Lisbon, Casa Fernando Pessoa, 2003.
– *Fernando Pessoa, a penumbra do génio.* Lisbon: Livros Horizonte, 2002.
– *O hábito de beber no contexto existencial e poético de Fernando Pessoa.* Porto: Laboratórios Bial, 1995.
Ferreira, Luzilá Gonçalves. *A antipoesia de Alberto Caeiro: Uma leitura de "O guardador de rebanhos".* Recife: Associação de Estudos Portugueses Jordão Emerenciano, 1989.
Filipe, Sinde. *Fernando Pessoa.* Lisbon: Dinalivro, 2008.
Finazzi-Agrò, Ettore. "Il volo della farfalla: Fernando Pessoa, il tempo e la storia. *Revista da Biblioteca Nacional, Lisboa* #3, Sep.-Dec. 1988.
– "Pessoa trivial: a viagem, o roubo, a troca". In: Minutes, 4th International Congress of Pessoan Studies, Porto, Eng. António de Almeida Foundation, 1988.
Fonseca, Cristina (org.). *O pensamento vivo de Fernando Pessoa.* São Paulo: Martin Claret Editores, 1986.
Fonseca, Edson Nery. *Três poetas brasileiros apaixonados por Fernando Pessoa: Cecília Meireles, Murilo Mendes, Lúcio Cardoso.* Recife: Editora Massangana, 1985 (reprint, 2005).
Fontenla, J. L. "Pessoa e a Galiza". In: Minutes, 4th International Congress of Pessoan Studies, Porto, Eng. António de Almeida Foundation, 1988.
França, Isabel Murteira. *Fernando Pessoa na intimidade.* Lisbon: Publicação Dom Quixote, 1987.
Franco, Gustavo. *A economia em Pessoa.* Rio de Janeiro: Reler, 2006; 2nd ed., Rio de Janeiro:

Zahar, 2006.
Freire, Luiza (edition and translation). Alexander Search: Poesia. Lisbon: Assírio e Alvim, 1999.
– *Fernando Pessoa: Entre vozes, entre línguas*. Lisbon: Assírio e Alvim, 2003 (reprint, 2004).
– *Fernando Pessoa: Poesia inglesa (1)*. Lisbon: Assírio e Alvim, 2000.
– *Fernando Pessoa: Poesia inglesa (2)*. Lisbon: Assírio e Alvim, 2000.
– "Fernando Pessoa retraduzido". In: Minutes, 4th International Congress of Pessoan Studies, Porto, Eng. António de Almeida Foundation, 1988.
Freitas, Ana Maria (Ed.). *Quaresma, decifrador, as novelas policiárias*. Lisbon: Assírio e Alvim, 2008.
Frcitas, Lima de. "Fernando Pessoa e o paradigma hermético". In: Fernando Pessoa e a Europa do século XX. Porto: Fundação de Serralves, DL. 1991.
Freitas, Marcus Vinicius de. "Um rubai de Ricardo Reis". *Tabacaria*, v. 5, Casa Fernando Pessoa, 1997.
Galhoz, Maria Aliete. "A fortuna editorial de Fernando Pessoa". In: Minutes, 4th International Congress of Pessoan Studies, Porto, Eng. António de Almeida Foundation, 1988.
– "Canções de beber na obra de Fernando Pessoa: Rubai e Rubaiyat na poesia ortónima". *Revista da Biblioteca Nacional, Lisboa,* #3, Sep.-Dec. 1988.
– (Ed.). *Fernando Pessoa: Canções de beber*. Lisbon: Assírio e Alvim, 2003.
– (anotações). *Fernando Pessoa: obra poética*. 3rd ed. Rio de Janeiro: José Aguilar, 1969.
– (anotações). F*ernando Pessoa: poemas dramáticos, poemas ingleses, poemas franceses, poemas traduzidos*. 3rd ed. Rio de Janeiro: Nova Fronteira, 1983.
Garcez, Maria Helena Nery. "Fernando Pessoa leitor de Mário de Sá-Carneiro". In: Minutes, 4th International Congress of Pessoan Studies, Porto, Eng. António de Almeida Foundation, 1988.
Garcia, José Martins. Fernando Pessoa: "Coração despedaçado". Ponta Delgada: University of the Azores, 1985.
Germain, Gilles. "La dernière apparition de Fernando Pessoa", undated.
Giannetti, Eduardo. "Periferias invisíveis". Braudel Papers, São Paulo, 2006.
Gil, José. *Fernando Pessoa ou a metafísica das sensações*. Lisbon: Filosofia, 1996.
Gomes, Augusto Ferreira. "Fernando Pessoa e os seus heterônimos". *O Mundo Ilustrado,* Lisbon, (Christmas) 1952.
– *Quinto Império*. Preface by Fernando Pessoa. Lisbon: Parceria António Maria Pereira, 1934.
Gomes, Francisco Casado. "A estrutura formal da Mensagem de Fernando Pessoa". In: Minutes, 4th International Congress of Pessoan Studies, Porto, Eng. António de Almeida Foundation, 1988.
Gonçalves, Robson Pereira. "A questão do sujeito em Fernando Pessoa". In: Minutes, 4th International Congress of Pessoan Studies, Porto, Eng. António de Almeida Foundation, 1988.
Gonçalves, Zetho Cunha. *Fernando Pessoa, contos, fábulas e outras ficções*. Lisbon: Bonecos Rebeldes, 2008.
Gotlib, Nádia Battella. "De Fernando Pessoa a Clarice Lispector". In: Minutes, 4th International Congress of Pessoan Studies, Porto, Eng. António de Almeida Foundation, 1988.
Grama, João. "A Lisboa de Pessoa". *Essencial* #12, Lisbon, 2006.
Guerra, Maria Luísa. "Bernardo Soares: A teoria do desconhecimento". In: Minutes, 4th International Congress of Pessoan Studies, Porto, Eng. António de Almeida Foundation, 1988.
Guerreiro, Ricardina. *De luto por existir, a melancolia de Bernardo Soares à luz de Walter Benjamin*. Lisbon: Assírio e Alvim, 2004.
Guibert, Armand. "Un demi-siecle de passion". *Europe* #s 710/711, Paris, 1988.
Guimarães Fernando. "Fernando Pessoa e o movimento saudosista". *Vila da Feira* #7, Feira (Portugal), 2004.
– "Fernando Pessoa, le symbolisme français et Max Nordau". *Europe* #s 710/711, Paris, 1988.
– *Simbolismo, modernismo e vanguardas*. Lisbon: Imprensa Nacional-Casa da Moeda, 1982.
Guimarães, Luis de Oliveira. Interview given to Fernando da Costa in *Público* newspaper (25/06/1995).

Gullar, Ferreira. "Fernando Pessoa: A razão poética". *Folha de S. Paulo, Caderno Mais,* 10/11/1996.
Hewitt, Júlia Cuervo. "Metafísica da navegação: A negação da metafísica na poesia de Alberto Caeiro". In: Minutes, 4th International Congress of Pessoan Studies, Porto, Eng. António de Almeida Foundation, 1988.
Hipólito, Nuno. *As mensagens da Mensagem.* Lisbon: Parceria A.M. Pereira, 2007.
Jabouille, Victor. "Materializações da mitologia clássica das odes de Ricardo Reis – Esboço de uma imagética mítica". In: Minutes, 4th International Congress of Pessoan Studies, Porto, Eng. António de Almeida Foundation, 1988.
Júdice, Manuela; Proença, Pedro. *O meu primeiro Fernando Pessoa.* Lisbon: Dom Quixote, 2006.
Júdice, Nuno. *A era do Orpheu.* Lisbon: Teorema, 1986.
Kamenezky, Eliezer. *Alma Errante.* Preface by Fernando Pessoa. Lisbon: Anuário Comercial, 1932.
Kovadloff, Santiago. "Vallejo y Pessoa: Lo poetico, lo político". In: Minutes, 4th International Congress of Pessoan Studies, Porto, Eng. António de Almeida Foundation, 1988.
Lancastre, Maria José de. *Fernando Pessoa.* Paris: Hazon-Lumière, 1997.
– *Fernando Pessoa: Immagini della sua vita.* Milan: Adelphi Edizioni, 1988.
– *Fernando Pessoa: Uma fotobiografia.* Lisbon, Imprensa Nacional-Casa da Moeda e Centro de Estudos Pessoanos, 1984.
Lanciani, Giulia. "Proposta per una edizione critico-genetica di pauis". *Revista da Biblioteca Nacional, Lisboa,* #3, Sep.-Dec. 1988.
Laranjeira, Pires. "Pessoa à procura de pessoa(s): dos ismos aos eus". In: Minutes, 4th International Congress of Pessoan Studies, Porto, Eng. António de Almeida Foundation, 1988.
Leadbeater, C. N. *Compêndio da teosofia.* Translation by Fernando Pessoa. Lisbon: Livraria Clássica Editora, 1921.
Leal, Raul. *Sodoma divinisada,* Lisbon, Olisipo, 1923.
Leme, Carlos Câmara. "Pessoa, o(s) outro(s) e as singularidades de uma rapariga loura". *Egoísta* #39, 2009.
Lima, José Lourenço de. "Fernando Pessoa e o culto ao idioma". *Estudos Portugueses* #5, Recife, Associação de Estudos Portugueses Jordão Emerenciano, 1995.
Lind, Georg Rudolf. *Estudos sobre Fernando Pessoa.* Lisbon: Imprensa Nacional – Casa da Moeda, 1981.
– "Fernando Pessoa e sua loucura". In: Minutes 1st International Congress of Pessoan Studies, Porto, Brasília Ed., 1978.
– "Les trois visages d'Alvaro de Campos". *Europe* #s 710/711, Paris, 1988.
– ; Coelho, Jacinto do Prado, (org.). *Fernando Pessoa: Páginas de estética e de teoria e crítica literária.* Lisbon: Edições Ática, 1973.
Linhares Filho. "A modernidade da poesia de Pessoa". In: Minutes, 4th International Congress of Pessoan Studies, Porto, Eng. António de Almeida Foundation, 1988.
Lisboa, Eugênio e Taylor, L. C. *A Centenary Pessoa.* Manchester: Carcanet, 1995.
Lopes, Teresa Rita. "A Europa de Pessoa e a de Sá-Carneiro". In: Fernando Pessoa e a Europa do século XX. Porto: Fundação de Serralves, DL, 1991.
– (introduction, organization and notes). *Álvaro de Campos, livro de versos.* Lisbon: Editorial Estampa, 1993.
– *Álvaro de Campos: Vida e obra do engenheiro.* Lisbon: Editorial Estampa, 1990.
– *Et le drame symboliste.* Paris: Éditions de La Differénce, 2004.
– *Fernando Pessoa, a biblioteca impossível.* Lisbon: Empresa Litográfica do Sul, 2001.
– *Fernando Pessoa, a hora do diabo.* 2nd ed. Lisbon: Assírio e Alvim 2004.
– (coord.). *Pessoa inédito.* Lisbon: Livros Horizonte, 1993.
– *Pessoa por conhecer: Roteiro para uma expedição,* v. I and II. Lisbon: Editorial Estampa, 1990.
– ; Abreu, Maria Fernanda de (orgs.). *Fernando Pessoa, hóspede e peregrino.* Lisbon: Instituto Português do Livro, 1983.

Lourenço, António Apolinário. *Fernando Pessoa*. Lisbon: Edições 70, 2009.

Lourenço, Eduardo. "A imagem à procura de Pessoa". In: Fernando Pessoa e a Europa do século XX. Porto: Fundação de Serralves, DL. 1991.

– "Apoteose ou segunda morte de Fernando Pessoa". *Expresso*, Lisbon, 13th of July 1985.

– "Cisão e busca do sentido em Pessoa". *Tabacaria* #2, Casa Fernando Pessoa, 1996.

– *Fernando Pessoa, rei da nossa Baviera*. Lisbon: Gradiva, 2008.

– "O jogo de Pessoa". *Tabacaria* #11, Lisbon, Casa Fernando Pessoa, 2003.

– *O lugar do anjo: Ensaios pessoanos*. Lisbon: Gradiva, 2004.

– "Pessoa e o tempo". Minutes, 4th International Congress of Pessoan Studies, Porto, Eng. António de Almeida Foundation, 1988.

– "Pessoa et le temps". *Europe* #s 710/711, Paris, 1988.

– *Pessoa revisitado: Leitura estruturante do drama em gente*, 17th volume of Civilização Portuguesa collection. Porto: Editora Inova, 1973; 4th ed. Lisbon: Gradiva, 2003.

– *Poemas de Fernando Pessoa*, Paço d'Arcos. Visão JL, 2006.

– "Portugal: identificação e imagem". *Expresso*, Lisbon, 4th of July 1987.

– ; Oliveira, António Braz de. *Fernando Pessoa no seu tempo*. Lisbon: Biblioteca Nacional, 1989.

Lourenço, Jorge Fazenda (presentation and notes). *Fernando Pessoa: Poemas escolhidos*. Lisbon: Editora Ulisseia, undated.

Lucas, Flávio. "O drama do ser em Fernando Pessoa". In: Minutes, 4th International Congress of Pessoan Studies, Porto, Eng. António de Almeida Foundation, 1988.

Lyra, Pedro. "O Ultimatum como fundamento da poética de Pessoa". In: Minutes, 4th International Congress of Pessoan Studies, Porto, Eng. António de Almeida Foundation, 1988.

Macedo, Helder. "A Mensagem de Fernando Pessoa e as mensagens de Oliveira Martins e de Guerra Junqueiro". In: Minutes, 4th International Congress of Pessoan Studies, Porto, Eng. António de Almeida Foundation, 1988.

Machado, Luis. *À mesa com Fernando Pessoa*. Lisbon: Pandora Edições, 2001.

– *Era uma vez um café*. Lisbon: Ed. Café Martinho da Arcada, 2004.

Mãe, Valter Hugo; Reis-Sá, Jorge (org.). *A alma não é pequena*. Famalicão: Centro Atlântico, 2009.

Malpique, Celeste. *Fernando em Pessoa, ensaios de reflexão psicanalítica*. Lisbon: Fenda, 2007.

Marmelo, Manuel Jorge. *Os fantasmas de Pessoa*. Porto: Edições Asa, 2004.

Marques, Paulo. *Fernando Pessoa (cadernos biográficos)*. Lisbon: Parceria A.M. Pereira, 2008.

Martín, José Luís Garcia. "Fernando Pessoa y Miguel de Unamuno: Las razones de un desencuentro". In: Minutes, 4th International Congress of Pessoan Studies, Porto, Eng. António de Almeida Foundation, 1988.

Martinho, Fernando. "O menino da sua mãe: Poema figurativo". In: Minutes, 4th International Congress of Pessoan Studies, Porto, Eng. António de Almeida Foundation, 1988.

Martinho, José. *Pessoa e a psicanálise*. Porto: Almedina, 2001.

Martins, Fernando Cabral (coord.). *Dicionário de Fernando Pessoa e do modernismo português*. Lisbon: Caminho, 2008.

– (coord.). *Dicionário de Fernando Pessoa e do modernismo português*. São Paulo:
Leya, 2010.

– (org.). *Ficções do interlúdio*. Lisbon: Assírio e Alvim, 2008.

– (org.). *Mensagem*. Lisbon: Assírio e Alvim; 4th ed., 2004; 15th ed., 2007.

Matos, José Sarmento de. "Lisboa, Pessoa e outros". *Tabacaria* #5, Casa Fernando Pessoa, 1997.

Matos, Maria Vitalina Leal de. *A paixão segundo Fernando Pessoa*. Lisbon: Edições Colibri, 2009.

– "A vivência do tempo em Fernando Pessoa". *Estudos Portugueses* #5, Recife, Associação de Estudos Portugueses Jordão Emerenciano, 1995.

Melcer, Ioram. "Mar oculto em Portugal". Originally published in Hebrew in *Dimuí* magazine,

2005.
Meller, Vilson Brunel. "Fernando Pessoa: A epifania do racional". *Estudos Portugueses* #5, Recife, Associação de Estudos Portugueses Jordão Emerenciano, 1995.
Mendes, Firmino Ribeiro. "Walt Whitman e Álvaro de Campos". *Tabacaria* #6, Lisbon, Casa Fernando Pessoa,1998.
Mendes, Joaquim; Dionísio, João. "A ortografia segundo Pessoa e opções editoriais: alguns elementos". *Revista da Biblioteca Nacional, Lisboa* #3, Sep.-Dec. 1988.
Mendes, Pedro Rosa. "As más caras". *Tabacaria* #11, Lisbon, Casa Fernando Pessoa, 2003.
Mendonça, Fátima; Costa, Nuno Félix. "O quarto de Fernando Pessoa". *Tabacaria* #6, Lisbon, Casa Fernando Pessoa, 1998.
Meneses, Philadelpho. "Sobre a tradução dos 35 sonetos ingleses de Fernando Pessoa". In: Minutes, 4th International Congress of Pessoan Studies, Porto, Eng. António de Almeida Foundation, 1988.
Miguel, Ruy. *Fernando Pessoa, o antidemocrata pagão.* Lisbon: Nova Arrancada, 1999.
Miraglia, Gianluca. "The case of the science master". *Revista da Biblioteca Nacional* #3, Lisbon, 1988.
Miranda, Wander Melo. "Fingimentos da memória: A biografia ficcional de Ricardo Reis". In: Minutes, 4th International Congress of Pessoan Studies, Porto, Eng. António de Almeida Foundation, 1988.
Moisés, Carlos Felipe. *Roteiro de leitura: Mensagem, de Fernando Pessoa.* São Paulo: Ática, 1996.
Mongelli, Lênia Márcia de Medeiros. "A Mensagem e o espírito de cavalaria". In: Minutes, 4th International Congress of Pessoan Studies, Porto, Eng. António de Almeida Foundation, 1988.
Monteiro, Adolfo Casais. *Fernando Pessoa: Poesia.* 45th ed. Rio de Janeiro: Agir, 1968.
– *Fernando Pessoa, o insincero verídico.* Lisbon: Inquérito, 1954.
– ; Sena, Jorge de. *Tradução de alguns dos 35 Sonets de Fernando Pessoa.* São Paulo: Clube de Poesia, 1954.
Mordoro, Rául. *Fernando Pessoa y otros precursores de las revoluciones nacionales europeas.* Madrid: Biblioteca Nueva, 2005.
Monteiro, George. "A presença de Pessoa no mundo da língua inglesa". *Tabacaria* v. 3, Lisbon, Casa Fernando Pessoa, 1997.
– *Fernando Pessoa and nineteenth-century Anglo-American literature.* Kentucky: The University Press of Kentucky, 2000.
– "Pessoa: Discípulo de Robert Browning". In: Minutes, 4th International Congress of Pessoan Studies, Porto, Eng. António de Almeida Foundation, 1988.
Mota, Pedro Teixeira da. Fernando Pessoa: *Moral, regras de vida, condições de iniciação.* Lisbon: Edições Manuel Lencastre, 1988.
Mourão Ferreira, David (organização e notas). *Fernando Pessoa, Cartas de amor a Ophelia Queiroz.* Lisbon: Edições Ática, 1978 and (with preface) 2009.
Mucznik, Lúcia Liba. "A morte de Fernando Pessoa e as notícias que teve". *Revista da Biblioteca Nacional, Lisboa* #3, Sep.-Dec. 1988.
Negreiros, Almada. *A invenção do dia claro.* Lisbon: Olisipo, 1921.
Nemésio, Jorge. *A obra poética de Fernando Pessoa.* Salvador: Progresso, 1958.
Neves, João Alves das. "A correspondência de Fernando Pessoa com o ocultista Aleister Crowley". *Livros e Leituras, Estudo de Comunicação*, v. 2, #5, Lisbon: Universitária Editora, 2006.
– "Dois poetas: Pessoa e Lorca, o inexplicável desencontro das duas joias da Ibéria". *Jornal da Tarde*, São Paulo, 5th Jun. 1999.
– (introduction). *Estatização, monopólio, liberdade de Fernando Pessoa.* Lisbon: Editora Universitária, 2004.
– *Fernando Pessoa, poesias ocultistas.* 4th ed. São Paulo: Editora A, 1995.
– "Os estudos pessoanos no Brasil". In: Minutes, 4th International Congress of Pessoan Studies,

Porto, Eng. António de Almeida Foundation, 1988.

Nogueira, Lucila. *A lenda de Fernando Pessoa.* Recife: Associação de Estudos Portugueses Jordão Emerenciano, 2003.

Nogueira, Manuela (org.). *Fernando Pessoa – Correspondência (1905, 1922),* Lisbon, Assírio e Alvim, 1998.

– *Fernando Pessoa, imagens de uma vida.* Lisbon: Assírio e Alvim, 2005.

– *O melhor do mundo são as crianças: Antologia de poemas e textos de Fernando Pessoa para a infância.* Lisbon: Assírio e Alvim, 1998.

– "Sobre a exposição 'Uma memória familiar'". *Tabacaria* #1, Lisbon, Casa Fernando Pessoa, 1996.

– ; Azevedo, Maria da Conceição. *Cartas de amor de Ofélia a Fernando Pessoa.* Lisbon: Assírio e Alvim, 1996.

; Zilhão, Teresa; Ferin, Madalena; Núncio, José. *Quarteto a solo.* Lisbon: Hugin Editora, 2000.

Ocidente #s 77 to 80, Lisbon, Editorial Império, 1944.

Oliveira, Maria de Lourdes Abreu; Pereira, Maria Luiza Scher. "Fernando Pessoa: O amor interdito?". In: Minutes, 4th International Congress of Pessoan Studies, Porto, Eng. António de Almeida Foundation, 1988.

Ordoñez, André. *Fernando Pessoa, um místico sem fé.* Rio de Janeiro: Nova Fronteira, 1994.

Orpheu #1, Lisbon, Tipografia do Comércio, 1915 (Ática, 4th reprint, 1984).

Orpheu #2, Lisbon, Tipografia do Comércio 1915 (Ática 3th reprint, 1984).

Orpheu #3, Lisbon, Edições Nova Renascença, undated (Ática, 1984).

Osakabe, Haquira. "Fernando Pessoa e a tradição do Graal". In: Minutes, 4th International Congress of Pessoan Studies, Porto, Eng. António de Almeida Foundation, 1988.

Padrão, Maria da Glória. "Actualidade europeia de Fernando Pessoa". In: *Fernando Pessoa e a Europa do século XX.* Porto: Fundação de Serralves, DL. 1991.

Pais, Amélia Pinto. *Fernando Pessoa, o menino de sua mãe.* Porto: Ambar, 2007.

Paiva, José Rodrigues de. Fulgurações do labirinto. Recife: Associação de Estudos Portugueses Jordão Emerenciano, 2003.

– "Pessoa/Soares: Uma poética do desassossego". *Estudos Portugueses,* Associação de Estudos Portugueses Jordão Emerenciano, Recife, 1995.

Pámpano, Ángel Campos. *Fernando Pessoa, un corazon de nadie.* Spain: Galaxia Gutemberg, 2001.

Parreira da Silva, Manuela. *Realidade e ficção, para uma biografia epistolar de Fernando Pessoa.* Lisbon: Assírio e Alvim, 2004.

Paz, Octavio (org.). *Fernando Pessoa, antologia.* Barcelona: Laia, 1984.

– *Fernando Pessoa, o desconhecido de si mesmo.* 2nd ed. Lisbon: Veja, 1992.

Pedrosa, Inês. "A carta do serralheiro para a corcunda". Lisbon: Egoísta, 2008.

– (org.). Os lugares de Pessoa (exhibit). Lisbon: Leya, 2008.

Peixoto, Francisco Balthar. "Fernando Pessoa: Os caminhos da estreia". *Estudos Portugueses* #5, Recife, Associação de Estudos Portugueses Jordão Emerenciano, 1995.

Peloso, Silvano. "A 'Figuração irônica' e a lógica da negação em Fernando Pessoa". In: Minutes, 4th International Congress of Pessoan Studies, Porto, Eng. António de Almeida Foundation, 1988.

Penteado Filho, José Roberto Whitaler. "Fernando Pessoa como precursor do marketing moderno". In: Minutes, 4th International Congress of Pessoan Studies, Porto, Eng. António de Almeida Foundation, 1988.

Pereira, Edgar. "Camões e Pessoa: Sugestões a partir de dois nocturnos". In: Minutes, 4th International Congress of Pessoan Studies, Porto, Eng. António de Almeida Foundation, 1988.

Pereira, Maria Helena da Rocha. *Temas clássicos na poesia portuguesa.* Lisbon: Editorial Verbo, 1972.

Perrone-Moisés, Leyla. "Costa Pinheiro: Uma leitura plástica de Fernando Pessoa". In: Minutes, 4th International Congress of Pessoan Studies, Porto, Eng. António de Almeida Founda-

tion, 1988.
– *Fernando Pessoa: Aquém do eu, além do outro.* São Paulo: Martins Fontes, 1982.
– "Les amours painnes". *Europe* #s 710/711, Paris, 1988.
– "O futurismo saudosista de Fernando Pessoa". In: Minutes, 4th International Congress of Pessoan Studies, Porto, Eng. António de Almeida Foundation, 1988.
Pessoa, Fernando. *35 Sonnets.* Lisbon: Monteiro e Co., 1918.
– *A maçonaria vista por Fernando Pessoa.* Lisbon: Secretariado da Propaganda Nacional, 1935.
– *À memória do presidente rei Sindónio Pais.* Lisbon: Editorial Império, 1940; Lisbon: Nova Ática, 2007.
– *A nova poesia portuguesa.* Lisbon: Editorial Inquérito, 1944.
– *A quintessência do Desassossego.* Porto Alegre: Artes e Ofícios, 2007.
– *Alguma prosa.* Rio de Janeiro: Nova Aguilar, 1976.
– *Antinous.* Lisbon: Sociedade Tipográfi ca Editora, 1918.
– *Apreciações literárias.* Porto: Editorial Cultura, 1951; Aveiro: Editora Estante, 1990.
– *Aviso por causa da moral.* Europa, tip. Anuário Comercial, 1923.
– *Barão de Teive a educação do estoico.* São Paulo: A Girafa, 2006.
– *Contos.* São Paulo: Edições Epopeia, 1986.
– *Contra Salazar.* Coimbra: Angelus Novus, 2008.
– *Defesa da Maçonaria.* CEP, s.d.
– "Deux poémes indédits d'Álvaro de Campos". *Europa* #s 710/711, Paris, 1988.
– Dialogues sur La Tyrannie. França, Anabolia Editores.
– *Elogio da indisciplina e poemas submissos.* Lisbon: Páginas Livres, s.d.
– *English Poems I.II.* Lisbon: Olisipo, 1921.
– *English Poems III.* Lisbon: Olisipo, 1921.
– *Faust, tragédie subjetive.* France, Titres, 2008.
– *Ficções do interlúdio.* Rio de Janeiro: Record, 1980.
– Inédito, sem título sobre a Cabala. *Cadernos de Literatura* #4, Coimbra Instituto Nacional de Investigação Científica, 1979.
– *Le gardeur de troupeaux.* Paris: Gallimard, 2007 (and 2009).
– *Mensagem.* Lisbon: Parceria Antonio Maria Pereira, 1934.
– *Mensagem.* Lisbon: Agência Geral das Colônias, 1941.
– *Mensagem.* 7th ed. Lisbon: Ática, 1963.
– *Mensagem.* São Paulo: Martin Claret, 1998.
– *Mensagem,* edição clonada. Lisbon: Guimarães Editores, 2009.
– *O banqueiro anarquista.* Lisbon: Edições Antígona, 1981.
– *O caso mental português.* Lisbon: Padrões Culturais, 2007; Lisbon: Centauro, 2008.
– *Ode marítima, Ode triunfal, Opiário, Tabacaria.* Porto: Livraria Científi ca, 1997.
– *O eu profundo e os outros eus.* Rio de Janeiro: Nova Fronteira, 2001.
– *O interregno.* Lisbon: Offis. da Sociedade Nacional de Tipografia, 1928.
– *O guardador de rebanhos.* São Paulo: Landy, 2006.
– *O poeta fingidor.* São Paulo: Globo, 2009.
– *Obra poética e em prosa.* Porto: Lello e Irmãos, 1986.
– *Ode triunfal.* Porto: Civilização Editora, 1997.
– *Odes de Ricardo Reis.* Lisbon: Ática, s.d.
– *Os preceitos práticos em geral e os de Henry Ford em particular.* Lisbon: Centauro, 2008.
– *Poemas dramáticos, poemas ingleses, poemas franceses, poemas traduzidos.* Rio de Janeiro: Nova Aguilar, 1976.
– "Poemas Inéditos Destinados ao no 3 de Orpheu". Lisbon: Inquérito, 1953.
– *Poemas ingleses.* Lisbon: Imprensa Nacional; Casa da Moeda, 1993.
– *Poèmes páiëns.* Paris: Points, 2008.
– *Poesia: Ricardo Reis.* São Paulo: Companhia das Letras, 2000.
– *Poesia completa de Alberto Caeiro.* São Paulo: Companhia de Bolso – Editora Schwarcz, 2005.

– *Poesias de Álvaro de Campos.* Lisbon: Ática, s.d.
– *Quando fui outro.* Rio de Janeiro: Objetiva, 2006.
– *Rebanho.* Ilust. Luci Sciasciã Cruz. São Paulo: Massao Ohno Editora, 2000.
– *Santo António, São João, São Pedro.* Lisbon: Edições A Regra do Jogo, 1986.
– *Selected Poems.* Traslated by Jonathan Griffin. 2nd ed. London: Penguin, 1982.
– *Sensacionismo e outros ismos.* Lisbon, Imprensa Nacional – Casa da Moeda, 2009.
– "Sobre um Manifesto de Estudante". Lisbon, Tip. Anuário Comercial, undated (1923).
– *Sociologia do comércio.* Brasil, JCTM, s.d.
– *Tabacaria, Bureau de Tabac.* Lisbon: Guerra e Paz, 2006.
– "Textes inédits et tradictions nouvelles". *Europe* #s 710/711, Paris, 1988.
– *Textos de críticas e de intervenção.* Lisbon: Ática, 1980.
– *Ultimatum.* Porto: Editorial Cultura, D.L., 1951,
– *Ultimatum de Álvaro de Campos.* Lisbon: Editorial Nova Ática, 2006.
– *Ultimatum de Álvaro de Campos, Sensacionista.* Separata de Portugal Futurista, Lisbon, tip. P. Monteiro, 1917.
Petrus (presentation). *A maçonaria vista por Fernando Pessoa.* Porto: Almagráfica, undated.
_____ (presentation). *Almas e estrelas.* Porto: Arte e Cultura, undated.
Picchio, Luciana Stegagno. "L'aff aire Pessoa", *Arquivo la Repubblica*, 2nd of Dec. 1991, (p. 36), Sec. Cultura.
Pires Filho, Ormindo. "Caeiro: Paganismo em prosa e verso". *Estudos Portugueses* #5, Recife, 1995.
Pizarro, Jerónimo (org.). *A educação do estoico.* Lisbon: Imprensa Nacional – Casa da Moeda, 2007.
– *El "Supra-Camões" – y todas las otras alegrias (sobre los artículos de Pessoa en a Águia).* Author's edition, 2001.
– "Fernando Pessoa: Auctor in fabula", master's thesis for the New University of Lisbon, 2002.
– (org.). *Fernando Pessoa, escritos sobre génio e loucura,* v. I and II. Lisbon: Imprensa Nacional – Casa da Moeda, 2006.
– "Fernando Pessoa, o génio e sua loucura". *Leituras* #s 14-15, Lisbon, 2005.
– (org.). *Fernando Pessoa: o guardador de papéis.* Alfragide: Texto, 2009.
– "Los robaiyat de Fernando Pessoa: Antologia de um Libro Inconcluso". Lisbon: Author's edition, 2001 (and separata of *Revista Romântica*, Dec. 2003).
– ; Dix, Steffen. *A arca de Pessoa.* Viseu: ICS, 2007.
– ; Ferrari; Patrício; Cardiello, Antonio. *A biblioteca particular de Fernando Pessoa.* Lisbon: Dom Quixote, 2010.
Poppe, Manuel. *Temas de literatura viva: 35 escritores contemporâneos,* Lisbon, Imprensa Nacional – Casa da Moeda, 1973.
Portela, Celestino. *Fernando António, o Pessoa.* Vila da Freira: LAF, 2003.
Porto, Carlos. "Pessoa no palco: Um teatro improvável". In: Minutes, 4th International Congress of Pessoan Studies, Porto, Eng. António de Almeida Foundation, 1988.
Portugal Futurista #1, Lisbon, 1917.
Portugal, José Blanc de. *Tradução e notas de Fernando Pessoa: O louco rabequista.* Lisbon: Editorial Presença, 1988.
Posada, Tarcísio Valencia. *Fernando Pessoa el angel marinero.* Colômbia: Taller El Angel Editor, 1996.
Presença, complete series, Coimbra, from 1927 on.
Prieto, Sonia. "Mensagem e Os lusíadas: Convergências e divergências". *Estudos Portugueses* #5, Recife, 1995.
Quadros, António. *Fernando Pessoa.* Lisbon: Editora Arcádia, 1960.
– Fernando Pessoa: *Vida, personalidade e génio.* 3rd ed. Lisbon: Publicações Dom Quixote, 1988.
– *Ficção e teatro.* Lisbon: Publicações Europa-América, 1987.
– *Mensagem e outros poemas afins.* 3rd ed. Portugal: Publicações Europa-América, 1990.

– "O poeta Pessoa, introdução à bibliografia e à obra". In: *Homenagem a Fernando Pessoa.* Editora António Almeida, 1991.
Queiroz, Carlos. *Carta à memória de Fernando Pessoa.* Lisbon: Centauro, 2008.
– *Desaparecido e Breve Tratado de não versificação.* Lisbon: Edições Ottiva, 1984.
– *Homenagem a Fernando Pessoa.* Coimbra: Editorial Presença, 1936.
Queiroz, Maria da Graça. *Cartas de Amor de Fernando Pessoa.* Lisbon: Ática, 1978.
Ramos, Auxilia; Braga, Zaida (introduction and organization). *Fernando Pessoa, poesias heterônimas.* Porto: Porto Editora, 2009.
Real, Miguel. *A morte de Portugal.* Porto: Campos das Letras, 2007.
Rebelo, Luís de Sousa. "Paganismo versus cristianismo em Fernando Pessoa". In: Minutes, 4th International Congress of Pessoan Studies, Porto, Eng. António de Almeida Foundation, 1988.
Rego, Thiago. "Identidades, modernidade e ambiguidade em Fernando Pessoa". *Espaço Acadêmico* #35, 2004.
Reis, Vasco. "A Romaria". 2nd ed. Braga: Ed. Missões franciscanas, 1936.
Ribeiro, Anabela Mota; Sena, Susana. "O senhor Pessoa". *Tabacaria* #11, Lisbon, Casa Fernando Pessoa, 2003.
Ribeiro, Maria Aparecida. "Fernando... enfim no palco". In: Minutes, 4th International Congress of Pessoan Studies, Porto, Eng. António de Almeida Foundation, 1988.
Rivas, Pierre *et alii.* "Veilleuraux confins". *Europe* #s 710/711, Paris, 1988.
Rosa, João Maria Nogueira. "Fernando Pessoa: Como eu o conheci". *Ocidente*, November, undated.
Roza, Miguel. *Encontro Magick, Fernando Pessoa e Aleister Crowley.* Lisbon: Hugin, 2001.
Sábat, Hermenegildo. *Anónimo transparente, uma interpretação gráfica de Fernando Pessoa.* Lisbon: Assírio e Alvim, 2008.
Sacramento, Mário. *Fernando Pessoa: Poeta da hora absurda.* Porto: Editora Inova, 1970.
Santos, Gilda. "As Lisboas de Duas Pessoas". *Revista do Núcleo de Estudos de Literatura Portuguesa e Africana da UFF*, v. 2, #2, Apr. 2009.
Santos, Irene Ramalho. *Poetas do Atlântico: Fernando Pessoa e o modernismo anglo-americano.* Belo Horizonte: Ed. UFMG, 2007.
Santos, Maria Laura Nobre dos; Cruz, Alexandrina; Montenegro, Rosa Maria; Pimenta, Lídia. "A inventariação do espólio de Fernando Pessoa: Tentativa de reconstituição". *Revista da Biblioteca Nacional* #3, Lisbon, Sep.-Dec. 1988.
Saraiva, Arnaldo. *Conversa acabada (sobre Fernando Pessoa e Mário de Sá-Carneiro).* Lisbon: Edições V.O. Filmes, 1982.
Saraiva, Mário. "A heteronímia de Pessoa". *Brotéria* #138, Lisbon, 1994.
– "Fernando Pessoa e a crítica recente (breve balanço)". In: Fernando Pessoa e a Europa do século XX. Porto: Fundação de Serralves, DL, 1991.
– *Fernando Pessoa poeta e tradutor de poetas.* Rio de Janeiro: Nova Fronteira, 1999.
– *Poemas com sentidos portugueses.* Porto: Câmara Municipal, 2001.
– *Correspondência inédita de Mário de Sá-Carneiro a Fernando Pessoa.* Porto: Centro de Estudos Pessoanos, 1980.
– "Anotação ao Sebastianismo", Separata from Boletim da Sociedade de Geografia de Lisboa, Lisbon, Jan.-Jun. 1985.
– *O caso clínico de Fernando Pessoa.* Lisbon: Edições Referendo, 1990.
– *Pessoa ele próprio.* Lisbon: Clássica Editora, 1992.
Saramago, José. "Da impossibilidade deste retrato". In: Fernando Pessoa e a Europa do século XX. Porto: Fundação de Serralves, DL, 1991.
– *O ano da morte de Ricardo Reis.* São Paulo: Companhia das Letras, 1988.
Saúte, Nelson. "Carta de Arthur William Bayly a João Miguel Rosa". *Tabacaria*, v. 11, Lisbon, Casa Fernando Pessoa, 2003.
Scherner, Leopoldo. "O número 3 n'O mostrengo da Mensagem de Fernando Pessoa". In: Minutes, 4th International Congress of Pessoan Studies, Porto, Eng. António de Almeida

Foundation, 1988.
Seabra, José Augusto. "Fernando Pessoa: Uma anarquia poética". In: Fernando Pessoa, e a Europa do século XX. Porto: Fundação de Serralves, D.L., 1991.
– "Pessoa et la 'nouvelle renaissance' de l'Europe". *Europe* #s 710 /711, Paris, 1988.
– "Poética e filosofi a em Fernando Pessoa". In: Minutes, 4th International Congress of Pessoan Studies, Porto, Eng. António de Almeida Foundation, 1988.
Segolim, Fernando. "Caeiro e Nietzsche: da crítica da linguagem à antifilosofi a e à anti-poesia". In: Minutes, 4th International Congress of Pessoan Studies, Porto, Eng. António de Almeida Foundation, 1988.
Sena, Jorge de. Fernando Pessoa: *Poemas ingleses.* Lisbon: Ática, 1974.
– *Fernando Pessoa & C a heteronímia.* 3rd ed. Lisbon: Edições 70, 2000.
– (organization and notes). *Páginas de doutrina estética.* Lisbon: Ed. Inquérito, 1946.
Severino, Alexandrino E. "Fernando Pessoa e William Shakespeare: Um estudo comparativo de heteronímia". In: Minutes, 4th International Congress of Pessoan Studies, Porto, Eng. António de Almeida Foundation, 1988.
Silva, Agostinho da. *Um Fernando Pessoa.* Lisbon: Guimarães Editora, 1996.
Silva, Deonísio. "A vitória de Fernando Pessoa". *Jornal do Brasil,* Rio de Janeiro, 28th of Dec. 2005.
Silva, José Luis da. "Que importa quien habla – Una mirada sobre la poesia heteronímica de Fernando Pessoa a partir de las ideas de Michel Foucault sobre el discurso y el autor", thesis for Universidad Católica Andrés Bello, Caracas, 2004.
Silva, Luís de Oliveira e. *O materialismo idealista de Fernando Pessoa.* Lisbon: Clássica Editora, 1985.
Silva, Manuela Parreira da. *Fernando Pessoa: Correspondência 1905-1922.* Lisbon: Assírio e Alvim, 1999.
– Fernando Pessoa: *Correspondência 1923-1935.* Lisbon: Assírio e Alvim, 1999.
– Fernando Pessoa: *Correspondência inédita.* Braga: Livros Horizontes, 1996.
– "Fernando Pessoa, jornalista anônimo". *Tabacaria,* v. I, Casa Fernando Pessoa, 1996.
– *Realidade e ficção, para uma biografia epistolar de Fernando Pessoa.* Lisbon: Assírio e Alvim, 2004.
– ; Freitas, Ana Maria; Izine, Madalena. *Poesia de Fernando Pessoa, 1902-1917.* Lisbon: Assírio e Alvim, 2005 (São Paulo, Cia. das Letras, 2005).
Silva, Paulo Neves da. *Citações e pensamentos de Fernando Pessoa.* Alfragide: Casa das Letras, 2009.
Silva, Teresa Cristina Cerdeira da. "De Pessoa a Saramago, as metamorfoses de Ricardo Reis". In: Minutes, 4th International Congress of Pessoan Studies, Porto, Eng. António de Almeida Foundation, 1988.
Silveira, Pedro da; Portugal, Idalina. "Fernando Pessoa: A sua estreia aos 14 anos e outras poesias de 1902 a 1905". *Revista da Biblioteca Nacional* #3, Lisbon, Sep.-Dec. 1988.
– ; – "Subsídios para uma bibliografia de Henrique Rosa". *Revista da Biblioteca Nacional,* Lisbon, #3, Sep.-Dec. 1988.
Silveira, Yvonne de Oliveira. "O marinheiro". In: Minutes, 4th International Congress of Pessoan Studies, Porto, Eng. António de Almeida Foundation, 1988.
Simões, João Gaspar. *Fernando Pessoa, escorço interpretativo de sua vida e obra.* Lisbon: Inquérito, s.d.
– "Nos noventa e oito anos de Fernando Pessoa". *Diário de Notícias,* 15th of Jun. 1986.
– *Vida e obra de Fernando Pessoa: História de uma geração.* 2nd ed. Lisbon: Editora Bertrand, 1970
– *Vida e obra de Fernando Pessoa: História de uma geração.* Rio de Janeiro: Nova Aguilar, 1976.
Soares, Fernando Luso. *A novela policial-dedutiva em Fernando Pessoa.* Lisbon: Diabril, 1976.
Souza, Eneida Maria de. "A escrita emblemática de Mensagem". In: Minutes, 4th International Congress of Pessoan Studies, Porto, Eng. António de Almeida Foundation, 1988.
Souza, João Rui de. "Fernando Pessoa: Um poeta para todo o papel". *Revista da Biblioteca*

Nacional, Lisboa #3, Sep.-Dec. 1988.
Souza, João Rui de. *Fernando Pessoa, empregado de escritório.* 2nd ed. Lisbon: Assírio e Alvim, 2010.
Souza, Maria Leonor Machado de. *Fernando Pessoa e a literatura de ficção.* Lisbon: Nova Era, 1978.
Stefan, Jude. "Qualquer música". *Europe* #s 710/711, Paris, 1988.
Steiner, George. "Quatro poetas, A arte de Fernando Pessoa". *Tabacaria* #1, Lisbon, Casa Fernando Pessoa, 1996.
Stoker, Michaël. Fernando Pessoa: *De fictie vergezelt mij als mijn schaduw.* Utrecht: Vitgeuerit Ijzer, 2009.
Suassuna, Ariano. *Olavo Bilac e Fernando Pessoa: Uma presença brasileira em Mensagem?* Lisbon: Arion Publicações, 1998.
Sudoeste, complete series, Lisbon, Editora SW, from 1935 on.
Tabucchi, Antonio. "Ce qu'a vu Pessoa". *Europe* #s 710/711, Paris, 1988.
– *Os três últimos dias de Fernando Pessoa: Um delírio.* Rio de Janeiro: Rocco, 1997.
– *Pessoana mínima: Escritos sobre Fernando Pessoa.* Lisbon: Imprensa Nacional; Casa da Moeda, 1984.
– *Une malle pleine de gens.* Paris: Christian Bourgois Éditeur, 2002.
Teixeira, Ana Lucia de Freitas. "Álvaro Campos ele mesmo", post-grad thesis in Sociology for the University of São Paulo, São Paulo, 2003.
Teixeira, Luís Filipe B. *A Mensagem do encoberto: Fernando Pessoa à luz do paradigma sebástico.* Lisbon: Edições Salamandra, undated.
– "Ciência e esoterismo em Fernando Pessoa". *Tabacaria* v. 0, Lisbon, Casa Fernando Pessoa, 1996.
– *O nascimento do homem em Pessoa.* Lisbon: Edições Cosmos, 1992.
– *Pensar Pessoa.* Porto: Lello Editores, 1997.
Toledo, Marleine Paula Marcondes. "À margem do génio ou o poeta marginal: Preparativos de Fernando Pessoa para a posteridade". In: Minutes, 4th International Congress of Pessoan Studies, Porto, Eng. António de Almeida Foundation, 1988.
Trigo, Salvato. "O construtivismo poético ou o mythos aristotélico em Fernando Pessoa". In: Minutes, 4th International Congress of Pessoan Studies, Porto, Eng. António de Almeida Foundation, 1988.
Trigueiro, Luiz Forjaz e Carlos Lacerda. *Ode marítima de Fernando Pessoa (com 15 desenhos a cores de Otávio Araújo).* Rio de Janeiro: Nova Fronteira, 1975.
Ulacia, Manuel. "Octavio Paz y Fernando Pessoa". In: Minutes, 4th International Congress of Pessoan Studies, Porto, Eng. António de Almeida Foundation, 1988.
Valdemar, António. "Pessoa no Ministério das Finanças". *Diário de Notícias*, Lisbon, 10th of Mar. 1996.
Vargas, Milton. "Pessoa: Personagens e poesia". *Revista USP* #50, São Paulo, 2001.
Various. *Fernando Pessoa e a Europa do século XX.* Porto: Fundação Serralves, 1991.
Various. *Fernando Pessoa revisitado.* Recife: Associação de Estudos Portugueses Jordão Emerenciano.
Vasconcelos, Taborda. "Antropologia de Fernando Pessoa". *Ocidente* #367, Lisbon, Nov. 1968.
Vega, Hugo Gutiérrez. "Por la carretera de Sinta". *Jornada Semanal*, 25th of Mar. 2003.
Velter, André. "Nada, fado pour un faust portugais". *Europe*, #s 710/711, Paris, 1988.
Viana, Antonio Fernando. *Vida e outras vidas em Fernando Pessoa.* Recife: Editora Nova Presença, 2004.
Vícola, Daniel; Oliveira, Jane Kelly de. "Marinheiro à deriva e os ventos pessoanos: uma interpretação dos símbolos em 'O Marinheiro', de Fernando Pessoa". *Boletim do Centro de Estudos Portugueses Jorge de Sena* #22, Araraquara, Unesp, Jan-Dec. 2004.
Vieira, Joaquim. *A governanta.* 3rd ed. Lisbon: A esfera dos livros, 2010.
– ; Zenith, Richard. *Fotobiografia de Fernando Pessoa.* Lisbon: Círculo de Leitores, 2008.
Vieira, Márcia Maria Rosa. "Fernando Pessoa e Jacques Lacan, constelações, letra e livro",

post-grad thesis in Letters (UFMG), 2005.
Vieira, Monsenhor Primo. "Fernando Pessoa e o hai-kai". In: Minutes, 4th International Congress of Pessoan Studies, Porto, Eng. António de Almeida Foundation, 1988.
Vieira, Yara Frateschi. "Pessoa, leitor da antologia grega". In: Minutes, 4th International Congress of Pessoan Studies, Porto, Eng. António de Almeida Foundation, 1988.
Villanueva Collado, Alfredo; Núñez, Santos Abersio. "El antinous de Fernando Pessoa: Una relectura", Associação Internacional de Amigos da Universidade Livre Iberoamericana em Galicia, 14/2/2005.
Vouga, Vera. "Pessoa: Versos, verso". In: Minutes, 4th International Congress of Pessoan Studies, Porto, Eng. António de Almeida Foundation, 1988.
Waldman, Berta. "Via de mão dupla". In: Minutes, 4th International Congress of Pessoan Studies, Porto, Eng. António de Almeida Foundation, 1988.
Willemsen, August. "Fernando Pessoa, o sincero mentiroso". In: Homenagem a Fernando Pessoa, Portugal, Fundação Eng. António Almeida, 1991.
Yahn, Gersey Georgett Bergo. "Cronos-Saturno: Uma leitura de Álvaro de Campos e de Luís de Camões". In: Minutes, 4th International Congress of Pessoan Studies, Porto, Eng. António de Almeida Foundation, 1988.
Zenith, Richard. "A heteronímia: muitas maneiras de dizer o mesmo nada". *Tabacaria,* v. I, Casa Fernando Pessoa, 1996.
– (organization and presentation). *Aforismos e afins.* Lisbon: Assírio e Alvim, 2003.
– (organization). *Cartas.* Lisbon: Assírio e Alvim, 2007.
– *Fernando Pessoa: A máscara e o espelho.* Lisbon: Instituto Camões, 2004.
– (organization and preface). *Fernando Pessoa: Escritos autobiográficos, automáticos e de reflexão pessoal.* Lisbon: Assírio e Alvim, 2003.
– (org. and preface). *Fernando Pessoa: Escritos autobiográficos, automáticos e de reflexão pessoal.* São Paulo, A Girafa, 2006.
– (organization). *Fernando Pessoa, Heróstrato e a busca de imortalidade.* Lisbon: Assírio e Alvim, 2000.
– (org.). *Fernando Pessoa, A little larger than the entire universe.* New York: Penguin, 2006.
– (org.). *Livro do desassossego.* 4th ed. São Paulo: Companhia das Letras, 2001.
– (org.). *Livro do desassossego.* Lisbon: Assírio e Alvim, 2006.
– (preface). *Mensagem, de Fernando Pessoa. Ilustrações de Pedro Souza Pereira.* Lisbon: Oficina do Livro, 2006
– "O meu coração um pouco maior do que o universo inteiro". *Tabacaria,* v. 13, Lisbon, Casa Fernando Pessoa, 2004.
– "O pré-heterônimo de Boston". *Revista Ler*, Sextante Editora, Edição 99, 2011.
– (org.). *Poesia do eu.* Lisbon: Círculo dos Editores, 2006.
– (org.). *Poesia dos outros eus.* Lisbon: Assírio e Alvim, 2007.
– (org.). *Poesia inglesa.* Lisbon: Assírio e Alvim, 2007.
– (org.). *Prosa íntima.* Lisbon: Assírio e Alvim, 2007.
– (org.). *Prosa publicada em vida.* Lisbon: Assírio e Alvim, 2006.
Zilberman, Regina. "Vanguarda e subdesenvolvimento: Respostas de Fernando Pessoa e Mário de Andrade". In: Minutes, 4th International Congress of Pessoan Studies, Porto, Eng. António de Almeida Foundation, 1988.

MIMESIS GROUP
www.mimesis-group.com

MIMESIS INTERNATIONAL
www.mimesisinternational.com
info@mimesisinternational.com

MIMESIS EDIZIONI
www.mimesisedizioni.it
mimesis@mimesisedizioni.it

ÉDITIONS MIMÉSIS
www.editionsmimesis.fr
info@editionsmimesis.fr

MIMESIS COMMUNICATION
www.mim-c.net

MIMESIS EU
www.mim-eu.com

Printed by Digital Team, Fano (PU) – May 2019